SUFFOLK AND THE TUDORS

Suffolk and the Tudors

*Politics and Religion in an
English County 1500–1600*

DIARMAID MacCULLOCH

CLARENDON PRESS · OXFORD
1986

Oxford University Press, Walton Street, Oxford OX2 6DP
Oxford New York Toronto
Delhi Bombay Calcutta Madras Karachi
Petaling Jaya Singapore Hong Kong Tokyo
Nairobi Dar es Salaam Cape Town
Melbourne Auckland
and associated companies in
Beirut Berlin Ibadan Nicosia

Oxford is a trade mark of Oxford University Press

Published in the United States
by Oxford University Press, New York

British Library Cataloguing in Publication Data
MacCulloch, Diarmaid
Suffolk and the Tudors: politics and religion
in an English county 1500–1600.
1. Suffolk—History
I. Title
942.6'405   DA670.S9
ISBN 0–19–822914–3

Library of Congress Cataloging in Publication Data
MacCulloch, Diarmaid.
Suffolk and the Tudors.
Includes index.
1. Suffolk—History. 2. Suffolk—Church history.
3. Reformation—England—Suffolk. 4. Great Britain—
History—Tudors, 1485–1603—Case studies. I. Title.
DA670.S9M28 1986   942.6'405   85–21770
ISBN 0–19–822914–3

Set by Hope Services, Abingdon, Oxon
Printed in Great Britain
at the University Printing House, Oxford
by David Stanford
Printer to the University

PAUL MARTIN HIS BOOK

Preface

CHOOSING to study Suffolk rather than any other county might be considered foolhardy by those familiar with the sources of local history. Researchers into the early modern history of Suffolk can only envy their colleagues across the county borders. We enjoy little to compare with the wealth of private papers surviving from fifteenth- and sixteenth-century Norfolk, and have none of the quarter sessions and assize material which enriches understanding of late Tudor Essex; nor have we a county history to equal the labours of Morant for Essex, Blomefield for Norfolk, or of the twin efforts made by the recent editors of the Victoria County History and the Royal Commission on Historical Monuments for Cambridgeshire. Before entering the world of modern research, students of Suffolk must be their own Morant or Blomefield, and resign themselves to basic prosopography.

As an adopted son of the county, I feel ample compensation for this handicap. The world around the country parsonage of my childhood retained much of the shape of its Tudor predecessor, and my experiences in that world have, I hope, given me a sharper ear for the resonances of the documents that I have been able to use than if I had come to the subject as an outsider to East Anglia. Two of the underlying themes of this work, the age-old relationship of Suffolk and Norfolk, and the sense of difference within Suffolk itself between the communities of east and west, have always been commonplaces for one brought up on the very border of the two regions; nor has the Puritanism already so strong in Elizabethan Suffolk entirely departed from the outlook of one of the most Protestant of English counties.

Since the sources that I have used appeared so unpromising when I tackled them, I have been particularly fortunate to have been guided in their use by Professor Geoffrey Elton; I have greatly appreciated his expertise and friendship over the years, and he has done much to punch this work into shape. Over the years I have benefited from the shared expertise of friends in the Tudor world, as the footnotes in this work reveal. I have been made particularly welcome at the Centre for East Anglian Studies in the University of East Anglia, and profited much from informal discussion and encouragement there with Dr Hassell Smith and Victor Morgan; my debt to Dr Smith's splendid trailblazing research will be apparent in this book. Among local historians in Suffolk who have long acted as a stimulus to my research on the county, I owe a great deal to my father, the Revd Nigel MacCulloch, Miss Joan Corder, Dr John Blatchly, Mrs Margaret Statham and Mr Norman Scarfe; Dr Blatchly has done me particular service in the illustrations with advice and with his own photography.

Of the many custodians of records that I have encountered, I am happy to acknowledge the help and courtesy offered me by the staff of the following institutions: the Public Record Office, the British Library, the House of Lords Record Office, the College of Heralds, the History of Parliament Trust, the National Register of Archives, Cambridge University Library, the Bodleian Library, the Inner Temple Library, Ipswich Borough Library, the Joseph P. Regenstein Library in the University of Chicago, the Pierpont Morgan Library, Bristol University Library, the Record Offices of Suffolk at Bury St Edmunds and Ipswich, and of Norfolk, Northamptonshire, Kent, and Essex, and the archivist of the Marquis of Salisbury at Hatfield House. The Town Clerk and Honorary Archivist of the Borough of Beccles were generous enough to place their borough muniments at my disposal, while the Earl of Iveagh and his staff at Elveden Hall and the Lord Walpole at Wolterton gave me welcome hospitality as well as access to their manuscript collections.

I am grateful to the Cambridge Historical Society, the Archbishop Cranmer Prize Fund of the University of Cambridge, and the Twenty-Seven Foundation of the University of London for their generous financial assistance for my work, to the Master and Fellows of Churchill College, Cambridge for electing me to a Research Fellowship, and to all members of Churchill who made my nine years' association with the College such an agreeable one. I owe an equal debt to my colleagues at Wesley College, Bristol, for putting up with me and for giving me the opportunity of sabbatical leave to further this book. Dr John Guy provided me with invaluable last-minute help. Of all those who have given me shelter over the years of my research, Katy and Roo deserve special mention. My final debt is to my parents for providing me with so enviable a boyhood in Suffolk and for kindling my interest in its history.

DIARMAID MacCULLOCH

Wesley College, Bristol, 1985

Contents

PART IV: POPULAR POLITICS

LIST OF PLATES

(between pp. 200 and 201)

LIST OF MAPS

LIST OF TABLES

Abbreviations and Conventions
used in the Notes

All printed works are published in London unless otherwise stated.

APC	*Acts of the Privy Council of England* (1890–1907).
Aylsham	NRO, Aylsham MS collections (with piece number).
Bacon	Nathaniel Bacon, *Annalls of Ipswiche*, ed. W. H. Richardson (1884).
Bacon Papers	*The Papers of Nathaniel Bacon of Stiffkey*, ed. A. H. Smith and G. M. Baker (2 vols. to date, Norwich, 1979–83; NRS, vols. XLVI, XLIX).
Bald	R. C. Bald, *John Donne and the Drurys* (Cambridge, 1959).
Baskerville, 'Married Clergy'	G. Baskerville, 'Married clergy and pensioned religious in Norwich diocese, 1555', *English Historical Review* XLVIII (1933), pp. 43–64, 199–228.
Bateson, 'Original Letters'	'Collection of original letters from the bishops to the Privy Council, 1564 . . .', ed. M. Bateson, *Camden Miscellany* IX (CS New Series, LIII, 1893).
Bec.	Beccles Corporation muniments, with piece number.
BIHR	*Bulletin of the Institute of Historical Research.*
Bindoff	S. T. Bindoff, *Ket's Rebellion* (Historical Association Pamphlets, general series, no. 12), 1949.
BL Add.	British Library, Additional MSS.
BL Add. Ch.	British Library Additional Charters.
BL Cott.	British Library Cottonian MSS.
BL Harl.	British Library Harleian MSS.
BL Harl. Ch.	British Library Harley Charters.
BL Lansd.	British Library Lansdowne MSS.
Bodl.	Bodleian Library, Oxford.
Boynton	L. Boynton, *The Elizabethan Militia 1558–1638* (1967).
Bury Wills	*Wills and inventories from the registers of the Commissary of Bury St Edmunds and the Archdeacon of Sudbury*, ed. S. Tymms (CS Old Series, xlix, 1850).
Butley Chronicle	*Register or Chronicle of Butley Priory, Suffolk, 1510–35*, ed. A. G. Dickens *et al.* (Winchester, 1951).
CCC	Corpus Christi College, Cambridge, MS no. 114.
CCN	NRO, Consistory Court of Norwich, wills.
CCR Henry VII	*Calendar of Close Rolls, Henry VII* (2 vols., 1954–63).

'Chitting'	'Henry Chitting's Suffolk Collections', ed. D. N. J. MacCulloch, *PSIA* XXXIV (1978), pp. 103–28.
Chorography	*The Chorography of Suffolk*, ed. D. N. J. MacCulloch, SRS XIX (1976).
Chorography of Norfolk	*The Chorography of Norfolk*, ed. C. M. Hood (Norwich, 1938).
CJ	*Journals of the House of Commons*, from 1542.
Clark	P. Clark, *English Provincial Society from the Reformation to the Revolution. Religion, Politics and Society in Kent, 1500–1640* (Hassocks, 1977).
Cockburn	J. S. Cockburn, *A History of English Assizes, 1558–1714* (Cambridge, 1972).
Collinson, 'Classical Movement'	P. Collinson, 'The Puritan Classical Movement in the Reign of Elizabeth I' (Univ. of London Ph.D., 1957).
Collinson, *Puritan Movement*	P. Collinson, *The Elizabethan Puritan Movement* (1967).
Collinson, *Religion of Protestants*	P. Collinson, *The Religion of Protestants* (Oxford, 1982).
Committee Book	Committee Book of the Deputy Lieutenants for the eastern division of Suffolk, 1608–24, *penes* Lord Tollemache, Helmingham Hall, Suffolk.
Copinger, *Manors*	W. A. Copinger, *The Manors of Suffolk* (7 vols., 1905–11).
Corder, *Dictionary*	J. Corder, *A Dictionary of Suffolk Arms*, SRS VII (1965), numbered by column.
Corder, *1561 Visitation*	*The Visitation of Suffolk 1561 Part 1*, ed. J. Corder (Harleian Society, New Series XI, 1981).
CPR Edward VI	*Calendar of Patent Rolls, Edward VI* (6 vols., 1924–9).
CPR Eliz.	*Calendar of Patent Rolls, Elizabeth I* (10 vols., 1939–date).
CPR Henry VII	*Calendar of Patent Rolls, Henry VII* (2 vols., 1956–63).
CPR Philip and Mary	*Calendar of Patent Rolls, Mary I, Philip and Mary* (4 vols., 1936–9).
Crawford, 'John Howard'	A. Crawford, 'The Career of John Howard, Duke of Norfolk 1420–1485' (Univ. of London M. Phil., 1975).
Crawley, *Trinity Hall*	C. Crawley, *Trinity Hall* (Cambridge, 1976).
CRS	Catholic Record Society publications.
CS	Camden Society publications.
CSPFor.	*Calendar of State Papers, Foreign, Edward VI, Mary, Elizabeth* (25 vols., 1861–1950).
CSPSpan.	*Calendar of State Papers, Spanish* (13 vols. and 2 supplements, 1862–1954).
CUL	Cambridge University Library.
Davis	J. F. Davis, *Heresy and Reformation in the south-east of*

	England, 1520–1559 (Royal Historical Society studies in history no. 34, 1983).
Dedham Classis	*The Presbyterian Movement in the reign of Queen Elizabeth, as illustrated by the minute book of the Dedham Classis, 1582–9*, ed. R. G. Usher, CS 3rd Series VIII (1905).
D'Ewes, *Autobiography*	*The Autobiography and Correspondence of Sir Simonds D'Ewes Bart.*, ed. J. O. Halliwell (2 vols., 1845).
D'Ewes, *Journals*	*The Journals of all the Parliaments during the Reign of Queen Elizabeth . . .*, ed. S. D'Ewes (1682).
DNB	*Dictionary of National Biography.*
Dugdale	W. Dugdale, *Monasticon Anglicanum*, ed. J. Caley, H. Ellis, and B. Bandinel (8 vols. 1817–30).
EANQ	*East Anglian Notes and Queries*, Old and New Series.
Elton, *Policy and Police*	G. R. Elton, *Policy and Police* (Cambridge, 1972).
Elton, *Reform and Reformation*	G. R. Elton, *Reform and Reformation* (1977).
Emden, *Cambridge*	A. B. Emden, *A Biographical Register of the University of Cambridge to 1500* (Cambridge, 1963).
Evans, 'South Elmham'	N. Evans, 'The Community of South Elmham, Suffolk, 1550–1640' (Univ. of East Anglia M.Phil., 1978).
Everitt, *Suffolk*	*Suffolk in the Great Rebellion*, ed. A. M. Everitt, SRS III (1960).
1524 Subsidy	*Suffolk in 1524: being the return for a subsidy granted in 1523, with a map of Suffolk in Hundreds*, ed. S. H. A. Hervey (Suffolk Green Books X, Woodbridge, 1910).
1568 Subsidy	*Suffolk in 1568: being the return for a subsidy granted 1566 . . .*, ed. S. H. A. Hervey (Suffolk Green Books XII, Bury St Edmunds, 1909).
Fletcher	A. Fletcher, *A County Community in Peace and War: Sussex 1600–1640* (1975).
Folger	Folger Shakespeare Library MSS, with piece number.
Ford, *Mary Tudor*	F. Ford, *Mary Tudor* (Bury St Edmunds, 1882).
Foster	*Alumni Oxonienses, 1500–1714*, ed. J. Foster (4 vols., Oxford 1891–2).
Foxe	J. Foxe, *Actes and Monuments*, ed. S. R. C. Cattley and G. Townsend (8 vols., 1837–41).
Gee	H. Gee, *The Elizabethan Clergy and the Settlement of Religion 1558–1564* (Oxford, 1898).
Gerard	*John Gerard: The Autobiography of an Elizabethan*, ed. P. Caraman (1956).
Gottfried	R. S. Gottfried, *Bury St Edmunds and the Urban Crisis: 1290–1539* (Princeton, 1982).
Griffith	The Chronicle of Ellis Griffith, described in *HMC*,

	MSS in the Welsh Language I (1898). I am indebted to Dr Peter Gwyn for this reference.
Gurney, 'Household Accounts'	'Extracts from the Household and Privy Purse Expenditure of Le Strange of Hunstanton, 1519–78', ed. D. Gurney, *Archaeologia* XXV (1834), pp. 411–569.
Guy, *Cardinal's Court*	J. A. Guy, *The Cardinal's Court* (Hassocks, 1977).
Guy, *More*	J. A. Guy, *The Public Career of Sir Thomas More* (Hassocks, 1980).
Harrison	G. B. Harrison, *The life and death of Robert Devereux, Earl of Essex* (1937).
Hall	E. Hall, *The Union of the two noble and illustre Famelies of York and Lancaster . . .*, ed. H. Ellis (London, 1809).
Hatfield	MSS of the Marquis of Salisbury, Hatfield House, Herts.
Haydn	*The Book of Dignities*, ed. J. Haydn (1894).
Heal	F. Heal, *Of Prelates and Princes* (Cambridge, 1980).
Hengr.	Hengrave Hall MSS, in custody of CUL.
Hirst	D. Hirst, *The Representative of the People?* (Cambridge, 1975).
History of Parliament 1509–1558	*The History of Parliament: The House of Commons 1509–1558*, ed. S. T. Bindoff (3 vols., 1982).
History of Parliament 1558–1603	*The History of Parliament: The House of Commons 1558–1603*, ed. P. W. Hasler (3 vols., 1982).
HLRO	House of Lords Record Office.
HMC	Historical Manuscripts Commission Reports.
HMC Salisbury	*Calendar of the Manuscripts of the Marquis of Salisbury, HMC* (1883–date).
Holmes	C. Holmes, *The Eastern Association in the English Civil War* (Cambridge, 1974).
Hoskins	W. G. Hoskins, *The Age of Plunder* (1976).
Houlbrooke, *Church Courts*	R. Houlbrooke, *Church Courts and the People during the English Reformation 1520–1570* (Oxford, 1979).
Houlbrooke, 'Persecution of Heresy'	R. Houlbrooke, 'Persecution of Heresy and Protestantism in the Diocese of Norwich under Henry VIII', *NA* XXXV (1970), pp. 308–26.
Howard	*The Visitation of Suffolke*, ed. J. J. Howard (2 vols., Lowestoft, 1867).
Iveagh	MSS *penes* the Earl of Iveagh, at present at Elveden Hall, Suffolk.
James	C. W. James, *Chief Justice Coke* (1929).
James, 'Obedience and Dissent'	M. E. James, 'Obedience and Dissent in Henrician England: the Lincolnshire Rebellion', *PP* XLIII (Aug. 1970) pp. 1–78.

Jeayes — *Letters of Philip Gawdy, of West Harling, Norfolk, 1579–1616,* ed. I. H. Jeayes (Roxburghe Club, 1906).

Jessopp, *Visitations* — *Visitations of the Diocese of Norwich, 1492–1532,* ed. A. Jessopp (CS New Series, XLIII, 1891).

Knowles — D. Knowles, *The Religious Orders in England* (3 vols., 1948–59).

Lehmberg, *Reformation Parliament* — S. E. Lehmberg, *The Reformation Parliament 1529–1536* (Cambridge, 1970).

Leicester *Correspondence* — *Robert Dudley, Earl of Leicester. Correspondence during his government of the Low Countries ...,* ed. J. Bruce (CS XXVI, 1844).

Le Neve, *Fasti* — J. Le Neve, *Fasti Ecclesiae Anglicanae ...,* ed. T. D. Hardy (3 vols., Oxford, 1854).

LJ — *Journals of the House of Lords,* from 1509.

Loades — D. M. Loades, *The Reign of Mary Tudor* (1979).

Lobel — M. D. Lobel, *The Borough of Bury St Edmunds* (1935).

LP — *Letters and Papers, Foreign and Domestic, of the reign of Henry VIII, 1509–47,* ed. J. S. Brewer *et al.* (21 vols. and 2 vols. addenda, 1862–1932).

MacCulloch, 'Catholic and Puritan' — D. N. J. MacCulloch, 'Catholic and Puritan in Elizabethan Suffolk', *Archiv Für Reformationsgeschichte,* LXXII (1981).

MacCulloch, 'Kett's Rebellion' — D. N. J. MacCulloch, 'Kett's Rebellion in Context', in *Rebellion, Popular Protest and the Social Order in Early Modern England,* ed. P. Slack (Cambridge, 1984), pp. 39–76, repr. from *PP* LXXXIV, XCIII (Aug. 1979, Nov. 1981).

MacCulloch, 'Power, Privilege and the County Community' — D. N. J. MacCulloch, 'Power, Privilege and the County Community: County Politics in Elizabethan Suffolk, (Univ. of Cambridge Ph.D., 1977).

McGrath and Rowe, 'Cornwallis' — P. McGrath and J. Rowe, 'the Recusancy of Sir Thomas Cornwallis', *PSIA* XVIII (1958), pp. 226–71.

Machyn's Diary — *The Diary of Henry Machyn, citizen and merchant-taylor of London, 1550–63,* ed. J. G. Nichols (CS Old Series XLII, 1848).

Metcalfe — *The Visitations of Suffolk,* ed. W. C. Metcalfe (Exeter, 1882).

Miller, 'Henry VIII's unwritten will' — H. Miller, 'Henry VIII's unwritten will', in *Wealth and Power in Tudor England,* ed. E. W. Ives *et al.* (1978), pp. 87–105.

Morant — P. Morant, *History and Antiquities of the County of Essex* (2 vols., 1768).

More, *Dialogue concerning Heresies* — T. More, *A Dialogue concerning Heresies*, ed. T. M. C. Lawler *et al.* (Complete Works of St Thomas More, vol. VI, pt. i), (Yale, 1981).

Morrill — J. S. Morrill, *Cheshire 1630–1660: County Government and Society during the English Revolution* (Oxford, 1974).

Muskett — J. J. Muskett and F. Johnson, *Suffolk Manorial Families* (2 vols. and 3 parts, Exeter, 1900–14).

NA — *Norfolk Archaeology* (1849–date).

Narratives of the Reformation — *Narratives of the days of the Reformation . . .*, ed. J. G. Nichols (CS Old Series LXXVII, 1859).

Neale, *Commons* — J. E. Neale, *The Elizabethan House of Commons* (1949).

NRO — Norfolk Record Office, Norwich.

NRS — Norfolk Record Society publications.

Original Letters — *Original Letters relative to the English Reformation . . .*, ed. H. Robinson (2 vols., Parker Society, 1846–7).

Oxley — J. E. Oxley, *The Reformation in Essex to the death of Mary* (Manchester, 1965).

Palliser — D. M. Palliser, *Tudor York* (Oxford, 1979).

Parker Correspondence — M. Parker, *Correspondence*, ed. J. Bruce and T. T. Perowne (Parker Society, XXXIII), (Cambridge, 1853).

Parkhurst — *The Letter Book of John Parkhurst*, ed. R. A. Houlbrooke (NRS XLIII, 1974–5). In quotations I have sometimes preferred my own transcriptions of the original.

'Parkyn' — 'Robert Parkyn's narrative of the Reformation', ed. A. G. Dickens (*English Historical Review* LXII, 1947), pp. 58–83.

Paston Letters — *Paston Letters and Papers of the Fifteenth Century*, ed. N. Davis (2 vols., Oxford, 1971–7).

Payne Collier, *Household Books* — *Household Books of John, Duke of Norfolk, and Thomas, Earl of Surrey, 1481–90*, ed. J. Payne Collier (Roxburghe Club, 1844).

PCC — PRO, Prerogative Court of Canterbury, probate copies of wills, by volume.

PCC Adm. — Administrations in the PCC, by book.

Peet, 'Parish Clergy' — D. J. Peet, 'The mid-sixteenth century Parish Clergy, with particular consideration of the dioceses of Norwich and York' (Cambridge Ph.D., 1980).

Petyt — Inner Temple Library, Petyt MSS.

PP — *Past and Present* (1952–date).

PRO — Public Record Office, with piece number of document.

PSIA — *Proceedings of the Suffolk Institute of Archaeology* (1848–date).

Redgr.	Redgrave Hall papers, Joseph P. Regenstein Library, University of Chicago.
Registrum Vagum	*The Registrum Vagum of Anthony Harison*, ed. T. F. Barton (NRS XXXII, 1963).
Richmond	C. Richmond, *John Hopton. A Fifteenth Century Suffolk Gentleman* (Cambridge, 1981).
Rose	E. Rose, *Cases of Conscience* (Cambridge, 1975).
Rowse	A. L. Rowse, *Tudor Cornwall: portrait of a society* (1941).
Rushbrook Registers	*Rushbrook Parish Registers, 1567–1850, with Jermyn and Davers Annals*, ed. S. H. A. Hervey (Suffolk Green Books VI), (Woodbridge, 1903).
Russell	F. W. Russell, *Kett's Rebellion in Norfolk* (1859).
Ryece	*Suffolk in the XVIIth Century. The Breviary of Suffolk by Robert Reyce*, ed. Lord Francis Hervey (1902). Despite the spelling 'Reyce' adopted by Hervey, I have adopted Ryece's habitual spelling of his own name.
Sayer, 'Norfolk Involvement in Dynastic Conflict'	M. Sayer, 'Norfolk Involvement in Dynastic Conflict 1469–1471 and 1483–1487', *NA* XXXVI (1977), pp. 305–26.
Scarfe	N. Scarfe, *Suffolk* (Making of the English Landscape, 1972).
Scott Thomson, 'Lord Lieutenancy'	G. Scott Thomson, 'The Lord Lieutenancy of Suffolk under the Tudors', *PSIA* XX (1929), pp. 227–31.
Seconde Parte	*The Seconde Parte of a Register*, ed. A. Peel (2 vols., Cambridge, 1915).
Simpson	A. Simpson, *The Wealth of the Gentry, 1540–1660: East Anglian Studies* (Chicago, 1961).
Smith	A. H. Smith, *County and Court. Government and Politics in Norfolk 1558–1603* (Oxford, 1974).
Somerville	R. Somerville, *History of the Duchy of Lancaster. Vol. i. 1265–1603* (1953).
SROB	Suffolk Record Office, Bury St Edmunds branch.
SROI	Suffolk Record Office, Ipswich branch.
SROI, Blois	SROI, GC 17/755, church notes of William Blois, *c.* 1650.
SRS	Suffolk Records Society publications.
Stat. Realm	*Statutes of the Realm*, ed. A. Luders *et al.* (11 vols., 1810–28).
STC	*A Short-Title Catalogue of books printed in England, Scotland, and Ireland, and of English Books printed abroad, 1475–1640*, ed. A. W. Pollard, G. R. Redgrave, *et al.* (2 vols., 1926; vol. II of revision so far issued, 1976).

Strype, *Annals*	J. Strype, *Annals of the Reformation ... during Queen Elizabeth's happy reign ...* (4 vols., Oxford, 1820–40).
Strype, *Parker*	J. Strype, *The Life and Acts of Matthew Parker ...* (3 vols., Oxford, 1821).
Suckling	A. I. Suckling, *History and Antiquities of ... Suffolk* (2 vols., 1846–8).
Tanner	Bodl., Tanner MSS.
Thirsk	*The Agrarian History of England and Wales, vol. iv*, ed. J. Thirsk (Cambridge, 1967).
Tittler	R. Tittler, *Nicholas Bacon. The Making of a Tudor Statesman* (1976).
Tudor Royal Proclamations	*Tudor Royal Proclamations*, ed. P. L. Hughes and J. F. Larkin (2 vols., New Haven, 1964).
VE	*Valor Ecclesiasticus*, ed. J. Caley and J. Hunter (6 vols. 1810–34).
Venn	*Alumni Cantabrigienses. Part I, from the earliest times to 1751*, ed. J. and J. A. Venn (4 vols., Cambridge, 1922–4).
Virgoe, 'Crown, Magnates and Local Government'	R. Virgoe, 'The Crown, Magnates and Local Government in Fifteenth-Century East Anglia', in *The Crown and Local Communities*, ed. J. R. L. Highfield and R. Jeffs (Gloucester, 1981), pp. 72–87.
Virgoe, 'Recovery of the Howards'	R. Virgoe, 'The Recovery of the Howards in East Anglia, 1485–1529', in *Wealth and Power in Tudor England*, ed. E. W. Ives *et al.* (1978), pp. 1–20.
'Vita Mariae'	'The *Vita Mariae Angliae Reginae* of Robert Wingfield of Brantham', ed. D. N. J. MacCulloch, *Camden Miscellany XXVIII* (CS 4th Series, XXIX, 1984).
Weever	J. Weever, *Ancient Funerall Monuments* (1631).
White	W. White, *History, Gazetteer and Directory of Suffolk* (1844 edn., repr, New York, 1970).
Williams, 'Maritime Trade'	N. J. Williams, 'The Maritime Trade of the East Anglian Ports, 1550–1590' (Univ. of Oxford D.Phil., 1952).
Williams, *Thomas Howard*	N. Williams, *Thomas Howard, Fourth Duke of Norfolk* (1964).
Winthrop Papers	*Winthrop Papers*, ed. J. Winthrop (Massachusetts Historical Society, 1929).
Woods, 'The Rioting Crowd'	R. L. Woods, 'Individuals in the Rioting Crowd: a New Approach', *Journal of Interdisciplinary History XIV* (1983), pp. 1–24.
Woodworth	A. Woodworth, *Purveyance for the Royal Household in the Reign of Queen Elizabeth, Transactions of the American Philosophical Society XXXV* (1945).

Wnothesley's Chronicle	Charles Wnothesley, *A Chronicle of England*, ed. W. D. Hamilton (2 vols., CS New Series, *XI*, pts. i and ii, 1875–7).
Zurich Letters	*The Zurich Letters* . . ., ed. H. Robinson (2 vols., Parker Society, 1842–5).

In the text, all dates are given New Style. In making quotations, I have extended abbreviations wherever possible, and have regularized capitalization and spelling.

Introduction

THIS study of Tudor Suffolk leaves much unsaid. Its themes are those of power, politics, and religion: there is little consideration of social structure, policing, agriculture, industry, education, art and building, poverty and wealth. Many themes, therefore, have been neglected in order to trace political and religious developments over a century timespan. Not many county studies so far have covered more than half a century, while the bulk of work has concentrated on illuminating the local impact of the Civil War, or on examining the later Tudor period.[1] There are good archival reasons for this: the vastly increased survival of informal papers from the 1560s onwards makes it much easier to construct rounded pictures of the men who mattered in the later world; even peers of the realm are generally shadowy personalities in the England of Henry VII and Henry VIII, with leading clerics only a little more garrulous in their legacy to us.

To take the period 1500–1600 might be characterized as either cowardly or old-fashioned. At one end, it can be said to avoid the question of continuity between the world of the Tudors and late medieval England, a notorious evasion by Tudor historians; at the other end, it can be criticized as ignoring the insight provided by so much research in recent years that it was a late-Tudor world that confronted a Stuart king in 1640. In my judgement, a century is the minimum period needed to make sense of local politics in early modern England. The sharp contrasts between the early and the later Tudor period which this study attempts to illuminate are lost in any lesser timespan. On the other hand, the daunting mass of original record material becomes difficult to cope with effectively for any period of more than a century. Even after a decade of work on manuscripts with the single theme of Tudor East Anglia, I am painfully conscious of what resources in particular the diocesan, exchequer, and

---

[1] For studies with a century-long timespan, cf. Clark; Rowse; C. Haigh, *Reformation and Resistance in Tudor Lancashire* (Cambridge, 1974). Studies with a shorter timespan are now so numerous that the following can be only a selection of some of the more significant: Smith; Holmes; Fletcher; Morrill; T. G. Barnes, *Somerset, 1625–1640* (1961); A. M. Everitt, *The Community of Kent and the Great Rebellion* (Leicester, 1966). One of the few early Tudor studies is R. B. Smith, *Land and Politics in the England of Henry VIII. The West Riding of Yorkshire 1530–1546* (Oxford, 1970).

common law court records still have to offer the Stakhanovite scholar.

Another line of criticism might cavil at the plan of taking a single county for study. The pioneers in the field of local history made much of the concept of the county community; more recent work has reacted against this notion, pointing out that regions in England might be either greater than the county, form a genuinely coherent region within it, or straddle county boundaries for geographical or economic reasons.[2] Undoubtedly the arrangement of the public records has encouraged historians to focus on the county as a unit: the pioneering studies of Dr Rowse, Professor Everitt, Dr Barnes, and Dr Smith might without too much offence be said to have been shaped by the accounting practices of the twelfth-century Exchequer, with its constant reference to counties or groups of counties in its organization, and by the persistence of this phenomenon down to the record calendars of the nineteenth and twentieth centuries.

The aim of the first part of this study, therefore, is to examine Suffolk as a county unit. Was there any perceptible development in the notion of community within the county, and what were the greater and smaller units which provided alternative identities and structures of life for the people of the region? I contend that despite competition from these other identities, there was a sense of county identity already perceptible in the fifteenth century; this came into its own when the great noblemen of East Anglia departed the scene with the fall of the fourth Duke of Norfolk in 1572, and Suffolk became a relatively coherent and well-governed county, whose leading men had a common mind on how to conduct their affairs.

After the Reformation, this common mind would have to deal with choices as to what sort of religion to accept. Part Two of the work examines the way in which the robust Catholic piety of early Tudor Suffolk was transformed into well-entrenched Protestantism by the end of the sixteenth century: a Protestantism which did not exactly coincide with the wishes of central government. Relations between the centre and the county are the theme of Part Three: this charts the growth of a traditionalist-minded spirit of independence which was particularly difficult for the government to deal with once there were no leading peers to mediate the wishes of the Court to local men. Part

---

[2] Cf., e.g. A. M. Everitt, 'The County Community', in *The English Revolution, 1600–1660*, ed. E. W. Ives (1968) and Everitt, 'The Local Community and the English Civil War' (Historical Association Pamphlet G70, 1969), with C. Holmes, 'The County Community in Stuart Historiography', *Journal of British Studies* XIX (1980), pp. 54–73.

Four deals with a different sort of politics, turning from the gentry who are the main actors in the earlier sections of the book to the lesser sort. They had minds and ideas of their own, and they were capable of expressing themselves forcefully and often effectively. Sometimes, particularly in the period 1525–70, their expressions of discontent were violent enough to be labelled rebellion, particularly if the authorities mishandled the situation; later in the century, their energies might be released more peacefully through suits at law or through activism in religion.

To begin with, then, we set the scene by looking at the landscape both natural and man-made. This attempt at 'chorography' (to use the term invented by Tudor antiquaries) will enable us to assess the real identity of the community which lived in and around the great houses of Suffolk, and which gathered in its towns for market days and court days, festivals, and sermons.

PART I

WAS THERE A COUNTY COMMUNITY?

I

Alternative Communities

(a) Suffolk and Norfolk

IF the term 'East Anglia' means anything, it refers at least to the two counties of Suffolk and Norfolk. They form its heartland, the two divisions of the Anglo-Saxon kingdom, and their links are strong and obvious: even today, the two counties seem to have an external frontier of significance. In the early sixteenth century, the memory of the East Anglian kingdom was more alive than today because of the popular legend and cult of St Edmund, the king of East Anglia who had been martyred by the Danes in 870, and whose body was still honoured in one of Europe's most magnificent Romanesque pilgrimage churches at Bury St Edmunds. Edmund had once bid fair to maintain a position as England's patron saint against St George, and in the decoration of the churches being so assiduously beautified and extended throughout Norfolk and Suffolk into the 1530s, his image was still a favourite; his coat armour, or that of the great abbey which bore his name, shone down from stained glass or poked out from carving in stone or wood.[1] In the Tudor period there remained administrative links in the two counties, in the diocesan boundaries, and in the shrievalty. All important ecclesiastical cases and much routine administration had to be transacted with reference to the diocesan bureaucracy in Norwich.

Despite its decline from its high medieval estate, the shrievalty was still an essential link of central legal administration with the localities, quite apart from the traditional Crown revenues that it still accounted for. There was one good reason why the shrievalty stayed undivided, despite the great distances involved in administering it: the existence of the privileged ecclesiastical Liberties of St Audrey in the east and St Edmund in the west. With only the ten hundreds of the Geldable to interest him, the sheriff had a comparatively minor administrative task to undertake in pre-Dissolution Suffolk. In the fifteenth century, the East Anglian shrievalty had fluctuated between more or less total outsiders from the Court and henchmen of the Dukes of Norfolk,

---

[1] Cf., e.g. index reference to St Edmund in M. R. James, *Suffolk and Norfolk* (1950).

depending on the balance of local power and the desire and capacity of the Crown to put its own men in.[2] However, the last purely Court figure to be pricked as Sheriff of Norfolk and Suffolk was Humphrey Catesby in 1500—probably a reflection of the crisis which led to the final flight of the Earl of Suffolk in 1501. After that, the choice of genuinely East Anglian gentlemen seems to have reflected the Crown's confidence in the reliability of the three noblemen who successively dominated the region until 1546, the thirteenth Earl of Oxford and the second and third Dukes of Norfolk. During this period, the ratio of Norfolk to Suffolk men reflected the greater workload that the sheriff suffered in Norfolk: twenty-nine sheriffs were from Norfolk out of a total of forty-eight.

The shock of the breakdown of élite control in Kett's stirs of 1549 brought a tidying of the system; henceforth, sheriffs were chosen in strict alternation from either county, perhaps reflecting the greater potential role of the sheriff in Suffolk now that the Abbot of Bury's great liberty was in the hands of the Crown. Nevertheless, it may have still been because the sheriff's task was light in Suffolk that the East Anglian shrievalty was not included in the experiments in splitting up unwieldy shrievalties in the 1560s.

However, the inconvenience which this shrievalty involved for either a Suffolk or a Norfolk man remained manifest. The difficulties of administering county elections for two large counties at Parliament time in such widely-separated centres as Ipswich and Norwich must have been considerable, and the distances for general business were equally daunting: three different assize centres to get ready during the year, for instance.[3] Accordingly, when the Bill for continuing the experimental division of other English shrievalties was introduced into the 1571 Parliament, a 'Bill for the severance of Sheriffs in the Counties of Norfolke and Suffolke' was also introduced. The first Bill passed; the second was 'dashed, upon the Division of the House' on its third reading.[4]

Why did the House go to the length of a division and a rejection of this apparently logical and overdue measure? The answer may lie in the confused atmosphere in the two counties, with two insurrections

---

[2] Sayer, 'Norfolk Involvement in Dynastic Conflict', pp. 305–26, and Virgoe, 'Recovery of the Howards', p. 7.

[3] Dr Smith (*Bacon Papers* I, p. 301) suggests that before 1575 there was a deputy sheriff for the county in which the sheriff himself did not reside, but I have found no evidence for this.

[4] *CJ* I, pp. 89–90.

recently crushed and the fourth Duke of Norfolk still under house arrest—we shall see how two new boroughs managed to find their way into this Parliament from two different interests within Suffolk.[5] The question of a sensible size for the shrievalties may have become inextricably mixed with local faction and with the Duke of Norfolk's continuing struggle to maintain his position. Alternatively the rejection may have been a symptom of stubborn East Anglian conservatism, a witness to the tenacity of the links which joined the two counties. There is no record of a further severance Bill in the next Parliament, yet in November 1575 the shrievalty was finally split and the first two sheriffs for the two counties were picked. The new office of lord lieutenant continued to echo the old association by joining the two counties while the lieutenancy was in operation.

Administratively, then, Suffolk and Norfolk had strong traditional links; these links also existed in the intermarriage of their ruling élites. It was true that Norfolk men in search of a bride outside the county had little choice but to pass through Suffolk unless they wanted to brave the Fens to their west; true also that Suffolk could claim many links with the gentlemen of Essex, for county boundaries are not exclusive frontiers. Nevertheless, consideration of the sample of gentry marriages given in Appendix IV indicates that the Norfolk links were stronger than any other. The proportion of Suffolk gentry who found a bride in Norfolk was, indeed, larger than the proportion who crossed into or out of the Liberty of St Edmund within the county to find a partner, and it was also larger than the combined total of marriages across the borders of the neighbouring counties of Essex and Cambridgeshire. Dr Holmes demonstrates the way in which this Suffolk/Norfolk distinctiveness among the social élite persisted into the seventeenth century by considering the antiquity of East Anglian gentry of political eminence in 1642; 42 per cent of Norfolk and 30 per cent of Suffolk families could trace their roots in the county before 1485, in contrast to 15 per cent of those in Essex and 10 per cent of those in Hertfordshire.[6] As early as the fifteenth century there are traces of a perceived East Anglian identity among the gentry of the region: in 1419, a childless Norfolk knight, Sir Thomas Erpingham, gave a stained glass window to the Austin Friars in Norwich commemorating those lords and knights of Norfolk and Suffolk who

---

[5] Below, pp. 25–6. The representation of the two boroughs was challenged in the Commons (*CJ* I, p. 83).
[6] Holmes, p. 231.

had died without male issue between the coronations of Edward III and Henry V.[7]

In the same way, the evidence of 'intercommissioning' among that part of the élite who served as JPs indicates the greater degree of exchange between the justices of Suffolk and their Norfolk neighbours than with those of Essex, Cambridgeshire, or the Isle of Ely (see Table 1).[8] At no time was intercommissioning a common feature of the East Anglian benches, except in the case of Cambridgeshire and the Isle of Ely, miniature commissions which with their high degree of overlap in membership, were more like two halves of a single commission than separate counties. The table shows clearly how the number of justices sitting on one commission at a time declined in step with the number of East Anglian noblemen, who were generally appointed to several county commissions. In the first half of the century those outside the peerage who sat on more than one commission were either relatives or retainers of noblemen and bishops, or East Anglian residents who were also great lawyers or officers of state.

The decline in intercommissioning was least steep in Suffolk and Norfolk; indeed, if one further breaks down instances of inter-commissioning from 1558 to 1603, cases between Essex and Suffolk were largely confined to the first half of Elizabeth's reign; with Norfolk, they continued throughout the reign, and if anything, tended to become more common. The contrast between the totals of men sitting for both Suffolk and Norfolk and Suffolk and Essex is also striking. To underline this difference, one should note that the Norfolk and Essex commissions were of much the same size throughout most of the century, until the Essex Bench began swelling with commuters from the Court in the 1590s, and became almost twice the size of that in Norfolk.

The Benches of Cambridgeshire and the Isle of Ely were much smaller. The JPs who sat on both Suffolk and Cambridgeshire Benches up to 1558 included that great East Anglian magnate the thirteenth Earl of Oxford, the Bishops of Ely and two relatives of Bishop Goodrich, the lawyer Thomas Lucas and the diplomat and steward of Cambridge University, Sir Richard Wingfield. From 1558, the Suffolk JPs who also sat on the two smaller commissions included three members of the family of the Cambridgeshire noblemen the

---

[7] Richmond, p. 15 n.

[8] Throughout this book, discussion of the appointment and dismissal of justices of the peace is based on statistics in Appendices I and II, with the lists of sources given there.

Table 1. Cases of East Anglian intercommissioning 1500–1603

		1500–58	1558–1603	Total
Suffolk/Norfolk	A	36	21	57
	B	22	16	38
Suffolk/Essex	A	21	11	32
	B	11	5	16
Suffolk/Cambridgeshire	A	12	6	18
	B	4	4	8
Suffolk/Isle of Ely	A	—	6	6
	B	—	3	3
Norfolk/Essex	A	5	4	9
	B	3	1	4
Norfolk/Isle of Ely	A	—	2	2
	B	—	2	2
Cambridgeshire/Isle of Ely	A	—	17	17
	B	—	14	14
Cambridgeshire/Essex	A	3	0	3
	B	3	0	3
Suffolk/Norfolk/	A	5	0	5
Essex/Cambridgeshire	B	1	0	1
Suffolk/Essex	A	—	1	1
Cambridgeshire/Isle of Ely	B	—	0	0
Suffolk/Norfolk/	A	7	4	11
Essex	B	3	1	4
Suffolk/Norfolk/	A	3	1	4
Cambridgeshire	B	2	1	3
Suffolk/Norfolk/	A	—	1	1
Isle of Ely	B	—	1	1
Suffolk/Cambridgeshire/	A	—	2	2
Isle of Ely	B	—	1	1
Norfolk/Cambridgeshire/	A	—	1	1
Isle of Ely	B	—	1	1
Essex/Cambridgeshire/	A	—	1	1
Isle of Ely	B	—	1	1
Cambridgeshire/Norfolk/	A	—	1	1
Isle of Ely	B	—	1	1

Key
A = total number of cases occurring among resident JPs.
B = number of cases not including peers and bishops.
Connected statistics cannot be compiled for the Isle of Ely before 1564.

Lords North, and two local officials of the Crown and University. Instances of intercommissioning between East Anglian counties not involving Suffolk are insignificant. Moreover, it is particularly noticeable for the period 1558–1603 that the Norfolk and Suffolk justices tended to be active on both Benches at the same period, while the examples of intercommissioning with all other counties were on the whole honorary appointments or the results of changes of residence. The general picture to emerge is that with the eclipse of the Dukes of Norfolk and the Earls of Oxford, the decline in the East Anglian influence of the Earls of Sussex and the lessening of the temporal power of the Bishops of Norwich and Ely, the commissions of Norfolk and Suffolk were settling down to become a collection of leading gentlemen whose links with each other were strong and more routine than their contacts with their neighbours in Cambridgeshire, the Isle of Ely, and Essex. Many of them would give ample proof of this alliance in their skirmishing with bishops and with central government during Elizabeth's reign (below, Chs. 6 and 9).

The sense of community between Norfolk and Suffolk was not merely confined to the magisterial élite. One of its most striking manifestations came in the popular stirs of 1549. If one pieces together the scraps of evidence, it is clear that the outbreak of disturbances and the setting-up of a quadrilateral of camps within the two counties took place within a week, between 8 and 15 July; parallel disturbances in Cambridgeshire and Essex did not succeed in establishing camps. It is difficult to believe that such a rapid success, which brought normal government within the region to a standstill, was not achieved without some co-ordinated planning. The sporting competitions, markets, and fairs of Norfolk and Suffolk provided plenty of ordinary occasions on which folk met from far and wide; for instance, men from West Walton in the Norfolk fenland and from Belchamp in north Essex were doing business at the Suffolk fairs of Cowlinge and Woolpit in 1519, while a gentleman's farm on the Wash at Hunstanton was buying its Northern steers at the cattle fair at Hoxne in Suffolk in 1538.[9] It is worth noting that butchers were among the known leadership in three out of the four centres of the Norfolk and Suffolk stirs: butchers were men who might travel long distances and make varied contacts in pursuit of their trade. It is only the sudden shafts of light provided by such exceptional events as the drama of summer 1549 which illuminate patterns of

⁹ PRO, C1/563/35; Gurney, 'Household Accounts', p. 552.

everyday behaviour and assumption otherwise only partially and gradually recoverable.[10]

A community of interest and acquaintance, or frequently and just as importantly, a community of clashes of interest and personal quarrels, gave Norfolk and Suffolk a distinctive quality among their neighbours. Repeatedly we will return to this theme, and note the way in which the affairs of the two counties became entangled.

(b) The county and its internal boundaries

This Country delighting in a continuall evenes and plainnes is void of any great hills, high mountaines, or steep rocks, notwithstanding the which it is nott always so low, or flatt, butt that in every place, it is severed and devided with little hills easy for ascent, and pleasant ryvers watering the low valleys, with a most beautiful prospect which ministreth unto the inhabitants a full choyce of pleasant situations for their seemly houses.

When in the last years of Elizabeth's reign, Robert Ryece began his description of Suffolk with a survey of the county's rivers, he was displaying a sound understanding of his homeland.[11] In default of any more imposing natural features, rivers have defined Suffolk's external boundaries with remarkable permanence from the early Saxon settlement to the present day: the Little Ouse and the Waveney to the north, the Stour in the south. In the east, the sea provides an absolute, if occasionally a mobile, frontier: only in the west are there no natural features to mark off the county, yet even here the variations in the county border have amounted to a handful of miles only, over ten or more centuries.

Within the county the rivers are equally important. The typical Suffolk landscape is one of gentle undulation, of water-cut valleys. The Roman communication system tended to avoid the lines of the watercourse system; later settlers both capitulated to the valleys and conquered them, and the settlements which dominated tenth-, sixteenth-, and twentieth-century Suffolk were connected largely by valley-bottom roads whose seasonal foulness Ryece somewhat cynically

[10] MacCulloch, 'Kett's Rebellion', p. 52 and *passim*: cf. below, Ch. 6.
[11] Ryece, pp. 7, 25. The anonymous Chorographer of Norfolk and Suffolk also gave high priority to his description of the counties' rivers: *Chorography* pp. 20–2, and *Chorography of Norfolk*, p. 68. Scarfe's work is an invaluable modern survey of the county's topography. On the Chorographies, see A. H. Smith and D. MacCulloch, 'The Authorship of the Chorographies of Norfolk and Suffolk', *NA* XXXVI (1977), pp. 327–41.

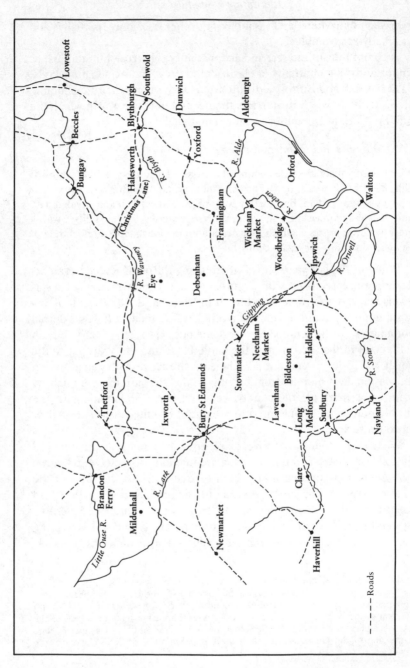

I. Suffolk: rivers, roads, and towns

Lowestoft

Southwold

Blythburgh

Dunwich

Beccles

Halesworth

Yoxford

Aldeburgh

Bungay

(Christmas Lane)

R. Blyth

R. Alde

Orford

Walton

R. Debben

Framlingham

Wickham Market

Woodbridge

R. Waveney

Eye

Debenham

Ipswich

R. Orwell

Thetford

Stowmarket

R. Gipping

Needham Market

Hadleigh

Bildeston

R. Stour

Ixworth

Bury St Edmunds

Lavenham

Long Melford

Sudbury

Nayland

Little Ouse R.

Brandon Ferry

Mildenhall

R. Lark

Clare

Newmarket

Haverhill

– – – – Roads

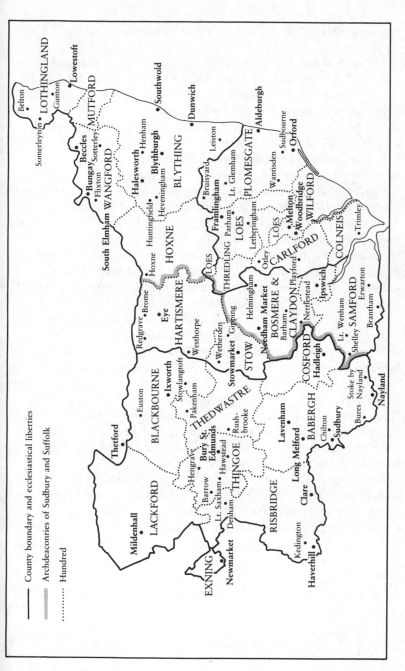

II. Suffolk: boundaries 1500–1600

— County boundary and ecclesiastical liberties
▨ Archdeaconries of Sudbury and Suffolk
········ Hundred

LOTHINGLAND
Belton
Somerleyton
Gunton
Lowestoft

MUTFORD
Beccles
Bungay
Flixton
Sotterley
WANGFORD
South Elmham

Lowestoft

Halesworth
Henham
Blythburgh
Southwold
Dunwich

Huntingfield
Heveningham
HOXNE
Hoxne
BLYTHING

Bruisyard
Leiston
Framlingham
Lt. Glemham
PLOMESGATE
Aldeburgh
Sudbourne
Orford
Wantisden

Redgrave
Brome
Eye
HARTISMERE
Westhorpe
Wetherden
Westthorpe

LOES
THREDLING
Parham
Letheringham
LOES
Otley
CARLFORD
Melton
Woodbridge
WILFORD
COLNEIS
Trimley

Thetford
Euston
BLACKBOURNE
Ixworth
Stowlangtoft
Pakenham

Gipping
Stowmarket
STOW
Needham Market
Helmingham
BOSMERE &
CLAYDON
Barham
Playford
Nettlestead
Ipswich
SAMFORD
Erwarton
Brantham

Mildenhall
LACKFORD
Hengrave
Barrow
Bury St. Edmunds
Rush-
brooke
THEDWASTRE
Hawstead
Lt. Saxham
Denham
THINGOE

Lavenham
COSFORD
Hadleigh
Lt. Wenham
Shelley
Stoke by Nayland
Nayland

Newmarket
EXNING
RISBRIDGE
Clare
Long Melford
BABERGH
Chilton
Sudbury
Bures

Kedington
Haverhill

regarded as one of the county's best insurances against foreign invasion.[12]

All these rivers take their source in 'the Woodlande and High Suffolck', that expanse of heavy soils which occupies most of the county: 'wood–pasture' country, in Dr Thirsk's phrase.[13] The name 'High Suffolck' applies to the eastern part of the region, but it has always been so vaguely used in the county that it seems best to stick to the alternative and less misleading title of 'Woodland'. It is the Woodland that produces the 'typical Suffolk landscape', but there are other natural divisions in the county. The heavy soils are flanked by 'sheep–corn' country, two areas of lighter, sandy soils, suitable for sheep, professionally-managed coney-warrens or the cultivation of corn, and only transformed in modern times by the introduction of sugar-beet. One area, known as the Sandlings, stretches along the entire coast from the River Orwell in the south through to Lothingland in the north: heathland widely devastated by the dust-bowl effect of prehistoric agriculture, whose Tudor inhabitants otherwise turned their interests from agriculture to the sea. At the other end of the county is the Fielding, another area of heathland, sheepcourses, and warrens, from Bury St Edmunds and Newmarket up to Thetford, part of the great circle of Breckland stretching deep into Norfolk, and still liable to disastrous sandstorms in its most barren areas at the end of the seventeenth century.[14] To complete the county picture, the very north-west corner of the county beyond these light soils is a limb of the Fens mainly comprising the monster parishes of Mildenhall and Lakenheath; while the coast from Landguard Point up to the River Alde at Aldeburgh was still fringed by undrained marsh in the sixteenth century.

The county was therefore dominated by a farming area which should have given rise to a classic wood–pasture economy; the two sheep–corn areas described above make up only a quarter of the county's land, and in any case, the Sandlings were not a corn-growing area of significance. The county's leaders frankly recognized that their wealth lay in dairy-farming and that their corn supply needed supplementing from the neighbouring 'great corne countreys' of Norfolk and Cambridgeshire. In Norfolk, the sheep-corn country

[12] Ryece, p. 14.
[13] Thirsk, pp. 41–9; the description above is from *Chorography* p. 20.
[14] White, p. 559.

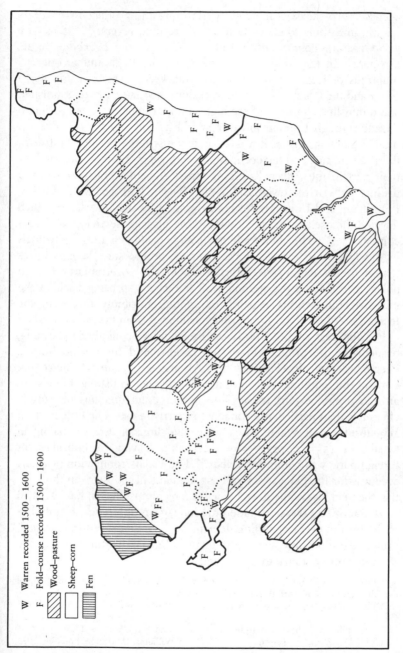

III. Suffolk: soil-types—distribution of fold-courses and warrens

W   Warren recorded 1500 – 1600
F   Fold-course recorded 1500 – 1600

Wood–pasture
Sheep–corn
Fen

occupied two-thirds of the county's farming and produced most of its wealth; in Suffolk, the situation was more than reversed.[15] It was the wood–pasture country of Suffolk which was the backbone of its prosperity. In the south of the county, in the large and prosperous hundreds of Cosford and Babergh, and stretching down into north Essex and the Colchester–Maldon region, the manufacture of finished and unfinished cloth was of the highest importance, tying the region to a trade through London to the rest of England and abroad. Even in these regions, however, it was a patchily distributed trade; the lists in the 1524 subsidy and the occupations of those in the area pardoned for their part in the Amicable Grant furore the following year reveal a distinct pattern of towns and large villages like the Waldingfields, Lavenham, and Long Melford, surrounded by smaller villages which devoted themselves purely to agriculture, perhaps servicing the larger communities.[16] The cloth trade made huge profits for a few individuals in the first two decades of the century, and despite serious crises thanks to the extraneous interference of the government's foreign policy, it remained prosperous until the 1620s, proving itself in the mid-sixteenth century capable of enough flexibility to accept the techniques of the 'New Draperies' introduced from the Netherlands.[17]

For the rest of the wood–pasture country, commercial farming, particularly the production of the famous and formidable Suffolk cheese, was well-developed by the early sixteenth century. The coastal ports of the Sandlings were not merely engaged in fishing, but also in an agricultural export trade. The monumental qualities of Suffolk cheese made it particularly suitable for garrison use. The little ports of Woodbridge and Walberswick were vital links in the victualling of Calais; in 1551/2, practically every ship leaving Woodbridge for foreign parts was bound for Calais.[18] The Calais connection probably accounts for the persistence of East Anglians in the garrison there, so that the final loss of the town comes to look almost like an East Anglian conspiracy. The disaster made little long-term difference to Suffolk's trade, for the ever-expanding demands of London saved the farmers' profits: so not only cloth production but agriculture linked the wood–pasture country to the capital.

[15] PRO, SP 14/128/65; A. H. Smith and D. N. J. MacCulloch, 'The Authorship of the Chorographies of Norfolk and Suffolk', *NA* XXXVI (1977), p. 333.

[16] PRO, KB 29/157, mm. 5–6; Woods, 'The Rioting Crowd', pp. 15–16, and below, Ch. 6.

[17] J. E. Pilgrim, 'The Cloth Industry in Essex and Suffolk 1558–1640' (Univ. of London MA, 1939), pp. 17–59.   [18] Williams, 'Maritime Trade', p. 130.

However, the whole picture is more complex than a contrast between two areas differentiated by soil-type and land-use. To begin with, it was important that the county's boundaries to south and north were rivers: frontiers, but also lines of communication and trade, with a string of market towns along them—Clare, Sudbury, and Nayland on the Stour, Thetford, Bungay, Beccles, and Great Yarmouth on the Waveney. In a similar way, Suffolk's western border boasted Newmarket, a typical example of a market town owing its existence to its position straddling a county boundary, with all the advantages of a confusion of jurisdictions that this provided.[19] All these markets had hinterlands which embraced two counties. Particularly significant was Sudbury, the only real rival to Bury St Edmunds as a town in the west of the county, whose market served the wood–pasture country of north Essex as well as south-east Suffolk; Great Yarmouth provided a unifying force for the valleys of the Waveney and Yare, uniting them into a single market area with the Norfolk Broadland. Thetford served the whole Breckland area. Such regions might blur the sense of distinction between one county and the next, but there were also further divisions within the county itself. The landscape of Tudor Suffolk was as man-made as it was natural. On the landscape were superimposed four different patterns of administration, all of venerable antiquity by the sixteenth century: the Anglo-Saxon county divisions, the feudal liberties, the chartered boroughs, and the structures of the diocese of Norwich. None of these coincided, and none of them coincided with the soil-types. All would have a claim to shape the lives of the county's people.

Until the reorganization of 1974, Suffolk had never been an administrative unit; in the sixteenth century it was divided into three, two of these divisions having been in the hands of great Benedictine monasteries since the Anglo-Saxon period. The smaller of the two, the Liberty of St Audrey, may also have been the older: it consisted of the five-and-a-half hundreds in the south-east corner of the county which in the seventh century had formed the Wicklaw, one of the heartlands of the East Anglian kingdom, and which had possibly been given by the king's daughter Etheldreda herself to her frontier foundation at Ely. The monks of Ely were far away, and their actual estates as opposed to their jurisdiction in the area were not substantial. They seem to have been absentee landlords; the local monastery of Butley, five lesser

---

[19] P. May, *Newmarket Medieval and Tudor* (Newmarket, 1982).

monasteries, and the nunneries of Bruisyard and Campsey were probably more significant religious houses to local people, while throughout the Middle Ages a series of secular magnates had been active in the Liberty: the Earls of Suffolk and the Lords Willoughby. Although the new Dean and Chapter of Ely were regranted St Audrey's Liberty when Henry VIII dissolved the Cathedral Priory, they continued the pattern of absenteeism: their leading officials in the Liberty before and after the regrant of 1541 were servants of the Duke of Norfolk, as one might expect, since the great Howard castle of Framlingham stood in St Audrey. Throughout the rest of the century, the stewardship was in the hands of a resident local notable.[20] The 'capital' of the Liberty by the reign of Elizabeth was the little estuary port of Woodbridge, with its bustling trade in dairy produce and grain. With the building of a Shirehouse at Woodbridge in 1578, the town had supplanted the former centre in the nearby village of Melton, although Melton Gaol continued in use for some time longer (see Plate 4b).

In the west were the eight-and-a-half hundreds which only in 1974 surrendered their separate existence as West Suffolk: the Liberty of St Edmund. Even in 1974 the amalgamation was not uncontested, while the previous attempt of tidy-minded outsiders to achieve the same result in 1882 had met with such opposition that the proposal had been abandoned.[21] More than a thousand years of separate identity were involved: the Liberty was probably a venerable administrative unit when Edward the Confessor's mother presented it to the expanding Benedictine abbey of Bury St Edmunds, and unlike the county as a whole, it was a unit of remarkable coherence. Its capital was geographically and economically unmistakable; the west Suffolk road system converges in a star pattern on Bury, a town laid out on a broad valley side, watered by a navigable stream. The monks did their formidable best to maintain and improve this coherence; they excluded all but the most insignificant of rival monasteries and markets and kept

[20] The Duke's servant John Sone of Wantisden was bailiff of St Audrey in 1540 (PRO, C244/177/39). His steward Robert Holdich held the hundreds of the Liberty when they were regranted in 1541 (*LP* XVI, no. 1226/12). Stewards under Mary and Elizabeth were successively Sir Robert Wingfield of Letheringham and his relative Thomas Seckford the younger of Woodbridge and Ipswich.

[21] J. H. Whitfield, 'The Evolution of Local Government Authorities and Areas in Suffolk 1555–1894' (Univ. of Kent MA, 1970), p. 147. By the sixteenth century there were in fact only seven-and-a-half hundreds, but Babergh was still reckoned as two hundreds and kept two separate hundred courts (PRO, E134/20 James I/Easter 3).

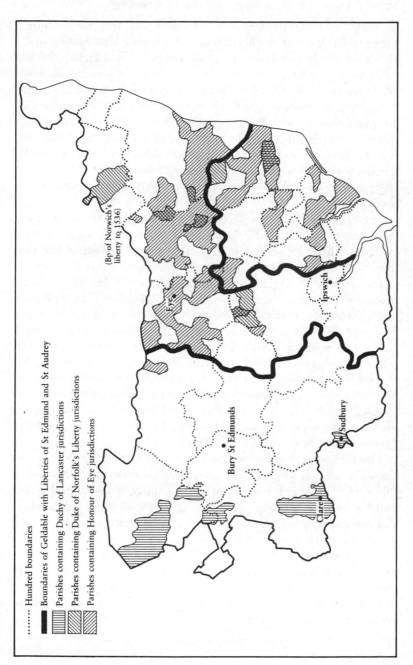

Hundred boundaries

Boundaries of Geldable with Liberties of St Edmund and St Audrey

Parishes containing Duchy of Lancaster jurisdictions

Parishes containing Duke of Norfolk's Liberty jurisdictions

Parishes containing Honour of Eye jurisdictions

(Bp of Norwich's liberty to. 1536)

Eye

Ipswich

Bury St Edmunds

Sudbury

Clare

IV. Suffolk: the ecclesiastical and feudal liberties

all early medieval noblemen, with their penchant for nurturing alternative liberties, to the borders of their domain. With his seat in the House of Lords and his wide estates outside the Liberty, the late medieval Abbot of Bury was a person of great consequence; his disappearance left Bury suddenly 'provincial',[22] the abbey ruins dominating the town as negatively as the Abbots had once done with positive authority. Administratively, the Liberty and the Crown lessees who replaced the Abbot as Steward were shadows of the old regime. Nevertheless, the caucus of local gentry who were to take up the threads of the Abbot's old authority as the Liberty's JPs in Elizabeth's reign were to show themselves as strong-willed as any of their mitred predecessors.

The remaining ten hundreds in the centre and north-east of the county were known as the Geldable, a name which suggests their character as the remnant left over from the ecclesiastical liberties; these were the only hundreds from which the Crown had been able to extract geld, or in which the sheriff could exercise his full authority before the dissolution of the monasteries. The east of the county thus had a double geographical incoherence when compared with the west; it was split between the Geldable and the Liberty of St Audrey, and it lacked a conveniently placed 'capital'. Ipswich, by far the largest town of the area, was sited in the extreme south-east of the county, and the major road to Norfolk from the south passed on a route fringing the Sandlings which went through Ipswich, Woodbridge, Blythburgh, and Beccles, but which ignored the coastal towns and other significant market towns of the area such as Stowmarket, Framlingham, Eye, and Bungay, in the heart of the Woodland.

These ancient divisions of the county had been taken over as the Crown developed its system of administration through the justices of the peace in the later middle ages; after all, the divisions formed a good practical basis for splitting up the county. By the mid-fifteenth century, and probably much earlier, the justices had adopted an adjournment system for quarter sessions.[23] Each quarter they met for one or two days each in four different centres; the total number of days grew with the growth of sessions business as the sixteenth century wore on. By Ryece's time, the schedule was standardized: on the Monday the JPs started at either Beccles on the Norfolk border or Blythburgh on the coast with sessions for the northern and coastal hundreds of the

---

[22] The adjective is Norman Scarfe's: Scarfe, p. 155.
[23] Cf. John Hopton's part in it in 1464: Richmond, p. 49.

Geldable; on Wednesday they met at Woodbridge for St Audrey, on Friday at Ipswich for the southern and western Geldable hundreds, and after a Sunday rest, at Bury St Edmunds for the Liberty of St Edmund on the Monday.[24] Hardly any justices attempted to follow the whole of this marathon circuit, with results that will be discussed below (see pp. 35–42).

The ancient divisions were also useful for fiscal purposes; they were subdivided for the collection of fifteenths and tenths and subsidies with little variation from collection to collection. For local taxes, an increasingly frequent phenomenon in the Tudor age, there was a customary division of the county whereby the Geldable paid half, St Audrey one-sixth and St Edmund a third; this reflected and was presumably based on the proportion of parishes in each division, a calculation within the capacities even of Tudor administrators.[25] The leading gentlemen of St Edmund referred to this division as 'comendable custome' when engaged in delicate negotiations over ship money in 1596.[26] It was a comment characteristic of the antiquarian constitutionalism displayed by the men who dominated East Anglian politics at this time, and it conveniently ignored the fact that the 'custome' underestimated both the acreage of St Edmund and the proportion of the county's gentry who lived in the Liberty: both around 40 per cent of the whole. Some of that acreage, admittedly, was barren heath and drowned fen, but commercial sheep farming and fen drainage were both reinforcing the Liberty's prosperity by the mid-sixteenth century.

Despite Ipswich's geographical inconvenience at the south-east of the county, Ryece noted without comment that it was 'the County towne', on the grounds of long prescription rather than because of the vigorous Tudor prosperity which had made it a suitable candidate for schemes to site a new Antwerp-style international mart.[27] It was here that county elections always took place. However, the assizes 'in respect of the conveniency of the judges circuitt from Cambridg to Suffolk and Norfolk' were normally held at Bury, occasionally at Newmarket. Less convenient for the assize judges up to the dissolution of Bury Abbey was the fact that the Abbot emphasized his dominance in Bury by excluding the assizes and forcing them to meet on

---

[24] Ryece, p. 83. Before the Dissolution, the JPs at Bury had met at Henhow, like the assize judges (e.g. PRO, KB 9/533, m. 239, 31 May 1535), but they also moved into Bury to sit at the Angel Inn later on (BL Eger. 1693, fo. 92ᵛ).
[25] Committee Book, fo. 1ʳ.　　　　　　　　　　[26] BL Add. 34564, fo. 16.
[27] Ryece, p. 87; PRO, SP 12/88/22, and cf. *PSIA* VII (1891), pp. 288–98.

heathland a mile outside the town, first at Great Barton and later by an ancient burial mound called Henhow at a place which came to be known as 'the gret felde' or Shirehouse Heath.[28] This strange variety of legal garden fête can hardly have been a particularly attractive prospect for litigants and justices at the Lent assizes at least, but once the Dissolution had marked the successful storming of the ancient monastic liberties, the assizes were able to move into more comfortable surroundings in the town itself. Easterners still chafed at the distance involved in going to Bury. In 1616 Sir Lionel Tollemache, an east Suffolk knight who was Sheriff that year, secured a royal letter to the justices of assize recommending that Ipswich should become the assize town, but it was no doubt his absurd claim of 'the equall distance thereof from all places of the said countie' that ensured that this proposal was never adopted.[29]

The relatively simple pattern of Anglo-Saxon administration was complicated by the later feudal liberties centred on the castle of Norman magnates. Some, like the mid-Suffolk honour of Haughley, had lacked late medieval nourishment and for all practical purposes had faded from the scene, but three were sustained by great noblemen or the Crown into the Tudor period: the Honours of Eye and Clare and the Liberty of the Duke of Norfolk. The Honour of Eye had jurisdiction over seventy-two townships, virtually all in east Suffolk, but scattered rather incoherently through the coastal Sandlings and High Suffolk; indeed, it has been suggested that the rather puzzling adjective 'High' derives from the title of the Honour, and therefore indicates that area of the Woodlands in the north central part of the county around Eye.[30] The Honour's association with the Earls and Dukes of Suffolk survived the extinction of the De Uffords in the fourteenth century and the disgrace of the De la Poles in the reign of Henry VII, and it was granted to Charles Brandon in 1515 after Henry VIII had created him Duke of Suffolk. When the King dismantled Brandon's East Anglian power once more in 1537–8, Eye went back to the Crown, and apart from a partial life grant to Anne of Cleves, stayed in royal hands for the rest of the Tudor period.

The Honour of Clare had extensive estates in Essex and significant

---

[28] PRO, E134/20 James I/Easter 3, deposition of John Mallowes; PRO, SP 1/131/149 (*LP* XIII pt. i, no. 838). The Bury quarter sessions also met at Henhow from 1469, when the Abbot reaffirmed his exclusion of them from the town (HMC XIV pt. viii, p. 139).

[29] Committee Book, introductory folios (unfoliated).

[30] HMC X pt. iv (Eye), pp. 513–16.

property in the south of the Liberty of St Edmund built up by the De Clare family and confirmed to them in the thirteenth century in the face of strenuous opposition from Bury Abbey. In 1460 the Honour came to Edward IV through the female line, and it was perhaps this origin which prompted successive kings to make life grants of the Honour to various female members of the royal family, including Katherine of Aragon and her daughter Mary, Anne Boleyn, and Katherine Parr. It was Mary as Queen who in a curious piece of neo-feudalism brought the practice to an end by annexing the Honour, including the borough of Sudbury, to the Duchy of Lancaster, together with miscellaneous Suffolk manors, the most important of which was the manor of Mildenhall: Sudbury began returning members to Parliament in 1559.[31]

The final complication to the feudal picture was another medieval liberty created as late as 1468, that of the Duke of Norfolk, fifteen of whose 139 parishes spilled over the Norfolk border into Suffolk. They included the ancient castle of the Earls of Norfolk at Bungay, but excluded their even more significant estate at Framlingham Castle and the property which the Howards had brought to the ducal title around Stoke by Nayland in the Stour Valley.

Scattered as islands of privilege across the Suffolk landscape were the chartered boroughs, widely differing in their significance and development of status. There were only three parliamentary boroughs in the earlier part of the century: Ipswich, Orford, and Dunwich. 'Had Ipswich (the onely eye of this Shire) beene as fortunate in her surname, as she is blessed with commerce and buildings, shee might well have borne the title of a Citie; neither ranked in the lowest row.'[32] Very different were the other two, Orford and Dunwich. Both were coastal towns in continuous decay through the century: the debris which the sea swept away from the heart of Dunwich was deposited in front of Orford, ruining its harbour.

Two further boroughs besides the Duchy of Lancaster borough of Sudbury achieved Parliamentary representation during Elizabeth's reign: Aldeburgh and Eye. Aldeburgh was another coastal town, but one whose rising fortunes contrasted with the decline of Orford and Dunwich. Aldeburgh had been the property of the small and undistinguished Benedictine priory at Snape, suppressed by Cardinal Wolsey in 1525, and it seems to have come into its own when it was

[31] *CPR Philip and Mary* IV, p. 50; PRO, DL 1/190/S9, and see below, Ch. 5.
[32] Weever, p. 750.

acquired by the Dukes of Norfolk: particularly the fourth Howard Duke, who both here and at Great Yarmouth showed a vigorous interest in the commercial development of ports within his sphere of influence. The Duke procured the removal of the lucrative customs house for the lesser coastal towns from Orford to Aldeburgh in 1565, and in 1568 he obtained a charter for a new market: the final step, although obtained only in the time of the Duke's disgrace and on the eve of his final destruction, was the parliamentary enfranchisement of the borough in 1571.[33] Naturally, even at this critical point in the Howard fortunes, the first two MPs for the borough were ducal nominees. The Duke's execution in 1572 did not affect Aldeburgh's prosperity; later in the century it specialized in very substantial ships for the Iceland trade, boasting more ships of over 100 tons than Ipswich, Bristol, Southampton or Hull in 1582.[34] Parliamentary patronage was taken over by the Exchequer along with control of the Howard estates, until the family's lawyers regained the borough along with much else in legal action in time for the 1588 election (below, Ch. 8).

Eye was a less obvious candidate for parliamentary enfranchisement: a borough near the Norfolk border given a certain traditional prestige through its Honour, but owing more in 1571 to the fact that it was dominated by the Lord Keeper of the Great Seal, Sir Nicholas Bacon. Bacon spent the 1550s rebuilding the Abbot of Bury's lodge at nearby Redgrave as his main East Anglian base, and no doubt appreciated the value of a new pocket parliamentary borough as much as did the Duke of Norfolk at Aldeburgh in the turbulent political atmosphere of 1569–71; the Bacons continued to dominate borough elections into the seventeenth century.

There were lesser corporations without burgesses of Parliament. The little coastal borough of Southwold had somehow achieved its own commission of gaol delivery, and was unique in Suffolk in that its incorporation had been achieved by Act of Parliament, in 1488/9, as one episode in its long-drawn-out conflict with its dying neighbour of Dunwich.[35] Hadleigh, always a substantial market town, benefited from deliberate discrimination in favour of its market at the expense of

[33] PRO, SP 46/33, fo. 254ʳ; *CPR Eliz.* IV, no. 1183; *History of Parliament 1558–1603* I, p. 246. On Yarmouth, Smith, pp. 28–30. All subsequent details of parliamentary representation and constituencies are corroborated by the *History of Parliament* volumes unless otherwise stated.
[34] Williams, 'Maritime Trade', p. 254.
[35] *CPR Henry VII* I, p. 300; II, p. 429.

neighbouring Bildeston through its leading JP, Sir Henry Doyle, in the reign of Mary; however, it had to wait until 1618 to gain a full charter.[36] Beccles spent half a century fighting the resident gentry family of Rede in order to establish its corporate rights to its extensive common land, once Henry VIII had removed its monastic overlords from Bury (below, Ch. 11). The oddest of all the non-parliamentary boroughs was Bury St Edmunds. Despite its long history and its central position in the Liberty of St Edmund, the town was kept totally subordinate by the great abbey which had given it its distinctive grid-plan in the twelfth century. As a result it had its own commissions of the peace and gaol delivery without any corporation at all, and the townsfolk's toils to obtain a full charter lasted for more than sixty years from the dissolution of the Abbey (below, Ch. 11).

The tangled structure of county secular government, which even divided the county town, the sheriff's administrative centre, from the assize town, was made no more coherent by the diocesan divisions. Suffolk had not been a separate diocese since the early Saxon period; in the sixteenth century it merely formed the two most southerly Archdeaconries of the diocese of Norwich: Sudbury and Suffolk. These ignored secular boundaries, for Sudbury covered not only the Liberty of St Edmund but also a fringe of Cambridgeshire and that considerable part of north central Suffolk included in the Deaneries of Stow and Hartismere. During the medieval period the problems of administering the diocese, not least the problems of how to cope with the claims of the Abbey of Bury, had been so great that the Archdeacon of Sudbury had come to assume an unusual degree of autonomy within his jurisdiction; in the Elizabethan and early Stuart period, for instance, he was the only Archdeacon in eastern England issuing schoolmasters' licences in a quasi-episcopal manner, and his court was much more of a competitor with the diocesan court than was its fellow in the Archdeaconry of Suffolk.[37] Perhaps this development would have been curtailed if Henry VIII had acted to save Bury Abbey and remodel it as a Cathedral of the New Foundation; but Bury never made it past the shortlist. Henry VIII gave Suffolk a suffragan bishop of Ipswich in 1536, Thomas Manning, Prior of Butley, but he had no successors.

[36] *Chorography* p. 30; MacCulloch, 'Power, Privilege and the County Community', p. 301.

[37] D. A. Cressy, 'Education and Literacy in London and East Anglia 1580–1700' (Univ. of Cambridge Ph.D., 1972), p. 60; R. A. Marchant, *The Church under the Law* (Cambridge, 1969), p. 30.

(c) The impact of internal boundaries

What, then, was the effect on the rhythm of life in Suffolk of these various divisions: agricultural, Saxon, feudal, urban, diocesan? Consider first the agricultural divisions, and the contrast between wood–pasture and sheep–corn. The dominant Woodland area did indeed exhibit many of the characteristics which one would expect. Its landscape was one of non-nucleated villages, with scattered hamlets and farmhouses. Enclosure of the open fields was far advanced, enclosure disputes of the classic Midlands type being virtually unknown in the sixteenth century. For this reason, the manorial system was in steep decline except as a framework for regulating the descent of land; communal organization centred far more round the supervision of village commons, which since Suffolk rarely let arable land lie fallow or used harvested arable for grazing, formed an essential part of a village's economy.[38] Most parishes contained several manors, and of the two it was the parish which was the authentic unit of everyday life. The testimony of probate inventories and of contemporary commentators like Sir Thomas Wilson or the anonymous author of the *Chorography of Suffolk* is that the Woodland was the area of greatest prosperity within the county; its population was more dense than that of the sheep–corn areas, and if anything, the contrast in density grew during the century.[39] The prosperity of the Woodland attracted gentlemen; they were spread more densely through the Woodland than through either sheep–corn region. It was often difficult to find a resident gentleman of sufficient standing or legal expertise to be named in the commission of the peace in the Fielding hundreds of Lackford and Blackbourne or the Sandlings hundreds of Colneis, Wilford and Mutford.

The Fielding and the Sandlings provided a contrast of nucleated villages where a manorial system still dominated agriculture: and both sheep–corn areas exhibited that peculiar system of Norfolk and Suffolk sheep-farming, the fold-course, a system virtually unknown in the Woodland (see Map III). The fold-course was an exclusive right belonging usually to the lord of a manor to pasture a specified number of sheep over a particular area of land; that land might belong to the lord himself, but it might equally belong to someone else. In such a

---

[38] Evans, 'South Elmham', p. 73.
[39] *PSIA* XXXIV (1979), p. 183; T. Wilson, 'The State of England, Anno Dom. 1600', *Camden Miscellany* XVI (CS 3rd Ser. LII, 1936), p. 12; *Chorography* pp. 19–20; J. Patten, 'Population distribution in Norfolk and Suffolk during the sixteenth and seventeenth centuries', *Transactions of the Institute of British Geographers* LXV (1975), p. 58.

situation, enclosures would be an issue, but in precisely the opposite way to counties where the fold-course custom did not exist. Here, the tenant's instinct would be to enclose his land for cattle or for his own corn, since he was prohibited from keeping sheep; the manorial lord's instinct would be to oppose enclosure to preserve the fold-course. Two such disputes, from opposite ends of the county at Westley and Leiston, became mixed up in the great popular stirs of 1549, while several other similar disputes occupied the attention of the central courts throughout the century from both Fielding and Sandlings.[40]

Dominant though it was, the Woodland lacked sufficient unity to form the basis of a single society undergirding the county's community. To begin with, its fertility made its agricultural possibilities so great that it was not a homogeneous area. Ryece testified that in his day it was dominated by cattle-rearing in the east, corn-growing in the centre and sheep in the more open country towards the Fielding around Bury, but everywhere it was fruitful enough to make a living from any combination of the three. The contemporary Chorographer of Suffolk laid more stress on the exceptional quality of the pasture from 'oxen and kine' and the 'wonderful goodnes' of the butter and cheese made.[41]

A further remark of the Chorographer underlines the difference within the Woodland itself; he described the eastern part, High Suffolk, as containing 'very many yeomen of good credit and great liberalitie, good housekeepers', the implication being that this was a peculiarity of the eastern area. The only attempt so far to demonstrate this high density of yeomen in the sixteenth-century eastern Woodland is unfortunately based on distorted evidence, but an impressionistic confirmation of the general picture comes from the one surviving list of Tudor freeholders in the Geldable, taken in 1561.[42] From this list, certain parishes stand out as having a higher than average number of freeholders for their size, notably Wortham, Redgrave, Laxfield, and Fressingfield, all in the eastern Woodland hundreds of Hartismere and

---

[40] MacCulloch, 'Kett's Rebellion', pp. 54–5. For other cases, cf. PRO, REQ 3/33, complaint of John Bacon (Drinkstone, 1564); PRO, C2 ELIZ R3/60 (Burgh Castle, 1589); Somerville, p. 308 (Methwold, Norfolk, 1532).

[41] Ryece, p. 29; *Chorography* p. 19.

[42] BL Lansd. 5/7. Evans, 'South Elmham', p. 62, tabulates the differing distribution of yeomen in the Suffolk hundreds, but she works from the evidence of wills in the Consistory Court of Norwich only, ignoring the relative strength of the Consistory Court of the Archdeaconry of Sudbury compared with that of the Archdeaconry of Suffolk, and her picture must be incomplete, being thus weighted towards yeomen in the east of the county.

Hoxne. This is not to say that such men 'froze out' the gentry in their area; throughout the sixteenth century, this region contained many gentlemen of esquire or knightly status, while as the century proceeded, more and more yeomen would be regarded as joining the ranks of the minor gentry. Nevertheless, as we will see (below, Ch. 11), the presence of a self-confident yeoman class, well aware of its 'good credit' and used to the multifarious tasks of minor administration, meant that political life and participation in local government was not a monopoly of the gentry, particularly in the eastern Woodland. It was no coincidence that this area had a vigorous and widespread commitment to the reformed faith, apparently linking up with pre-Reformation Lollardy (below, Ch. 5).

Other features make the eastern and western divisions of the Woodland distinctive, while doing little to elucidate the distinction. Why, for instance, was the manorial custom of Borough English, or inheritance by the youngest son, so concentrated in the manors of the eastern Woodland and so uncommon in the west? Even more puzzlingly, why was the instability of surnames and the habitual use of aliases by certain families right up to the level of armigerous gentry so localized within the eastern Woodland? In the west and south of the county, the peculiarity was found mainly in towns and was probably the result of immigration; neither was it especially common in the Sandlings (see Map V). These are frail scraps from larger patterns of life, but they serve to indicate that the Woodland was not a coherent region in Suffolk and did not serve to unify it. How, then, did the various forms of administrative division already described affect the county? What reality did they have, and did they provide real alternatives to the county as a source of identity?

Probably least influential were the feudal liberties. While the Honour of Eye still served a resident Duke of Suffolk, as it did for a quarter of a century under Charles Brandon, there would be a substance to the Honour which would be lacking once it reverted to the Crown, and merely supplemented the ordinary jurisdiction of the sheriff. 'The Shreyffes turne . . . within the honor of Aye' continued to meet in a circuit of six different centres not only to decide on manorial cases but to deliberate on minor offences like failing to wear a hat in church: behaving, as indeed it ought to, as a superior leet court.[43]

What Eye lacked to give its Honour continuing life was access to a

[43] Iveagh 73/2, William Spurdaunce to Sir Thomas Cornwallis; PRO, STAC 5 C.49/12, interrogatories, description of a case in the tourn, 1574.

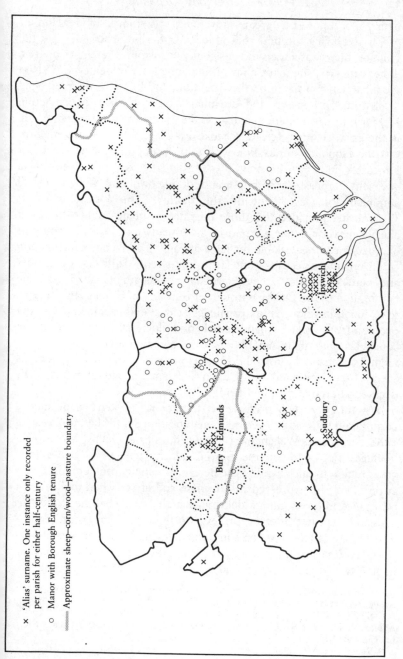

× 'Alias' surname. One instance only recorded
    per parish for either half-century

○ Manor with Borough English tenure

—— Approximate sheep-corn/wood-pasture boundary

Bury St Edmunds

Sudbury

Ipswich

V. Suffolk: 'alias' surnames and Borough English tenure—distribution

figure of real power. A greater advantage was enjoyed by the Honour of Clare. During the time that Queen Katherine of Aragon held the Honour, there was always the possibility of soliciting her active interest in her property; she made a favourable long lease of demesne lands to the inhabitants of Clare on their petition, and in 1526 she intervened to obstruct Bishop Nix and Cardinal Wolsey when their competing zeal for reform threatened to disturb the evenly strife-torn tenor of life in the great chantry college at Stoke-by-Clare.[44] Even more effective was the Honour's annexation with other properties to the Duchy of Lancaster in 1557–8; now these estates were appendages of a powerful corporation with a mind of its own and with a central administration based outside the county. The Duchy court at Westminster provided, for those litigants fortunate enough to owe it allegiance, yet another weapon in the already formidable armoury of alternative courts available for legal actions. The Duchy's jurisdiction could provide an escape-route from the sheriff's officers for debtors and petty criminals; it could provide a sympathetic hearing to the corporation of the Duchy borough of Sudbury in its constant struggle to maintain its mid-century privileges against encroachment, or to the people of the great Fenland parish of Mildenhall in their recurrent squabbles with their neighbours over common rights. The Duchy might be a channel for royal favour, as when in 1596 the Clare tenants successfully petitioned the Crown for material aid to repair their decayed church and ruined bridges.[45]

In return for such preferential treatment, the tenants of such a corporation were still expected to act corporately. In the crisis year of 1588, Sir Francis Walsingham, Chancellor of the Duchy, wrote to Sir Nicholas Bacon to tell the Suffolk Duchy tenants to give a joint contribution to raise cavalry, the perennial military problem for Tudor government; he expressed his surprise and anger when told of their reluctance to do so, and added menacingly 'theie shall finde mee (as occasion shall heerafter be proferd) to think of them accordingly'.[46] The Duchy had more success in influencing parliamentary elections at Sudbury. It probably did not even consult the borough when returning its first two MPs in 1559, but after that, it was not until 1593 that Sir

[44] *CPR Philip and Mary* II, p. 145; Jessopp, *Visitations*, p. 228, and cf. below, p. 152. Jessopp's interpretation of the affair is not to be trusted.
[45] Sudbury: PRO, DL 1/105/S6, DL 1/103/B32, DL 1/137/S10, DL 1/150/F7. Mildenhall: DL 1/73/S2, DL 1/109/A20, DL 1/113/P1, DL 1/204/N7. Clare: PRO, C2 ELIZ B5/58.
[46] Redgr. 4150A.

John Fortescue, then Chancellor of the Exchequer, decided to exact some return for the undoubted advantages that association with the Duchy conveyed on the town by nominating his son William Fortescue, a stranger to Sudbury, as second burgess for the town.[47] This cavalier disregard for Sudbury's *amour-propre* undoubtedly caused resentment, particularly since it involved the town in extra expense: the town accounts record with irritation the expenditure of 13s. 8d. because 'wee were drevne to send a letter of attorny to sware our other Burgges at London, apoynted by Sir John Fortescue'.[48] In 1597 the interference was repeated when John Clapham, an old servant of Lord Burghley, was nominated, with the son of an old friend of the town taking the other seat. A local gentleman, Thomas Blagg, claimed that he had been elected by the townsfolk, but he could not prevail against the Chancellor of the Duchy, Robert Cecil, who supported his father's servant up to the hilt. It is probably a significant indication of the passions that this disputed election aroused that the pages in the borough minute book relating to the business of 1597 have been torn out.[49]

The Crown tenants of lands administered by the Exchequer enjoyed the same rights of access to a special court in Westminster, and in return they could be expected to provide a bloc of votes like the blocs which many county gentlemen used in county elections. When surveying the scene before the 1572 election, Lord Keeper Bacon told his son Nicholas that the Crown Receiver and Surveyor, an old family friend, 'myght do sumwhat with the Esch. tenantes' for his candidature for Knight of the Shire.[50] Similarly, the Duke of Norfolk's Liberty had a life of its own; its tenants could look to the Duke's Council, an active body of lawyers and administrators which could tackle a serious dispute like that which polarized the Duke's town of Bungay in the second decade of the century.[51] The Duke's bailiffs had similar powers of returning writs and taking fines as the officers in the older liberties, and while there was a Duke of Norfolk, his immediate authority was

[47] *History of Parliament 1558–1603* I, p. 250.
[48] SROB, EE 501/3, fo. 161ʳ.
[49] Ibid. fos. 222, 224, 225 have been removed. The dispute is described in PRO, STAC 5 B31/3, Answer, interrogatories *ex parte* Thomas Eden and deposition of John Skinner. On Clapham, cf. A. G. R. Smith, *Servant of the Cecils. The Life of Sir Michael Hickes* (1977), pp. 31, 35, 42–3.
[50] Redgr. 4118.
[51] PRO, STAC 2/5/161, and cf. the buck provided for the Council, BL Add. Roll 17745, m. 7.

more impressive than, for instance, that of an absentee Dean and Chapter in St Audrey's Liberty.

Nevertheless, these were fading forces in the county. The Duchy and the Exchequer lands were not significant or coherent enough to form a power bloc in the county; the Norfolk Liberty was not extensive enough either, and in any case it was in the hands of the Exchequer or of family trustees after 1572. No piece of administrative apparatus was allowed to fade away: all provided official posts of one sort or another for the omnivorously occupied Tudor gentry and yeomanry. The leets and even the hundred courts continued to operate within the county beyond the end of the century. Yet real administrative power had passed elsewhere, to the justices of the peace and the assize judges. A sign of this was the usurpation from the leets by the JPs of the appointment of high constables to the hundreds, a process which proceeded piecemeal and with a certain amount of acrimony through Elizabeth's reign, but which was made official in a county meeting in 1615.[52] Only an exceptional situation, such as the sudden development of the great expanses of former waste fen at Mildenhall and the consequent need to find some corporate administration to deal with it, could give the leet any continuing significance and emotional resonance traceable in surviving literary evidence (below, Ch. 11). Otherwise quarter sessions and assizes would be the basis of county life by the end of the century.

This new ascendancy of the justices paradoxically gave continued life to one of the most ancient of the county's divisions, the great ecclesiastical Liberty of St Edmund. The antiquity and the geographical rationality of the Liberty have already been emphasized. Bury St Edmunds was not merely a natural capital of the Liberty because of geography and the transport system; it was also an attractive centre for the gentry. Politically, in contrast with Ipswich, it was open to domination by gentlemen because it had no form of chartered corporation; socially, only half a century after the death of Elizabeth, an antiquary noted that 'many of the Gentry buy or hire houses in Bury because of the pleasantnesse of the place'. This was no new development; in 1591, some Suffolk influence at Court procured a special licence for one Roger Wright to maintain 'one Tennys play, and one garden, with Bowling Alleyes, for the honest recreation of gentlemen' in Bury.[53]

---

[52] Committee Book, fo. 21ᵛ; MacCulloch, 'Power, Privilege and the County Community', p. 20.   [53] BL Add. 15520, fo. 70ʳ; PRO, SO 3/1, s.v. July 1591.

With such an agreeable centre, the Liberty was a viable focus indeed for local loyalties. To the east, the 'old ditch called the Franchise Bank', whose formidable remains survive in part today, served to divide the people of west from east Suffolk and to remind them of the venerable character of the division.[54] The Abbots of Bury had prided themselves on their thorough administration, claiming that their Liberty 'was noted and holden the most notable franchise of good rule in the land'.[55] Much of the glory of the Liberty departed with them, but the Franchise retained something of its old mystique, quite apart from its continued administrative independence of the sheriff in the serving of writs; as late as 1601, Henry Warner could write to the Abbots' successor, the lessee of the Liberty, Sir Nicholas Bacon, to 'send to your hundreds to be ther' at Ipswich to back the candidature of Sir Henry Glemham for Parliament.[56] Unlike the Liberty of St Audrey, that of St Edmund retained a separate grand jury at the assizes into the nineteenth century.[57]

Quite apart from the continued momentum of the Franchise's administration, was the effect that its existence and character had on the newer administrative structure of the sessions of the peace. The adjournment system by which the Suffolk Bench met in four different areas for each session has already been described; in theory every Suffolk JP could have attended sessions in all four areas. In practice few ever did. In the absence of extant records from Tudor sessions in the county, it is impossible to give detailed statistical evidence of JPs' movements for the period, but one can give a general picture by the use of two surviving sources. First, the sheriffs' claims for allowances on the Pipe Rolls give the number of days' wages for which the JPs who were not also peers or servants of the Crown were claiming. Using the attendance figures listed in these claims, it is possible to compare the attendance record of JPs resident in the Liberty of St Edmund with those resident outside it. Taking a ten-year sample of the attendances of all JPs resident in the county from 1537 to 1546, and averaging out average annual attendances of the west Suffolk and the east Suffolk JPs separately, one arrives at an average annual attendance at quarter sessions of 1.7 days for a JP within the Liberty and of 2.76 days for the JPs living in the east of the county. The Henrician attendance claims

---

[54] The name occurs on an estate map of the Wetherden/Elmswell/Woolpit area, belonging to Lord Stafford and reproduced in Scarfe, p. 195; the map was probably made in connection with a Requests suit of the 1590s (PRO, REQ 2/42/48).
[55] Bodl. MS Charters Suff. a. 1, 134, qu. Lobel, p. 115.   [56] Redgr. 4171.
[57] Cf. PRO, E134/20 James I/Easter 3, interrogatories, with Dugdale, IV, p. 272.

are not as systematically recorded as one would wish, but a sample of the more orderly Elizabethan returns, from 1578 to 1587, gives the same picture: 1.8 days in the west and 3.2 in the east. Why was a JP in east Suffolk almost twice as likely to attend quarter sessions as a JP in the west? It was not that he was disposed to be more conscientious in the performance of his duties; the evidence suggests that the leading justices of west Suffolk, in the Elizabethan period at least, had an unusually high conception of their duties as local magistrates. The difference was that east Suffolk justices were likely to attend quarter sessions in more than one of its eastern locations, while JPs in the Liberty habitually only attended their own sessions at Bury.

The few surviving records of which JPs attended which sessions, preserved among the estreats of fines at the sessions sent into the Exchequer, tend to bear out this conclusion. Four returns survive intact for the period, for 1551, 1560, 1564, and 1592, plus a fragment for 1507.[58] In 1507, only two of the sixteen justices recorded attended quarter sessions in both east and west, and one of them was the veteran lawyer Sir James Hobart, who was probably *custos rotulorum*. Out of the forty-three residents in 1551, no JP crossed the Franchise Bank in either direction; in 1560 only the assiduous new *custos*, Sir Clement Higham, and a couple of his west Suffolk neighbours, Sir Ambrose Jermyn and Robert Gurdon, did so, out of a total of thirty-one resident JPs. In 1564, for some reason best known to themselves, six out of twenty-six justices attended sessions in both east and west, and two, Laurence Meres (later to be an active member of the Council of the North)[59] and the lawyer Francis Nunn, achieved the highly unusual distinction of attending sessions in all its four county locations. Can the threat of the Privy Council's national purge of this year have produced this exceptional flurry of activity? In 1592 the picture was similar to the earlier returns; out of forty-three justices, only William Forth of Hadleigh ventured away from his home within St Edmund to attend sessions in the north-east of the county, no doubt while in transit to his second home at Raveningham, just over the Norfolk border from Beccles sessions.[60]

The estreats of fines also indicate that the other monastic liberty,

  [58] PRO, E137/42/4, E137/69 (unsorted material). Comparison between this material and the attendances listed on the Pipe Roll indicates that the Pipe Roll figures are accurate.
  [59] *History of Parliament 1558–1603* III, p. 43.
  [60] Forth probably married a Keen of Starston, Norfolk (Muskett, I, p. 119) and was described as of Raveningham in 1596 (PRO, REQ 2/56/24).

that of St Audrey, was not so exclusive as St Edmund in the composition of its Bench, even though its ancient administration continued to function in much the same way. Its Lords, after all, had always been the absentee monks, later the canons, of Ely, hardly such potent figures in Suffolk politics as the monks of Bury; St Audrey's Liberty was smaller and lacked the natural coherence of St Edmund, while its meeting-places for sessions, Woodbridge and Melton, were a mere eight miles' ride at most from the next sessions town and county capital of Ipswich. It is hardly surprising, then, that all five years in the estreats reveal east Suffolk justices who sat at both the Geldable sessions and in St Audrey, mostly St Audrey justices who were enjoying a day out in Ipswich: four in 1507, six in 1551, five in 1560, eight in the strenuous year of 1564 and three in 1592. Rather fewer JPs attempted the journey from the south of Suffolk to the northern sessions at either Beccles or Blythburgh, nor did many from the north travel south, despite the fact that Ipswich and the northern sessions were both held for parts of the Geldable, and occasionally both dealt with the same townships:[61] none in 1551, three in 1560, nine in 1564, but none in 1592. Indeed, if the latter year was typical of developments in Elizabeth's reign, then the whole Bench was settling down to a normal pattern of attending sessions in one area only; only four men out of forty-three attended sessions in more than one area during that year. This supposition is made more plausible by an odd feature of the Pipe Roll claims for 1600–1 and 1601–2; all the JPs listed as claiming wages came from east Suffolk. Whatever happened to the JPs and the sessions for St Edmund during those years, the *en bloc* omission on a geographical basis only, suggests that the Bury quarter sessions were becoming confined solely to JPs resident in the west.

All this rather complex juggling with figures indicates that the old exclusiveness of the Liberty of St Edmund was perpetuated in late Tudor administration, while for much of the century at least, the sessions system of the remainder of the county was still much more flexible; the area of the Geldable and St Audrey lacked the coherence which nature, early Anglo-Saxon monarchs, and the monks of the High Middle Ages had done so much to create in the west. The unified system of the commission of the peace was in effect a fiction as far as the quarter sessions were concerned, although the county's

[61] For example, PRO, E137/42/4; the October sessions at Ipswich in 1592 dealt with a Bungay case; the January sessions at Blythburgh and Ipswich both dealt with men from Westleton.

commission continued to meet together at the biannual assizes at Bury. The government appears to have been aware of this characteristic of the Suffolk Bench; otherwise it is difficult to account for the fact that from the 1520s until the very end of Elizabeth's reign, the Suffolk commission was consistently larger than the Bench in Norfolk, although Norfolk was the larger county. Norfolk did not operate an adjournment system, but moved the entire business of each session to various towns in rotation, with justices tending to follow the sessions; hence numbers on the Bench did not need to be as large as in Suffolk.[62]

The division between east and west was not merely a matter of history and of administrative practice; if anything, the division in the quarter sessions was a reflection of the fact that the Benches of east and west tended to be staffed by two distinct family structures. Because of the propensity of Tudor gentlemen to go a long way to find a good marriage, it is difficult to illustrate these structures with precision; however, the sample of gentry marriages for the period given in Appendix IV shows how separate the two halves were. Both halves of the county tended to contract about half their marriages within their own area; the rather larger percentage for the east than for the west, 54 per cent as opposed to 44 per cent, may be because there were more gentry available for local marriages in the eastern half of the county. However, each half regarded the other as no more significant than the neighbouring counties, Essex and Norfolk, when seeking a wife. No sense of a unified county community governed the choice of a bride; the view north and south was as important as the view east or west. Moreover, west Suffolk, bounded to the north by Breckland, a great expanse of barren heathland, and to the west by the Fens and the rather restricted gentry community of Cambridgeshire, tended to look south to Essex, while the east of the county was more interested in Suffolk's traditional links northwards with Norfolk.

It is also likely that the ruling 'establishment' of Elizabethan west Suffolk boasted a higher proportion of radical Protestants than east after a generation of older gentry had died off. Certainly leading west Suffolk men like Sir Robert Jermyn, Sir John Higham and Sir Edward Lewkenor were influential and outspoken patrons and supporters of Puritan ministers. An indication of this comes from the list of sixty-four Suffolk ministers who were resolved not to subscribe to

---

[62] Cf. Smith, pp. 89–90. I am indebted to Dr Victor Morgan for drawing my attention to the significance of this difference.

Archbishop Whitgift's Visitation Articles of 1584; of the forty-seven who can be traced as beneficed, twenty-nine were based within the Liberty, despite its smaller number of parishes, and seventeen in the rest of the county.[63] It is also noticeable that practically none of the group beneficed in east Suffolk held benefices in the Sandlings area or in the centre and north-east of High Suffolk. By and large, it was the local gentry who were the patrons of these clerics, often as lay impropriators, and it is likely that the distribution of uncompromising radical clergy is a reflection of the views of their patrons.

Further evidence of this comes from the distribution of charitable foundations in Suffolk. One of the convincing points to emerge from the relentless superlatives of Professor W. K. Jordan's work on the charitable institutions of early modern England, is that there was a strong correlation between the growth of institutionalized secular charities and the spread of radical Protestantism among the charitably inclined.[64] The distribution of such charities in Suffolk reflects the concentration of Puritanism among the élite of the western half of the county in Elizabeth's reign. Under Gilbert's Act of 1782 relating to charitable institutions and the Poor Law, a Commission of Enquiry listed all institutionalized benefactions surviving at that time.[65] If one takes the foundations recorded for the period 1558–1603 or with named benefactors likely to have given in this period, then the concentration within the Liberty of St Edmund is very striking. Although it is impossible to be precise as to date in cases where only a donor's name is given, the eight-and-a-half hundreds of the Liberty boasted seventy-one or more benefactors during the period, while the remaining fifteen-and-a-half hundreds had only thirty-four. Even as the impulse to institutional charity developed, and the number of benefactions in east Suffolk increased, the picture is not greatly altered; if one considers the late Elizabethan charitable donors who made their benefactions in the period 1603–1640, the figure for the Liberty of St Edmund is sixty-five, and that for the rest of the county, fifty-two. During the period 1558–1640, eight Elizabethan JPs left money for the foundations in the Liberty, and only five in the rest of

[63] *Seconde Parte* I, pp. 243–4. Cf. the discussion of clergy-gentry links in Collinson, *Religion of Protestants*, Ch. 4.
[64] Cf., e.g. W. K. Jordan, *Philanthropy in England, 1480–1660* (1959), pp. 159–239, on the literature of exhortation to charity, and pp. 281–2, 311–14.
[65] *Abstract of the Returns of Charitable Donations . . . 1786–1788* (Parliamentary Blue Book XVI, 1816).

the county, a virtual reversal of the proportion of resident justices in east and west.[66]

Did the sense of difference between east and west emerge in conscious attitudes to produce a sense of locality for each area? Certainly the cohesiveness of the Liberty of St Edmund resulted in its mid- and late-Elizabethan leadership forming firm and concerted lines of policy, as was instanced by the disputes over the repair of Christmas Lane and the collection of ship money in the last two decades of the reign (below, Ch. 9). The leading members of the Liberty's élite had a strong sense of corporate identity. In his will of 1614, the veteran Puritan magnate Sir Robert Jermyn bequeathed

> to my loving freindes, Sir Nicholas Bacon, Knight and Baronet, Sir Robert Gardiner Knight, Sir John Higham Knight, to every one of them one gould rynge with suche a devise and posey conteyned in yt as I shall hereafter set downe in token of my true love to them, hartelie praying them that as we have lyved together in sweete and christian societie and by oure unitie have muche furthered the peace and profitt of our countrye in the administracion of justice and other publicke dutyes, so they wilbe pleased to accept of this my last request, that they will maynteyne the same to the uttermost of theire power.[67]

All these men had been leading figures in the Liberty since the middle of Elizabeth's reign. Death had already snatched away a number of Sir Robert's erstwhile colleagues on the Bury Bench; otherwise such men as Robert Ashfield, Sir William Spring or one of the Cloptons might have been recipients of his memento of their years of friendly partnership.

Sir Nicholas Bacon, named first in Jermyn's list of his friends, had long been on the periphery of his chosen associates at Bury because his father the Lord Keeper had chosen to build his capital mansion just outside the Liberty. Clearly he felt the need to be more closely involved in the affairs of the Liberty; in 1585, at the end of the first great county furore which drew the west Suffolk leaders together in their opposition to Bishop Freke (below, Ch. 6), he bought Culford Hall, a brisk half-hour's ride from Bury St Edmunds, 'bestowed great cost' on rebuilding it, and gradually shifted the focus of his activities

---

[66] West: Sir Henry North, Sir Robert Jermyn, Sir Robert Gardiner, Sir William Cordell, Sir Thomas Kitson, Sir Nicholas Bacon the younger, and Edward Buckenham. East: Sir Nicholas Bacon the elder, James Rivett, Thomas Seckford the younger, and Sir Michael Stanhope. I am grateful to Mrs Nesta Evans for letting me know of a fifth, Sir John Tasburgh, as recorded in SROI, HA 12/C2/42.

[67] Pr. *Rushbrook Registers* p. 153.

there from Redgrave.[68] At the same time his efforts in 1586 to get the area round Redgrave included in the Liberty for administrative purposes provoked a storm of indignation from its traditionally-minded residents, who particularly resented being asked to contribute to the rebuilding of the Liberty's Bridewell. Tempers rose high; the leader of the opposition, a minor local gentleman, was reported as saying that Sir Nicholas was as good a justice as any hanged by the highways, while Sir Nicholas, with a remarkably elastic view of geography, claimed that Redgrave was less than half its actual distance from Bury St Edmunds.[69] His attempt does not appear to have met with success.

The difference between east and west, accentuated by the notoriously 'verye fowle and uncomfortable' roads of central Suffolk,[70] became of importance when it led to differences of opinion. In Sussex a similar cleavage had developed between the ruling élites of east and west, so that the Privy Council saw fit to reprimand the Sussex county leadership in 1584 for the lack of opportunities for 'generall conference and resolucion' that their arrangements provided, particularly after a muster certificate had been delayed as the muster commissioners argued by means of messages and letters.[71]

Although there is no similar extant letter of reproof to the leaders of Suffolk, the consequences of the division were the same. During July 1569, when peasant unrest in the county was at its height and was about to break into open rebellion, the seven muster commissioners were squabbling about where they should meet to discuss letters from the Privy Council. The commissioners from the Liberty of St Edmund wanted to meet at Stowmarket, a central point for the county just over the border of the Liberty inside the Geldable; the commissioners from the east refused, claiming that Needham Market was 'the most aptest place and best agreing with the nerest dwellynges of the moste comysshoners'.[72] The fact that the two towns under dispute were less than four miles apart along the Gipping Valley road shows that the disagreement was a symbolic rather than a rational one. At the end of August Sir Robert Wingfield wrote once more to the western commissioners, explaining with a candour that can hardly have proved

---

[68] PRO, C66/1278, m. 2; BL Add. 15520, fo. 72ʳ.
[69] PRO, STAC 5 B19/37, Answer and Replication.   [70] *Chorography* p. 19.
[71] BL Harl. 703, fo. 16, qu. Fletcher, pp. 134–5; Fletcher wrongly describes the division in Sussex administration as 'unique'.
[72] BL Harl. 286, fo. 2ʳ.

disarming, why the last combined meeting arranged as a compromise at Needham had been abortive: 'conceyve no other opinion in the slaknes of our metinge then forgettinge the tyme appoynted'. In the same letter he asked the westerners to send 'one of discretion unto us to fetche our bookes and also . . . make relation unto yo of our doinge', precisely the procedure for which the Privy Council were to reprimand the gentry of Sussex in 1584.[73]

Such squabbles between east and west continued into the seventeenth century despite the growing practice of meeting at Stowmarket, and they might easily resolve themselves into questions of principle; thus in 1589 when the deputy lieutenants in the west took a hostile line to the collection of money under special patent for the repair of Christmas Lane, the deputies in the east went on with the collection.[74] It is difficult to document the sense of difference between east and west below the level of the gentry, yet the furore of 1586 already described over Bacon's proposal to include Redgrave in St Edmund shows that sense was real enough; the various peculiarities of social structure in the eastern Woodland, such as the retention of Borough English manorial tenure and the persistence of 'alias' surnames, also testify to the fact that the Franchise Bank separated distinct societies. Yet people outside the magisterial class might not be so tied to the rhythms of the movement of the sessions as their social superiors; their lives might be more influenced by the catchment areas of the markets which lay outside the system of the five sessions towns. Two of East Anglia's great popular disturbances in the period once more illustrate everyday patterns of life and show how this might operate. In the successful near-rebellion over the levying of the Amicable Grant in 1525, the Suffolk protestors of Cosford and Babergh lobbied the people of north Essex when they came to Sudbury 'which is in Suffolk and is their market towne';[75] here was a market area also comprising the clothing production area, which transcended the county boundary and the division between east and west. Similarly, in the stirs of 1549, the people of north-east Suffolk round Beccles and Bungay, part of the Broadland market area of Great Yarmouth, took part in the gathering at Norwich on Mousehold Heath, rather than contributing to the main east Suffolk camp which assembled successively at the east Suffolk sessions towns of Ipswich and Melton.[76]

    [73] Ibid., fo. 12^r.   [74] See below, Ch. 9.
    [75] PRO, SP 1/34, fo. 192^r (*LP* IV pt. i, no. 1321).
    [76] MacCulloch, 'Kett's Rebellion', pp. 43, 46, 51.

These incidents are a further reminder that there was a world of county political involvement outside the relatively decorous transactions of the magisterial élite. Such involvement is glimpsed on the one hand in these recurrent outbreaks of popular unrest throughout the century, but it is most continuously seen in the day-to-day life of the chartered boroughs. All the ten boroughs already described could claim a degree of autonomy within the county structure, but their freedom of action differed widely.

As Suffolk's greatest borough, Ipswich represented one extreme of freedom from interference by outsiders. The two bailiffs who headed its administration were chosen from a tight little group of wealthy merchant families who tended to establish firm roots in the town; between 1485 and 1603, for the years when the bailiffs are traceable, 83 individuals drawn from 67 families filled 220 places; six families provided two individuals to be bailiffs during the period, and a further five provided three. Virtually none of the sixteenth-century bailiffs came from gentry families in the county, and despite the considerable wealth that many of them accumulated, very few of them chose to forsake the town and use their money to become county gentry.[77]

Throughout most of the sixteenth century, the town avoided the sort of uncomfortable association with a powerful outsider which (through the Duke of Norfolk's henchman Sir John Howard) had forced it into the Yorkist camp in the previous century;[78] neither Charles Brandon nor successive Howard Dukes of Norfolk attempted to exercise undue influence in Ipswich. When the corporation did turn to a great nobleman at the end of the century, it was as a deliberate gesture of independence against the leaders of the county: in 1590 it elected Henry, Lord Hunsdon as High Steward.[79] Hunsdon was Lord Lieutenant of Norfolk and Suffolk, but this hot-tempered military man was something of a contrast with Ipswich's previous High Steward, that judicious Puritan statesman Sir Francis Walsingham. The corporation's leaders cannot have been unaware that Hunsdon's relations with the Puritan magnates who had come to dominate East Anglian life were usually delicate and occasionally stormy. Hunsdon's death in July 1596 in the middle of a prolonged and bitter squabble between Ipswich and the leaders of west Suffolk over the financing of

---

[77] Most of the bailiffs will be found listed in Bacon, *passim*, on their election.
[78] W. I. Haward, 'Gilbert Debenham', *History* XIII (1929), pp. 308–11; Crawford, 'John Howard', p. 88.
[79] Bacon, p. 363.

ships in the Cadiz expedition led to another attempt to enlist an outsider among the peerage for the town against their gentry opponents; their new choice of a High Steward was the Earl of Essex, hero of the very expedition which had caused the dispute (below, Ch. 9).

Nevertheless, this return to an association with the nobility was a voluntary decision of the corporation, taken as an expedient in the troubles of the 1590s. In mid-century the town's leaders had sufficient independence of mind to stick to the borough's oft-reiterated rules on recommendations to borough office and to ignore commendatory letters from both the Duke of Norfolk and Lord Keeper Bacon in choosing a new Town Clerk in 1562.[80] In January 1566, at a time when it was particularly sensitive to infringements of its rights, the borough denied the Sheriff of Norfolk and Suffolk the use of the Town Hall for the county quarter sessions to demonstrate its annoyance at his officer's infringement of the borough's liberty of arrest.[81]

Few towns would be able to take such an independent line as Ipswich in their dealings with the county leaders. They lacked Ipswich's economic muscle, and they were therefore at a disadvantage in their relations with the gentlemen who were resident near or in the midst of every community. Right from the medieval period, Bury St Edmunds had a host of local great men who seemed to anticipate the town's Georgian function as the centre of a local 'season', not to mention its Abbot; Sudbury had the Waldegraves, the Edens, and the Cranes and Fortescues, Hadleigh the Doyles, the Tilneys, and the Forths, Orford the Willoughbys, the Sones, the Forths, and the Wingfields, Dunwich the Jennys, the Rouses, and the Wingfields, Beccles the Redes, the Brends, and the Colbys, Eye the Cornwallises and the Bacons: a formidable massing of coat armour, and one that might well be increased if some other gentleman decided that he too had some interest in a town with which to concern himself. Even Ipswich generally boasted a person of quality in its midst, although they tended to be newcomers to the county or younger sons who had made good, for there was no custom of town houses for the 'county' in this community of merchants and sailors. Early in the century, for instance, there was the Imperial count Lord Curzon and the successful

[80] SROI, HD 36/2672/33, 2781/124, both recommending Thomas Tose. John Hawes was in fact chosen (Bacon, pp. 265–6). For fifteenth-century regulation on this matter, see *History* XIII (1929), p. 308.

[81] Bacon, p. 271.

lawyer Sir Humphrey Wingfield; later the newly-wealthy Withipoll family, the career Crown servant, Edward Grimston, and another hard-working lawyer, Thomas Seckford the younger. At the end of the century Sir Philip Parker was exceptional as a county gentleman who rented Seckford's town house;[82] while Lord Wentworth's mansion at Nettlestead was within the sound of the church bells of Ipswich. The general theme of relations with these gentlemen was harmony. Admittedly, if any gentleman threatened the established liberties or the ambitions of a corporation, then the corporation would not hesitate to challenge them in litigation. Such legal conflicts were a recurrent feature of life in Suffolk particularly after the upheaval of the Dissolution, as we shall see (below, Ch. 11); boroughs could be both remarkably persistent and remarkably successful in them, even if they took half a century to achieve their results, as at Bungay, Beccles, and Orford. Nevertheless it would be unrealistic now, and it would have seemed sheer folly then, to assume that friction based on class and economic antagonism formed the norm of relations between boroughs and the county. For one thing, when conflict with a gentleman did occur, it would be highly advantageous for a borough to turn to other gentlemen for help in the struggle: at Beccles, for instance, the favourable intervention of county JPs was probably crucial for the townsfolk who opposed William Rede, also a Suffolk JP, in the 1580s. One could multiply examples of the acknowledgement of such good relations, from the spectacular feasting when the Duke of Norfolk was made free of Norwich's Guild of St George in 1563 to the sugar-loaf which Sudbury gave old Lady Paulet in 1592 in grateful if rather ungrammatical remembrance 'of hur favours toward our pore peepell as allsoo for that hir good knight Sir Edward Waldegrave who holpe us to our charter frome Queen Marye'.[83]

One useful index of this cultivation of mutual interest is to be found in an analysis of those elected by boroughs to Parliament (Appendix V). There is no doubt that boroughs were keenly interested in Parliament, which might provide them with an outside arbiter in disputes which could not be solved within the county. Orford Haven, for instance, was the subject of repeated legislation on the banning of stallboats for fishing and the use of a certain size of net, beginning in 1489; the competing interests of fishermen and of sailors in the coastal

[82] PCC 4 Rutland (will of Thomas Seckford).
[83] Norwich: Smith, p. 26, and NRO City Muniments case 18, shelf B, fo. 110. Sudbury: SROB, EE 501/3, fo. 161ʳ; cf. below, Ch. 11.

communities clashed bitterly for a century before an Act was finally passed in 1589, after much parliamentary discussion, which satisfied all parties concerned.[84] At Sudbury we can see how the town kept an eye on Parliament, in 1571 buying a copy of what its accounts describe as 'a bill that was enteryd against Corporacyons' and in 1584 conferring with its legal counsel 'for matters to preferr into the Parliament Howse'.[85]

The trouble with Parliament was that it was expensive to maintain burgesses there. Sir John Neale discussed the financial problems which might face a small borough unless it saved itself the charge of an MPs wages by electing a gentleman who was prepared to forgo his wage claims in return for a parliamentary seat; he cited the case of Dunwich to prove his point, without mentioning the Chancery suit which the town brought in indignation against its impecunious although resident MP Sir Edmund Rous, after he had reneged on his promise not to demand his wages for the second Parliament of 1554; there they bluntly stated that such a claim would be 'to the greate losse and damage of all the inhabitantes of the said towne'.[86]

Sympathetic representation in Parliament from a local gentleman would therefore be of mutual advantage. After all, three boroughs had secured their first representation in the sixteenth century through great men of the realm: Orford through Lord Willoughby,[87] Eye through Lord Keeper Bacon, and Aldeburgh through the Duke of Norfolk; everyone would correctly assume that the principle of 'Founder's kin' would operate in these cases. The ideal for a borough would be a local gentleman who also had some office at Westminster at Court or in the law; not merely would he be useful in the comparatively short periods for which Parliament sat, but with luck he would go on acting in the interests of his former seat for much longer.

The results of this alliance of borough and gentry are seen in Appendix V. Comparing the percentages of 'real' burgesses attending Parliament earlier and later in the century, it is clear that their numbers were dwindling, and that they must have often felt awkward

---

[84] *Stat. Realm* II, p. 544; D'Ewes, pp. 364, 393, 395, 403, 412–13, 424, 431–2, 438, 441; HLRO, 31 Eliz. 17.

[85] SROB, EE 501/1, fo. 109ʳ; EE 501/3, fo. 11ʳ.

[86] Neale, *Commons*, p. 155; PRO, C3/56/91. Rous in fact claimed in error for the 1553 Parliament, but the claim fits only the Parliament of 1554 for which we know he sat (I am grateful to members of the History of Parliament Trust for our discussions on this point).

[87] *History of Parliament 1509–58* I, p. 192.

outsiders in the gentlemen's club which was developing in the Commons; certainly, the gentlemen diarists seldom noticed such burgesses speaking in the House, and concentrated (perhaps somewhat misleadingly) on gentlemen's oratory.

Another noticeable feature of the comparative totals is the growth of influence from outside the county. Apart from Aldeburgh, where the Exchequer seems to have been putting in a nominee from the 1580s, this was overwhelmingly a development of the 1590s, perceptible in every borough except Eye, and it reflected the growing factionalism and turbulence of politics at Court. The Earl of Essex interfered at Dunwich to secure a friend's election in 1593, and also at Ipswich once he had become High Steward. More consistent was the influence of Edward Coke in the three coastal boroughs, while apart from an initial return of 1559, the Duchy of Lancaster started being active at Sudbury in 1593. Also in 1593, clearly a significant Parliament in this respect, Ipswich elected Zachary Lock, secretary to its High Steward Lord Hunsdon, in a move almost certainly intended to irritate the gentry leadership of the county: Lock was unique among Ipswich's sixteenth-century MPs in having no Suffolk roots or connections.

Nevertheless, even in the 1590s it was the local gentry rather than outsiders who were in the majority. Throughout the century even Ipswich was delighted to elect such influential local men as Solicitor-General John Gosnold or the Ipswich residents Sir Thomas Rush, Sir Humphrey Wingfield, Thomas Seckford, and Edward Grimston; these were ideal examples of good Suffolk men with plenty of contacts among the mighty and among the labyrinth of Westminster bureaucracy. Under Mary the borough seems to have gone out of its way to demonstrate its loyalty, perhaps somewhat suspect in view of the aggressive Protestant element in the town, by electing people who were associated with Mary's East Anglian *coup d'état* and Ipswich's loyal part in it, including three county gentlemen who had no great association with the town (see below, pp. 80–1). A more remarkable service for the county élite was the town's making one seat available as an insurance policy for a would-be knight of the shire in case of a contested election. Sir John Higham made this arrangement and used it in 1584; in 1588 he was again accepted by Ipswich, but this time gained his county seat, and the town elected its Recorder instead.[88] Sir William Waldegrave made the same provision in 1597, but also succeeded in his bid to be knight of the shire.[89]

[88] MacCulloch, 'Catholic and Puritan', pp. 282, 285.   [89] Bacon, p. 389.

For the little borough of Eye, there was no question of choice in the elections; its succession of MPs reads like the guest-list for a house-party at Redgrave Hall. At Orford things were more complex; although the Willoughbys had probably secured the borough's enfranchisement, the earliest returns reveal another association with John Sone, servant of Lord Willoughby's friend the Duke of Norfolk, which was to continue through John's son and through his Wingfield relations; Edward Grimston played a part, and Katherine, Duchess of Suffolk also used her claim to the Willoughby inheritance and the townsfolk's old affection for her mother probably in two or three mid-century elections. At Sudbury, Edens, Fortescues, and Waldegraves were elected beside the Duchy nominees, and at Dunwich there was a similar succession of local gentlemen.

The boroughs were worth co-operating with, and we misread Tudor politics if we regard their increasing representation in Parliament by gentlemen as mere exploitation. From the largest to the smallest, these corporations had a reality among the divisions which structured the county. Their privileges shaped the lives of their inhabitants and protected them from outside interference in their markets except in the times of most severe crisis in the food supply. They were complementary to the work of the countryside, whether they were merely servicing their own agricultural district, as in the case of Bury, Hadleigh or Sudbury, or whether like Ipswich and the coastal ports, their trade links stretched from Italy to Iceland.[90] The county's gentry could usually overawe them, and by sheer obstruction might outwit as great a town as Ipswich in its legitimate demands for financial help in the 1590s (below, Ch. 9), but the boroughs could never be ignored.

The final element in the superimposed jurisdictions of the county was the organization of the diocese of Norwich. As the century progressed, it was increasingly difficult for the diocesan administration to make an impact on Suffolk. It was serving one of the largest dioceses in the country, and the Reformation had done nothing to diminish its size, while considerably adding to the Bishop's troubles. The only simplification of his problems was the removal of the rival ecclesiastical jurisdictions of the monasteries, particularly the great house of Bury, which had been exempt from his jurisdiction. A most serious handicap on the other hand was the loss of property, which meant that the Bishop had a very restricted base for directly influencing the county

[90] Williams, 'Maritime Trade', p. 151.

later in the century. Richard Nix, bishop from 1501 until 1535, clearly enjoyed living at his north Suffolk palace of Hoxne, perhaps relishing its connections with East Anglia's patron saint Edmund, otherwise so much monopolized by the Abbey at Bury. It was from Hoxne that Nix generally addressed his correspondence in his last years, when despite his blindness he fought to preserve the Church as he had known and loved it, and he died at Hoxne. He also maintained the deer-park at the other episcopal palace in Suffolk further down the Waveney at South Elmham, and one of his household gentlemen who served as parker at Elmham was buried at Hoxne in 1517.[91]

Both these ancient properties of the diocese, so conveniently central to the whole East Anglian region, were lost by the exchange of lands which brought William Rugge to the see of Norwich as Nix's successor in 1536 Prior Manning's appointment as Bishop of Ipswich was part of the same deal, obviously intended to be some compensation for the loss of authority in the county. Although Manning was transferred to be master of the rich chantry college at Mettingham on the surrender of his Priory at Butley, and clearly meant to make this his permanent home, spending money on building works there,[92] he found himself once more forced to surrender his house after only five years; it is not certain where he lived after this. His death in the late 1540s left the county without effective episcopal supervision. The government of Northumberland was given due warning of the possible consequences of this vacuum, and of the ineffectiveness of Rugge the diocesan, by the explosion of Kett's Rebellion in 1549. Part of their work of reconstruction, which also included Rugge's forced retirement, was to provide Suffolk with a replacement episcopal palace sensibly sited at Ipswich, and to give the Bishop of Norwich a few other properties in the county.[93] In the long term this made little difference. Elizabeth took back Sudbourne, one of the best of the manors granted in Northumberland's time.[94] There is little evidence that the Bishops used their Ipswich palace. Mary's bishop, John Hopton, seems to have stayed there on his anti-heresy campaigns.[95] Elizabeth's first bishop,

---

[91] 'Chitting', p. 116 (Thomas Aschby). South Elmham was also an episcopal peculiar with its own court, but this special status came to an end in 1540, four years after the episcopal exchange (*PSIA* XIV, 1912, p. 326). A monument to one of Nix's relatives remained at Hoxne in the early seventeenth century ('Chitting', p. 116).

[92] *PSIA* XI (1903), p. 316.

[93] *CPR Edward VI* III, p. 287. For similar augmentations in other dioceses, see Heal, pp. 145–7.   [94] *CPR Eliz.* I, p. 444.

[95] For example, Foxe, VIII, pp. 223–5; HMC IX pt. i, p. 248.

John Parkhurst, may have used it particularly while his son Christopher was at school in Ipswich in the early 1570s, but the town records are silent on his presence.[96] He and his successors divided most of their time in East Anglia between their Norfolk country home at Ludham and the palace at Norwich. Edmund Scambler, bishop from 1584 to 1594, among his many inroads on the diocesan endowments, leased out the Bishops' little-used palace at Ipswich to his son James for three lives, 'and gave him leave to pull down what he wished, which he did'.[97]

Even before that, Bishops seem only to have ventured on occasional progresses into their Suffolk Archdeaconries, apart from when they were forced to pass through on their way to sessions of Parliament; otherwise they left Suffolk to the ministrations of their archdeacons and commissaries. Norfolk business dominates the surviving episcopal correspondence; in Norfolk the Bishops were active JPs and subsidy commissioners, in Suffolk, never.[98] In terms of property, the Dean and Chapter of Ely could make a better show in Suffolk than could the county's own Bishop. Small wonder, then, that John Parkhurst said of Suffolk's gentry that he had 'little accesse thither or acquaintance among them'.[99] It is true that he married the daughter of an east Suffolk gentleman, Thomas Garneys or Garnish of Kenton, but a bitter difference in religious outlook cut him off from contact with father-in-law, whom he satirized in one of his Latin poems as '*Crispus*'—a pastry garnish.[100] Of his successors, only Bishop Edmund Freke took any independent initiative among the Suffolk gentry, and he provoked a bitter reaction (below, Ch. 6).

The Bishops' difficulties were not simplified by the inferior jurisdictions of the diocese. In particular, the Archdeaconries suffered an anomalous situation by which the Eye–Stowmarket area was outside the Liberty of St Edmund in temporal affairs, but was comprehended by the western Archdeaconry of Sudbury rather than the eastern Archdeaconry of Suffolk. This may well have weakened the Archdeacon of Sudbury's control of the area in the late medieval period, and

---

[96] *Parkhurst*, p. 261. Anthony Harison, qu. *PSIA* VII (1891), p. 382, claims that Parkhurst was occasionally resident in the Ipswich palace. In 1561 he made his brother Christopher keeper of the Palace (ibid.).

[97] Bishop Richard Montagu, writing in 1638, qu. *EANQ* New Series VII (1891), p. 239.

[98] Cf., e.g. the episcopal correspondence preserved among the papers of Thomas Browne, secretary to Scambler and Redman, in the Aylsham collection, particularly bundles 176 and 347. Dr Houlbrooke endorses this judgement: *Parkhurst*, p. 49.

[99] Bateson, 'Original Letters', p. 48.   [100] *Parkhurst*, p. 21.

allowed the growth of religious nonconformity without too much restraint (below pp. 176–9). Yet the senior clerical staff of the county could be as troublesome to the Bishop as the laity. While the bishops of Norwich were doctrinal conservatives amid the ambiguities of the Henrician and early Edwardian church, there were important ecclesiastical peculiars at Hadleigh and Bury St Edmunds whereby Archbishop Cranmer could harass Bishops Nix and Rugge (below, Ch. 5). Hadleigh always had an able and resident incumbent who played an important part in the religious life of the county; from the 1570s until the 1590s it was personally united to the surrounding Archdeaconry of Sudbury because its incumbent was also Archdeacon, but this may not have ended the Bishops' problems. The Archdeacon of Sudbury's unusual degree of autonomy was calculated to bring him into conflict with his Bishop, particularly if they were not in theological sympathy. John Still, Archdeacon from 1577 to 1592, sided with the Puritan gentry of the Bury area in their struggle with Bishop Freke in the 1570s and 1580s, no doubt feeling additionally secure in his defiance because of his incumbency at Hadleigh. Like the gentry, Still doubtless resented the interference of the commissary for the Archdeaconry, who was the Bishop's personal officer and who struggled to maintain the Bishop's authority even though he doubled as the Archdeacon's own official.[101] It is noticeable that a decade later, when gentry and Bishop were on much better terms, Still's newly-installed successor as Archdeacon continued to wage legal warfare against the commissary's independent jurisdiction.[102]

During the century, more than forty religious houses had disappeared from the county, including the house whose authority in the Liberty of St Edmund rivalled that of the justices of the peace; the remainder of the Church's hierarchy was stripped of much of its former wealth. The Church was understaffed, and, with the delights of Reformation *odium theologicum* to add to its repertoire, even more internally quarrelsome than during the medieval period. The people of late Tudor Suffolk could therefore enjoy much more freedom from the Church's control. A considerable proportion of those who cared about the Church—and that would include anyone with an interest in the affairs of Church,

---

[101] PRO, SP 12/126/3; cf. Smith, p. 220. Houlbrooke, *Church Courts*, p. 32, shows that the Archdeacon of Norfolk claimed in 1572 to nominate the Bishop's commissary for his area; if this was so in Sudbury, it must surely have been one of Still's predecessors who nominated Commissary Day.

[102] Aylsham 180, Robert Redmayne to Bishop Scambler, 30 Aug. 1593.

state, and the welfare of their own soul—felt that the Church's reformation had gone too far; another group felt that it had not gone far enough. How could an Elizabethan Bishop of Norwich reconcile the Puritan gentleman who gloomily listed the 'dumbe and unpreachinge' ministers in his area with the prosperous yeoman and churchwarden who said that he 'had more pleasure and delyte to here the vyrgynalles than to here the scrypture'?[103] With his many financial and administrative worries, could a bishop even perceive this task of reconciliation as a pastoral problem? He could not rely on much automatic backing from the Suffolk gentry in his work; unlike the gentry in counties which contained a cathedral city, they were unlikely to develop close ties through family and acquaintanceship with higher ecclesiastics. Their tendency would be to see the ecclesiastical hierarchy as a hindrance to their particular view of the Church's task, whether it was to be reconciled to the Holy See or to be the handmaid of a truly godly Protestant commonwealth. Their Church would be the church of the parishes, the church of the incumbents whom they and their friends had appointed: and woe betide any higher ecclesiastic who tried to restore a broader vision of the Church's hierarchy to them. Charles I's clergy would discover this to their cost.

To sum up: geography and land-use did not form a particularly strong basis for division within Tudor Suffolk. The Woodland area was too dominant to produce a continuing rivalry in the county between wood–pasture and sheep–corn areas; while at the same time, the Woodland was not enough of a cultural and economic unit to unify the county. The feudal liberties were a fading force, the diocesan authorities remote and their local officials frequently divided. The boroughs were to a greater or lesser extent all capable of successfully defending their privileges against encroachment, but the hallmark of their relations with the magisterial élite was co-operation. The most potent line of demarcation within the county was the boundary of the ancient ecclesiastical Liberty of St Edmund, which produced two separate administrative structures and gentry societies for the east and the west of the county. Against these various divisions, we must set the county community as a whole. What was its nature, and how real was it? How was it affected by the presence of great noblemen whose interests transcended county boundaries, and how was it affected by their eventual disappearance?

---

[103] BL Add. 38492, fo. 90; PRO, STAC 5 C49/12, interrogatories.

2
Power in the County

(a) The early Tudors: noblemen in their counties

SINCE the Norman Conquest East Anglia had been dominated by a great nobleman or pair of great noblemen; the Tudor period saw this structure of power ended for good. At the beginning of Henry VII's reign, the De la Poles, the Howards, the De Veres, the Radcliffes, and the Willoughbys all had the potential to establish or re-establish power-bases in Suffolk; at the end of Elizabeth's reign, no aristocratic family of comparable significance remained, thanks to a combination of dynastic and political accident and deliberate Crown action. Suffolk became a community of gentlemen, who had lost the habit of deference to a great magnate in their midst.

In all this, the Crown's aim was not to destroy aristocratic power. During the sixteenth century it created a local power in the Brandons before removing them elsewhere, and it twice reconstructed the power of the Howards as well as twice destroying them; the De la Poles fell as much through their own folly as through the malice of central government. The ideal mediator between centre and locality was a reliable great nobleman, as both the thirteenth Earl of Oxford and (after his fashion) the third Duke of Norfolk demonstrated. However, East Anglia's stormy history in the fifteenth century, when its life was constantly disrupted by the rivalries of the Dukes of Norfolk and Suffolk, showed that it was difficult to find a reliable magnate for long, and the new religious divide from the 1530s made the task more difficult still. The institution of the lords lieutenant was the later Tudor solution; it was only partially successful in curbing the newly-emancipated gentry on the county Benches of Norfolk and Suffolk. The balance between a leading man who was a courtier subservient to the monarch's will and a man with a real following in his 'country' was hard to strike.

To begin with, however, the task of the Tudors was surprisingly easy in East Anglia. The Mowbray interest, for so long a powerful source of misrule throughout the region, had nothing to hold it together on the death of the last Mowbray Duke in 1476, and the first Howard Duke of Norfolk could do no more than begin to rebuild it on the basis of his share of the old Mowbray estates before his disgrace and death at Bosworth in 1485. Although Henry VII did not choose to destroy the Howards utterly after this catastrophe, the family's recovery would proceed to a timetable set by the Tudors.[1]

The De la Poles had not enjoyed as much power as the Mowbrays since the destruction of the first Duke of Suffolk in 1450, and it is noticeable that no East Anglian gentry accompanied the De la Pole Earl of Lincoln in attainder after his unsuccessful bid for power in 1487. Lincoln's father, John Duke of Suffolk, lived in such discreet obscurity during Henry VII's reign that it is not certain exactly when he died, beyond the fact that it was some time in 1491 or 1492. The fate of Lincoln's brothers Edmund and Richard was only gradually decided; after a partial restoration of the family lands to Edmund, with the reduced title of Earl of Suffolk, final shipwreck came to the family in 1501, after Edmund had fled the country for the second time in three years. This flight was probably hastened by deliberate government harassment in a lawsuit. The Earl had become locked in a struggle with William Rivet, a wealthy Rishangles yeoman whom he claimed as his villein; the case aroused the attention of the King's Council, and in 1501 it ended in a humiliating King's Bench defeat and heavy damages awarded against the Earl. Now the De la Poles would finally disappear from Suffolk, with Edmund kidnapped for the King and in 1513 executed in the Tower, and Richard killed fighting for another king in 1525.[2]

Otherwise the region provided few problems for Henry VII. Two royal servants, Gilbert Debenham of Wenham and John Lord Fitzwalter, were executed in connection with the Perkin Warbeck affair; another, Sir Robert Chamberlain of Gedding, was attainted of high treason and was executed in 1491; Sir James Tyrrell of Gipping was caught up as Captain of Guisnes in the De la Pole disaster and went to the block in 1502. Yet all these men were serving away from home when they were caught up in opposition politics, and all their

---

[1] Sayer, 'Norfolk Involvement in Dynastic Conflict', pp. 315 f.; see also Crawford, 'John Howard'.
[2] Sayer, 'Norfolk Involvement in Dynastic Conflict', pp. 319–20. Family details on peers unless otherwise stated are taken from G. E. Cokayne, *Complete Peerage* (13 vols., 1910–49). For the Rivet villeinage case, see Selden Society LXXV (1956), p. 30, and PRO, KB27/951, m. 66; cf. Rivet's enrolments of manumissions, *CPR Henry VII*, II, p. 58.

families secured the reversal of their attainders within a few years. Henry could afford to be generous. Looking after his interests in East Anglia was John de Vere, thirteenth Earl of Oxford, whose stormy career had been built on his Lancastrian loyalty and who owed the restoration of his fortunes to Henry VII's success. At the beginning of the reign, with the loyalty of the Howards still on trial, there was no one to challenge him in his control of the region, a fact emphasized by the various offices and lands granted to him which had lately been in the hands of John Howard.[3] The Sheriff of Norfolk and Suffolk had no doubt as to Oxford's authority in the crisis caused by Lambert Simnel's rising with the Earl of Lincoln in 1487: 'nexte to the Kynge I answered pleynly I was bownde to do him service and to fullfylle hys comawndment to the vttermest off my powere'. All the evidence suggests that Oxford used his power wisely and moderately; in particular, he showed no inclination to hit the Howards when they were down.[4]

As a magnate permanently to dominate East Anglia, however, Oxford suffered certain disadvantages. To begin with, his power base was concentrated on the old family home at Castle Hedingham in north Essex; his influence in Norfolk and Suffolk was concentrated (most unusually for an East Anglian nobleman) in the Liberty of St Edmund in Suffolk. Here the De Veres enjoyed the large and wealthy manor at Lavenham, where the thirteenth Earl left the most potent symbol of his power, the great church tower which looms over that early Tudor boom town. The Vere mullet and coat of arms spatter the tower in cheerful competition with the emblems of the fabulously wealthy clothier of Lavenham, Thomas Spring, to prove that this nobleman of ancient lineage was no snob. Oxford's widow retired to the west Suffolk village of Polstead, also in the hundred of Babergh.[5] To judge by the evidence of wills and feoffees, Oxford's social circle was drawn from north Essex and St Edmund, centring around such west Suffolk leaders as Sir William Waldegrave of Bures, Sir William Carew of Bury, Sir Robert Drury of Hawstead, John Clopton of Melford, Robert Broughton of Denston, Clement Higham of Barrow, and Thomas Sampson of Kersey.[6] Oxford certainly had a following in Norfolk, most obviously his councillor Sir John Paston, and his lands

---

[3] Virgoe, 'Recovery of the Howards', pp. 8–13.
[4] *Paston Letters* II, pp. 445, 453.   [5] PRO, KB 9/534, m. 75.
[6] *CCR Henry VII* I, no. 777; PCC 17 Horne (Clopton), PCC 11 Moone (Carew), PCC 29 Adeane (Broughton).

in west Norfolk were extensive, but he and his family were not destined to make a permanent mark there. The Earl had no sons. On his death in 1513, his title passed to his nephew, who showed no sign of taking on his uncle's regional role; neither did any of his successors, who are distinguished throughout the Tudor period by their increasing ineffectiveness and irresponsibility.

One significant indication of changing circumstances was the fourteenth Earl of Oxford's marriage to the daughter of Thomas, Earl of Surrey in 1511, disastrous though the marriage proved. Dr Virgoe has ably outlined the gradual progress of the Howards back into a position of leading authority in Norfolk and Suffolk: the first appearance of Surrey's servant and brother-in-law Philip Tilney in the commission of the peace for Suffolk in 1497 and the appearance of Surrey and his son in 1504: the piecemeal rebuilding of the Mowbray landed inheritance including the great castle at Framlingham, and the return of the Earl from his northern duties for the Crown after 1500.[7] Surrey regained the ducal title of Norfolk in 1514 after his military success at Flodden; all might seem set fair for the Howards to take up an unchallenged role as leaders of East Anglia, bolstered by the family alliance with the De Vere fortunes.

One curious ray of light shed on the Howard interest in these years is provided by the accounts of the keeper of Framlingham deer-park, preserved for 1508–13 and 1515–19, in which he meticulously recorded the deer slaughtered in the Castle park for presents or in the course of hunting by guests.[8] This was no trivial concern; even when in 1510 a disastrous winter killed no fewer than 1,307 deer in the park, it did not exhaust its resources, and in an ordinary year, between one hundred and two hundred deer would be given away to local gentry, churchmen, townships, friends of the family or Howard servants. Framlingham park was a potent symbol of the Howards' role in the county, with a catchment area for its gifts concentrating on St Audrey and all the Geldable except that part in the south which might look to the Howards' other deer-park at Stoke by Nayland. Richard Chamber, the keeper of Framlingham Park, was a proud man, dating his accounts not only by the regnal year of the king, but also by the year of his own reign amidst the Howards' bucks and does.

No doubt many of these gifts of deer represented customary payments: they included regular presents to various parsons on the

[7] Virgoe, 'Recovery of the Howards', esp. pp. 13–17.
[8] BL Add. 27451, fos. 11–25; Add. Ch. 16554; Add. Roll 17745.

Howard estates and to every significant religious house in the area, with the understandable exception of the De la Poles' old chantry college at Wingfield. Many gentry, too, received gifts which must have been traditional in the same way. Two features, however, stand out from the largesse bestowed on the gentry. First, the Howards dominated the Liberty of St Audrey in which their castle stood, but they dominated it in amicable partnership with the Liberty's other resident peer, William Lord Willoughby of Eresby. Willoughby, his brothers and his chief servants Thomas Rush and Christopher Harman were regular recipients of deer from Framlingham; during 1515, Willoughby even acted as the Duke of Norfolk's agent in delivering various requests for deer and in restocking another Howard park at Earsham in Norfolk.

Secondly, this sanguinary but cordial social contact stands in significant contrast to the silence surrounding another leading local family, the Brandons of Henham. Sir Robert Brandon only twice received a buck from Framlingham in ten years; his nephew Charles is only mentioned in 1516, the year in which he brought his bride, the French Queen, back to Suffolk for the first time. No other local family of consequence was so consistently ignored, and this paltry record of gifts stands beside the thirty-eight bucks and thirty-five does which represented ten years of friendship between the Howards and Lord Willoughby. Nor can it be objected that the Brandons already had three parks in the area; so had Lord Willoughby, and in any case, these gifts were as much of symbolic as of culinary significance.[9] The silence symbolizes a chill in relations which may have stretched back to the fifteenth century, when both families were in the circle of the Mowbrays; the Brandons had chosen the winning side and the Howards the losers at Bosworth Field.

The situation in East Anglia would therefore be a delicate one in the years when Charles Brandon rose from the ranks of the knightly families of Suffolk to become a Duke, through the sheer accident of Henry VIII's favour. The King not only created him Duke of Suffolk in February 1514, on the same day as Thomas Howard gained his ducal title, but granted Brandon either immediately or in reversion virtually all the lands formerly held by the De la Poles. Henry had thus recreated at a stroke the system of two great magnates which had

---

[9] Brandon parks at Rishangles, *LP* I, no. 682(40), and two at Henham, PRO, SP 1/242/1 (*LP* App. I pt. ii, no. 1311); Willoughby parks at Benhall and two at Parham, *LP* IV pt. i, no. 1857.

caused such trouble in East Anglia during the previous century. Tensions there certainly were at the outset: Howard and Brandon clashed in the squabbles surrounding the entourage of Princess Mary as she was crowned Queen of France, Brandon showing natural partisanship for his old love and future wife. Nevertheless, and fortunately for the peace of East Anglia, the second Duke of Norfolk was not a man to breed faction; perhaps Charles Brandon's former friendship with his son Lord Edward Howard, killed at sea in 1513, helped to ease the situation.[10] Like Oxford before him, Norfolk seems to have been determined in his last years to exercise restraint in the role which the Crown had allowed him to construct. He avoided conflict in East Anglia with Brandon and at Court with Cardinal Wolsey; he finally retired from Court in 1522 and died at Framlingham in 1524.

The new Duke of Norfolk had been co-operating with Brandon as early as January 1516, when Suffolk had settled an annual rent-charge of £413. 6s. 8d. on him out of manors in Oxfordshire and the West Country.[11] It is a mysterious transaction, which seems to reflect the fact that at this stage in his career, Brandon needed all the friends he could get; it was only a year since his clandestine marriage with the King's sister in France, which had aroused Henry's fury; the King's favour was still an uncertain quantity, and Brandon was already burdened with the massive debt to the Crown which would dog him for two decades. At the same time Brandon was busy currying Wolsey's favour in a constant effort to repair the damage caused by his marital adventure: above all, desperately trying to get back to Court to regain the access to the King's presence which was the only source of his newly-gained East Anglian power.[12]

In East Anglia Brandon remained the junior partner of the two Dukes into the 1530s; one sees this not only in the range of his patronage but also in his pattern of residence. Brandon's circle was narrowly based on east Suffolk and his relatives there: men like Sir Arthur Hopton, Sir Anthony Wingfield of Letheringham, Humphrey Wingfield of Brantham, or members of the families of Jenny, Cavendish, Seckford, and Glemham. Nor could such eminent men as

[10] On the French Queen, see LP I pt. ii, nos. 3555, 3556, 3376. Edward Howard: cf. Virgoe, 'Recovery of the Howards', p. 17.
[11] PRO, SP 1/141/86 (*LP* XIII pt. ii, no. 1215); HLRO, Original Acts 27 Henry VIII 35; PRO, C4/106, Answer of Elizabeth Gold to complaint of executors of third Duke of Norfolk.
[12] Cf. PRO, SP 1/13/251 (*LP* II pt. i, no. 2170).

Hopton or the two Wingfields really be regarded as clients of Suffolk, for all that the Duke secured the office of *custos rotulorum* for Sir Humphrey;[13] they were simply relatives. Howard, on the other hand, was heir to the Mowbray clientage of which Brandon's circle formed only a part. His associates included men from all over the East Anglian region: Suffolk men like John Cornwallis of Brome, Henry Everard of Denston, Sir Anthony Rous of Dennington, Sir Philip Tilney of Shelley, the Timperleys of Hintlesham, but also Norfolk men like Sir Thomas Wyndham of Felbrigg, Sir Roger Townshend of Raynham, or Sir Richard Southwell of Woodrising. The commissions of the peace in the two counties reflect the difference: although Charles Brandon had himself been in commission in both counties since 1512, there is no evidence that he had any influence in appointments to the Norfolk Bench, with the dubious exceptions of James Framlingham in 1514 and Sir John Jenny in 1534;[14] Howard, by contrast, was active in both counties. In 1531, for instance, when the tensions surrounding the burning of Thomas Bilney for heresy and the King's attack on Bishop Nix's conservative group may have prompted the government to look to Howard to supply reliable names for new justices, three of his associates were added in either county: John Cornwallis, Robert Crane, and Christopher Willoughby in Suffolk, and Nicholas Hare, Richard Southwell, and Roger Woodhouse in Norfolk. Even in Suffolk, so many of Brandon's circle were distinguished in their own right that it is difficult to be certain about the extent of his influence in their appointment: Thomas Seckford in 1535, Nicholas Bohun in 1539, and Richard Freston in 1543 were all in the Duke's service and are more likely cases than most others.[15]

In terms of residence, the contrast is also significant. The Howards had their own ancient family home at Stoke by Nayland in the Stour valley, together with the Mowbray castle at Framlingham. The third Duke had lived at Stoke while his father was living at Framlingham, but he recognized that this was not a suitable permanent base from

[13] Ibid.
[14] Framlingham made Brandon one of the supervisors of his will (CCN 73 Briggs) and his second wife Ann Mortimer was probably one of the daughters of Brandon's repudiated second wife, Margaret Mortimer (cf. SP 1/32/131–2, *LP* IV pt. i, nos. 736–7, with *LP* IV pt. iii, no. 5859).
[15] On Howard's servants, see Virgoe, 'Recovery of the Howards', pp. 16, 19. Brandon made Seckford keeper of Wingfield Park (PRO, C3/169/14). Bohun's service: Houlbrooke, *Church Courts*, pp. 193–4. Freston was comptroller of Brandon's household: PRO, SP 1/46/198 (*LP* IV pt. ii, no. 3884).

which to dominate East Anglia; when writing from Stoke in 1528, he reminded Wolsey that 'that litle poure that I may make, your grace doth well know is not within xxiiii or xxv myles of this howse'.[16] Such a distance encompassed Framlingham, but the Duke was probably thinking rather of his new palace at Kenninghall, begun in the 1520s and strategically sited at the very heart of East Anglia on the Norfolk–Suffolk border. It was an ideal centre from which to hold sway over the entire region, and it was to become the centre of the Howards' activities.

On the other hand, the Duke of Suffolk never achieved a permanent East Anglian base. His ancestral home at Henham was modest and he eventually rebuilt it, but the restlessness of his wanderings in the 1520s suggests a man without a home to go to. His surviving East Anglian letters in the State Papers between 1516 and 1528 are dated from Butley Priory, the Abbot of Bury's lodge at Elmswell, Castle Rising, Leiston Abbey, Eye, Wingfield, Norwich, and Bishop's Lynn, and of these, only Wingfield Castle seems to represent a house of his own.[17] Monasteries seem to have been particularly favoured as hosts; in 1536 Eye Priory boasted a room called the Queen's Chamber which had presumably housed Brandon's third wife, while the Chronicler of Butley has left a detailed account of how the Duke and the French Queen used Butley Priory as a base for a series of visits to their east Suffolk gentry friends during July and August 1527. During the 1530s Westhorpe Hall seems to have been rebuilt and to have become a favoured residence—the French Queen's entrails were to be buried in the parish church there—but by then, the Duke's East Anglian days were drawing to a close.[18]

In the one great East Anglian crisis which they both faced, the Amicable Grant affair of 1525, the two Dukes were careful to work together. By then their growing suspicions and jealousy of Wolsey had drawn them together; they were both away from Court, and from the beginning they realized that the levying of the grant so soon after previous heavy tax demands was going to cause problems. Neither

---

[16] PRO, SP 1/47/211 (*LP* IV pt. ii, no. 4192).

[17] PRO, SP 1/13/26, 1/13/251, 1/15/33, 1/17/7, 1/17/52, 1/17/64, 1/34/139, 1/34/143, 1/35/234, 1/36/37, 1/46/50, 1/46/107, 1/46/194 (*LP* II pt. i, nos. 1604, 2170; II pt. ii, nos. 3018, 4334, 4423, 4448; IV pt. i, nos. 1253, 1260, 1542, 1642; IV pt. ii, nos. 3760, 3811, 3883).

[18] *PSIA* VIII (1892), p. 106; *Butley Chronicle* pp. 51–2. Entrails: 'Chitting', p. 120. The Duke dated a patent to Richard Freston from Westhorpe in June 1537: PRO, REQ 3/36, unnumbered material.

could afford to see the other make a false move; the only person to gain from that would be Wolsey. From their first negotiations with the local gentry in March, they worked in close co-operation, taking care to synchronize the date for the public demand for the grant in the two counties 'to thentente that if it shall chaunce any to make denyall thothers shalhave noo knowledge of the same to take any evill ensample thereby'.[19] When the crisis broke, with open demonstrations against the Grant in west Suffolk in early May, they jointly gathered a force of gentlemen and their tenants to oppose the crowds; before they had come to a confrontation with the demonstrators, they combined to bypass Wolsey and write straight to the King, frankly advising him to be conciliatory.[20] Even when they had been successful in overawing the demonstrations, they were determined not to be separated, writing anxiously to Wolsey 'we beseche your grace not to send for the oon of us without thother for such a greate respecttes as we shall declare at our comyng'.[21]

The whole Amicable Grant fiasco reflected little but credit on the Dukes while representing a considerable setback for Wolsey; it was all very well for him to unite with the Duke of Norfolk in a theatrical gesture to be joint sureties for the chief demonstrators when they appeared in Star Chamber to face the Crown's wrath,[22] but the blame for the failure was firmly on the Cardinal's shoulders. It was the first stage in his progressive fall from the King's favour; when Wolsey's final fall came four years later, no one worked harder to see his ruin completed than the two Dukes. That was a contest at Court, not in East Anglia; Wolsey had no strong acquaintance among the Suffolk gentry, predictably enough as a former townsman of Ipswich, and indeed, apart from a triumphal progress through the region in 1517, he hardly ever visited the county of his boyhood during the years of his greatness (below, Ch. 7). His passing disturbed no local power structure.

The one change in local affairs to occur at the end of the 1520s was that the Duke of Suffolk was making a determined attempt to consolidate his position by seeking to annex the lands of the Howards' old friend William Lord Willoughby, who died in 1526. By involving himself in the affairs of the Willoughbys, the Duke became a partisan in a family dispute of unusual bitterness, centring on a clash between

---

[19] BL Cott. Cleop. F VI, fos. 336–8 (*LP* IV pt. i, no. 1235).
[20] PRO, SP 1/34/190 (*LP* IV pt. i, no. 1319).
[21] SP 1/34/196 (*LP* IV pt. i, no. 1329).   [22] Hall, p. 702.

the heirs male and the heirs general of Lord Willoughby's estates, and affecting not only Suffolk but Lincolnshire.[23] The heir male was Lord Willoughby's brother, Sir Christopher Willoughby, who for a long time had been his heir apparent. However, Lord Willoughby, childless in his first marriage, had married Mary de Salinas, one of Katherine of Aragon's Spanish ladies-in-waiting; she had produced a daughter Katherine. The properties settled on Mary included some lands previously entailed to Sir Christopher, and he was quick to contest her right to them.

Matters were already heated before the Duke of Suffolk stepped in. Sir Christopher's case was quite strong in law, but Lady Willoughby possessed the considerable asset of Queen Katherine's favour, which she had no scruples in exploiting to lobby Wolsey. Lord Willoughby had already enlisted Suffolk as one of the feoffees of his wife's life estates in 1517;[24] the Duke was granted the wardship of their daughter on 12 February 1529. As Queen Katherine's backing became a wasting asset amid the deepening crisis of the Divorce, Suffolk became a very useful substitute. The advantages for him were clear. Some of his De la Pole lands were in Lincolnshire, and his son had been given the title Earl of Lincoln in accordance with De la Pole precedent while still a boy in 1525; now a marriage alliance between the youth and Katherine Willoughby marked the chance of building up a substantial estate in Lincolnshire as well as Suffolk. This marriage was not to be, for Suffolk changed his strategy and in 1533 made the best of his recent widowerhood by the drastic step of marrying Katherine himself, a mere six weeks after the death of the French Queen. Despite the age difference, the plan worked, producing two talented and promising sons. It was hardly Suffolk's fault that six years after his death both of them died of sweating sickness and his dynastic ambitions were thwarted.

In the meantime the dispute produced tensions which Dr James has demonstrated fed into the Lincolnshire rising of 1536:[25] what was their effect in Suffolk? Just as in the Lincolnshire properties, Sir Christopher was forced by Lady Willoughby's consistent advantage at Westminster into direct action in the localities. He had already manœuvred himself into possession of the old family home at Parham, but a month after the Duke had secured the Willoughby wardship, Sir Christopher

---

[23] The best account of this dispute is to be found in James, 'Obedience and Dissent', pp. 38–48.
[24] PRO, STAC 2/19/241.   [25] James, 'Obedience and Dissent', p. 45.

staked his claim to Orford, Lord Willoughby's old headquarters in Suffolk. Despite taking along a sympathetic Suffolk JP, Sir Thomas Tey, he met with sullen resistance and fierce partisanship for Lady Willoughby from the townsfolk. Tey arrested one of her servants, and Sir Christopher had begun a feud which would last in Orford for some thirty years; it was noticeable that Thomas Rush, Lord Willoughby's old servant, was careful to keep out of Sir Christopher's enterprise, although he was also a justice for the county and lived only a couple of miles from Orford.[26] In August and September 1529 Lady Willoughby's men counter-attacked by reaping their harvest on the land which Sir Christopher claimed in Orford and by assaulting Sir Christopher's servants on another Willoughby estate at Combs, some twenty-five miles away. A second incident at Combs three weeks later again had Sir Thomas Tey on the scene, allegedly and somewhat implausibly bidding Sir Christopher to keep the peace.[27]

These ripples of violence seem to have been stilled as far as Suffolk was concerned by an interim decree in Star Chamber on 28 February 1531; until further evidence could be produced, Sir Christopher was to retain Parham and Bredfield in Suffolk and Roughton in Norfolk, while Lady Willoughby kept her life interest in Combs, Orford, and Ufford. The Duke of Suffolk had no inhibitions about sitting in the session of the Council which produced this decree. Similarly, when a settlement was hammered out for the whole range of Lord Willoughby's estates and embodied in an Act of Parliament in February 1536, Sir Christopher did not get all that his original entail had given him. He lost some of his prospective Lincolnshire manors for ever; nevertheless, his eventual prospects in Suffolk were good. The Act was silent about the East Anglian properties, for the settlement of 1531 was adhered to. Sir Christopher's descendants kept Parham; his son was in possession of Orford by 1540, and took his title from Parham when created a baron in 1547. Meanwhile, the Duke of Suffolk had secured a very satisfactory deal in Lincolnshire for himself and his young wife.[28]

The Duke of Norfolk cannot have been greatly pleased at Brandon's

---

[26] PRO, STAC 2/20/400. ·

[27] PRO, STAC 2/27/169, Complaint of Sir Christopher Willoughby; STAC 2/19/241.

[28] PRO, STAC 2/17/399; HLRO Original Acts 27 Henry VIII, 42. N. H. Nicholas, *Proceedings and Ordinances of the Privy Council of England 1386–1542* (7 vols., 1834–7), VII, p. 58. It is noticeable that the Master and Fellows of Mettingham College were still hedging their bets as to their Founder in 1535 when they told the *Valor Ecclesiasticus* commissioners that he was 'the heir to Lord Willoughby' (*VE* III, p. 431).

gaining a sizeable part of the Willoughby inheritance and thus greatly strengthening his position. There is some evidence that Howard was something of a partisan for Sir Christopher's claims. His father had headed the feoffees for Sir Christopher's marriage; Sir Christopher paid a fee to Howard's legal counsel, Edward White of Shotesham, who was appointed probably on Sir Christopher's part to assess Lord Willoughby's goods for his will.[29] When Sir Christopher wrote to Wolsey on 16 August 1527 to complain of Lady Willoughby's highhandedness, his letter was addressed from the home of Howard's servant William Rous at Dennington.[30] And was it a mere slip of the pen when on 7 December 1526 Howard referred to someone who can only have been Sir Christopher as 'my lorde Willoughby'?[31] Was it thanks to Howard that Sir Christopher was added to the Suffolk commission of the peace at the height of his dispute with Brandon?

At Court the two Dukes needed to act together throughout the 1530s because of their common detestation and fear of Thomas Cromwell, but in East Anglia their interests were liable to clash. The position cannot have been eased by the fact that Brandon's position continued to improve, even after the death of the French Queen in 1533. Particularly important was the cancellation in December 1535 of the remainder of the huge burden of debt to the Crown into which his marital escapade had dragged him.[32] In 1536 Brandon abandoned the old family home in Southwark to gain a more sumptuous residence in St Martin-in-the-Fields: appropriately, it had lately been the London home of the Bishop of Norwich until the royal looting of diocesan property which had followed the death of Bishop Nix.[33]

When the Lincolnshire Rising broke out in autumn 1536, Brandon was the obvious man to be sent as the King's lieutenant to suppress it, with his new-found active role in that county; his prestige demanded it, for his skirmishes with Sir Christopher Willoughby continued, and Sir Christopher commanded a good deal of sympathy among his fellow-gentry in Lincolnshire.[34] Brandon set out from East Anglia in October,

[29] PRO, SP 2/P(13) (*LP* VII, no. 224); Tanner 106, fo. 11.

[30] PRO, SP 1/43/43 (*LP* IV pt. ii, no. 3349) It is also notable that in 1532 Sir Christopher granted Norfolk the next presentation to a family chantry in Brundish Church (NRO, ACT 4b, fo. 4ᵛ).

[31] PRO, SP 1/45/144 (*LP* IV pt. ii, no. 3649). *LP* misdates this letter to 1527, but the content definitely assigns it to 1526. Lord Willoughby died on 19 Oct. 1526.

[32] *LP* IX, no. 1063/5; HLRO, Original Acts 27 Henry VIII, 28.

[33] HLRO, Original Acts 27 Henry VIII, 48.

[34] James, 'Obedience and Dissent', p. 45, and see PRO, SP 3/14, fo. 46 (*LP* X, no. 635).

and Howard hurried down to Suffolk, clearly chafing at not having a leading role. He emphasized to Cromwell that it was only his own presence in Suffolk that had prevented serious disturbances breaking out there as well, and gave details of his movements to underline the point; characteristically he boasted that 'it shalbe very herd for one to speke any unfittyng worde but that he shalbe incontynent taken and sent to me'. The following day he urged the King to realize that Brandon had inadequate forces with which to meet the rebels; he should not meddle with Howard's own men, and he should wait until Howard could join him before taking any action, notwithstanding 'I shalbe as glad to go under hym as the most poure servant ye have'. A second letter the same day badgered Cromwell to the same effect.[35]

In the event Howard would get his chance against the far more serious disturbances in Yorkshire from November to January; both he and Brandon proved themselves loyal lieutenants to the King despite the opportunity that the risings had afforded to destroy Cromwell, and despite the terrible blow that their suppression dealt to the cause of religious conservatism. Both noblemen would benefit from the share-out of monastic lands which was just beginning, and which had partly been responsible for triggering off the risings in the North; being based primarily on claims of founder's descendants, the grants in Suffolk during 1536, 1537, and early 1538 were more or less a straight share-out between the two Dukes, with no one else in the game. Even here, analysis of these grants suggests that Brandon enjoyed a greater initial success in the county than Howard.

This success is all the more remarkable because Howard seems to have been much more active in his moves against monasteries than Brandon. Already in 1531, while Brandon was still preoccupied in his skirmishes over the Willoughby property, Howard and his lawyer Lionel Tollemache had managed to pick up four out of the five little Suffolk monasteries which Wolsey had suppressed to finance his collegiate foundations at Oxford and Ipswich.[36] Howard's legal and administrative staff were well entrenched as officials in some Suffolk monasteries when the *Valor Ecclesiasticus* recorded their fees in 1535: Nicholas Hare at Bungay nunnery, Sir William Rous and John Holdich at Sibton Abbey, John Sone at Leiston Abbey, Robert Mills at Blythburgh Priory, Sir William Rous and John Sone at Bruisyard

[35] PRO, SP 1/107/83, 118, 120, 148 (*LP* XI, nos. 603, 625, 626, 659).
[36] *LP* V, nos. 220/3, 4, 11; PRO, SP 1/141/86 (*LP* XIII pt. ii, no. 1215). For the location of Suffolk religious houses, see Map VI (below, p. 134).

Nunnery, Richard Wharton and Robert Mills at Flixton Nunnery; even mighty Bury, where Howard was hereditary chief steward of the Liberty of St Edmund, had Sir John Cornwallis as steward of the cellarer's manors. Only one of Brandon's officials can be traced in a similar capacity: Thomas Beck at Redlingfield Nunnery.[37]

Moreover, Norfolk was not above using strong-arm tactics to secure his will with hapless religious houses. At Cistercian Sibton, a wealthy house which had fallen far from its noble early ideals, he engineered a straight sale of the whole house from Abbot Flatbury in 1536, much to the chagrin of Sir Arthur Hopton, who himself had been in the middle of similar negotiations with the unscrupulous Abbot; Howard's transaction was backed by an oral licence from the King and confirmed by a proviso attached to the general statutory confirmation of the King's title to monastic lands in 1539.[38] Howard persuaded the Prior of the Cluniac house at Thetford, where his father and royal son-in-law Richmond were buried, not only that he himself should have custody of the convent seal, but also that the 'misorder' of Thetford's Suffolk cell at Wangford was so great that it ought to be leased to a layman; the Prior 'of hym selfe without my motion' (said the Duke) granted the lease to the Duke's Treasurer.[39] At Bungay in 1536, the nuns discovered a sudden aversion to remaining in their house, and Howard entered as founder; however, a similar private transaction with the Austin Canons of Woodbridge at the same time failed to come off, for it was overtaken by the Act dissolving the smaller monasteries, and Woodbridge fell to the King.[40]

For all this activity, Howard's share of the Suffolk suppressions of 1536, 1537, and 1538 was not as impressive as Brandon's. Perhaps his continuing absence from Court, apparently thanks to Cromwell, hampered his efforts to lobby for lands. Apart from Sibton, Wangford, and Bungay, he only secured a Crown lease of Flixton Nunnery for his comptroller Richard Wharton, the house's former steward.[41] The total value of these properties in the *Valor* had been £366. 11s. 3½d. Brandon, on the other hand, saw his servant Richard Freston procure leases of most of Blythburgh Priory's lands from the Prior and

---

[37] *VE* III, pp. 430, 434, 437, 439, 443, 446, 463, 478. Beck was under-steward of Brandon's lands (*LP* XXI pt. i, no. 1538 I).

[38] PRO, C1/815/40; *Stat. Realm* III, p. 738.

[39] PRO, SP 1/117/96, 134, 263 (*LP* XII pt. i, nos. 737, 711, 836).

[40] SP 1/103/59, 1/104/226 (*LP* X, nos. 579, 1236); *LP* XIV pt. i, no. 1355.

[41] *LP* XIII pt. i, no. 1520: on Wharton, cf. PRO, E134/29 Eliz./Easter 3.

subsequently buy out the Crown lessee;[42] he himself picked up Butley, Eye, and Mendham, while his associate Sir Edmund Bedingfield (whom he had knighted in France in 1523) bought the Bedingfield family nunnery at Redlingfield. The grand total for these houses in the *Valor* had been £676. 16s. 9½d., excluding Mendham, which the *Valor* had not recorded.[43] Brandon's own acquisitions were easy targets for him, for they had all been in the patronage of the Earls and Dukes of Suffolk, and, as we have seen, had frequently provided him with hospitality in earlier years. Butley was the second richest house in Suffolk, and its Prior, the Bishop of Ipswich, was still making strenuous efforts to resist the overtures of the Duke of Suffolk's council for the house's surrender in December 1536. However, by March 1538 William Petre was reporting a textbook quiet surrender to the Crown.[44] The reason was clear; in the same month Brandon agreed to lease the Bishop two hundred marks' worth of land in Lincolnshire or Suffolk, and in the following year the Bishop became Master of the comfortable College at Mettingham, in Brandon's gift through his wife. At the same time the Bishop was further granted a Warwickshire manor, with reversion on his death to Brandon.[45] Brandon was responsible for the pensions at Butley, and did his best to commute them for presentations to secular benefices, as he did with Freston's tame Prior of Blythburgh, John Righton.[46]

These processes continued the steady build-up of Brandon's property; but in the summer of 1538 there came a dramatic change of direction. On 13 July 1538 Brandon sold to the Crown his ancestral home at Henham, together with Benhall Park and other manors and the rent-charge which he had reserved on selling Mendham Priory to his servant Freston. On 30 September 1538 he sold to the Crown the whole Honour of Eye in Suffolk and Norfolk, including his house at Westhorpe, and Leiston and Eye priories. Butley went back to the

[42] PRO, C4/113, Answer of Richard Freston to Sir Arthur Hopton; Hengr. 3, fo. 25.
[43] PRO, SP 1/242/1 (*LP* App. I pt. ii, no. 1311); *LP* XII, no. 1103/11; *CPR Philip and Mary* III, p. 195; *LP* XII, no. 795/39. Brandon claimed to have a Crown grant of Redlingfield: PRO, SP 1/141/190 (*LP* XIII pt. ii, no. 1269). All references to knighthoods are taken unless otherwise stated from W. A. Shaw, *Knights of England* (2 vols., 1906).
[44] PRO, SP 1/113/35 (*LP* XI, no. 1377); BL Cott. Vesp. F XIII, fo. 158 (*LP* XIII pt. i, no. 393).
[45] *LP* XIII pt. i, no. 553; XIV pt. i, no. 651/57; XIV pt. ii, no. 442.
[46] Baskerville, 'Married Clergy', p. 203. Righton was presented to the Duke of Suffolk's living of Stratford St Mary in 1536 (all details of inductions unless otherwise stated are taken from *PSIA* XXII (1936), pp. 33–85 and 294–320).

Crown some time later. In return he was granted properties in Staffordshire, Oxfordshire, Buckinghamshire and elsewhere, together with substantial monastic lands in Lincolnshire. Large grants of Essex lands were made to him in December, but he almost immediately sold them away.[47]

In effect, Brandon was stripped of virtually all his East Anglian property except that held in right of his wife, which after the parliamentary settlement of 1536 was not extensive. His large estates in other counties had hardly been affected. In a letter written in the autumn of 1538, with Henham and Westhorpe taken from him, he complained that he was 'left clerlle wyth howth ane howes trostyng that the kynges henes wyll consedar of hes goodnes and to relef me wyt some wat to helpe me to byeld some hows agayn'.[48] This touching picture of a peer on the streets was not quite accurate, for now Brandon had large plans in Lincolnshire. In April 1537 he had been granted Lord Cromwell's great fifteenth-century castle at Tattershall; he had ambitious schemes for rebuilding Lord Willoughby's old home at Eresby, according to John Leland, and on the death of the dowager Countess of Oxford in 1537 he had come into possession of Grimsthorpe Castle. Grimsthorpe, 'no great thing' before then, was hastily transformed to welcome the King on his progress north in 1541, probably with the building of the new second court which Leland mentions.[49] The agreement for his sale of Eye, perhaps in response to the Duke's plea for a new home, gave him permission to build and embattle three houses in Lincolnshire 'convenient for his degree'.[50] In effect, within four years Brandon had abandoned all pretence of being a power in East Anglia, and even determined in his will (ultimately in vain) to be buried among Willoughbys and Cromwells at Tattershall College, rather than amid his ancestors in Suffolk.[51] From 1538 there is no evidence that he played a part in Norfolk and Suffolk affairs apart from soliciting favours for friends and servants who lived there.

Why had this happened? We can be sure that it was not through any

[47] *LP* XIII pt. i, nos. 1328, 1182/18; PRO, SP 1/242/1 (*LP* App. I pt. ii, no. 1311) Essex grant and sale: Oxley, p. 251.
[48] PRO, SP 1/130/219 (*LP* XIII pt. i, no. 642).
[49] Tattershall: *LP* XII pt. i, no. 1103/5. Eresby: Leland, V, p. 34, where the editor mistakenly supplies the name of Lord Willoughby; the reference is clearly to Brandon. Grimsthorpe: Leland, I, p. 23; G. A. J. Hodgett, *Tudor Lincolnshire* (*History of Lincolnshire* VI) (Lincoln, 1975), p. 151.
[50] BL Harl. 6689, fo. 30ʳ.   [51] PCC 32 Alen.

initiative of Brandon's; within the decade he had spent large sums on rebuilding Henham and Westhorpe Halls in a fitting manner (see Plate 4a);[52] and why would he have gone to the trouble of buying Eye, Leiston, Mendham, and Butley if they were intended to return to the King so soon? Brandon must have been pressurized into abandoning his native county and extending his interests in Lincolnshire; that pressure can only have come from above. Brandon's removal from East Anglia predated the destruction of the nobility of the White Rose—Courtenays, Nevilles, and Poles—which began in late summer 1538; yet the action was just as much a product of royal policy.

The advantages of Brandon's move for the Crown were obvious. The Tudors, far from wishing indiscriminately to destroy a powerful nobility, preferred to rule the localities through reliable but hand-picked magnates; Lincolnshire had no such magnate, and the consequences had been only too obvious in the rising of 1536. East Anglia, on the other hand, had one magnate too many. The Duke of Norfolk had proved his loyalty in the very testing circumstances of the Pilgrimage of Grace; he and his father had built up their East Anglian estates at the expense of lands elsewhere, and he had developed an ideally-placed headquarters for the whole region at Kenninghall.

The King and Cromwell must have been aware of the strains to which two powerful noblemen were subject when they were in such close proximity as Brandon and Howard in the years after the restoration of the Dukedoms. The grim precedent of East Anglia in the fifteenth century was always there, and despite the two Dukes' co-operation in the crises of 1525 and 1536, there were signs of developing strain in the wake of the Willoughby inheritance dispute. Admittedly, the Dukes always behaved correctly to one another, but overt tensions arose with their associates. In 1532, Brandon's servants were reported as feuding with Norfolk's client Richard Southwell, although Brandon angrily denied any knowledge of such doings.[53] In 1537 the Duke of Norfolk faced harassment and lawsuits from Richard Cavendish of Trimley over property in Walton and Trimley and from Sir Arthur Hopton over the Sibton Abbey sale;[54] Cavendish was a relative of Brandon's, involved in his business affairs like many of his family, and he beseeched Brandon to keep an eye on his suit at

---

[52] PRO, SP 1/242/1 (*LP* Add. I pt. ii, no. 1311); White, p. 349.
[53] PRO, SP 1/70/165 (*LP* V, no. 1183).
[54] PRO, SP 1/115/36, 1/118/150 (*LP* XII pt. i, nos. 216, 917); PRO C1/815/40, C1/1211/16; PRO, STAC 2/17/356; PRO, E 111/11.

Court while he was on royal business in Suffolk.[55] Hopton was another close relation, serving under Brandon in France in 1523 and becoming one of the six knights chosen to escort the body of the French Queen at her funeral at Bury in 1533.[56] Accompanying Hopton in that duty had been Sir John Jenny of Brightwell, who had already distinguished himself as one of the leaders in defence of Orford for Lady Willoughby against Sir Christopher Willoughby and Sir Thomas Tey in 1529. He also became involved in litigation with Howard over former Sibton property, and Howard clearly detested him, spitefully referring to him in a routine business letter to the Privy Council in 1542 as 'as good a knight as ever spored a cowe and so welbiloved that he can get few hable men to serve the Kinge'.[57]

Such tensions as these would undoubtedly have intensified if the Duke of Suffolk had consolidated his East Anglian estates with large grants of monastic property in Suffolk. If he was moved to Lincolnshire and his estates there augmented, he would be well placed to repeat his success of 1536, should that become necessary. To move a Duke like a chess-piece might seem a bold game, but the King now had plenty of monastic land with which to be generous, and after all, Brandon was Henry's creation in both a technical and a general sense. Although the debts which Brandon and the French Queen owed the Crown had been pardoned, the Duke continued to owe the King large sums: in 1543, for instance, he paid Augmentations £1,986. 11s. 4d. owed for the year 1542.[58] The move to Lincolnshire was certainly a more calculated and statesmanlike act than the tyrannous caprices by which Henry or those manipulating him had destroyed the Duke of Buckingham or the Montagues, and would yet cast down the Duke of Norfolk; it was more akin to the strategy by which in the 1530s the Percys' northern patrimony was dismantled and transferred to the Crown. One suspects the calculations of Thomas Cromwell at work, safeguarding Lincolnshire and tidying up East Anglia just as at the same time he restructured the Council in the North and initiated the short-lived Council in the West under Russell to act as a more efficient and organized agent of Westminster's will. 1538, after all, saw the

---

[55] PRO, SP 1/84/147 (*LP* VII, no. 800); Cavendish was involved in Brandon's debts to the Crown (*LP* IX, no. 1063/5).

[56] *LP* II, no. 3288; Ford, *Mary Tudor*, p. 43.

[57] BL Add. 32647, fo. 117 (LP XVII, no. 753). Lawsuit: PRO, C1/1134/53; PRO, C4/48, Answer of Duke of Norfolk to Sir John Jenny. Orford case: PRO, STAC 2/27/169.

[58] PRO, E323/2B/1, m. 13d.

height of Cromwell's power and influence in the wake of the defeat of the Pilgrimage of Grace and the destruction of his enemies among the former supporters of Katherine of Aragon.[59] From Cromwell's point of view, the arrangement might have the additional advantage of keeping a dangerous opponent further away from the Court.

With Brandon effectively removed from the East Anglian scene by the end of 1538, the Duke of Norfolk became the leading magnate in the area. This is not to say that his power became absolute in Suffolk; it would hardly have suited Thomas Cromwell if that had happened. Howard's territorial base in Suffolk did not expand materially; he did not make any spectacular gains from the later stages of the Dissolution in the county during 1538 and 1539. In 1540 he gained the freehold of the cell at Wangford, which his Treasurer had been leasing for the past four years, as part of his acquisition of the Norfolk Cluniac priory at Thetford; in 1539 his lawyer Nicholas Hare bought Bruisyard Nunnery, but by then Hare was one of the masters of Requests and would have his own access to monastic spoils.[60] Norfolk seems to have gained very little from the remaining dissolutions, nothing from the sweeping-away of the friaries in 1538; most strikingly, he did not make extensive purchases at the break-up of the greatest house of all, Bury Abbey, after its surrender in November 1539. Those first off the mark there in February 1540 were wealthy gentlemen of the Bury area like William Drury, Thomas Jermyn, and Thomas Kitson, together with Nicholas Bacon, that shrewd local boy making good in the Court of Augmentations.[61] The Duke's Treasurer Anthony Rous stepped in in the same week to buy the west Suffolk manor of Icklingham and various outlying east Suffolk properties of the Abbey, but it was not until July 1540 (appropriately, after Thomas Cromwell's arrest) that the Duke invested in the Bury manor of Elveden, together with a substantial park on the Suffolk coast which he had himself sold to Butley Priory eleven years before. A later purchase of the Bury manor of Rougham did not come until 1545, and the Duke soon sold it.[62] The lands of Bury were destined to be split up without any one dominant purchaser, in contrast to the dissolutions of 1536–8, where the two Dukes had gobbled up the main monasteries to which they could lay claim as founders.

[59] Elton, *Reform and Reformation*, pp. 271–2, 279–81.
[60] *LP* XV, no. 942/43; XIV pt. i, no. 651/22.
[61] PRO, E323/1/2, mm. 12d–15, 39d (*LP* XIV pt. ii, no. 236).
[62] *LP* XV, nos. 436/88, 942/44; *Butley Chronicle*, p. 57; *LP* XX pt. ii, nos. 496/18, 496/68.

For all his repeated statements about his East Anglian power, the Duke of Norfolk did not enjoy the same sway in Suffolk that he might claim in Norfolk. One indication of the contrast between the two counties comes in the list of knights of the shire elected for the two counties under Henry VIII, incomplete though the returns are for the earlier years. In 1539 the Duke claimed that he had 'put such order that such shalbe chosen as I doubt not shall serve his highnes according to his pleassure' in the two counties.[63] In Norfolk, the knights were quite consistently Howard's associates; however, loyal servants of the King that the succession of Suffolk knights of the shire undoubtedly were, they mostly owed little to the Duke. Five men served in eight known results between 1529 and 1545: Sir Thomas Wentworth, created Baron Wentworth in 1529 in the very Parliament to which he had been elected, Sir Anthony Wingfield, Sir Arthur Hopton, Sir William Waldegrave, and Anthony Rous. Of these, only Rous was closely associated with the Duke, and all of them, Rous included, were tried men in the royal service, as well as being local men of impeccable Suffolk antiquity in lineage.

Lord Wentworth seems to have gained his barony for long-term Crown service and as part of the crop of secular peers by which the King robbed the peers spiritual of their majority in the Lords in 1529.[64] He was an unspectacular but wholly reliable minor peer, who in addition to his close family connections with Charles Brandon, was on excellent terms with the Duke of Norfolk; he served as a feoffee when Howard bought the interests of the two Cardinal Colleges in the lately-dissolved houses of Snape, Dodnash and Felixstowe between 1529 and 1532, and he was also a feoffee in the Earl of Surrey's marriage in 1532.[65] In October 1536, Howard recommended that Wentworth be put in charge of Suffolk if both Dukes were absent quelling the northern risings: 'sewerly ther is no man so mete for that purpose as he'.[66] Wingfield had started his court career as Esquire of the Body by 1509, and by 1536 was Captain of the Guard; Hopton had been a Knight of the Body since 1516.[67] They were all relatives and contemporaries of Brandon, even if they had not progressed quite so far in the Court as he had done. Sir William Waldegrave was a similar

[63] BL Cott. Calig. B VI, fo. 373 (*LP* X, no. 816).
[64] Lehmberg, *Reformation Parliament*, p. 46.
[65] *LP* IV pt. iii, no. 5985; V, nos. 220/3, 120₁/37; *LJ* I, p. ccxxvi.
[66] PRO, SP 1/107/148 (*LP* XI, no. 659).
[67] *LP* I, no. 20; Haydn, p. 298; *LP* II, no. 2735.

man, although younger; referred to by Leland as 'yong Walgreve of the courte', he was a man with a great popular following in his own county, and devoted himself to a military career, commanding part of the Suffolk contingent in the Scottish expedition in 1542 and eventually dying in the garrison at Calais in 1554.[68]

Such men as these did not form part of Howard's clientage, however much they might respect his position in East Anglia. We have noted Sir Arthur Hopton's conflict with Howard, and it is significant that like Brandon's formidable young fourth wife Katherine Willoughby, Wentworth and Waldegrave were already enthusiastic for the reformed religion in the 1530s, in contrast to the men surrounding the Duke of Norfolk (see below, Ch. 5). Here were the first signs of the new religious cleavage among the gentry of Suffolk which would fuse with family structures to produce a broad division among the county gentry by Elizabeth's reign. For the moment the county was united, partly by the strange atmosphere of inertia in religious policy that characterized the last seven years of Henry's reign, partly by the last joint military ventures of those ageing generals Brandon and Howard, despatched by their royal contemporary on fresh expeditions into Scotland and France. The Scots venture of 1542 sent the leading men of the Liberty of St Edmund north with Howard; the French venture of 1544 sent the largest cross-section of the leading men of Suffolk to be seen in military service abroad during the sixteenth century. Notable among them was Sir Anthony Wingfield, who in leading his forces to Boulogne was to continue the association of his friends and relatives with England's French possessions which had begun with his uncle Robert, would survive his death and would only end with the humiliation of the loss of Calais in 1558.[69] All the knights of the shire already mentioned took part in the French expedition under the indifferent generalship of Brandon and Howard; Sir Anthony Rous died at Boulogne in 1546.[70]

The great days of the Dukes were over in the 1540s. The Duke of Suffolk, already evicted from the county, died in 1545; the Duke of Norfolk was growing old and struggling alongside the other religious

---

[68] Leland, II, p. 17; *'Vita Mariae'*, pp. 259–60; BL Add. 32647, fo. 52 (*LP* XVII, no. 671); SROI, Blois, p. 295.

[69] BL Add. 32647, fos. 52, 85 (*LP* XVII, nos. 671, 731); *LP* XIX pt. i, nos. 273–5; PRO, C1/1141/9. A mark of the unity created by the Boulogne expedition was Sir Anthony Wingfield's election as MP for the Duke of Norfolk's Sussex borough of Horsham in 1545.

[70] PRO, REQ 3/31, depositions *ex parte* Thomas Rous.

conservatives on the King's Council to maintain his position against the reformist group gathering around the Seymours and the Parrs. The uneasy religious consensus of these years, and Howard's gradual loss of the initiative in events even in his native country, is symbolized by the change in the pattern of acquisitions of the remaining religious properties in Suffolk during the 1540s. A career civil servant in Augmentations of uncertain family origins, John Eyer, purchased half the former friaries in the county in 1545; a London merchant and an outsider to the county, Paul Withipoll, bought outright Ipswich's leading house, Holy Trinity, in 1546. Sudbury College went to another outsider, the courtier and gentleman of the Privy Chamber, Sir Thomas Paston, in 1545; while the substantial prize of Mettingham College had gone down in 1542 to Anthony Denny, another leading gentleman of the Privy Chamber with no real Suffolk connections and moreover a man of distinctly Protestant sympathies.[71] Apart from Eyer's friaries, these were all permanent acquisitions for those who bought them. The only Suffolk people to gain much were all outside the Howard circle: William Sabin at the Ipswich Blackfriars in 1541, William Forth at Butley and John Tasburgh at Flixton in 1544, this last undercutting an earlier lease to the Duke of Norfolk's steward Richard Wharton.[72] Various gentry families, also without close Howard connections, turned their leaseholds into freeholds: the Wingfields at Woodbridge in 1542, Sir Christopher Willoughby's son Sir William at Campsey in 1543, and the Jerninghams at their ancestral priory at St Olaves in 1546.[73]

The final defeat of the Howards in the factional struggles of Henry's last years came with as surprising rapidity as had Cromwell's defeat at the hands of Howard seven years earlier; both Howard and his son the Earl of Surrey were arrested on 12 December 1546, and while Surrey went to the block five weeks later, his father escaped death through the death of the King whom he had served so faithfully. Nevertheless, the Howards' power was shattered. The Duke's estates were dispersed among the men in the Council who had supervised his downfall; the intention was clearly to destroy the power of the Howards for good, with no possibility of the sort of reconstruction which Thomas Howard

[71] *LP* XX pt. i, nos. 282/37; XXI pt. i, no. 302/65; XX pt. i, no. 125/2; PRO, E323/2B/1, m. 31d (*LP* XVIII pt. ii, no. 231). .
[72] *LP* XVI, no. 1391/66; XIX pt. i, nos. 812/17, 1035/41, 610/114; XIII pt. i, no. 1520.
[73] *LP* XVII, no. 220/15; XIX pt. i, no. 278/31; XXI pt. ii, no. 771/30.

had undertaken during the reign of Henry VII.[74] This left the question of who was to govern East Anglia now that both its greatest noblemen had been removed from the scene.

Even in more tranquil circumstances, the problem would have soon posed itself, probably with the usual Tudor symptoms of a rash of disputes among the local gentry carried into the common law and equity courts at Westminster. However, in the troubled conditions of a government simultaneously trying to fight a ruinously expensive war on two fronts, to carry through a religious revolution and to make expansive gestures of social reform, the question took on an especial urgency. In July 1549 the ordinary folk of East Anglia staged a concerted and spectacular mass demonstration traditionally known as Kett's Rebellion. One strong element in this was a celebration of the passing of the Howard family, a point made clear by the most famous and at first sight the most anomalous of the demands which the demonstrators produced at their largest camp, Mousehold Heath: 'We pray thatt all bonde men may be made fre for God made all fre with his precious blode sheddyng.' This was no pious piece of peasant theology; it referred bluntly to the fact that the third Duke of Norfolk had been an unusually oppressive landlord who had made the most of his family's conservatism in estate management and had exploited the remaining serfs on his estates at a time when most East Anglian manors had freed their bondmen. Whatever the gentry of Norfolk and Suffolk had felt about the Howards' passing in 1547, the Duke's ordinary tenants had shed few tears, and a group of his bondmen from both counties had lost little time in petitioning Protector Somerset for their manumission now that they were Crown property. In 1549, their published demands sought to make the process mandatory. Once the rebellion took shape, it is noticeable how its chief centres or camps in Norfolk at least were associated with former Howard properties; the seat of the rebellion was in the centre of the Duke of Norfolk's liberty and close to the Duke's former capital mansion at Kenninghall; the assembly in the King's Lynn area chose first to camp on Rising Chase, lately one of the chief Howard lordships, and the Norwich insurgents made for the Earl of Surrey's former mansion on the edge of Mousehold Heath.[75]

If the actual origins of the 1549 stirs reflected the fall of the

---

[74] See Miller, 'Henry VIII's Unwritten Will', pp. 87–105.
[75] MacCulloch, 'Kett's Rebellion', pp. 58–60. The bondmen's petition is PRO, C1/1187/9.

Howards almost in the manner of a fiesta, the ruling classes' efforts to restore their control demonstrated the contrast between the power structures of Edwardian Norfolk and Suffolk. In both counties the gentry were initially paralysed, probably terrified by the ease with which the demonstrators had seized the initiative in the region; in both counties, representatives of leading families had been rounded up and imprisoned. Even the Sheriff, Sir Nicholas L'Estrange, had been forced to leave his brother and son with the rebels in order to retain his own freedom of movement. However, the measures which the government took to restore order in the two counties differed significantly. The aim was to restore order as cheaply and with as little fuss as possible. The precedent of the Amicable Grant troubles of 1525 suggested that the easiest way to achieve this was through some powerful local figure whom the government trusted; but where would the government of Protector Somerset find the equivalent of Brandon and Howard? Their first attempt was through the Sheriff of the two counties, who was a close associate of Somerset and who had been helping Sir John Thynne to suppress earlier disturbances in Hampshire; this duty had necessarily involved him in absence from East Anglia in the crucial months of the spring and early summer when his presence back home might have been useful. Now it was too late; although L'Estrange hurried up from London on 13 July and seems to have made contact with the rebels two days later at Downham Market, he did nothing to stem the tide of the protest. Efforts at conciliation with York Herald as the government's envoy at Norwich a week later only made the situation worse; Somerset's administration was no nearer regaining control in the region. Full-scale military intervention was at that time out of the question; most of the royal forces were tied up in Scotland or the West Country.[76]

It was at this stage that one perceives the contrast between affairs in Norfolk and Suffolk as they had been left by the fall of the Howards. For Suffolk, the government had at least three reliable men who were prominent at Westminster, who were all close relatives, and who were also local men who could reason with the rebels: Sir Anthony Wingfield, by now vice-chamberlain of the household and a privy councillor, Thomas Lord Wentworth, who was probably created a privy councillor specifically to meet this challenge, and John Gosnold, who was both solicitor of the court of Augmentations and *custos*

---

[76] MacCulloch, 'Kett's rebellion', pp. 41–5.

rotulorum for the county. For Norfolk, the problem was much harder, quite apart from the fact that the camp at Norwich was the largest of all those set up in the region. No Norfolk man sat on Somerset's Privy Council, and Bishop Rugge was a nonentity. The most eloquent testimony to the disruption which the Duke of Norfolk's fall had caused to the government of Norfolk was that two outsiders were sent to lead the negotiations with the camp leaders at Norwich: William Parr, Marquis of Northampton, and Lord Wentworth.[77] Somerset had appointed Parr Lieutenant for Essex, Norfolk, and Suffolk in 1547; Parr had done some work on improving coastal defences in the region, he had inherited the manor of Bildeston in Suffolk and he was a first cousin of Sheriff L'Estrange, but he had no real connection with Norfolk.[78] He turned out to be a highly unfortunate choice, and Wentworth, for all his newly-acquired status of councillor, was a Suffolk and not a Norfolk man. By contrast, Wingfield and Gosnold were wholly appropriate men to deal with Suffolk.

This team, backed up by as much military force as the government could spare, and suitably armed with promises of pardon for the rebels, set out from London around 26 or 27 July. They probably started by neutralizing the camp at Bury St Edmunds, which would be on their route to Norwich, but after that the result of the expedition in either county was very different. At Melton in east Suffolk, Wingfield and Gosnold succeeded in persuading the insurgents that the King really wanted to pardon them, and they were soon writing back to London for money to help the pacification. At Norwich the result was disastrous, thanks to Northampton's ineptitude in provoking a full-scale battle in which a peer of the realm was killed; it took a fresh expeditionary force under the Earl of Warwick to suppress the rebels with a ferocity which was applauded and exceeded by the demoralized local gentry.[79]

It may well have been Warwick's experiences in the East Anglian crisis of 1549 which encouraged him in his years of power as Duke of Northumberland to experiment with lords lieutenant. The system is first mentioned in the King's Chronicle for May 1550, although William Paget had already suggested something of the sort to

[77] Ibid., pp. 45–7.
[78] *APC* I, p. 118; PRO, C1/1317/1; PRO, SP 12/171/63; Gurney, 'Household Accounts', p. 419.
[79] MacCulloch, 'Kett's Rebellion', p. 46; Bindoff, p. 6; PRO, SP 10/8/55 I. Robert Parkyn, writing from news reaching the North, confirms that there was a 'treattie and ther pardon promisside': 'Parkyn', p. 70.

Somerset in February 1549; the first surviving commissions of a series renewed annually date from 26 May 1551.[80] That first commission had the familiar name of Sir Anthony Wingfield in combination with the Lord Chamberlain, Thomas Lord Darcy: the old Lord Wentworth had died at the beginning of the year. Darcy had been building up Suffolk estates and interests since the end of the 1530s; he had friends and relatives in the county, particularly in the west, and Somerset's regime had encouraged him in his local ambitions on Henry's death by granting him the Stewardship of the Liberty of St Edmund, confiscated from the Howards, together with the custody of all the Howards' Suffolk lands, and the keepership of Framlingham Castle and Park.[81] In 1552 the new Lord Wentworth was added to the Lieutenancy; with Lord Darcy's west Suffolk base and Lord Wentworth's interests in the east of the county, the lieutenancy was neatly balanced, and represented an aggregate of power and influence which might equal that of the Duke of Norfolk in his great days. In Norfolk, the government was clearly intending to make a fresh start out of the confusion which Kett's Rebellion had revealed. Bishop Rugge had been brusquely forced into retirement in 1550; his successor was the diplomat Thomas Thirlby, who although an almost permanent absentee, left the adminstration of the diocese in the hands of capable servants.[82] Northumberland's strategy here was to build up his own power base by establishing his son Robert as a local magnate. Robert had married the daughter of Sir John Robsart of Syderstone in 1550 and was becoming an active JP in the county by 1551.[83] The lieutenancy commission of May 1552 shows how the Norfolk system was developing, with Dudley and Sir John Robsart in partnership with the Earl of Sussex and Sir William Farmer, a leading county gentleman, but only established in Norfolk after one generation of riches.

    [80] M. L. Bush, *The Government Policy of Protector Somerset* (1975), p. 127. On the lieutenancy in Suffolk, Scott Thomson, 'Lord Lieutenancy', p. 228.
    [81] Suffolk lands and offices: *LP* XIV pt. i, no. 113/17; XVII, no. 362/62, 1258 I; XXI pt. i, no. 1537/23. Cf. the accounts of his ship at Dunwich, *Mariners Mirror* XXV (1939), pp. 170 ff. Lady Darcy lodged at Sir Thomas Tyrrell's house at Gipping (PCC 23 Bucke), and in 1569 the under-steward of Bury St Edmunds, John Holt, remembered his 'olde maister' Darcy with warm gratitude (PCC 11 Lyon). Somerset's grants: *APC* II, p. 19.
    [82] T. F. Shirley, *Thomas Thirlby, Tudor Bishop* (1964). Shirley is not quite correct in saying that Thirlby never saw the diocese during his episcopate (p. 106), for he was involved in a commission in Norwich in 1552 (BL Add. 27959, fo. 1).
    [83] Marriage agreement: PRO, E328/101; attendance at Norwich sessions, PRO, KB 9/581, m. 39.

The further development of this planned system of close personal supervision in the region was rudely interrupted by Edward VI's death from tuberculosis in July 1553. East Anglia then became the theatre of the last total defeat of the Westminster government by the provinces before 1642; the Princess Mary fled there from Hertfordshire, raised her standard and persuaded the entire gentry community of the region to support her. Mary's spectacular success in her *coup d'état* has ‧ obscured the scale of her achievement. Systematic suppresion of the evidence has concealed the fact that in counties as diverse as Cornwall and Suffolk, the first reaction of the county leadership was to obey Westminster's orders, as they had been doing for more than half a century, and proclaim Queen Jane. The gentlemen of Suffolk under Lord Wentworth's leadership met at Ipswich on 11 July to consider the situation, and after long and careful discussion they proclaimed Jane; the proclamation was made by the Sheriff, Sir Thomas Cornwallis, who was a lifelong devout Catholic. Despite Cornwallis's doubts about what he had done, he changed his mind only after an accidental meeting with a close friend who had just observed the popular hostility to Northumberland in London; Cornwallis returned to Ipswich on 12 July to proclaim Mary. Similarly, it was Mary's chance capture of the Earl of Sussex's son that brought the Earl hastening from his home at Attleburgh to her base at nearby Kenninghall to change his allegiance; the alliance between the Earl and Robert Dudley, who had previously persuaded him that Edward VI was still alive, came to an end. In Suffolk, Lord Wentworth took until 14 July to wrestle with his conscience and reject his oath to Queen Jane; when he did so, it was through the mediation of John Tyrrell and Edward Glemham, two members of the Wentworth–Wingfield family circle who had already gone over to Mary a couple of days before.[84]

The manner in which the *coup* had proceeded had a considerable effect on the reordering of East Anglian political life which characterized Mary's reign. First, it had been masterminded by Mary's Catholic household officers, who included a remarkably high proportion of East Anglians: eleven out of twenty-nine members listed by the contemporary chronicler of the *coup*, including its three leading men, Robert Rochester, Henry Jerningham, and Edward Waldegrave. All three

---

[84] '*Vita Mariae*' pp. 254–7. On Jane's proclamation, cf. Rowse, p. 300, Palliser, p. 52, 'Parkyn', p. 77, and for her proclamation at Bury St Edmunds, PRO KB 9/584, m. 100. Cf. also R. Tittler and S. L. Battley, 'The Local Community and the Crown in 1553: the accession of Mary Tudor revisited', *BIHR* LVII (1984), pp. 131–9.

would continue as leading figures in the Marian regime. No doubt they had laid good advance plans among their East Anglian relatives to receive Mary in the event of trouble, but the second stage of the *coup* had been to win over the uncommitted, like the county leadership which had proclaimed Jane at Ipswich. When this operation, based on a call to legitimism and a convenient silence on the subject of religion, had been successful, this group was added to Mary's council of war at her Framlingham headquarters: the Earl of Bath, Sir Thomas Cornwallis, Sir William Drury, Sir Clement Higham, Sir John Shelton, Sir Richard Southwell, the Earl of Sussex, Lord Wentworth. They remained privy councillors, but for the most part in an honorary capacity as a measure of the Queen's gratitude for their service in the heroic days of the triumph at Framlingham; they continued to make themselves useful in mostly secondary roles, often in their own country.[85] They became the backbone of administration in Norfolk and Suffolk, and ensured that there was a particularly effective Marian leadership in a region which was unusually divided and troublesome, and where a number of active Protestants had to be removed from the justices' Bench (see below, Ch. 7). Both the Earl of Bath and the Earl of Sussex were active in organizing East Anglian defence under Mary, Sussex lending particular support to Bishop Hopton in his campaign to eliminate active Protestantism.[86]

Parliamentary elections provide interesting proof of the continuing dominance of the men of the *coup* in the affairs of Marian Suffolk. The most emphatic demonstration comes from Ipswich, which repeatedly breached its long-established custom of choosing leading townsfolk or gentlemen closely connected with the borough, to honour the memory of the *coup* in four out of five of Mary's Parliaments. In October 1553 and October 1555 John Sulyard of Wetherden, standard-bearer of the Queen's pensioners and a member of her household before the *coup*, was chosen as one of the MPs;[87] in April 1554 there were elected Clement Higham of far-off Barrow in west Suffolk, a Framlingham councillor, and Thomas Poley, an intrepid servant of Mary whose claim to fame was that he had defiantly proclaimed her at Ipswich

[85] *'Vita Mariae'* pp. 189–91. Mary's privy councillors are listed in Loades, *Mary Tudor*, pp. 475–80. I am grateful to Prof. Dale Hoak for sending me a copy of his so far unpublished paper on Mary I's Privy Council.

[86] Hengr. 88/1/101, 103; 88/3/11; *CPR Philip and Mary* III, p. 554; *Original Letters* I, p. 179; BL Cott. Titus B II, fos. 142–3.

[87] PRO, LC 2/4(2), 2/4(3) (I owe these references to Dr W. J. Tighe); *'Vita Mariae'* p. 252.

while in another part of the town, Lord Wentworth's assembly of gentry was proclaiming Jane.[88] The most striking choice was in January 1558: Philip Williams, a mere innkeeper of the town and a Welshman into the bargain, who was celebrated both for his ardent Catholicism and for his crucial role on 14 July 1553 in letting Mary's forces know that Northumberland's naval squadron had mutinied in her favour while at anchor in the Orwell estuary.[89]

The county elections tell the same story. Sir William Drury and Mary's old servant Sir Henry Jerningham were knights of the shire for Suffolk in each of Mary's first four Parliaments. By the end of 1557, Sir William was sinking into his last illness, so there would have to be a change of representation. Sir Thomas Cornwallis and the Master of the Rolls, Sir William Cordell, sat in the Parliament of January 1558. A letter about this election from one of the county JPs, John Southwell of Barham, throws light on the cosy consensus politics within the Marian county oligarchy; there is no suggestion that a contested election might be a possibility, nor that serious disagreement could arise among the men of the Framlingham adventure.[90] Southwell told his servant in this letter to sound out Sir Thomas Cornwallis:

> at the tyme of takinge your leve of Sir Thomas knowe whither he will be contented in case we chose hym one of the knights of the Shire, and also whome he wolde have more chosen with hym, and whether he thinke that Sir Henry Bedingfeld, Sir Henrye Jernyngham is desierus to have it orelles if none of them, whether he be content Sir John Suliard should have it with hym. Sir William Drurie is verye weke and whether Sir Ambrose Jermyne is desierus to have it or not, I knowe not, nor yet whether Sir Thomas will write that any of his brotherne or I should speke to Mr. Shrive and other gentlemen in this case and howe his plesure is we shall procede with towchinge hym I and my frindes shall to the uttermoste of my power followe.

A significant feature of the letter is the assumption that Sir Thomas Cornwallis would be the natural knight of the shire for the county. Why should this be, when he had not previously sat for the county or in any Suffolk borough? It was not because of his service at Court, but rather the reflection of a force in East Anglian politics which had been gathering strength during Mary's reign: a new recovery for the Howard family. Sir Thomas was the leading servant of Thomas Howard, fourth Duke of Norfolk.

[88] *'Vita Mariae'* pp. 255–6.
[89] Foxe, VIII, pp. 219, 598; *'Vita Mariae'* pp. 258–9. Williams may have been French rather than Welsh (ibid. p. 297, n. 39). [90] Hengr. 88/3/26.

Mary's first East Anglian headquarters had been the former Howard palace at Kenninghall, and her second, their ancient castle at Framlingham: both understandable choices, since these were both properties which the Edwardian regime had granted her, but also a tribute to the sound geographical strategy of the Howards in making these their principal East Anglian residences. Mary's success inevitably involved the restoration of the Howards. The third Duke was waiting for Mary at the Tower on her first entry into London, and immediately regained his freedom; the Parliamentary repeal of his attainder followed naturally. To reconstruct the Howard inheritance was a rather more complex matter. Despite the Duke's pleas that his estates should be kept together even if they were confiscated, his enemies had dispersed them, so two years were spent hammering out a settlement with those who had bought former Howard lands in good faith by letters patent and who now found themselves deprived of their property. Not everyone was satisfied, and at least one former patentee, the unscrupulous and disreputable Suffolk knight Sir Edmund Rous, revived his claims at the time of the next Howard disaster in 1572.[91]

The impact of the Howard recovery was at first muted. The third Duke had recovered all his former lands and dignities, but he was approaching eighty, and, as John Foxe, who knew the family at first hand, recorded, he was a shadow of his former self. His last military command, the leadership of a force against the Kentish rebels of Sir Thomas Wyatt in 1554, was an unqualified disaster, and within the year he was dead.[92] His successor, his grandson Thomas, was then only sixteen years old. Only gradually would the new Duke take on the role in local and national affairs to which his rank and favour from the Queen entitled him. At a local level, his first royal service out of many came in January 1558, on the eve of his twentieth birthday, when he was put in charge of levying fresh troops in Norfolk and Suffolk to aid Calais; the whole levy was abandoned in less than a month when the hopelessness of the situation became apparent.[93] In June 1558 he was in London, writing to the Earl of Bath to levy a further two hundred men from the two counties, and flexing his muscles to a man forty years his senior in the traditionally peremptory Howard epistolary

---

[91] *'Vita Mariae'* p. 272; Miller, 'Henry VIII's Unwritten Will', pp. 99–100; *HMC Salisbury* II, p. 5. We await Mr Gary Hill's Oxford dissertation on the Howard lands dispute.
[92] Foxe, V, p. 553; *'Vita Mariae'* pp. 280–1.
[93] PRO, SP 11/12, fos. 23, 50, 54, 56, 78, 83.

style: 'I shall further desier your good L. to se that al thinges be well ordered in the Shire . . . as my trust ys in yow'.[94]

Here was the authentic note of the 'high and mightye Prynce Thomas Duke of Norfolk' who was to be the leading figure of East Anglia until the crisis of 1569–72; but before the Duke's adult career was fully under way, Queen Mary was dead. Inevitably this would have an effect on the balance of power in the region. With the coming of a determinedly Protestant ruling clique around the new Queen, the men of Mary's *coup* were yesterday's men in national affairs, but what would happen to them in their own countries? Might they continue to dominate the region in the manner described in the epitaph of Sir Clement Higham of Barrow? Sir Clement continued as *custos rotulorum* for Suffolk up to his death in 1571, despite being a convinced Catholic; he had been Speaker of the 1555 Parliament and Lord Chief Baron of Mary's Exchequer

> The which advauncement ended by Queene Maries death: and hee
> Retorninge unto private state, contynude in degree ·
> Of worshippe in his country still, as Justicer of Peace.
> And from his vertues here reherst, till death he ded not cease.
>
> . . . .
>
> By this his knowledge in those lawes, he ded still peace preserve,
> When quarrels causd his neyghbors ofte, from unitye to swerve.
> His country may full well bewaile, the loss of such a guyde:
> Who ready was as rightfull iudge, their strife for to decyde.[95]

(b) The reign of Elizabeth: the Duke's departure

In his study of Elizabethan Norfolk, Dr Hassell Smith provided a detailed picture of the Duke of Norfolk's pre-eminence in that county during the first decade of Elizabeth's reign. Howard was too young to have been damagingly compromised by too close an association with the Marian regime; he was England's premier peer, Earl Marshal by hereditary right and after 1562, a privy councillor; in his home county he enjoyed a position which could give substance to his later boast to Queen Elizabeth: 'I count myself, by your Majesty's favour, as good a prince at home in my bowling-alley at Norwich as . . . [Mary Stuart] is, though she were in the midst of Scotland'.[96] Like his grandfather and great-grandfather before him, he was a great man in Suffolk too, and he was the obvious person to be appointed as Lord Lieutenant for the

---

[94] Hengr. 88/3/10.   [95] Monumental brass, Barrow.
[96] Smith, p. 25, and Ch. 2 generally; see also Williams, *Thomas Howard*, Chs. 3 and 5.

two counties in 1559. In 1566 he emphasized the point to Secretary Cecil: 'I wold have been sorye that my cuntrye men schuld have hade cawse to have iudge that enye matter concernyng the quenes maiestyes sarvys in Norfolke or Suffolke shulde rather have bene comyttyd off trust to others than to me'.[97]

The Duke's influence in Suffolk may be gauged, as in Norfolk, by an examination of the county commissions of the peace during the 1560s. Like the Marian regime before it in 1553, the government did its best in 1558 to eliminate men who would oppose a change in direction in religious policy. Nevertheless, it would have been folly to disrupt local government overmuch, and the commission remained fairly evenly balanced between conservatives and Protestants; it would be up to the government to shift the balance in favour of the new religious settlement if it could over the next few years.[98] Over the next two or three years, various Catholic JPs who had been retained at first were excluded: Sir Henry Doyle, Sir Henry Jerningham, Robert Rookwood (a royal official under Mary), Thomas Rous (generous with financial help to exiled Catholics during the 1560s), Sir John Sulyard, Thomas Timperley.[99] Two other conservatives, the Earl of Bath and Sir John Jerningham of Somerleyton, had been removed from the commission by death. Yet despite the Privy Council's repeated attempts to identify conservative justices on a nationwide basis and purge the Benches accordingly, the proportion of conservatives on the Suffolk Bench in 1564 remained much the same as it had been five years earlier: about half, with a minimum of eighteen out of thirty-six. In the intervening period the number of Suffolk JPs had been reduced by three, the total number of identifiable conservatives by two.[100]

The responsibility for this strange state of affairs can only lie with the Duke of Norfolk. Even if he himself always claimed to be a good Protestant, and gave a place in his household to his old tutor, the martyrologist John Foxe, his circle of client gentry in Suffolk was consistently conservative.[101] Michael Hare, son of the Howard family

[97] Scott Thomson, 'Lord Lieutenancy', p. 229; PRO, SP 15/13/52.
[98] MacCulloch, 'Power, Privilege and the County Community', pp. 40–3, and below, Ch. 8.
[99] Rookwood was described as a servant of the late Queen in a case of 1561, PRO, DL 1/50/S4; cf. *CPR Philip and Mary* I, p. 305. Rous was discovered to have sent £19 to Louvain in 1568 (Strype, *Annals* I pt. ii, p. 261) and was accused of maintaining his brother, a doctor of civil and canon law, at Rome, *c.*1570 (PRO, SP 15/19/58, qu. Trimble, p. 53).
[100] MacCulloch, 'Power, Privilege and the County Community', p. 50.
[101] On Foxe, Williams, *Thomas Howard*, pp. 47–8, 253.

lawyer, became a justice against the odds in 1559; in 1560 the Duke's chief agent, Sir Thomas Cornwallis, reappeared briefly in commission despite his earlier removal.[102] By 1564 Cornwallis's son-in-law Thomas Kitson, who had served in the Duke's household at Kenninghall, was on the Bench, and the conservative Kitson family lawyer Henry Payne of Bury had only a few months to wait before he was restored to the commission after the 1559 purges.[103] In 1564 Thomas Steynings, who had been a steward of the Howard estates and who had married the Duke's widowed mother, appeared on the Bench, and in the same year Sir John Tyrrell, who seems to have had links with the Duke, made a brief reappearance in commission.[104] The head of the Tollemaches of Helmingham, a family with long-standing Howard links, was in commission up to the crisis of 1569, and John Blennerhasset of Barsham, the Duke's steward, seems to have remained in commission in Suffolk up to his death in 1573.[105] This bloc counterbalanced the losses that the conservatives had suffered in the commission in 1559; in general those who were then dismissed and did not reappear were from those families who do not seem to have had close links with the Howards, such as the Rookwoods, the Bedingfields and Jerninghams, the Kempes and Clerkes.

In 1564 the new Protestant Bishop of Norwich, John Parkhurst, was told by the Privy Council to report on the religious views of the justices of Norfolk and Suffolk as part of a national campaign to purge the Benches of conservatives by consulting the bishops. Dr Smith has emphasized the strangeness of the Norfolk section of the report, coming from a radically Protestant cleric who nevertheless named only four justices who were 'not thought by common fame to be so well bent as the other' and did not suggest a single Protestant replacement; the Suffolk section of his report is equally odd.[106] Commendably, Parkhurst decided to rely on the reports of his officers in the county for greater impartiality rather than listen to any gentleman. Their efforts produced the names of seven justices who 'are not so well bent unto the advauncement of the godlie procedinges of this realme in cawses ecclesiasticall as other the justices of that shire be'—an even more

---

[102] Attendance at Ipswich quarter sessions, January 1560: PRO, E137/42/4.

[103] Hengr. 88/1/159, 72, 93.

[104] Steynings: *PSIA* XXVI (1955), pp. 146–7. In November 1559 it was said of the two rich manors of Cotton parish that 'my lord of Norff. meaneth to obteyne them for Sir John Tyrrell in recompens of the manor of Kanhams' (PRO, SP 12/7/36), which the Duke did the following year (*CPR Eliz.* I, p. 260).

[105] Hengr. 18, fo. 28ʳ.   [106] Bateson, 'Original Letters', p. 48; Smith, p. 35.

elaborately soothing circumlocution than the formula that Parkhurst used in his Norfolk report. Although Sir John Tyrrell, Lionel Tollemache, and Henry Payne from among the Howard circle appeared on the list, there was no mention of Michael Hare, John Blennerhasset, Thomas Kitson, Thomas Steynings or Sir Thomas Cornwallis's lawyer, John Thurston of Hoxne, all men with Howard connections: hardly surprising omissions when Parkhurst noted in his Norfolk report that he had consulted with the Duke in the matter.[107] Among the four other justices on the list, Parkhurst qualified his remarks still further: 'I must testefie as in my certificat of Norffolk that I nether know nor yet can lerne probablie of anie fact, that eyther Sir Clement Higham or Mr. Gosnoll are to be charged withall . . .': this of one of Mary's chief officials and of one of the villains of Foxe's *Acts and Monuments*.[108]

It is perhaps not unexpected that Parkhurst's information had little effect on the composition of the Suffolk Bench; of the seven JPs that he named, only three, John Southwell, William Foster, and Sir John Tyrrell, were dismissed, the two latter having apparently only come into commission that year, for they appear as Elizabethan justices in no other source besides the Bishop's report. Parkhurst's native Protestant zeal counted for less in his report than the wishes of the Duke. When the composition of the commission of the peace could be swayed so much by the Howard interest, it was an easy task for the Duke to perform lesser favours for his Suffolk clients while he was at Court; when, for instance, Thomas Kitson was appointed a captain of the local military levies, his wife wrote off to the Duchess of Norfolk to ask the Duke to procure Kitson's discharge by special letters from the Privy Council 'lest peradventur in thabsence of my L. Grace from the Court or in the want of some other appoynted to be in readynes by the L. Wentworth, ther shall seme some necesitie to contynue ther former determination towardes my sayd husband, contrary to my L. Grace's good meanyng towardes hym . . .'[109]

Nevertheless, the degree of the Duke's influence in Suffolk was different from that portrayed by Dr Smith in Norfolk. He could wield considerable authority within the bounds of his own Liberty, but only fifteen of its 139 townships lay in Suffolk, the rest in Norfolk. In Norfolk the Duke's influence was decisive in nominating at least one MP for each of the county's boroughs in nearly every parliamentary

---

[107] On Thurston, see Hengr. 88/1/159.
[108] Foxe, VIII, p. 433.   [109] Hengr. 88/2/46.

election up to 1572, and his influence seems traceable in the elections of some of the knights of the shire as well;[110] in Suffolk there is no evidence for the Duke having any effect on any election either for a county or a borough seat until his seigneurial borough of Aldeburgh was enfranchised in 1571.

The Duke could bring much influence to bear on the composition of the Suffolk commission of the peace and on certain other types of patronage because of his influence on the Bishop of Norwich, who fell within the scope of his powerful Norfolk patronage, and because he could use his position at Court to obtain favours for his clients, even when his Court position became threatened as the decade wore on and he withdrew increasingly into his East Anglian domains. Because this was the character of his patronage, he could not bring influence to bear on the more local workings of Suffolk parliamentary elections in the same way as in Norfolk; at a local level, there was still a substantial number of Suffolk gentry who stood outside the Howard clientage, a group that had no equivalent in Norfolk.

Most prominent among these gentry was now Elizabeth's first Lord Keeper of the Great Seal, Sir Nicholas Bacon. Denied the Lord Chancellorship itself and the chance of a peerage probably because of royal prejudice against his yeoman background, he was nevertheless to have a burial-space reserved next to that of John of Gaunt in Old St Paul's, and through judicious use of his various official positions under Henry VIII, Edward VI, and Elizabeth, he had built up extensive estates in his native Suffolk.[111] In 1555 this son of the Abbot of Bury's sheepreeve scored a local coup by acquiring the Liberty of the town of Bury St Edmunds from Lord Darcy, thereby becoming the successor of generations of Abbots: he picked up the stewardships of seven-and-a-half out of the eight-and-a-half hundreds within the Liberty of St Edmund by stages up to 1562, taking good care to prove his claim to the financial perquisites appertaining to these offices before the officials of the Exchequer.[112] He also came to monopolize most of the stewardships of the Duchy of Lancaster within the county, and was granted the stewardship of the Honour of Eye; on the death of Sir Clement Higham in 1571, he extended his conquests in the Liberty by

[110] Smith, pp. 36–41.
[111] See Simpson, pp. 1–139, for a concise biography and economic study of Bacon.
[112] *CPR Eliz.* II, p. 256. Bacon had already leased the Liberty before Lord Darcy acquired it in 1553 (SROB, Accn. 449/5/31/31, contemporary copy of Darcy's letters patent. Cf. PRO, E368/346, m. 20).

having his eldest son appointed chief bailiff of the liberty of the town of Bury.[113]

Such offices were honorific and profitable; positions on the commission of the peace and on the diocesan ecclesiastical commission were incidental rights of Bacon's eminence; but that eminence within the county stemmed from his role at Westminster at the heart of the formal agency of Court patronage in Chancery. Considering that the commissions of the peace were made up in Chancery, it is surprising that there is little evidence of Bacon's use of this most obvious form of patronage. Bacon's servant John Eyer returned to the commission in 1559, but he had a certain claim to do so as a former JP dismissed by the Marian regime; Henry Chitting may have been a protégé of the Lord Keeper.[114] By 1569 Bacon's servant Thomas Andrews, and by 1575 John Le Hunt, was in commission; both men, however, were lawyers of some distinction and might have justified their position on the Bench on their own merits, while Le Hunt had other connections at Court.[115]

The evidence is better for Bacon's influence in Parliamentary elections. In 1571 the borough of Eye near his home at Redgrave was enfranchised, and it became a safe seat for any nominee of the Bacon family, as no doubt the Lord Keeper had intended; in 1603 Philip Gawdy, a relative of the Bacons and already MP for the borough in 1593, could write from Court to his brother Bassingbourn in Norfolk, 'I pray make suer with Sir Nicholas Bacon that I may be burgesse of Aye'.[116] At Sudbury Bacon's influence is traceable in 1563 and 1571, perhaps because of his involvement with the local administration of the Duchy of Lancaster, perhaps also because of his friendship with William Waldegrave, the borough's long-standing patron; he may also have had a hand in the parliamentary enfranchisement of the borough with the confirmation of its new charter in 1559.[117] In the 1563

---

[113] *CPR Eliz.* II, p. 256; IV, no. 2575; V, no. 1792.

[114] MacCulloch, 'Power, Privilege and the County Community', p. 42.

[115] Frequent mentions of Andrews occur in the Bacon correspondence, Redgr. 4065–4178. He was Assize Clerk on the Western Circuit 1560–9 (Cockburn, pp. 77, 318). Le Hunt was described as Bacon's servant in a Chancery case of 1577 (PRO, C2 ELIZ M10/48) and was himself a D.Civ.L. (cf. e.g. PRO, C66/1329, m. 25d); he was a Master in Chancery from 38 to 45 Eliz. (Haydn, p. 395). He was also a great-nephew by marriage and 'espetiall good friend' of the Essex Gentleman Pensioner Henry MacWilliam, whose wife, the widow of Sir John Cheke, was a lady of the Queen's Privy Chamber (PCC 50 Strafford).   [116] Jeayes, p. 127.

[117] Waldegrave was active in the Bacon cause in the 1572 county election (Redgr. 4118). The charter, an *inspeximus* of that of 1554, does not mention the right to return members to Parliament (*PSIA* XIII, 1909, pp. 263 ff.).

election, the second MP for the borough was Thomas Andrews, while in 1571 the town sent its mayor off to Redgrave expressly to confer with 'my Lorde Keper for the appoyntinge of too Burgesses for the parliament'.[118] The first man that they chose was clearly a nominee of the Lord Keeper, John Le Hunt; the second was a more local gentleman, John Gurdon of Assington.

There is no evidence of a similar involvement in the 1572 election, but in that year the Lord Keeper had other worries. His eldest son Nicholas, only newly a justice of the peace for the county, decided to put himself forward for election as knight of the shire, a move which the Lord Keeper, always conscious of the proprieties in local politics, considered premature. It was all very well for Nicholas to have sat for the newly-enfranchised borough of Beverley far away in Yorkshire in 1563, at the age of twenty, but the county election was a different matter.[119] 'I had no greate desyre to have you delt in yt at thys tyme, but seyng you have gon so far I wold not have you yeld for feare of charge', he wrote from London to his rash offspring. The Bacon family honour was at stake, and the Lord Keeper resigned himself to participating, promising his son one hundred pounds and more to back up his campaign, enlisting the support of the Master of the Rolls (Cordell), setting out the possible sources of support and opposition within the county and unsuccessfully attempting to form an election partnership with the respected county magnate Sir Owen Hopton, Lieutenant of the Tower and knight of the shire in 1559 and in the previous Parliament. He emphasized that he wished to carry a low profile in the election campaign: 'you must take great hede that my name be non otherwyse usyd then you have wreton.'[120]

In the event, however, the Bacon name carried the day, and young Nicholas made his debut in county politics as first knight of the shire, with Sir Robert Wingfield, county MP in 1563 and one of the potential opposition noted by the Lord Keeper, in second place. The compromise was a significant one, for it is likely that just as in the election for the January 1558 Parliament, this election owed more to discussions among a gentry oligarchy in county politics than to the

[118] SROB, EE 501/1, fo. 108ʳ.

[119] The younger Nicholas was 44 in 1587 (PRO, E134/29 Eliz./Trinity 2). Besides various other serious errors in his account of the 1572 election campaign, Tittler (pp. 163–4) confuses Nicholas with his younger brother Nathaniel.

[120] This paragraph is based in Redgr. 4118, which Sir Nicholas misdated 1571; the date Thursday 24 April can only be of 1572. Bacon's negotiations with Hopton are outlined in Redgr. 4117 (17 Apr. 1572).

outcome of a contest at the polls. At the beginning of the month the Privy Council had written to the Lord Keeper and Lord Wentworth to 'have good choyce' in the election of the Suffolk knights of the shire, no doubt mindful of the Duke's execution; hence, perhaps, the Lord Keeper's embarrassment at the repercussions for his reputation in the county of his son's electoral initiative.[121] After the political storms of the previous three years, this was no time to be having open disagreements at the polls, and it was presumably the consultations of Wentworth and Bacon rather than the untrammelled choice of the county electorate, which made Sir Robert Wingfield content to yield first place to the younger Nicholas Bacon with a good grace. After all, Wentworth was in a good position as Sir Robert's father-in-law to exert a little influence and smooth over potential trouble. The Lord Keeper's promise of a hundred pounds and more, if it was ever anything more than a rhetorical flourish, is unlikely to have been called upon.

The Lord Keeper could exercise his patronage in other directions; it can only have been through him, for instance, that in 1575 Eye became one of the few places to gain exemption from purveyance demands during the reign.[122] Bacon servants and associates played a major part in the day-to-day administration of the county during his lifetime: John Eyer as Receiver-General of Crown Revenues until his death in 1561 with his nephew Thomas Badby succeeding him, John Southwell the elder, Francis Boldero and Thomas Andrews as successive feodaries, various High Collectors of subsidies who executed this office more regularly than was normal in the county: Edward Bacon, Francis Boldero, William Corbould, Robert Thorpe.[123]

Bacon's influence was especially predictable in the Court of Wards and Liveries, over which he presided until 1561; it can hardly be coincidence that of the nineteen individuals who held the office of escheator of Norfolk and Suffolk from 1559 to 1579, no less than fourteen were Suffolk men. Curiously, the tally is even more strikingly weighted before the Duke of Norfolk's fall than after: eleven out of

---

[121] BL Add. 48018, fo. 282ᵛ.

[122] Woodworth, p. 35, and cf. the Eye charter, *CPR Eliz.* VI, no. 2190.

[123] Succession of Receivers: PRO, E401/1794–1797, fo. 98ᵛ; *CPR Eliz.* II, p. 33; PRO, WARD 13/3, Answer of Sir Ambrose Jermyn to a debt in the Court (1562). John Southwell's son John served the Lord Keeper in his youth (Candler MS, qu. Iveagh/Phillips 4, fo. 21ʳ). Feodaries: PRO, SP 15/21/87; *CPR Eliz.* VII, no. 91. High Collectors are derived from PRO, E401, Receipt Rolls and Books. Corbould was Bacon's steward of the manor of Burgate (Redgr. 4123).

thirteen between 1559 and 1571.[124] Of these, three (Francis Boldero, Augustine Curtis, and George Nunn) who held the office in succession from 1561 to the end of 1564, were in Bacon's retinue, while George Waller of Wortham (1564/5), Edmund Ashfield, and George Chitting of Wortham and Milden (successively November 1566–November 1568) had homes close to Redgrave; Chitting was the son of the late JP Henry Chitting and Boldero's brother-in-law, and the Ashfields were close friends of the Lord Keeper.[125] Edmund Wright of Bradfield Combust, escheator in 1553/4 and 1560/1, was Chitting's brother-in-law: altogether a cosy little group of administrators under Bacon's aegis.

No doubt if more could be discovered about the lesser officials of the county, Sir Nicholas's role would become even clearer; in 1570 he wrote to his son Nicholas of one of their household servants 'Tell George Nunne . . . his sonne is undershiref but not without much ado', the 'ado' presumably being to persuade his friend Edmund Withipoll to accept this candidate for his year of shrievalty.[126] It is noticeable that John Bacon, the Lord Keeper's distant cousin from the old gentry family of Hessett, was under-sheriff in 1574, and possibly also again in 1581, in the latter case to the younger Sir Nicholas; he was also escheator in 1574/6.[127] However, the statesman whose motto was '*mediocria firma*' was content to use his opportunities for patronage with restraint. 'Yo writt for my lettere in favor of one to be undershireve', he wrote severely to his son Nicholas in 1569, 'and yo tell me not his name, whereby I must writt for one that I knowe not, which I use not to do.' The following year, after another request from his son for a friend, he 'lett Mr Cowte to understand that albeit I have refused to all men to deale in such suytes as his is, yit upon yor lettere I was contented to writt to Mr. Secretary in his favor'.[128]

A man with such formidable access to the springs of patronage, a

---

[124] *List of Escheators for England and Wales*, List and Index Society LXXII, pp. 91–2.

[125] Curtis, Boldero and Nunn were among Bacon's feoffees in 1566 (*CPR Eliz*. III, no. 2241). Cf. Waller's will, CCN 170 Bate, and the letters between Bacon and Robert Ashfield, BL Harl. 286, fo. 8, and Redgr. 4089. Wright: Metcalfe, p. 14, and *1568 Subsidy* p. 250.

[126] Redgr. 4109, and cf. Redgr. 4090. Nunn was presumably under-sheriff of Norfolk, as Henry Hannam of Ipswich is recorded as under-sheriff of Suffolk for this year (*HMC Various Collections* IV, p. 275; Webb, *Poor Relief*, pp. 15 n., 100).

[127] PRO, SP 46/15, fo. 77; PRO, E401/1834, *s.v.* 21 February. John Bacon was involved in the Lord Keeper's business affairs (cf. PRO, E134/24, 25 Eliz./Michaelmas 5, deposition of John Bumpstead).

[128] Redgr. 4099, 4104.

man who was received at the county border by the leading gentlemen
of the Liberty of St Edmund as if he were a monarch on progress,[129]
inevitably provided a challenge to the Duke of Norfolk's position, quite
apart from the fact that the Lord Keeper was one of the architects of
the new settlement in religion that was anathema to so many of the
Duke's clientage. Yet Bacon's restraint, perhaps partly the respect of a
parvenu for England's only Duke, characterized his relations with
Thomas Howard as much as it did his electioneering and his use of
patronage; there is no hint of trouble between the two magnates. A
potential source of friction was their dual jurisdiction within the
Liberty of St Edmund, for while Sir Nicholas was lessee of most of the
Abbot of Bury's former rights within the Liberty, the Duke was its
hereditary Steward; the Steward and the Abbots had often been at
loggerheads before the Dissolution.[130] However, there seems to have
been a satisfactory arrangement between Bacon and the Duke, for the
Liberty was administered by servants of the Lord Keeper, successively
Robert Thorpe and Thomas Andrews, who exercised their jurisdiction
in the Duke's name.[131] This arrangement seems to have survived
Norfolk's fall, for the younger Sir Nicholas Bacon's lawyer Robert
Mawe was still acting as under-steward to the Earl of Arundel's
steward Edward Coke in 1594.[132] The inclusion of the Duke among
the notables chosen to be the feoffees of Bacon's family settlement in
1566 was perhaps an inevitable courtesy, but the Duke and the Lord
Keeper were on sufficiently good terms to effect a major exchange of
properties on the Suffolk border in 1565.[133] Aspirants for office in both
counties certainly realized that the two magnates had complementary
roles to play in the East Anglia of the sixties; thus in 1563, Thomas
Tose obtained letters of recommendation from both Duke and Lord
Keeper in his unsuccessful effort to become Town Clerk at Ipswich,
while two years later, Edmund Ashfield did the same when seeking an
under-shrievalty in either county from the sheriff-elect.[134] No doubt
many others followed their example.

---

[129] Hengr. 88/2/40, and a reference to Bacon's reception into Bury in the 1560s,
PRO, C4/160, Answer of Henry Payne to John Chetham.
[130] Ryece, p 266 n.
[131] Hengr. 91, bond of Thorpe as deputy steward to Sir Richard Fulmerston, the
Duke's under-steward for the Liberty; SROB, Accn. 449/7/2, deed of deputation of the
Stewardship jointly to Thomas Kitson and Thomas Andrews, 1567.
[132] PRO, DL 1/166/S30, and cf. PRO, E134/22 James I/Michaelmas 40.
[133] *CPR Eliz.* III, no. 2664; Williams, *Thomas Howard*, p. 113.
[134] On Tose, see above, Ch. 1, n. 80. Ashfield: BL Add. 27447, fo. 110^r.

Through his office and his wealth, Lord Keeper Bacon could easily play a leading role in western Suffolk, but in the east there were other leading men who stood outside the conservative circle who looked to the Duke of Norfolk. In particular, there were those gentry who centred on the families of Lord Wentworth and the Wingfields of Letheringham, whom we have already met in the reigns of Henry VIII and Edward VI. A snapshot of the group is conveniently provided by a list of the gentlemen who accompanied Lord Wentworth to do their fealty to Mary at Framlingham in 1553 and 'who were wont to go in his company': Sir Richard Cavendish of Trimley, Sir Henry Doyle of Hadleigh, Robert Wingfield of Letheringham, Lionel Tollemache of Helmingham, Edward Withipoll of Ipswich, John Southwell of Barham, Francis Nunn of Martlesham, John Colby of Brundish, and Robert Wingfield of Brantham, son of Sir Humphrey and the chronicler who provided us with this roll-call. The group was linked even in death, for several of them patronized the same London firm for their family funeral monuments.[135]

This group represented the shadow of Charles Brandon's East Anglian associates, and just as the Duke's household had tended towards Protestantism in the years of his fourth marriage to Katherine Willoughby, so these gentlemen and their families were predominantly Protestant in contrast to the religious conservatism so common in the Duke of Norfolk's circle. It would have been an exaggeration to describe the leading men among them as Brandon's clientage even in the great days of his East Anglian activity, and this was even more true of their relationship with the second Lord Wentworth. Wentworth's career was blighted by the fact that he had been Deputy of Calais at the time of its fall in 1558; although subsequent enquiry showed that he had warned the government of Calais' weaknesses and he was absolved from the charge of treasonable surrender, he never developed a career in national politics thereafter.[136] Although a peer of the realm, in his county he was first among a number of equals.

Shadow of the Brandon days the 'Wentworth–Wingfield' group might be, but it was a shadow with substance. Apart from Wentworth himself, the most prominent Elizabethan member was Sir Robert Wingfield, son of old Sir Anthony, and head of a family whose forest of

---

[135] *'Vita Mariae'* p. 259; cf. the monumental brasses of the Colbys and Glemhams at Brundish, of the Glemhams at Little Glemham and of Philip Parker the younger at Erwarton.

[136] *DNB* s.v. Wentworth, Thomas, 2nd Baron Wentworth.

ancestral tombs in the little priory church at Letheringham was already becoming a tourist attraction in the 1560s.[137] Sir Robert could expect to and did play a leading part in county administration; one of the most frequent recipients of Privy Council directives in the county, a muster commissioner and deputy lieutenant and an ecclesiastical commissioner for the diocese from the 1570s to the 1590s, on more than one occasion he found himself so weighed down with special commissions from central authority that he was at a loss as to how to perform them.[138]

Closely associated with Sir Robert Wingfield was his relative and near neighbour Thomas Seckford the younger, of Ipswich and Woodbridge, one of the Masters of Requests. Seckford was a younger son who had made a successful effort to restore the decayed fortunes of his house with his Court career under Elizabeth; in 1563 he acquired the Stewardship of the Dean and Chapter of Ely's Liberty of St Audrey from Sir Robert and was thus able to emulate Sir Nicholas Bacon's position in St Edmund on a smaller scale.[139] Together, Wingfield and Seckford combined county prestige with Court influence, and it was the intentions of this formidable pair that gave the Lord Keeper most apprehension for his son's candidature in the 1572 parliamentary election.[140] Both of them were firm supporters of the Elizabethan regime, Seckford among the first of Elizabeth's appointments in central government in 1558, and Wingfield one of the signatories of a protest letter about the suspension of the leading Protestant preacher John Laurence in 1567, besides having been a victim of the Marian purges of the Bench.[141] Such men as these could provide a focus of leadership for those lesser men who were of different sympathy from the Norfolk–Cornwallis alignment. The fact that the Wentworth–Wingfield group enjoyed a virtual monopoly on the county seats in Parliament from 1559 to 1572 underlines the Duke's lack of influence

---

[137] W. Bulleine, *A Comfortable Regiment, against . . . Pleurisi* (1562), STC 4035, sig. A ii. Cf. J. Blatchly, 'The lost and mutilated memorials of the Bovile and Wingfield families at Letheringham', *PSIA* XXXIII (1974), pp. 168–94.

[138] BL Harl. 286, fo. 12 (August 1569); PRO, SP 12/119/6 (1577).

[139] He left his nephew and heir Charles a third of his lands 'in augmentation of the revennews of our said howse by some of our auncestors greatlie decayed' (PCC 4 Rutland); cf. his concern to perpetuate the name of his family in his memorial inscription at Woodbridge, *Chorography* p. 92. Wingfield last appears as bailiff in PRO, E401/1801, s.v. 12 May; Seckford took a fifty-year lease of the Dean and Chapter on 3 March 1563 (PRO, E134/44, 45 Eliz./Michaelmas 39, deposition of William Carr).

[140] Redgr. 4118.

[141] Laurence: CCC, p. 647; on Marian purges, see below, Ch. 5.

on the freeholder electorate and their social superiors when compared with Norfolk.

There were thus two forces of much the same strength in Suffolk in the 1560s. One was distinctly conservative and based largely on the Duke of Norfolk's clientage and estates. The other force was entirely Suffolk-based, predominantly Protestant, and more or less independent of the Duke. There was no major group corresponding to this second group in Norfolk. Such a balance of forces in Suffolk would inevitably cause tension. It is therefore not surprising that while Dr Smith found little evidence of conflict in Norfolk during the years of the Duke's dominance, Bishop Parkhurst spoke of 'discention as well for religion as otherwise' among the gentry of Suffolk in his 1564 report to the Privy Council.[142] It was during the 1560s that the only certain sixteenth-century instance occurred of a Suffolk JP being dismissed from the Bench for riotous behaviour, when Francis Jenny was convicted in Star Chamber in 1561 of leading a riot on the Coddenham land of his fellow-JP Robert Crane.[143] The crisis of 1569–72 was crucial in altering the balance of power between these forces and hence the political atmosphere within the county.

Two different convulsions disturbed Suffolk's political life in summer and autumn 1569, well before the rebellion in the north; apart from both being symptoms of the general political malaise in England, they had no traceable connection with each other. One was an attempt at a popular rising in the style of Kett's Rebellion which took place in July and which will be considered elsewhere (below, Ch. 10); the other was the flight of the Duke of Norfolk to Kenninghall in late September. By then the Duke had become deeply embroiled in the intrigues around Mary Queen of Scots, and in the increasingly strained atmosphere of the Court, his nerve had broken. In the four days after he arrived at Kenninghall, he was visited by a remarkable procession of gentry, remarkable because it was not simply a collection of the area's leading conservatives.[144] Predictable figures were there: Sir Thomas Cornwallis, as was to be expected, even if he subsequently rather implausibly claimed to the Privy Council that he had met the Duke on his arrival by chance when he was out hunting near Diss;[145] he was soon followed by his son-in-law Thomas Kitson and his cousin

---

[142] Smith, p. 157; Bateson, 'Original Letters', p. 48.
[143] PRO, STAC 5 A3/12, A57/31; PRO, STAC 7/9/26; BL Harl. 2143, fo. 21. For a possible earlier instance, see below, p. 108.
[144] *HMC Salisbury* I, pp. 438–9.   [145] Ibid., p. 438.

Michael Hare. There were a number of figures from the Marian past, elderly gentlemen: Sir John Sulyard, Sir Ralph Chamberlain of Gedding (yet another of the Suffolk team who had been involved in the loss of Calais), the veteran courtier John Paston of Huntingfield; Sir Henry Jerningham sent his son, while Lord Morley, who later fled the realm for his Catholic religion, appeared in person. Yet among these names, what does one make of the appearance of the Lord Keeper's eldest son Nicholas, his Protestant neighbour and friend Bassingbourn Gawdy the elder, the equally Protestant Edward Grimston the elder, or the Keeper of the Town of London (soon to be the Duke's involuntary host), Sir Owen Hopton?[146] This was no gathering of potential rebels; it was the last manifestation of the deep-seated East Anglian reflex action of looking to the Duke for an initiative in a time of crisis, the last expression of the Duke's power among the gentry of the two counties before his arrest. There was no train of client supporters as he made his abject way back to London; the Lord Lieutenant's hasty soundings among 'such as loved the Queen' on the Duke's arrival had proved unnecessary.[147]

The Howard cause was not yet completely finished; there were worse and more irreversible fates in Tudor politics than being sent to the Tower, and indeed, the Duke was released to live in his own London house under house arrest by August in the following year. Yet there was no mass uprising to take the Duke from the Tower, however much his arrest offended East Anglian *amour propre*, and the rebellion in the north provided little spark for Norfolk and Suffolk. After the agitation expressed in Lord Wentworth's summons to the muster commissioners on 16 November, the situation at large was sufficiently calm by Christmas Eve for the Lord Keeper, with characteristic pennywise attention to detail, to tell his son Nicholas to break off his purchase of pistols now that better weapons could be bought at cheaper rates. Guerau de Spes's hopeful reports to the King of Spain of preparations in Norfolk and Suffolk a month later bore no fruit.[148]

The summer of 1570 brought a renewal of unrest, but this time it was led by a group of gentry with conservative associations from the Norwich area and the north-east corner of Suffolk, including John Jerningham of the cadet branch of that family established at Somerleyton and Christopher Playters of Sotterley, who may have

---

[146] Chamberlain: Ryece, p. 152. Paston: cf. his monumental brass, Huntingfield. Morley: Trimble, p. 65. Gawdy: Smith, p. 178.
[147] *HMC Salisbury* I, p. 427.

been the member of the Playters family who had come to see the Duke the previous autumn at Kenninghall. The would-be rebels concentrated their attention mainly on Norfolk, but it is significant that even there they did not use the Duke's name as the main rallying call for their attempt, except (hardly surprisingly) in the village of Kenninghall itself; elsewhere they appealed to one of the themes of the peasant risings of the previous summer, 'to expulse and dryve all the Duchemen and straungers owt of Norwiche'.[149] Their efforts met with no more success than had those of the rebels the previous year; both Jerningham and James Hobart of Hales Hall received pardons, however, and survived to be a source of worry to security-conscious Protestant JPs in a later military crisis.[150] The government perhaps exercised clemency in the knowledge that the lesson of Kett's Rebellion twenty years earlier had been learnt, and that firm, prompt action combined with efficient intelligence, was capable of effectively suppressing such unrest before it had gathered any momentum.

These events, culminating in the Duke's execution in 1572, destroyed the power of the conservatives in Norfolk and Suffolk; they showed that few were prepared to take the step of actively seeking the overthrow of the Elizabethan regime. No doubt the spectre of social unrest conjured up by the popular stirs of July 1569 was an aid in curbing the enthusiasm of potential gentry rebels. At the beginning of the crisis of November 1569, the Privy Council sent a circular letter to all sheriffs ordering that all present and former JPs should sign an acknowledgement of their duty to observe the Act of Uniformity. In Suffolk such known Catholics in retirement as Sir John Sulyard, Sir Ralph Chamberlain, Sir John Tyrrell, and William Foster signed without demur; only two elderly gentlemen who were no longer justices, Thomas Rous and Sir Henry Bedingfield, refused the declaration.[151]

Three of the leading visitors to the Duke at Kenninghall, Sir Thomas Cornwallis, his son-in-law Kitson, and Michael Hare, had already been arrested with their patron. Recognizing Sir Thomas's importance in East Anglian politics, the government used their best resources to reconcile him to the Anglican Settlement by peaceful

---

[148] BL Harl. 286, fo. 14ʳ; Redgr. 4100; *CSPSpan.* II, p. 255.

[149] *CPR Eliz.* VI, no. 1230; V, no. 1343. For details of the conspirators, see PRO, SP 12/71/61.

[150] Report on the defences of Lothingland, 1584, PRO, SP 12/171/63, and see MacCulloch, 'Catholic and Puritan', pp. 244–6.

[151] PRO, SP 12/60/61, 62.

means, and after he had spent several months in the company of Bishop Jewel and Dean Goodman of Westminster, their efforts met with some success, in the shape of a rather guarded declaration of Cornwallis's conformity.[152] Kitson was more pliable material, as he had already demonstrated in 1565, when the report of the Lord Keeper's displeasure at his Catholic leanings had been enough to send him chasing up to Redgrave in a flurry of protestations and explanations; now he made an explicit declaration of loyalty not only to the Crown, an easy task, but also to the Established Church 'without any scrowpelouse conceite (which I muste confess hath heretoffore accombred me)', and he was sufficiently overawed by his ordeal to retain an outward conformity for most of the rest of his life.[153] Hare was less ready to conform, and as a result he spent three years in the Tower while the Duke remained alive.[154]

An entire local power bloc had lost its power, and had also demonstrated that it was unwilling to put up a fight to retain that power. The Howards were finished as a force in local politics for a generation. The Norfolk Liberty and those estates which had survived the Duke's own sales and Crown confiscation were in the hands of family trustees, in some cases as tenants of the Crown. Philip, Earl of Surrey and later of Arundel, rarely visited East Anglia, and in any case his estates were burdened with the financial problems inevitable after the spectacular fall of a great dynasty. 'We bestowed money aswell for the funerall of my lady his graundmother which myght very well have bene spared as for my lord his own use', lamented the Earl's hard-pressed East Anglian steward Robert Buxton, after the dowager Countess's death in 1577;[155] by 1584 one of the Earl's trustees and financial advisers, William Dix, told him that sales of the rich manor of Narborough in Norfolk and of lands in Suffolk near Ipswich were imperative if debts running into thousands of pounds were to be paid off, and the Earl had already made extensive sales of Suffolk lands.[156] Only in the late eighties did the Howards beat off a royal claim to most

[152] Cornwallis's accounts for this period are Iveagh, Cornwallis MS 1/3, pr. McGrath and Rowe, 'Cornwallis', pp. 264–71. They point out (ibid., p. 235, n. 35) that Dean Goodman's covering letter (PRO, SP 12/43/9) for Cornwallis's declaration (SP 12/43/10) is dated 1567, which must be a mistake.

[153] Hengr. 88/2, fos. 40 f., is an undated draft letter to the Duke of Norfolk, dateable on internal evidence to 1565. Declaration: Hengr. 88/3, fo. 27ʳ.

[154] PRO, STAC 5 H45/39, Answer of John Burlingham.

[155] CUL, MS Buxton 96/25.

[156] Folger Ld 260; for Suffolk sales, see PRO, SP 12/99/34; PRO, C66/1204, m. 10, 1207, m. 23, 1250, m. 18. Cf. Williams, *Thomas Howard*, pp. 119–20.

of their remaining Suffolk lands and liberties.[157] Arundel's lack of involvement in East Anglian affairs, in later years caused by his imprisonment in the Tower under suspicion of treason, is reflected by his brief appearance in the East Anglian commissions of the peace: in Essex from 1581 to 1585 and in Cambridgeshire, Norfolk, and Suffolk from 1583 probably up to 1585.

The Howard clientage remained a recognizable group in East Anglia after the disappearance of its patron. Many gentry among the group turned to Catholic recusancy, following the example of the most prominent gentleman among them, Sir Thomas Cornwallis; it was no coincidence that totals in lists of recusants consistently indicated that throughout Elizabeth's reign, the Diocese of Norwich contained the largest number of recusants in the Province of Canterbury outside London.[158] However, many in the group conformed to the Established Church with good will; it remained an association of acquaintance and family connection as much as one of religious distinctiveness. Thus the would-be East Anglian magnate Sir Arthur Heveningham of Ketteringham in Norfolk and Heveningham in Suffolk, son of one of the third Duke of Norfolk's servants, was a good conformist to the 1559 Settlement, but he had close and friendly links with his conservative cousins the Rous's of Henham and Badingham, and with the leading Catholic recusant Michael Hare, who even acted as his business agent while up at Court.[159] Heveningham also took one member of the embarrassingly large family of the recusant Henry Everard of Linstead into his household, and he could call one of Sir Thomas Cornwallis's sons 'cousin' when trying to raise money from him in 1591.[160] Ties of friendship might date from university days and before: the conformist Gawdy brothers, Bassingbourn and Thomas, had been up at Cambridge with Bassingbourn's future brother-in-law Henry Everard, the young Thomas Cornwallis and his brother, and four members of the Hare family, including Michael.[161] The Inns of Court provided

[157] PRO, E134/22 James I/Michaelmas 40, deposition of Sir Edward Coke, and see below, Ch. 5.
[158] This point was first made by Dr. Smith: cf. Smith, pp. 201–2.
[159] On Heveningham's father Sir Anthony, cf. PRO, STAC 2/10/201; on Sir Arthur's conformity, MacCulloch, 'Power, Privilege and the County Community', p. 248. Aylsham 16, letters of Reynold Rous and Sir Philip Parker to Heveningham, Aylsham 180, Hare to Heveningham, 1589.
[160] Aylsham 175, Hare to Everard, 1595; ibid., Heveningham to Cornwallis (copy), 1591.
[161] Unless otherwise stated, all references to Cambridge careers are from Venn, under the appropriate name.

similar links: Sir Arthur's son John and the younger Thomas and Reynold Rous of Badingham went up to the Inner Temple, as successive members of the Hare, Gawdy, and Everard families had done, following in the distinguished footsteps of the lawyers who had founded the Gawdy fortunes and of Michael Hare's father Sir Nicholas.[162]

In contrast to the Wentworth–Wingfield group, we can characterize this association as the 'Cornwallis–Heveningham' group. The alignment was rarely made explicit in the courtesies of county life, and it took a newcomer to the area, the courtier Sir Michael Stanhope, bluntly to expose it in a letter to the Sheriff of Norfolk in 1592: Stanhope was concerned in a legal case, and urged the Sheriff to impanel an indifferent jury, 'nott sutche as stande in fear of Sir Arthur Hynnenghame or that lyve under anye of the Cornewalleses'.[163] Since this affinity had strong links with the Howard family, it was not surprising that leading members of the group tried to salvage something of the Duke's power from the wreck of his fortunes. During the late 1570s and early 1580s Sir Thomas Cornwallis entered into a bizarre alliance with the Anglican Bishop of the diocese, Edmund Freke, against the convinced Protestant gentry who sought to take up the reins of authority in the region (below, Ch. 6); at much the same time, and continuing right into the seventeenth-century, Sir Arthur Heveningham took on much the same combination of opponents in his effort to establish himself as the man to whom the Court naturally looked in East Anglia. In Norfolk, where the fourth Duke's power had been at its greatest, Sir Arthur contributed materially to the factionalism which increasingly disfigured county life in the last decades of the century; in Suffolk he was less disruptive, as we shall see (below, Ch. 9).[164]

Such bids for power on the part of leading gentlemen were possible because there was no resident peer of significance in either county by the end of the century to take on the Howard mantle. As early as the year of the fourth Duke's execution Bishop Parkhurst was lamenting the lack of a resident peer who might give him backing in furthering godly reformation.[165] Charles Brandon's widow, bereaved of her two Brandon sons, devoted much of her considerable energies to

---

[162] *Students admitted to the Inner Temple 1547–1660* (1877), pp. 4, 6, 10, 11, 51, 80, 102, 140, 162.

[163] BL Eger. 2713, fo. 294.

[164] See Smith, esp. Chs. 8–13.   [165] *Parkhurst* p. 112.

establishing her second family as peers of the realm, but they were not to be Suffolk men; the Willoughby lands dispute was finally laid to rest with a settlement between her and William Lord Willoughby of Parham, Sir Christopher's son, 1565.[166] In her later years, the Duchess's contacts with her native county were minimal: some signs of electoral influence at Orford before the 1565 settlement, one or two Suffolk gentlemen in her household at Grimsthorpe, a rare visit to the county to see old friends and occasional correspondence with her old chaplain Parkhurst, now Bishop of Norwich.[167] Nor was her old adversary Lord Willoughby any more resident; although he maintained the ancestral home at Parham and his widow retired there, he lived largely on his Lincolnshire estates, and by the end of the century the Suffolk antiquary Robert Ryece could regard the Willoughby family as non-resident.[168]

Even the leading figure of the Wentworth–Wingfield group, Lord Wentworth, was a fading force in the county. He was at his most active while the Duke of Norfolk was still alive, succeeding the Duke as Lord Lieutenant of the two counties in 1560 and again in the crisis of 1569–70, supervizing the Suffolk military preparations himself;[169] at that time he could be called on to sort out serious local disputes and he would turn up at Ipswich quarter sessions.[170] However, he spent less time at the family home in the upland village of Nettlestead as Elizabeth's reign wore on, and he died in 1584 at his Middlesex home at Stepney. His son Henry was made *custos rotulorum* in 1587; Thomas had never held the office, and it is unlikely that Henry regarded his position as anything other than honorific. He died six years later, and his son remained a minor for the rest of the reign.[171] The Lords North sat on the Suffolk Bench throughout Elizabeth's reign, owning the old episcopal manor at Elmham and estates at Mildenhall, but their main property and interest lay in Cambridgeshire, a small county which they

---

[166] E. Read, *My Lady Suffolk* (New York, 1963), *passim* and p. 170.
[167] Laurence Meres, MP for Orford 1563, had connections with the Duchess (*History of Parliament 1558–1603* III, p. 43). The Jennys were connected with the Suffolk household (PRO, C2 ELIZ 12/52, 4/40). In 1580 the Duchess visited Ipswich, Seckford the Master of Requests and the Feltons of Playford (*HMC* IX, pt. i, p. 250). Cf. *Parkhurst* pp. 112, 224–5.
[168] PCC 25 Martyn; Ryece, p. 76.
[169] *HMC Salisbury* I, p. 253 (1560); PRO, SP 12/59/57 (1569; Wentworth had two deputies for Norfolk); Hengr. 88/2, fo. 46ʳ and BL Harl. 309, fo. 99ʳ.
[170] PRO, STAC 5 A3/12, A57/31; PRO, STAC 7/9/26; attendance as JP 2/3 October 1562 (PRO, E137/42/4).
[171] On the Wentworths, see *EANQ* New Series II (1886), pp. 193 ff.

could dominate more effectively. John Earl of Bath had lived at Hengrave Hall until his death in 1561, but he was only a Suffolk man by marriage and his heir moved back to the West Country when he had obtained his majority. Other peers, such as the Darcys of Chiche or the Rich's, continued to hold minor estates in Suffolk and were therefore appointed to an honorific place on the Bench from time to time, but they played no active part in county life.

Similarly in Norfolk there were no peers of distinction after 1572. Lord Morley became a Catholic fugitive; Lord Cromwell 'appears to have been impecunious and commanded little political influence'.[172] The Earl of Sussex still had estates at Attleborough in Norfolk and lesser Suffolk properties which gave him a place on the Norfolk and Suffolk Benches, and gave the central government a useful excuse for intruding him into East Anglian defence administration when necessary as late as the 1580s, but he was now seldom resident in the area.[173]

The one person who might have emerged as the founder of a ruling dynasty for the region was Lord Keeper Bacon. However, he himself chose to spend most of his later years when in the country at his Hertfordshire home, nearer the activity of London, and he had both too many sons and too much affection for them to allow his great estates throughout the south-east of England to remain as a unit. It is true that he gave the three sons of his first marriage a rigorous training in the running of county affairs, sending letters to fellow-Suffolk gentry via his son Nicholas with instructions to read them before sending them on as if they had come straight from the Lord Keeper;[174] however, Nicholas, Nathaniel, and Edward were not of the same calibre as their quite exceptional younger half-brothers Francis and Anthony.

Nathaniel Bacon inherited his father's capacity for hard work and attention to detail, while his sense of duty made him one of the leading administrators of Elizabethan Norfolk and the chief opponent of Sir Arthur Heveningham's ambitions. Nicholas was to achieve the honour of becoming Premier Baronet of England under Elizabeth's successor, but one suspects that he was something of a disappointment to his father: he was not the material for a statesman, and he was rather a slow pupil in his training for the duties of a county magnate. 'And [i.e.

---

[172] Smith, p. 27.

[173] Thomas, Earl of Sussex was a muster commissioner through the 1570s (BL Harl. 309, fo. 197 and PRO, SP 12/133/14) and commissioner for horse provision in the Eastern Counties in 1580 (PRO, SP 12/143/26).

[174] Redgr. 4126.

If] you had bene at the Assises as you showld have bene, yf you had done well, you might have enformed me of this of yor owne knowledg', wrote his father tartly to him when seeking information about an assize case, two years after getting Nicholas appointed to the Suffolk Bench; Nathaniel never needed the frequent reminders that Nicholas received from the meticulous statesman to write to him, and to 'wryght at large and not scantly'.[175] Neither did Edward, the lawyer, show any exceptional qualities, despite his spells as MP for the family seat at Eye and for the county; he was noted as 'very silent' by his relative Philip Gawdy during his first Parliament in 1589.[176] Eventually Nicholas, like Nathaniel, played a prominent part in the government of his county, but neither they nor Edward showed a disposition to demand pre-eminence among the magnates of their counties; the Lord Keeper's rise to power had been too recent for him to bequeath to his eldest son a clientage of any but the most minor of Suffolk gentry. The two Suffolk Bacons were content to form part of the partnership which ran their county. 'Mediocria firma' was a lesson that they had learnt well from their father; indeed, the whole ruling élite of Elizabethan Suffolk might well have adopted the Lord Keeper's motto for its own.

By the latter half of Elizabeth's reign East Anglia became an area made safe for county gentry. Within Suffolk, three distinct groupings could be discerned, despite all the imprecision which intermarriage and relationships outside the county might impart. In the west there were the gentlemen of the Liberty of St Edmund, whose contacts with a peer of the realm had been small since the great days of the Abbots of Bury; Lord Darcy's influence among them in the 1540s and 1550s had been shortlived. In the east of the county were the two legacies of the two noble families which had once been dominant: the Wentworth–Wingfield and the Cornwallis–Heveningham alignments. How could Westminster organize its contacts with them to produce the atmosphere of consent and co-operation which made early modern government function? The Tudors had themselves made and unmade the nobility of the area; now the results of their efforts were seen when the Elizabethan government revived the lieutenancy in 1585 on a more permanent basis. The man that they chose for Norfolk and Suffolk was Henry Carey, Lord Hunsdon, a cousin of the Queen who had been given a substantial Suffolk estate at Huntingfield;[177] yet Hunsdon was

[175] Redgr. 4125, 4115.   [176] Jeayes, p. 45.
[177] Grant *inter alia*, 1559, *CPR Eliz.* I, p. 115; on Hunsdon's East Anglian acquaintanceship, see below, Ch. 8.

an outsider to the region whose social contacts there were dangerously unbalanced in favour of the Cornwallis–Heveningham alignment. Hunsdon and the central government needed a wider range of contacts than this. Before seeing how a Tudor government might make those contacts, we need to examine how a county community developed in Suffolk in the face of aristocratic dominance and of the geographical, administrative, and familial divisions within the county.

3
The County Community Displayed

CAN one trace a sense of county community before the Tudor period? Did such a sense transcend the internal divisions of the county and give it an identity distinct from that of the East Anglian region as a whole? For neighbouring Norfolk, the fifteenth-century evidence is clear, in that unrivalled informal source, the Paston Letters, which offer us one or two hints for Suffolk as well. The letters reveal a community in the county which knew that it was of Norfolk and proud of it, and which was ready to express community opinion, particularly if it was righteous indignation. At its most basic, the sentiment might seem mere tribalism, as when in 1455 John Howard faced a rough ride in the election for knights of the shire, despite his backing from the Duke of Norfolk and the Duke of York; Howard was a Suffolk man. 'It is a evill precedent for the shire that a straunge man shulde be chosyn ... for yf the jentilmen of the shire will suffre sech inconvenyens, in good feithe the shire shall noght be called of seche wurshipp as it hathe be.'[1] The picture in John Jenney's mind when he wrote to John Paston was clearly one of a whole assembly of county communities, before whose opinion the gentlemen of Norfolk stood marshalled at the bar to preserve their good name and independence.

At the head of this assembly of communities stood the King; if counties were to compete together, it would be with him as audience and as referee. A royal progress would be something like a modern trades fair for the county: William Paston wrote to his brother John of Henry VII's progress in 1487 that the Earl of Oxford was gathering the gentlemen of Essex at Chelmsford to meet the King, to impress not only their royal master but also the men of Lancashire who were to accompany him 'that the Lankeschere men may see that ther be gentylmen of so grete sobestaunce that thei be able to bye all Lankeschere'. Norfolk men must do the same, urged William: 'Your contre is gretely bostyd of, and also the jnabytours of the same'. Perhaps this might imply a serious political purpose to overawe

---
[1] *Paston Letters* II, p. 120.

turbulent Northerners with southern prosperity, but county sentiment was also an enjoyable game: the Earl of Oxford had 'made grete boste of the fayre and goode gentylwomen' in Norfolk 'and so the Kynge seyd he wolde see them sure'; a suitable assemblage of ladies must be gathered.[2] The Pastons loved their county, half in earnest, half in joke; the affectionate tone comes out in a letter of September 1465 from John to Margaret Paston as from his London exile he considered clothing for the onset of the cold weather. 'I wold make my doblet all worsted for worship of Norffolk rather thanne like Gonnores doblet.'[3]

In times of stress this community feeling could cease to be mere fun and turn to purposeful anger. In 1451 the two counties of Norfolk and Suffolk were bitterly polarized about the conduct of the Duke of Suffolk's protégés Sir Thomas Tuddenham and John Heydon, sworn enemies of the Pastons. John Paston's servant William Wayte took great glee in reporting the forthright language of the bailiff of Swaffham to no less a person than the Lord Chancellor on the crimes of Tuddenham and Heydon:

yf the Kynge pardoned Syr Thomas Tudenham and Heydon here issewes . . . the shire of Suffolk wold paye no taxe; for what nedyth the Kynge for to have the taxe of hese pore puple whanne he wyll not take hese issues of thoo ryche extorssioners and oppressours of hese puple . . . ther was vp in Norffolk redy to ryse v m¹ and moo yf they have not execucion of the oyre and terminer.[4]

This is a partisan report of a partisan statement, but it reveals that counties were conceived of as having opinions, and as taking action together to remedy injustice if the King's government would not. Moreover, this community action could come from a county which thought of itself as acting in opposition to the great noblemen of the area, if they were offending against a communal sense of custom and justice. The Duke of Norfolk was as vulnerable as the Duke of Suffolk; in 1452 there was great indignation at least among the Pastons' friends and probably throughout Norfolk when the advisors of the Mowbray Duke contrived to have the quarter sessions called at an extraordinary date: not only in the middle of harvest-time, but also at short notice, simply for factional reasons—to injure those who opposed their 'oppynyons'. The plan was wrecked by the sessions jury: 'whiche malysiows purposid oppynyon the jantylmen of the seyd shyere that were sworyn att the seyd sescions kowd not fynde in her conciens

---

² Ibid., I, p. 654.   ³ Ibid., I, p. 140.
⁴ Ibid. II, p. 60.

to observe, but dede the contrarye as it apperyth be here verdyte if itt be shewed . . .'⁵

Already in the fifteenth century, therefore, the gentry of Norfolk and Suffolk were capable of seeing themselves as distinct communities with a self-esteem to be preserved or trespassed against, in the face both of the Crown and of great noblemen. What happened to this county sentiment in the early sixteenth century? Is it merely the lack of surviving evidence which accounts for its apparent absence? The silence might just as plausibly be explained by the character of the successive magnates who dominated the whole region of East Anglia from the beginning of Henry VII's reign to the death of Henry VIII: the thirteenth Earl of Oxford, the Howard Dukes of Norfolk, and Charles Brandon were peers whose influence crossed county boundaries and who exercised that influence in a far more reasonable way than their Mowbray and De la Pole predecessors; there was less cause for the gentry of the region to remember their role as defenders of the shire when their social superiors united the entire East Anglian area in a reasonably statesmanlike manner. This was demonstrated in 1525, when a tax strike threatened just as it had done in 1451; this time the line-up of forces was very different. Instead of an open expression of gentry approval of the idea of five thousand people ready to take arms, the gentry were solidly behind the region's two Dukes in doing their best to quell a popular expression of outrage and to act in defence of the peace of the realm imposed from Westminster (below, Ch. 10).

It was only later in the sixteenth century, with the effective disappearance of the powerful noblemen from East Anglia, that a strong sense of county community came into its own once more. Particularly striking is the growing contrast in political behaviour in the two counties of Norfolk and Suffolk; despite the similarities in their economies and despite the close links of their leading families, the fall of the fourth Howard Duke of Norfolk drove politics in the two counties in precisely opposite directions. Dr Smith's work on Norfolk after 1569 has revealed a picture of mounting conflict which became acute in the 1590s. For Suffolk in the same period, the evidence is all the other way.

One useful as well as entertaining index of the political peace of a Tudor county is to be found in the number of major conflicts which

⁵ Ibid., I, p. 72. Cf. discussion of this point in Virgoe, 'The Crown, Magnates and Local Government', pp. 82–3.

reached the prerogative courts in Westminster. Each dispute represented a failure for the county; it meant that outsiders would have to adjudicate in a matter which the men of the county should have solved for themselves. Such outside intervention ought to be avoided at all costs. Thus that experienced county politician Sir Thomas Cornwallis advised his son-in-law Thomas Kitson in 1572 that his wholly legitimate grievances against Thomas Poley, a neighbouring JP, should not be taken to the Privy Council before he had approached the other local JPs; such a move would 'geve the justyces your neyghbors iuste cause of offence', for it might give the Council a low opinion either of Kitson's local standing or of the Suffolk Bench's impartiality.[6]

Nevertheless in Norfolk the later part of the sixteenth century was marked by a series of set piece struggles in the court of Star Chamber between men in the county commission of the peace, those who in theory should have been setting an example of harmony to their neighbours: for example, the conflicts between Sir Arthur Heveningham and Edward Flowerdew in the 1580s, Thomas Farmer and Martin Barney in the 1590s, or the case of the Martham parsonage dispute in the same decade.[7] No really comparable material exists for Suffolk, in the sense that there appears to be nothing surviving from suits between members of the magisterial élite in the prerogative courts, where one would expect to find it.

This is of particular significance when one notes that this was not the case earlier in the century. We have already considered the disputes over the Willoughby inheritance which convulsed the county at the end of the 1520s, and noted the disputes of the 1530s and 1540s between the Duke of Norfolk and various associates of the Duke of Suffolk (above, Ch. 2), but these were not isolated examples. Some years before, the old Lord Willoughby had been drawn into a violent dispute with his fellow-JP John Glemham, which resulted in at least two assaults on Glemham's servants and property at Little Glemham, and which may have been reflected in the exclusion of both men from the commission of the peace some time after 1515.[8] The first Lord Wentworth also appears to have been possessed of an imperious temper; on one occasion in the 1530s, he had an open quarrel in the middle of Ipswich sessions with Sir Thomas Tey, who had indicted Wentworth's servants for forcibly resisting his entry as a JP into the

---

[6] Hengr. 88/2, fo. 65.   [7] Smith, esp. Ch. 9 and pp. 268–75.
[8] PRO, REQ 3/7, Bill of John Glemham and Answers of George Willoughby and others.

disputed manor of Copdock; Wentworth successfully obstructed the indictment, and with 'great manesshyng and unfyttyng wordes', according to Tey in his complaint to Star Chamber.[9] In 1545 Wentworth waš so furious when his cousin Mary Barnes married his close relative and fellow-JP Edward Glemham, 'whome he toke to be hys enemye', that he withdrew his promise of a twenty-pound annuity to her and caused a row which resulted in his being summoned before the Privy Council.[10]

It is surely no coincidence that all these examples involved a member of the peerage. Once Suffolk became a county made safe for knights and mere gentry after the fall of the fourth Duke of Norfolk, this aggressive style was not how the county's leading men chose to conduct their affairs. That is not to say that there were no major lawsuits in the county; it would be asking too much of the Suffolk gentry to suppose that they did not display the normal Tudor qualities of quarrelsomeness and litigiousness. The county had its share of gentlemen who were either eager participants in lawsuits or else litigation-prone; the most notorious Elizabethan example was the lawyer Thomas Okeley of Friston, close to the coast, whose influence can be traced in a variety of lawsuits in his area, and who was eventually denounced (with good reason) to the Privy Council 'for troubling his neighbors and others with unjust suites and vexacions'.[11] Francis Bohun, from Westhall twelve miles to the north of Friston and briefly a JP from 1589 to 1591, was another man who for one reason or another was frequently to be found involved in some suit in the Westminster courts.[12]

These two can reasonably be regarded as fomenters of litigation, but the saga of John Gardiner of Stowupland shows that it was possible to be a less culpable victim of major lawsuits. Gardiner was to become a JP for the last three years of his life from 1592, but by then the worst was over of a marathon legal dispute which had lasted more than thirty years from the reign of Queen Mary and which had involved him almost from the outset. Gardiner had been lucky or unlucky enough to

[9] PRO, STAC 2/17/125, and cf. STAC 2/19/394.
[10] PRO, REQ 3/15, Bill of Edward and Mary Glemham, Answers of Lord Wentworth and associated papers.
[11] PRO, STAC 5 F12/20; STAC 5 C16/34; PRO, C3/215/10; C3/210/85; PRO, C2 ELIZ 14/40; C2 ELIZ M7/59, M2/44; PRO, REQ 2/73/81; *APC* XXII, p. 266.
[12] *APC* XIV, p. 109; PRO, STAC 5 B37/24; STAC 5 B30/18; STAC 5 F20/38; PRO, C3/31/8; C3/204/41; PRO, C2 ELIZ A1/14; C2 ELIZ G3/44; C2 ELIZ W10/55.

buy Columbine Hall, Stowupland, from its mortgagee, a London
merchant called Thomas Stambridge, in 1559; he thus incurred the
wrath of the Tyrrell family, late owners of the Hall, who claimed that
Stambridge had gained absolute possession by dishonest manipulation
of their mortgage.[13] With such formidable local figures as Sir John
Tyrrell and Tyrrell's relative Sir John Sulyard united against him, it is
not surprising that Gardiner, an outsider to the county, had an
uncomfortable time of it in the Stowmarket area, and he was constantly
facing lawsuits from the Tyrrells and the clothiers who lined up with
the old-established families of the area against the upstart. As early as
1562, the yeoman oligarchy of Stowupland was objecting to his
inclusion among the charity feoffees for the township, while the
Tyrrells bombarded him with Chancery suits;[14] by the 1580s Gardiner
was complaining openly of the enmity of the clothiers and of one
Henry Gilbert, a local man who had become wealthy as a London
goldsmith and had married into the Howes, one of the leading yeoman
families of Stowmarket.[15] It was just as well for the balance of forces in
the area, and doubtless a deliberate move, that a year after Gilbert had
been appointed to the Suffolk Bench, Gardiner was appointed as well;
it was the exception for the half-hundred of Stow to boast one JP, let
alone two during Elizabeth's reign. Gardiner clung to his hard-fought
purchase, and though childless, he tried to make sure that the Tyrrells
never regained it by making Sir Robert Carey, a cousin of the Lord
Lieutenant, his heir, a move which Carey's son, reminiscing long after
the end of the dispute, found it difficult to account for.[16]

The Columbine Hall affair was the nearest approximation in Suffolk
after 1572 to a *cause célèbre* involving two justices; the tangled half-
century of conflict at Beccles over common rights might at first sight
appear to be another, for it involved JPs of the county in dispute with
the gentry protagonist, their fellow-JP William Rede. Nevertheless,
this was essentially a crusade led by the townsfolk themselves. The
Beccles dispute is in fact symptomatic of the contrast between Norfolk

---

[13] PRO, STAC 5 T2/7.

[14] PRO, C3/7/37, C3/179/14, C3/181/4, C3/108/5, C3/106/13.

[15] Gardiner's Complaint: Hengr. 15, fo. 92^r—a paper in a Chancery suit und. but
referred to in PRO, STAC 7/2/41 as of 1582. The Howe family also included a London
goldsmith, and John Howe's daughter had married Thomas Tyrrell (Metcalfe, p. 97;
PSIA XII, 1905, pp. 166–7).

[16] Copinger, *Manors*, VI, p. 233. The Tyrrell party gained an eventual revenge when
Sir John Poley, who married Henry Gilbert's granddaughter, obtained the Hall
(Metcalfe, p. 158).

and Suffolk. There were indeed set piece conflicts from Suffolk which reached the level of Star Chamber during the reign of Elizabeth, but they were not between magistrate and magistrate, but between a gentleman and a chartered corporation: Rede and Beccles, Edmund Withipoll and Ipswich, Thomas Eden and Sudbury (below, Ch. 11).

What is striking about Suffolk is that such venom was not allowed to disrupt county government; it is likely that Francis Bohun's survival as a JP was shortlived precisely because he was recognized as being too contentious to fit the role. There is evidence to suggest that even fiery-tempered individuals were aware of the need to preserve the proprieties in the conduct of the county's affairs. The case of Sir Charles Framlingham of Debenham, JP from 1578 until his death in 1595 is instructive. Sir Charles was a naturally aggressive man, with a particular dislike of Catholicism; a Catholic turned government informer said that Catholics numbered him with the Earl of Leicester and the Norfolk knight Sir William Heydon as 'most cruell tirantes . . . and . . . a very plague unto all Catholickes'.[17] It is not surprising after this to find Sir Charles engaged in a dispute over rival manorial jurisdictions at Snape and Sternfield with one of Suffolk's leading recusants, Michael Hare, in the early 1580s.[18] It is equally under-standable that Sir Charles should have engaged in a bitter feud with the Catholic-sympathizing churchwardens of Debenham in 1587, culminating in a pitched battle in the churchyard for custody of the lead from the vestry roof which he had chosen to remove, or that his efforts to protect a leading Puritan preacher of east Suffolk from his opponents should have caused a political storm at Woodbridge Sessions in 1592; these incidents all ended in Star Chamber.[19] However, some of the suits which involved him have no obvious religious background: disputes, for instance, over the ownership of various tenements with his gentry neighbours, the Blowers, Brookes, and Garneys, leading in the latter case to a Star Chamber accusation against him of perjury.[20]

In view of his active involvement in litigation both as complainant and as defendant, it is interesting to note that even Sir Charles

[17] PRO, SP 12/169/19 (confession of Richard Lacey).
[18] PRO, STAC 5 F12/20, F21/31; PRO, STAC 7/2/37; PRO, STAC 5 H45/39.
[19] Vestry dispute: PRO, STAC 5 J6/29; PRO, STAC 7/24/1; Aylsham 176, Framlingham to Bishop Scambler, 1588. Woodbridge: PRO, STAC 5 M26/3, 7; cf. *APC* XXII, p. 287.
[20] PRO, C3/63/3; C3/30/16; PRO, C2 ELIZ F9/34; PRO, STAC 5 G12/22, 19/16.

exercised restraint in dealing with his fellow-magistrates in the interests of good county government. In 1593 he wrote to his son-in-law Bassingbourn Gawdy to use his influence with Sir Nicholas Bacon to secure the removal of Taylor, an unsatisfactory Head Constable probably conservative in religion, and to make sure that Taylor did not insinuate a puppet substitute into his place if he were dismissed. His fellow-justices, he wrote, knew of Taylor's unsuitability; he wished Sir Nicholas to speak with Sir Robert Wingfield, also a JP of the area, about the necessity of the High Constable's dismissal. Debenham lay only seven miles from Sir Robert's home at Letheringham; Sir Nicholas lived nearly twenty miles from Sir Robert. However, the only way to achieve Taylor's removal was indirectly 'by Sir Nicholas Bacon's meanes not letting Sir Robert Wingfield to knowe my forwardnes to remove this bade man, for then I know he would rather continue him'.[21]

Such elaborate scheming might seem inefficient, and it was unfortunate that two neighbouring JPs disliked each other enough to make direct co-operation so difficult; nevertheless it is a remarkable contrast with the style of Norfolk politics that a justice of so choleric a temperament as Sir Charles Framlingham should go to such lengths to keep up the appearance of harmony in county administration. Once again, a member of the Suffolk Bench had demonstrated his conviction that the county's reputation for unity was not lightly to be imperilled.

All the evidence presented so far has necessarily been impressionistic, and indeed it could be considered an impossible task to describe a political atmosphere in terms of statistics. However, statistical evidence can at least be compiled on various aspects of the magisterial élite in the county to throw light on political conditions at a local level. Comparison with Dr Smith's work on Elizabethan Norfolk reinforces the impression of the gentry of two similar counties acting in precisely contradictory ways. Both the development of the late Elizabethan county military organization and the characteristics of the county commissions of the peace provide such evidence.

Consider first the deputy lieutenancy and the Muster Commissions for the two counties. From the time of Lord Hunsdon's appointment

[21] BL Eger. 2713, fo. 310. Eight years earlier, Framlingham had lost his temper with Taylor sufficiently to threaten in public to strike him (PRO, STAC 5 R29/1, Bill). Taylor is probably also to be identified with the foreman of the Grand Jury which in 1592 had preferred an indictment against the Puritan preacher favoured by Framlingham (STAC 5 M26/7, Answer of William Goodwyn).

as Lord Lieutenant for Norfolk and Suffolk in 1585 until his death in 1596, Hunsdon kept the number of his deputies in the counties small, although the Suffolk deputies included Sir Robert Jermyn and Sir John Higham, who had little sympathy with some of their superior's interventions in local politics, as instanced in his support for patentees within the county (below, Ch. 9). However, on Hunsdon's death, the lieutenancy was put into commission, and with no resident peer of consequence to dominate their proceedings, the leading magnates of the two counties were more or less their own masters. In Norfolk this meant that the Muster Commission provided yet another arena for conflict; from 1596 to 1602 the Norfolk Commission doubled its numbers from six to twelve as each of the two main factions in the county tried to bring in its own supporters by using influence at Court.[22] In Suffolk the increase was only from five to six in the same period. The veteran trio of Sir Robert Jermyn, Sir John Higham and Sir Philip Parker continued to irritate the government with their own conception of their military duties, and they were joined by their like-minded friend Sir Nicholas Bacon when the lieutenancy was put in commission; as their old colleague Sir Robert Wingfield reached extreme old age, he had been replaced by his eldest son Anthony in peaceful hereditary succession. Newcomers were in 1598 Sir Henry North, younger son of Roger, Lord North, a peer long on good terms with this coterie of county leaders, and in 1601 the only possible outsider, Sir Henry Glemham; Glemham was perhaps an unwelcome arrival to Jermyn and Parker, but he was Wingfield's cousin and friend.[23] The contrast between this comfortable little group of Suffolk magnates and the ill-will and swollen numbers of the Norfolk Commission could hardly be greater.

In his study of Norfolk, Dr Smith brought detailed evidence to disprove earlier assumptions that the number of candidates for a place on the justices' Bench was much the same as the actual number of justices; in the sixteenth century people were usually eager to become JPs, a prospective JP was a buyer in a seller's market, and office was frequently uncertain and prone to interruption. A justice's insecurity of tenure could be exploited by his opponents at a local level for factional ends, and therefore interrupted or brief tenures of a place on the

[22] Smith, p. 288.
[23] Bacon: *APC* XXVI, p. 51. Wingfield: BL Harl. 6996, p. 128. North first appears as a commissioner on 9 Dec. 1598 (*APC* XXIX, p. 343). Glemham was appointed 5 June 1601 (*APC* XXXI, p. 400). On Glemham and the 1601 election, see below, pp. 335-6.

Bench to some extent reflected the degree of faction within a county.[24] If we examine the commissions of the peace in the two counties in this light, they yield further evidence of the growing contrast in political behaviour between Norfolk and Suffolk. It is significant that although the Norfolk Bench had been consistently smaller than that of Suffolk since the 1520s, probably because of the difference in administrative needs and practices already outlined (above, Ch. 1), it overtook its neighbour in numbers in 1595 and remained either the same size or larger for the rest of the reign of Elizabeth. Just as with the Muster Commission, Norfolk's troubled politics led to greater pressure for a place on the Bench.

In the same way, interrupted careers and dismissals from the Bench became much more common in Norfolk than in Suffolk after the Duke of Norfolk's fall in 1572 (see Appendix III). Some of these were thanks to the round of nationwide 'purges' instituted at intervals by the government for its own political or administrative ends, but we are concerned here with the other dismissals, which are more likely to have been caused by local initiative of one sort or another. It is difficult to provide satisfactory details of these before 1558 because of the fragmentary nature of the sources, but the total number of dismissals of JPs in the county between 1485 and 1558 is roughly comparable, at seventy-seven for Suffolk and seventy-four for Norfolk, as it is between 1558 and 1584, at forty-five and forty-three respectively. After the departure of Bishop Freke from the Diocese of Norwich in 1584, on the other hand, Norfolk achieved fifty-three dismissals from the Bench against Suffolk's thirty-eight, with more than twice as many dismissals for the second or even the third time. The impression of greater instability in Norfolk is reinforced by considering the JPs who were local men but who were removed after four years or less on the Bench: from 1558 to 1572, six in either county, and from 1572 to 1603, twenty in Norfolk and eleven in Suffolk. More men were going and more men were arriving in Norfolk. When we can finally get a precise picture of the number of commissions of the peace issued annually, through the inauguration of a docquet book of commissions in 1595, we find that 'at least six' commissions were issued annually for Norfolk between 1595 and 1603, but the average for Suffolk was rather less than three.[25] Fewer comings and goings meant less paperwork.

[24] See esp. Smith, Ch. 4, 'A Place on the Bench'.
[25] PRO, C231/1; Smith p. 74.

There is therefore ample evidence to suggest that Norfolk and Suffolk developed radically different political atmospheres. The explanation for this, after the 1569 crisis as before it, lies in the differing degrees of influence which the fourth Duke of Norfolk had exercised in the two counties. In Norfolk, where he had reigned supreme before 1569, his execution left a far more serious political vacuum than in Suffolk; the structure of political life was far more seriously disrupted. It is likely that Sir Arthur Heveningham was well aware of this contrast between the two counties when he chose to make Norfolk the focus of his bid to assume the mantle of the Howards. Although the Heveninghams had owned their Norfolk estate at Ketteringham since the fifteenth century, they were a Suffolk family who had seldom before figured in Norfolk politics.[26] Sir Arthur himself was appointed to the Suffolk Bench in 1578, a year before his appointment in Norfolk; he continued the traditional family interest in Suffolk affairs, particularly in military matters, and throughout his career he continued to attend quarter sessions in Suffolk with unusual assiduity.[27] However, he came to attend sessions in Norfolk even more frequently than in Suffolk, and his surviving correspondence and the letters which his secretary used to compile a precedent book for local administration are largely to do with Norfolk.[28] An attempt to dominate Suffolk politics would have been a far more difficult task than it was in Norfolk; even there it proved difficult enough. The Duke's influence in Suffolk had been a disruptive one; on his departure from the scene, leadership of the county passed easily to a group of men who had never been numbered among the Duke's clients. The gentry of Suffolk had little use for the sort of single, all-powerful patron that Thomas Howard had been to Norfolk; the days of Charles Brandon were long over, and after 1572 the days of the Howards were over as well, while Queen Elizabeth lived. The time had come for the sort of county community attitudes displayed by the Pastons a century earlier to come into their own.

The county leaders of Elizabethan Suffolk were well aware of their county's tranquillity, and they could afford to look over the border into turbulent Norfolk with a certain complacent pride. We have already

---

[26] Ibid., p. 157.
[27] Cf. a bundle of certificates for the view of armour in the hundred of Blything in 1584, Aylsham 181; he continued to command one of the Suffolk bands through the 1590s (Aylsham 16, deputy lieutenants to Heveningham, 22 Sept, 1590).
[28] Precedent book: Aylsham 129.

seen a hint of this county pride in Sir Thomas Cornwallis's advice to Thomas Kitson in his quarrel of 1572 with Thomas Poley; his private grievance should not be a means of sullying the good name of the county's justices before the Privy Council if it could possibly be helped. Sir Thomas was not alone among Suffolk's leading men in prizing the county's good reputation. In June 1588, when the contrast between Norfolk and Suffolk had become more obvious than it had been in 1572, the four deputy lieutenants for Suffolk, two from the west (Sir Robert Jermyn and Sir John Higham) and two from the east (Sir Robert Wingfield and Sir Philip Parker), heard that Sir Nicholas Bacon was discontented because his fellow-captain in the hundred of Hoxne had twenty more troops under his command than Bacon had, and they urged him to be reasonable: 'our contry hath for many yeares caryed great credyt for the good agrement emongest the gent., and lamentable yt were that so small a cause shuld be the begynnyng of any disagrement.'[29]

Sir Philip Parker repeated the same sentiments ten years later, more in anger than in sorrow, to a quarrelsome female relative of his—an outsider to the county—to whom he attributed responsibility for the recent unseemly brawl between his two cousins, Anthony Felton, JP, and Edmund Withipoll: 'neyther do I knowe of anye contention for place in this sheire, but where yourself is a partye.'[30] No gentleman of Norfolk could have made such an observation about his own county with a clear conscience. Queen Elizabeth herself could be brought in as a witness in the county's collective memory; eighty years later, as the Interregnum drew to its close, the minister of Lavenham could remind his congregation of what he had heard of her words on her 1578 progress: 'Now I have learned why my country of Suffolk is so well governed, it is, because the magistrates and ministers go together.'[31]

Suffolk therefore prided itself on its good government and tranquillity, with the awful warning of Norfolk on its doorstep: but every county at least in the lowlands of England must have had its particular point of pride. How far outside the Lowland zone did this county community sense extend? We have seen that already in 1487, at least in the eyes of an East Anglian, 'the Lankeschere men' were a recognizable unit. Perhaps in their own region, the Lancashire men

[29] Redgr. 4150.
[30] Tanner 283, fo. 24, Parker to the wife of Sir Henry Grey, 31 Apr. 1598.
[31] W. Gurnall, *The Magistrates Portraiture* (1656), pp. 37–8. I owe this reference to Dr Blair Worden.

would not have felt this to be such a compelling identity, although there are signs of it in neighbouring Cheshire throughout the fifteenth and sixteenth centuries.[32] In the north and in Wales, the comparative weakness of county structures and the continuing importance of great aristocratic families may have made the alternative identity provided by the county of less importance than in the south-east, even at the close of the sixteenth century.[33]

An important witness to the new strength of county pride throughout the lowland zone during Elizabeth's reign was the growth of antiquarian studies on a county basis. Antiquarian studies were by no means new in the late sixteenth century, but their concentration on the county was a genuine novelty. Fifteenth- or early sixteenth-century antiquarians had either worked within a traditional monastic framework, like Thomas Elmham at St Augustine's, Canterbury, or for a great noble family, like John Rous for the Earls of Warwick, or in a nationwide omnivorous manner, like Rous, William of Worcester or John Leland.[34] Now there was a proliferation of county studies, beginning with William Lambarde's *Perambulation of Kent* in 1570, which took for granted the fact that the county was a coherent and interesting unit. Even William Camden's *Britannia* of 1586, although in theory adhering to a fashionably humanistic arrangement by the Celtic tribes of Roman Britain, was in reality a county by county gazetteer, and must have owed much of its popularity and frequent new editions to this fact.

It is not surprising that a county with a strong corporate sense among its élite like Suffolk produced examples of the county history genre by the end of Elizabeth's reign. It is interesting to note a minor Puritan gentleman of Suffolk, Adam Winthrop of Groton, lending out his copy of Lambarde's *Perambulation* in 1597.[35] The prime concern of these works was the gentry, their possessions, their ancestors and their tombs; the earliest example of which fragments remain, perhaps dating from the 1580s, appropriately concerns itself wholly with the current

---

[32] P. Williams, *The Tudor Regime* (Oxford, 1981), p. 450, and Morrill, pp. 2–4.

[33] However, for the view that the distinctiveness of the north has been much exaggerated, see B. W. Beckingsale, 'The Characteristics of the Tudor North', *Northern History* IV (1969), pp. 67–83.

[34] Cf. A. Gransden, 'Antiquarian Studies in Fifteenth-Century England', *Antiquaries Journal* LX (1980), pp. 75–97. However, Virgoe notes that Worcester also compiled notes for the history of Norfolk gentry families: Virgoe, 'The Crown, Magnates and Local Government', p. 83.

[35] *Suffolk Review* (September 1983), p. 23.

ownership and descent of the lands owned by the county's gentry.[36] The next, cut into fragments by the same eighteenth-century vandal as the former, was compiled between 1600 and 1604 and models itself consciously on the contemporary published 'Chorographies' of the surveyor John Norden; it seems to have been compiled by a clergyman associated with the gentry circle of Sir Arthur Heveningham and, significantly, is one of a pair with a volume still intact describing Norfolk: East Anglian regionalism allied to county particularism.[37] Like most of Norden's own work, this is primarily a gazetteer, but the almost contemporary *Breviary of Suffolk* by Robert Ryece is a more ambitious work. Started in 1603, the *Breviary* unites an extended thematic essay on the county and its historical worthies with topographical notes on churches.[38] A further Suffolk-born antiquary, the herald Henry Chitting, wrote up topographical collections on Suffolk churches in the second decade of the seventeenth century, in effect celebrating places which were associated with his family and his family's patrons, drawn from such diverse religious backgrounds as the Bacons of Redgrave, the Kitsons of Hengrave, and the Cornwallises of Brome.[39] None of these manuscripts were published at the time, and they were probably not intended to be: the tradition of passing manuscripts round circles of acquaintance was still strong, and would be adequate to satisfy the interest of the restricted gentry circle within the county whom the works celebrated. Indeed, one of the surviving copies of Ryece's *Breviary* is a transcript of a gift copy which the antiquary made in 1618 for his friend Sir Robert Crane of Chilton.[40]

The concerns of the new antiquaries with heraldry and genealogy underlined the nature of a strong county community like Suffolk: it was an association of gentlemen. Genealogy was no mere academic interest or pastime; it gave established families a sense of security in the face of the unprecedented albeit in modern terms hardly very dramatic social mobility of Tudor England; it underpinned the dignity of the county's élite, sometimes by bending the facts. The knightly family of Hopton disguised the fact that they had come into their very extensive fifteenth-century estates in Suffolk and Yorkshire in an illegitimate line by faking both their pedigree and their coat armour

---

[36] Cf. a fragment in Hengr. 18, fo. 53, on William Roberts of Beccles. The work was dismembered by the eccentric herald, Peter Le Neve (1661–1729).

[37] *Chorography* Introduction, esp. pp. 10–16.

[38] For discussion and biographical details of Ryece, see G. C. Harlow, 'Robert Ryece of Preston', *PSIA* XXXII (1970), pp. 43–70.

[39] 'Chitting', pp. 104–5.   [40] BL Harl. 3873, fos. 10 ff.

during the Tudor period.[41] Venal heralds and unscrupulous genealogists could find an eager market among thè gentry for their talents.

Similarly, heraldry was the ritual language of power. The county community could be depicted far more effectively and immediately by massing its coat armour than by the portraits of its members. One of the most interesting and comprehensive displays of this sort was created by Sir Robert Jermyn at his west Suffolk home of Rushbrooke Hall. Who better than Sir Robert? He personified the dedicated Puritan county magnate who by the end of Elizabeth's reign was the dominant force in Suffolk; his grandfather Sir Thomas seems to have pursued an active policy of seeking marriages for his family from all corners of the county, and so Sir Robert had a formidable array of close cousins throughout Suffolk, maintaining genuinely friendly relations even with that very different East Anglian magnate Sir Arthur Heveningham (below, pp. 258–9). The motto '*nec ab oriente nec occidente*' which adorned Sir Robert's portrait may well have been an expression of his determination to build on his grandfather's strategy and create a Suffolk community which had no segregation into east and west;[42] be that as it may, he chose to decorate Rushbrooke with a display of the coat armour of the families of the whole county as they existed in the latter half of Elizabeth's reign—139 shields with the proud inscription '*Qui sumus*'. He further underlined the historic continuity of this body by a further marshalling of 109 coats of extinct families, significantly labelled '*qui fuimus*'—'who *we* were', not 'who they were'.[43] A good deal of patient historical research lay behind this iconography of the Suffolk gentry.

Robert Ryece also used his antiquarian expertise to create an heraldic shrine of county gentlemen in his parish church at Preston, where much of it can still be seen. Ryece, a firm Puritan who had been educated in Geneva under Theodore Beza, purified the church of Popish relics and provided instead decoration suitable for a Protestant county gentleman in the form of heraldry in paint and stained glass. The ensemble provides a striking visual presentation of the ideals of this fairly minor member of the Suffolk county community—Ryece was never a JP—loyalty to the God of scripture, loyalty to the English Crown and pride in its antiquity and achievements, combined with a fierce attachment to the gentry of Suffolk. Painted wooden triptychs,

---

[41] Richmond, p. 6. [42] *Rushbrook Registers* p. 422.
[43] SROI, GC 17/755, Blois's Church Notes, pp. 354–6.

apparently Ryece's own handiwork,[44] survive, severally depicting scriptural texts, the Ten Commandments, and the royal arms of Elizabeth quartered with an astonishing display of bogus coat armour back to the arms of King Brutus of Troy; the doors of the latter triptych, with unconscious irony, contain stern exhortations against image-worship. A further triptych, alas long perished, contained a long Latin commemoration of the defeat of the Armada.[45] In the windows of the body of the church, Ryece marshalled the arms of the Suffolk gentry. With exquisite snobbery, he relegated the arms of the county's lawyers to the west window in the tower, to the chagrin of an antiquary of the next generation, Sir Simonds D'Ewes; Sir Simonds's father, a professional lawyer who had become one of the Six Clerks of Chancery, had been an incomer to the county, but D'Ewes later insisted that the family coat should be moved into the body of the church near the impeccably ancient heraldry of his wife's family, the Cloptons.[46]

It was appropriate that Ryece's *Breviary* should put this iconography into words. Ryece has left us a most thoroughgoing description of the ideals of an English county community in his description of his fellow-gentry. In the following paragraph, Ryece's friends could see themselves not as others saw them, but as they would wish to see themselves: members of a common fellowship to whom division was a sin.

as they visitt one another much, meett often conversing most familyarly together, which so winneth the good will one of another with all reverent regard of the meaner sort, true love and unfeyned affection of their neighbours, that if differences doe arise which are very seldome, such is the great discretion ever tempered with love and kindnes among them, that these devisions are soon smothered and appeased. So againe what with the enterlacing of houses in marriage (a practice at this day much used for strengthening of families thereby) such is the religious unitie wherewith in all good actions they doe concurre, that whatsoever offendeth one displeaseth all, and whosoever sattisfieth one contenteth all.[47]

Once more, we hear the complacency of success: a county which had

[44] Ryece bequeathed his 'boxes of painting colours' to a Lavenham painter for touching up the display: *PSIA* XXXII (1970), p. 61.

[45] Cf. an English translation of the inscription in H. M. Cautley, *Royal Arms and Commandments in our Churches* (Ipswich 1934), pp. 125–6. Cautley also illustrates the surviving work: ibid., pp. 38, 43, 111.

[46] SROI, GC 17/755, p. 293.   [47] Ryece, p. 60.

succeeded at least more than its neighbours in achieving an appearance of peace against forces which would disturb it from without and within, Ryece's verbal picture made explicit the essential equality of the heraldry he had depicted, for (*pace* the Suffolk lawyers!) one man's coat armour is no more honourable than another's: no nobleman has a more honourable heraldic achievement than a mere gentleman. In this way, the displays of heraldry which Jermyn and Ryece constructed were symbols of a commonwealth which knew itself, and which treasured its identity in the face of its sovereign monarch and in the face of the great noblemen who appeared and disappeared in the region over the years.

This county pride was not merely stimulated by the disappearance of leading aristocrats during Elizabeth's reign, but was also encouraged by the development of the county's institutions of government against the various divisions within the county. The office of sheriff was a symbol of this development; even if the sheriff had fallen from his high medieval estate in terms of real power, he was still an officer of great prestige, and there is good evidence that gentlemen often competed eagerly to obtain the office.[48] The dissolution of the monasteries had provided the Sheriff of Norfolk and Suffolk with a chance to extend his attenuated role in the county against rival jurisdictions. The Crown now became direct Lord of the Liberty of St Edmund, which seems to have encouraged the Sheriff to make an assault on its Steward's privileges of returning royal writs within the Liberty. On at least two occasions in Elizabeth's reign, the under-steward of the Liberty, Thomas Andrews, entered Complaints into Chancery about the attempts of the Sheriff's officers to serve writs within the Liberty; he was no doubt encouraged by the knowledge that the Lord Keeper to whom he was appealing in Chancery was his own master, Sir Nicholas Bacon, himself Crown lessee of most of the Abbot's rights in the Liberty.[49] From the other side, a litigant in 1579 challenged Andrews's right to return writs within the Liberty and hence to impanel a jury on a writ of waste granted out of Chancery.[50] There is no record of similar trouble between the Sheriff and the officers of St Audrey, still responsible to an ecclesiastical lord after the Dissolution, who seem to have exercised their rights as before; however, the Sheriff's officers did attempt to assert their rights in the 'rival' Crown franchises of the Duchy of Lancaster; in 1559 the Mayor of the Duchy borough of

[48] Smith, pp. 139, 146–8, 153–4, 312, and Jeayes, pp. 23–4, 42.
[49] PRO, C3/4/18 (und.), C3/4/102 (10 Feb. 1570).   [50] C3/210/27.

Sudbury complained that the under-sheriff had made a seizure within the bounds of the borough. In 1567 the Sheriff sent his officer to make an arrest in the west Suffolk manor of Hundon, traditionally privileged from all officers except the Bailiff of the Honour of Clare, now part of the Duchy, and in any case (like Sudbury) deep inside the Liberty of St Edmund. At the other end of the county a similar complaint was made in 1576 by the inhabitants of the Duchy manor of Iken near Orford.[51] The formation of a separate shrievalty for Suffolk in 1575 must have encouraged this perhaps rather surprising revival in the position of the sheriff in the county.

County administration also benefited from the provision of new architectural symbols in the form of new buildings in Elizabeth's reign. In the Liberty of St Audrey the Liberty's steward, Thomas Seckford, organized a general rate to finance the building of a sessions house and gaol at Woodbridge in 1578,[52] while in the northern Geldable at Beccles, the decay of the sessions house which the townsfolk blamed on their lifelong enemy William Rede necessitated rebuilding there in the 1580s.[53] The JPs of the southern Geldable also seem to have made provision for new accommodation after their temporary eviction from the Town Hall by the borough of Ipswich in 1566; it is probable that the later arrangement by which they occupied part of the former Ipswich Blackfriars originated soon after 1569, when the premises were bought by the town for various public purposes.[54] A scheme sponsored by Edward Grimston the elder to build an entirely new sessions house and gaol at Ipswich for which a rate was levied in 1580 seems to have collapsed, with a distinct odour of scandal hanging about it.[55]

One might argue that these buildings were symbols of local particularism rather than of county unity, but it is likely that they had less impact on their areas than the new Elizabethan arrangements for holding Bury assizes had for the county as a whole. Once Shirehouse Heath had been abandoned after the Dissolution, the assizes were convened in the converted monastic schoolhouse on the edge of the great abbey churchyard, finally conveyed to the town feoffees of Bury just before Queen Elizabeth's visit in 1578.[56] The inconveniences

---

[51] Sudbury: PRO, DL 1/43/M6. Hundon: DL 1/74/T4. Iken: DL 1/103/A9.
[52] Bodl. MS Top. Suff. d. 7, p. 656; SROB, E2/41/8b, fo. 339ᵛ.
[53] Bec. A4/31; PRO, E134/28 Eliz./Easter 21, interrogatories *ex parte* defendants, depositions of Thomas Colby and John Rede.
[54] Dugdale, IV, p. 297.
[55] *APC* XXVI, pp. 38, 402.   [56] *Rushbrook Registers* p. 446.

imposed by the Abbot of Bury's independence of mind were at an end; once the assizes had moved into the agreeable surroundings of the town of Bury, they could better fulfil their political, social, and ceremonial role in uniting the county. No other institution so effectively gathered the Suffolk gentry from either side of the Franchise Bank; after all, it was an obligation for all justices of the peace to attend the assizes, and as the commission of the peace so markedly expanded in numbers from the 1530s, most of the leading gentlemen of the county would need to be there. As a social occasion, the assizes had become so successful by the end of the century that in 1600 the Privy Council used the assize judges to communicate its growing alarm at the scale of feasting on these occasions, seeing it as a temptation to some to curry favour among the freeholders and a discouragement to others to take office.[57] By 1612 it was a commonplace for the justices to use the assizes, 'where moste of the gentlemen of the countye meett as alsoe the chiefe yeomen and ffearmers', as an opportunity to ascertain the county's mind on grain prices and the feasibility of moving grain elsewhere, while the assizes also provided a chance for the muster commissioners to meet and agree on policy.[58]

These developments were all in existing institutions, but such was the pressure of government business in both military and civil spheres that local rulers all over England were forced to experiment with new methods of coping with the burden. One method widely used was the introduction of petty sessions for minor business, but petty sessions were not of much significance in Suffolk. The name was not new; we find it being used for the sheriff's tourn held for Ixworth, an island of the shrievalty's responsibility in the middle of the Liberty of St Edmund, around 1515, but this clearly referred to an older form of institution than that of the justices of the peace.[59] No records survive to show whether Suffolk adopted the provisions of the highly unpopular and ultimately unsuccessful Act of Parliament of 1542 establishing petty sessions,[60] but there survive two references from 1560, one to sessions for Blything and one to the 'receyte of the petycessyans boke' by the churchwardens of Metfield in the Hundred of Hoxne.[61] This

---

[57] Cf. the list of JPs present at and absent from the 1579 summer assizes, PRO, SP 12/133/13, fos. 29 f. Council's letter: Tanner 76, fo. 40.
[58] PRO, SP 14/128/65; BL Harl. 309, fo. 231.   [59] PRO, STAC 4/9/122.
[60] S. E. Lehmberg, *The Later Parliaments of Henry VIII* (Cambridge 1977), pp. 151–2.
[61] PRO, E137/42/4, bond of John Pryme of Halesworth, 1560; *PSIA* XXIII (1938), p. 143.

suggests that the county was operating a regular system at this date, but the solitary later reference to petty sessions at Stoke by Nayland in 1598 suggests that unlike other counties, Suffolk did not find them a useful expedient.[62] Probably the well-defined system of demarcation in the four meetings of quarter sessions made the addition of supplementary petty sessions unnecessary.

More significant were the general county meetings supplementing the assizes which became a feature of the county's administration during Elizabeth's reign. We have already noted the muster commissioners squabbling in 1569 about where they should meet when neither assizes nor quarter sessions afforded them an official meeting-place (above, Ch. 1). Although Needham Market had then been agreed on, following the wishes of the commissioners from the east, the leaders of the Bury Bench eventually got their way in this as in so much else and secured Stowmarket as the usual venue; henceforward, apart from occasional meetings at Bury, Stowmarket was to be the place where the muster commissioners and deputy lieutenants of east and west met.[63] During the 1570s and early 1580s all or most of the JPs were also on the muster commission, and it was hardly surprising that civil as well as military affairs should come to be discussed at such meetings at Stowmarket. When the new organization for purveyance was set up in the 1590s, Stowmarket was the obvious place for the annual meetings of the JPs who regulated the composition and chose the purveyance commissioners for the coming year.[64] By 1615, general meetings of the justices at Stow to discuss any sort of county administrative business could be referred to as a matter of routine.[65]

Professor Everitt has seen these meetings as providing a heritage of administrative experience for their direct successor, the County Committee of the Civil War and Interregnum; Suffolk's continuity of personnel with the pre-war county leadership had few parallels in other counties.[66] The County Committee was an appropriate offspring for an institution whose origin owed nothing to the initiative of royal central government, but which was a local response to the ever-increasing demands made by Westminster. Particularism was still a strong force in the Suffolk of 1603, in the Liberties, in the Geldable, in

---

[62] PRO, STAC 5 J15/10, Answers of Ralph, Robert, and Thomas Agas.
[63] Cf., e.g. BL Harl. 309, fo. 204; Harl. 286, fo. 42; Aylsham 17, Deputy Lieutenants to Heveningham, 19 Oct. 1590, 7 May 1601.
[64] Ryece, pp. 15–17.
[65] Committee Book, fo. 14^r.   [66] Everitt, *Suffolk*, pp. 17, 22.

the half-hundred of Lothingland; yet the demands of central government forcing local administration to work as a unit, the elaboration of organization for military affairs and for purveyance, continued the erosion of lesser institutional loyalties and strengthened county unity. Paradoxically, it would be central government which would ultimately suffer from this development, as a result of its own demands.

PART II

CHANGING PATTERNS OF RELIGION

Introductory

AT both an official and a popular level, the Reformation changed the character of East Anglian piety to a degree which would have been inconceivable in 1500. At the beginning of the century, most religious practice expressed itself within an institutional structure which was virtually unchanged from the thirteenth century; it centred on some of the most splendid and lavishly-furnished churches in England, theatres for a liturgical cycle of the year which provided the framework for everyday life. By the end of the century this framework was largely dismantled; what remained of the institutions of the pre-Reformation Church was being put to strikingly different religious purposes, and the wealth of art, music, and decoration which had been built up without significant pause into the 1530s counted for very little. The old piety became the property of an embattled gentry minority, sheltering as best they could a few humbler folk; in such circumstances the extrovert devotional life which the old religion fostered was necessarily a thing of the past, and the Roman Catholicism which emerged from the devoted salvage work directed from abroad during Elizabeth's reign was almost as different in character from pre-Reformation religious practice as the Protestantism of the new establishment. The death of Queen Mary saw the passing of a religious world of visual impression, of sound, smell, colour, of hallowed things; the settled, stable confusion born of centuries of accretions to a complex system of devotion gave way to a new confusion, born of uncertainty as to the future shape of the Church in England. However, the man who most personified the old system for East Anglians had died two decades before the death of the queen who gave Catholicism its last taste of establishment.

4

Richard Nix and the Old World
1501–1535

CONSIDER first the personalities and institutions around which the old world of devotion was organized. The medieval diocesan structure in the county has already been described (above, Ch. 1); over it Bishop Nix presided from 1501 until his death amid the destruction of the old order at the end of 1535. Although Nix had the makings of a career in royal service under Henry VII, even briefly holding the Keepership of the Great Seal in 1500, he seems to have abandoned any further progress in that direction after his consecration to Norwich, and he spent his time in his diocese. Most unusually among his colleagues, he had spent much of his time in diocesan administration before he was consecrated bishop.[1] The impact of his three decades in East Anglia would considerably outlast his death, through the influence which he wielded over protégés and associates (below, pp. 187–8).

Few of Nix's subordinates as Archdeacons of Sudbury and Suffolk can have provided much support for him. His first Archdeacon of Sudbury, John Fineux (1497–1514) was at least resident in his archdeaconry, with a base as Master of Sudbury College and finally a tomb in St Mary's Bury St Edmunds, but Thomas Larke (1517–22) and Richard Wolman (1522–37) are unlikely to have taken much interest directly in archidiaconal affairs. Larke was a Cambridge man of Thetford origins who had risen to be chaplain to Henry VII and subsequently Master of Trinity Hall, supervising various royal building schemes; he was confessor to Wolsey, whose mistress was his sister.[2] His career may have started through the Howard family, given their links with Thetford; Wolman's almost certainly did, for his father was in the service of the first Howard Duke of Norfolk. His subsequent career was founded on his chaplaincy to Henry VIII and his steadfast support for the King in his Great Matter, and in the midst of his numerous preferments it is a moot point whether he was more of an

[1] P. Hughes, *The Reformation in England* (3 vols., 1954), I, p. 76.
[2] Crawley, *Trinity Hall*, p. 26.

absentee from his Archdeaconry of Sudbury than from his Deanery of Wells.[3]

In the Archdeaconry of Suffolk the Bishop inherited Nicholas Goldwell, Master of the wealthy college of Chapel in the Field in Norwich, and a great man through being the brother of the late Bishop Goldwell; his death in 1505 may well have been something of a relief to Nix.[4] Little is known of his successor, John Dowman, but his London rectory and prebend at St Paul's suggest that his interests lay elsewhere;[5] when he resigned in 1526, he was replaced by Thomas Winter, Cardinal Wolsey's bastard son and nephew of Larke, the former Archdeacon of Sudbury. Winter's main distinction appears to have been his beautiful italic handwriting. When Winter was transferred to the Archdeaconry of Norwich in 1529, Nix at last got the chance to put in his own man in the shape of his chaplain, Edmund Steward, whose later preferment as Chancellor of Winchester and Gardiner's right-hand man suggests that he would be a soulmate for the aged bishop; however, once more Wolsey interfered, and intruded his own chaplain Richard Sampson to replace Steward despite Nix's protests and pleas. Sampson was to remain Archdeacon until 1536, and if his subsequent career as Bishop of Chichester is anything to go by, he can have taken little interest in his duties in Suffolk.[6]

If there was little to be said for most of his archdeacons, who were the outstanding personalities in Suffolk under Nix? Two priests stand out from the records: Dr John Bailey and Dr Thomas Pells, both Suffolk-born. Bailey, the son of a former bailiff of Ipswich, had a Cambridge career as Fellow of Pembroke besides six years' study abroad, and he was one of the benefactors of Gonville Hall, whose master he made one of his executors.[7] In 1510 he was presented by the King to St Matthew's Ipswich, a wealthy suburban church important because it was in charge of the well-known shrine of our Lady of

[3] Lehmberg, *Reformation Parliament*, pp. 73–4.
[4] C. Harper-Bill, 'A late medieval visitation—the Diocese of Norwich in 1499', *PSIA* XXXIV (1977), p. 45.
[5] Dowman: cf. *Butley Chronicle* p. 45 n.
[6] On Steward at Winchester, R. Fritze, 'Faith and faction: religious changes, national politics and the development of local factionalism in Hampshire, 1485–1570' (Cambridge Ph.D. thesis 1982), p. 471. On Sampson, PRO, SP 1/50/19 (*LP* IV pt. ii, no. 4659), and on his career at Chichester, *Continuity and Change. Personnel and Administration of the Church in England 1500–1642*, ed. R. O'Day and F. Heal (Leicester, 1976), pp. 229, 233.
[7] Emden, *Cambridge to 1500*, p. 46, s.v. Bayly, John; *PSIA* VII (1890), pp. 160–2. The will of his father Richard Bailey is at PCC 40 Holgrave.

Grace (Gracechurch); Bailey was to play a part in the dramatic events of 1516 there (below, pp. 144–6). He was clearly the leading cleric in Ipswich, while his brother Robert was among the fellows of Mettingham College up in the Waveney Valley; Richard Weybread the Master of Mettingham was also a relative, and in 1507 John Bailey was the man chosen to preach a series of sermons in towns and villages throughout Norfolk and Suffolk on the bequest of the late Master of Mettingham, Richard Braunch.[8] He was wealthy enough to be named specifically as one of the clergy to contribute to the loan of 1522 for the French War. It is worth noting that he is recorded as crossing swords with Wolsey over the endowment of Wolsey's Cardinal College, Ipswich with revenues of St Matthew's; this would no doubt have appealed to Bishop Nix, who had his own bones to pick with Wolsey. On Bailey's death in 1525, Wolsey made sure that a successor would not interfere further with his plans to make a daughter-church of St Matthew's into part of the nucleus of Cardinal College by arranging that the same Thomas Winter who became Archdeacon of Suffolk was presented as rector of St Matthew's.[9]

Thomas Pells, like so many able clerics in the middle ranks of the Church, was of prosperous yeoman stock; his family had comfortable property in east Suffolk at Clopton and Sudbourne.[10] One of his earliest pieces of preferment, freeing him from his Benedictine priory at Norwich, was his appointment in 1509 as Prior of the little Norwich cell at Hoxne, near Nix's favourite residence; in effect, the Bishop was giving him room to turn to the career of a secular priest. He was one of Nix's right-hand men, becoming Official of the Diocese in the Bishop's last years and a prominent 'Aragonese' Leader in Convocations' rearguard action against the imposition of the Royal Supremacy in 1531–2.[11] Pells had a strong position in Suffolk; as Chancellor of the Diocese of Ely from 1515, he gained two Ely livings at Glemsford and Hitcham, lavishly rebuilt Glemsford rectory, and combined all this with the Chancellorship of the Diocese of London.[12] As forceful a character as Nix his patron, he threatened in 1526 to execute a sentence of excommunication on anyone who fished the waters belonging to the parsonage of Glemsford; it is significant to note

[8] BL Add. Ch. 63062; BL Add. 40070, fo. 58ᵛ; Add. 40061, fo. 73ʳ.
[9] Loan: *LP* III, no. 2483. *PSIA* VII, pp. 161–2.
[10] PRO, REQ 2/9/97; *1524 Subsidy* p. 269.
[11] Guy, *More*, pp. 142, 167–71, 176.
[12] Venn, III, p. 338, s.v. Pelles, Thomas; on rectory, CCN 163 Corant; on an inscription for Pells now at Hawkedon near Glemsford, *PSIA* XIX (1927), p. 346.

Wolsey taking an interest in the depositions of this case, in the same year that the Cardinal was skirmishing with Bishop Nix over jurisdiction in the College of nearby Stoke-by-Clare, consolidating his hold on the Archdeaconry of Suffolk and St Matthew's Ipswich, and pressing ahead with his college-building plans.[13]

Apart from these leading Suffolk clerics, Nix had to deal with a network of religious houses. At the beginning of his episcopate, Suffolk boasted twenty monasteries, five nunneries, and ten friaries, together with six colleges of secular priests. These had been the spiritual power-houses of previous centuries; what was their state in the early Tudor period? The visitations by successive Bishops of Norwich, which leave out certain monasteries and all friaries, do not reveal any spectacular areas of scandal to compare with the consistently deplorable examples of Walsingham Priory or Norwich Cathedral Priory in Norfolk; the general picture is one of conscientious if uninspired and pedestrian observance of the Rule, marred by occasional minor scandal and a good deal of run-of-the-mill ill-nature in the cloister.[14] Suffolk religious houses were no exception to the rule that there was little sign of falling-off in numbers or entrants to the monastic life until it became obvious that the Dissolution was a real threat. Of all the religious houses, only two secular Colleges seem to show any noticeable decline in numbers during the half-century before the Dissolution: Sudbury and Wingfield. Sudbury was a late fourteenth-century foundation which had no contemporary active patron to take an interest in it; Wingfield's decline might be expected after the eclipse of its De la Pole patrons, but even here, the evidence is uncertain.[15]

Occasional scandals erupt from the records; the greatest corporate disaster was Butley Priory's unsuccessful attempt at a takeover bid for the small neighbouring house of Snape in 1508, plunging Butley into catastrophic debt and probably causing the suicide of its Prior in the following year; the constitutional crisis which ensued had to be sorted out by the intervention of the Bishop, who deposed the Butley Canons' first choice of a successor to the unhappy Prior Brommer.[16] The prize

[13] PRO, SP 1/40/77–80 (*LP* IV pt. ii, no. 2710).

[14] For a brief summary of the material printed in Jessopp, *Visitations*, see Knowles, III, pp. 73–5.

[15] The contrast in recorded names of staff at Wingfield in 1532 and 1534 (cf. Jessopp, *Visitations*, p. 296 with *Report of the Deputy Keeper of the Public Records* VII App. ii, 1846, p. 305) indicates that not all the names are recorded in the visitations. Oxley, Ch. III, offers a contrasting and probably unnecessarily gloomy picture of Essex religious houses.

[16] *CPR Henry VII* II, p. 625; *LP* I pt. i, nos. 132(76), 289(28); *LP* II, p. 1483; *Butley Chronicle* pp. 25–7.

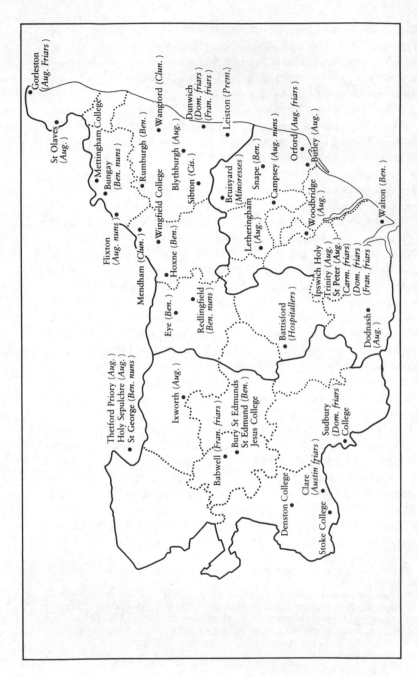

VI. Suffolk: religious houses in 1500

for most disreputable cloistered priest in the county must go to
Thomas Whitehead, prebendary of the College of Stoke-by-Clare
from about 1497, who enlivened his perpetually disruptive career in
the College by large-scale agricultural trade, fornication, and on one
occasion, the manslaughter of a passing beggar; none of this prevented
him seeing the final dissolution of the College in 1548 at the age of 75,
still a prebendary.[17] Against such stories must be balanced the austere
piety which in 1531 made Abbot Green of Leiston forsake his house
for a hermit's life in the marshes by the sea, or the evident pride and
loving care with which the Canons of Butley maintained their round of
sacred music in the years after the Snape fiasco.[18]

It is difficult to gauge what impact these houses continued to make
on the world around them. Some impression can be gained from the
legacies which they received from the laity, nearly all soliciting
requiem masses or prayers. A sample of the wills of thirty-eight
members of the county magistracy from 1485 to 1539 shows seventeen
making some gift to one monastery or another, and considerably more
(twenty-six) making bequests to friaries. Such élite figures as knights
and noblemen would naturally tend to remember monasteries more
than other people, for they included families like the Willoughbys who
had traditional connections with several houses. In general, lay
generosity to monasteries and friaries revealed a much greater gap
than this. For instance, a sample for the same period of a lesser élite
group, twenty-two individuals who served as bailiffs of Ipswich, reveals
nine testators making bequests to monasteries and precisely double
that figure for friaries—in nearly every case, the three friaries of
Ipswich.[19] Professor Gottfried's sample of wills in the Peculiar Court
of Bury St Edmunds from 1440 to 1530 shows that 56·8 per cent of
testators made bequests to the local friary at Babwell and 30 per cent
to the Abbey of St Edmund. Dr Peet's examination of the same
sources indicates a remarkable decline in goodwill towards the Abbey
in the second half of the period: only six direct bequests to it out of 118
wills made in Bury between 1512 and 1539.[20]

---

[17] PRO, C244/162/83; PRO, SP 1/40/165–73 (*LP* IV pt. ii, no. 2752); *LP* I pt. ii,
no. 3107/37; Jessopp, *Visitations,* pp. 82–3, 153, 195; *PSIA* XII (1904), p. 40.
[18] Green: *Butley Chronicle* p. 59. Butley: ibid., pp. 28, 66; Jessopp, *Visitations,* p. 131.
[19] Sample of wills drawn from PCC and CCN.
[20] Gottfried, p. 183. Gottfried's remarks about differences of popularity between the
various orders should be treated with caution; the prominence of the Franciscans which
he notes is surely the result of the fact that theirs was the only house of friars easily
within reach of Bury. Peet, 'Parish clergy', p. 55.

The slump in giving by the townsfolk of Bury to their Abbey is an extreme case, reflecting the resentment of a growing and prosperous town at the continuing power of this great house. In wealth it easily outclassed any other foundation in the county: its annual income in the *Valor Ecclesiasticus* was five times that of its nearest Suffolk rival, Butley Priory. Despite arguments recently and rashly advanced by Professor Gottfried, there is no good evidence that the Abbey's last half-century was anything but a time of continued prosperity and success.[21] At the Dissolution it was owed much greater sums than it owed others;[22] intellectually, too, it was no backwater. At the beginning of the century, its library was probably still second only to that of Oxford University; it continued to fulfil its obligation to train various members of the house at university, and at least two of the early sixteenth-century members of the house went as far afield as Louvain in their training. The intellectual liveliness of the monks is attested by the interest which several of them showed in the teachings of Luther.[23]

The Abbot from 1513 until the end was John Reve alias Melford, no great saint or scholar, but a capable administrator who delighted in building schemes, on which he employed the Bury-born John Wastell, one of the most talented master masons of the day.[24] Some time between 1515 and 1520 Reve became the first and only regular to sit on the county commission of the peace; it was a somewhat ironical honour in view of the fact that he and his predecessors had excluded the quarter sessions from the town of Bury at least since the mid-fifteenth-century. Moreover, it only supplemented his far older powers within the Liberty of St Edmund. Reve's relatives were prosperous west Suffolk yeomen, including the clothier Thomas Smith of Melford, one of the richest men in Suffolk in the 1524 Subsidy, but by

---

[21] Gottfried's contention that the Abbey was selling off substantial parts of its landed endowment in its last years (pp. 239, 241–2) is based on no stated firm evidence, and rather seems to be founded on a misunderstanding of L. J. Redstone's edition of the first Ministers' Account of Bury lands, made in 1540 *after the Crown* had sold off substantial parts of the Abbey estates (above, Ch. 2, nn. 61, 62; cf. *PSIA* XIII, 1909, pp. 311–66). The same fault, and further misinterpretations, seems to lie behind his conclusion (pp. 38–45) that the centre of the town of Bury was in decay on the eve of the Dissolution: an intrinsically unlikely surmise.

[22] Cf. payments of its debts in 1539 (*LP* XVI, no. 745 iv) with the debts owing it (PRO, E323/2B/1, m. 14, *LP* XVIII pt. ii, no. 231).

[23] Library: G. McMurray Gibson, 'Bury St Edmunds, Lydgate and the N–Town Cycle', *Speculum* LVI (1981), p. 69. Foxe, IV, pp. 585, 681; V, pp. 28, 43.

[24] On Reve's building, PRO, SP 1/73/91 (*LP* V, no. 1719), BL Cott. Cleop. E IV, fo. 145 (*LP* IX, no. 772). On Wastell, J. H. Harvey, *English Medieval Architects* (1954), pp. 279–87.

the Abbot's death, the circle of friends revealed in his will was more exalted: the world of his gentry colleagues on the Suffolk Bench, Highams, Drurys, Somersets, Jermyns.[25]

Abbot Reve promoted the interests of his house as vigorously as any of his predecessors. Just as in the thirteenth and fourteenth centuries, the Abbot clashed with the people of Bury, and he won this conflict just as previous Abbots had done. A series of disputes about jurisdictions and the payment of tax came to a head when the Abbot sought Wolsey's help on his East Anglian tour of 1517; the Abbey's leading opponents were summoned into the Cardinal's presence at Ipswich and forced to swear not to challenge the Abbot's title further.[26] This set the seal on Reve's previous victories over the townsfolk; his legal case was unanswerable until the destruction of his house. Small wonder that eighty years after the Dissolution, a Bury townsman could recall his mother saying that 'manie of the inhabitaunts . . . had greved at some speeches of the last Abbott used (vizt.) he said, he was lord and kinge within the said towne'.[27]

There can be little doubt that this is an accurate reflection of the Abbot's imperious tone. Many of the complaints in the Bury disputes running up to 1517 were of his partisanship for his officers and servants even when they were in the wrong, and two separate sources testify to his support for his pugnacious servant and relative Richard Smith, son of the clothier Thomas, at Long Melford.[28] Nevertheless, outside the traditional battleground of Bury, there is some evidence of a different spirit. At Beccles, the embattled inhabitants looked back with nostalgia in 1586 to the fifteenth-century agreement which they had worked out with Bury Abbey over the administration of their common lands, and tried to incorporate as much of it as possible in their latest attempt to solve their legal problems. At the Bury manor of Hessett, the parish church retains much of the rich decoration which made it a symbol of the co-operation between successive abbots, abbey officers, and the village leadership from the fifteenth to the early sixteenth century, and under one of the stone tombs in the churchyard lies Robert Bacon, Abbot Reve's sheepreeve and hundred bailiff,

[25] On Smith, *1524 Subsidy* p. 30, and PRO, C1/758/25; Reve's will pr. Muskett, II, pp. 3–4.
[26] PRO, E135/2/11; PRO, SP 1/232/43 (*LP* App. I pt. i, no. 197); PRO, STAC 2/1, fo. 23, 2/7/159–65, 2/16/9, 2/22/6, 2/26/220.
[27] PRO, E134/20 James I/Easter 3, deposition of John Hill.
[28] PRO, C1/758/25; PRO, SP 1/240/258 (*LP* App. I pt. i, no. 1190), and cf. PRO, E135/22/5.

father to Queen Elizabeth's Lord Keeper of the Great Seal.[29]

No other house could hope to wield the same influence as Bury; indeed, the paucity of evidence about lawsuits with their secular neighbours suggests that Suffolk monasteries were more peaceable outside than inside the cloister. Most of them were small and not especially well-endowed; few of their leaders emerge clearly from the general obscurity. Thomas Manning, Prior of Butley from 1529 and subsequently Bishop of Ipswich, stands out because he was in Thomas Cromwell's circle of East Anglian acquaintance (below, Ch. 7); otherwise the most interesting figures come from the larger secular colleges. Most exalted was Richard Eden, Clerk of the King's Council from 1512 and Master of Sudbury College from 1516; he shared origins in Bury St Edmunds and Cambridge connections at Trinity Hall with Archdeacon Larke and Stephen Gardiner, and it was probably Eden's family friendship with the Gardiners that started young Stephen on his exalted career.[30] As a senior civil servant, Eden was a pluralist and a habitual absentee from Sudbury who never deigned to turn up for Nix's visitations of the College,[31] but nevertheless his family settled in the town and would clash with the townsfolk in later years (below, Ch. 11). Richard Shelton, Master of Mettingham College from 1517 to his death in 1539, was exceptional among Suffolk heads of houses as a member of the local gentry; his elder brother Sir John was twice Sheriff of Norfolk and Suffolk and married Anne Boleyn's aunt. Shelton seems to have done much to reform a College which had been in serious disorder (see below, p. 155), and was locally noted for his skill in hydraulics, being consulted in the attempts to improve Yarmouth Haven in 1528.[32] His successor as master was Bishop Manning.

Stoke by Clare, the richest of Suffolk colleges and little less wealthy than Butley Priory, had developed into a country retreat for Cambridge dons and other deserving clerics. From 1497 all five successive deans had been or were currently masters or fellows of Cambridge colleges;[33]

[29] Beccles: PRO, E134/28 Elizabeth/Easter 21. Hessett: 'Chitting', p. 110.

[30] Crawley, *Trinity Hall*, p. 45, although he does not complete the identification between the cleric and the Council Clerk. Eden was presented as rector of Sudbury St Gregory, which went with the College, in 1516.

[31] Jessopp, *Visitations*, pp. 150, 225, 298.   [32] BL Add. 33990, fo. 145[r].

[33] John Edenham, fellow of Clare Hall 1473–87; Robert Bekinsawe, President of Queens' 1508–19; William Grene, fellow of Pembroke from 1515 and Vice-Chancellor 1524–5; Robert Shorton, Master of St John's 1511–16 and of Pembroke 1518–34; Matthew Parker, Master of Corpus 1544–53.

in 1526 the fellows included the then Vice-Chancellor of Cambridge and the Master of St Katherine's-by-the-Tower in London, while the Master of St Catherine's Hall, Cambridge was among the fellows at the dissolution of the College in 1548.[34] The last Dean from 1535 was the future Archbishop Matthew Parker; for all the constant problems caused by the deficiencies of the statutes and by the presence of such horrific colleagues as Thomas Whitehead, Parker loved the place as 'a pleasant solitary retirement . . . from the Court or University', and his friend Walter Haddon used to nickname Stoke 'Parker's Tusculanum'. On Stoke's dissolution, Parker took away a stained glass panel with the founder's arms and set it up in the Master's Lodge at Corpus, Cambridge.[35]

Such was the state of the county's ecclesiastical machine on the eve of the Reformation: there was much that was good, much that was indifferent, and little that was catastrophic. The Bishop was resident, strong-willed and conscientious after the fashion of piety of one who had been born when Henry VI was still in his twenties. For many layfolk, this would be a devotional style which met their own understanding of the faith, whether simple or sophisticated. It was a style which owed little to the humanism of an Erasmus or a Colet; that was a piety which both nourished a new brand of Catholicism and lay behind much of the zeal of the English Protestant reformers. The main focus of the older devotion was the life of the parish church. Suffolk was ideally suited to develop a vigorous parochial life; with slightly more than five hundred parish churches and relatively few chapelries, it was well-provided without being over-provided. In the wood–pasture country which dominated most of the county, the parishes were compact units, mostly of pre-Conquest origin and usually predating the much more subdivided manorial network, which was increasingly a weak competitor in the organization of local affairs.

The enthusiasm of people for their parish churches shines out from the legacies in their wills. The great majority of them ignored the monasteries in their giving, and about half of them ignored the friaries, but close to 90 per cent left something to the parish church, even if it was just a nominal sum to the high altar for tithes forgotten; this is as true for the population at large as it is for our half-century sample of sixty members of the bailiff leadership of Ipswich and the county

---

[34] Respectively Dr Burton (*LP* IV pt. ii, no. 1229), Gilbert Latham (PRO, DL 1/42/L2) and Reynold Bainbridge (*PSIA* XII, 1904, p. 41; Venn I, p. 69, s.v. Bainbridge, Reynold).　　　　　　　　[35] Strype, *Parker*, I, pp. 15, 45.

magistracy.[36] The wills fill in the details of the picture created by the magnificence of the many buildings that have survived subsequent inconoclasm and misguided restoration. Take a single decade, the 1520s, and a single item of church furniture, the rood screen and its loft: the wills show that in the Archdeaconry of Sudbury alone, no fewer than fifteen parishes were undertaking new work on their rood screens.[37] Although the peak of building activity was in the third quarter of the fifteenth century, the tale of refurnishings and extensions went on into the 1540s; the Edwardian churchwardens' returns of 1547 reveal many parishes in the Archdeaconry of Suffolk, mostly the larger ones, which were still completing church building schemes.[38] The tower of East Bergholt was caught in the forties, when bitter lawsuits and religious uncertainty put a stop to work for ever; the great church of St James Bury St Edmunds and the Howards' extensions at Framlingham were luckier, for they were completed in the reign of Mary.[39]

How was all this activity paid for? Surviving parochial records for pre-Reformation Suffolk are pitifully scanty, but the picture which emerges is of a large amount of corporate giving and fund-raising quite apart from the generosity of exceptionally wealthy families like the Springs of Lavenham or the Cloptons of Melford. Typical seems to have been the effort described by an Elizabethan parish clerk at Eye, who looked through his late fifteenth-century records to see how the superb church tower there had been financed within a single year: the churchwardens

receiving but £1. 6s. 2d. of the former churchwardeyns gatheryd that yere partly with the plowgh, partly in churchales, partly in legacies given that waye, but chiefly of the frank and devowte hartes of the people the some of xl li and litell odde money . . .[40]

---

[36] Gottfried, p. 127, and see above, p. 135.
[37] PCC 20 Maynwaring; SROB, Sudbury Archdeaconry Wills, Brydon fos. 5, 20, 39, 100, 256, 258, 324A; Johnson fos. 124, 159, 220, 226; Newton fos. 39, 52, 71, 72, 87; Brett fos. 30, 46.
[38] *Suffolk Churches. A Pocket Guide*, ed. J. Corke *et al.* (Lavenham, 1976), pp. 24–7. Building works in or just before 1547 at Beccles, Bergholt, Gorleston, Cratfield, Framlingham, Fressingfield, Halesworth, Hopton St Margaret, Huntingfield, Marlesford, Saxmundham: see *EANQ* New Series I (1885), pp. 69, 83, 102, 186, 236, 285–6, 343; II (1887), pp. 43, 124. For similar instances in Essex, see Oxley, pp. 167, 170–1.
[39] Bergholt: PRO, C1/789/43; C1/994/39; C1/1099/5; C4/45, answer of Robert Crane. Bury: PRO, C1/1402/97. Framlingham: *EANQ* New Series I, p. 236.
[40] *HMC* X pt. iv, p. 531. Cf. P. Northeast, 'Church fund-raising in Suffolk before the Reformation', *Suffolk Review* (Sept. 1983), pp. 15–19.

One successful means of fund-raising not included in this list was the village play. The churchwardens' accounts for Boxford, for example, show that in 1535 they staged a play which they seem to have toured round twenty-six neighbouring towns and villages—interestingly enough, a circuit showing considerable overlap with the group of parishes which were at the centre of the Amicable Grant protest ten years earlier (below, Ch. 10). Between front-of-house sales and bar takings, they made the very substantial profit of £19. Other enterprises of other villages are mentioned in these accounts and elsewhere.[41] Such a successful production as this did not merely raise money; it brought the parish together and in the religious content of the play, reaffirmed the parish's commitment to traditional devotion.

Equally important and more permanent in the organization of the parish's life were the guilds; most parishes would have at least one guild, providing its members with entertainment in this life and assistance in the life to come. The guild records of St Peter of Bardwell survive from 1511 to 1547; here was a typical guild for a middle-rank village in the hundred of Blackbourne, named after one of the patron saints of the parish church, and possessing its own guildhall and fee'd musicians and cook for social occasions—the building as well as the archive happily survives into the twentieth century. Its membership seems to have included nearly all the adult population of the village, and its impressive collection of cutlery, all gifts, would have coped with most of them at table; on one occasion the guild was able to run to the extravagant outlay of £10. 19s. on silver, presumably for a loving-cup or a chalice.[42]

In the towns, religious and social guilds shaded off into those with trading and restrictive craft functions; at Bury St Edmunds, hamstrung in self-government by the Abbey's ancient supremacy, the Candlemas or Alderman's Guild took on a particular importance as the main institution whereby the leading townsfolk sought to regulate their own affairs; by the early sixteenth century it had lands in four counties and in more than two hundred parishes.[43] At Ipswich there was no such external rivals as Bury Abbey in town government to give the leading guild of Corpus Christi such an important role, and it is interesting to

---

[41] *Boxford Churchwardens' Accounts 1530–1561*, ed. P. Northeast, SRS XXIII (1982), pp. 2, 8, 11, 15, 18–20. Mr Northeast interprets the means of staging the play differently.

[42] Accounts edited with commentary by F. E. Warren, *PSIA* XI (1901), pp. 81–147; cf. particularly p. 109.

[43] Gottfried, p. 187.

note that despite being the oldest known guild so dedicated, it was beginning to languish in the early sixteenth century. In particular, the pageant associated with it on Corpus Christi day enjoyed chequered fortunes. M. E. James has argued that such pageants were valued in communities wracked by tension, where they were seen by the élite as an affirmation of order and unity, and that they were correspondingly irrelevant in towns where there was no such problem of authority.[44] The evidence from Ipswich, a borough where the merchant oligarchy virtually never lost control, lends plausibility to this thesis. There were already rumblings of trouble for the pageant in 1502, when the borough court ordered that no bailiff should 'interrupt or hinder' it; in 1511 it was replaced by a requiem mass for 'the soules of all the brothers and sisters of the said Towne'. The following year, the wealthy and pious Ipswich merchant Thomas Drayll was clearly doubtful about the future of the whole guild, making a £5 bequest to it 'yf it prosper and goo forthe to effect to the pleasure of god'; although the guild survived, the pageant was not revived until 1520, and then only for a year, after which it seems to have disappeared for ever.[45]

Perhaps such extrovert devotion was past its peak by the early sixteenth century. If it is true that the high-point of building was in the 1460s and 1470s, it is also noticeable that the most extravagant provision for funeral masses and doles came in wills of the 1480s and 1490s, and the cynicism of testators seems finally to have stemmed their giving to crusades soon afterwards.[46] The curious phenomenon of Ipswich merchants and other people given to risky enterprises mentioning their 'avowers' among the saints in their wills must have been a fashion of devotion learnt at the end of the fifteenth century, for it occurs almost exclusively among elderly people making their wills in the 1520s.[47] It is also worth observing that devotion to the life of the parish guilds and to the fabric of the parish church did not necessarily imply excessive affection for the clergy who staffed them. The parson might be regarded (as is often still the case) as a temporary intruder

---

[44] M. E. James, 'Ritual, drama and social body in the late medieval English town', *PP* 98 (Feb. 1983), pp. 3–29, esp. pp. 4, 23–8.

[45] Bacon, pp. 175, 184, 186–91, 193, 195, 202, 204; PCC 9 Fetiplace.

[46] The last I have come across was Drayll in 1512: ibid.

[47] PCC 20 Holder (Edmund Dandy, 1515); CCN 81 Briggs (Sir John Timperley, 1521); PCC 3 Bodfelde (Sir Thomas Wyndham, 1522); CCN 108 Briggs (Sir Edmund Jenny, 1522); PCC 39 Bodfelde (John Forgan, 1525); PCC 15 Porch (William Hall, 1526); PCC 28 Porch (Sir Edward Echingham, 1527); CCN 72 Attmere (William Stisted, 1528).

into the unchanging structure of village life. The frequent friction over tithe and dues like mortuaries, seen at its most extreme in the national outcry over the Hunne case in 1514, goes far to explaining the apparent paradox of English popular anti-clericalism running side by side with English popular Catholic piety. A forthright and wealthy cleric like Thomas Pells could split his parish apart by vigorous action to defend the rights of his benefice: no Chaucerian parish priest he, 'full looth . . . to cursen for his tythes'.[48] Apart from such very traditional grievances, conservative anti-clericalism might equally be fed by indignation that the clergy failed to live up to their self-proclaimed standards of celibacy. John Bale in the course of his Protestant polemic, gleefully reported how the prominent religious conservative and JP Richard Wharton had in disgust 'brought once to the duke of Northfolke, a wenche clothed in mannes apparell, wyth iiii waiting chaplaines, good curates, whiche had one after an other, bestowed their chastity upon her'.[49]

Nevertheless, there was life still in the whole system, both in the newly-completed parish churches and in the shrines which provided a wholly random supplement to the ecclesiastical structure of East Anglia. Some of these shrines were comparatively obscure, like the image of the distinctively East Anglian St Petronilla in the parish church of Stanton All Saints; Our Lady of Woolpit, with her holy well, had attracted the devotion of the first Howard Duke of Norfolk, but does not seem greatly to have interested his successors.[50] Apart from St Edmund, Suffolk's star cult was that of Our Lady of Ipswich, who in 1516 was to demonstrate just how much life remained in the old piety.

The story of the Ipswich miracle of 1516 was the last great set piece of English devotion before the Nun of Kent irretrievably mixed up such wonders in the politics of the Reformation. Thomas More gave a long description of it in his *Dialogue concerning Heresies* of 1529 as the best example of a modern miracle in England.[51] The fullest account of it was written for Henry VIII by no less a person than Robert, Lord Curzon, an Imperial count who had retired from a not wholly unspotted military career to live in Ipswich, and who had played a

---

[48] Pells: PRO, SP 1/40/77–80 (*LP* IV pt. ii, no. 2710). *The Complete Works of Geoffrey Chaucer*, ed. W. W. Skeat (Oxford, 1915), p. 425.

[49] J. Bale, *A declaration of Edmonde Bonners articles* (1561, *STC*. 1289), fo. 20ʳ.

[50] Stanton: BL Lansd. 64/28. Woolpit: Payne Collier, *Household Books*, p. 57, but see also the gift of a buck from Framlingham Park to the parson of Woolpit in 1509, BL Add. 27451, fo. 15ʳ.

[51] More, *Dialogue concerning Heresies*, pp. 92–4.

leading part in the affair.[52] This was no plebeian marvel; its impact derived from the fact that it involved the children of one of the leading knights of Essex and was witnessed by virtually the entire magistracy of Suffolk.

Curzon's narrative begins in November 1515, when the twelve-year-old daughter of Sir Roger Wentworth of Gosfield in Essex started suffering violent fits. These continued to torment her until the following Lady Day (25 March 1516), when a persistent vision of the Virgin 'in the picture and stature of our Lady of Grace in Eppeswyche' put an end to her trouble for the time being. No other Our Lady would do; she insisted on being taken to the chapel at Ipswich. When she was ceremoniously escorted there three weeks later, word had got around; a thousand people waited to receive her at the chapel. She spent several days there, summoning Curzon and the town bailiffs to pray for her; soon Abbot Reve of Bury arrived, having travelled the thirty miles from his house on foot 'of pylgremage', and vowing to do the same yearly if Our Lady would effect a cure for the girl. Duly delivered, the girl led the great crowd of clergy and laypeople in prayer and left for home, promising to return in eleven days.

Alas, in the familiar manner of fairy-tales, her parents delayed the return to Whitsun in order to gather 'the moste part of the worsschipfull of the contrey'; further fits and some (presumably) divinely-inspired rudeness from the young lady brought the day forward and ensured not simply the leading knights and clergy of the shire, but an estimated crowd of four thousand when she arrived once more at Gracechurch. After devotions in the shrine and admonitions to the crowd to be 'mor stedfaste in the fayth', she apparently retired for the night, but at midnight she suddenly summoned the bailiffs of Ipswich, the county magistracy, Dr Bailey, and other worthies to her lodgings. She then launched on a two-hour sermon to the bleary-eyed company; she gave a sharp response to her mother's embarrassed admonition 'A dowther ye muste take hede to the grette clerkes and of ther sayyng' and emphasized her retort by falling into another fit. Curzon successfully intervened by thrusting his cross decorated with a Pietà into her hands, but an hour later, her sisters and a cousin burst from their beds in a demented state. Cured in their turn, they gave place to her brother John, whom she cured of two raving fits, the second before the image of Our Lady in the shrine itself. After this

[52] BL Harl. 651, fos. 194ᵛ–196ᵛ, a contemporary clerk's copy initialled 'W. H.s' but narrated in the first person by Curzon. On Curzon, see *PSIA* IX (1896), pp. 271–8.

night of excitement, Dr Bailey brought the proceedings to a decorous end the following Sunday afternoon with an edifying sermon, obviously delighted that his own shrine had witnessed such an event that 'syth that England was crystened were never schewed suche meracles'.

The story is a classic case of child hysteria and manipulation, reminiscent of, though happier in its results than, the Salem witch trials; nearer home, it bore a remarkable resemblance to a Protestant miracle at Norwich witnessed and narrated by Bishop Parkhurst fifty-eight years later. It is also fascinating in its interplay between hierarchy and anarchy, Our Lady's gentle misrule giving *carte blanche* to this twelve-year-old publicly to be rude to her parents, to dispute with Cambridge doctors and to order around the leading men of the county. Traditional religion could find an unchallenging place for all this disorder—integrate it with the picture of devotion presented by Abbot Reve on his pious tramp from Bury to Ipswich and on to the Good Rood of Dovercourt, and with Lord Curzon himself pushing a way for the Abbot into the crowded shrine church. The girl herself remains significantly anonymous throughout the whole account, for all the temporary power that she wielded; More tells us that she became a nun in the Minories in London, and with that she vanishes from history—no honours of a Ste Bernadette for her. It is also worth pointing out that her brother John, so dramatically affected by the affair, does not seem to have been permanently enough marked by it to resist conforming to the Henrician, Edwardian, and Elizabethan Settlements when he became head of the family.[53] Nevertheless, the Gracechurch miracle created an immense sensation at the time. Both Queen Katherine and Cardinal Wolsey paid visits to Ipswich and to the shrine in particular in the following year; it is possibly in connection with the miracle that John Wentworth entered Wolsey's service.[54] Wolsey's statutes for his new college at Ipswich would make a particular point of its association with Gracechurch, enjoining a solemn annual procession on the Marian feasts from the college to the nearby shrine, and the Cardinal took especial pains to secure a new papal indulgence for Gracechurch in 1526.[55] So Wolsey's showpiece

---

[53] See *Parkhurst* p. 86, on the Norwich miracle. There were two John Wentworths who were brothers, and one cannot be certain which was the subject of the miracle (W. L. Rutton, *Three Branches of the Family of Wentworth*, 1891, pp. 150, 153, 193).

[54] Ibid., p. 153.

[55] BL Cott. Titus B I, fo. 281 (*LP* IV pt. ii, no. 4778); *LP* IV pt. i, no. 2108.

of humanist education would honour this focal point of traditional piety.

Humanist Catholicism, which under a more sympathetic regime might have revitalized the old faith in the long term, has left rather fragmentary traces in the county's records. There is some evidence that it affected the greater colleges in the county; one would expect this of Stoke, with its strong Cambridge connections, but we have no information as to how the canons of Stoke made use of the up-to-date collection of written and printed books augmenting their library, bequeathed to them by Dean Edenham in 1517.[56] More positive are the signs at Mettingham, where we have already noted the Master's bequest for sermons in 1507, to be carried out by the much-travelled ex-Cambridge don Dr Bailey; it is interesting to note the Ipswich notable Thomas Drayll, an old friend of Bailey's father, five years later making a bequest to Mettingham and also a provisional bequest for a similar course of sermons to be preached in Ipswich and the surrounding villages and for a scholarship to Cambridge.[57] Ipswich merchants like Drayll would also be in touch with humanism through their trade contacts with the Low Countries; thus the merchant Thomas Pounder had the good taste to go to a Flemish firm to buy an exquisite monumental brass in the most up-to-date Renaissance style for himself and his family some time before his death in 1525 (see Plate 1).[58]

Also associated with Ipswich was the county's most remarkable exhibit of humanist learning, the private school organized by Sir Humphrey Wingfield of Brantham.[59] Sir Humphrey was a great figure in Suffolk, one of the twelve sons of Sir John Wingfield of Letheringham; as a younger son, he had to make his own way to success, but became 'one of the ablest lawyers at Gray's Inn'.[60] Through a fortunate marriage to a widow, he set himself up as a country gentleman at Brantham in the Stour valley, but also built a fine house in Ipswich, some four miles from Brantham; from early on in his career he had much to do with the town, being appointed one of its counsel in 1507 and serving as its MP in 1523. High in Wolsey's favour, he became *custos rotulorum* for Suffolk through the good offices

[56] Emden, *Cambridge to 1500*, p. 205, s.v. Edenham, John.
[57] PCC 9 Fetiplace: cf. Richard Bailey's will, PCC 40 Holgrave.
[58] Brass formerly in St Mary Quay, Ipswich, now in the Borough Museum.
[59] The following paragraphs unless otherwise stated are based on my introduction to the *'Vita Mariae'* pp. 183–5, 193, where the references will be found.
[60] Griffith, p. iv.

of his cousin the Duke of Suffolk, and eventually replaced Thomas Audley as Speaker in the Reformation Parliament.

Although so much a man of affairs, Sir Humphrey was keenly interested in scholarship, and took it upon himself to educate a whole succession of promising young men from all over England for careers in the Church and in academic and public life. Some of the work was done at Brantham, some at Wingfield House in Ipswich, which boasted a 'chamber sometyme called the scole howse' at his death in 1545; his boys learnt their Latin and Greek from a priest named Robert Bond—probably the Cambridge graduate of that name—who held several Suffolk livings and whom Sir Humphrey regarded as so indispensable to his enterprise that he secured permission for the priest to remain in the Wingfield household when he was a royal chaplain in 1532.

We know little of the pupils at the school, but one of the most distinguished of them was the classicist and tutor to Elizabeth I, Roger Ascham, who has left us an enthusiastic description of the enlightened combination of academic work and physical exercise prescribed by Sir Humphrey. Another pupil was the Marian bishop of Chichester, John Christopherson; his stay at Brantham was less happy, since it included the fatal stabbing of a fellow-pupil, a catastrophe which an inquest jury and a commission of oyer and terminer including Sir Humphrey himself were careful to accept as killing in self-defence. Ascham and Christopherson both went on to St John's Cambridge, that centre of early Tudor humanist studies; it is likely that this was the normal pattern with Sir Humphrey's brighter pupils. Apart from Ascham's numerous works, we have a testimony to the effectiveness of the school's classical education in the form of a treatise on Princess Mary's seizure of power in 1553, written by Sir Humphrey's own son Robert Wingfield; the work's content is that of a conscientious plodder, but the style is showpiece humanist Latin, delighting in classical archaisms and recondite phrases. Not only did the school breed good Latin, but also in Christopherson and Robert Wingfield at least, a robust Catholic piety which would no doubt have been echoed in the Cambridge college whose fellows were to brave the wrath of Henry VIII in showing their sympathy for their co-founder, Bishop John Fisher, in his last imprisonment.[61] Yet Humphrey Wingfield's own Catholic convictions did not prevent him presiding over the later

[61] C. Read, *Mr Secretary Cecil and Queen Elizabeth* (1955), pp. 24–5.

sessions of the Reformation Parliament with apparent equanimity. Alongside the richly complex structure of the old faith and the gradual infiltration of humanist ideas into it, the evidence for the survival of the earlier East Anglian Lollard tradition is patchy, and most of the evidence has to be read back from after the coming of Lutheranism, in particular in the Marian persecution. A handful of religious dissidents is recorded as having been burnt before the Lutheran explosion, more from Norfolk than from Suffolk: in 1511 one man from Bungay, which had been in the centre of Lollard prosecutions in the early fifteenth century, and between 1512 and 1515, two more from Eye and Earl Stonham, which were in the mid-Suffolk heart of radical religion right into the reign of Elizabeth. The trouble with this evidence is that in the manner of so much of our information on early Tudor Lollardy, it is entirely based on two passages in Foxe's *Acts and Monuments,* and it may simply reflect the preservation of hagiographical traditions which related only to their own area, ignoring Lollard groups which had staggered into the sixteenth century and then found no successors. Foxe, for instance, got his account of the Earl Stonham man from an inhabitant of Winston, a village with a strong group of Marian Protestants from whom he derived a good deal of his Suffolk anecdotal material.[62]

What is nevertheless clear from Foxe's narratives is that Lollard groups were capable of keeping in touch with each other over a wide area. Thomas Man was a Lollard preacher who before his execution in 1518 had made contact with and sustained a whole spectrum of groups in Buckinghamshire, Oxfordshire, London, Essex, Norfolk, and Suffolk, and when he fled from the Lincoln diocesan authorities, he could go to East Anglia and seek out the 'godly professors of Christ's gospel'. John Hacker was revealed in Bishop Tunstall's London clamp-down of 1528 as having contacts over a very similar area, from Buckinghamshire to Norfolk; Dr Davis sees Man and Hacker as closely linked.[63] Such a wide network of relationships has interesting implications, for it is very reminiscent of the hints that the purely political expressions of dissent in 1525 and 1549 linked up a whole

---

[62] Foxe, IV, p. 773; V, p. 254. Houlbrooke, 'Persecution of heresy', p. 323, adds Thomas Gold, a Stowmarket man prosecuted in 1511, from the Norwich Institution Books, although the outcome of this case is uncertain. Foxe's account of Peke of Earl Stonham in the above two passages is confusing, and has misled Houlbrooke into giving Peke a second martyrdom in 1537 (ibid., p. 324). It can be securely dated to *c.*1515 by the names of the JPs involved in the case.

[63] Foxe, IV, pp. 208–14; Davis, p. 57.

range of politically-aware and geographically-mobile people across south-east England (below, Ch. 10).

The story of fugitive groups and of persecution that emerges from Foxe and from the intermittent court records of the Norwich diocese in the first two decades of the century is so fragmentary that it is hardly possible to estimate the scale of the Lollards' survival. Lollardy was still capable of producing quite heavy-handed reactions in a touchy and energetic bishop like Nix; Dr Houlbrooke draws attention to the fact that a failure to confess or receive the sacrament at Easter was by itself enough to bring a suspicion of heresy on one unfortunate in 1511.[64] Nix's reaction was similarly extreme four years later, when in the middle of the national row about the case of Richard Hunne, he heard that many at Ipswich were asserting that 'no busshop within his diocesse shalle reserve thabsolution of any certeyn cryme to hym selff'; in a menacing letter to the bailiffs of the town, he declared that this somewhat esoteric attack on the Church's jurisdiction 'savorithe of heresy', and urged that stern warnings should be delivered. The letter suggests a hypersensitive intransigence typical of the episcopate's reaction to the Hunne and Standish affairs.[65] This in turn may show that the lack of evidence about repressive measures in Norwich diocese—no clamp-down in the general flurry of episcopal activity in 1527–8, for instance—is a good indication that Nix did not see the Lollards as of much significance.

In the ensuing years, however, Nix's troubles would grow steadily worse; now he was assailed not merely by the lower-class remnants of a heresy repeating hundred-year-old formulae or by impudent Ipswich anti-clericals, but by the new dynamism of Lutheranism. Norwich diocese was vulnerable to Lutheranism because it was so near Cambridge; as early as 1521, a Norfolk incumbent was confessing that he had possessed and surrendered various books by Luther in the University.[66] It was particularly galling for Nix that Gonville Hall, the college with the strongest Norfolk links, should in his celebrated phrase, savour of the frying pan;[67] nor was Trinity Hall, like Gonville actually founded by one of Nix's predecessors and also the subject of his own generous benefactions, much better, for Nix's future victim Thomas Bilney was a Hall man.

[64] Houlbrooke, *Church Courts*, p. 223.
[65] SROI, C5/12/7, fo. 220ʳ; cf. Elton, *Reform and Reformation*, pp. 51–8.
[66] Houlbrooke, *Church Courts*, p. 226.
[67] BL Cott. Cleop. E V, fo. 389 (*LP* IV pt. iii, no. 6385).

Bilney was from Norfolk; besides being the protomartyr of the English Reformation, his role in the early stages of the Reformation in East Anglia was probably unique. One wonders whether he would have caused trouble for Nix even if Luther had never lived; rather than being Lutheran, his views seem to have been a fusion of a reforming brand of Cambridge Erasmianism with Lollard ideas from his native county, and if this is so, this rare escapee from the proletarian ghetto of Tudor Lollardy did their cause sterling service.[68] By 1527, fired by his own discovery of the implications of justification by faith, the little Cambridge don was preaching extensively in his home diocese, particularly in the archiepiscopal peculiar to Hadleigh where he was beyond Nix's clutches. Foxe pays particular tribute to the results of his work there, and a shoemaker of Eye, some twenty-two miles away, was to testify to the lasting effect of one of those Hadleigh sermons on him, when he was examined by the Bishop five years later.[69]

Within a year or two, Bilney had widened his activity to take in the capital as well as East Anglia. Thomas More devoted much energy in *The Dialogue concerning Heresies* of 1529 to attacking his work and career; in the face of Bilney's consistent criticism of images and pilgrimages, it was probably a deliberate gesture for More to give prominence in the *Dialogue* to his account of the Gracechurch miracle, a proof of the efficacy of Our Lady's wonders in the middle of Bilney's East Anglia.[70] However, it was not simply avant-garde clerics or humble folk who were giving Bishop Nix cause for concern in the 1520s; in 1525 he forced Anthony Yaxley of Rickinghall Superior, one of an energetic and quarrelsome gentry family whose professional members included lawyers, clerics, and an eminent medical doctor, to abjure his Lutheran views. The abjuration had little long-term effect; Yaxley was to continue to rebel against the marked Catholic piety of his family, taking an obvious delight amid the changed atmosphere of the 1540s in denouncing the guild of St Thomas Becket in Yaxley parish.[71]

Perhaps almost as vexing for Nix in this busy decade was the erratic but intimidating interference of Cardinal Wolsey in diocesan affairs.

[68] On Bilney's career, and for convincing evidence that his views were not Lutheran, see J. F. Davis, 'The Trials of Thomas Bilney and the English Reformation', *Historical Journal* XXIV (1981), pp. 775–90.

[69] NRO, ACT 4b, fo. 34ᵛ; cf. below, p. 155.

[70] More, *Dialogue concerning Heresies*, pp. 92–4, and index references to Bilney, Thomas.

[71] Abjuration pr. *Eastern Counties Collectanea* (Norwich, 1872–3), p. 42; cf. PRO, C4/46, answer of Yaxley to Thomas Sherman and John Newman.

Wolsey seems to have had little to do with his county of origin in the years when he was capturing Henry VIII's favour, but his triumphal progress through Norfolk and Suffolk in 1517 seems to have marked the beginning of a new involvement in the area which was to culminate in his plans for Cardinal College, Ipswich. We have already seen how his arrival at Bury dragged him into disputes between the Abbey and the townsfolk; he also launched himself with energy into the long-standing warfare between the leading figures in Bungay and the officials of the Duke of Norfolk who ran the town, showing a concern to establish indifferent justice there which did not endear him to the Howard administrative machine.[72]

Wolsey's enthusiasm for his grandiose plans at Ipswich managed to earn him the enmity of many who should have been his natural allies in defending the traditional Church against the menace of Lutheranism. We have already noted how he clashed with Dr John Bailey (undoubtedly a childhood acquaintance) over the use of revenues at St Matthew's Ipswich for his new College. His suppression of the small Suffolk monasteries of Dodnash, Snape, Rumburgh, and Felixstowe between 1525 and 1528 seems to have aroused the same sort of local antagonism as his other suppressions elsewhere. The Chronicler of Butley Priory, a sturdily conservative commentator on the religious turmoil of his day, described Wolsey's suppressions as being to the shame, scandal, destruction and ruin of all the monks and nuns of England. Not only was the Chronicler later to describe the Cardinal's fall with satisfaction, but he was also to note with pleasure the King's resumption of the lands of houses dissolved by Wolsey—a sad irony, if he lived to see the surrender of his own house.[73]

Wolsey's ruthless pursuit of his plans by imposing his nonentity of a son both on the Archdeaconry of Suffolk and the rectory of St Matthew's Ipswich—a bizarre successor to the worthy Dr Bailey—cannot have failed to raise eyebrows in the county. The suppression of Rumburgh Priory brought the agitated but vain pleas of the Abbot of its mother house, St Mary's York, for its preservation; more dangerously for Wolsey, in the very year of his fall he managed to irritate the Duke of Norfolk, founder by descent of Felixstowe, with the manner of his suppression of the house.[74] The dowager Countess

---

[72] PRO, STAC 2/34/29, particularly letter, Sir Thomas Wyndham to Wolsey.

[73] *Butley Chronicle* pp. 47, 58–9; cf. Clark, p. 22, for similar feelings about Wolsey's dissolution in Kent etc.

[74] York: BL Cott. Cleop. E IV, fo. 58 (*LP* IV pt. ii, no. 4762). Norfolk: PRO, SP 1/53/174 (*LP* IV pt. iii, no. 5458).

of Oxford, widow of the formidable thirteenth Earl, also had her feathers ruffled when Wolsey imperiously pressed a demand for stone for Ipswich College from her cliffs at Harwich, accusing her of making excuses to avoid yielding it. Most astonishingly of all, the Cardinal pressurized that pious old soldier Lord Curzon into agreeing to an exchange involving the surrender of his large Ipswich house to form the basis of a palace for Wolsey in the town; the plan was however nullified by the Cardinal's fall.[75]

However, such was Wolsey's abrasive style in his years of greatness that it was not merely his schemes for his college which antagonized local notables. One of the pillars of west Suffolk society, Henry VII's old solicitor, Thomas Lucas, was humiliated by being committed to the Tower for scandalous words against the Cardinal in 1517, and was dismissed from the commission of the peace for several years. The Cardinal's financial exactions on the spectacularly wealthy clothier Thomas Spring of Lavenham were a common enough matter of gossip in East Anglia to reach the ears of the poetical rector of Diss, John Skelton, just across the Norfolk border, and to find a satirical place in 'Why come ye nat to Court?'[76] Bishop Nix was frequently forced into confrontation. Already in the early 1520s, the Bishop took offence at Wolsey's brusque application of common sense to the interminable dispute over jurisdiction between the city and the cathedral priory of Norwich.[77] In 1526 Nix was conducting his visitation of Stoke College, at that time in a state of serious crisis, when he was abruptly interrupted and overriden by Wolsey's visitors; he carried on regardless, sending a somewhat evasive letter to stave off the Cardinal's wrath, but he subsequently pronounced the Dean of Stoke contumacious for not appearing at the episcopal visitation and for postponing his appearance until Wolsey's officers were to appear.[78] Wolsey's eventual retort was three years later to engineer the appointment of one of his officers who had carried out the 1526 visitation, Robert Shorton, as Dean of the College.

A similar unexpected intervention by the Cardinal interrupted the

---

[75] Oxford: PRO, SP 1/49/92, 136 (*LP* IV pt. ii, nos. 4484, 4548). Curzon: BL Cott. Vesp. F XIII, fo. 142 (*LP* IV pt. iii, no. 5505).

[76] Lucas: BL Lansd. 639, fo. 47ʳ. Spring: *John Skelton: the Complete Poems*, ed. J. Scattergood (1983), pp. 302–3.

[77] *Biographical Register of the University of Oxford to 1500*, ed. A. B. Emden (3 vols., Oxford, 1957–9), II, p. 381; Guy, *Cardinal's Court*, pp. 68–9.

[78] Jessopp, *Visitations*, pp. 226–39, 254–9. Jessopp's commentary on these events should largely be ignored.

election of a new prior at Butley in 1529, and Nix at his most silver-tongued added his pleas to those of the canons that Wolsey should allow their choice.[79] Occasionally, however, the Bishop's mask dropped; after a whole series of snubs and humiliations, his letter of May 1529 to the Cardinal was a pathetic mixture of anxiety, resentment and injured pride.[80] Nor can Wolsey's good-humoured treatment of Thomas Bilney have failed to incense the aged bishop; despite all Bilney's disruptive activities in London, East Anglia, and Nix's own Trinity Hall, the Cardinal had dismissed him in 1527 with nothing more than a genial warning.[81]

There is every sign that after all this, Nix echoed the Chronicler of Butley's satisfaction at Wolsey's fall; certainly he lost no time in citing Archdeacon Winter before him in January 1530, as Wolsey's credit collapsed—a revenge for the humiliation of seeing this young man financing his Continental education with Archdeaconry of Norfolk revenues.[82] However, Wolsey's fall produced far more problems than it solved. Already by May 1530, as the Cardinal was making his way north and as the first and last Dean of Wolsey's Ipswich College was miserably struggling to keep the College alive, Nix was lamenting to Archbishop Warham that it was now beyond the power of him or any cleric to suppress heretical opinions and books, for a new and sinister reason: 'dyverse saith openly in my diocesse that the kinges grace wolde that they shulde have the saide arronious bokes.'[83] Even if such claims were not as yet strictly true, they reflected an awareness of the current diplomatic flurry between the King, the Pope, and the Emperor, and the likelihood of a new session of Parliament; above all, it would soon become apparent that Wolsey's former servant Thomas Cromwell was gaining ground among Henry's councillors, along with the alarming novelties of thought on England's imperial status which Cromwell was to manipulate with such devastating effect.[84] On 11 July 1530, Nix found himself along with Abbot Reve of Bury among a select company of senior clerics on a *praemunire* charge of having abetted Wolsey in his legatine powers; the irony is unlikely to have amused him. The two men appeared together in King's Bench on 17

---

[79] PRO, SP 1/52/122 (*LP* IV pt. ii, no. 5158); BL Harl. 604, fo. 61 (*LP* V, App. no. 230).
[80] PRO, SP 1/54/29 (*LP* IV pt. iii, no. 5589).
[81] More, *Dialogue concerning Heresies*, p. 268. [82] *LP* IV pt. iii, no. 6139.
[83] BL Cott. Cleop. E V, fo. 389 (*LP* IV pt. iii, no. 2867).
[84] Guy, *More*, pp. 127–36.

October, but for the moment they were saved from further harassment by the grander design of the Crown to indict the whole body of clergy; the clergy quickly caved in to this attack when it came in the following January.[85]

The next few years represented a desperate rearguard action to defend the old Church by Nix and like-minded conservatives. On a national level, the struggle was effectively over by May 1532, when Thomas More resigned as Lord Chancellor; in Norwich, Nix only seems finally to have been cowed by his exemplary fine of ten thousand marks on a fresh charge of *praemunire* in February 1534.[86] Throughout 1531, Nix and his henchman Pells were still on the offensive; it was their destruction of Nix's old adversary Thomas Bilney in August 1531 which provided the major confrontation between the 'Aragonese' party round More and the radicals round Thomas Cromwell. Bilney was only the most important among five victims of conservative bishops in this struggle, one of the others being a renegade monk of Bury burnt by one of Nix's conservative colleagues in London.[87] However, the issue of whether Bilney had recanted at the last became one of national importance as leaders of the city of Norwich, furious at the execution of a popular and respected local boy, threatened to raise the affair in the imminent session of Parliament.[88] It was dubious whether Bilney was in any strict Catholic sense a heretic, and his death was no doubt seen at the time as a riposte to Cromwell's indictment of Pells on a *praemunire* charge two months before; Pells was determined to show that he and the leaders of the 'Aragonese' opposition in the Lower House of Convocation were not thus to be intimidated.[89] Pells indeed secured a pardon on 15 November 1531, making doubly sure by a corrected pardon eleven days later, and at much the same time he went on the attack once more by putting a Bill of complaint to the Lord Chancellor, his ally More, against the Mayor of Norwich who was leading the protest about Bilney.[90]

On the other side, it was probably in a deliberate reaction to Bilney's death that a wave of iconoclasm hit East Anglia; the main target of his campaign of preaching had been the practice of pilgrimage and the invocation of saints. No one seems to have dared to tackle St Edmund

---

[85] Ibid., pp. 137–8, 148–9.   [86] *Butley Chronicle* p. 61.
[87] Guy, *More*, p. 164; on Richard Bayfield, see Foxe IV, pp. 680–8.
[88] Guy, *More*, p. 168.   [89] Ibid., p. 142.
[90] *LP* V, no. 559/22, 36; Foxe IV, Appendix, no. vi. Pells was one of the signatories in support of the conservative friar Stokes in his battle of 1537 with Matthew Parker: PRO, E135/8/39.

in his well-defended monastery, but both Foxe and the Chronicler of Butley record from very different points of view a campaign of violence in 1531 and 1532 against the more vulnerable outposts of the old religion's love of sacred places: attacks on the cross at Gracechurch and on more than one image of the favourite East Anglian saint St Petronilla, a St Christopher near Sudbury, and a cross and images in the Duke of Norfolk's park at Stoke by Nayland.[91] Most serious of all, and apparently the centrepiece of this terrorism, was the theft and burning of the Good Rood of Dovercourt in Essex, the goal of Abbot Reve's pilgrimage after his witnessing the Gracechurch miracle a dozen years before; was the rood's fate a deliberate reminiscence of the fate of Bilney? The inspiration of this attack, and possibly of several others, came from the priest Thomas Rose, who was one of Bilney's associates working at Hadleigh.[92] In his summer visitation of 1532, Bishop Nix caught up with four Eye shoemakers, one of whom threatened in a similar manner to burn the rood in Eye Priory church besides proposing rather more earthy insults to it; all of them made iconoclastic remarks, and once more the name of the dead Bilney surfaced as the source of it all.[93] It was not surprising, after the appalling public relations blunder that Bilney's death represented for the world of shrines and images, that the accounts of Gracechurch showed at June 1534 that there 'was never soo lityll devotion' at the shrine.[94]

Even if More was a spent political force after May, throughout 1532 Nix continued to operate a 'business as usual' policy in face of the growing unrest in his diocese. Though long blind, and by now perhaps eighty-five years old, he insisted on carrying out most of his summer monastic and diocesan visitations in person, and these were no mere ineffectual formalities. At Mettingham we can catch a rare glimpse of him at work the day before the official visitation, using the opportunity to hear depositions in a diocesan testamentary case and witnessing the Master's quitclaim of all debts owed him by the College; this resulted in the first *omnia bene* result in the recent history of this financially troubled house.[95] The last two sessions of the visitation he left to his chancellor Dr Spencer, being himself involved in other diocesan business, which included backing the parish priest of Wissett in

[91] Foxe, IV, p. 707; *Butley Chronicle* p. 60.
[92] Foxe, VIII, p. 581, which seems to place the Dovercourt outrage in late 1532.
[93] NRO, ACT 4b, fos. 33^v–37^r.　　[94] PRO, SP 1/84/159 (*LP* VII, no. 803).
[95] NRO, ACT 4b, fos. 70 f; BL Add. Ch. 63068; Jessopp, *Visitations*, p. 317.

Suffolk in his defiance of Cromwell's wishes in a dispute over parish tithes.[96]

Significantly, however, by December 1533, Nix was giving way in the Wissett affair; he received Cromwell's letter 'whyche for fere he ded obey', but he was still secretly working to thwart Cromwell in this and other former properties of Rumburgh Priory, trying to enlist the Duke of Norfolk in his support.[97] Such intrigue was too late. The *praemunire* charge of February 1534, despite his speedy pardon, was a personal shock and a public humiliation, and in the following month, 12 March, he swore to recognize the royal supremacy.[98] Even then, his radical enemies did not leave him alone; when Cranmer began his metropolitical visitation in 1534, the aged bishop was pronounced contumacious for non-appearance, and was belatedly forced into making a personal appearance before the metropolitan commissary for the diocese.[99] In January 1535 he was summoned into Star Chamber, but made the excuse of illness; by now the end was near.[100] One of the acts of his last summer was to forward prayers for Queen Anne through the diocese, something which can have given him little pleasure.[101] In his last months he determined to dissipate all his fortune in good works through the diocese, but even in this, he was to be thwarted by the intervention of the Duke of Norfolk. At his death, his household, perhaps conscious of the end of an era, did their best to strip the palace of Hoxne bare.[102]

[96] Ibid., pp. 318–19; PRO, SP 1/69/80, 1/70/223 (*LP* V, nos. 769, 1263).
[97] SP 1/80/198 (*LP* VI, no. 1534).
[98] *Foedera* . . ., ed. T. Rymer (20 vols., 1704–35), XIV, p. 484; *Butley Chronicle* p. 61 n.
[99] Ibid., p. 66.   [100] PRO, SP 1/89/130 (*LP* VIII, no. 159).
[101] *Butley Chronicle* p. 68.
[102] PRO, SP 1/99/120, 1/101/58 f. (*LP* IX, no. 978; X, no. 79).

5

The Years of Uncertainty 1536–1572

NIX'S successor was the infinitely less impressive William Rugge, who presided over the dismemberment of the diocesan estates in exchange for the retention of his abbey lands of St Benet's Hulme. Like so many former heads of religious houses promoted to the episcopal bench by Henry, Rugge turned out to be a total nonentity; most unusually in Tudor Norfolk and Suffolk, he was never appointed to the commission of the peace in either county, at a time when Bishop Goodrich of Ely was continuously on both commissions. After Nix's intransigence, it no doubt suited Cromwell to have a weakling in the see of Norwich, particularly since the new Suffragan of Ipswich, Thomas Manning, was the Secretary's close associate. Rugge's conservatism in theology would please the Duke of Norfolk while representing little threat to Cromwell; the bishop proved easy enough to bully.[1]

What was the balance of religious forces in the diocese presided over by Bishop Rugge? Certainly religious radicalism had moved on from the clandestine groups of humble folk sporadically revealed by the records in the first two decades of the century. When Nix was rather gloomily surveying the state of his diocese in 1530, he saw the main areas of disaffection as being among clerics from Cambridge and 'marchantes and suche that hath ther abyding not ferre from the see'.[2] Overseas infiltration of Protestantism may in fact have been more localized than this suggests. There is good evidence that Ipswich, with its many Low Countries contacts, its early hints of anti-clericalism, the long-standing interest of some of its leading merchants in humanism and its later nucleus of opposition to the Marian reaction, conformed to Nix's diagnosis; one could probably build up a similar picture for major ports like Lynn or Yarmouth. However, many of the lesser ports of Suffolk looked to Iceland as much as the Low Countries for their main overseas contacts, and Iceland was hardly in the vanguard of

[1] Houlbrooke, 'Persecution of Heresy', p. 310.
[2] BL Cott. Cleop. E V, fo. 389 (*LP* IV pt. iii, no. 6385).

Reformation thought.[3] The Suffolk coast was in fact remarkable by its consistent absence from the areas demonstrably enthusiastic for radical religious ideas, and the most pronounced evidence of any religious views on the county's coast during the sixteenth century is of the persistence of religious conservatism in Lothingland during Elizabeth's reign (below, pp. 212–15).

Nix's opinion in 1530 was that as yet 'the gentilmen and the comentye be not greatly infect'. This situation was to change over the next decade, when the gentry support vital for sustaining (although not necessarily for creating) a vigorous grass-roots Protestantism began to emerge. Central to this was the growing sympathy of the Duke of Suffolk for reformist ideas in religion after his marriage to the young Katherine Willoughby in 1534. Earlier in his career, Brandon's religious practice was predictably and conventionally Catholic; in 1518, in an unprecedented move, he and his wife the French Queen were made brothers and sisters of the Augustinian Order along with the King and Queen, Princess Mary, and Wolsey.[4] The French Queen is unlikely to have been anything other than traditionalist in her piety; the couple spent a good deal of their East Anglian married life enjoying the hospitality of various religious houses, and at her death in 1533, Mary was buried in Bury Abbey with every traditional splendour—the last great public ceremony which that prodigious church was to witness.[5] Brandon's book of devotions survives, obviously a cherished personal possession, for it has little beauty in itself, but it is a perfectly unoriginal blend of psalms and prayers. Brandon also seems to have been fond of church music, for he maintained his own itinerant choir whose leadership provided at least two Suffolk gentlemen with their first stepping-stone in their careers.[6]

Alongside this, however, Brandon's views on religion included a pronounced version of the anti-clericalism often to be found among the early Tudor gentry. As early as 1525, he was making a point of reporting to Wolsey popular indignation that the Suffolk clergy seemed neither to be contributing to the Amicable Grant nor leading

---

[3] Nevertheless, one should note the three early sixteenth-century carved floor-slabs to parishioners in Walberswick parish church; these must have been ordered in the Low Countries.

[4] *Butley Chronicle* p. 21.

[5] See Ford, *Mary Tudor*, and *Butley Chronicle* p. 60.

[6] Brandon's book of devotions is BL Harl. 1664. On the choir's stay at Butley, *Butley Chronicle* p. 68; Henry Munnings and Nicholas Cutler had successive charge of the choir (Muskett, I, p. 106 and BL Harl. Ch. 47 A 49).

services to intercede for the success of the King's affairs, and he said that he had assured the complainers that the clergy should pay double.[7] In the crisis of the Divorce, he was constantly in the forefront of those urging an attack on the Church's institutions; it was this clash which wrung from him the only memorable thing that he ever said: 'It was never merry in England whilst we had cardinals among us.'[8] Katherine Willoughby, who became Brandon's fourth wife, was a quite exceptional young lady, and it was possibly she who developed this strong prejudice against clerical pretensions into a more general interest in reformed theology. During the later 1530s and 1540s, the Brandons included among their chaplains a number of definite reformers, such as the Scots ex-friar Alexander Seton, or the first Elizabethan Bishop of Norwich, John Parkhurst.[9] It is significant to find Thomas Rose finding a haven for his Protestant preaching in Stratford St Mary, a benefice of the Duke's, from 1534, and Friar John Bale leaving his order to marry and act as a secular priest at Thorndon, another Brandon manor.[10] By 1540 Brandon could be noted as one who took the Protestant part in the King's Council, and at his death, John Hooper numbered him among those whose departure was a grievous blow to the Protestant cause.[11]

Since Brandon changed his views gradually, one would not expect to find a firm bloc of Protestants emerging fully-armed in his circle. Among his household officials and servants there remained religious conservatives like Richard Freston, his comptroller, Thomas Seckford, keeper of his castle of Wingfield, and Kirk, the bailiff of his manor of Thorndon who caused serious trouble for Bale in 1537.[12] However, formidable early support for Protestantism came from gentlemen

[7] PRO, SP 1/34/143 (*LP* IV pt. i, no. 1260).

[8] Guy, *More*, pp. 107, 110; G. Cavendish, *The Life of Cardinal Wolsey*, ed. S. W. Singer (2 vols., 1825). I, pp. 167–70.

[9] Seton: Foxe, V, p. 449; M. Bowker, *The Henrician Reformation* (Cambridge, 1981), p. 171. Parkhurst: *Parkhurst* p. 21.

[10] Rose: Foxe, VIII, p. 581. Bale: Knowles, III, p. 57. The churchwardens of Stratford later claimed that their predecessors had dissolved a village guild to found a school as early as 1534 (PRO, E178/2121), and another priest of Stratford was indicted for radical words about confession in 1540 (PRO, KB 9/97⁸, m. 11). Stratford introduced English into the Mass by 1538 (*Wriothesley's Chronicle* I, p. 83).

[11] Foxe, V, p. 439; *Original Letters* p. 36. However, Brandon was sufficiently traditional in outlook to order masses and dirige at Tattershall College in his will (PCC 32 Alen).

[12] Freston: PRO, SP 1/140/16 (*LP* XIII pt. ii, no. 964). Seckford: PRO, C3/169/14; he was removed from the commission of the peace under Elizabeth. Kirk, bailiff of Thorndon: BL Cott. Cleop. E IV, fo. 167 (*LP* XII pt. i, no. 307).

among Brandon's friends and relatives, gentry who would remain in the county after his removal to Lincolnshire in 1538. Most important was Thomas Lord Wentworth; throughout the 1530s, he acted as a willing agent for Protestant policies and for the harassing of conservative clergy in the county.[13]

Wentworth lived near Ipswich and was much involved in its affairs; it is likely that he was a decisive influence in establishing the Protestant tone of the town. He acted as Cromwell's agent in the secret removal of the image of Our Lady of Ipswich for destruction at London in 1538, and he pacified the conflicts which broke out in the town as a result.[14] As founder by descent of the Ipswich Greyfriars, he was distinctly lacking in fatherly concern for his charge, expressing satisfaction in 1538 that the friars found it almost impossible to live since the inhabitants of Ipswich had perceived 'by godes worde' that it was more meritorious to give alms to the poor than 'to suche an idell neste of drones'. Such a perception may well have been at Wentworth's prompting, since having taken into account that the mendicant orders were nothing but 'a Ipocritall wede planted of that stordy nembrot [Nimrod] the bishope of Rome', he induced the unfortunate friars to surrender the house to himself.[15] Convenient as such Protestant considerations may have been in this case, Wentworth's zeal for reform was genuine; John Bale, former Prior of the Ipswich Whitefriars, attributed his own conversion to Protestantism from orthodox Catholicism to Wentworth's influence. If Wentworth could so affect Bale, it was small wonder that his effect in Ipswich was so decisive. Miles Coverdale would preach at his funeral in 1551.[16]

Also in Brandon's circle was Edward Grimston of Rishangles, who was one of the two Suffolk gentlemen appealed to for corroboration by Bale in his Thorndon troubles of 1538, the other being Lord Wentworth himself.[17] Grimston did not become a justice in the county until the reign of Edward VI, but this was probably because of his frequent absences from the county as a gentleman pensioner of Henry VIII. Like Wentworth, he had much to do with the borough of Ipswich, acting three times as its MP and maintaining a town house there; in 1549 the town schoolmaster dedicated a translation of the works of

---

[13] Cf. PRO, SP 1/92/40, 179; 1/115/91; 1/137/150 (*LP* VIII, nos. 570, 770; XII pt. i, no. 257; XII pt. ii, no. 571).
[14] SP 1/242/5 (*LP* App. I pt. ii, no. 1313).
[15] SP 1/130/239 (*LP* XIII pt. i, no. 651).
[16] Bale: Knowles, III, p. 57. Funeral: *Machyn's Diary* p. 3.
[17] BL Cott. Cleop. E IV, fo. 167 (*LP* XII pt. i, no. 307).

Zwingli to him.[18] Sir William Waldegrave, who was to be associated with Grimston and the second Lord Wentworth in the administration of Calais in its last English days under Mary, was a courtier likewise. Waldegrave has no obvious links with Brandon; his links seem rather with Essex gentry. His Essex father-in-law Sir John Rainsford was instrumental in backing the efforts of the men of Hadleigh to regain the services of their Protestant preacher Thomas Rose, and it may well have been Rose, originally brought to Suffolk from Devon by a clerical relative of Waldegrave, who was responsible for converting this member of a normally rather conservative family to enthusiasm for reform.[19] It may be indicative of his alignments among the factions at Court that Waldegrave was knighted amid the festivities surrounding Anne Boleyn's coronation; by 1538 he was having to be restrained in his enthusiasm for promoting services in English in the area of his home at Bures, and he had no compunction in denouncing his own grandmother's chaplain to Cromwell as a papist and a bad influence on her.[20] Such men as Waldegrave, Wentworth, and Grimston, together with Wentworth's associate and relative Sir Anthony Wingfield (still apparently a sympathizer with traditional religion under Henry VIII) would be the willing local agents of the regimes of Edward VI.[21]

Among the clergy, the spread of religious reform was equally patchy. The bulk of the clergy remained hostile to such opinions: Cromwell's papers include a number of cases of Suffolk priests opposing religious change, mostly in words spoken in the heat of the moment which they subsequently tried to explain away.[22] When in 1537 the vicar of Yoxford expressed his enthusiasm for Cromwellian reform in a series of propaganda plays, he found himself ostracized by most of the country clergy.[23] Dr Peet has shown how the commendation formulae of wills in the diocese reveal a greater persistence of traditionalism

---

[18] R. Argentine, *Certeyne preceptes gathered by Hulrichus Zwinglius . . .* (Ipswich, 1548/9, *STC* 26136).

[19] Rose in his life history (Foxe, VIII, pp. 581–90) says that he was brought to Polstead by Fabian, the incumbent; Thomas Fabian was nephew to Sir William Waldegrave, the younger Sir William's grandfather (PCC 29 Porch), and the Waldegraves had estates near Rose's birthplace at Exmouth.

[20] PRO, SP 1/140/223 (*LP* XIII pt. ii, no. 1179).

[21] Wingfield was noted as a papist in divisions of the King's Council in 1540 (Foxe, V, p. 439), and in 1537 he could commend a conservative priest to Wriothesley (PRO, SP 7/1/84, *LP* XII pt. i, no. 10, and cf. SP 1/113/44, *LP* XI, no. 1393).

[22] Cf. last reference and SP 1/92/179, 1/130/214, 1/142/62 (*LP* VIII, no. 770; XII pt. i, no. 256; XIII pt. i, no. 633; XIV pt. i, no. 76).

[23] SP 1/116/157 (*LP* XII pt. i, no. 529).

among the clergy than among the laity, who in the reign of Edward VI were quicker to abandon the Catholic formulae and under Mary slower to readopt them than their clerical neighbours; one would expect this of the clerical body, with its sense of professional *esprit de corps* based on a traditional training.[24]

However, radical clergy succeeded in securing some significant footholds. Some, as we have seen in the case of Bale, Seton, and Parkhurst, came through patronage from interested laypeople; such was the case with Stoke College. Here Anne Boleyn exercised the patronage of the house that lay in the Queens of England by appointing her chaplain Matthew Parker as Dean in 1535; the prime mover in this may well have been Cromwell, who had taken an interest in tackling the long-standing problems in the College statutes in the time of the previous Dean.[25] In 1537 Parker faced a trial of strength with local conservatives when he was faced by accusations of disloyalty and unorthodoxy from local gentry, who with the friars of nearby Clare were backing Dr Stokes, head of the sister-friary at Norwich in his traditionalist preaching at Clare. With Cromwell's help, Parker vindicated himself and secured Stokes's imprisonment and humiliation; it was a major triumph for the radical cause at a time when public confrontations between radicals and conservatives in the county were becoming frequent occurrences.[26] Over the next decade, Parker devoted a good deal of energy to the place between his Court and Cambridge duties, finally recasting the statutes, organizing a school from which bright boys might go to his Cambridge college of Corpus Christi, and using the place as a base for spreading his gentle version of the reformed faith through preaching and hospitality.[27] Even though he never succeeded in getting rid of that hardened survivor Thomas Whitehead from among the prebendaries, the turnover of staff in the College between Nix's visitation in 1532 and the dissolution in 1548 is noticeable, and Parker used the College resources to benefit his reforming friends in other ways; thus in 1545 he granted the presentation of a Stoke living which he had formerly held himself to his friend and Cambridge colleague, the prominent Protestant William May.[28] It was no doubt this strategy of using Stoke as a bastion for

---

[24] Peet, 'Parish clergy', pp. 222–3.   [25] *LP* VIII, no. 934.

[26] PRO, E135/8/39; *Parker Correspondence* pp. 7–14; Strype, *Parker*, I, pp. 23–4.

[27] Strype, *Parker*, pp. 15–17, 25, 45–6.

[28] PRO, C1/1367/16; cf. *Parker Correspondence* p. vii, for Parker's time as rector of Ashen, Essex, the benefice concerned, and also Oxley, p. 181.

reformed doctrine which enabled Parker to stave off the College's dissolution in 1545 through the good offices of Queen Katherine Parr, the patron, and the Protestant gentleman of the Privy Chamber Sir Anthony Denny; by this means, the College was preserved until 1548, the last of all the religious houses of East Anglia.[29] When destruction became unavoidable, Denny was instrumental in securing a good pension for Parker, even though he was by now also Master of Corpus; through Parker's influence, the College itself briefly continued to combine its traditional function as a Cambridge country retreat and its more recent role as a support for Protestant scholarship by becoming the country house of his friend Provost Cheke of King's.[30]

Of even greater significance for the nurturing of Protestantism in the county was the Archbishop of Canterbury's important peculiar parish of Hadleigh. Even in the time of Archbishop Warham, an unlikely patron for dissent, we have seen Hadleigh serve as a refuge from Bishop Nix for the preaching of Thomas Bilney and his iconoclastic associate Thomas Rose. Foxe particularly praised Hadleigh after Bilney's efforts as one of the first towns 'that received the word of God in all England . . . the whole town seemed rather a university of the learned, than a town of cloth-making or labouring people'. Hadleigh continued to spearhead the work of reform, being noted in London in 1538 as one of the places which were introducing English into the Mass.[31] Cranmer built on the work of Bilney and Rose in his appointments for the town. When Nicholas Shaxton resigned the bishopric of Salisbury on the passing of the Six Articles, it was in Hadleigh that Cranmer found him a refuge.[32] Shaxton's immediate superior, the rector William Rivet, was probably also a sympathizer with reform; he was a royal chaplain who in 1540 was appointed Archdeacon of Suffolk by royal letters patent rather than by Bishop Rugge, and also in that year we find him witnessing the will of the head of a prominent Protestant family of the town.[33] His successor as rector in 1544 was Rowland Taylor, a noted Protestant preacher.

Bishop Rugge would not have viewed such appointments with enthusiasm, and particularly in the Archdeaconry of Sudbury, the

---

[29] *Parker Correspondence* pp. 31–3.   [30] Strype, *Parker*, p. 44.
[31] Foxe, VI, p. 676. English service: *Wriothesley's Chronicle* I, p. 83. The other place named was undoubtedly Stratford St Mary, Suffolk, not the Essex place of the same name (cf. above, p. 159). For Waldegrave's advocacy of the English service in the Stour valley in 1538, see PRO, SP 1/140/223 (*LP* XIII pt. ii, no. 1179).
[32] *DNB*, s,v, Shaxton, Nicholas.
[33] *LP* XV, no. 1027/21; will of Robert Forth, Muskett, I, p. 109.

Bishop's subordinates were equally unsympathetic to reform. From 1536 the Archdeacon of Sudbury was Miles Spencer, a nephew of Cardinal Bainbridge who had appeared on the historical scene in 1513 in a fashion which was to become characteristic of a cleric who enjoyed his comforts; at the age of nineteen he had obtained a papal dispensation for pluralism to support his education.[34] He was to survive as Archdeacon, a monstrous pre-Reformation anachronism and an obstacle in the path of reform, down to his death in 1570. His assistants as commissaries were successively John Bury and Thomas Symonds, clerics whom Foxe was to single out as playing a particularly active and enthusiastic role in the Marian persecution. Spencer was also Rugge's Chancellor: altogether a harmonious team. In the Archdeaconry of Suffolk, Dr Rivet was succeeded in 1542 by Giles Ferrers, ex-Abbot of Wymondham, who had assisted Bishop Nix in visitation work before Nix's world had collapsed,[35] and his successor in 1548 was one of Bishop Rugge's numerous relatives, Robert Rugge.

For all Cranmer's efforts, the administration of the diocese thus remained in the hands of conservatives not only in the reign of Henry but also under Edward, and there would therefore be little disruption to the ecclesiastical hierarchy when Mary came to the throne. Under Henry, men like Spencer felt constrained to enforce what legislation remained as the tattered remnant of Cromwell's attempts at reformation; the one surviving court-book for Sudbury Archdeaconry, for instance, shows Spencer's court officials between 1544 and 1546 pursuing clergy for not providing a Bible or quarterly sermons in parish churches.[36] Nevertheless, much more congenial to them was the business of attacking further manifestations of Protestantism, as and when the government let them. One weapon beyond the traditional ecclesiastical courts was the commission set up to enforce the Act of Six Articles of 1539, doing its work on jury presentments of offenders; Spencer was among those who sat on this, with the *custos rotulorum* and various leading JPs, and we catch a rare glimpse of their work in the proceedings against an adulterous priest of Chelsworth on 28 May 1540. We cannot be certain how frequently such sessions were held in subsequent years, but they re-emerge in 1546, when the commission

[34] *LP* I, no. 2236.
[35] Cf. e.g. Jessopp, *Visitations*, pp. 285, 290.
[36] SROB, IC 500/5/1, fos. 26ʳ, 31ʳ, 62ʳ, 71ʳ. Lack of provision for sermons was also being presented in the neighbouring Archdeaconry of Colchester in 1545 (Oxley, p. 146).

was used to condemn two Protestants, Kirby and Clarke, burnt respectively at Ipswich and Bury.[37]

The destruction of Kirby and Clarke marked the local manifestation of a government reaction in favour of conservatism, perhaps motivated by the wish to neutralize hostile reaction to the statute providing for the dissolution of the chantries. The former sexton of Bury Abbey, Dr Rougham, preached the sermon at Kirby's burning. Swept up in this act of government policy despite his reformist views was Lord Wentworth, naturally forced to preside over Kirby's burning as Suffolk's leading JP, but according to Foxe, moved to tears of pity and shame by the experience. However, central government did not confine itself to making examples of such humble victims, traditional targets for drives against heresy. Parallel with attacks on prominent Protestant figures at Court like Anne Askew came an onslaught on the clerics whom Cranmer had infiltrated into Suffolk: Rowland Taylor and his assistant at Hadleigh Nicholas Shaxton. The impression is of local conservative forces eagerly taking the opportunity to rid themselves of these troublesome clerics; the same Dr Rougham who had preached at Kirby's death was jointly responsible with the former Warden of Babwell Friary (just outside Bury) a month later for reporting to the Privy Council on a sermon which Taylor had preached at Bury.[38] The Council had sent for Shaxton on the same day that they ordered Kirby's arrest, and the conservative bailiff of Hadleigh had to be restrained in his enthusiasm by a further Council order from confiscating Shaxton's goods.[39] Faced with this arrest and perhaps mindful of Kirby's fate, Shaxton's morale collapsed. By the autumn he was negotiating abjectly for some small piece of East Anglian preferment, having gained a pardon for heresy; his recantation was the subject of a reproachful letter from his Protestant friends at Hadleigh, but he never seems to have regained his reformer's faith.[40]

This was a notable triumph for the conservative group, but the destruction of the house of Howard and the death of the King both showed how insecure the Catholic position was. Now the local ecclesiastical hierarchy, whatever its own preferences, would have to

[37] PRO, C244/177/19; Foxe, V, pp. 530–2. Foxe misdated this latter case to 1545, but cf. *APC* I, p. 417.

[38] *APC* I, p. 443.   [39] *APC* I, pp. 417, 492.

[40] PRO, SP 1/225/6–13 (*LP* XXI pt. ii, no. 134); pardon, *LP* XXI pt. i, no. 1383/49; R. Crowley, *The Confutation of xiii Articles, wherunto Nicholas Shaxton ... subscribed* (1548, *STC* 6083), sig. A iiii; Foxe VII, p. 404. For a similar onslaught on Essex Protestants in 1546, see Oxley, p. 147.

enforce a policy moving well beyond anything that Henry VIII had contemplated, and with no prominent secular figure to look to as a brake on the enforcement of the central government's wishes; indeed, the leading men of the county were now sympathetic to reform. Most prominent now that the Duke of Norfolk was in the Tower was Lord Wentworth, no longer constrained to go against his Protestant conscience; Suffolk gained a second peerage title in the initial shareout of spoils by Edward's councillors when Sir William Willoughby was promoted to be Baron Willoughby of Parham. Sir Anthony Wingfield served both Somerset and Northumberland as courtier and county magnate until his death in 1552. Sir William Waldegrave was now free to express his long-standing Protestant enthusiasm; we catch a glimpse of this in action in 1548, when his order to a conservative incumbent to appear before him to be examined about disobedience to royal injunctions led to brawls and a suit in Chancery against Waldegrave's servant.[41]

There was as yet no recognizable grouping among the county magistracy to counterbalance these magnates. Whatever faction fighting took place at Court during the 1540s, Henry VIII's hybrid Church had enjoyed more passive support in the country than the Church of England has ever done since; papalist opposition had been cowed by the defeats of the 1530s and by the capricious official terrorism surrounding the destruction of the Pole–Courtenay circle in 1538. Religious conservatives among the gentry, schooled in obedience to the Crown, took a long time to realize that obedience might sometimes prove impossible. The piecemeal changes of Edward's brief reign seem to have left most of them confused and lacking in leadership; as yet the party lines had hardly been drawn up. One mark of this was that there was apparently no major purge of the East Anglian commissions of the peace on ideological lines when Somerset manœuvred his way to power on Henry's death; by contrast, both the Marian and the Elizabethan regimes did their best to strip the commissions of troublesome men when they came to power (below, Chs. 7, 8). The evidence for the Suffolk commission in the 1540s is fragmentary, but the surviving commission of May 1547 does not have many noticeable omissions of earlier JPs; two associates of the fallen Duke of Norfolk, Thomas Tilney and Robert Downes, were omitted, together with the conservative Sir Richard Freston who was probably already in the

[41] PRO, C1/1309/74.

Lady Mary's service, but of the other five left out, two were back by 1550.[42] Indeed, the batch of new names in this commission which may represent fresh arrivals is split quite evenly between pillars of conservatism and those with reforming sympathies.[43] By the standards of thirty years later, the Edwardian commission was remarkably mixed in religious outlook.

The reluctance of conservative JPs to show opposition to the regime is also illustrated by the way in which they acted as agents of the government's reforming policies. In May 1552 the regime issued commissions to inventory church plate, bells, and other items, ostensibly to check on embezzlement, but clearly part of the new stages of reform which brought in the second Prayer Book. Among the commissioners named for Suffolk and Ipswich beside obvious favourers of reform were men who were soon to emerge as enthusiastic partisans for Mary's religious reaction and as opponents of the Elizabethan changes: in the county, Sir John Jerningham, Sir Thomas Cornwallis, and Sir William Drury; in Ipswich, Sir Nicholas Hare, Sir Henry Doyle, Lionel Tollemache, and William Foster. Nor were these men necessarily sleeping partners in the commission: at Ipswich, Hare and Foster were among those signing the return.[44] It is also significant that Northumberland's government was sufficiently trustful of Sir William Drury and Sir Henry Bedingfield to recommend them as knights of the shire for Suffolk in January 1553; both men became pillars of the Marian regime, and Sir Henry Bedingfield survived into Elizabeth's reign to be an obstinate Catholic recusant.[45] The point is made all the more strongly by Cornwallis's initial obedience to Westminster's order to him as Sheriff to proclaim Queen Jane in 1553 (above, p. 79).

There was therefore no rallying-point for conservatives to oppose

---

[42] Tilney was son of the Duke's late leading household official and brother-in-law Sir Philip Tilney. Downes was involved in the Duke's legal business (e.g. *LP* V, nos. 220/3, 4, XX pt. ii, no. 496/68). On Freston, see '*Vita Mariae*' p. 204; he was already hosting Mary in 1548 (BL Add. 24124, fo. 5^r); on his conservatism, PRO, SP 1/140/16–17 (*LP* XIII pt. ii, no. 964). Robert Rookwood and Sir Thomas Barnadiston were restored by 1550.

[43] Reformers: Nicholas Bacon, Henry Gates, John Lucas, Christopher Goldingham, Robert Gurdon. Subsequent conservatives: Sir Edmund Bedingfield, Thomas Cornwallis, John Eyer, Alexander Newton, Henry Payne, Nicholas Hare, Francis Nunn, George Colt. Uncertain: James Downes, Sir John Jenny, Robert Ashfield, Thomas Lord Burgh, Sir Anthony Heveningham.

[44] *CPR Edward VI* IV, p. 393; *EANQ* New Series (1885) I, p. 7.

[45] BL Lansd. 3/19, fo. 36.

the religious changes of the Edwardian regime; it is noticeable that the East Anglian rebels of 1549 exhibited no signs of Catholic partisanship even for Henrician Catholicism, perhaps associating it with the religious sympathies of the disgraced and unlamented Howards.[46] The best that the conservative operators of the diocesan bureaucracy like Miles Spencer could do was to restrain the enthusiasm of Protestant activists as much as the new regime allowed them, and they faced open abuse from their opponents as they did so.[47] Moreover, they faced official moves which undermined their position; in September 1547, a royal visitation temporarily overrode the whole diocesan jurisdiction and pressed forward the work of Reformation.[48] Cranmer was clearly trying to emulate the success of his earlier manipulation of a peculiar jurisdiction at Hadleigh when in 1548 he turned his attention to the town of Bury St Edmunds. This had long been in the hands of the Abbot of Bury for purposes of ecclesiastical administration, and was thus exempt from the control of the Bishop of Norwich. Now this peculiar, which had lapsed to the Crown on the Dissolution, was given its own Archdeacon by letters patent, and the man chosen was none other than Suffolk's leading Protestant cleric, Cranmer's protégé at Hadleigh Rowland Taylor.[49] Here was a challenge to Bishop Rugge and his subordinates in the heart of Miles Spencer's archdeaconry of Sudbury. Mary's replacement for Taylor as Archdeacon of Bury would be a fitting symbol of his fall: his old adversary Dr Rougham, the former sexton of Bury Abbey.[50]

In the fragmentary state of the evidence, it is difficult to gain a coherent picture of the grass-roots effectiveness of Edwardian attempts at reform. The impression given by the narrative of the conservative northern priest Robert Parkyn is that the various Edwardian orders to dismantle the scenic apparatus of the old order were obeyed promptly even by those who, like Parkyn, profoundly disapproved of the changes; moreover Parkyn, gazing sourly on events in the realm from his Yorkshire parsonage, noted Suffolk as among various counties in the 'sowth parttes' which were especially quick to abandon traditional customs like the use of hallowed bread and holy

---

[46] MacCulloch, 'Kett's Rebellion', pp. 58–61.
[47] Houlbrooke, *Church Courts*, p. 245.
[48] Ibid., p. 36, and cf. *EANQ* New Series, I, pp. 252–3.
[49] *CPR Edward VI* II, p. 5.
[50] Rougham occurs as Archdeacon in 1555 (PRO, C85/215/8). He died in 1556 and was buried in his eponymous village of Rougham (PRO, E178/3251); I have not come across references to subsequent Archdeacons.

water in the first year of the reign.[51] Certainly the surviving churchwardens' returns to the order of November 1547 to detail sales of church plate show that the vast majority of parishes had already hastened to make sales; indeed, they reveal that the process had already started earlier in the 1540s.[52] Many parishes had been pushed into sales by the heavy financial demands of Henry VIII's last French campaign, but some of the largest sales in Henry's reign had been in parishes which wanted to finance some local worthy cause: church extension at Bungay St Mary, sea defences at Dunwich, town lands at Blythburgh. After 1547, a number of parishes spent their gains specifically on such government demands for church reordering as whitewashing over wall-paintings and removing 'superstitious' stained glass windows; the parishes of Ipswich were notably active in this respect, with the churchwardens of the central and influential parish of St Laurence showing themselves zealous in selling valuables and in purging their richly-beautified church of superstition. Similar moves came in some of the parishes of central east Suffolk which were to be in the centre of resistance to the Marian reaction: Chediston, Laxfield, Stonham Aspall.[53]

Elsewhere, village leadership may not have been so receptive to the change of official atmosphere in 1547. While the firmly Protestant churchwardens of Ipswich St Laurence had already given the cloths before their rood away to the poor by November 1547, the churchwardens of Bungay St Mary, home of the conservative JP Richard Wharton, were still paying to have the curtain before the rood washed two years later.[54] The furniture of the rood and its screen was one of the most prominent features of the medieval church, and with its symbolic position separating the priest's chancel from the people's nave, the screen was a natural focus for Reformation conflicts which might split a village. The parish of Wortham had already been the centre of trouble savouring of religious dissidence in the early 1540s, when the two parsons of the village sued certain parishioners for refusing to offer them the traditional 'hallybred' candle on a rota basis Sunday by Sunday, and for otherwise causing 'moche grudge murmor

---

[51] Parkyn, pp. 66, 68.
[52] The returns pr. *EANQ* New Series, I–II.
[53] Ibid., I (1885), pp. 252–3, 159, 362, 49; II (1887), p. 366. The concentration of activity in country parishes round Ipswich is also notable, e.g. Little Bealings, Freston, Playford, Rushmere, Sproughton, Stratford St Mary, Whitton (ibid., I, pp. 67, 251; II, pp. 106, 145, 170, 283).
[54] *EANQ* Old Series, II (1866), p. 227.

and debates'. Under Mary, one of the same parsons joined with leading parishioners in suing former churchwardens for over-zealous attention to the Edwardian reordering of the church, including the destruction of the roodloft. It emerged that many Suffolk parishes had done the same, and that this had worried the county establishment as going beyond the requirements even of Edward's second Prayer Book; in 1552 or 1553 the second Lord Wentworth as Lord Lieutenant had ordered several of the enthusiasts 'to make uppe agayne the same rodeloftes at their owne costes and charges which by his commandement were so made uppe agayne.[55]

The accession of Mary was a renewed chance for the conservative diocesan hierarchy and its supporters among the gentry to assert themselves after their confusion and loss of nerve under Edward. In 1554 their hand was particularly strengthened when the Catholic but almost permanently absentee Bishop Thirlby was promoted to Ely and replaced by John Hopton, a trusted chaplain of the Queen who was to prove himself energetic in promoting the restoration of the old faith. Even before Hopton's consecration in October 1554, the work of depriving the large numbers of clergy who had married in Edward's reign had been virtually completed: a huge task, which in Suffolk meant the deprival of more than a quarter of all clergy, although nearly all of them soon found other livings.[56] His consecration was closely followed by the reconciliation with Rome and the parliamentary reimposition of the old anti-Lollard legislation. It was his diocese which was to be one of the most seriously affected by the Marian programme of persecution; over thirty people were to be condemned to death, and most of them, some twenty-seven, came from Suffolk. It was in Suffolk that the most distinguished victim of persecution after the Oxford martyrs, Dr Rowland Taylor, was to suffer; not surprisingly, this prime clerical assailant of the old order in East Anglia was the first to be burnt in the diocese.

The parson of Hadleigh was already marked out as an enemy of the new regime while it was still establishing itself; while the Queen was still at Ipswich receiving late converts from Northumberland's supporters, on 25 July 1553, her Council ordered Taylor's arrest, and three days later he was committed to the custody of the Sheriff of Essex as the

[55] PRO, C1/982/69, C1/1340/17–19. There were two medieties of the parish of Wortham, hence two parsons.
[56] Baskerville, 'Married Clergy', p. 45. The proportion in Essex was very similar: Oxley, p. 180.

Queen progressed in triumph through that county.[57] However, if Taylor had become involved in the Lady Jane Grey débâcle, he escaped serious consequences for the moment, for he was at liberty in his benefice until the following Holy Week, ostentatiously maintaining the still legal Edwardian service and assiduously preaching against the steady Catholic takeover in the surrounding countryside.[58]

Palm Sunday was an obvious time for the situation at Hadleigh to come to the boil, for it was in the ceremonies of Holy Week that the traditional liturgy showed itself most remote from the world of reformers like Taylor. For all Foxe's eulogies of Hadleigh, all had not been sweetness and light there in Edward's reign; the clash between leading Protestant supporters and Catholic opponents of Taylor was exemplified in the ostensibly secular violence and lawsuits between the Protestant gentleman William Forth and the Catholic Walter Clerke which came to a head in 1552.[59] Clerke and his brother John had long been vigorous opponents of reform, having been instrumental in Thomas Rose's arrest in 1533;[60] now John Clerke combined with the Ipswich lawyer and JP William Foster to bring in the parson of the neighbouring village of Aldham to attempt to say mass on the Monday and Tuesday in Holy Week. This provoked a direct confrontation with Taylor and his supporters which enabled a complaint to be made to Lord Chancellor Gardiner. On Easter Monday the Council ordered Foster and Hadleigh's leading JP Sir Henry Doyle to arrest Taylor; it looks as if Clerke and Foster had prepared the ground well at Westminster.[61] Taylor's burning came in February 1555, dismaying even many of the conservative gentry of the county, who tried to persuade him in his last days as he stayed at Lavenham to abjure Protestantism.

Few of the Suffolk clergy followed Taylor's example in making a stand for Protestantism. The large number of clergy who had married do not seem to have felt that the other results of the Edwardian Reformation were worth a martyrdom. Only Robert Samuel, formerly curate of East Bergholt and then leader of a clandestine Protestant congregation at Ipswich, withstood official pressure sufficiently to result in his death at the stake in August 1555; Taylor's former curate

---

[57] *APC* IV, pp. 418, 421.
[58] The following account of Taylor's arrest is taken from Foxe, VI, pp. 676–703, unless otherwise stated.
[59] PRO, STAC 10/16/212, 224; PRO, KB 9/579, m. 239.
[60] Foxe, VIII, p. 581.   [61] *APC* V, p. 3.

at Hadleigh, Richard Yeoman, was burnt at Norwich in 1558, after wandering in Kent.[62] It was the laity who would take up Taylor's example of self-sacrifice; news of the death of the first layman, a shoemaker called James Abbes, reached the London diarist Henry Machyn from Bury St Edmunds at the beginning of August 1555.[63] Most of those who were forced into confrontation with the government over religion were humble people; a few strong-minded gentry widows faced harassment by the authorities, and half a dozen gentry had to face the Privy Council on charges concerned with conspiracy, but no one of gentle status died for heresy.[64] Among those sixty-four persecuted or burnt for whom occupation or status can be assigned, the number of those involved in the leather trade, particularly shoemakers, is remarkable: fifteen, as opposed to nine people connected with the cloth trade and eleven labourers or smallholders. It is a figure reminiscent of the connection between activists in the 1549 stirs and the butcher's trade (below, Ch. 10); earlier examples can be found of heretical shoemakers, as part of the chain of independent thought which seems to distinguish the trade in an extraordinary variety of western historical settings.[65]

Almost from the beginning of the campaign of burnings, the government was confronted with the unpalatable fact that its efforts were frittering away the regime's initial propaganda advantage, and not merely in the case of a well-known and popular cleric like Taylor; they had to step in during May 1556 to order a search for two men who were promoting the Protestant cause in the Sudbury area by the somewhat paradoxical means of exhibiting the calcined bones of the Essex martyr William Pygott as relics.[66] Yet the burnings continued. Taylor had been condemned out of the diocese as he had been beneficed in an archiepiscopal peculiar, but the sort of appeal made by Clerke and Foster to the Lord Chancellor was not necessary in subsequent cases; the local machinery could cope. Dr Houlbrooke points out that the work of persecution in the diocese was spasmodic, coming in four phases: spring to summer 1555, in connection with

---

[62] Foxe, VII, pp. 371–4; VIII, pp. 486–7.   [63] *Machyn's Diary* p. 92.

[64] BL Harl. 421, fo. 181ʳ; Foxe, VIII, p. 147 (Ursula Garneys and her sister Mrs Thwaites); Foxe, VIII, pp. 599–600; *APC* IV, p. 409; V, pp. 66, 100, 106, 171.

[65] E. J. Hobsbawm and J. Wallach Scott, 'Political Shoemakers', *PP* no. 89 (1980), pp. 86–114. Names and occupations of Marian martyrs and confessors are derived almost entirely from Foxe and from BL Harl. 421.

[66] *APCV*, p. 20. This can only refer to William Pygott: cf. Foxe, VI, p. 740, with ibid., VII, p. 405.

Bishop Hopton's primary visitation, spring 1556, associated with the metropolitical visitation, winter 1556/7 and spring 1558.[67] The burnings which resulted from these initiatives stayed much the same in number each year: five Suffolk people in 1555, seven in 1556, eight in 1557, and seven in 1558—five of the latter, as Foxe grimly emphasized, in the fortnight before the Queen's death.[68]

Foxe's point was that the official responsible for this last piece of pointless thoroughness was no ecclesiastical official, but the prominent local JP and Chief Baron of Mary's Exchequer, Sir Clement Higham. It was not simply the obvious targets among the clergy like Bishop Hopton and Archdeacon Spencer who came in for Foxe's abuse; he records eleven of his twenty-seven Suffolk martyrs as trapped on the initiative of committed conservatives among the laity, and names many more among the county's Marian magistracy who took an active part in the proceedings of persecution. Proceedings to secure Catholic uniformity went forward partly through the customary work of the diocesan courts, but partly through the efforts of a secular commission; the presence of so many nominal members of the Privy Council in the region, the group who had steered Mary's East Anglian *coup*, encouraged the government to appoint a special commission of councillors to suppress heresy. Foxe prints a long and courageous petition addressed to these commissioners from 'the lovers of Christ's true religion in Norfolk and Suffolk' pleading for the restoration of Protestantism, but no doubt more characteristic of the commissioners' work was the 1556 list of accused Ipswich Protestants which he also preserves.[69]

There is little evidence that the Suffolk laity played much part in the more positive side of restoring Catholicism, beyond the activity demanded of churchwardens in bringing back church interiors to their old state. Mary's reign was too short for the laity to feel encouraged to spend good money on the Catholic revival. No Suffolk gentlemen seem to have followed the examples of their Essex neighbours Sir Robert Rochester, Sir William Petre, Sergeant William Bendlowes, and Lord Rich in founding chantries for themselves, and no religious house was to be refounded in East Anglia;[70] the only Suffolk lands to be restored to the regular life were among those granted by the Queen

---

[67] Houlbrooke, *Church Courts*, p. 232.   [68] Foxe, VIII, p. 497.
[69] Foxe, VIII, pp. 121–30, 598–600, and cf. Houlbrooke, *Church Courts*, p. 233.
[70] On Essex, see Oxley, pp. 183–5. For clerical provision for obits at Hepworth and Elmswell, see Peet, 'Parish clergy', p. 269.

to the Knights of St John of Jerusalem, although the Bedingfield family seem to have sheltered a number of ex-religious around their Norfolk and Suffolk homes.[71] The Catholic laity were not anxious to disgorge their former ecclesiastical property, as debates in the Marian Parliaments demonstrated. Sir Nicholas Hare was unusual in returning purchased church lands to the parish of Homersfield to be used for their former spiritual purposes by his will of 1557; he was also paying annuities to the surviving nuns of Bruisyard Abbey, now his principal residence. Sir Thomas Cornwallis, who had been up at Cambridge with Hare's sons, was among various English Catholics to come to a private agreement with the Pope over the holding of monastic lands, but that was not until 1579.[72]

The heresy which the machinery of discipline was trying to eliminate was remarkably localized within the county, and the evidence both before and afterwards suggests that this was no mere temporary quirk of Marian administration. Martyrs and victims of persecution were limited virtually exclusively to the town of Ipswich and to parts of the Woodland area in the county. Dr Houlbrooke points out that Ipswich was the only large town in the diocese to cause Bishop Hopton serious trouble, to the extent that he seems to have quitted the town without completing all the work of his visitation in 1556.[73] Evidence of Protestant sympathies at Ipswich suggested by the 1547 churchwardens' returns combines significantly with the story which reached London in September 1554: 'in Ypswich, being a xj parish churches, there was but ij preistes to serve them.' In 1555 three parishes in the town were still vacant, and in 1556, four.[74]

Parish vacancies were of consequence at Ipswich, because the town had a tradition of choosing many of its parish clergy; seven out of the town's twelve parishes had been appropriated to religious foundations and so became impropriate livings, five of which were in the hands of the parishioners themselves. In fact, because the pre-Reformation appropriations had nearly all been to houses within the town itself, the

---

[71] Grant to Hospitallers: *CPR Philip and Mary* IV, p. 313. Bedingfields: an ex-monk and an ex-nun died at Denham, home of Lady Bedingfield, in the 1560s (PRO, E178/3251), and an ex-nun was still living at Oxborough, the main Bedingfield home in Norfolk, during the 1570s (MacCulloch, 'Catholic and Puritan', p. 249).

[72] Hare's will, PCC 46 Wrastley. Cornwallis: *Miscellanea*, ed. C. Talbot, CRS LIII (1960), p. 230. Sir William Petre obtained a dispensation during Mary's reign (Oxley, pp. 184–5).

[73] Houlbrooke, *Church Courts*, p. 237; Foxe, VIII, p. 225.

[74] *Narratives of the Reformation*, p. 289; NRO, VIS I, unpag. consignation books, 1555, 1556.

parishioners would probably long have had the decisive voice in parochial appointments. An instance of this is recorded in the parish of St Clement, legally appropriated to St Peter's Priory, where the inhabitants before the Dissolution had demonstrated not only their independence by choosing a secular priest, 'little Sir John', to serve them, but also their concern for clerical quality by dismissing him for his incontinent life.[75] Such vigorous involvement in parochial life and the humanist connections of the town's early sixteenth-century leadership need not have produced Protestantism, but the influence of the first Lord Wentworth and of Edward Grimston had probably been decisive in channelling this religious vigour in a Protestant direction. The strength of Ipswich Protestantism in Mary's reign is unmistakable. The result was that in 1556, Catholic partisans at Ipswich could produce a list of ninety-eight inhabitants who were in hiding for or otherwise exhibited Protestant sympathies, including five clergy.[76]

In secular terms too, Ipswich was a constant worry to the government, with reports of Protestant activity, conspiracies, and seditious language making the town's enthusiastic reception of the victorious Mary in July 1553 seem a little ironic.[77] It was perhaps because of all this that the borough leadership was so anxious to demonstrate its loyalty in its choice of MPs (above, Ch. 1), and in its creation of the new office of High Steward of the borough in 1554; the first Steward was a sound Catholic, the Duke of Norfolk's lawyer and Master of the Rolls, Sir Nicholas Hare.[78] Yet only one of the Marian leaders of the town, Richard Smart, is recorded by Foxe as being an enthusiast for the programme of reaction, and he apparently became a sincere and remorseful Protestant in the next reign.[79] The leadership of Elizabethan Ipswich would overwhelmingly follow the tendency to committed Protestantism already so much in evidence.

Elsewhere in the county, the patterns of Protestant activism revealed in the Marian persecution are confirmed by earlier evidence. Of particular interest is the one surviving courtbook of Sudbury Archdeaconry for 1544–6. Miles Spencer, John Bury, and their officials waged war on a whole variety of petty acts of religious deviance: refusal

---

[75] PRO, E134/28 Elizabeth/Easter 29.   [76] Foxe, VIII, pp. 598–600.

[77] *APC* V, pp. 65–6, 70, 88, 105; *CPR Philip and Mary* III, p. 257. Cf. *'Vita Mariae'* pp. 220–1.

[78] Bacon, p. 242; Hare is not actually named as High Steward in Bacon's extracts, but there is mention of a gift from 'Mr. Steward' in 1556 (ibid., p. 246), and on Hare's death in 1557, William Cordell was specifically chosen as High Steward.

[79] Foxe, VIII, p. 223.

to attend services or to carry out traditional observances in thirteen parishes, use of a Tyndale Bible by a parishioner at Clare, fomenting of disturbance and discussion at Brent Eleigh by reading injunctions in taverns, or the happy but unorthodox belief of a Lidgate man that there is no devil in Hell.[80] Spencer's oficials had still been concerned in this time of anti-chantry legislation to uphold the provision of prayers for the dead, but the five prosecutions that they brought for refusal to fund obits or items of liturgical use may have been the result of testamentary disputes rather than of Protestant views.[81] Among all the offenders, only one case involves someone who was to run into trouble with the Marian authorities: William Hammond of Haverhill refused to genuflect to the rood in 1546 (again, one notes the symbolic importance of this feature of the church), and a decade later, he was refusing to go to a priest to be confessed and was affirming a Cranmerian spiritual presence in the Eucharist.[82]

The continuities in three main areas of the wood–pasture country are clear: the Stour valley, the area round Hadleigh, and the 'High Suffolk' country in the centre of the county (the hundreds of Hartismere, Hoxne, Thredling, and Bosmere and Claydon). In the Stour valley, the cloth trade occasionally created spectacular fortunes, but more ordinarily brought widespread modest prosperity and greater mobility of labour than in more purely agricultural regions. Prosperity could create leisure and stimulus to lively devotion which might result in a more than conventional commitment to Catholic piety as expressed in the lavish churches of the valley; however, particularly in common with mobility of labour, it might equally well create a tendency towards independence of mind and an interest in dissident ideas. No doubt Parker's proselytizing at Stoke College also played an important part, but ten years before his arrival, this area was at the heart of the vigorous popular protest which helped to see off the Amicable Grant. Likewise, Hadleigh was a clothing town, but here the main stimulus to religious dissidence was the succession of charismatic reformist clerics from Bilney onwards, combined with the protection from diocesan interference through Hadleigh's peculiar jurisdiction. In the north central region, the open structure of many villages, the large number of prosperous yeomen and the weakness of the manorial

[80] SROB, IC 500/5/1, fos. 15ᵛ, 19ʳ, 20ᵛ, 21ʳ, 23ᵛ, 26ʳ, 29ʳ, 34ʳ, 40ʳ, 43ᵛ, 44ᵛ, 45ʳ, 46ᵛ, 48ʳ, 51ʳᵛ, 60ᵛ, 70ᵛ; 23ᵛ, 29ᵛ, 50ᵛ.
[81] Ibid., fos. 21ʳ, 24ʳ, 26ʳ, 20ᵛ.
[82] Ibid., fo. 60ᵛ; BL Harl. 421, fo. 186ʳ; Davis, p. 114.

system may have produced an atmosphere of relative religious freedom, reinforced by the anomalous administrative status of the area already noted (above, Ch. 1): the hundreds of Hartismere and Stow looked eastward in temporal administrative affairs to the quarter sessions at Beccles, Blythburgh or Ipswich, but in ecclesiastical affairs westward toward the court of the Archdeaconry of Sudbury.

The character of the laity in these areas seems to have influenced at least some of their clergy. Among clerical offenders recorded in the 1544–6 proceedings, the vicar of Edwardstone in the Stour valley was allowing a preacher in his church who had no licence from Bishop or Archbishop; this is reminiscent of the ex-cleric turned mercer at Nayland, five miles away, who a decade later maintained that it was not contrary to Scripture for a layman to preach and 'that he maye preache by the lawes of the realme'.[83] Significant also was the case of the rector of Palgrave in Hartismere, who neglected his cure to go preaching elsewhere.[84] Of three prosecutions for clerical incontinence, two were from the parishes of Wetheringsett and Rishangles, likewise in the heart of the north central Suffolk area which was to provide so many victims of Marian persecution, and lying either side of the parish of Thorndon, where ten years before, Bale had scandalized the local gentry by marrying; it is likely that even if the diocesan hierarchy believed that here was incontinence, the ladies involved would have thought themselves as good a wife as in any lay marriage.[85] By 1554, the incumbents of Wetheringsett and a cluster of villages round about—Winston, Stonham Aspall, Stonham Parva, Thwaite, Cotton, Bacton, Wyverstone, and Westhorpe—were all married.[86] The tradition of clerical radicalism and confrontation in this area persisted through the Marian troubles into the 1570s, when the Marian persecutor Sir John Tyrrell was still harassing the Puritan clergyman Roger Nuttall to stop him succeeding to his father's benefice of Bacton; Nuttall, born of pugnacious Lancashire gentle stock and backed by hundred and village constables, was not to bullied, despite the five-day siege and subsequent capture of his parsonage.[87] The same radical strain can be traced in the 1580s: of the seventeen traceable beneficed clergy of east Suffolk who refused to subscribe to Whitgift's Articles of 1584, eight

[83] SROB, IC 500/5/1, fo. 68ʳ; BL Harl. 421, fo. 186ʳ; Davis, pp. 113–14.
[84] SROB, IC 500/5/1, fo. 41ʳ.   [85] Ibid., fos. 14ʳ, 40ʳ.
[86] Peet, 'Parish clergy', p. 342.
[87] PRO, STAC 5 N10/19, T25/33. Thomas Nuttall was inducted to Bacton in 1564; cf. his monument there, *Chorography* p. 75. Cf. Roger Nuttall's subsequent clash with Sir Thomas Cornwallis, PRO, SP 15/25/119, p. 11.

(including Roger Nuttall) came from this area, with four more further south close to the old radical stronghold of Hadleigh.[88]

Certain parishes stand out as particularly striking in their continuity of religious dissent. The classic central Suffolk case is Mendlesham in the hundred of Hartismere, the neighbouring parish to Wetheringsett. This was a large village with several prosperous yeomen; the gentry landlords of the village, the Knyvetts, had long been absentee, living at Buckenham Castle in Norfolk. It was perhaps this which enabled the village to develop a startling radical organization, which horrified Edmund Knyvett when in the early 1530s he responded to a plea for help from the parish priest and rode over to investigate matters. The dissidents were holding regular meetings of up to a hundred people, and had elected officers 'for a gostly purpose to be done by us crysten brothers and systers'; they had already intimidated Knyvett's leading tenant into doing nothing, and their attitude to Knyvett himself was one of taciturn independence which must have infuriated that irascible gentleman.[89] Knyvett would maintain a feud with one Mendlesham yeoman, Robert Shepherd, for more than a decade in the 1530s and 1540s, personally beating him up at Buckenham in 1538.[90] Another member of the Shepherd family made his will in 1537, making no mention of the local church or parish priest, giving a long exposition of his reformed faith and once more using the significant phrase 'Crysten bretheryn'; one of the victims of the 1546 conservative purge was a Mendlesham man.[91] Nor were the Mendlesham Christian Brethren isolated either locally or on a wider scale. Dr Peet has teased out the network of links with surrounding villages revealed in wills like that of Shepherd and in Foxe's stories of Marian persecution. In 1536 a priest was married in Mendlesham church to a girl from the reformers' south Suffolk haven at Hadleigh, no doubt at the hands of the then parish priest of Mendlesham, whom a scandalized local gentleman reported in the same decade as openly living with his wife and children.[92] Most remarkably of all, the exposition of faith contained in William

---

[88] *Seconde Parte* I, pp. 242–3.

[89] PRO, SP 1/65/191 (*LP* V, no. 186). *LP* without explanation dates this 1531, which is surely too early, but it must be before 1536, when the parish priest was Protestant enough to preside at the wedding of the priest Adam Lewes: PRO, SP 1/123/224 (*LP* XII pt. ii, no. 450).

[90] PRO, C1/903/32, C1/1184/26, C1/1266/23; PRO, STAC 2/26/349, 2/29/9, 46.

[91] *Bury Wills*, pp. 130–3; Foxe, V, p. 530.

[92] Peet, 'Parish clergy', pp. 212–15; PRO, SP 1/123/224 (*LP* XII pt. ii, no. 450); BL Cott. Cleop. E IV, fo. 151 (*LP* XII pt. ii, no. 81).

Shepherd's will of 1537 contains precise verbal correspondences with the formulae in the will of a Yorkshire Protestant eleven years later.[93] In the 1560s, Edmund Knyvett's Catholic-minded son Sir Thomas would again be involved in a major legal campaign against the villagers to recover the status of demesne land at the former family home; one of his opponents would be William Whiting, prominent among those Mendlesham Protestants harassed by Mary.[94]

If Mendlesham lay at the heart of dissident religious activity in Hartismere and Hoxne, Stoke by Nayland was equally prominent in the Stour valley. All along the Suffolk Stour valley border there is evidence of religious dissidence during the 1540s and later, from Haverhill in the extreme west to East Bergholt in the extreme east, and Stoke, a large village which was almost a town, was perched right in the middle. The tendency to religious independence of mind there may have been encouraged by the removal in the late 1520s of the Howards from their old home at Stoke Park up to the new ducal palace at Kenninghall; it is worth noticing that a cross in Stoke Park and two images in a chapel there were among the victims of the campaign of iconoclasm in 1531–2, and one doubts that they would have suffered if the Duke of Norfolk had still been in residence.[95] There do not seem to have been any other prominent gentry in the parish up to the reign of Elizabeth, and the Protestant enthusiast Sir William Waldegrave was on the doorstep. By 1538, royal surveyors were reporting that the people of Stoke were 'not of so good inclynation' as their neighbours, a remark which in its context might suggest that they were papists until one looks at the evidence of the 1540s and 1550s.[96] A Stoke man was pardoned for heresy in the clamp-down of 1546, two different priests of the parish found themselves in trouble with the Archdeacon's court in 1545 and 1546, one for contumacy, and from Denston, a dozen miles off, John Abbot tried to justify his failure to offer a candle at Candlemas because he had heard that no parishioner had offered it in Stoke.[97] Stoke showed similar group resistance, according to Foxe, in the reign of Mary; as late as 1556 the bulk of the inhabitants refused to receive the Easter eucharist in the Catholic manner, and the

[93] Peet, 'Parish clergy', p. 217: cf. *Bury Wills*, pp. 131–2, with A. G. Dickens, *Lollards and Protestants in the Diocese of York 1509–58* (Oxford, 1959), p. 217.
[94] PRO, C3/47/23, C3/77/19, C3/96/43; C4/41, replication of Robert Crane, James Rivett, and Elizabeth Reve to Knyvett; PRO, KB 9/622, mm. 21–2 (Whiting). Knyvett's religion: Smith, p. 69. On Whiting, cf. Foxe, VIII, p. 147.
[95] Foxe, IV, p. 707.   [96] PRO, SP 1/242/1 (*LP* App. I pt. ii, no. 1311).
[97] *LP* XXI pt. ii, no. 332/71; SROB, IC 500/5/1, fos. 31^r, 68^r, 70^v.

authorities were reluctant to force a confrontation; the parish priest, Robert Cotes, was willing covertly to provide an Edwardian service for those who wanted it.[98] However, James Abbes, a former Stoke shoemaker, had already been burnt in Bury in 1555, among the first laypeople to suffer, and in 1557 the authorities clamped down in the village, arresting and eventually burning four Arian believers who caused Foxe some little trouble in turning them into acceptable godly martyrs.[99]

Just as notable as these continuities of activity are the continuities of deafening silence. In the Archdeaconry of Sudbury, the fen and sheep–corn area to the north of Bury St Edmunds was almost as completely absent from presentations for religious dissidence in the 1544–6 court book as it was to be from the records of Marian persecution, while the two names which emerge from Bury itself as espousing reforming ideas in Mary's reign form a remarkable contrast with over a hundred confessors and martyrs at Ipswich. The sheep–corn area along the coast was equally absent from Marian persecution, with the exception of three women from Orford and Aldeburgh; it had shown little previous trace of heresy and would show little inclination to Protestant activism under Elizabeth.[100] Perhaps the light-soil communities, with their sparser population and tighter manorial structure, were easier to control than the tough-minded yeoman farmers of the wood–pasture country, although one finds this difficult to believe of the coastal villages. In the corner of fen which made up the north-western parishes of Mildenhall and Lakenheath, the fen reclamation boom may have left the Tudor inhabitants little time for radical spiritual interests. An Elizabethan Puritan incumbent of Mildenhall acidly remarked of his parishioners that 'their large Fen' was their god.[101]

Bishop Hopton died in August 1558. He had been energetic during his short episcopate, pushing forward the restoration of the old religion, but he was not merely a mindless conservative bureaucrat. He conscientiously argued at length with the heretics brought before him;

[98] Foxe, VIII, pp. 556–7.

[99] Abbes: Foxe, VII, p. 328; cf. Foxe, VIII, p. 492, with BL Harl. 421, fo. 169ʳ, and Davis, p. 146: Foxe dated the burning of the four in error to 1558. It is interesting to find Abbes's name in the county election indenture for 1545 (PRO, C219/18C/110) next to the name of John Mannock, the Stoke man pardoned for heresy in 1546.

[100] Bury: BL Harl. 421, fo. 186ᵛ; *EANQ* New Series, I (1885), p. 99. Aldeburgh, Orford: BL Harl. 421, fos. 193ʳ, 195ʳ; Davis, p. 115.

[101] T. Settle, *A Catechisme*, qu. Collinson, 'Classical Movement', p. 767.

his will reveals two Greek bibles and a de luxe edition of the plays of Aristophanes in Greek as among the books which he had borrowed from his beloved Queen Mary. Aristophanes must have been a relaxation from a gruelling programme of work in his diocese which went beyond the work of basic reconstruction; Hopton was the first and only Tudor Bishop of Norwich to make a determined attempt to deal with the problem of simony.[102] However, his vision of a reformed Catholic church was to come to nothing: his bequest of half his library to the Norwich Dominicans 'yf they be restored' was a futile gesture of generosity. Within three months the Queen was dead, and the burnings which would be the main memory of all Hopton's pious energy were at an end.

The new regime would have to tread carefully. Although Elizabeth's advisers were determined to impose a Protestant settlement, and spent their first six months ensuring that this was pushed through Parliament, they were keenly aware that a large body of influential opinion was still unenthusiastic for reform; this was particularly true in East Anglia, where the Marian regime had enjoyed such powerful support among the county magistrates. Their greatest asset was the general weariness about religious controversy and the fear of rocking the boat to let in religious extremism. It was no coincidence that the government quickly raised the menace of Anabaptism, a nightmare threat calculated to keep conservative magnates on the side of the new regime. That sound Catholic and conscientious Marian official the Earl of Bath received a letter from the Lord Lieutenant, the young Duke of Norfolk, in June 1559, requiring him 'to have a deligent eye and regard to the dew observation of all good lawes and statutes now made for the advauncement of religion and uniformyte common prayers as for the suppressinge and puniss [. . .] of all souche as have the name of Anabaptistes [. . .] Lybertines [. . .] suffer them [not to] assemble nor resorte together'; we may be sure that it was the second half of this request rather than the first which raised his enthusiasm.[103] A year later, Lord Wentworth was still preoccupied with the same amorphous menace; in his capacity of Lord Lieutenant, he wrote to the Privy Council, he had had good success in keeping the county in due order, except for a few persons, 'which yet are rather doubted, than certainly known to be Anabaptists and Libertines', which sects being

[102] Hopton's will, PCC 62 Chayney; on simony, Houlbrooke, *Church Courts*, pp. 192–3.
[103] Hengr. 88/3, fo. 84^r.

most dangerous, he had paid especial attention to them.[104] Catholic and Protestant alike could unite in their fear of another Münster latent in their midst.

With the county élite in this state of cautious compromise, it is not surprising that the county as a whole accepted the new developments on Elizabeth's accession with reasonable grace. The parish priest of the veteran JP Sir John Brewse at Little Wenham, one Ralph Backhouse, uttered words seditious enough to merit a Privy Council order that he be pilloried at Ipswich and his ears cut off, in March 1559; in the same year Gavin Hodson, parish priest of Rougham, the home of a branch of the conservative Drury family, found himself deprived of his living.[105] Apart from these two, however, only six incumbents of Suffolk livings appear to have been deprived for any reason between 1559 and 1563.[106] On the whole, the conservatively-minded seem to have taken the passive attitude of the parishioner of Eye, who when making his will two days after Elizabeth's accession, left his parish church twenty ounces of silver towards making a new cross, 'yf the lawes of the realme will permyth and suffer the same'. Many, too, must have behaved like John Chapman alias Barker, who as churchwarden of Sibton hid various 'popyshe bookes' belonging to the church and persuaded his vicar to make a presentment to the ecclesiastical commissioners that there were no such books in the parish, in the hope that there might be yet another turn to the caprices of the central government.[107]

Nevertheless, the Marian experience had been a trauma which had forced people to take sides in a way that even the disturbances of Edward's reign had not achieved; it was bound to have left dangerous tensions. Suffolk experienced an explosion of these tensions straight away, in the shape of a furious row over iconoclasm in the church of Bures. Bures was the obvious place for religious conflict to come to a head; it was in the centre of the Stour area of reformist activism, the next parish to Stoke by Nayland, and no doubt conservative spirits in the village fiercely resented the dangerous posturings of their

[104] *HMC Salisbury* I, p. 253.

[105] On Backhouse, see *APC* VII, p. 71, although he was prepared to subscribe to the Acts of Uniformity and Supremacy at the general visitation six months later (Gee, p. 109). Hodson: *CPR Eliz.* I, p. 414.

[106] Gee, pp. 252 f., 267, 281–2, lists eight, but two of these cannot count: cf. Baskerville, 'Married Clergy', p. 48 n.

[107] Eye: *PSIA*, II (1854), p. 142. Sibton: PRO, STAC 5 C49/12, interrogatories for Chapman ex parte Copland.

neighbours. Its church had been lavishly furnished by the piety of prosperous clothiers in the parish and by the ancient and knightly family of Waldegrave, whose splendid tombs crowded the building. The arrival of commissioners for a royal visitation of the diocese at Bury in September 1559, bearing orders for the demolition of 'Images, Roodes, Roodloftes and other superstitius monumentes' gave the radical Protestants of Bures the excuse that they needed; probably they remembered the setback which reformists had suffered in demolishing roodlofts under Edward VI earlier in the decade.[108] Once more the roodloft became the focus of religious division. While the visitors were still in the county, about twenty radicals hacked down all the screens of Bures church to waist height, destroyed the Easter Sepulchre canopy over the finest of the Waldegrave tombs and damaged another monument. The conservatives of Bures were outraged, not least William Siday, longstanding servant of the Waldegraves, former steward of Stoke College and a champion of resistance to religious innovation since the 1530s.[109] He made sure that young William Waldegrave, present head of the family, was 'moche offended' particularly at the damage done to his ancestors' memorials. It is an indication of the strength that the conservatives still enjoyed in county administration that Siday and Waldegrave should turn without hesitation to Bury general sessions to indict the radicals for their vandalism; but then Sir Clement Higham, the new *custos rotulorum* and newly-retired Marian official, was Waldegrave's uncle. The indictment for destroying the screens and monuments was found.[110]

Nevertheless, the conservatives were not content with this local humiliation of their opponents: in Hilary Term 1560 they complained to the Privy Council. The Council viewed the potentially disruptive effect of the dispute with sufficient seriousness to send quite a high-powered commission of Suffolk JPs to view the damage; of the three, two (Thomas Seckford, one of the Masters of Requests, and John Eyer, one of the Masters in Chancery) would be busy about legal business, and only Robert Gurdon of Assington lived at all near at

---

[108] Gee, p. 96. The desecration took place on 29 September.

[109] Siday was already servant to Waldegrave's great-grandfather in 1524 (*1524 Subsidy* p. 2); he was auditor and steward of Stoke at the Dissolution (*PSIA* XII, 1904, p. 41, and cf. note on his pension, PRO, E164/31, m. 14ᵛ). As Chancellor Audley's servant in 1538, he was recorded as obstructing Cromwell's Injunctions (PRO, SP 1/140/223, *LP* XIII pt. ii, no. 1179).

[110] The story is told in PRO, STAC 5 U3/34; the Bury indictments are in PRO, KB 9/604, m. 23.

hand. The commission backed up the findings of Bury sessions. It was probably the Bures case which gave rise to the issuing of a proclamation against the destruction of monuments and memorial glass in September 1560.[111] Even this was not the end of the matter. A year later, when the Queen was on progress through the county and stayed with the Waldegraves at Smallbridge Hall in Bures, Sir William Cecil himself was taken across to the church to view the damage; he agreed with the commissioners 'and thought the Reavers therof worthy to make it ageyn at their own charges'. There is no record of what happened to the radicals of Bures after this august pronouncement, but the affair demonstrates that innovation in religion did not always have the final say in these confused opening years of Elizabeth's reign even in such a nursery of Puritanism as the Stour valley.

Clearly it would be a delicate task to find a bishop to suit this large and unruly diocese, and the government dithered, meanwhile leaving diocesan administration in the unsympathetic hands of Miles Spencer.[112] Their first choice was the prominent reformer and Marian exile Richard Cox, who was nominated in June 1559 but transferred to the richer and less demanding see of Ely in December; the Calvinist divine Thomas Sampson, himself from an ancient Suffolk gentry family, refused the see.[113] In March 1560 the choice eventually fell on John Parkhurst, another exile who had vigorously resisted being nominated to a bishopric, but he was not consecrated until 1 September.[114] The delay worried Lord Wentworth as Lord Lieutenant for the county; in May 1560 he wrote to the Archbishop of Canterbury urging that the new bishop or some substitute should come down as soon as possible to sort out the confusion and shortage of suitable ministers in the county. It would not be an easy task: three years later the new bishop would have to report that out of 510 parishes in Suffolk, 172 were still void of an incumbent.[115]

Parkhurst's *'nolo episcopari'* was an honest judgement of his own capabilities.[116] A kindly and scholarly man, he was to prove a hopeless administrator and a poor judge of subordinates; for many years he

---

[111] *Tudor Royal Proclamations* II, pp. 146–8, and cf. F. A. Youngs, *The Proclamations of the Tudor Queens* (Cambridge, 1976), p. 193.

[112] Cf. his returns of significations of excommunication into chancery 1558–60, PRO, C85/142/1–4.

[113] *DNB* s.v. Sampson, Thomas.

[114] Parkhurst's reluctance: *Zurich Letters* I, p. 61.

[115] Wentworth: CCC no. 78. Parkhurst's report: BL Lansd. 6/60.

[116] *Parkhurst* pp. 17–57, is the best biography.

would allow himself to be hamstrung by the local political situation in attacking conservatism in his diocese, while his own reforming convictions made him reluctant to discipline the Protestant activists whom he considered the main hope of reform. A year after his appointment, the Queen was infuriated during the course of her East Anglian progress by the 'undiscreet' behaviour of the Suffolk ministers, and Cecil, desperately trying to prevent her taking action against the inchoate Protestant ministry, wrote to Archbishop Parker from Bures, fresh from his visit to the wreckage in the parish church, lamenting the laxity of Parkhurst which had aggravated the situation:

the bishop of Norwich is blamed even of the best sort for his remissness in ordering his clergy. He winketh at schismatics and anabaptists, as I am informed. Surely I see great variety in ministration. A surplice may not be borne here. And the ministers follow the folly of the people, calling it charity to feed their fond humour. Oh, my Lord, what shall become of this time?[117]

Parkhurst's response to the frosty atmosphere of this royal progress was not quite to the point: three weeks later he wrote to his old Swiss friend Heinrich Bullinger, delightedly telling him that he had ordered all the ministers of Norfolk and Suffolk to read Bullinger's sermons on the Apocalypse, newly translated and published in Ipswich.[118]

It is not difficult to imagine the feelings of old Archdeacon Spencer when he received this instruction from his new diocesan. Parkhurst would have to face the fact that the majority of the diocesan hierarchy was markedly out of sympathy with his reforming theology, and one can understand him feeling that they constituted a greater threat to the newly-established church than the Protestant enthusiasts of the Stour valley. Spencer was perhaps the most obvious foe of reform, thoroughly enmeshed as he was in the Marian circle who would form the basis of Catholic recusancy in the diocese; his nephew William Yaxley, a wealthy young Suffolk gentleman, would become one of the county's chief recusants, and Suffolk's leading Catholic layman Sir Thomas Cornwallis would buy Spencer's splendid Norwich house, Chapel in the Field, by a previous agreement at his death. Spencer's will of 1570 revealed a formidable array of conservative associates, including John Hoo, who would be one of the leaders of the Catholic strong-arm regime in the Suffolk hundred of Lothingland in the 1580s (below, pp. 212–15), and Miles Yare, who as Sir Thomas Cornwallis's rector at Stuston would cheerfully combine the functions of Anglican

---

[117] *Parker Correspondence* p. 149.   [118] *Zurich Letters* I, p. 99.

incumbent and mass priest for the area round Sir Thomas's home, well into the 1580s.[119]

However, Parkhurst's other Archdeacons were not much better than Spencer. Nicholas Wendon was made Archdeacon of Suffolk in April 1559, but he did not take deacon's orders until the following year, obstinately remained a deacon only, spent most of his time on the Continent and was not ejected until 1570, when Parkhurst was at last getting a grip on his diocese. Wendon ended his days in Roman orders as Provost of Cambrai.[120] Richard Underwood, Archdeacon of Norwich, was a Marian appointment, presented by his brother on an old grant from the feckless Bishop Rugge; he was a member of the generally conservative household of the Duke of Norfolk which so impeded Parkhurst's work of reformation during the 1560s, and he witnessed Archdeacon Spencer's will. Matthew Carew, Archdeacon of Norfolk, shared Wendon's penchant for foreign travel.[121] Parkhurst termed all his pre-1572 Archdeacons 'popish lawyers or unlearned papists'. Apart from the Archdeacons, Parkhurst was on bad terms with his diocesan registrar, William Mingay, another Marian survivor with conservative associations, and he quarrelled with or mistrusted all his four successive diocesan Chancellors, two of whom were also conservative sympathizers.[122]

To crown this tale of untrustworthy colleagues, there was the Dean of Norwich, John Salisbury. Salisbury, originally a monk of Bury, had founded his career on compliance with Cromwell's wishes and become first Prior of Horsham St Faith and later Bishop of Thetford, at the same time as that other creature of Cromwell's, Bishop Manning of Ipswich, in 1536; as late in his career as 1570 he would be made absentee Bishop of Sodor and Man.[123] His religious views had not moved far beyond Henrician Catholicism, and are sufficiently indicated by his successful recommendation of Spencer's Catholic friend John Hoo as undersheriff for Suffolk in 1565; Hoo was the son of his old priory auditor from Horsham days.[124] Parkhurst discreetly detested Salisbury, and could not conceal his glee at his success when with studied courtesy, he insisted on supplanting the Dean as preacher

---

[119] Spencer's will, PCC 8 Lyon. Yare: PRO, SP 12/169/19.

[120] Le Neve, *Fasti* II, p. 489; *Miscellanea*, ed. C. Talbot, CRS LIII (1960), p. 193.

[121] Underwood: *Parkhurst* p. 104 n; PCC 8 Lyon. Carew: BL Lansd. 6/60.

[122] *Parkhurst* pp. 27, 30–2, 38.   [123] Knowles, III, p. 350.

[124] BL Add. 27401, fo. 7; for Hoo as under-sheriff, see PRO, DL 1/67/F2. Richard Hoo was auditor of Horsham in 1535 (*VE* III, p. 366), as well as auditor of Wymondham and steward of Rushworth College (ibid. III, pp. 317, 323).

at the funeral of the Duke of Norfolk's second wife in 1564. This important public occasion for East Anglia was something of a victory for Parkhurst and the godly cause in the diocese in terms of its restraint on traditional ceremony, *'sine crux, sine lux'*, as he wrote in boyish delight to John Foxe; he repeated his satisfaction in a letter to Simler in Zurich.[125]

The Bishop's confrontation with conservatism was as much with the strong caucus among the East Anglian gentry as with these clergy, and principally with the group which formed such a large proportion of the Howard clientage. We have already seen the link between conservatism and the Howard circle (above, Ch. 2), but why should this link exist? And why should it continue in the time of the fourth Duke, who quite sincerely maintained that he was a Protestant, even in his last letter warning his children to beware of papistry?[126] The key to the ideological stance of the group, and thus to the eventual survival of a sizeable Catholic minority among the East Anglian élite, lies with the long shadow cast by a powerful man of the past: Bishop Nix. The link is clear enough among the clergy. Spencer in particular had been Nix's Chancellor and close associate in the blind bishop's last years; he had been named as one of his executors, and was devoted to his memory, stipulating a grave near that of his old master in Norwich Cathedral.[127] Thomas Symonds, rector of Thorndon, commissary in the Archdeaconry of Sudbury during the 1550s, and an enthusiastic persecutor in the Hartismere–Hoxne area under Mary, had been Nix's chaplain.[128]

Yet the link is also traceable among the gentry, notably in the family of Sir Thomas Cornwallis. Nix had granted Sir Thomas's father Sir John the next presentation of the Archdeaconry of Norwich, and Sir John had presented his brother, another Thomas.[129] The Cornwallis connection brought with it a network of gentry families prominent under Mary and conservative under Elizabeth: Sulyard, Jerningham, Bedingfield, Yaxley, Rous, Tyrrell, Kitson. It was reinforced by Nix's family connections with the Essex family of Rochester, Sir Robert Rochester being one of Queen Mary's most loyal servants, and with

---

[125] BL Harl. 416, fo. 75; *Zurich Letters* I, p. 137, where the editors have misunderstood the reference to 'the dean of Christ Church' in the letter to Foxe; the context makes it clear that it was Christ Church Cathedral, Norwich, not Oxford, which was intended.

[126] Williams, *Thomas Howard*, p. 242.

[127] As executor: PRO, SP 1/101/180 (*LP* X, no. 220). Cf. PCC 8 Lyon.

[128] PRO, C1/1146/14.

[129] PCC 11 Pynnyng; Corder, *1561 Visitation*, I, p. 150.

the wealthy Suffolk clan of Rookwood; one of the Euston Rookwoods married Sir Thomas Cornwallis's brother Henry.[130] The gentry and clergy conservatives built on these links; we have already noted some of Spencer's gentry connections. Not surprisingly, John Foxe's abusive stories about Thomas Symonds contrast sharply with the high esteem in which he was held by the conservative gentlemen of his area. In 1551 he witnessed the will of Sir Thomas Tyrrell, father of his collaborator in Marian persecution Sir John; he was executor of another persecuting JP of the same area, Robert Kene, in 1558, and in 1569 he was bequeathed a ring by the ex-JP Alexander Newton of Braiseworth, brother-in-law of the stridently Catholic chronicler of Mary's *coup d'état*, Robert Wingfield of Brantham.[131]

Links with Nix were reinforced in the same circle by other connections with the last generation of pre-Reformation churchmen. The Cornwallises had also been on cordial terms with Abbot Reve of Bury. Sir John Cornwallis had been steward of the cellarer's manors, and Reve granted him and his clerical brother the next presentation of St John's Chapel at Palgrave, near their family home; they appointed Sir Thomas Cornwallis's brother Henry, although he was a layman.[132] Affectionate memories of Abbot Reve were probably a significant factor in disposing gentry in the west of the county to religious conservatism in mid-century (below, Ch. 7). It is noticeable that those gentry families who still had a representative among the local clergy in the confused mid-century years were more likely to retain a conservative outlook on religion than others. The Cornwallises had Archdeacon Cornwallis and Sir Thomas's brother William; the conservative Elizabethan JP Lionel Tollemache had his uncle William, commissary of the Archdeaconry of Suffolk from the days of Nix until William's death in 1558; the Bedingfields could still put a member of the family into their living at Bedingfield in the first decade of Elizabeth's reign, and earlier on, they had given the living to one of their Yaxley relatives, a former Norwich monk and still a minor canon of Norwich Cathedral in the 1560s.[133] Anthony Goldingham was presented by his mother to the family living at Belstead in 1562, but found the Elizabethan Settlement too much to take and fled to the

---

[130] PRO, SP 1/101, fo. 64ᵛ (*LP* X, no. 79); Corder, *1561 Visitation*, I, p. 151.

[131] Tyrrell: PCC 23 Bucke. Kene: PCC 75 Noodes. Newton: PCC 20 Sheffield.

[132] *VE* III, p. 463; BL Harl. 308, fo. 84ᵛ; *PSIA* XII (1904), p. 32.

[133] On Francis Yaxley, see Baskerville, 'Married Clergy', p. 60; he was inducted to Bedingfield in 1541.

Continent; she was a Rous of Dennington.[134] Such gentlemen clergy were becoming rarer in the troubled state of the mid-century Church, and would become rarer still in Elizabeth's reign.

Who could Parkhurst look to as a counterpoise to this formidable network? Among the gentry of east Suffolk, he could rely on the long-standing inclination to Protestant views of the 'Wentworth–Wingfield' grouping; in west Suffolk, some of the leading conservative gentry had produced sons whose religious enthusiasm ran to the opposite extreme of enthusiastic reformism. Sir Ambrose Jermyn's son Robert, for instance, must have imbibed his lifelong radical Protestantism when up at Parker's Corpus, Cambridge, from 1550, and he may well have been one of Parker's Stoke protégés. Robert Ashfield may also have been influenced by his time at St Edmund's Hostel in the 1550s. Sir Clement Higham, mindful of his friendship with Bishop Gardiner,[135] sent his son John to conservative Trinity Hall, but that did not stop the boy becoming as thoroughgoing a radical in religion as Jermyn and Ashfield; these three would champion Puritan causes as they took their place in local affairs from the 1570s.

Among the clergy, it would take time to bypass Spencer and his fellows to develop an effective leadership for the motley crew of clerics which had so infuriated Queen Elizabeth in 1561. The great problem was to provide for preaching, the essential basis for any thoroughgoing imposition of Protestantism on a largely indifferent population; less than ten per cent of the clergy of Norwich Diocese could be returned to Archbishop Parker as preachers in the 1560s, and not all these would be friendly to Protestantism.[136] Thomas Spencer, successor to the Marian rector of Hadleigh, did a herculean job of preaching in the county from 1560 to 1571, having leisure enough from his fairly nominal duties as Archdeacon of Chichester, but there was a limit to what he could achieve single-handed.[137] In the hundred of Bosmere and Claydon, for instance, local tradition preserved the memory that there had been no preacher between Elizabeth's accession and the coming of a new incumbent to Swilland in 1573, and in 1567 the Protestant gentry of east Suffolk, in the course of a protest against the suspension of their hero John Laurence, made the point that there was

---

[134] Corder, *1561 Visitation*, I, pp. 196–7; Goldingham's flight: PRO, E178/2133.
[135] Cf., e.g. *Chorography* p. 57.
[136] Houlbrooke, *Church Courts*, p. 203.
[137] *Zurich Letters* I, p. 255; he was inducted to Hadleigh in 1560. On archdeacons in Sussex, see Manning, p. 21.

no preacher in the whole of the coastal zone from Blythburgh to Ipswich, an area of two hundred square miles.[138]

For all its irregularity, the work of Laurence was at least one answer to Parkhurst's problems.[139] Laurence never seems to have been ordained, starting life as a prosperous yeoman in the north Suffolk village of Fressingfield, in the zone of early Protestant activism. He led a clandestine congregation during Mary's reign, and seems to have felt no need to regularize his status on Elizabeth's accession; naturally this worried the authorities, and he was twice ordered not to preach by diocesan and archiepiscopal officers during the 1560s. However, he was a firm favourite among the local Protestant gentry, and the fair-minded Bishop Parkhurst recognized his worth in the fight against conservatism, employing him to preach to clergy of old-fashioned views. Despite predictable further harassment by Parkhurst's successor, Cornwallis's ally Bishop Freke, Laurence continued to enjoy a special status and affection in Suffolk throughout Elizabeth's reign, leaving a memory green among the godly into the days of the Interregnum.

Tensions did not cease in the county with the conclusion of the row over Bures church; the 1560s were the years when Suffolk was disturbed by 'discention as well for religion as otherwise'. Fuel was added to the fire by John Foxe, whose investigative journalism pitilessly exposed the Marian record of the conservative circle in *Acts and Monuments*. Foxe was in a good position to be accurately informed about East Anglian events; he himself had been the fourth Duke of Norfolk's boyhood tutor, and he was on corresponding terms with Bishop Parkhurst; among his many East Anglian contacts was his publisher John Daye, who had set up as a Suffolk gentleman at Little Bradley. The 1570 edition of Foxe's work doubled the number of references to prominent living East Anglians, once the Howard circle had been humbled in the Duke of Norfolk's fall, but the first English edition of 1563 already contained explosive attacks on people who remained in prominent positions. Among those indicted for their Marian activities were Francis Nunn and Lionel Tollemache, both still active JPs, and the county *custos rotulorum* himself, Sir Clement Higham; retired justices, Sir John Tyrrell and Sir John Sulyard, also came under fire, together with Thomas Symonds, still rector of

---

[138] On John Clyatt at Swilland, see Hengr. 4, fo. 77; on Laurence, CCC, no. 237.
[139] On Laurence, see MacCulloch, 'Catholic and Puritan', pp. 265–7.

Thorndon.[140] Foxe did not escape unscathed from conservative indignation. One lawsuit arose out of a story of a supposed martyr of Wattisham who turned out to have been a common criminal, while Francis Nunn was not a Fellow of Gray's Inn for nothing; a strong attack on his fitness to be a JP quietly disappears from sight after the 1563 edition of *Acts and Monuments*.[141] By contrast, Archdeacon Spencer was one of those spared major attack until the 1570 edition, in the year of his death.[142]

A consistent picture emerges from the 1560s of a conservative gentry circle based on the clientage of the Duke of Norfolk and in particular on the lively and attractive figure of Sir Thomas Cornwallis, retaining its close links with the clerics who had been trained under Bishop Nix. If Catholicism was to survive as a major force in East Anglian life after this, it would be dependent on powerful sympathizers among the leading men to remain at the centre of local affairs and sustain it: hence in considering religious life in the rest of Elizabeth's reign, we will be paying particular attention to the efforts of Cornwallis and his circle to retain their active place in local politics. Cornwallis would remain at the centre of his grouping until his death at an advanced age a year after Queen Elizabeth, his intellectual curiosity and independence of mind preserved to the last:[143] yet by then, he and his acquaintance had lost the battle to remain at the centre of East Anglian life. Although the group was on the defensive throughout the 1560s, it still had the crucial advantage of the Duke of Norfolk's protection; the difference that this made became clear after his fall in the political crisis of 1569–70. Thereafter, despite the temporary success of the conservative rearguard action fought in co-operation with Bishop Edmund Freke during the 1570s and 1580s, the period of uncertainty and religious confusion was over. The established Church had become decisively Protestant, and the main disagreement was on the exact form that this Protestantism should take.

[140] References to standard edition, with page numbers of 1563 edn. in brackets: Foxe, VIII, pp. 493 (1670), 158 (1528), 497 (1672), 462 (1655), 146 (1521), 466 (1657).
[141] John Cowper of Wattisham: cf. Foxe, VIII, pp. 630–1, with BL Harl. 416, fo. 174. Nunn: Foxe, VIII, p. 788.
[142] Foxe, VIII, pp. 492, 496 (1570 edn. pp. 2247–8).
[143] See McGrath and Rowe, 'Cornwallis', and MacCulloch, 'Power, Privilege and the County Community', pp. 139–40.

6

A New World: Recusant and Puritan
1572–1603

In the beginning of the eleventh yeare of her raigne, Cornewallys, Beddingfield, and Silyarde were the first recusants, they absolutely refusing to come to our churches. And untill they in that sort began, the name of recusant was never heard of amongst us.

Thus Lord Chief Justice Coke in reminiscent mood at Norwich in 1606; Coke knew what he was talking about, because his mother-in-law married a Bedingfield and he himself had been brought up in the Cornwallis–Heveningham circle.[1] One should note his precise dating, unexpectedly confirmed as it is from a very different standpoint by Father Robert Parsons, SJ:[2] recusancy emerged before, not as a result of, the political débâcle of 1569, and it was a sign that the tension growing in Suffolk during the 1560s had finally grown too great further to sustain the fiction that all Englishmen were part of a single national church. Henry VIII's dream was shattered for ever. Once the Duke of Norfolk ceased to be able effectively to intervene in East Anglian affairs after his arrest in October 1569, Parkhurst was at last free to respond to the conservative challenge, and he met its new openness with an unwonted vigour of his own. In 1570 he secured the ejection of Archdeacon Wendon for not being in priest's orders, and in the same year came the bonus of Archdeacon Spencer's death. An extraordinary crop of no fewer than seventeen inductions in the Archdeaconry of Sudbury during 1571 must be an indication that Parkhurst was introducing new blood to Spencer's former fief in co-operation with his new Archdeacon, Thomas Aldrich, a reassuringly Protestant academic from Corpus, Cambridge.[3] Going on the

---

[1] *A Charge delivered to the grand jury at the Assizes holden at Norwich 4th August 1606 . . . by the great Lord Coke* (2nd edn. 1813), p. 20. I owe this reference to T. B. Trappes-Lomax, 'Catholicism in Norfolk, 1570–1780', *NA* XXXII (1961), p. 27. On Coke, see below, Ch. 8.
[2] CRS XXXIX (1942), p. 58.
[3] SROB, IC 500/5/1, fos. 236–9ʳ. Aldrich supported Thomas Cartwright in his Cambridge controversies (*Parkhurst* p. 129 n.).

offensive in conservative circles, Parkhurst snubbed Cornwallis when approached for a favour for a Catholic kinsman, Michael Hare's brother, and he lectured young William Playters on the need for conformity to the Elizabethan Settlement. Leading conservative gentlemen like Michael Hare and Cornwallis's son-in-law Thomas Kitson found their candidates for benefices rejected by the Bishop's veto, although Parkhurst's enthusiasm ran away with him when he tried to deprive the geriatric former physician to Anne Boleyn of his rich benefice at Aldeburgh for non-subscription to the Thirty-Nine Articles: Queen Elizabeth was not amused.[4]

Parkhurst was probably responsible for the new effort to staff the East Anglian justices' Benches with reliable Protestants. In Norfolk there is direct evidence for the Bishop's activities; in Suffolk the names tell their own story. Such stalwarts of Elizabethan Puritanism as Roger Lord North, Nicholas Bacon the younger, John Higham, Philip Parker, William Spring, and Robert Forth appeared in commission at this time, and of the remaining seven appointed between 1571 and 1575, only one (Philip Tilney) had Catholic sympathies.[5] Meanwhile both the Bench and the county scene were losing their leading conservatives by a process of attrition. Sir Clement Higham and Lionel Tollemache died in 1571, Thomas Rous and John Blennerhasset in 1573, Robert Gosnold, Sir John Sulyard, and Sir John Tyrrell in 1574, Sir Ralph Chamberlain in 1575. Soon, it might seem, death would remove all the conservative leadership.

However, the situation changed drastically, bringing new hope for the conservative group, when Parkhurst died and was succeeded by Edmund Freke as Bishop. Freke had not shown any marked hostility to Puritanism in his previous see of Rochester, but he was appointed to Norwich with instructions to bring the Puritan movement within bounds.[6] He took to his duties with enthusiasm. It was perhaps hardly surprising that in looking for an ally in his campaign he should turn to the most prominent anti-Puritan in his diocese, Sir Thomas Cornwallis. The 'Anglican' position as such hardly existed in the mid-1570s outside a minority of the clergy; the only definite allies that Freke could hope for against Puritan activists were the conservative gentry. However, the link between Freke and Cornwallis may have been less fortuitous than this. Freke himself was no stranger to East Anglia,

---

[4] On all these moves of Parkhurst, see n. 8 below and *Parkhurst* pp. 122, 188, 146, 148, 243–4.
[5] MacCulloch, 'Catholic and Puritan', p. 234.   [6] Smith, p. 214.

being Essex-born; from the uncanonical age of twelve he had been a
Canon of the Essex Augustinian priory of Leighs, assisting in
alchemical experiments there, and he had been sufficiently enthusiastic
for the monastic life to transfer to the last house to survive in all
England, Waltham Abbey. It is noticeable that among the witnesses of
Archdeacon Spencer's will were his chaplain Thomas Freke and his
servant Michael Freke; what relation did they bear to the then Bishop
of Rochester? The Puritans may not have been so far from the truth
when in a long report of 1579 they depicted the Bishop as being
dominated by Catholic sympathizers.[7]

Certainly the alliance began bearing fruit for the conservative group
soon after Freke's arrival in East Anglia. It was in 1575 that Thomas
Atkinson, a Marian priest who was Thomas Kitson's protégé, was able
to enjoy the second benefice in Kitson's gift to which Parkhurst had
refused to institute him; he would continue on his hedonistic clerical
career there into the 1590s, the only parson of the district to carry on
being addressed in the medieval usage as 'Sir Thomas'. In the same
year, Michael Hare saw his clerk John Spink instituted to the rich
benefice of Saxmundham in his gift, five years after Spink had been
rejected as unsuitable by Parkhurst; in order to clear the way for Spink,
Hare frightened away the substitute minister whom Parkhurst had
presented by lapse.[8] At the same time the new Bishop scandalized the
Bury St Edmunds Bench by showing favour to Sir Thomas
Cornwallis's efforts to get the case of Henry Gibbons dropped;
Gibbons was a bigamous ecclesiastical lawyer who had already been
characterized as 'an enymy to the Gospell' by the Bury JPs before
Parkhurst's death.[9] The infuriated justices claimed that the conduct of
the case before the diocesan ecclesiastical commission had been
designed 'to disgrace the gentlemen of Suffolk' together with
Archdeacon Still of Sudbury, who sympathized with them, and they
noted 'the frowninge displeasure and mischieff afterwards of them that
discharged their duty plainly at the commissioners bord'. To make the
insult plainer, it was claimed that 'Gybons to wynne favour openly at
the bord protested he was sought for Sir Thomas his cause'. The affair
still rankled more than five years later, when the JPs aired their sense

[7] On Freke at Leighs, see Oxley, p. 57. Waltham: Venn, II, p. 176. Spencer's will:
PCC 8 Lyon. Report: PRO, SP 15/25/119. For further convincing proof of Freke's
tolerance of Catholic activity, see *Bacon Papers* II, pp. 274–6.

[8] Atkinson: *Parkhurst* pp. 98–100; PRO, C2 ELIZ A9/64; Hengr. 88/3/32. Spink:
PRO, STAC 5 H45/39, Answer of John Burlingham.

[9] BL Harl. 286, fo. 22ʳ (22 November 1574).

of grievance over the Gibbons case in their reply to the charges brought against them by Freke.[10]

Such were the direct favours which the Bishop performed for the recusant and conservative group in Suffolk in the early years of his episcopate, at the same time as he launched a fierce attack on Puritan preachers particularly in the city of Norwich. Like his predecessor, he also sought to build up a party on the East Anglian Benches favourable to his aims. Not all the appointments during Freke's episcopate could have been in accordance with his plans, for his dubious reputation quickly reached the ears of central authority; however, the additions to the Suffolk Bench in the first three years of the new regime were in marked contrast to those of Parkhurst's last years. In 1575 one of the two new JPs was William Rede, the nourisher of the conservative faction in the great conflict at Beccles over the ownership of common land; in the following year there appeared Sir William Drury, a courtier who would become the scourge of the non-conforming ministers in the Bury area a few years later, John Jerningham of Belton, who was to spend his career on the Bench making the half-hundred of Lothingland safe for recusancy, and Edward Bocking, who during his time on the Essex Bench had been noted as both crypto-Catholic and corrupt.[11] 1577 saw the arrival of Thomas Rivett, a successful local boy turned London merchant who had married the sister of the Catholic Lord Paget.[12] The succession in the same year of firm Puritan Robert Jermyn to his father's place on the Bench was hardly a balance for all these appointments.

By 1578 the government could hardly ignore the fact that Freke's appointment to the diocese of Norwich had succeeded in exacerbating rather than easing its turbulence. The Puritan group in the diocese had plenty of exalted contacts in the Court, and it was at a high level in the Court that a counter-attack was mounted on Freke's activities. This took the form of a royal progress through East Anglia; all such progresses were exercises in propaganda, but this one more than most seems to have been stage-managed from beginning to end as much for the Queen's edification as for her subjects'. The suddenness of the announcement took everyone by surprise; even Lord Keeper Bacon

---

[10] PRO, SP 15/25/119, fo. 9ʳ; BL Eger. 1693, fo. 92ᵛ. NB also that in 1576 Freke's officer licensed the marriage of Anne Moulton and the prominent recusant Edmund Bedingfield, a ceremony performed by a Marian priest according to traditional Catholic rites (PRO, STAC 5 B79/38).

[11] Bateson, 'Original Letters', p. 62.   [12] Metcalfe, p. 205.

sounded confused about it when writing to Cecil. The Puritan group later gave Cecil the credit for engineering the event, although it is likely that the Earl of Leicester also had a hand in it.[13] The Queen's route from Audley End to Norwich through Suffolk was a peculiarly devious one, designed to take her to as many great houses as possible across the confessional spectrum from convinced Puritans to out-and-out recusants.

The Queen's methods of returning thanks for this varied hospitality were the most didactic elements of the progress. The most theatrical episode outside the planned pageantry occurred at Euston, where after Elizabeth had given Edward Rookwood thanks for his entertainment, the Lord Chamberlain berated him for his recusancy, and an image of Our Lady was found hidden, allegedly during a search for a piece of plate, dragged out and burnt in the Queen's presence. The dénouement took place at Norwich, where twenty-three prominent Catholic gentlemen of Norfolk and Suffolk were made to appear before the Council. All but one refused to conform and were subjected to various degrees of confinement, including two of the Queen's Suffolk hosts, Rookwood and Henry Drury of Lawshall.[14] By contrast, Suffolk's five leading Protestant gentlemen, Parker, Jermyn, Higham, Spring, and the younger Nicholas Bacon, received knighthoods, as did the conformists, however lukewarm in their conformity, who entertained the Queen in the journey: Thomas Kitson, Thomas Rivett, and George Colt. The message was clear; conformity was worth the effort. At the same time the Puritan preachers whom Freke had suspended were reinstated, 'a greater and more universal joy to the countries, and the most part of the Court, than the disgrace of the Papists; and the gentlemen of those parts, being great and hot Protestants (almost before by policy discredited and disgraced) were greatly countenanced . . .'. Thus exulted the Protestant fanatic Richard Topcliffe, but Sir Thomas Heneage, who was more likely to understand the manœuvrings of Court life, more pointedly hinted to Walsingham that the Queen was as much under tactful instruction in the progress as her undutiful subjects:

. . . by good meanes her Majesty is brought to beleeve ryght and intreate well

---

[13] For a more detailed account of the progress, see MacCulloch, 'Catholic and Puritan', pp. 237–9. Dr Simon Adams makes the point to me that Leicester was probably involved in the planning of the summer's progress.

[14] Richard Topcliffe to the Earl of Shrewsbury, pr. E. Lodge, *Illustrations of British History* (3 vols. 1838), II, p. 119; *APC* X, pp. 310 ff.

dyvers most zealous and loyall gentlemen of Suffolk and Norfolk whome the foolysh Bisshoppe had malysiously complayned of to her Majesty, as hynderers of her proceedynges and favourers of precyssness, and purytanes, as he calls them . . .[15]

The whole progress represented a serious setback for the Catholic group and for Freke's policy of attacking Puritanism while turning a blind eye to much recusant activity; it is hardly surprising that Sir Charles Framlingham, a fervent anti-Catholic, and Sir Robert Gardiner, who was to become a staunch member of the Bury Protestant 'establishment', first appeared on the Suffolk Bench in this year of humiliation for Freke, while the only new justice in 1579 was Robert Wrott of Gunton, who was eventually to prove one of the agents of the downfall of the Catholic JP John Jerningham of Belton.

The progress represented only one round in the bitter warfare waged by Freke and his conservative allies against the Puritan group, who were well represented in the diocesan ecclesiastical commission (probably thanks to Lord Keeper Bacon), for control over the hearing of ecclesiastical causes in the diocese. This struggle ended in a certain degree of success for Freke in 1580, when his threat to resign the see drove the Privy Council to find an honourable place elsewhere for Freke's front-running enemy, the Puritan Chancellor of the diocese John Becon; the Bishop's nominee William Masters was reappointed.[16] However, the Puritans' guerrilla warfare against their father-in-God was being subsumed into wider conflicts. By 1580, the polarization of the 1560s was returning; the decade would witness a bitter series of conflicts over religion, with the novelty that now they would involve an increasingly influential Puritan group among the county magistracy clashing not only with the bishop but with the central government. The deteriorating foreign situation certainly encouraged opinion in the Council and in Parliament to harden against Catholicism; symptoms of this were seen in the setting-up in 1580 of a state prison for recusants and seminary priests, symbolicly at Framlingham Castle commandeered from the Earl of Arundel,[17] and in the framing of the first draconian statutory penalties for recusancy in 1581. Nevertheless, a disciplinarian group, of whom Bishop Whitgift of London was the most prominent, was increasingly gaining the Queen's ear with its conviction that Puritan deviations were just as harmful to the life of her Church as was Catholicism.

---

[15] PRO, SP 15/25/113.
[16] Smith, pp. 208–28.   [17] *APC* XII, p. 82.

By now clergy and laity with Puritan views on the nature of the church and the world were well established throughout the county. In east Suffolk John Laurence had done his unofficial work well. In Ipswich there seems nothing to suggest that the town's one leading outspoken Elizabethan conservative, William Barber, had much support among his peers. Barber was one of the bailiffs during 1564 and was noted as conservative in religion by Bishop Parkhurst in his Privy Council report on the Suffolk magistracy in that year; in 1568 he refused to pay any contribution to the maintenance of the town's stipendiary preacher, Mr Kelke, and sued one of the town's serjeants who distrained some cloth for Kelke's wages; the corporation had no hesitation in fighting the suit for their officer.[18] When tempers were short in the 1580s over matters of religion, some anonymous opponent of the godly witnessed to the identification of the town's governing élite with the Puritan ministers by producing 'seditious libelles . . . touching the bayliffes portemen prechers and other of this towne', while Professor Collinson's work has produced ample evidence of the enthusiastic support which several leading Ipswich merchants such as John Moore and Robert Barker the younger gave to the Puritan cause.[19] In 1571 the town leadership, no doubt spurred on by the recent unpleasantness over William Barber's intransigence, decided to give statutory authority to previous practice by adding to their Parliamentary Bill for the better paving of Ipswich streets a rather incongruous clause which empowered the churchwardens within the town to levy rates with powers of distraint for the maintenance of parish clergy and church fabric, with the bailiffs as auditors. By the 1580s the borough was maintaining a second preacher out of its rates. This was all part of a tidy scheme of town government also including an elaborate system of subsidized employment and poor relief which was gradually implemented during the second half of the sixteenth century, and which was designed, with considerable success, to turn Ipswich into the model of a well-regulated and godly self-governing community.[20]

In west Suffolk, the leadership of the Bury Bench had swung strongly in favour of radical reformation by the 1580s; after Spencer's

---

[18] Bateson, 'Original Letters', p. 62; Bacon, pp. 276, 278.
[19] *HMC* IX pt. i, p. 255; Collinson, 'Classical Movement', pp. 864–5.
[20] *Stat. Realm* IV, pp. 559–60; Bacon, p. 329; *Poor Relief in Elizabethan Ipswich*, ed. J. Webb, SRS IX (1966). On the Ipswich town preacher's role, see Collinson, *Religion of Protestants*, pp. 170–3.

death, Archdeacons Aldrich and Still were both in succession kindred spirits in their enthusiasm for godly reformation, and they were partnered by Puritan parish clergy of more than local significance like John Knewstub of Cockfield. Why was it, then, that when the struggle over Puritanism developed in the 1580s, it was centred so much in the Bury area rather than in the east? The answer lies in the degrees of religious polarization in all three areas. The Archdeaconry of Suffolk was not coherent enough geographically for its conservative or radical gentry to form parties round a single issue; even the tense atmosphere of the eighties produced only a series of localized clashes, as apparently abstract questions of land and title took on a bitterly sectarian aspect.[21] The only real centre of the east, Ipswich, was firmly under the control of one party and is remarkable by its absence from the battles of Bishop Freke's days. The town's astute choice of Sir Francis Walsingham as High Steward on the death of Sir William Cordell in 1581 contributed to this immunity; Walsingham was naturally fully in sympathy with the radical opinions of the town's oligarchy, no doubt looked after their interests at Court when necessary, and even recommended them a new town preacher when they were looking for someone sufficiently 'godly and learned' in 1585.[22] In Ipswich no real contest was possible, as William Barber had discovered in the 1560s. It is a paradox that conflict centred on the Bury area not because of the strength of the Puritan party there, strong though it was, but because of the strength and coherence of the opposition.

In summer 1582 the Puritan party in Bury collected 174 signatures of inhabitants of Bury to a long and extravagantly worded petition to the Privy Council claiming that their two town preachers, Handson and Gayton, had been harassed out of their cures. In this they named no specific opposition, but spoke vaguely and darkly of 'enemyes' who had sought to remove the ministers by 'a moste subtile and dangerous devise'. This 'devise' was simply that attempted by William Barber in Ipswich some years before: a refusal to contribute to the fund which maintained the two ministers. Its subtlety may therefore have not been very great, but its effect was more significant and more 'dangerous' than at Ipswich; the petitioners had to admit that the plan had been 'verie likelie to have taken effecte, yf god by some good meanes'—no doubt more specifically by some judicious lobbying by the local Puritan

---

[21] See MacCulloch, 'Power, Privilege and the County Community', pp. 150–1.
[22] Bacon, p. 329; *HMC* IX pt. i, p. 252 (1585).

gentry—'had not moved your honnorable affections, by your moste godlie lettres directed to our Justices, and their paineful travailes in the execucion by waie of prevention'. Clearly the opposition to the Puritan party in Bury was far more powerful than at Ipswich if it could nearly succeed in bringing Handson and Gayton down by crippling the collection of their salaries.[23]

Who was leading the opposition in Bury? An obvious front-runner was Bishop Freke's commissary for the Archdeaconry, Dr John Day, who in his efforts to maintain the Bishop's legal jurisdiction in Bury against the encroachments of gentry and archdeacon alike was to suffer insults and the threat of imprisonment. Behind Day there was Thomas Andrews, former servant of the Lord Keeper and a lawyer of some distinction as Clerk on the Western Assize Circuit and from 1578 to 1581, Solicitor to Cambridge University; he was a JP resident in Bury itself. Several sarcastic references in Puritan JPs' vindication of their conduct at the beginning of 1583 testify to their annoyance at Andrews' opposition to their policies after he had put his signature to their stringent local by-laws four years earlier.[24] However, the opposition was wider than that, and related to the constitutional confusion of a town which had never had a proper corporation thanks to the existence of the abbey. The Dissolution had made things worse rather than better, because the second phase of assaults on guilds and chantries had destroyed the Candlemas Guild which the townspeople had developed into a substitute communal organization. The inhabitants had retained a body of feoffees, which had spent the reign of Edward VI buying back as much as possible of the medieval town lands, while at the same time the townsfolk secured the refoundation of the dissolved grammar school in the name of the King.[25] The town's only legal organization was therefore in the hands of the feoffees and of the school governors, despite the quite separate existence of a commission of the peace for the medieval area of the borough, and despite the organization of an informal caucus for 'common conference' from 1570; the consequent constitutional disputes into which Bury fell in the 1580s became inextricably tangled with the county's religious squabbles.[26]

[23] PRO, SP 12/155/5.

[24] BL Eger. 1693, fos. 87–100; on Andrews, see above, Ch. 2, n. 115.

[25] See the papers and accounts of the feoffees, BL Harl. 4626; chantries were granted to the town in 1549 (*CPR Edward VI* II, p. 218), and the new school was founded in 1550 (ibid., III, p. 436). Andrews was a founder governor.

[26] SROB, C2/1, last folio.

PLATES

1. *Brass of the Pounder family, c.1525, Ipswich St Mary Quay*

Thomas Pounder, bailiff of Ipswich 1523–4, d.1525, commissioned this splendid brass from Flanders. His widow Emma survived him until the early 1560s: hence, perhaps, the impossibility of inserting the date of her death in a compatible style. Emma might also by then have objected to being associated with the prominent rosary swinging at her belt, for in 1556 she was scorning the elevation of the Host at Mass (Foxe VIII, p. 599); she was in fact buried at St Clement's Church. St Mary Quay now being redundant, the brass is in High Street Museum, Ipswich. Rubbing by Dr John Blatchly.

2a. *Abbot Reve's Drinking Cup*

This elaborate cup was made for John Reve, last Abbot of Bury, bearing his arms on the shield held by the wild man who forms the knop of the cover; a suitable memorial for a prelate who left a large quantity of wine to various gentlewomen acquaintances in his will of 1540. The present whereabouts of the cup is unknown; this drawing seems to be a copy by Henry Davy made c.1830 from a drawing by the Revd Henry Uhthoff of Huntingfield, when the cup was owned by a descendant of the Reve family, Rowland Burdon of Castle Eden, Co. Durham (BL Add. 19177, fo. 173^r; reproduced by permission of the Trustees of the British Library).

2b. *S. Ward, 'Woe to Drunkards', title-page*

Samuel Ward (1577–1640) was town lecturer at Ipswich 1605–35, and was founder and first custodian of the town library whose first benefactor was William Smart, besides being an original Fellow of Sidney Sussex College; he became a prominent target for William Laud's campaign for conformity in the 1630s. The title-page appeals to its Suffolk audience's vision of a heroic and martial (and, ironically, pre-Reformation) past, and the text is replete with lurid local examples, some supplied to Ward by local JPs. Ward sees towns with zealous preachers as safe from the hazards of drunkenness, but it is also noticeable that he is prepared to quote from the Catholic writer Nicholas Harpsfield. Title-page from first edition of 1622 (STC 25055); a second edition came out 1627.

2c. *Rushbrooke Hall*

Shown here before eighteenth-century alterations, the home of the Jermyns was burnt down during demolition in 1961, and only a well-house remains. Sir Thomas Jermyn's will of 1552 (PCC 33 Powell) mentions 'the newe work' at

Rushbrooke, suggesting that this building was largely of the late 1540s and 1550s; but it was here that Sir Robert Jermyn installed his display of Suffolk heraldry c.1580 (see Ch. 3). This painting, formerly at Hardwicke House, now at the Athenaeum, Bury St Edmunds, is reproduced by permission of St Edmundsbury Borough Council. Photograph by Mr Oswald Jarman.

3. *Monument of Sir John Sulyard d.1574, St Mary's Wetherden*

Sir John was in the Lady Mary's household before her 1553 *coup*, and became Mary's standard-bearer of the Gentlemen Pensioners; his continuing Catholic convictions under Elizabeth are boldly proclaimed by the 'CUIUS ANIME PROPITIETUR DEUS' which ends his tomb's inscription. Some later Puritan zealot, possibly William Dowsing on his destructive official visit of 1643, has rather ineffectually chipped away these words. Sir John kneels in armour in front of his three wives and their children, all thoroughgoing Catholic recusants despite the family's continuing use of this private aisle which they had built for Wetherden church eighty years before. To the east of Sir John's tomb is the tomb-chest of his grandfather, an earlier Sir John (d.1488)—a politic lawyer who served as Chief Justice of the Common Pleas to both Richard III and Henry VII and who had founded the family fortunes at Wetherden. Photograph by Dr John Blatchly.

4a. *Henham Hall: gate façade*

Rebuilt by Charles Brandon, Duke of Suffolk; described in 1538 as 'a faier newe howse well buylded with tymber and fayer lyghtys and at the cummyng in to the Cowrt a faier yate howse of breake newly buylded with iiij turrettes' (PRO, SP 1/242/1, *LP* App. I pt. ii, no. 1311). Burnt down in 1773; its successor was demolished in 1953. This drawing is a copy by Mrs Ann Mills (c.1820) of a drawing by Joshua Kirby, c.1750 (BL Add. 19176, fo. 64; reproduced by permission of the Trustees of the British Library).

4b. *Melton Gaol, 1850*

The building of the gaol for St Audrey's Liberty still survives at Melton, though altered since this water-colour. Structurally it may be fourteenth century. Here the Orford rebels of 1549 brought Thomas Spicer, Lord Willoughby's bailiff, probably alongside many gentry prisoners; Marian martyrs were also brought here, and presumably it also housed the St Audrey quarter sessions before they moved to Woodbridge. Painting by Henry Davy, 1850 (BL Add. 19181, fo. 85; reproduced by permission of the Trustees of the British Library).

1 Brass of the Pounder family, *c.*1525, Ipswich St Mary Quay

2a Abbot Reve's Drinking Cup

2b S. Ward, 'Woe to Drunkards', title page

2c Rushbrooke Hall

3 Monument of Sir John Sulyard *d*.1574, St Mary's Wetherden

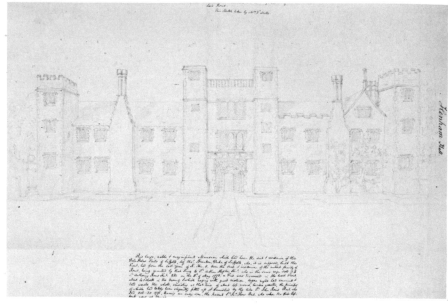

4a Henham Hall: gate façade

4b Melton Gaol, 1850

The conflict came into the open in Bury when in 1581 the Puritans went on the offensive in the Liberty of St Edmund, with Sir Robert Jermyn and his fellow-JPs harassing Dr Day for trying to hold his commissary court; while Gayton preached sermons against the commissary, the JPs bound over Day's brother-in-law, rector of Great Bradley, to keep the peace because he had attempted a counter-attack from the pulpit.[27] During the year, the Puritan group on the Bury Bench was reinforced by the appointment of the young Thomas Crofts, newly out of Lincoln's Inn, to be a justice. Simultaneously one of the leading Puritan ministers of the neighbourhood, Oliver Pigg of Rougham, secured the humiliation before the Privy Council of his unsympathetic patron, Robert Drury, who was withholding tithe in an effort to get rid of him, and it was also at this time that the Council ordered the resumption of the contribution to the Bury preachers' stipends.[28] As yet the justices of assize had not decisively entered the conflict against the Puritans on their visits to Bury, confining themselves during 1581 and 1582 to disciplining Puritan extremists like Robert Browne.[29]

The link with Bury's constitutional problems soon emerged. At the beginning of 1581 Jermyn and Sir John Higham had procured a letter from Burghley to the governors of Bury Grammar School, obliquely criticizing Thomas Andrews's conduct as the leading Governor and adding that the two ministers of the town were reputed to be far less satisfactory than the two preachers, and should be removed if necessary.[30] The relevance of these two issues is not apparent until one appreciates that both the school governors and the town feoffees were the centre of opposition to Puritanism in the town; both were dominated by Andrews and like-minded men. It is noticeable that Sir John Higham ceased to sign the feoffees' accounts between 1580 and 1585, the years when tensions in Bury were at their height, and it was the whole body of school governors headed by Andrews who launched a counter-attack after Burghley's letter.[31] Ostensibly acting as private individuals, they put a Bill of Complaint into Chancery against Andrews's fellow-resident JP, the Puritan champion Thomas Badby.[32]

[27] BL Eger. 1693, fos. 87–100; BL Lansd. 33/20–2.
[28] *APC* XIII, pp. 46, 133; PRO, SP 12/155/10.
[29] BL Lansd. 33/20; *HMC Salisbury* II, p. 509.   [30] SROB, E5/9/103.
[31] Feoffees' account-book, SROB 1150/1, unfol. (on loan only). I am most grateful to Mrs Margaret Statham for our discussions of the constitutional position in Bury.
[32] PRO, C3/205/104. For a detailed account of the case, see MacCulloch, 'Catholic and Puritan', pp. 271–2.

Badby, with a certain symbolism, lived in a mansion converted from part of the massive ruins of the Abbey which remained the physical focus for the town, and the issue at stake had nothing to do with the running of Bury Grammar School; it concerned the high-handed manner in which he had misused the great town churchyard and the outbuildings of the two parish churches which flanked it in front of the ruined west front of the abbey church. Andrews and his fellows were successful in their aim; it was with this case in the background as well as for the accusation that he had harassed a conformist minister out of Bury that Badby was dismissed from the commission of the peace in 1582. He was never to be reappointed before his death in December 1583, when he was buried in Sir Robert Jermyn's parish church at Rushbrooke with a memorial brass that still survives.[33]

Badby's humiliation was one indication that things were beginning to go badly wrong for the Puritans during 1582. Their covert moves to set up a 'presbytery in episcopacy', planned at a meeting this year at Knewstub's parsonage at Cockfield, were now being countered by Whitgift's growing power.[34] In contrast to the Puritan success in adding an ally to the commission of the peace in 1581, Freke and his associates now excelled themselves, not only getting rid of Badby but adding Sir Thomas Kitson's newly-wed son-in-law Charles Cavendish, the Howard Earl of Arundel's legal adviser and family friend Sir Thomas Gawdy, and Robert Gosnold, heir of a former conservative on the Elizabethan Bench. In the same year, with what can only have been intended as a deliberate insult to the Bury Puritans, Bishop Freke placed Giles Wood, Sir Thomas Cornwallis's rector at Brome, as minister at St James Bury St Edmunds to replace the Puritan nominee. It is odd that the Puritans should not have pointed out Wood's Cornwallis connection when justifying their opposition to him rather than merely castigating him as 'a very simple yonge man' established by 'diverse irreligious persones of the towne'.[35] Possibly they felt that while attacks on Thomas Andrews as an active combatant were permissible, there was no point in breaching the county gentry's reputation for courtesy if Cornwallis was not openly involved in their affairs. Yet worse was to come for them; most significant index of the

---

[33] *HMC Salisbury* II, p. 536. It may also be significant that Sir Nicholas Bacon the younger does not appear to have been immediately reappointed to the commission of the peace after his shrievalty year of 1581–2.

[34] Collinson, *Puritan Movement*, pp. 218–20.

[35] BL Eger. 1693, fo. 91ᵛ. Wood was rector of Brome 1582–1600 (Venn IV, p. 451).

fact that they had lost the initiative in lobbying at Court was the pricking as sheriff on 5 December 1582 of Sir William Drury of Hawstead.

Sir William was head of the only major family group of the Bury area which was neither Puritan nor wholly recusant in sympathy, grandson of the earlier Sir William who had been one of the leaders of Marian Suffolk.[36] He married one of Elizabeth's Ladies of the Bedchamber and besides being a trusted military commander he was a familiar figure at Court, regularly exchanging New Year presents with the Queen; this eminence may explain why there are so few open references to him in the war of words over Bury. His uncle Henry Drury was the only out-and-out recusant of the family, while his near neighbour, uncle by marriage and distant cousin Robert Drury of Rougham was a stern foe of Puritan ministers. Robert's appearance at the Council Board for his persecution of the minister Oliver Pigg had been one of the Puritan successes of their year of aggression in 1581, and it is interesting to note that when a servant of Sir Thomas Kitson was reminiscing about the Bury stirs of the early eighties in a West Country inn at the end of the decade, he made the hostility between Drury and Pigg into the centrepiece of the whole conflict, implying that Sir Robert Jermyn's humiliation at the Bury assizes of summer 1583 was the result of his championship of Pigg.[37] This may have been an exaggeration encouraged by the remarkable coincidence of meeting the ex-minister of Rougham in a Dorset town, but it may also suggest that the Drurys' part in the Bury stirs was larger than appears at first sight. Henry Drury of Lawshall was likewise the *éminence grise* of the parish conflict at Lawshall; here the conservatism of the rector appointed by Henry had driven the Puritan party in the parish to start their own lecture in 1582, while at the same time crypto-Catholics monopolized parish offices. The struggle at Lawshall was to follow much the same lines in miniature as that at Bury, with increasing harassment of the godly party in the courts prolonged at least into early 1585.[38]

With a certain inevitability, Sir William's cousin Robert Drury appeared in commission in 1583, despite his recent admonition by the

[36] On the Drurys, see J. Cullum, *The History and Antiquities of Hawsted . . .* (1813).

[37] PRO, SP 12/223/83. It is interesting to note that Robert Drury had a copy of the epitaph of Sir William's grandfather, the elder Sir William, hanging in his parlour at Rougham: 'Chitting', p. 119.

[38] BL Add. 38492, fos. 107–8, and MacCulloch, 'Catholic and Puritan', p. 254.

Privy Council, while on his appointment as Sheriff, Sir William brought that pioneer of the art of detection, Richard Bancroft, back to Bury. Bancroft had already been a shocked witness of the humiliation of Dr Day's brother-in-law in 1581, and it was probably Day who recommended him to Sir William; Day and Bancroft had worked together on an archiepiscopal visitation of the diocese of Peterborough.[39] It was Bancroft who pointed out the extraordinary biblical quotation painted round the new set of royal arms, symbol of the Act of Supremacy, in St Mary's church. The inscription, from Revelation 2, was a description of the Laodicean Church as neither hot nor cold, but it was soon discovered that the original intention had been to put up a quotation from the following chapter, an even less flattering character-ization of the Church at Thyatira. There could have been nothing more calculated to infuriate the Queen than a double insult both to her religious settlement and to her coat armour. The outrage had been paid for by a Bury bookbinder, Thomas Gibson, who turned out to be a follower of the separatist minister Robert Browne, and an associate of other sectaries, Henry Copping and Elias Fawker, in distributing Brownist books.[40] It was the perfect opportunity for the anti-Puritan party to exploit; for years there had been trouble with sectaries at Bury, Copping and another having been in prison for separatist activity since 1578. They were an embarrassment to the orthodox Puritans of the Bury area; Sir Robert Jermyn had sent for Browne on one of his visits to Bury in 1581 to warn him to show care in his proceedings. Nevertheless, Jermyn emphasized in his report to Burghley that there were many godly and reasonable points in Browne's views.[41] However, the extremists had remained extremists, whose activities were worthy of suppression but whose conventicles could not readily be connected with the Puritan leadership. It was only when the extremists moved into the public arena and into the parish church itself that the opposition could represent the Puritan justices as endangering local order by their countenancing of such men.

With Sir William Drury as the willing agent of discipline within the county, the stage was set for the opponents of the Puritans to turn their

---

[39] Bancroft's account of the Bury stirs is to be found in *Tracts ascribed to Richard Bancroft* p. 71 (qu. Collinson, 'Classical Movement', pp. 902, 918). Details of a case in Chancery over the excommunication of Bancroft while on the Peterborough visitation with Day were reused for notes on one of the Beccles law-suits of the 1580s, Bec. A4/46.

[40] BL Lansd. 36/65.

[41] BL Eger. 1693, fo. 91^r; BL Lansd. 33/13. Jermyn: Lansd. 33/67.

reverses of 1581 into a strong offensive. In January 1583 Bishop Freke drew up a list of complaints against the high-handed administration of the Bury Puritan JPs stretching back over five years.[42] This was not so serious for Jermyn and his fellows; Freke's independent credit at Court was low, and over the previous months Burghley and Walsingham had lent sympathetic ears to the complaints which they had made.[43] Even while the Puritan gentry were answering Freke's articles at least to their own satisfaction, in February the Privy Council could still send a letter to Freke's anti-Puritan diocesan Chancellor ordering him to treat the case between Robert Drury and Oliver Pigg fairly, using language distinctly hostile to Drury.[44]

However, more powerful forces than Freke were at work. Professor Collinson pointed out that of the assize judges who rode the Eastern Circuit during Elizabeth's reign, Edward Anderson was the only one to be appointed while still only a serjeant; he can only have been chosen for his resolution against the Puritan cause. His colleague Sir Christopher Wray was equally concerned for the suppression of nonconformity, and obviously found Sir William Drury a congenial figure; years later his son would marry Drury's daughter. Anderson joined Wray for the Eastern Circuit in the tense year of 1581, and Bishop Freke was already expressing his gratitude for their work in disciplining the followers of Browne in the summer assizes that year.[45] Nevertheless the assize judges had avoided direct confrontation with the Puritan élite during 1581 and 1582. In the summer of 1582 Wray took the most unusual step of ordering the Sheriff to make preparations to hold the summer assizes at Newmarket rather than Bury; afterwards the judges travelled directly up the Mildenhall road to the Thetford assizes without ever visiting Bury, presumably to avoid any trouble that their presence might have caused in the explosive state of Bury politics.[46] There is no record of unusual disciplinary proceedings at these assizes.

After Bancroft's discoveries and the discrediting of Thomas Badby, the atmosphere was different at the Lent assizes of 1583. The

---

[42] BL Eger. 1693, fos. 89–100, with the géntry's answers; another copy is to be found in BL Lansd. 37/28.

[43] BL Eger. 1693, fo. 87; *HMC Salisbury* II, p. 535.

[44] PRO, SP 12/158/79.

[45] BL Lansd. 33/20; for the Wray/Drury marriage, see C. Dalton, *History of the Wrays of Glentworth* (2 vols., 1880), I, p. 67.

[46] Hengr. 15, fo. 63, and see MacCulloch, 'Catholic and Puritan', p. 276 n. The possibility that this evasive action was to avoid plague does not seem likely.

separatists Copping, Fawker, and Gibson were tried for dispersing Browne's books and Gibson for setting up the inscription in St Mary's, but while Oliver Pigg managed to secure a conditional discharge from a suit of Robert Drury, several other ministers were indicted or bound over. The situation was to worsen for the Puritans. Even before Whitgift's final capture of the see of Canterbury in August and September 1583 on the death of the unhappy Grindal, the summer assizes had witnessed an extraordinarily dramatic humiliation for the Suffolk Puritan ministers and their gentry allies at the hands of Wray and Anderson.[47] As far as the ministers were concerned, five of Suffolk's leading clergy found themselves imprisoned on a variety of charges of nonconformity. At least three of them, Oliver Pigg, William Fleming of Beccles, and John Knight of Palgrave, were involved in fierce local disputes which had escalated far beyond religious controversy, but that did not prevent the five being incarcerated with an extremist minister whose wild words Lord Chief Justice Wray quoted to Burghley with gloomy relish and who was regarded by his more conventional fellow-prisoners with embarrassment and alarm lest 'his doinges shalbe reported to our discredit'.[48] Many other ministers and laymen were indicted but not imprisoned; Copping, Fawker, and Gibson were convicted and the first two summarily executed.

Robert Drury celebrated a triple triumph, for not only had he finally secured Pigg's imprisonment, Sir William Drury as Sheriff steadfastly ignoring Pigg's pleas for liberty, but he had also at last obtained Pigg's removal from Rougham and the induction of his own nominee, Richard Garnet; most spectacularly of all, he joined the Bury leaders on the justices' Bench. 'O it is a wofull thing to our contrie that Mr. Drurie is in the comission of the peace', lamented Pigg to Walsingham from Bury Gaol.[49] If this were not galling enough for Drury's new colleagues, Sir Robert Jermyn and Sir John Higham were made the scapegoats for the confusions of recent years in the Bury area and left

[47] On the two assizes, see BL Lansd. 38, fo. 162; PRO, SP 12/161/63. The proclamation of 30 June declaring books by Browne and Harrison seditious and schismatic (*Tudor Royal Proclamations* II, pp. 501–2) was clearly designed to strengthen the hands of Wray and Anderson. As a souvenir of the affair, Bancroft treasured a copy of one of Browne's works given him by Wray the day after the second execution: S. L. Babbage, *Puritanism and Richard Bancroft* (1962), p. 21 n.

[48] PRO, SP 12/161/33. On these ministers, cf. *Seconde Parte* I, pp. 160–4.

[49] PRO, SP 12/161/63. Garnet had been mentioned by the Privy Council as Drury's nominee at the beginning of the year (PRO, SP 12/158/79). John Jerningham of Belton was restored to the commission at the same time as Drury was introduced.

out of the new commission of the peace;[50] worse still, Judge Anderson made Jermyn serve on a jury in a *nisi prius* case before him. It is true that this was a preliminary to a nationwide effort in 1584 to encourage men of substance to sit on trial juries,[51] but in the circumstances it cannot have been taken as anything else than the humiliation which was intended. The fact that seven leading recusant gentry were also disciplined by Wray and Anderson can have been little consolation.

The events of 1583 produced an unwonted county-wide sense of solidarity. Primarily this was brought about by the justices of assize themselves shifting the focus of attention away from the internal quarrels of the town and district of Bury St Edmunds and onto the assizes, the two occasions in the year when the county gentry united across the boundary between east and west to participate in three days of ceremonial, socializing, and legal business. The Lent assizes of 1583 had shown the county justices the way that matters were tending, for at the beginning of the summer assizes the assize judges were visited by a high-powered delegation of fifteen 'principall men of Suffolk' headed by Lord North and including seven of the thirteen knights in commission in east and west. The group asked Wray and Anderson to 'handell trifling matters the more kindly' for their sakes, 'not willing to cross them'. The judges, perhaps resenting the slight hint of menace in the gentlemen's reminder that the JPs' Bench had 'equall auctorite' with themselves, 'did not only uncurteusly denie all oure requests, but handeled all those causes with most severite', as we have already seen. Lord North, himself smarting with indignation from the assize judges' public reproof to the Cambridgeshire Bench for wrongly condemning a petty thief to death, reported all this to Burghley, adding that if the judges were to 'hold on their former cowrce, no dowt yt ys like to breke to some sutch unkindnes as will not be liked'.[52] The very awkwardness of his phrase gives some indication of how dangerous the atmosphere had become among the Suffolk JPs after their outrageous treatment.

Neither the vicissitudes of John Laurence in the east nor of the Bury ministers in the west had produced protests outside the areas in which they operated, but the assize judges had attacked on a county-wide front. The first sign of the county leaders' new unanimity came in the shape of a letter of protest about the assizes to the Privy Council; it was

---

[50] PRO, SP 12/223/83.
[51] M. Campbell, *The English Yeoman* (1960), p. 304.
[52] BL Harl. 6993, fo. 61; see MacCulloch, 'Catholic and Puritan', p. 278 n.

signed by ten leading Suffolk gentlemen including seven of the fifteen muster commissioners, five names from west Suffolk, five from east. The document was widely circulated at the time and predates the rush of petitions from all over south-east England which resulted from Archbishop Whitgift's drive against Puritan ministers; its highly emotional tone reflected the overwrought state of the Suffolk magistracy.[53] Nevertheless the impassioned outburst did not go unheard at the Council Board, where, if contemporary gossip reported in an Ellesmere MS account can be believed, Burghley and other leading privy councillors were doing their best to assuage the Queen's wrath against the Suffolk Puritan élite.[54] At no stage had the Council lost its sympathy for the Suffolk Puritans, and now its response was to send a letter to Wray and Anderson suggesting that the charges against the ministers had been produced by informers and inquests 'not so well disposed in religion' and 'in love with the licence of former times'. The assize judges were told to examine the motives of such informers and to treat the ministers 'according to ther quality, not matching them at barr or in the indightment with roges, fellons, or papistes', a clear echo of a phrase in the Suffolk justices' letter and as such an implied reproof to Wray and Anderson.[55]

After this Council letter, the main impetus of the attack on the beleaguered Puritan gentry and their ministers no longer came from the assize judges, although the Ellesmere account already cited suggests that they were responsible for the executions of two more separatists at the summer assizes of 1584, but rather from the newly-appointed Archbishop of Canterbury. Whitgift's wholesale suspension of ministers for refusal to subscribe to his articles at the beginning of 1584 brought a storm of protest and a further series of petitions, including one from the recalcitrant ministers of Suffolk, and led to his

---

[53] BL Harl. 367, fo. 24; BL Lansd. 109/10; Petyt 538 vol. 47, no. 20; PRO, SP 12/243/25; All Souls' College Oxford MS 150, fo. 24; Bodl. MS Douce 393, fo. 129; Anon., *A Parte of a Register* (1593, *S.T.C.* 10400), pp. 128 f. The copies contain quite substantial variations, but BL Harl. 367 gives the signatures, albeit in garbled form. Signatories from the west: Sir Robert Jermyn, Sir John Higham, Robert Ashfield, William Clopton, Thomas Poley. From the east: Sir Robert Wingfield, Sir Nicholas Bacon, Sir Philip Parker, Robert Forth, and Richard Wingfield. For further discussion, see Conclusion below.

[54] Huntington Library Ellesmere MS 2067C, fos. 34^v, 50^v, pr. *Transactions of the Congregational Historical Society* XV (1945–6), p. 65.

[55] Petyt 538, vol. 47, no. 20; other copies are to be found in All Souls' College Oxford MS 150, fo. 24 and pr. in *A Parte of a Register* p. 131 (I owe these latter two references to Collinson, 'Classical Movement', p. 912).

celebrated quarrel with Robert Beale, the Puritan secretary of the Council.[56] By the summer, the efforts particularly of Burghley, 'whome God hath stirred up to be a meane for the ministers of Norfolk and Suffolke' had secured a compromise which freed practically all the ministers from suspension, but at least two, William Fleming of Beccles and John Holden of Bildeston, went on to face deprival in July; of these two, Fleming at least was the victim of the passions engendered in the old disputes which racked his town.[57]

Compromise there may have been by the summer, but neither ministers nor gentry were any less indignant at their treatment over the previous two years. It is during this summer that the first evidence appears of the great Puritan surveys of the Church's ministry which were to be compiled over the next few years to reveal the inadequacies of the established religion: on 23 August 1584 two members of the Dedham Classis reported to their brethren that they had 'delt with the gentlemen in Suffolke about the number of ill mynisters as it was before appointed'.[58] The only part of this survey surviving from Suffolk, for the hundred of Risbridge, is less detailed than those from other counties, but like them, it was not merely an attack on supposedly inadequate clergy; it also reflected on the patrons who had chosen them.[59] In effect the Puritans were doing the same thing that Freke and Whitgift attempted when they sought to discipline radicals in the ministry: interfering, as spiritual and geographical outsiders, in the affairs of gentlemen. Conformist patrons suffered implied criticism just as much as papist-sympathizing patrons: John le Hunt, for example, brother-in-law of Foxe's publisher, contributor to *Acts and Monuments* and proud owner of 'The Rhenishe Testament well and worthely answered by that learned and grave man Mr. Doctor Fowlke', was by implication responsible for the 'scandalous' minister in his living of Little Bradley.[60] The whole exercise constituted a belligerent statement that those who were not with the Puritans were against them, and this was bound to strike home.

[56] Collinson, *Puritan Movement*, pp. 249–72; *Bacon Papers* II, p. 282.

[57] *Seconde Parte* I, pp. 241, 244. On Fleming and Beccles, see MacCulloch, 'Power, Privilege and the County Community', pp. 306–7.

[58] *Dedham Classis*, p. 38.

[59] BL Add. 38492, fo. 90, among the papers of Edward Lewkenor of Denham, which Collinson cites as a typical file of papers for the 1584 Parliament: Collinson, *Puritan Movement*, p. 280. Cf. MacCulloch, 'Catholic and Puritan', p. 281, for details of patronage, but NB that it was the Peyton and not the Kitson family who presented Oliver Phillips at Great Bradley.

[60] Metcalfe, p. 146; Foxe, V, p. 345; PCC 50 Strafford.

The whole course of the stirs in west Suffolk implies this. Religious conservatives were thrown into alliance with anti-Puritans. One or two papist sympathizers can be identified among the town feoffees and school governors at Bury; of those who brought the 1581 Chancery suit against Thomas Badby, Anthony Payne was the brother of the deceased conservative JP Henry Payne, and Roger Potter was an absentee from church and communion during the 1570s. However, Thomas Andrews himself was no Catholic, directing in his will of 1585 that he should be buried in the churchyard of St James 'without any superstition or sumptuous pompe'; what seems to have united them was resentment that others were trying to interfere with the town institutions which they had so painstakingly rescued from the Dissolution wreckage.[61] The same group of Puritan local gentry against whom they combined would later join in obstructing their successors' attempts to secure a true corporation on the basis of these institutions (below, Ch. 11). Similarly, the Bury conflicts reveal an interesting degree of co-operation between a new generation of anti-Puritan clergy and Catholic sympathizers among the Suffolk gentry.

Leading Catholics like Michael Hare, Sir Thomas Cornwallis, and Sir Thomas Kitson had inherited considerable parish patronage; they used this not only to appoint Marian clergy whom they could regard as in valid orders, but also new clergy who might be seen as the first Anglicans. Nicholas Cannop, for instance, was inducted thanks to Michael Hare to a Howard living at Rendham in 1571, and he then replaced Hare's clerk John Spink at Hare's living of Saxmundham in 1584; he named one of his own sons Michael, and qualified for a bequest of a ring in Hare's will of 1611. Hare's servant Henry Cannop, who was bequeathed Hare's library of theological and other books, may well have been Nicholas's son Henry, a Caius graduate who was incumbent of Hare's own home parish of Bruisyard from 1598.[62] It was notorious, claimed Bishop Freke's opponents in 1578, that Cornwallis bestowed his benefices 'upon papish idiotes, non residentes or unlerned instrumentes'; it is not certain into which category we should fit Giles Wood, Cornwallis's rector at Brome from 1582, and long a trusted figure in the Cornwallis family circle.[63] Wood stood

[61] Potter: *Miscellanea*, ed. C. Talbot, CRS LIII (1960), p. 110. Andrews's will: Muskett III, p. 25.
[62] Venn I, p. 288; Hare's will, PCC 38 Wood.
[63] PRO, SP 15/25/119, fo. 14^v; for Wood's attendance on one of the Cornwallis family in 1594, Hengr. 88/2/85.

surety for Dr Day when the Puritan justices bound him to good behaviour in 1581, and Bishop Freke put him in the thick of the Bury conflict, but as a Cambridge graduate and apparently the holder of a doctorate, he was hardly 'an unlearned instrument'.[64] Similarly Oliver Phillips, the Cambridge don who was Dr Day's brother-in-law and who so infuriated the Puritan justices by his sermon in St Mary's in 1581, spent much of his career in Kitson livings: Westley in 1587 and Fornham All Saints, at the gates of the Kitson family home, in 1618. In view of these conjunctions, the future Archbishop Bancroft's links with Day and Phillips become all the more significant. The long-term reaction within the Church of England against Calvinist orthodoxy and against the godly establishment of Elizabeth's day may not have been as far from the shadowy world of Catholic recusancy as has sometimes been imagined.

The capabilities of Puritan and anti-Puritan groups after five years of growing conflict would be put to the test in the campaigning which took place for the elections to Parliament during autumn 1584. This is the first county election for Suffolk in which there is good evidence of a genuine contest at the polls.[65] Evidently Jermyn and Higham stood against their Bury opponent of 1583, Sir William Drury, and the various elements backing Drury—his friends, his tenants, perhaps a hint of Court interest, those who resented the Puritan group in the county—proved stronger; Drury came first in the poll, Jermyn second. Higham had to console his prestige a fortnight later with election as one of the two MPs for the county's leading parliamentary borough Ipswich—doubtless a pre-arranged provision for defeat in the county. The other boroughs had also delayed their elections until after the county contest, perhaps so that their patrons could see the result, and they seem to have taken their cue from the partial Puritan reverse. In this county which was supposed to be the heartland of Puritanism in eastern England, where so many gentry were enthusiastic for radical reformation and which had perhaps given the government more trouble in this respect than any other county, the Suffolk boroughs produced only one other well-known Puritan name as an MP: Sir Robert Jermyn's half-brother Henry Blagg at Sudbury. Edward Lewkenor of Denham, one of the sponsors of the surveys of the ministry, had to find a seat at Maldon in Essex, and it is notable that in

[64] BL Lansd. 33/21; Venn IV, p. 451.
[65] For a detailed reconstruction of events, see MacCulloch, 'Catholic and Puritan', pp. 282–3.

'Puritan' Essex too, the Puritans suffered a reverse in the shire election.[66] Their activity had stirred up no mean opposition.

Nevertheless, Blagg, Higham, and Jermyn were safely in Parliament, and there they proved themselves active members—more so than Sir William Drury, who is only recorded as sitting on the Committee to consider a Bill for Suffolk cloths, a measure which would automatically demand his attention as knight of the shire, and the Committee for continuing various statutes. Blagg's abuse of a speech of Archbishop Whitgift caught the attention of one Parliamentary diarist; Higham concerned himself, predictably, with committees considering such subjects as impropriate parsonages, Jesuits, and the seizure of recusant armour—appropriate concerns for the Governor of the recusant prison at Wisbech Castle and a county recusant commissioner—besides a committee dealing with a bill for the preservation of grain and game. Both he and Jermyn were among a delegation sent on 15 February to discuss a dispute over business with the Lords. Jermyn showed his interest in ecclesiastical reform by sitting on committees considering pluralities and marriage licences as well as the two committees of which Sir William Drury was member, but in early March he had to retire home to recover his never very robust health.[67]

The shifting fortunes, moves and counter-moves in the Bury stirs are reminders that there was always more than one road to Westminster in the Tudor period. Jermyn and Higham might have been publicly humiliated at the 1583 assizes, but they had become too central to local administration to be dispensed with entirely; the weird result was that while they spent most of the next decade excluded from the commission of the peace, they remained commissioners for musters and subsequently became deputy lieutenants, more exalted places than those of mere JPs. They also remained commissioners for examining recusants;[68] most ironically of all, in 1584 Jermyn was included in the commission for examining the defences of Lothingland which secured the removal of the crypto-Catholic John Jerningham from the commission of the peace in the following year.

The coastal half-hundred of Lothingland provides a microcosm of the changing fortunes of Catholicism in Suffolk during Elizabeth's

[66] Collinson, *Puritan Movement* p. 278.

[67] D'Ewes, *Journals*, pp. 334, 337, 343, 349, 352, 360, 363, 368. On Blagg, see J. E. Neale, *Elizabeth I and her Parliaments* (2 vols., 1953–7), II, p. 66.

[68] BL Harl. 474.

reign.[69] It was practically an island, projecting north-east of Suffolk along the Norfolk border, an ideal place for piracy and clandestine activities with a centuries-old tradition of enmity between its chief town Lowestoft and the port of Yarmouth facing Lothingland across the river estuary in Norfolk. It was dominated by the great clan of Jerningham, who leased it from the Crown and who like many of the leading gentry of the Yare and Waveney basins, remained overwhelmingly Catholic in sympathy throughout Elizabeth's reign. Death and judicious weeding of the commission of the peace had removed the Jerninghams from the justices' Bench during the 1560s, but that left a vacuum which worried Bishop Parkhurst in his later emancipated years: 'ther is a place in Suffolk called Lothinglande where are many stubborne people neither religious nor otherwise wel disposed, the cause is (as I take it) the wante of a good justice'. Parkhurst's own suggestion to fill the gap, Edward Spany, was not taken up, either because of the Bishop's death or because Spany's foothold in Lothingland rested on a shady and sharply contested title at law; Bishop Freke was to find a characteristically different answer to the problem by seeing to the appointment of John Jerningham of Belton, younger son of the deceased JP Sir John, and a royal pensioner under a grant from Queen Mary.[70]

In 1579 Jerningham's monopoly of influence was challenged by the appointment of Robert Wrott of Gunton as JP: an unusual appointment, for Wrott was the son of a mere husbandman and was the only non-armigerous man to be appointed to the Suffolk Bench during Elizabeth's reign. The explanation is that he was the heir of Parkhurst's former nominee Edward Spany, and was currently engaged in complex litigation with the Jerninghams over Lothingland common land.[71] With these two as JPs, the situation rapidly deteriorated; in 1581 the Privy Council ordered a county-wide commission of JPs, excluding both Jerningham and Wrott, to examine a riot on the disputed common land, and did their best to detect and

[69] For a detailed account of Lothingland, see MacCulloch, 'Catholic and Puritan', pp. 241–6.

[70] On Spany, *Parkhurst* p. 159, and his title: PRO, C2 ELIZ D5/28. Jerningham: *CPR Philip and Mary* I, p. 318.

[71] Wrott's father John described as husbandman of Bungay, 1542: PRO STAC 2/27/132; his grant of arms 1581 (Corder, *Dictionary*, col. 418). He refers to his mother as Bridget Spany in his will (PCC 91 Leicester), although she was the daughter of John Hervey of Ickworth. Wrott was a client of Leicester's, receiving a grant of the fines of the Hanaper with Thomas Dudley in 1586 (*ex inf.* Dr Simon Adams); he should not be confused with the better-known Robert Wroth of Middlesex.

break up a recusant communications system based on the island.[72] In the following year on the same common, John Jerningham was alleged to have personally assaulted the Protestant ex-High Constable John Arnold whom he had earlier dismissed; this may have led to his temporary suspension from the commission of the peace. With its close proximity to the port and magazine of Yarmouth, Jerningham's turbulent fief was becoming an obvious security risk, more reminiscent of the situation in parts of Lancashire than anywhere in the Lowland zone.

The Privy Council finally took action in May 1584 by ordering a report on the defences of the island of Lothingland. The opportunity was gleefully seized by three of west Suffolk's leading Puritans, Sir Robert Jermyn, Robert Ashfield, and Thomas Poley, reinforced by Robert Wrott, to prepare a devastating indictment of Jerningham's misgovernment.[73] They took care to expose the leading Catholic sympathizers in Lothingland, including Spencer's old associate John Hoo and the estate management of Henry Jerningham, the head of the family, who still presided at a distance over the island from his Norfolk residence at Costessey. The Jerningham group must have put up a struggle to avoid nemesis, but in the next year, with support no longer available from Freke, a follow-up letter from the enquiry commissioners was enough finally to ensure Jerningham's removal from the Bench.[74] Perhaps understandably, Wrott preferred to live outside the island at Bungay towards the end of his life, but that did not save him from a violent death in 1589.[75] Despite the renewed outbreak of lawlessness after his death he was not replaced as a JP until 1596, by John Wentworth, a wealthy self-made lawyer who although he owed his rise and residence in the island to the patronage of the Earl of Arundel and the local Catholic network, never showed any tendency away from conformity in later life. Under the early Stuarts his son Sir John succeeded where Elizabethan administration had failed; he 'brought good preachers into that Island of Lothingland, and ther was the chief patron of religion and honestye in his time'.[76] Lothingland's deep-seated alliance of archaic localism and religious conservatism could only be tamed, and the area brought within the bounds of the maturing

---

[72] *APC* XIII, pp. 143, 299.
[73] PRO, SP 12/171/63, extensive extracts of which are pr. *PSIA* XX (1928), pp. 1 ff.
[74] PRO, SP 12/178/63.
[75] SP 12/281/88. He was described as of Bungay in his will.
[76] BL Add. 15520, fos. 21ᵛ–22ʳ. On the elder John, see *Chorography* p. 118.

county community, by an energetic local gentleman who was prepared to challenge the old ways.

Freke's departure had been the turning-point in the fortunes of Lothingland Catholicism, and so it proved elsewhere. Worn out by the struggles in his diocese and increasingly outmanœuvred at Court, he was finally heeded in his pleas for an easier place in autumn 1584 and was safely translated to Worcester in December.[77] His successor, Edmund Scambler, had been the leader of a clandestine congregation in London in the time of Queen Mary, and was unlikely either to be well-disposed to the Catholic group or to wish to antagonize the Puritan gentry; for all his heroic past, he was now an old man whose main concern was to set up his family as gentry at the expense of the diocesan revenues.[78] Besides wanting a quiet life generally, Scambler took much less interest in Suffolk than in Norfolk; on a request from the Privy Council in 1587, he gave a detailed report on the religious views of Norfolk JPs, but simply reported that as far as Suffolk was concerned, all was well.[79] There does not seem to have been any systematic effort to rid the Bench of Freke's former nominees.

Another enemy to the Puritan group was soon to disappear, for the summer assizes of 1585 were the last at which Sir Edward Anderson appeared on the Eastern Circuit. Although Wray continued until the Lent assizes of 1592, the hated Anderson, 'the hottest mane that I did ever se sitt in Judgment' in the view of Lord North,[80] was replaced by William Periam, who had married Lord Keeper Bacon's daughter; he was a decidedly more sympathetic figure. Periam was to support the Bury JPs in their opposition to Sir Arthur Heveningham's schemes for county road repair in the 1590s, and one of Periam's last acts as circuit judge was to secure a place on the Bench for his brother-in-law Edward Bacon, the least distinguished of the old Lord Keeper's sons; indeed in his will Edward left a bequest 'to my most lovinge and deere Sister the Ladie Peryam to whome I have been bound above all

---

[77] There were already reliable rumours of his going in March 1584 (*Bacon Papers* II, p. 286).

[78] *DNB*, s.v. Scrambler, Edmund; on his depredations and nepotism, see Bodl. MS Gough Norfolk 43, fo. 3, and Heal, pp. 229, 340. Scrambler's refusal of a licence to travel to the confined recusant Henry Hobart in 1588 shows that he was not inclined to do favours for the Catholic group (PRO, STAC 5 H5/12, Complaint of James Hobart).

[79] BL Lansd. 52, fos. 200–1; ibid., 53, fo. 187ᵛ.

[80] BL Harl. 6993, fo. 61. But Anderson continued to be named to the Cambridgeshire and Norfolk commissions of the peace between Wray and Periam until at least 1591, and quite probably 1592, the year that Periam left the circuit. What does this imply?

others'.[81] Within a year both bishop and assize judges had become less of a threat to the integrity of the county community.

There was a further source of distraction from the troubles of the county. At the end of 1585, the Puritans discovered a cause still greater than the griefs of the English Church: Leicester's expedition to the Low Countries. Jermyn and his half-brother Blagg sailed with Leicester's forces, accompanied by their brother William Jermyn and the veteran west Suffolk Protestant Thomas Poley; Sir Robert was commanding one of the troops of horse and Lord North was also among the commanders. This was no ordinary campaign, as Oliver Pigg reminded his erstwhile champion, Jermyn: 'the cause which yow have in hande, I nothing doubt is the Lordes'; the war would safeguard not only the Dutch Protestants but also the English Church 'now in som sort florishing'—quite a generous assessment on Pigg's part of the church presided over by Whitgift.[82]

Once more Jermyn's health betrayed him after nine months of campaigning, and although the Earl of Leicester noted when sending Jermyn home to recover that he was reluctant to leave the fighting, his return was conveniently less than a month before another general election.[83] His prestige must have been high in the county—Pigg had reminded him of 'the praiers of so many faithful servauntes of the Lord' at home sustaining his efforts—and Sir William Drury (apparently) did not try to repeat his victory of the previous election. This time Jermyn and Sir John Higham were duly elected for the county ready to press forward the continuing Puritan campaign in Parliament, and Higham did not require his insurance policy of the Ipswich seat; the townsmen had to declare their election of him void when the result of the county election was declared, and choose their Recorder in his place.[84] Once more the complaisant capital burgesses of Sudbury elected Henry Blagg, this time in first place.

Whitgift's harassment of godly ministers continued, and Sir Robert Jermyn continued to be recognized as one of their chief champions in Suffolk and Essex; presumably this was the reason for his consistent exclusion from the commission of the peace, for initiatives by Leicester

---

[81] On Christmas Lane, see below, Ch. 9. Bacon's appointment recommended, BL Harl. 286, fo. 197; his will: PCC 112 Meade,

[82] PRO, SO3/1, s.v. 1 December 1585; *HMC, Lord De Lisle and Dudley* III (1936), p. xxxiii; *Leicester Correspondence* pp. 75, 114, 195, 411, 417. Pigg's letter: CUL MS Dd. II. 75, fos. 21–5. I owe this reference to Collinson, 'Classical Movement', p. 995, although Collinson is more tentative than I would be in identifying the recipient with Jermyn.

[83] *Leicester Correspondence* pp. 114, 410.   [84] Bacon, p. 347.

and Burghley to have him restored along with Higham and Robert Ashfield do not seem to have succeeded.[85] In 1587 Jermyn was the obvious person for the Dedham Classis to suggest as a messenger to the Privy Council on behalf of the ministers suspended for refusing to wear the surplice; in 1590 he was acting as go-between with the central authorities for the restoration of the preaching licence of Richard Rogers, vicar of the Essex village of Wethersfield.[86] Yet despite this continuing activity, the county was no longer rent by the religious quarrels which had distinguished the episcopate of Bishop Freke. Significantly, the constitutional wrangling in Bury came to an end with an agreement arbitrated by the local Puritan gentry on an order from the Privy Council in January and April 1585.[87] The main figures were ageing; in east Suffolk John Laurence was by now a very old man; that veteran Protestant Sir Robert Wingfield was sixty-seven in 1590 while Sir Thomas Cornwallis was seventy-one. In the west Thomas Badby had died at the height of the stirs in 1583, Thomas Andrews in 1585, while Sir William Drury, a fighter to the last, was to perish in a duel while governor of Bergen-op-Zoom in 1589. It was a strange indicator of changed times that Sir Robert Jermyn should be one of the team of leading knights of the Liberty of St Edmund who tried to sort out the financial chaos left by Sir William's death in the Drury family estates.[88] With the main opposition figures either dead or growing old and the Catholic community a spent political force, the Puritan leadership could dominate the life of the county with little challenge.

It is likely that as far as the county community was concerned, Jermyn's exclusion from the commission of the peace meant little in later years; certainly when in 1588 the village of Brandon petitioned the justices of the Liberty of St Edmund to approach Bishop Scambler to have their unsatisfactory incumbent removed, it was Jermyn who wrote to the Bishop and headed the six signatories.[89] However, by the summer of 1593, a decade of exclusion from the county Bench was over, and by the end of the summer there came a further honour which underlined the absurdity of that decade. The incumbent *custos*

---

[85] *CSPFor.* Sept. 1585–May 1586, p. 379; *HMC Salisbury* III, p. 133.
[86] *Dedham Classis* p. 61; on Rogers, *Two Elizabethan Puritan Diaries*, ed. M. M. Knappen (Chicago and London, 1933), p. 99.
[87] [F. K. Eagle], *Report of the Finance Committee of the Town Council of Bury St. Edmunds, upon the Charity in that Borough, called the Guildhall Feoffment* (Bury St Edmunds, 1839), pp. 37–9.
[88] Redgr. 4158.
[89] Aylsham 176, Jermyn *et al.* to Bishop Scambler, 3 June 1588.

rotulorum, Henry Lord Wentworth, died on 16 August; six days later the Earl of Essex recommended Jermyn for the post and by the end of the year he had been appointed as the acknowledged president of the county Bench.[90] One may suspect that it was Essex, playing at being the godly nobleman, who secured Jermyn's restoration to the commission of the peace. Sir Robert's son Thomas had been one of Essex's companions-in-arms at the siege of Rouen and had been knighted by him there; he was to be Essex's companion again in the Azores expedition and in Ireland.[91] Jermyn's prolonged exclusion can only have been thanks to the hostility of the Queen, Whitgift and perhaps Lord Chief Justice Wray; who better to remove the Queen's prejudice against the ministers' champion than the young Essex, if for a decade Burghley had failed?

For all their shortcomings, Bishops Scambler and Redman were different men from Bishop Freke. The Brandon incident demonstrates that the Bury JPs felt that they were not merely wasting their time if they approached Scambler. In contrast to the bad old days of the eighties, Bishop Redman's tone was unmistakably friendly when he wrote to the Bury justices in 1596 commending their 'Godlie and Christian care' in seeking an extraordinary public fast, and telling them that he would recommend their request to the Archbishop.[92] It was clear from this that despite the changed times the Bury Bench had lost none of its old zeal for promoting godly religion, even if it was now prepared to act more discreetly. However, when the Bury justices took it upon themselves to recommend their own candidate for the see of Norwich on the death of Redman, they were 'perhaps taking themselves too seriously', as Dr Smith comments on a parallel move from the Norwich justices, and neither recommendation was acted on by the authorities at Westminster.[93]

By the late 1580s the Protestant élite of Suffolk was sure enough of itself to be able to dominate county administration with little interference once the ecclesiastical authorities and the assize judges had ceased to harass it. Freke's departure had meant the end of the last chance for Catholics to play any significant part in the running of the county; henceforth the only development for the Catholic group was to be in its increasing identifiability against the background of conformist

---

90 BL Harl. 6996, fo. 27.   91 Harrison, pp. 168, 240.

92 BL Add. 38492, fo. 100.

93 *HMC Salisbury* XII, p. 523, and cf. Cecil's tactful reply, Tanner 76, fo. 166. Smith, p. 101.

and radical Protestant neighbours. The last decade of Elizabeth's reign saw the fading of religion as a major divisive issue among Suffolk's ruling gentry, just as it did on a national level; the Puritan justices who had battled for godly causes in earlier years with enemies both internal and external to the county had emerged as the acknowledged leaders of county society and would carry their view of the role and character of the national Church through into the next century to confront the dangerous novelties of Arminianism. However, this did not imply that all conflict in the county was at an end. Even while the religious struggle was still developing and before bishop and assize judge had ceased to be seen as a threat, new conflicts had been beginning in a new direction. During the 1590s these would develop into a confrontation with the Privy Council which would have seemed unthinkable in the years of the Bury stirs when Burghley and Walsingham battled at Court for the interests of the county's Puritan leaders.

PART III

THE COUNTY AND THE CROWN

Introductory

TUDOR government, for all its increasingly extravagant expressions of deference to the monarch, was an exercise in obtaining consent from the governed. Henry VII knew that his title to the throne was shaky, and that the minority of his subjects who mattered politically were fully aware of this. If he was to found a lasting dynasty, he and his progeny must show that they could achieve results and bring a lasting end to governmental instability; the nobility and gentry of East Anglia, so profoundly affected during the fifteenth century by the factional struggles of aristocrats, would be particularly sensitive to this need. His successors had to cope with the new problems of a nation which for the first time since the early fifteenth century faced serious division over religion, a division which successive governments themselves made worse; in addition, Henry VIII fought expensive wars which had to be financed largely by the consent of the taxpayer. Northumberland shrewdly withdrew from such adventures, but Mary's regime was drawn into even more disastrous albeit mercifully curtailed enterprises. By the 1580s, all Elizabeth's natural caution could not prevent her regime in turn becoming committed to increasingly ruinous military expenditure, just at a time when her government was establishing a sufficient working measure of consent to the Elizabethan Settlement of religion in the localities.

All these different issues needed intelligent management if the government was not to lose the confidence of the people in the localities who provided it with most of its money and the vast majority of its armed force. Sustained terror was out of the question; individual members of the defeated dynastic grouping of the White Rose might be destroyed by Henry VII and Henry VIII, individual religious dissidents of all descriptions might be destroyed by successive regimes, but conciliation, mediation, rather than coercion, must be the basis of any Tudor attempt to impose policy. To enforce its will, the government must seek effective collective bargaining with the most influential people of the localities who could sympathize with and explain its intentions. Ideally these would be people with a foot in both camps: familiar faces at Court or in central administration, but also trusted and respected members of the county Bench. Such people would be the prime candidates for election as knights of the shire, or additionally later in the century, for appointment as lords lieutenant, muster commissioners or deputy lieutenants.

7

Co-operation and Rebellion 1485–1558

IN Chapter 2 we saw the pattern of domination by great noblemen in the county up to 1572: the thirteenth Earl of Oxford, the Howard Dukes of Norfolk, the Duke of Suffolk. It was these figures who were relied on by the government to mediate its policies to East Anglia. During the reign of Henry VII it was the Earl of Oxford, with his power base in Essex and west Suffolk, to whom the King first looked. It is noticeable that of ten known results for the election of knights of the shire during Henry's reign, seven were of men from the west Suffolk circle round Oxford. Most regular of all, at least four times MP for the county, was Sir Robert Drury of Hawstead. In Sir Robert, the government found almost the ideal as intermediary: nationally he was one of the leading figures of Lincoln's Inn, Speaker of the Commons in 1495, one of the King's Councillors under Henry VII and VIII, and frequently engaged in royal diplomacy and ceremonial attendance on the King. Locally he survived Oxford to die at an advanced age in 1535, an active JP and perhaps *custos* to the last, still the most influential layman in the west of the county and still concerning himself with the increasingly troubled affairs of the Vere family.[1] William Carew of Bury St Edmunds, second knight in 1490, had one of the Drurys as his first wife,[2] while Drury's colleague in the Commons in 1495 was his brother-in-law Sir William Waldegrave of Bures, an experienced soldier who was likewise involved in Council business under Henry VIII. Drury and Waldegrave would long continue to lead affairs in west Suffolk.

When Waldegrave died in 1527, the Oxford circle had been dispersed by death and by the emergence of the new powers in the region, the Dukes of Norfolk and Suffolk. Significant of the change was the fact that whereas Sir Robert Broughton of Denston, knight of

---

[1] On Drury, see *DNB*, s.v. Drury, Robert. PRO, REQ 3/25, *Wright, Lincoln and Neve v. Kempe and Brett*, Replication, suggests that Drury was *custos* in the early 1530s, although it is possible that Sir Humphrey Wingfield may have been *custos* then: Wingfield may have stepped down while he was Speaker of Parliament. On Drury and the Veres in 1528, see PRO, SP 1/236/2 (*LP* App. I pt. i, no. 607).

[2] Corder, *1561 Visitation*, I, p. 69.

the shire in 1489, made his 'especiall and singuler goode lorde' the Earl of Oxford supervisor of his will in 1507, by 1517 it was the Duke and Duchess of Norfolk who were given the same address and made executors by his brother John Broughton.[3] The two Dukes' success in stifling a major popular rebellion in the Amicable Grant affair was a proof of their ability to control the region, and it was probably their blunt advice to Wolsey and the King in the middle of their pacification that some sort of government climb-down on the demand was essential which produced this remarkable reversal of Westminster's policy.[4] In 1528, another year of acute economic distress, the Duke of Norfolk acted swiftly in co-operation with Sir Robert Drury to preempt further unrest, urging Wolsey to convey appropriate thanks to Drury, calling together the Suffolk gentry to determine a fair price for the sale of corn commandeered to meet the crisis, and summoning the leading clothiers of the county to prevent them repeating the blunder of 1525 by sudden lay-offs of their workers.[5] It was not simply that the Duke took the initiative in this emergency; it was to him that a deputation of east Suffolk notables and yeomen turned when they wanted someone to convey to the King and Wolsey the urgency of a resumption of normal trade with Flanders. The Duke of Suffolk was approached at the same time, and sent a similar if less cogently expressed appeal to Wolsey.[6]

A useful if rather less serious illustration of the role of the Duke of Norfolk and his household as a clearing-house for East Anglian business in London comes from the sad story of the men of Westleton.[7] Through a series of blunders and misunderstandings, three inhabitants of this east Suffolk village had forfeited bonds for their vicar and a neighbour which by 1532 had resulted in them all running up a debt to the King of sixty pounds. Although the Duke of Norfolk had no property in their village, their instinct was to turn to him for help; the first stage was to toil for a 'token' from the bailiff of the Duke's Norfolk manor of Forncett, some twenty miles north, to get access to the Howard household at Court. They took their token to a groom of the Duke's chamber in Greenwich Palace, and he in turn got

    [3] Sir Robert: PCC 29 Adeane. John: *Collectanea Topographica et Genealogica* V (1838), p. 89.
    [4] PRO, SP 1/34/196ʳ (*LP* IV pt. i, no. 1329); BL Cott. Cleop. F VI, fos. 325 f. (*LP* IV pt. i, no. 1323).
    [5] PRO, SP 1/47/59 (*LP* IV pt. ii, no. 4012).
    [6] PRO, SP 1/45/144–6 (*LP* IV pt. ii, no. 3649); SP 1/46/50 (*LP* IV pt. ii, no. 3760).
    [7] PRO, REQ 3/25, *Wright, Lincoln and Neve* v. *Kempe and Brett*.

them a letter to see the Duke. The Duke did not succeed in persuading the King to pardon the bonds, and later the group came back to his groom promising a substantial reward to anyone near the King who could get them relieved of their forfeiture; the groom did a deal with them to take a consignment of their corn when he was back in Norfolk to finance a handsome tip to his friend the King's cook, who would approach his royal master direct. The Westleton men failed to complete the deal, and it took a third visit to the Duke's groom before they were presented to the King in person in the Greenwich tiltyard. To crown this tale of incompetence and indecision, even then they succeeded in forgetting to collect the bill describing their case from the Dean of the Chapel, to whom the King had passed it on, and having exhausted all the unofficial channels that they could try, they ended up with a collusive action in the Court of Requests.

The ducal machine thus failed to deliver the goods for the Westleton unfortunates, but it is significant that they turned to the Duke and his household as a key to the maze of central government. A delicate web of personal links could carry them from their coastal heathland eventually into the King's presence; no great man who was not an East Anglian could hope to rival the Howards' and the Brandons' mastery of such webs. In particular, neither Wolsey nor Cromwell could claim a particularly strong acquaintance among the early Tudor notables in the county.

Wolsey's lack of Suffolk gentry contacts may seem surprising at first sight in view of his origins at Ipswich, but it was in fact precisely those origins which meant that he would have no natural contact with the county gentry. Wolsey's family had a rather minor foothold in the little group of merchant families which ran the borough of Ipswich; one of the town's greatest merchants and benefactors, Edmund Dandy, would remember Wolsey's parents among those for whom he founded a family chantry in St Laurence's church in 1510, while the future Cardinal was still only Dean of Lincoln.[8] This borough élite was on the whole quite separate from the world of the landed gentry beyond the town ditch, and Wolsey's whole career in his years of power seems marked by the independent attitudes which characterized the Ipswich merchants' relations with their gentry neighbours. His long absence in Oxford and his later employment at Court did nothing to build up alternative contacts in the county; he never had substantial personal

[8] *LP* I, no. 381(69).

property in the area. None of those Suffolk men who can be reckoned as among his followers were important enough in the county to be JPs in his lifetime; they were all men who made their mark away from the county in Wolsey's own service, like the future bishops Stephen Gardiner and John Clerk, or laymen like Anthony Hansard, Thomas Alvard (son of an Ipswich bailiff and customer at Ipswich from 1524), or Richard Cavendish of Trimley, downstream from Ipswich.[9]

It was also in the service of Wolsey that another great minister of Henry VIII, Thomas Cromwell, would build up his Suffolk contacts. Cromwell seems first to have come to Suffolk in 1525 as part of Wolsey's team to begin the suppression of various small East Anglian monasteries,[10] and it was in this East Anglian coastal area, particularly in the Ipswich-based Wolsey circle, that his acquaintance remained based. In the following years his private legal practice included several cases from around Ipswich; when he made a will in July 1529, it included bequests not only to his colleague Thomas Alvard but also to Alvard's father-in-law, the Suffolk JP Thomas Rush. It was to Rush that Cromwell first turned when looking for a parliamentary seat in 1529: he considered using Rush's share of the Willoughby influence at Orford.[11] Rush was repeatedly MP for Ipswich, and Alvard joined him at a by-election there in 1534; however, he normally lived in the Sandlings area near Orford at Sudbourne, and a close neighbour of his there was the Augustinian Priory at Butley. Its Prior from 1529 was Thomas Manning, a child of Sudbourne who had become a Canon of the house and who was a personal friend of Alvard and Rush; Rush was instrumental in writing to Cromwell to persuade Wolsey to allow Manning's election after the Cardinal had interfered with the house's deliberations on a new Prior.[12] The acquaintance developed sufficiently over the next three years for the future Bishop Manning to be writing chatty letters to Cromwell about a local legal dispute and incidentally passing on his greetings to Rush. In the following year, Rush was knighted at Anne Boleyn's coronation, and it was to Rush that Miles Spencer repeatedly looked as a mediator with Cromwell in the course

[9] *DNB*, s.v. Gardiner, Stephen; Clerk, John. Hansard: PRO, SP 1/27/149 (*LP* III pt. ii, no. 2932(2)). Alvard: *History of Parliament 1509–58* I, p. 315. Cavendish: PRO, SP 1/42/201 (*LP* IV pt. ii, no. 3276).

[10] *LP* IV pt. i, nos. 1137/6, 13.

[11] Legal practice, e.g. PRO, STAC 2/17/252; PRO, C1/484/11, C1/648/37, C1/667/9. Orford seat: BL Cott. Cleop. E IV, fo. 211 (*LP* IV pt. ii, App. no. 28, although Orford is there wrongly described as Oxford). 1529 will: *LP* IV pt. iii, no. 5772.

[12] PRO, SP 1/236/67 (*LP* App. I pt. i, no. 632).

of his vain attempts to secure his title to the Archdeaconry of Suffolk.[13]

Another Suffolk friend of Cromwell's whom he probably met through the Wolsey dissolutions was Richard Wharton, bailiff of the Duke of Norfolk's important manor of Bungay since the opening years of the century. Wharton served as one of Cromwell's business agents in East Anglia during the 1530s, but the relationship was one of genuine friendship as well, with frequent mentions of exchanges of hospitality and gifts; on one occasion Cromwell even made a remembrance to pursue a request of Wharton's to the bailiff's own master the Duke of Norfolk.[14] Wharton was involved with the same Ipswich circle which formed the basis of Cromwell's Suffolk acquaintance; an old friend of his was Cromwell's servant Robert Hogan, who had started his career as apprentice to an Ipswich pewterer, and whose cousin Robert Basse was not only Cromwell's chaplain but also for a time parson of the central Ipswich parish of St Mary Quay.[15] In 1537, at the height of Cromwell's influence, Wharton became a JP for the county.

In the days of Cromwell's greatness, his contacts naturally became rather wider than this circle of acquaintance from Wolsey days. Richard Southwell, who became his son's tutor, Edmund Bedingfield, Richard Freston, and Sir Anthony Wingfield of Letheringham were all East Anglians with positions at Court who at one time or another gained favours through Cromwell;[16] yet of all these, Wingfield was the only one sufficiently eminent in the county life to sit on the Suffolk justices' Bench during Cromwell's years of power, and his eminence in the county long predated 1529, owing little if anything to the Lord Privy Seal. The fact remains that Cromwell's special acquaintance in the county, men who could get things done for him as opposed to the constant stream of those seeking bounty from the current favourite, was a narrow circle developed in earlier years and confined almost

[13] Manning: PRO, SP 1/70/148 (*LP* V, no. 1153). Spencer: SP 1/107/123 (*LP* XI, no. 629).
[14] PRO, SP 1/69/80, 1/77/82, 1/80/198, 1/91/74, 1/101/125, 1/114/92 (*LP* V, no. 769; VI, nos. 709, 1534; VIII, no. 372; X, no. 162; XII pt. i, no. 83). Remembrance: PRO, E36/143, p. 70 (*LP* VI, no. 1371, but there wrongly dated; the memorandum relates to a letter of Robert Hogan, ibid., no. 709).
[15] Wharton: PRO, SP 1/241/76 (*LP* App. I pt. i, no. 1228). Apprenticeship in will of Nicholas Winter, 1489 (PCC 32 Milles). Basse: PRO, SP 1/65/221 (*LP* V, no. 205); rector of St Mary Quay 1528 (*PSIA* XXII, 1934, p. 36).
[16] Southwell: BL Cott. Cleop. E IV, f. 274 (*LP* X, p. 507). Bedingfield: PRO, SP 1/110/96 (*LP* XI, no. 946). Freston: SP 1/117/263 (*LP* XII pt. i, no. 836). Wingfield: SP 1/153/160, 1/154/50 (*LP* XIV pt. ii, nos. 224, 370).

exclusively to the coastal zone of the county. Perhaps most significantly of all, Cromwell had no estate in the county on which to base his influence.

Equally striking among Cromwell's friends was their general lack of interest in religious reform; in no sense did they constitute a reformist-minded Cromwellian 'party' such as Dr Clark has postulated for Kent.[17] Of all those discussed above, only Sir Anthony Wingfield developed Protestant sympathies, and that was not until at least the late 1540s. On the contrary, Richard Freston was informed against in 1538 for papalist words, and Wharton, Bedingfield, and Southwell were all definite religious conservatives.[18] The party of religious reform in the county owed little to Cromwell and much to the circle of the Duke of Suffolk who contributed to his destruction; if my reconstruction of the Duke's removal from the area in 1538 through Cromwell's good offices is correct, then the gap between the two groups is only too easy to understand (above, Ch. 2).

The great noblemen of East Anglia were thus unrivalled in their control of Suffolk's access to the world of Westminster and the Court; not even Henry VIII's two most powerful ministers were either able or disposed to build up any rival network of patronage. The point is given interesting confirmation by the curious disproportion between east and west in the number of those who played a prominent or even a minor part in administrative, legal or Court office in the capital. In Henry VII's reign, the Bury area had boasted great men like Sir Robert Drury, Sir William Waldegrave or Jasper Tudor's servant and the King's solicitor, Thomas Lucas;[19] as they died off in Henry VIII's reign they had no successors. Although the gentry of the Liberty of St Edmund were fewer in numbers than those of the east, the difference in numbers is much more pronounced than this would suggest. The men who succeeded the thirteenth Earl of Oxford in his earldom could not provide the same access to Court for western gentry as he had done, but in the east, many of the circle of Charles Brandon and Thomas Howard followed them to the King's presence. The Wingfields, for instance, boasted several representatives about Henry

[17] Clark, pp. 43, 50–7, 419 n.
[18] Freston: PRO, SP 1/140/16 (*LP* XIII pt. ii, no. 964). On Wharton, see the dedication of G. Marshall, *A compendious treatise in metre declaring the firste originall of sacrifice . . .* (1554, *STC* 17469a), sigs. A ii–A iiii. Bedingfield: cf. Nicholas L'Estrange's remarks about him and his associates, PRO, SP 10/8/60. Southwell: *Narratives of the Reformation* pp. 45–6, 140.
[19] Cf. Lucas's will, PCC 14 Thrower.

VIII's Court; Sir Anthony rose the highest, becoming a privy councillor and eventually Comptroller of the Household under Edward VI, but Henry VIII esteemed Wingfield's son Anthony enough to give him the lease of the chief manor in Woodbridge as a wedding present.[20] Sir Richard Wingfield, Christopher Garneys, and Edward Jerningham were all east Suffolk gentry who held Court office close to the King.[21]

Successive magnates were able to manage the gentlemen of Suffolk and render them docile. There was no hint, for instance, in the troubles of the Amicable Grant that there was any gentry participation in the protest; the affair was far too much of a popular expression of fury for that. The result was that the Dukes could report with satisfaction that within two days they had gathered a force of four thousand from Norfolk and Suffolk to overawe the protestors.[22] Similarly, during the disturbances in the North of 1536–7, there was no suggestion that the gentry would lend any encouragement to the unrest among Suffolk clothworkers; the Duke of Norfolk had far fewer worries than about Norfolk, but in any case, was able confidently to leave both counties in the hands of the leading JPs.[23] Even when the Edwardian regime began imposing sweeping religious changes, the Wentworth–Wingfield alignment which represented the ghost of Brandon's affinity was able to implement them in the county without serious challenge; conservatives remained in disarray (above, Ch. 5).

The East Anglian opposition to Northumberland's attempted *coup* in 1553 was the first time that the gentry of the area resisted the will of central government in the Tudor period. We have already outlined the crucial role of the East Anglian members of Mary's household in organizing her counter-*coup*, and their successful initiative in capturing the sympathy of the less committed among the landed élite; it was the leadership of these two groups which formed the bulk of the Council which Mary put together at Kenninghall and Framlingham, although they did not go on to take the leading role at a national level when the *coup* had succeeded.[24] Power shifted away from the Wentworth–

---

[20] *Chorography* p. 70; cf. PRO, SP 10/2/27.

[21] Cf. Weever, p. 769, and *LP* I, no. 20.

[22] BL Cott. Cleop. F VI, fos. 325–6 (*LP* IV pt. i, no. 1323), and cf. PRO, SP 1/34/143 (*LP* IV pt. i, no. 1260).

[23] SP 1/107/83, 118 (*LP* XI, nos. 603, 625).

[24] Above, Ch. 2. I am grateful to Professor Dale Hoak for sending me a draft of his paper 'Another Tudor Revolution? The Formation and Organisatin of Mary I's Privy Council', to be published in *Revolution Reassessed*, ed. C. Coleman and D. Starkey (Oxford).

Wingfield alignment as a result of the *coup*. Wentworth himself had been sworn of the Council at Framlingham, but he was removed from active participation in county affairs after the opening months of 1554 by being shipped off to the thankless task of governing Calais.[25] Perhaps it was a relief to him to escape participation in the East Anglian campaign of burnings; it is noticeable that already in August 1553 he deliberately avoided active participation in the examination of the Protestant Edward Underhill at the Council Board.[26] His responsibility for the loss of Calais brought further humiliation on the Wentworth circle, with the arrest in summer 1558 of his wife on Privy Council orders, for religious offences; instructions were given that his sisters and children should be given a good Catholic education.[27] Sir Anthony Wingfield's heir Robert had already been removed from the commission of the peace in 1553, making Mary's reign the only time since the reign of Richard III and the only time during the sixteenth century that there was not a Wingfield on the Suffolk Bench.

Wingfield's dismissal was part of a systematic remodelling of the East Anglian Benches in 1553; the Marian regime was the first since the fifteenth century to undertake such sweeping changes, with the aim not merely of getting rid of those who had supported Northumberland at the time of the 1553 *coup*, but also of stripping the commission of Edwardian appointments and convinced Protestants (see Appendix III). Nothing on this organized scale took place at the beginning of Edward's reign, although since the ideological barriers were now going up irrevocably, it would happen again when Elizabeth came to the throne. Sixteen resident JPs were dismissed in Suffolk, about one-third of the residents: of these, eleven had either been first appointed by the Edwardian regimes or were compromised by involvement with Northumberland. Another, Francis Clopton, was later to be arrested in connection with a Suffolk and Essex conspiracy, another was Henry Goodrich, protégé of the disgraced Bishop Goodrich of Ely, and another was the well-known Protestant in the Wentworth circle, Edward Grimston; only Sir George Somerset and Henry Hobart cannot easily be accounted for.[28] The picture is the same for the other

---

[25] He was appointed in December 1553 (*CPR Philip and Mary* I, p. 67), but was still writing from Suffolk in January 1554 (PRO, SP 46/8, fo. 13).

[26] *Narratives of the Reformation* p. 139.

[27] *APC* VI, pp. 376–7, 387–8.

[28] Eleven dismissed: James Downes, John Eyer, William Forth, Henry Gates, Christopher Goldingham, Robert Gurdon, John Lucas, Robert Southwell, Robert Wingfield, Thomas Playters, Alexander Newton. On Clopton, cf. *APC* V, pp. 165, 171.

East Anglian Benches: in Norfolk, of sixteen JPs dismissed, twelve can be identified as Edwardian appointees or Northumberland supporters, and of the eight in Cambridgeshire, all were Edwardian appointees except Henry Goodrich.[29] In Essex, there were fifteen dismissals of Edwardian appointees or Northumberland supporters, with two further dismissals less easy to explain.[30]

There was no shortage of adequate gentry to replace the gaps thus created. One or two appointments were obviously exceptional ones, made to cope with the religious revolution which the government was pressing forward. It is unlikely that in other circumstances the Bailiff of Hadleigh, Walter Clerke, would have been appointed a JP, for he was no more than a clothier, and one of probably only two non-armigerous men to be named in the Suffolk commission during the entire century; however, his JPs authority would be useful in the government's planned destruction of his rector, Rowland Taylor, and in the management of a troublesome town.[31] The appointment of Archdeacon Miles Spencer in 1556 was also unusual, for he was the only Suffolk cleric apart from successive bishops to be included in the county commission of the peace after the Dissolution. Otherwise, of eighteen resident JPs whose names appear in commission for the first time in 1554, twelve were leading men who had either been in Mary's household before her *coup* or who had been associated with her in the *coup*'s early days.[32] There is no evidence that any of them displayed positive enthusiasm for the reformed religion on Elizabeth's accession to the throne, and several of them would become obstinate Catholic recusants. In Suffolk at least, the Marian government could pick and

[29] Norfolk: William Butts, John Clere, Thomas Clere, Thomas Guybon, Lord Robert Dudley, Thomas Hollis, Nicholas L'Estrange, William Hunston, Robert Southwell, Ralph Symonds, Robert Robsart, John Plumstead. Cambridgeshire: Nicholas Bacon, Henry Pigott, Thomas Bowles, Thomas Wakefield, William Walpole, Richard Wykkes, Thomas More. Cambridgeshire and Essex figures are derived from the same range of sources as Norfolk and Suffolk figures.

[30] Francis Jobson, Roger Cholmeley, William Norris, George Foster, Anthony Cooke, Francis Wyatt, William Latham, Edward Bury, Thomas Golding, George Browne, John Tey, John Lucas, Robert Darkenall, Peter Meutas, Thomas Lord Darcy. The other two were Robert Mordaunt and Thomas Josselyn.

[31] Cf. *LP* II, no. 4096; Clerk's son matriculated arms in 1556 (BL Harl. 1507, fo. 404). The other non-armigerous JP was Robert Wrott, product of a precisely opposite religious emergency in the reign of Elizabeth (above, Ch. 6).

[32] Nicholas Rookwood (son of Lady Burgh), John Sulyard, Sir John Tyrrell, Henry Jerningham, Richard Freston, Ambrose Jermyn, Lionel Tollemache, John Earl of Bath, John Brend, Henry Earl of Sussex, Sir Henry Bedingfield, Sir Edward Waldegrave. Cf. *'Vita Mariae'* pp. 204–13.

choose whom it wanted in commission to carry out its policy of Catholic restoration.

By contrast to the Wentworth–Wingfield alignment, the men who governed Suffolk for Mary were concentrated in the west of the county. In the absence of the Earl of Bath, who divided his time between west Suffolk, the Court and the West Country and who was sent off to be governor of Beaumaris in 1558, the most prominent '*coup* councillors' normally resident in the county were Sir William Drury of Hawstead, Sir Clement Higham of Barrow, and William Cordell of Melford, all westerners; it is their names which occur most frequently in Privy Council letters concerning business in all parts of the county, often coupled with cordial thanks for their efforts. On one occasion these thanks were coupled with a sour warning to the justices of oyer and terminer in Essex to emulate the diligence of their Suffolk neighbours, with the addition of three Suffolk men to the Essex commission.[33]

Was it merely coincidence and the eclipse of the Wentworth–Wingfield grouping which resulted in this concentration of the Marian government's most active agents in the west? Perhaps their conservative sympathies may also have been the result of nostalgia for the area's old association with Bury Abbey, and regret at the policies which had led to its destruction. Sir Clement Higham had been Abbot Reve's chief steward, and he and his wife had been left affectionate bequests in Reve's will; indeed, the old Abbot's legacies of a formidable quantity of wine to the wives of prominent local gentry must have left sunny memories of that epicurean prelate. Among the beneficiaries were Sir William Drury's mother and the mother of that enthusiastic Marian persecutor Sir John Tyrrell of Gipping; Reve's links with the Tyrrells were particularly close, with a Tyrrell servant in his household and a Tyrrell godson.[34] Furthermore, the conservative gentry of the Bury area had an active friend in Lord Chancellor Gardiner, who came from a Bury family and had no doubt known many of them when they were boys. He probably owed his first steps on the ladder of success to his links with the Clerk of the King's Council, Richard Eden, also from a Bury family, and in later years Gardiner would return the

---

[33] *APC* V, pp. 105, 171, 236, 246, 310; VI, p. 85.

[34] Muskett III, p. 3. The Tyrrells were also closely linked with Sir Thomas Cornwallis, Sir Thomas Tyrrell being godfather to Thomas's fourth child in 1545 (MS transcript by Francis Blomefield of Cornwallis christenings and confirmations, in a folio volume on the Cornwallises formerly *penes* Sir Thomas Phillipps and now *penes* Mr Tony Copsey, Ipswich.).

compliment to the Edens, making Richard's nephew George Eden his secretary; George and his brother Thomas, now in his turn Clerk of the Council, would both first appear in the Suffolk commission of the peace during Gardiner's time as Chancellor. Thomas was MP for the Bishop of Winchester's borough of Taunton in November 1554.[35] The Jermyn Gardiner who was among Gardiner's longstanding servants was probably named after the Rushbrooke family, and it was through Gardiner's 'ayde and meanes' that Sir Clement Higham came to the gift of the rich manor of Nedging from Queen Mary.[36]

We have already observed the way in which the men of Mary's *coup* dominated the parliamentary returns for the county and for the borough of Ipswich (above, Ch. 1), but an even more striking proof of the Marian regime's high regard for its Suffolk supporters can be seen in the number of Suffolk men who sat for parliamentary seats outside the county during Mary's reign. In the whole of the reign of Henry VIII, only eleven known election results outside the county involved Suffolk men; for Edward's reign five, and for Elizabeth's forty-five years, thirty-three, but for Mary's six years, the total was no fewer than thirty-seven. It is particularly significant that a much higher proportion of the Marian results came in seats which were under the control of a department of royal administration: 65 per cent under Mary compared with 27 per cent under Henry VIII and 27 per cent under Elizabeth I. Mary's regime provided a haven for East Anglian gentry. Apart from Gardiner, various East Anglians who had been members of Mary's household before her *coup* were given positions in central administration for old times' sake and for their conspicuous enthusiasm for the old faith: Robert Rochester, Comptroller of the Household and Chancellor of the Duchy of Lancaster, Henry Jerningham, Captain of the Guard and later Master of the Horse, Edward Waldegrave, who succeeded his uncle Rochester as Chancellor of the Duchy of Lancaster, Richard Freston, Cofferer of the Household, John Sulyard, Standard-Bearer of the Gentlemen Pensioners, and Henry Jerningham's nephew George, one of the Sewers of the Household. One could add to these Sir Thomas Cornwallis, whose defection as Sheriff of Norfolk and Suffolk had been an important stage of the *coup*, and who became Comptroller of the Household in succession to Rochester in 1557;

---

[35] Cf. above, Ch. 4, n. 30; on George, PRO, DL 1/50/S4.
[36] Jermyn: *Rushbrook Registers* p. 341. Higham: *Chorography* p. 57.

Ladies Waldegrave, Jerningham, and Cornwallis were also ladies of the Queen's Privy Chamber.[37]

The connection with the Duchy of Lancaster through Rochester and Waldegrave was of particular significance, because the Duchy came to play a new role in the county. The survival of the Duchy and of the Court of Wards in 1554, when virtually all the other recommendations of the Edwardian commission on the reorganization and amalgamation of central government departments were implemented, has long seemed a puzzling anomaly. Professor Elton ascribed Wards' survival to the Queen's personal favour for its newly-appointed master, Sir Francis Englefield, but explained the Duchy's retention as the result of successful opposition by conservative civil servants; in fact, it is likely that the same motivation applied as in Wards.[38] One might see both survivals as a reflection of the tensions within Mary's Privy Council. Dr Hoak has shown how as the *coup* came to a successful conclusion towards the end of July 1553, old hands in government like Paget, Arundel, and Winchester took over the dominant role in the Council from the councillors of Kenninghall and Framlingham, Catholic zealots like Rochester, Waldegrave, and Englefield; for the rest of the reign, even '*coup* councillors' like these three, who remained genuinely active in Council business, played a secondary role to the more experienced group: 'Mary's "first" privy council was composed of men who had given her England, the second of men who governed England.'[39] In this situation, Englefield and Rochester may well have regarded their administrative departments as power bases which they could ill afford to lose, and they put up a stiff fight for their retention. In the final debates that saved the Duchy, the Council took a great deal of convincing by the arguments of civil servants that it should be retained;[40] does this reluctance to preserve the Duchy reflect the common-sense view of experienced government operators on the Council like Paget and Winchester coming into conflict with the group round Rochester?

[37] I am grateful to Professor Dale Hoak for this latter information; cf. '*Vita Mariae*' pp. 204, 207–8.

[38] G. R. Elton, *The Tudor Revolution in Government* (Cambridge, 1953), pp. 238–44. Professor Elton (ibid., p. 242) also makes the point that the mesne tenants of the Duchy were reluctant to lose their mesne tenancy relationship to the Crown and thus to incur the feudal incidents consequent on tenancy-in-chief; they would add their weight to the opposition to Duchy abolition.

[39] The phrase is Professor Hoak's, from the unpublished paper mentioned above, n. 24.

[40] Elton, *Tudor Revolution in Government*, pp. 242–3.

Catholic fervour and personal loyalty to the Queen not only saved the Duchy and Wards for Rochester and Englefield, but also provided a reason actually to strengthen the Duchy's position. In 1555 an Act of Parliament authorized the augmentation of Duchy lands, partly by the resumption of former grants, but more importantly by authority to annex new lands up to the annual value of £2,000. The last augmentations to the Duchy, in Henry VIII's reign, had logically enough been in the North, but the very substantial increases which now followed, yielding a net income of £1,176 in 1558–9, were nearly all in the South.[41] In particular, in 1556 or 1557, important estates were added to the Duchy in Suffolk, a county where there had previously been little Duchy property: the entire Honour of Clare with the borough of Sudbury, the site of the College at Stoke by Clare and the very extensive and increasingly prosperous manor of Mildenhall, formerly owned by Bury Abbey. Sudbury returned members to Parliament from 1559, a move immediately exploited by the Duchy (above, pp. 32–3). Behind this augmentation, at first sight a pointless piece of antiquarianism, one sees the councillors of the *coup* further strengthening their position in Suffolk and north Essex. Sir Edward Waldegrave, Chancellor of the Duchy by 1557, took a special interest in Sudbury, which was only a mile or two from his Essex home at Borley; in 1554 he was instrumental in getting the town a generous new charter which made particular mention of its loyalty in resisting Northumberland's attempted takeover of 1553, and the town was not quick to forget his help.[43] Waldegrave became steward for the Honour of Clare jointly with Sir John Leigh, also in 1554.[44] At Mildenhall, Sir Clement Higham had been associated with the manor since the 1520s because of his chief stewardship of Bury Abbey; he retained property in the parish in the 1540s and was certainly steward for the Crown by 1555.[45] Higham was to sit as MP for the Duchy borough of Lancaster in Mary's 1558 Parliament, while for other councillors of the *coup*, the Duchy found a seat for John Sulyard at Preston in November 1554 and for Sir William Drury's son Robert at Thetford in three successive

---

[41] *Stat. Realm* IV, pp. 294–5; Somerville, pp. 286, 302–3.
[42] The formal grant is of 15 April 1558 (*CPR Philip and Mary* IV, p. 50) but PRO, DL 1/71/F21, suggests that Mildenhall at least became part of the Duchy in 3 & 4 Philip and Mary.
[43] *CPR Philip and Mary* I, pp. 141–3; above, p. 45.
[44] Somerville, p. 602.
[45] Property: PRO, C1/1110/29–30; PRO, C4/144, Replication of Richard Codington to Higham, Steward to Crown: Foxe, V, p. 359.

Marian Parliaments. Half a dozen other Suffolk men would sit for Duchy boroughs during Mary's reign.[46]

---

[46] Sir Giles Alington (Liverpool October 1553), Robert Barker (Thetford 1555), George Eden (Knaresborough 1555), Thomas Poley (Ripon 1555), Thomas Seckford (Ripon November 1554), Nicholas Rookwood (Thetford April–November 1554, 1555). Barker is admittedly difficult to identify with certainty, but it is likely that he was the prominent Ipswich merchant of that name.

8

The Elizabethan Regime: Contrasts and Contacts

THE Elizabethan government, committed from the outset to very different goals of policy from its predecessor, would face delicate problems in constructing a set of local governors in Suffolk who would be as willing agents of the change in direction as Mary's followers had been. The task would not be made easier by the fact that the Duke of Norfolk had now come to maturity and was ready to fulfil the local role which his grandfather had played in the reign of Henry VIII, since so many religious conservatives were prominent in the Howard clientage. The difficulty was lessened by the deaths of Sir William Drury and Bishop Hopton, victims both of the extraordinary providential wave of mortality among prominent Marians which heralded and accompanied the death of Mary herself. The government otherwise undertook a partial purge of its likely opponents. Just as in 1553, about a third of resident JPs were omitted from the first surviving Elizabethan commission of the peace: a group of sixteen, all obvious conservatives, headed by Sir Edward Waldegrave and Sir Thomas Cornwallis. Cornwallis, for all his significant role in Elizabethan Suffolk, was only going to reappear in commission for a few months of 1560.[1]

To balance these losses, twenty new justices appeared. They included no fewer than thirteen JPs who had no previous experience on the Suffolk Bench, together with victims of Marian purges. Most noticeable was the return of the Wentworth–Wingfield alignment: Richard and Robert Wingfield were named in commission, together with their associate Thomas Seckford, a younger son who was appointed one of the Masters of Requests by Elizabeth and who was replacing his aged father as a JP. Although so many new faces appeared, they did not represent a discontinuity in county government; only four had not previously had a relative on the Suffolk Bench, and two of these, Sir Giles Alington and Edward Lord North, were from well-established magisterial families of Cambridgeshire with substantial

---

[1] Attendance at Ipswich quarter sessions, January 1560, PRO, E137//42/4.

Suffolk estates.[2] There was no need for the regime to introduce large numbers of outsiders to the county leadership; like the Marian regime, Elizabeth's ministers found that the surplus of candidates for the Bench even in its greatly expanded post-Reformation state gave them the chance to effect a major change of personnel in the commission without too much disruption to local administration.

Nevertheless, common sense and the presence of the Duke of Norfolk prevented a total clean sweep of the Bench, and not all the new arrivals were good Protestants. Edward Lord North, newly appointed in 1559, opposed the Act of Uniformity in the Lords and stuck obstinately to a Catholic formula for commending his soul in his will of 1565;[3] Michael Hare, son of Mary's Master of the Rolls, was to become one of Suffolk's leading recusants later in Elizabeth's reign, and his inclusion can only have come from his family's long-standing links with the Howards. If anything, the conservatives still had the edge in numbers on the Bench, with twenty identifiable conservatives or definite Catholics out of thirty-nine resident justices.[4] No doubt recognizing this fact of administrative life, the government appointed the religiously undemonstrative Sir Ambrose Jermyn to be the first Elizabethan Sheriff of Norfolk and Suffolk, taking good care to congratulate him only five days after his appointment when he 'stayed' one John Sheparde from exercising his unpopular inquisitorial powers for the execution of various penal statutes under a commission from the late Queen: a curious little anticipation of the rows over administration and patentees which would disrupt East Anglian county government later in the reign.[5] Sir Clement Higham, newly retired from his position as Chief Baron of the Exchequer, was given a consolation prize as *custos rotulorum* for the county, an office which he seems to have exercised with exemplary assiduity.[6]

Higham's demotion was symptomatic of the fact that of all the Marian county leadership, so strongly based in the west of the county, only Sir William Cordell retained his office in central government on Elizabeth's accession. In the changed circumstances of the new regime

[2] MacCulloch, 'Power, Privilege and the County Community', pp. 41–2. On Norfolk, cf. Smith, p. 32, and A. H. Smith, 'The personnel of the commissions of the peace, 1554–1564: a reconsideration', *Huntington Library Quarterly* XXII (1959), pp. 301–12.
[3] D'Ewes, *Journals*, p. 30; PCC 7 Morrison.
[4] MacCulloch, 'Power, Privilege and the County Community', p. 43.
[5] *CPR Philip and Mary* IV, pp. 148–9; *APC* VII, p. 9, and cf. the patentees' internal wrangles in PRO, REQ 2/104/13.
[6] MacCulloch, 'Power, Privilege and the County Community', p. 44.

a number of these leaders viewed with dismay the prospect of representing Suffolk at Elizabeth's Court before the Prince of Sweden in 1560. Sir Thomas Cornwallis made great play with his harvesting commitments and his plans for a visit to his Yorkshire coal-mines when obtaining a discharge from this imposition through a neighbour who was Clerk of the Signet; Sir Ambrose Jermyn put forward 'his want of experyence in that kynde of servys . . . the which he hath alweys fledde from beyng a great enemye to his helth' to explain his 'mislikyng of the attendens in the Court'.[7]

The shift of power back towards the Wentworth–Wingfield alignment may help to explain why just as in the reign of Henry VIII, the west of the county was much less directly in contact with the Court than the east. The east's stronger commercial links with the capital may have encouraged this process, but additionally men like Higham and Jermyn may have conveyed their distaste for the ways of the new Court to their heirs, even if they did not succeed in passing on their preferences in religion. The only magisterial family to retain a place in Court affairs in the Liberty was the Drury family of Hawstead, who had no Marian magnate to guide it through the opening years of Elizabeth's reign, thanks to old Sir William's death; his grandson William remained a minor for some years before marrying one of Elizabeth's Ladies of the Bedchamber and embarking on his distinguished military career.[8] Lord Keeper Bacon might have provided the link between the Liberty and the Court, and as we have seen, his voice seems to have been decisive in choosing Crown financial officers in the county, particularly from among the gentry members of his household based in the Bury area (above, Ch. 2). However, he himself was normally resident in Hertfordshire, and his Suffolk home was just outside the Liberty at Redgrave; in any case he had few strong links with the family network of the Bury area. Moreover, by inclination Bacon was not a courtier but an administrator, albeit a very exalted one. No attractive honorific posts lay in his gift for aspiring courtiers; recipients of his bounty were more likely to be seeking financial posts within Suffolk, or, like his cousin John Bacon,

---

[7] PRO, SP 12/13/9, 12.

[8] *History of Parliament 1558–1603* II p. 58; he was still a royal ward in 1567 (PRO, WARD 13/6, bill of Lady Drury). The Herveys of Ickworth were also heavily involved in Court affairs for several generations, but to such an extent that they made no traceable impact in their own locality during the sixteenth century (cf. W. J. Tighe, 'The Harveys: three generations of Tudor courtiers', *PSIA*, paper unpublished at time of my writing).

such unglamorous but profitable positions as that of Chafewax in Chancery.[9]

By contrast, the gentry of east Suffolk appear to have been more ready to seek the rewards of office at the Elizabethan Court. At the heart of the Wentworth–Wingfield network was Thomas Seckford, supposedly celebrated for his ability to banter successfully with the Queen;[10] his brother Henry became Groom of the Privy Chamber, and his cousin Anthony Wingfield carried on the family involvement with the Court as a Gentleman Usher. Seckford may also have been responsible for bringing the Woodbridge boy Robert Beale to Court and starting him on the career which led to the Clerkship of the Privy Council.[11] Sir Owen Hopton, Elizabeth's Governor of the Tower of London, and his brother Robert, Knight Marshal, were of nearly comparable stature. Thomas Cornwallis of the Shotley branch of the family became Groom-Porter, and no Elizabethan gentleman of the Liberty of St Edmund is recorded as having the drive or the success of John Gosnold of Otley, who borrowed £500 from his father to buy the office of Gentleman Usher.[12]

In addition to all this, Elizabeth's government retained estates in east Suffolk which were available to be granted or leased to men at Court, thus increasing the number of courtier-gentlemen involved in the area's affairs. William Honnings, Henrician Clerk of the Signet, leased the royal manor of Sudbourne, resumed from the diocese of Norwich in 1560, and he married into a family called Cutler who were the lessees and stewards of the demesne lands of the Honour of Eye.[13] John Paston, an old Gentleman Pensioner, settled at Huntingfield, while Michael Stanhope, a protégé of Cecil and another Groom of the Privy Chamber, finally bought Sudbourne manor outright from the Crown in 1591 and used it as the nucleus of an extensive new estate in the area. At a slightly lower level in the social scale, William Page, Gentleman Harbinger, picked up morsels like the lease of the royal rectory of the coastal parish of Middleton.[14]

In contrast to the gentry of the west, who formed a single community clearly based on Bury St Edmunds, the family structures of the east were divided into two groupings. We have seen how the Wentworth–

[9] *CPR Eliz.* I, p. 348.   [10] Neale, *Commons*, p. 180.
[11] Metcalfe, p. 184.   [12] PCC 101 Rudd.
[13] *CPR Eliz.* II, p. 128.
[14] Paston's memorial brass, with an interesting rhymed inscription, remains at Huntingfield. Stanhope: PRO, STAC 5 S42/16. Page:PRO, SP 46/39, fo. 6.

Wingfield and Cornwallis–Heveningham family connections developed; for all the imprecision and overlap which intermarriage and inter-relations within a comparatively small area produced, one can see these alignments persisting throughout the sixteenth century. Each would have to find its own access to Court; for the Cornwallis–Heveningham group, so seriously affected by the downfall and death of the fourth Duke of Norfolk, there was the task of building up a new structure of contacts at the top—all the more necessary since so many members of the grouping were involved in Catholic recusancy from the 1570s, and needed to find ways of mitigating the burdens which this created. The shreds of evidence which enable us to reconstruct east Suffolk's relationship patterns also suggest that as Elizabeth's reign went on, the two sides of the eastern gentry developed different sets of contacts at Court. The Wentworth–Wingfield group cultivated links with Thomas Lord Buckhurst, while the Cornwallis–Heveningham group not only maintained its contacts in a traditional way with the surviving leaders of the Howard family, but also became associated with Lord Hunsdon, Lord Lieutenant of Norfolk and Suffolk for the decade after 1585, the man whom the government put up as a replacement for the power and Court contacts of the fallen Duke. Here again, as a caution against drawing these lines too precisely, it is worth noting that Lord Thomas Howard was Buckhurst's nephew by marriage, while it was Lord Howard of Effingham who knighted a key figure of the Wentworth–Wingfield alignment, Henry Glemham, at Cowdray in 1591.[15]

The complexity of groupings in the county was paralleled by the range of contacts open to the local gentry at Court. Among those early in the reign of Elizabeth were men who themselves came from East Anglia: the Duke of Norfolk, the area's patron *par excellence*, with such lesser figures as Sir Thomas Cornwallis's brother Henry or Francis Yaxley, Clerk of the Signet; representing a rather less conservative viewpoint were the two Seckfords and Lord Keeper Bacon. However, members of the county élite might also go beyond these men who were already enmeshed in local politics to the twin giants of the Elizabethan regime, the Earl of Leicester and William Cecil.

In their own areas Leicester and Cecil were as much local magnates with local followings as the Duke of Norfolk in East Anglia; in a national setting, however, their patronage was characterized by a desire

---

[15] Manning, p. 232, n. 4; on Glemham: Shaw II, p. 88.

to embrace as many strands of opinion and personality as possible, for reasons both of self-interest and of statesmanship. Thus Leicester was not merely the great Puritan patron, source of comfort for the Bury radicals and their ministers, the godly commander in the Netherlands. Sir Thomas Cornwallis could also call on his acquaintance when necessary; William Cavendish of Trimley could approach him when seeking influence at Court in his lawsuit with a local Exchequer official.[16] Likewise Cecil could prove useful not only to Puritans but also to Sir Thomas Cornwallis and Kitson relatives when their conservative religious views ran them into trouble; he might even be drawn into local disputes on the side opposite to the Puritans, as in his unfavourable comments on the depredations in Bures church in 1561 or in the Exchequer suits in Beccles in the 1580s.[17] His links with the Wentworth–Wingfield group in the east were as strong as with the Puritans in the west; they were cemented by his daughter's marriage to Lord Wentworth's heir in 1582, although the young man died before his father.[18]

The varied nature of Cecil's and Leicester's contacts was particularly important in the west, where their continued efforts together with Sir Francis Walsingham on behalf of the Puritan gentry prevented a complete breakdown of communication between central government and local leaders during the religious crisis of the 1580s. However, towards the end of the reign these contacts were to be severed by death; Leicester had died in 1588, Walsingham two years later, while Burghley's health and energy progressively failed him up to his death in 1598. Death had already proved unkind to the west in depriving it of the voices at Court of Lord Keeper Bacon in 1579 and Sir William Cordell in 1581. The east made up for the loss of Thomas Lord Wentworth in 1584 and of Thomas Seckford in 1587 by its sustained contacts with Lord Buckhurst, Lord Thomas Howard, Sir Edward Coke, and Lord Hunsdon; the governing élite of the west developed few such links, although one of Sir John Higham's sons continued in the service of Lord Burghley in the nineties.[19] It is hardly surprising, therefore, that the leaders of the west took the dominant part in

---

[16] On Leicester as Puritan patron, see Collinson, 'Classical Movement', Ch. 11. Cornwallis: PRO, SP 12/7/33; Iveagh, Cornwallis MS 1/8; BL Lansd. 33, fo. 185; Longleat, MS Dudley II, fo. 54 (I owe this last reference to Dr Simon Adams). Cavendish: PRO, SP 46/28, fo. 101.

[17] On Bures, see above, Ch. 5; Beccles: Bec. A4/36, and below, Ch. 11.

[18] Strype, *Annals*, III pt. ii, p. 110.

[19] BL Eger. 2713, fo. 452r.

obstructing the initiatives of the central government and the central government's patentees towards the end of the reign; their contacts with the centre were lapsing and their suspicion of its intentions no doubt growing in proportion. It was a dangerous situation indeed for the delicate balance of relationships between the Liberty of St Edmund and the centre when the Privy Council began to have almost as 'little accesse thither or acquaintance' as the Bishop of Norwich.

Since the Sackvilles had practically no estates in east Suffolk it is difficult to see why Lord Buckhurst should have built up relationships with the gentry there. However, the contacts had been established by 1586, when Buckhurst referred to Francis Colby of Brundish as 'a frende of myne' in soliciting favour for him in a lawsuit. In 1592 Buckhurst was one of the two peers called in to arbitrate in a major row in the Forth family since Charles Forth was his servant, while in 1601 Buckhurst's daughter married Henry Glemham: the Colbys, Forths, and Glemhams were a tightly-related little group of east Suffolk families.[20] The Howard contacts with east Suffolk were more to be expected. Lord Henry Howard paid high tribute to his old family friend Sir Thomas Cornwallis when regretting to Lady Kitson that he could not accompany Lady Howard on a visit, for 'I holde it halfe a paradise to live with your good wise father'. Michael Hare used a phrase characteristic of his doughty traditionalism when he made 'the Righte Honorable and my special good Lorde Henry nowe Earl of Northampton' supervisor of his will in 1611, but the Howard links were not merely with such defenders of the old religion; Lord Thomas Howard addressed Sir Arthur Heveningham as his 'lovinge cosen' when asking him for the loan of a couple of hunting-dogs.[21]

It was revealing that Howard's note to Heveningham was dated from Chesterford, the Cambridge home of John Carey, Lord Hunsdon's son.[22] Hunsdon's links with Sir Arthur became notorious in the faction fighting which disrupted Norfolk in the 1580s and 1590s. Dr Smith was not quite correct in asserting that Hunsdon 'had no lands in East Anglia and knew little of its society and political undercurrents'; Hunsdon might have been more acceptable to the various East Anglian

[20] Colby: PRO, SP 46/34, fo. 101. Forth: PRO, REQ 2/27/45, Complaint of Robert Forth, and details of the case in MacCulloch, 'Power, Privilege and the County Community', p. 174. Glemham: Metcalfe, p. 140, and cf. below, pp. 335–6.

[21] Cornwallis: Hengr. 88/2, fo. 71. Hare: PCC 38 Wood. Heveningham: Aylsham 182, Howard to Heveningham, 1 July *s.a.*

[22] For Carey's residence, PRO, C66/1308, m. 1d.

gentry who resented his stance in local politics if this had indeed been the case. It would be truer to say that he had no property in Norfolk; in Suffolk he was a muster commissioner from at least 1579, while the Queen had made him various grants of land to support his barony in 1559, one grant being of the important manor, park, and advowson of Huntingfield.[23] Huntingfield lies within a mile of Sir Arthur Heveningham's ancestral home at Heveningham, and it was probably this which provided the initial contact between Heveningham and the future Lord Lieutenant. In this, the heart of the Cornwallis–Heveningham country, Hunsdon's local agents cannot have been looked on with much favour by the godly-minded, for they included a notorious local conservative and tenant of the Earl of Arundel, John Chapman alias Barker of Sibton.[24] In Norfolk too, the same link was made explicit. When William Dix, one of the Howards' family trustees, was restoring his parish church at Wickmere in 1592, he beautified the nave with wall-paintings massing the heraldry of his friends and acquaintances; at the height of the squabbles which were disrupting Norfolk's leadership, the people of Wickmere would see the arms of the Lord Lieutenant alongside those of such allies of Sir Arthur as Sir Edward Clere.[25] Hunsdon's links with local conservatism could hardly escape the notice of Heveningham's largely Puritan opponents on the East Anglian Benches.

It may seem surprising that Sir Edward Coke's early links were also with the Howard-inclined group in east Suffolk, for his career would take a rather different direction in the long term. Coke was a Norfolk man by origin, but through his first marriage to Bridget Paston, he came into substantial Suffolk estates centring on Huntingfield, where he was tenant to lord Hunsdon.[26] Bridget's father had been the old courtier John Paston, a stray from the great conservative Paston family of east Norfolk, and her mother had taken as her third husband one of Suffolk's leading recusants, Edmund Bedingfield, thereby occasioning a major dispute about dower with one of her Bedingfield stepsons, who

[23] Smith, p. 242. Muster commissioner: PRO, SP 12/133/14. Grant: *CPR Eliz.* I, p. 115.
[24] PRO, STAC 5 T24/22, deposition of Robert Purdye; CUL MS Buxton 96, Dix file no. 23, and cf. PRO, STAC 5 C49/12. Hunsdon's son was to be pressed into Lady Kitson's service to quash the charge of recusancy against her (Hengr. 88/2, fo. 66ʳ).
[25] One complete shield remains amid other evidence of the restoration, and the sequence of shields is described in church notes probably by Robert Kemp, MS *penes* Lord Walpole, Wolterton Hall, Norfolk, fo. 25 (cf. 'Chitting', pp. 103–4).
[26] Cf. SROB Accn. 449/5/31/36 with *CPR Eliz.* I, p. 115, and *Chorography* p. 37.

was able to prove that the marriage had been undertaken by a Marian priest with Catholic rites.[27] Coke retained a great affection for and sense of obligation towards his mother-in-law, to whom he owed the Huntingfield estates, and he lived at Huntingfield up to her death in 1595. Before 1595 most of the godparents for his children were from the Cornwallis–Heveningham circle, and he even chose Sir Arthur Heveningham to be godfather for his son Arthur in 1588.[28] Pursuing the same connections, Coke was of counsel to the Earl of Arundel, and one of his early coups was successfully to prove the Earl's rights to his remaining liberties, including the Stewardship of the Liberty of St Edmund, and certain manors, in the face of strenuous efforts by Exchequer officials and the then Attorney-General to prove that they had been forfeit to the Crown by the Duke of Norfolk's attainder. In 1590, as a result of this triumph, the Earl leased Coke the stewardships of St Edmund and the Duke of Norfolk's Liberty, and Coke sublet them on Arundel's instructions to the family solicitor John Wentworth of Somerleyton as a reward for Wentworth's part in the recovery.[29]

Wentworth and Coke maintained a lifelong friendship; Wentworth was godfather to Coke's third child, and left twenty marks to his 'most true frend' in his will in 1619.[30] However, Coke would not remain trapped in the ghetto of East Anglian conservatism for life; his ambition demanded wider contacts. The child named Arthur had as two of its other godparents members of the Wentworth–Wingfield grouping, Francis Colby and the wife of Sir Robert Wingfield's heir. Coke kept up his friendship with the Colbys of Glemham, and also became friendly with the Warners of Mildenhall, a family who were based in west Suffolk, but who tended to be at loggerheads with the Bury Puritan oligarchy and look to the east.[31] The Warner friendship was an interesting hint that Coke stayed close enough to his origins to keep at arm's length from the leaders of the Bury Bench, a hint which

---

[27] PRO, SP 12/189/30; PRO, STAC 5 B67/1, 79/38; *APC* XIV, p. 117.

[28] On Coke's mother and family, see BL Harl. 6687, fos. 10–12.

[29] PRO, E134/22 James I/Michaelmas 40, and Aylsham 16, Coke to John Browne, 27 May 1612. Wentworth and Coke can also be found acting for the conservative Rede family in the Beccles Fen dispute during the 1580s (cf. Bec. A4/39 and PRO, E134/28 Eliz./Easter 21).

[30] PCC 51 Parker. John Wentworth of Somerleyton had no connection with the baronial family of Nettlestead; his father was an Ipswich joiner (Muskett III, p. 17). Like Coke, he moved away from his conservative background: cf. *Chorography* pp. 11, 62, 118.

[31] James, pp. 23–4, qu. visits in 1597 listed in Holkham House MS 724; Coke supervised Warner's will (PCC 65 Weldon). On Warner, see below, p. 336, and MacCulloch, 'Power, Privilege and the County Community', p. 299.

may be reinforced by the fact that that *éminence grise* of Bury conformity, Sir William Drury, made him one of the supervisors of his will in 1587. It is notable, too, that when in 1601 Sir Robert Jermyn and Sir John Higham were opposing the Bury townsfolks' agitation for a borough charter, they reported to Cecil that 'it is given out that Mr. Atturney inclineth towards' the townsmen's aims.[32]

By the 1590s Coke was developing his national career and becoming a figure to attract patronage in his own right. In the process he had moved far enough away from the Cornwallis–Heveningham alignment to become a consistent opponent of Sir Arthur Heveningham's Norfolk schemes.[33] By 1601 he was influential enough to get his brother-in-law Robert Barker of Parham appointed to the Suffolk Bench,[34] but over the previous decade he had also built up a useful network of electoral patronage in the Suffolk coastal boroughs. One of his initial benefits from the Earl of Arundel's recovery of the family's Suffolk liberties was his return to the 1588 Parliament as one of the burgesses for the recaptured Howard seigneurial borough of Aldeburgh. As in other boroughs formerly controlled by the Duke of Norfolk, parliamentary patronage at Aldeburgh seems to have lapsed to the Exchequer nominee.[35] Now the Howard family celebrated its victory Osborne had sat for the borough in 1584 and 1586, and it may be suspected that Francis Beaumont, a career lawyer who had no traceable Suffolk connections, burgess in 1572, had also been an exchequer nominee.[35] Now the Howard family celebrated its victory over Westminster by returning its champion as member for Aldeburgh together with a genuine burgess, William Bence. The Howard electoral influence there was to endure until overwhelmed by popular fervour in the turbulent elections of 1640.[36]

Coke never subsequently sat for Aldeburgh, although as we shall see, it is possible that he secured the election for the borough in 1593 of Thomas Knyvett of Ashwellthorpe; at the same time his independent influence was spreading to the other coastal boroughs.[37] In 1593 Orford elected him Recorder on the death of Sir Gilbert Gerrard, and it is possible that in the same year he procured the election of Thomas

---

[32] Drury: PCC 40 Scott. Jermyn, Higham: Hatfield 88/68.
[33] Smith, pp. 123, 273, 284, 299, 302, 325.   [34] PRO, C231/1, fo. 100ᵛ.
[35] Cf. the career of Thomas Fanshawe, Remembrancer of the Exchequer, at Rye (1571) and Arundel (1572–93).
[36] Holmes, p. 23.
[37] For Coke's arbitration in disputes over jurisdiction among the coastal communities, see PRO, STAC 5 B96/39 interrogatories, and ibid., S42/16, Answer.

Corbet as second burgess for Dunwich; certainly Dunwich gave him the nomination of one member in 1597 'in respect of his former and continued friendship many ways'.[38] Again in 1601 Coke was given one nomination there, choosing Francis Mingay, a close relative from Norfolk, while the borough showed itself aware of the local gentry's relationship with Lord Buckhurst by electing John Suckling, Buckhurst's secretary, as the other member.[39] Orford, which had adhered to its established choice of local gentlemen in 1593 and 1597, in 1601 showed itself more sensitive to its Recorder's wishes by electing Sir John Townshend, whom Coke was supporting in the faction-fighting of Norfolk politics, and another Coke relation, Sir Richard Knightley.[40] Coke may even have been responsible for the election of another member of the Corbet family at Aldeburgh in the same year. Seven Norfolk men sat for Suffolk borough seats during Elizabeth's reign, apart from Coke himself, all in the coastal towns.[41] The fact that six of these seven were elected in the 1590s is partly a tribute to the spreading ripples of Norfolk's political dislocation, but it is also likely to be thanks to Coke's efforts to use his influence in Suffolk on behalf of his Norfolk compatriots. In these efforts his new friendly contacts with the Wentworth–Wingfield group would have been important in gaining him a place in the affairs of Dunwich and Orford, two boroughs where the electoral influence of Hopton and Wingfield was strong.

The rise of the Earl of Essex and his clumsy attempts to win supremacy for himself at Court had little effect on Suffolk politics. By contrast, Dr Smith comments that in Norfolk the gentry's divisions were 'heightened by the Essex–Cecil conflict at Court', but Norfolk politics lead one to suspect that the gentry there welcomed any excuse to heighten their divisions.[42] It is true that Essex was instrumental in restoring Sir Robert Jermyn to pre-eminence on the Suffolk Bench and that Jermyn's son was among his clientage; it is also true that the Earl was unlikely to make any headway in the east of the county, where

---

[38] Orford: *HMC Various Collections* IV, p. 270; Dunwich nomination: *HMC Various Collections* VII, p. 85.

[39] Ibid., p. 87; on Mingay, cf. James, p. 3.

[40] *HMC Various Collections* IV, p. 270; James, pp. 2, 26. On Townshend, cf. Smith, p. 304.

[41] Roger Woodhouse (Aldeburgh 1571), Thomas Knyvett (Aldeburgh 1593), Thomas Corbet (Dunwich 1593), Francis Corbet (Aldeburgh 1601), John Suckling, Francis Mingay (Dunwich 1601), Sir John Townshend (Orford 1601).

[42] Smith, p. 303.

the two main groupings looked either to his implacable foes the Howards or to Lord Buckhurst, a man at best above Court faction or at worst a sympathizer with the Cecilian party.[43] The Devereux estates in east Suffolk were to insignificant to give Essex the basis for any rival clientage. However, any attempt to argue from this that Essex sought to provide a west Suffolk contact with the Court as opposed to the east Suffolk contacts outlined above founders on the rock of the Earl's political incompetence. At the same time as Essex was performing favours for Jermyn and thus apparently aligning himself with the opponents of local patentees and of Sir Arthur Heveningham, he was becoming a partisan for the Exchequer patentees who were seeking with Heveningham's support to overthrow the title of the Dean and Chapter of Norwich to the Chapter estates.[44]

Essex's involvement with local politics was indiscriminate and irrational, a sorry parody of the wide contacts cultivated in earlier years by Leicester and Cecil. His following in Suffolk consisted of young men who had not achieved a place in the county magistracy, companions-in-arms whom he had knighted like Sir Thomas Jermyn, Sir Robert Drury of Hawstead, Sir William Poley of Boxted, Sir John Poley of Stowupland, or men with Court ambitions like Robert Gosnold, Robert Naunton or Lord Keeper Bacon's two youngest sons.[45] Of these only Gosnold achieved inclusion in the county commission of the peace during Elizabeth's reign, probably at Essex's prompting, and the other names are a motley collection drawn from families of all shades of religious opinion and from all sides of the county.

With the boroughs Essex made a little more headway. At Dunwich, having secured the election of his friend Henry Savile in 1593, he wrote demanding both parliamentary seats in 1597, but the borough gave him only one nomination and granted the other to his bitter foe Edward Coke: a dangerous game for a little town to play in the 1590s! Aldeburgh also elected a close associate of Essex, Francis Hervey, in 1597.[46] Ipswich was placed in a similar dilemma in 1596 when

---

[43] R. Naunton, *Fragmenta Regalia* (1824), p. 129; Manning, p. 231; Harrison, p. 277.
[44] Smith, p. 270.
[45] Shaw, II, pp. 89, 93, 96; Venn, III, p. 232; *DNB* s.v. Bacon, Anthony, and Francis.
[46] Dunwich: *HMC Various Collections* VII, p. 85. *History of Parliament 1558–1603* II, p. 266, identifies Francis Hervey with the son of Stephen of Cotes, but this is surely wrong. I owe the identification of this MP with Francis Hervey of Cressing Temple to W. J. Tighe, 'The Harveys: Three Generations of Tudor Courtiers' (unpublished article), and offer Dr. Tighe my thanks.

choosing a new High Steward. Sir Robert Cecil had put forward the candidature of his friend Michael Stanhope, a newcomer among the county gentry who had done the borough a number of favours at Court in the past, but Essex, his prestige at its zenith after his spectacular if useless triumph at Cadiz, had been elected by popular demand despite the intention of the senior burgesses to choose Stanhope. Such at least was the story of the town's bailiffs, who wrote an abject letter of apology to Cecil after the Common Council's election meeting and Essex's subsequent acclamation among the commonalty.[47] It sounds an unlikely tale in view of the tight control which the town's oligarchy normally exercised over its government. Ipswich was then at the height of its quarrel with the county leaders over their refusal to pay an adequate sum towards the expenses of two ships in the Cadiz expedition, and the town leaders probably decided that Essex as commander-in-chief of the Cadiz venture would be more use to them in their lobbying at Court than Stanhope; Sir Robert Cecil's wrath therefore seemed worth risking, particularly if fair words might turn it away.

As it had done with Lord Hunsdon for the previous Parliament, Ipswich offered Essex one of the nominations for its members in the 1597 Parliament, and he chose Francis Bacon. On the withdrawal of Sir William Waldegrave junior from the other seat after his election for the county, the burgesses found the ideal solution to make their peace with Michael Stanhope by electing him as a colleague for Bacon.[48] Evidently this solution was a success, for Bacon and Stanhope were re-elected even after Essex's execution, for the 1601 Parliament; on this occasion Bacon preferred his Ipswich seat to a family nomination at St Albans. The servant proved more satisfactory for Ipswich than the master; like everyone else who pinned their faith to Essex, the burgesses of Ipswich found little comfort and much embarrassment in their decision. If their choice of Essex had been something of an affront to the gentry alignments of east Suffolk, his successor as High Steward after his disgrace was a suitable symbol of the borough's contrition: Thomas Lord Buckhurst.[49] Otherwise, because he had never made much impact on the county, Essex's fall left few traces there. Of all Essex's Suffolk clients only his secretary Robert Gosnold

[47] *HMC Salisbury* VI, p. 332; on Stanhope, cf. BL Add. 34564, fo. 10[v].
[48] Bacon, p. 389.
[49] Bacon, p. 406.

was implicated in his pathetic insurrection, and he escaped with a £40 fine.[50]

Humbler contacts in the Westminster bureaucracy might prove safer than exalted but maverick figures like Essex. In particular, the conservative gentry of East Anglia seem to have maintained useful links with officials in the Exchequer which served them well in the years when central policy was pressing ever harder on convinced Catholics. These links may have originated with Robert Hare, brother of Michael, one of the most prominent of Suffolk recusants; Robert was an Exchequer Teller from 1560 to 1570 and seems to have maintained a subsequent connection;[51] later the connections concentrated especially on the conservative families in Lothingland and the Waveney and Broadland basins. It had been from these families that the abortive rising of 1570 had sprung, and it is puzzling how lightly they had escaped; John Jerningham of Somerleyton and James Hobart of Hales were both given pardons despite their leading part in the unrest.[52] Jerningham's subsequent career was remarkable, and does not make sense until it becomes clear that he was recruited as an English spy on the Spanish armies, spending time with the King of Spain in ostensible self-imposed exile during the 1570s and sending information from Parma's army in the Netherlands in 1583–4.[53] At the same time he became involved in Exchequer affairs, standing surety for a debt of Thomas Gardiner, a bankrupt Teller of the Exchequer, in 1578; in 1581 he was openly described as a royal servant.[54]

Another Exchequer link with the Jerningham circle in Lothingland comes through John Hoo, Miles Spencer's old friend, who leased all Henry Jerningham's courts in Lothingland and Mutford and who was numbered by the defence commissioners of 1584 as among the 'evyll men' of the island much favoured by the Catholic JP John Jerningham of Belton, the other John Jerningham's uncle.[55] He had an uncle, John Gamage, who was an attorney in the Queen's Remembrancer's Office of the Exchequer; his father-in-law also had influence in the

[50] *APC* XXXI, pp. 159, 275, 314, 356; PRO, C231/1, fo. 117ᵛ.

[51] *DNB*, s.v. Hare, Robert.

[52] PRO, SP 12/171/63.

[53] Hatfield 2/21; PRO, SP 12/168/8; *CSPFor.* Jan.–June 1583, pp. 412–13; ibid., July 1583–July 1584, pp. 23, 35–6, 39–40, 77–8 (I am indebted to Dr W. J. Tighe for drawing my attention to these references).

[54] PRO, SP 46/31, fo. 193ʳ (1578); *APC* XIII, p. 284 (1581); he was granted two successive periods of freedom from arrest for debt, 1582 (ibid., pp. 361, 381).

[55] PRO, SP 12/162/40, SP 12/171/63.

Exchequer, for it was to him that Hoo wrote to obtain the lease of the issues and post-fines of Lothingland from the Queen.[56] Similarly, Hoo's father Richard appears to have had Exchequer connections, for his papers ended up among the Exchequer correspondence. Richard Hoo also had strong links with the great East Anglian Catholic family of Bedingfield, and one might notice Thomas Bedingfield of that same family, who obtained his celebrated monopoly of the manufacture of playing cards with Ralph Bowes.[57]

One of the conservative gentlemen of Lothingland listed in the 1584 report was George Hervey of Oulton, ex-steward of the Catholic Lord Morley, and an open recusant in the 1570s; yet in the very year of the report, this associate of John Jerningham of Somerleyton was chosen escheator for Suffolk, an office in the gift of Exchequer officials.[58] Thomas Tasburgh, who became a Teller in the Exchequer, was another north-east Suffolk man, a younger son of the family of Flixton-by-Bungay; his first wife was sister of Sir Thomas Kitson.[59] Although Tasburgh's elder brother John was a strong Protestant, John's daughter-in-law was so staunch a Catholic as to bring all her children back to the old faith, and it needed the intervention of their relative Lord Buckhurst to save Mrs Tasburgh from the consequences of recusancy on at least one occasion.[60]

The results of these links are not far to seek. Such contacts with central government may well have helped to prolong the extraordinary regime of Catholic sympathizers in Lothingland constructed by John Jerningham of Belton and not exposed until 1584, but equally striking is the absence of all but one of the conservative families of north-east Suffolk from regular and concentrated occurrence in late Elizabethan

[56] Gamage's papers form PRO, SP 46/60, and cf. SP 46/31, fo. 3. SP 46/31, fo. 250, is a letter from Hoo to his 'loveing father Mr. Wyskerd at Framsham' (Fransham, Norfolk).

[57] Richard Hoo's papers, SP 46/9. Thomas Bedingfield: *APC* XI, p. 172, and *HMC Salisbury* II, p. 144.

[58] PRO, SP 12/171/63: lease from John Jerningham of Somerleyton, *Calendar of Charters, Rolls, etc. in the Bodleian Library* (Oxford, 1878), p. 448. Recusancy: CRS LIII (1961), p. 109; Hatfield 139/215.

[59] Howard, II, p. 103.

[60] MS Collections of Brigadier T. B. Trappes-Lomax, Jesuit Library, Farm St., London: Suffolk file s.v. Flixton, qu. Louvain Chronicle I, pp. 253–6. For the later recusancy of the Tasburghs up to the eighteenth century, see Suckling, I, pp. 198–200, and cf. Sir John Tasburgh's letter to his sister, *s.a.* (SROI, HA 12/unlisted material/76). On Buckhurst and Mrs Tasburgh: *HMC Salisbury* V, p. 198. I am indebted to Mr Christopher Coleman for our discussions about the Elizabethan Exchequer, and in particular for this reference.

recusant lists and on the Recusant Rolls; the Tasburghs, for instance, are never mentioned. Even among those who were pursued, Dom Hugh Bowler remarks on the 'astonishing laxity' displayed by the Exchequer nationwide in collecting recusant fines.[61] Such laxity was openly discussed in East Anglia. In 1616 Thomas Scot, rector of St Saviour's Norwich, produced a series of elaborate allegorical verses with explanations of the meaning, one of which was a bitter attack on church papists and the ease with which they escaped trouble; if Catholics did get as far as being prosecuted, said Scot, 'there are pillars in the Exchequer: or if these faile, a friend or kinsman in Court makes all sure'. In view of Sir Arthur Heveningham's family connections and his long association with the Exchequer and the Court, Scot's dedication of this verse and diatribe to him 'and his truely religious lady' can only have been a piece of heavy-handed irony.[62]

Scot could have looked back over decades of Exchequer involvement in East Anglian affairs. Sir William Drury, the scourge of Bury Puritanism in the 1580s, became an Exchequer official, and the military service in the Netherlands in which he met his death in 1589 was as much an escape from his disastrous financial commitments in the Exchequer as anything else.[63] The Exchequer also supported the conservative faction in the Beccles Fen dispute in the 1580s, while Sir Arthur Heveningham was to play a major role in defending the Exchequer in the great quarrels over the ownership of Martham parsonage in Norfolk in the 1590s.[64] The Martham conflict was part of the wider confrontation over concealed lands and patents generally; in this the Exchequer ran up against the Puritan group in East Anglian politics which was so opposed to patentees and the policies of central financial organization. It was not surprising that East Anglian Puritans were so suspicious of central government's intentions in local affairs, when a significant group of medium-rank officials in the Exchequer were so plainly opposed to everything which they held dear in religion.

To approach a great patron or friend at Court or a lesser contact in the Westminster bureaucracy was one way for the local gentleman to

---

[61] CRS LVII (1965), p. cxii. The Jetters of Lowestoft were the only family of the area regularly to be noticed.

[62] T. Scot, *Philomythie or Philomythologie* . . . (1616, *STC* 21869), Sig. E. Cf. *DNB*, s.v. Scot, Thomas.

[63] *History of Parliament 1558–1603* II, p. 58.

[64] On Beccles, see MacCulloch, 'Power, Privilege and the County Community', p. 305. Martham: Smith, pp. 265–75.

achieve his ends; another was to enter Parliament. Parliament was not merely a forum for conflict, but was also a vehicle for co-operation with central authority; certain leading county figures among those regularly returned to Parliament were clearly valued for their expertise in drafting everyday legislation, men who were skilled not merely in articulating grievances in the Commons chamber, but also in reconciling the interests of government and people. The development of the Commons Journals in the later sixteenth century gives us a chance for the first time to see these men at work. Although it is dangerous to assume that an MP automatically attended every Commons committee to which he was appointed, four Suffolk men all with interests in central government stand out as being chosen for committees of the House strikingly more often than their fellows: Sir Owen Hopton, Thomas Seckford the younger, Edward Grimston, and William Humberston.

Hopton as Governor of the Tower, knight of the shire for Suffolk in 1559 and 1571 and for Middlesex in 1572, was the prime example of the mediator between the centre and local interests: the Commons Journals record him as sitting on thirteen committees discussing bills on such varied subjects as the repression of seminarists, shipping, the Merchant Adventurers, clerks of the market, and the Court of Common Pleas, while predictably in view of his office, he was one of the commission of members of the Commons who met to discuss the fate of Mary Queen of Scots in 1572.[65] Seckford is recorded on sixteen committees in the Parliaments of 1563 to 1571, besides being one of those conferring with the Lords over the succession in 1563; because of his legal expertise as one of the Masters of Requests, it was not surprising that seven of the sixteen committees were concerned with law reform: such matters as conveyancing, actions upon the case, common recoveries or grants by corporations. However, as one of the quorum of High Commission he also sat on committees dealing with recusancy and church discipline, and in 1576 he was the obvious person to deliberate on the Suffolk and Essex Cloths Bill, although like Sir Owen, he was no longer the county member.[66]

Edward Grimston with his interests in concealed lands, royal salt-houses, and the alnage for Suffolk was a useful man for specialist committees on commercial matters. He was a recorded member of

---

[65] *CJ* I, pp. 83, 87–8, 91, 95–6, 106, 112, 120, 125, 127, 129–30, 134.
[66] *CJ* I, pp. 66, 78–9, 83–5, 96, 99, 104–6, 108–9, 112, 127–8, 133. On High Commission, Gee, p. 147.

twenty-three committees in four Parliaments, and of these, fourteen concerned commerce in various ways ranging from local issues like the improvement of Orford Haven through bills for leather manufacture and broggers and drovers to his particular interests in the alnage and wool manufacture; no doubt self-interest as much as the House's desire for specialist knowledge compelled him to membership of such committees.[67] William Humberston was Crown Surveyor and also acted for the Duchy of Lancaster in Suffolk; he sat on seven recorded committees in the Parliaments of 1571 to 1572 including two in which he would have had a particular concern, dealing with exchequer frauds and outlawry proclamations.[68]

These men had one thing in common; they all came from the east of the county, for although Humberston had lived with the Springs at Lavenham and Pakenham in the west during the sixties, he was associated with Dunwich in later years.[69] Two of the four, Hopton and Seckford, were members of the Wentworth–Wingfield group; indeed, it is worth noting that of the twenty knights of the shire elected during Elizabeth's reign, eleven were associated with this alignment: Hoptons and Wingfields on three occasions each (1559, 1563, 1571, 1572, 1588), William Cavendish (1559), Thomas Seckford (1571), Henry Warner (1597), Henry Glemham (1601) and Calthorpe Parker (1601). By contrast, the leaders of the Bury Bench, Sir John Higham and Sir Robert Jermyn, were elected for the county only at the height of the Puritan agitation of the 1580s and were still not capable of a landslide victory at the polls at their first attempt in 1584. Although Sir John Higham's son Clement secured election for the county in 1593, it is surely significant that the group which provided the largest number of knights of the shire was also that with the closest and most enduring contacts with the Elizabethan Court and central government. Higham and Jermyn had been the bearers of the county's protests into the Commons in a time of exceptional religious tensions: the Wentworth–

---

[67] *CJ* I, pp. 83, 86, 88, 92, 103, 105–6, 108, 112, 125, 127–8, 134; D'Ewes, *Journals*, pp. 247, 431, 441, 445, 477. On his commercial interests, see PRO, SP 12/43/1; PRO, SP 46/38, fo. 10.

[68] *CJ* I, pp. 88–9, 92–4, 96. On Humberston, cf. *CPR Eliz.* IV, no. 1452; Somerville, pp. 446, 450.

[69] *CPR Eliz.* I, p. 363, III, no. 59; he married Dorothy, da. of Robert Spring (Metcalfe, p. 146) and was named executor of Thomas Spring in a Pakenham case (PRO, C3/131/17). He bought land in Dunwich in 1561 (PRO, E401/1798, fo. 30ʳ), was MP for Dunwich in 1571, and was described as of Dunwich at his death (PCC Adm. II, p. 75).

Wingfield representatives are unlikely to have seen their parliamentary role in such dynamic terms. Similarly, it was the leaders of the west and not the east who were to be the focus of opposition to central interference in local affairs when secular grievances began replacing religious disagreements during the 1580s.

9

Civil and Military Controversy 1582–1603

IN his study of Norfolk, Dr Smith saw the 1580s and 1590s as the
time when 'two conflicting views of county government tended to
polarize the gentry into coherent and reasonably stable groups', when
gentry like Nathaniel and Nicholas Bacon and Francis Wyndham took
issue with the adherents of Sir Arthur Heveningham and Lord
Hunsdon on a wide range of local issues both administrative and
military, championing the well-established powers of the justices'
Bench against the innovations of the lieutenancy and royal patentees.
Smith sees the 'point at which opponents of those who abused patents
and licences began to oppose the grants themselves' as occurring
somewhere around the period in the mid to late eighties when the
lieutenancy became a permanent part of the apparatus of local
government; faction was becoming principled. The contrasts in the
development of Norfolk and Suffolk suggest a modification of this
view, and emphasize his observation that 'not for the first time,
perhaps, the self-justification of one generation has provided the
political maxims of the next'.[1] Ideology alone cannot explain the
contrast between the later Elizabethan politics of Norfolk and Suffolk.
Tempers were certainly raised on religious issues in Suffolk during the
1580s, but the outcome of the Puritan débâcle of 1583–4 was in the
long term to unite the county leaders; while tensions lessened in
Suffolk during the nineties, in Norfolk they increased to fever-pitch.
Why then did Sir Arthur Heveningham's activities not lead to disputes
as bitter in Suffolk as in Norfolk? It was not merely that he was more
active on the Norfolk Bench; although to judge from his surviving
papers he spent much more time on Norfolk affairs, his attendance at
Suffolk quarter sessions as recorded on the Pipe Rolls was in most
years well above the county average, and one would have thought that
there would have been ample opportunity for equally serious friction to
arise.

Dr Smith comments with relation to Norfolk that although
Heveningham had many relatives in the county, he himself married the

[1] Smith, pp. 333, 246, 333.

daughter of a Hertfordshire squire, and none of his twelve children married into a Norfolk family until 1601. In Suffolk, by contrast, the Heveninghams were one of the county's oldest surviving magisterial families, traditionally regarded as of knight banneret status, and still one of the most important in east Suffolk.[2] One of their alliances was of particular significance: the marriage of George Heveningham's daughter to the west Suffolk squire Sir Ambrose Jermyn, Sir Robert's father. It was a relationship which did much to blunt the edge of the conflicts between Heveningham and his opponents in Suffolk, for it was Sir Robert who took it upon himself at several stages of the Christmas Lane controversy to write to his cousin to explain the attitudes of those opposing the repair patents; at the same time he did his best to provide mediation in the bitter clashes between Sir Arthur and the Norfolk lawyer Edward Flowerdew. Sir Robert's characteristically earnest but kindly and moderate admonitions came from a 'lovinge and sure frend and kynsman', 'lovinge bothe your sealff and your name', and they were a far cry from the acrimony of the Norfolk Bench; by 1594 Sir Arthur had recovered sufficiently from any pique that he might have felt against his cousin's stance on patents to give Jermyn some useful help in his efforts to defend his old clerical friend Clement Paman, earning some grateful thanks from Sir Robert.[3]

In Norfolk Sir Arthur's links with the Jermyn family would carry little weight. We have already seen that Heveningham's close acquaintance in Suffolk included the Cornwallises and the arch-recusant Michael Hare and his relatives; when, therefore, Sir Arthur antagonized such Norfolk justices as Nathaniel Bacon, Edward Flowerdew or Francis Wyndham, they saw him as a new representative of that particular family grouping in East Anglian politics, a grouping which recalled the old dominance of the Howards so recently ended. The etiquette of local politics and the plain fact of Sir Arthur's consistent conformity to the Established Church prevented any open use of this connection in the arguments used by his opponents; it was much more feasible to oppose his schemes in terms of constitutional or legal theory.

In Suffolk the opposition to Sir Arthur was not only muted by his family contacts but was also weakened by the historic division of the county. Even in the later nineties, when Sir Arthur and Lord Hunsdon had ceased to be the front-line 'antagonists' and the Privy Council

---

[2] Smith, p. 159; on the Heveninghams, see *NA* III (1852), p. 285.
[3] Aylsham 16, Jermyn to Heveningham, 8 June 1583; 23 April 1589; 29 April 1594.

came into more direct conflict with the county leadership, it was still the leaders of the west who took the initiative. Moreover, the controversies in Suffolk consistently lack a constitutional edge, perhaps because the lesser internal tension of Suffolk did not demand the sophisticated political arguments employed by Sir Arthur's Norfolk opponents, and in particular by that almost obsessive constitutionalist Nathaniel Bacon. Dr Smith reminds us that 'behind most disputes between "Court" and "county" justices lurked the issue of who paid for what'; in Suffolk this issue was unashamedly in the forefront of debate on both civil and military matters throughout the last two decades of Elizabeth's reign.[4]

In Norfolk the 'civil' issues in local politics had three main focuses: patents for local administrative purposes, the furore over concealed ecclesiastical lands, and purveyance compounding. In Suffolk, as we will see, only the first engendered much controversy: the dispute over the Christmas Lane and Sheringham Pier patents which also disrupted Norfolk political life. However, in the beginning, the repair of Christmas Lane was a non-partisan issue in Suffolk. The JPs of north-east Suffolk were well aware of the consistent difficulty of this stretch of main thoroughfare through the parish of Metfield, 'very noysome and combrous to thenhabitaunce of the whole contrye there aboute', and those who were regular attenders of the Beccles quarter sessions put their signatures to a petition by the inhabitants of Metfield for a county-wide system of collection for the road's repair, in March 1581; the nine signatories were headed by that future champion of the Suffolk Puritans, Roger Lord North, followed by Sir Arthur Heveningham himself, and they included those bitter enemies John Jerningham of Belton and Robert Wrott.[5]

There was therefore good reason for a commission to be granted some fourteen months later for the diverting of two days of the county labour obligations for road repair to the repair of Christmas Lane with the alternative of a money commutation for those who did not fulfil their service in person.[6] However, already the supporters of the project were making some tactical errors. Most importantly for its future success, the patent enlarged the area affected by the obligations in a manner that had not been suggested in the Beccles justices' petition; as well as Suffolk it included the hundreds of Norfolk which lay nearest to Metfield and were most likely to benefit from any improvement in

⁴ Smith, p. 334.   ⁵ Hengr. 12 pt. ii, fo. 77.
⁶ PRO, C66/1218, m. 38.

Christmas Lane. This was only logical, but while no doubt the Beccles JPs would have felt it a breach of etiquette to suggest a charge on the neighbouring county in their petition, the project's sponsors seem to have made no effort to remedy the effect of this display of good manners by consulting the justices of south Norfolk; certainly the letters patent referred only to petitions from Suffolk. Perhaps Sir Arthur felt that tensions were already too high in Norfolk for him to secure the same comfortable unanimity there that he had achieved in Beccles.

The second tactical error provides further evidence that this was the case. Three weeks after the grant of the Christmas Lane patent, on 11 July 1582, Lord Chancellor Bromley sent a circular letter to eight leading East Anglian gentlemen asking them to see to the assistance of the commissioners appointed by the patent. Of these, seven names were predictable, the leading knights of Suffolk administration together with the *custos* for Suffolk and one of the signatories of the original petition, Bassingbourn Gawdy; these were the obvious choices to represent Suffolk.[7] However, apart from Gawdy, who had residences in both counties, Norfolk was represented solely by Sir Roger Woodhouse of Kimberley, hardly the happiest choice for winning over suspicious opponents of Heveningham. Woodhouse leant towards conservatism in religion, while significantly on his death his secretary entered the service of Sir Arthur.[8] It was an astonishing snub for the other JPs of south Norfolk.

Bromley's hand had no doubt been guided by Heveningham in his circular, and Sir Arthur was soon to reap the results of his egregious lack of tact towards the Norfolk Bench. 'Bitter debates' followed at Norwich sessions, and both sides appealed to the Privy Council. However, opposition was not confined to Norfolk; Suffolk justices had also written to the Council remonstrating against the patent.[9] It is not difficult to guess that the initiative came from the Bury Bench, where the Puritan leaders were still locked in conflict with their local religious opponents, and where Nathaniel Bacon had the advantage of contact with his brother Nicholas in order to spread the opposition to Sir Arthur's schemes. The Liberty of St Edmund would be less concerned

---

[7] BL Eger. 2713, fo. 133; the knights were Robert Wingfield, Nicholas Bacon, Robert Jermyn, John Higham, and William Spring.

[8] *Chorography* p. 14, and cf. Smith, p. 222. Sir Roger also gave support to the conservative faction in the disputes at Beccles (Bec. A4/52).

[9] Smith, p. 232.

with the maintenance of Christmas Lane than were the JPs of the east; the Metfield route was merely one among many routes for their commerce with the coast, whereas justices around the hundreds of Hoxne and Hartismere knew how vital a road it was for that area. In June 1583 Sir Robert Jermyn stressed to Sir Arthur that he should have his demands sanctioned 'at the Assises or when some solempne assemblye is: for sure it maye not be undertaken by one or two but by manye'.[10] However, as he went on to say that the Suffolk justices had already expressed their disapproval of the project in writing and would be unlikely to want to change their minds, his proposal must have seemed like sheer time-wasting to Heveningham. Since the west of the county would never be sympathetic to a proposal so purely for the benefit of the east, any move to get a road-repair approved by the whole county Bench would almost certainly have been hamstrung by the justices of the Liberty of St Edmund.

We have no information as to the outcome of this first round of the patents dispute. Dr Smith suggests that in Norfolk Sir Arthur may have had enough support on the Bench to get the patent enforced; likewise in Suffolk the discomfiting of the Puritans at the July 1583 assizes might have worked in Heveningham's favour. However, the first patent expired in May 1585 and does not seem immediately to have been renewed, so it is possible that for the time being Sir Arthur had given up the struggle; in any case he was occupied elsewhere with the Norfolk ramifications of a parallel dispute over the repair of Sheringham Pier. Whatever the outcome of the 1583 disputes, Christmas Lane still needed repair. Encouraged by the backing which he was now receiving from his old neighbour Lord Hunsdon, Lord Lieutenant from 1585, Heveningham made a fresh attempt at the end of 1587, and with judicious assistance from Hunsdon in the form of letters to Burghley he secured a new commission in April 1588.[11] This time the obscure men who had been named commissioners in the 1583 patent were replaced by Heveningham himself, Lord Hunsdon's son John Carey and Edward Honnings of Darsham and Eye, a gentlemen of esquire status from a family which had intimate connections with central administration.[12] Moreover this patent was a

---

[10] Aylsham 16, Jermyn to Heveningham, 8 June 1583.
[11] BL Lansd. 55/40; PRO, C66/1308, m. ld.
[12] His father William had been Clerk of the Signet: he leased Crown estates at Eye with his relatives the Cutlers, who were stewards of the royal park there (*CPR Eliz.* II, p. 128; PRO, C66/1266 m. 14), and he would become Receiver of the Crown lands in

far more sweeping document which proposed to give the commissioners powers to see the highways and roads of Norfolk, Suffolk, Norwich, King's Lynn, Ipswich, Bury St Edmunds, Sudbury, and Newmarket repaired by such persons as were chargeable to do so, and in particular it was directed not only to the repair of Christmas Lane but to the equally noisome stretch of the main Norwich road north of Attleborough.

Nearly a year elapsed before Heveningham brought this new patent before the justices at Norwich in January 1589; even he must have realized that the crisis year of 1588 was no time to start a major campaign for road maintenance. Nevertheless his proposal sparked off immediate opposition. While a subsequent attempt at compromise by the Privy Council divided the objectors on the Bench at Norwich, perhaps because the inclusion of a Norfolk road in the patent had made it more attractive to the Norfolk magistracy, opposition remained firm at the Lent assizes at Bury and Thetford thanks to the advocacy of Sir Nicholas Bacon; the Suffolk Bench was persuaded to put its signatures to 'a lettre to the Counsell to shewe the dislyking of the contry'.[13] The odds happened to be weighted at Bury against the patentees, for in the absence of Sir Arthur there was no one to rally his sympathizers like Philip Tilney, the Sheriff, and Sir William Waldegrave (both, significantly, JPs with discreet conservative leanings in religion). Edward Honnings was present, but he was worse than useless. He was not to become a JP until 1596 and so he could hardly address members of the Bench on equal terms; besides, he was in a particularly unhappy position as a near neighbour and tenant of Sir Nicholas Bacon's at Eye. His consistent timidity as a patentee aroused the fury of John Carey and may well have earned him his parliamentary seat at Eye at the hands of Sir Nicholas Bacon in 1593.[14] Against his feeble attempts to put forward the case for Christmas Lane to the blandly patronizing Bacon was ranged the leadership of the Bury Bench, backed up by Sir Nicholas's brother-in-law, the circuit judge William Periam. Small

Suffolk in May 1589 (PRO, SO 3/1 s.v. May 1589) probably through the good offices of John Carey on Heveningham's request (cf. Aylsham 180, Michael Hare to Heveningham, 12 April 1589).

[13] Smith, pp. 257–8; information on events at the Lent assizes comes from Aylsham 17, Edward Honnings to Heveningham, und. but of spring 1589.

[14] Aylsham 17, Carey to Heveningham, und. and 16 May 1590. Honning's uncle Charles Cutler had been one of Eye's first MPs in 1571 and again in 1572, but the Cutlers' official position at Eye which gave them a claim to one of the borough seats was in any case subordinate to the Bacons' stewardship of the Honour of Eye.

wonder that in April Lord Hunsdon should vent his spleen on Bacon for obstructing his son's patent at Bury and Thetford.[15]

Faced with this setback, Sir Arthur must have realized the futility of trying to get the Suffolk Bench to change its mind once publicly expressed; as Sir Robert Jermyn had reminded him at an earlier stage in the affair, having stated a position 'we maye not shewe so great a contraretye'.[16] He therefore turned to the deputy lieutenants to enforce his warrants for levying repair money, and it was at this stage that the Suffolk leadership began to split on regional lines. It is likely that during the 1583–4 dispute over Christmas Lane, disagreement among the county leaders had been set aside in their united stand against the assize judges' assault on Puritan 'ministry and magestracye', but tempers had cooled on that issue; now the deputy lieutenants of the east could show their sympathy for the repair of Christmas Lane, an issue which vitally concerned the transport network of their part of the county. To the annoyance of the Bury leadership, their fellow-deputy lieutenants in the east agreed to Sir Arthur's request: 'that which Sir Robert Wyngfeld and Sir Phillip Parker have done we presume thei ded as havinge rather regard unto ther office of Justices, then as deputie Lieutenantes' wrote Sir Robert Jermyn and Sir John Higham to emphasize that they were not going to demonstrate cabinet responsibility in the lieutenancy and follow suit.[17]

Sir Arthur wrote once more to Sir Robert before the summer assizes of 1589, and presuming on the fact that he was able to satisfy one of his kinsman's requests unconnected with the patent affair, Jermyn in his reply offered yet another admonition on this issue. 'It is a greater and a more weightie cause then I thinke is considered of, all circumstances regarded . . . but the president is it that is so offensive', he began in true constitutional style; but his subsequent remark revealed the context of the opposition: 'are speciallie at this tyme after so mani impositions as (as you can not but knowe) late drawne the contrie drie of monye'.[18]

The affair dragged on through 1590: Lord Hunsdon sent down letters backing Heveningham's demands; the justices of Suffolk retracted enough to offer a composition which Sir Arthur considered quite inadequate, and in Norfolk the conflict grew ever more bitter, resulting in extraordinary scenes at the January Norwich sessions of

---

[15] Redgr. 4152 and Bacon's draft answer, ibid., 4153.
[16] Aylsham 16, Jermyn to Heveningham, 8 June 1583.
[17] Ibid., same to same, 23 April 1589.   [18] Ibid., same to same, 6 July 1589.

1591 and a letter on 15 January complaining of Heveningham's conduct to the Privy Council. The one immediate result of this was a notably unsuccessful meeting for reconciliation between Lord Hunsdon and Francis Wyndham, but by early summer Heveningham was up in London, no doubt bearing the petition of his supporters then presented to the Council.[19] His visit bore good fruit, for he secured a Council letter on 27 June 'to the Shrive and Justices of the Peace of the countie of Suffolke and Norffolke'.[20] This rather peculiar form of address reflected the fact that the letter was in reality addressed almost exclusively to Sir Arthur's opponents in Norfolk rather than to the Suffolk Bench: it commented on 'the devision and faction growen amonge you that are gentlemen and of the comyssion of the Peace of that countie' and found 'by that which hath ben delivered before us that the actions of the said Sir Arthur have in some pointes receaved worse construction then there was cawse, and that his endevour for the repairing of the high waies aforesaid hath tended to the good and service of the countrey'. The Council said that if certain places had been unfairly rated, adjustments should be made to allow the work to go ahead, and it claimed that in the conflict between Heveningham and Francis Wyndham 'we have reduced them to good termes of love and frindshipp'. Sir Arthur was also exonerated from any discredit attached to his extraordinary humiliation at the January Norwich sessions, when the justices had granted the peace against him; this represented a decided snub for his opponents on the Bench.

It is hardly surprising that this rather one-sided attempt at compromise did not succeed in ending controversy in Norfolk, as Dr Smith explains; in Suffolk events were rather different.[21] Ipswich in particular had always displayed support for the Hunsdon–Heveningham party and its efforts for road repair, reflecting a growth of strained relations with the leading gentry of the west of the county at least. On the death of the former High Steward Walsingham at the height of the Christmas Lane controversy, Ipswich gave an emphatic demonstration of its partisanship by electing Lord Hunsdon in Walsingham's palace, a choice which can hardly have pleased the Bury Bench, while at the end of September 1591 the town sent twenty marks direct to Sir

---

[19] Smith, pp. 263–4. Suffolk offer: Aylsham 17, Heveningham to Sir Thomas Gawdy (copy), 23 July 1590. London: ibid., Richard Wright to Heveningham, 8 June 1591.

[20] *APC* XXI, p. 244. He probably also used this London visit to lobby for the grant of the patent to licence London brewers made him on 16 November 1591 (BL Add. Ch. 67530).

[21] Smith, pp. 264–5.

Arthur Heveningham 'towards the reparation of Christmass Lane, by a Commission to him granted'.[22] In the first parliamentary election after the Christmas Lane furore, in February 1593, the townsfolk of Ipswich gave yet another demonstration of where their sympathies lay by electing as their second MP Zachary Lock, Lord Hunsdon's secretary; such a step was without precedent in the borough. Lock was a London man with no Suffolk connections apart from his employment by Hunsdon and his links with Sir Arthur Heveningham: 'he is a very discrete and kind frind of your worshipps', Michael Hare had said of Lock when on Sir Arthur's business at Court in 1589.[23] The election was in direct contrast to the election of Edward Bacon and Clement Higham for the shire, yet this was the borough which only five years before had been prepared to give Sir John Higham an insurance seat when he was standing for the county election in the Puritan interest: a remarkable indication of how the issue of religion had faded and how the division over patents had taken its place in Suffolk politics.

In the west of the county, in contrast to Norfolk, no further references to the Christmas Lane affair have survived after the Council's compromise letter of 27 June 1591. The whole business had not solved the problem of Christmas Lane, as frequent later references to its lack of repair indicate,[24] and in any case the patent expired in 1593. However, in 1591 the Bury Bench became involved in a parallel controversy hitherto confined to Norfolk, the dispute over the patent for the repair of Sheringham Pier also sponsored by Sir Arthur Heveningham, granted in 1583 and renewed in 1590.[25] Although there were good grounds for alleging corruption in the administration of this patent, the west Suffolk JPs characteristically entered the fray only on the issue which concerned their particular area: according to the patent, the repair work was to be financed by fines on those landowners who offended against the statute for encouraging the sowing of flax and hemp. The men of the Franchise of St Edmund knew that its predominantly light soils were generally useless for the growing of flax, and in autumn 1591 they petitioned the Privy Council to this effect. It is likely that their interest in the question had been kindled by a fresh demand from the patentees, for after an initial

---

[22] Bacon, pp. 363, 366.
[23] Aylsham 180, Hare to Heveningham, 12 April 1589, and cf. various letters of Lock to Heveningham in Aylsham 16. Lock reveals no Suffolk links in his will, PCC 27 Bolein.
[24] *PSIA* XXIII (1939), pp. 144–5; *Chorography* p. 55.
[25] Smith, pp. 247–53.

payment of £20 in 1583, the Franchise does not appear to have been troubled again for some years.[26]

This petition formed part of a more general agitation from Norfolk which led to the setting-up of a bipartisan commission of enquiry including both Sir Arthur Heveningham and his Norfolk opponents into the administration of the Sheringham patent; in the following month the commissioners were sent a letter by nine justices of the Bury Bench underlining the unfairness of the flax penalty device.[27] This was no party issue, but a simple local grievance; although the letter's signatories were headed by Sir Nicholas Bacon, they included that veteran anti-Puritan Robert Drury of Rougham, the conservative-minded Sir William Waldegrave, and Henry Gilbert, whose son John was to marry one of Sir Arthur Heveningham's daughters eighteen months later.[28] It is perhaps hardly surprising that Gilbert's name dropped out of the subsequent letters, but the certificate of April 1592 to the commissioners giving detailed reasons for the unsuitability of the Liberty's soil still bore the signatures of Drury and of Waldegrave. Despite Dr Smith's interpretation of this correspondence, there are no grounds for supposing that the Bury justices took any wider view of the Sheringham Pier issue than a resentment at the agricultural absurdity of their liability to the flax penalty; they had taken no part in the vigorous agitation which had been raised in Norfolk against both the principle and the application of the patent in the years when the Liberty was apparently not being charged by the patentees.[29]

The flax patent was annulled when the 1593 Parliament allowed the thirty-year-old flax-growing statute to lapse; it was therefore no longer possible to collect such fines. Dr Smith considers that 'Kirk's patent provided one of the issues in the 1593 election in Norfolk', and while this is unlikely for the sister-county, it is worth noting that the knights of the shire elected were Sir John Higham's son and Edward Bacon, younger brother of Nicholas and Nathaniel, both of whom would be marked out as partisans against the Heveningham group and its predilection for the use of patents in local affairs.[30] However, one can discern a more indirect effect on the 1593 elections in Suffolk from this and another controversy involving Sir Arthur, indirect because this

[26] Petition: *APC* XXII, p. 87; cf. *NA* X (1888), p. 248. It is surprising in view of Sir Arthur's background that the accounts there printed reveal no payments from east Suffolk.
[27] Commission: *APC* XXII, p. 87; letter: *NA* X (1888), pp. 229–30.
[28] *NA* III (1852), p. 284.
[29] *NA* X (1888), pp. 232–3; Smith, p. 250. [30] Smith, pp. 252–3.

other controversy was primarily a Norfolk issue and hardly affected Suffolk: the dispute over the 'concealed lands' status of the lands of the Dean and Chapter of Norwich.

'Concealed lands' provided another example of the use of patents by central authority to shift burdensome administrative tasks onto private individuals: the grantees or their assigns at their own costs made the inquiries necessary to prove that certain lands were former ecclesiastical lands wrongfully concealed from the Crown, in return for a grant, lease or sale of the lands concerned; the device was also a useful way of rewarding the deserving by grants of what were in effect other people's lands.[31] In Suffolk Lord Wentworth had secured a grant of the right to two hundred pounds' worth of concealed lands in 1570, which he then regranted to various dependents or speculators; Edward Grimston and his son also went into partnership in the concealed lands business with Sir William Drury of Hawstead and a Crown servant of East Anglian origins during the 1570s.[32] They were predictable figures to engage in such traffic, Drury with his interests at Court and Grimston with his complex concerns with the Crown's financial business; predictable also because Wentworth, Drury and Grimston have already been identified as among the leading gentry of the county with particularly strong links with the Court and central administration.

Such activities were unlikely to arouse widespread controversy in the county, although Grimston found himself embroiled in the Beccles Fen dispute as a grantee of part of the Fen as concealed lands, and the claim to the Fen as concealed lands became one of the gambits by which the conservative JP William Rede sought to maintain his authority there.[33] The Dean and Chapter controversy in Norfolk was on a different scale altogether, for thanks to the inept way in which the Chapter had been set up on the surrender of Norwich Cathedral Priory and the equally inept efforts made later to remedy the initial mistake, it was possible to argue that the entire Chapter lands were being wrongfully withheld from the Crown. It was the assignees of the

---

[31] For a useful general treatment of the subject, see C. J. Kitching, 'The Quest for Concealed Lands in the reign of Elizabeth I', *Transactions of the Royal Historical Society*, 5th Series XXIV (1974), pp. 63–78.

[32] Wentworth: *CPR Eliz.* V, nos. 1900, 2724; VI, no. 109; VII, no. 3714. Grimston: *CPR Eliz.* IV, no. 2106; V, no. 2447; VI, no. 1563; VII, no. 2180; VIII (in preparation, PRO), no. 1235.

[33] Cf. ibid., no. 2106, and Bec. A4/52. For a concealed lands dispute on Grimston's patent in Benhall and Farnham, PRO, STAC 5 C16/34, C74/8, H62/37, H75/38, and for another in St Clement's parish Ipswich, PRO, E134/28 Elizabeth/Easter 29.

remainder of Lord Wentworth's patent who successfully argued this before the Exchequer Court, itself hardly a disinterested party, in 1583.

The subsequent conflict resolved itself into the familiar party lines of Heveningham supporters against his opponents, with Heveningham predictably taking the part of the Exchequer and its patentees against the capitular tenants. Since the Dean and Chapter had little property in Suffolk the struggle was confined almost exclusively to Norfolk and in particular to a long-drawn-out and sometimes violent test-case as to the ownership of the parsonage of Martham in the Norfolk Broadland.[34] The furore was at its height in Norfolk when the 1593 Parliament was summoned; there had been previous attempts to establish the title of the Dean and Chapter by Act of Parliament in 1576,[35] 1584 and 1588, and Dr Smith considers that the renewed effort to give the Dean and Chapter statutory existence was another of the major issues of the 1593 Norfolk election. The candidates involved are a measure of the polarization which had developed in the county at this time: Sir Arthur Heveningham, Edward Coke and Nathaniel Bacon. News of 'a great deale of unkyndenes about the chosinge of the Knights of the Shire' reached Court circles, while the result was a decisive defeat for Heveningham: Coke and Bacon were elected, Coke becoming Speaker of the Commons.[36] Coke was by now a national figure, and his Cornwallis–Heveningham links in Suffolk counted for less than his strong partisanship for the Dean and Chapter's title. Indeed, the issue of the capitular lands was a singularly unfortunate one for Sir Arthur to have taken a stand on; a wide variety of county gentry and yeomen were tenants of the Dean and Chapter, including the family of Sir Arthur's own secretary, John Browne of Poringland,[37] and it is hardly surprising that the Norfolk freeholders voted so firmly for the supporters of the Chapter.

However, it is likely that Coke did not confine himself to a triumph in the Norfolk election; every vote which could be mustered for the Dean and Chapter in the Commons would prove useful in the subsequent debates. We have already seen how Coke was gaining electoral influence in the Suffolk coastal boroughs; it cannot be coincidence that the 1593 election was the first in which two Norfolk men sat for Suffolk boroughs, Thomas Knyvett of Ashwellthorpe for Aldeburgh and Thomas Corbet for Dunwich. Knyvett was the son of

---

[34] Smith, pp. 265–75.   [35] *CJ* I, p. 107.
[36] Smith, p. 273.   [37] *Chorography* p. 14.

the bibliophile Sir Thomas Knyvett, a particular enemy of Hunsdon and Sir Arthur Heveningham, Corbet the son of a strong supporter of the Dean and Chapter, and both were close relatives of the Bacon brothers who were championing the capitular cause in the Norfolk county election.[38] Such was the effect of this Norfolk dispute on a county which had little direct interest in the affair.

The Act passed by the 1593 Parliament which quashed the legal technicality threatening the Dean and Chapter of Norwich and certain other Henrician corporations was singled out for particular praise by Speaker Coke in his closing oration; its successful passage led to Suffolk's one traceable involvement in the Dean and Chapter case when in 1596 the notoriously litigious Francis Bohun of Westhall, uncle by marriage to Coke, attempted apparently without success to overthrow the Queen's title to the rectory of Westhall, which had formerly been the property of Norwich.[39] This, however, was a very minor affair in the light of the passions which divided Norfolk society. The patentees were not daunted by their parliamentary defeat and found a new legal technicality which had to be dealt with by a fresh act of Parliament in 1597.[40] Once again Edward Coke intervened successfully against Heveningham's electoral aspirations at the Norfolk election for this Parliament; it is interesting to note Henry Warner, knight of the shire for Suffolk and himself of Norfolk origins, as chairing the heavily pro-capitular committee which considered the Bill after its second reading, for as has been noted above, Warner was a close friend of Coke's. This time the Exchequer admitted defeat and gave judgement in favour of the Dean and Chapter in the Michaelmas Term of 1598.[41]

The third issue of civil administration which disrupted Norfolk politics was that of purveyance. The Elizabethan government fully realized that the royal rights of purveyance provided one of the most dangerous sources of grievance to the country as a whole, and throughout the reign Burghley devoted much energy to persuading the counties to minimize the possibilities of friction with central government by regularizing their purveyance contributions. By 1580 at least fifteen

[38] On Knyvett and Corbett, see Smith, pp. 242–3, 270, 272. Corbet's father was an 'especial good friend' of Coke (*History of Parliament 1558–1603* I, p. 657).
[39] PRO, STAC 5 F20/38; Bishop Redman still considered Bohun's opponent to be farmer of the rectory at his 1597 visitation (NRS XVIII, 1948, p. 132). Cf. the boastful genealogical brass for Bohun's son, Westhall church. Coke's oration: Smith, p. 273.
[40] 39 Elizabeth, cap. 22.
[41] Smith, pp. 275, 325. On Warner, D'Ewes, *Journals*, p. 562.

shires had negotiated compositions for purveyance with the government and by 1597 practically all had done so. On a national scale Burghley could claim a considerable success; there was no more parliamentary agitation about purveyance after 1589 until the accession of James I, with his much increased requirements.[42] However, in Norfolk purveyance was too closely involved with Sir Arthur Heveningham, who was involved enough in its administration to include at least one purveyor among his servants, for a composition to work. A county-wide composition with the Board of Green Cloth was negotiated at Heveningham's insistence in 1593, but several JPs were still refusing to levy a county rate under its terms in 1602.[43]

In Suffolk the purveyance composition was far more successful. This is not to say that it was popular: Robert Ryece sarcastically headed the section on purveyance in his *Breviary of Suffolk* 'The discommodities of the soyle' since he regarded the county's fertility as a sure magnet for dishonest purveyors.[44] However, the machinery of purveyance never became the property of a factional interest as it did in Norfolk; the preliminary meeting to negotiate an agreement took place in September 1592 at Stowmarket, by now the accepted meeting-place for east and west when a general county decision had to be made (above, Ch. 3), and the first compounder in July 1593 was that established leader of the Bury Bench, Sir Robert Jermyn, soon to become *custos rotulorum*. Here was a mark of confidence in the new system from the group on the county Bench which would have been most likely to oppose it; it was a particular contrast to the choice of Sir Arthur Heveningham and his like-minded colleague Sir John Peyton as the first compounders in Norfolk. The compounders who succeeded Jermyn in 1595 were an equally appropriate symbol of the county's determination to keep partisanship out of purveyance: from the east Sir Philip Parker, both a veteran deputy lieutenant and a friend of Sir Arthur Heveningham, and Edward Grimston; from the west, Sir Robert Jermyn's old colleague Sir John Higham. Meetings at Stowmarket continued to regulate the system, and as Ryece commented after the Queen's death, 'after divers consultations the composition still continueth'. Perhaps the example of Norfolk served as an awful warning to the gentry over the border.

[42] Woodworth, pp. 4–5.
[43] Smith, pp. 296–302. Heveningham's servant was Thomas Southalls (Aylsham 16, Southalls to Heveningham, 20 February 1597).
[44] My account of purveyance is based on Ryece, pp. 15–17.

Such were the three areas of civil administration in which Heveningham played such a disruptive role in Norfolk. By contrast, Suffolk's rather muted internal controversies over civil administration faded as the national military situation grew more critical and the central government's military needs became more and more urgent in the later nineties. In Norfolk the increased importance of military administration was twofold in its effect on county politics: military organization provided yet another forum for conflict, while at the same time much the same group of gentry who were opposing Sir Arthur began directly to oppose the military demands of the Privy Council. In Suffolk only the latter strain of opposition is at all noticeable. Although we will note signs of a regional split among the deputy lieutenants over the ship money issue of 1596–7, in a rather similar manner to the split which occurred over the Christmas Lane dispute in 1589, this was no serious breach; despite any differences which might have arisen over ship money, Sir Robert Jermyn and Sir Philip Parker were still close enough to form a joint interest in the county election of 1601 in opposition to Henry Glemham and Henry Warner (below, pp. 335–6). The relative unity of the muster commissioners made it all the harder for the Privy Council to secure its demands in the face of local opposition; in Norfolk they could at least attempt a policy of divide and rule.

There had been a certain amount of friction between the Privy Council and the muster commissioners ever since the reorganization of the counties' military forces in the 1570s. In 1577 the Council had to reprove the commissioners for not sending up the muster certificates of 1573, and later in the same year it noted the negligence of several shires when sending out a certificate in standard form for the commissioners to use.[45] In 1580 the commissioners agreed that the Council's demand for the 'furnyture' of 5,000 troops in the county militia was too high and petitioned it to that effect; similar complaints came in from Lincolnshire and Huntingdonshire.[46] It was probably because of such displays of recalcitrance on the part of county muster commissioners, who still included most JPs on the county Benches, that the Council felt encouraged to attempt a further reorganization of the county military organizations in 1585. For the first time Privy Councillors were appointed as permanent lieutenants of counties or

---

45 BL Harl. 309, fos. 119ʳ, 203ʳ.
46 Ibid., fos. 231–2; Harl. 366, fo. 37; Boynton, pp. 76, 83.

groups of counties with a much smaller group of local deputies to assist them.

The Lord Lieutenant for Suffolk and Norfolk was Lord Hunsdon, an appropriate choice for Suffolk in view of his lands in the county and his previous membership of the muster commission, but a less acceptable figure for the gentry of Norfolk, particularly in view of the way in which his local acquaintanceship was linked to a particular section of the region's gentry. His choice of deputies in Suffolk was, however, hardly likely to ensure any easier co-operation with the Council's orders, and one suspects that as with the appointment of Sir Thomas Knyvett in Norfolk, Hunsdon was not given a free hand on his choice.[47] Sir Robert Wingfield was a predictable figure among the deputies in view of his county eminence and experience in administration, as was Sir Philip Parker, but Sir Robert Jermyn and Sir John Higham, still thrust out of the commission of the peace, were strange choices dspite Jermyn's military experience. What of Sir William Drury, Sir Owen Hopton, Sir William Waldegrave; what, indeed, of Sir Arthur Heveningham, who seems never to have been a deputy in Suffolk?

The crisis year of 1588 was chiefly remarkable for the extraordinary degree of squabbling which the government's unprecedented emergency demands for cash precipitated; one is reminded of the muster commissioners' bickering over a meeting-place in the other Elizabethan crisis year of 1569 (above, p. 41). The noisiest arguments came from the coastal towns, always ready to quarrel with each other, over the Council's requirement that they should supply certain ships for defence; Aldeburgh, Orford, and Dunwich could find no basis of agreement for apportioning the cost between themselves until the Council intervened; they could concur only in demanding that Woodbridge should be included in their contribution rather than that of Ipswich, while Sir Robert Wingfield wrote up that the inhabitants of Orford were trying to shift part of the burden onto those who were already charged in land service.[48] Meanwhile Mistley, East Bergholt, and Manningtree were protesting that they should not be liable to part of the cost sustained by Ipswich and Harwich in setting forth three hoys on the grounds that their occupation was the cloth trade rather than the sea; a previous memorandum by certain east Suffolk JPs to the Council had requested that Bergholt be exempted from Colchester's

---

[47] Cf. Smith, pp. 242–3.
[48] Council intervention: *APC* XVI, p. 93. Woodbridge: PRO, SP 12/209/96. Orford: SP 12/209/95.

charge of two ships 'that we maye not weaken our contrye to strengthen an other'.[49] This egregious piece of local patriotism a fortnight before the Armada set sail is unlikely to have impressed the Privy Council. At the end of the year the Council decided to cut the Gordian Knot of expense accumulated in the building of the coastal towns' ships by ordering the deputy lieutenants to levy the deficit of £500 from the landward hundreds of the Geldable on the basis of subsidy ratings. It was an ominous precedent for the attempts to collect ship money in 1596, and if the bailiffs of Ipswich sourly recalled their expenses of 1588 in that subsequent clash, it is unlikely that the deputy lieutenants had forgotten either.[50]

Disagreements were not confined to coastal defence, however; we have already noted how the tenants of the Duchy of Lancaster in the county refused to supply horse for defence in the national emergency on Sir Francis Walsingham's request (above, Ch. 1, n. 46). Nor were the gentry captains of the county defence forces exempt from petty quarrels; at the height of the crisis, on 27 June, the deputy lieutenants had to write to Sir Nicholas Bacon to calm a 'contraryety' which had arisen between him and Robert Forth over the apportionment of men and armour in the hundred of Hoxne between their respective bands.[51] In the light of this quarrel it was perhaps significant that the exigencies of 1588 produced a new agreement over the apportionment of horse between captains of divisions which was still appealed to in the early seventeenth century. It was against a background of widespread and sordid squabbles that the county's 2,500 men marched to Tilbury to hear Queen Elizabeth at her dramatic best.[52]

If the county could be so affected by disagreement over the financing of defence in the face of the Armada, it was not surprising that it showed even greater disinclination to foot the bill for naval defence eight years later. The euphoria of the 1588 victory brought about a distinct slackening of local interest in military preparedness: Dr Boynton noted the marked deterioration in muster returns on a nationwide scale after 1588, and the virtual disappearance of the well-to-do from the trained bands.[53] It was in this situation, after a petition from the port towns, that the Privy Council wrote to the deputy

[49] *APC* XVI, p. 58; PRO, SP 12/209/102.
[50] Council order: *APC* XVI, p. 399. Ipswich: BL Add. 34564. fo. 1ᵛ.
[51] Redgr. 4150.
[52] Agreement: Committee Book, fo. 5ᵛ. Armada: Ryece, p. 92.
[53] Boynton, p. 173.

lieutenants in January 1596 asking them to levy a county rate to assist
the port towns in the charges of providing two ships for the Cadiz
expedition. By the beginning of March it was clear that some at least of
the deputies were reluctant to levy any such rate.[54]

Who among the deputies was displaying such reluctance? The
Council's letter of 8 March 1596 makes it clear that some at least of
the deputies had 'showed good forwardnes' in the business, and
among these latter was probably Sir Philip Parker, who rented a house
in Ipswich and had maintained a long tradition of friendly relations
with the borough; the leaders of Ipswich were the chief movers in the
petition for county aid.[55] If Parker was not sympathetic to Ipswich's
cause it is difficult to account for the presence of one confidential letter
from Jermyn and Higham to him together with certain other
lieutenancy correspondence in the letter-book which is our main
source of information on the dispute, and which was clearly compiled
by a partisan of Ipswich.[56] As in the Christmas Lane dispute, it is likely
that the deputy lieutenants of the east could sympathize with the plight
of the coastal towns, while throughout the affair it was the leaders of
the west who took a hard line. Before the Privy Council had fixed an
exact sum for the county to contribute to the ships, Sir Robert Jermyn
wrote to Burghley asking that the contribution should not exceed
£400. His letter revealed an extraordinary degree of antagonism
towards Ipswich which calls to mind the town's gestures in support of
the Christmas Lane patentees a few years earlier; he accused Ipswich
of profiteering in building the ships, of unjustly taxing gentlemen who
came to live for short periods in the town, and of engrossing corn for
export in years of dearth. Perhaps recognizing the animus in this
appeal, the Privy Council rejected the deputy lieutenants' revised offer
of £600 on 28 March and told them to collect £900.[57]

So far the deputy lieutenants had been hampered in their opposition
to the levy by the oversight of Lord Hunsdon, who both as Privy
Councillor and as High Steward of Ipswich was a strong supporter of
the Council's demands; he had already written one hortatory letter to

[54] *APC* XXV, p. 276.
[55] Parker's house was rented from the Seckfords: cf. PCC 4 Rutland. He was made
free of the town in 1585 (Bacon, p. 343), and his daughter was given a wedding present
by the borough in 1593 (ibid., p. 373).
[56] BL Add. 34564, fos. 3[v], 4[v], 8[r], 9[r], 14[v], 15[v], 16[r], 18[r]. At fo. 7[r] of the volume is a
signature in a legal hand: 'Will'm Hawys nuper de Gipp'o': this was the son of John
Hawes, a former town clerk of Ipswich (PRO, STAC 5 D28/35, deposition of Hawes).
[57] Jermyn: *HMC Salisbury* V, p. 556; *APC* XXV, p. 315.

his deputies on 10 February.[58] However, fate dealt a cruel blow to Ipswich's cause in July when Hunsdon died; Essex proved no substitute to the town as High Steward despite his generalship at Cadiz. The four deputy lieutenants were reappointed as muster commissioners, their freedom of action and personal prestige much enhanced; within a month they had been joined in commission by Sir Nicholas Bacon who had been excluded from the lieutenancy administration by Hunsdon's consistent hostility, and who was to give strong support to the opposition to the ship money levy.[59] In Norfolk his brother Nathaniel was providing characteristic leadership to similar opposition to a much smaller proportional levy for ships furnished by King's Lynn and Yarmouth, and he was likewise included in the new Norfolk muster commission.[60]

The Privy Council was still writing to the newly-appointed commissioners in fairly polite terms when on 12 September it gave them good reason for acceding to the county rate and told them to confer with the bailiffs of Ipswich. It was more than a month before the two sides met at Stowmarket and little seems to have emerged from the meeting; by late November the Council's letters to the commissioners were assuming a threatening tone as a result of the delays.[61] On 29 November Jermyn and Higham wrote to their fellow-commissioners in the east, and having got some routine militia business out of the way sent the clerk out of the room and continued with a frank summary of their attitude to Ipswich's demands:

We are willinge to yeld to any reasonable order for there Releife, but we would not be overreached with a crooked measure, and therfore we praye you to intreate Mr. Roberte Forthe and Mr. Edward Bacon to take paynes to examyne the Ipswich accomptes, and what they shall sett downe to be the one halfe of the chardge allotted to this countie, we wilbe content to make out our warrantes for the thirde parte allotted by comendable custome to this Franchise of Burie.[62]

Here was a combination of the west's long-standing suspicion of Ipswich's motives with an insistence on 'comendable custome' in levying the rate; if the levy was going to be made it must follow the traditional apportionment of local taxation in the county between the Geldable and the two franchises, an apportionment which would be

[58] BL Add. 34564, fo. 4ᵛ.   [59] *APC* XXVI, pp. 51–3.
[60] Smith, pp. 282–3, 288.
[61] *APC* XXVI, pp. 171, 321; Bacon, p. 385.   [62] BL Add. 34564, fo. 16ʳ.

reaffirmed by the county Bench twenty years later.[63] The letter's tone confirms one's impression that the differences of opinion among the muster commissioners were not serious enough to create bad feeling; Jermyn and Higham ended up with some London gossip and a joke about a flood around Westminster Hall.

Jermyn and Higham had thus committed themselves at least in private, and with proviso, to accepting the Privy Council's demands. However, two months later Jermyn and Sir Nicholas Bacon sent out a form of warrant for levying the money which verged on insolence in its equivocation.[64] This extraordinary document described for the benefit of the high constables how the commissioners had met the Council's demands for half the costs of the ships with 'sondrie reasons of importance to the contrarie'; nevertheless, they said,

in dischardge of our humble dueties to ther honors we are herebie to require you and eyther of you that together with the signification of there honorable pleasures in this behalfe you will use your best indevor to perswade all persons of the better sort of habilitie within your hundred to yelde ther willinge benevolence and voluntarie contribution towardes which payement . . .

If, therefore, the Council were to get its money, it would only be with an implied rebuke to its authority; contribution was to be 'voluntarie'. In any case, with such a backhanded warrant directed on the initiative of only two of the commissioners, it was unlikely that many constables would make much effort in the collection.

The Council reacted with predictable fury when news reached it in March of the issue of these warrants, 'aggravatinge the matter and dyswadinge the same by perrillous arguments, meeter to move the people to dyscontentment then to concur in her Majesty's service'; hardly surprisingly it summoned Jermyn and Bacon to appear at the Council board. However, the appearance was something of a triumph for the two commissioners. Far from being dismissed, by promptly submitting themselves to the Council's direction in the matter and by 'earnest intreaty' they secured pardon of their proceedings and a reduction of the remaining £740 owed by the county to £500.[65] The Council may have been influenced by news of the Norfolk Bench's continued refusal to levy funds for King's Lynn,[66] but the outcome of the affair gave extraordinary testimony to its lack of sanctions in the face of determined opposition from local magnates who had made

---

[63] Committee Book, fo. 13ᵛ.   [64] BL Add. 34564, fo. 16ᵛ.
[65] *APC* XXVI, p. 553, XXVII, p. 49, XXVIII, p. 137.   [66] Smith, p. 282.

themselves wellnigh indispensable in government. Nor, despite their promises at the Council board, were the commissioners any more ready with their payment.

There was a distinct note of weariness in the Council's letters to the commissioners seeking action in the cases of refusals to pay ship money from the town of Lowestoft and from a prominent Ipswich merchant in early 1597, yet by the end of the year it was clear that the principal offenders were Jermyn and Bacon themselves.[67] By now the other muster commissioners seem to have faded out of the dispute and the initiative was entirely with these two; it was to them that the bailiffs of Ipswich wrote in November complaining that they had received a mere £136 of the £500 laid down by the Council in the spring. The desperate obsequiousness of the bailiffs' letter veiled a renewed threat to write to the Council, which prompted Jermyn and Bacon to promise satisfaction and to call them to a meeting with the master and owners of the ships concerned.[68] As an indication of where the advantage now lay, the meeting was to be at Bury rather than Stowmarket; there was no concession to the convenience of the Ipswich men.

Such was the situation on 21 November 1597; on 27 August 1598 the Council menacingly reminded Jermyn and Bacon that £300 of the £500 was still outstanding. On 5 April 1599 the bailiffs of Ipswich wrote once more, this time to all the muster commissioners.[69] They were still unsatisfied of part of their £500, and threatened in much less polite terms than before to bring the Council back into the dispute. Yet no satisfaction emerged; conference with the assize judges at the Lent assizes of 1600 produced a warrant from the commissioners for a levy.[70] The Council noted that such was the mood of the county that only 'strict order' would produce any results, and told the commissioners to deal severely with any defaulters; since it was the commissioners themselves who had consistently encouraged such default the Council's letter was a rather empty gesture, as it must have realized. In Norfolk King's Lynn was still vainly soliciting money from Nathaniel Bacon's part of the county in June 1601;[71] the missing ship money was a lost cause. Charles I's regime was to learn a short-term if not a long-term lesson from the affair by entrusting a new ship money collection to the personal liability of an annual officer rather than to

[67] *APC* XXVII, pp. 98, 126, 153, 236.
[68] BL Add. 34564, fos. 22ᵛ, 23ʳ.
[69] *APC* XXIX, p. 105; BL Add. 34564, fo. 25ʳ.
[70] *APC* XXX, p. 146.   [71] Smith, p. 282.

such a firmly-entrenched clique of local magnates as the Suffolk muster commissioners; and indeed, in the short term, Charles was to enjoy more success in his collection than had Queen Elizabeth.

Throughout the dispute the commissioners had displayed the same traditionalist attitude towards the levy of money as the opponents of Christmas Lane; when Jermyn and Bacon spoke in their circular to the constables of 'the wayte of the burden so unusuall in sea service to be layde uppon the Inland partes and the danger of the president hereof in future tymes' they were precisely echoing Jermyn's letter to Sir Arthur Heveningham about Christmas Lane eight years before even to the idiosyncratic spelling of 'precedent'.[72] In the extraordinary conditions of the 1590s any 'burden' laid upon the county was likely to be unusual compared with the 'commendable custome' of years past, but the leaders of the Bury Bench in particular, with their attenuated contacts with the Court, were unlikely to share the Privy Council's awareness of changed times any more than they had been able to see any virtue in Sir Arthur Heveningham's solutions to the difficulties of local administration.

Although the resistance to ship money in Norfolk and Suffolk was undoubtedly concerted, the opposition displayed an interesting difference of approach in the two counties which underlines the unity of the Suffolk leadership compared with that of Norfolk. In Norfolk the dispute was fought throughout at quarter sessions, among the whole body of the justices;[73] in Suffolk there is no single mention of the justices' sessions as playing any part in the affair, and throughout it was the muster commissioners who were in the forefront of the dispute. In Norfolk Lord Hunsdon had been able to exploit the county's divisions to create for himself a reasonably compliant body of deputy lieutenants, including Heveningham; in Suffolk he was faced by a generally harmonious group of independent-minded deputies. The result was that while the Norfolk deputies found their powers and prestige attenuated by the loss of Lord Hunsdon, and their ranks gradually invaded by Heveningham's opponents,[74] the Suffolk deputies had owed much less of their county influence to their lord lieutenant and were able to keep the initiative in the ship money dispute from passing to the wider body of JPs. Since Sir Philip Parker and Sir Anthony Wingfield seem to have been prepared to keep their sympathies for Ipswich within the bounds of virtual abstention from

[72] Aylsham 16, Jermyn to Heveningham, 6 July 1589.
[73] Smith, pp. 282–3.   [74] Smith, pp. 283, 288.

the commissioners' policy of confrontation with the borough and the Privy Council, their colleagues could act as a dynamic leadership for the county and sway county opinion into an appearance of unanimity.

One's impression of Suffolk as a county made safe for 'country-minded' gentlemen in the late 1590s is strengthened by considering the fortunes of the muster-mastership in the county. It was at this time that two views tended to develop on the role of the muster-master in county military organization. Professional soldiers argued that for efficiency's sake the muster-master should be a paid professional soldier commanding small companies of men who would be better able to perform the new methods of manœuvre than the old large, unwieldy county companies; the county gentry, however, tended to object strongly to these ideas. Since the 1580s the muster-masters had been paid exclusively out of county funds but the counties had no say in choosing the officers whom they paid; the appointment was in the hands of the lords lieutenant. Moreover gentry who had invested much emotional capital in their local military commands objected to the idea of reducing the size of their companies and to the consequent admission of lesser gentry to captaincies on the same basis as themselves; Sir John Smyth and Sir Henry Knyvett produced pamphlets to argue the case for large companies commanded by leading local gentlemen and for a muster-master who was 'a knight or an esquire of great worship of the same shire'.[75]

In Suffolk the death of Lord Hunsdon which freed his erstwhile deputies from irksome supervision also freed them to reorganize the county's military organization as they pleased. Only six months after Hunsdon's death they secured the removal of the professional muster-master, Allen Lewis, when Sir Clement Higham, Sir John's eldest son, knight of the shire in 1593, and also a soldier of 'verie good experience', offered to perform the service free of charge. Sir Clement was already in charge of the company previously commanded by his father.[76] Here was the ideal man from the county gentleman's point of view, and it was well worth raising a county contribution to pension off Captain Lewis. When Sir Clement decided to leave the post in 1601 it only required a letter on the part of his relative Serjeant Yelverton to Sir Robert Cecil to secure the appointment in his place of his cousin, veteran captain in both county and overseas service, Thomas Higham of Wickhambrook.[77] Under the two Highams there was no question of

[75] Smith, p. 286.   [76] APC XXVI, pp. 371, 485.
[77] PRO, SP 12/116/9; PRO, SO 3/1, s.v. June 1592; HMC Salisbury VI, p. 361.

the proposals for smaller companies being implemented, as Hevening-ham had managed to do in Norfolk between 1596 and 1599.[78] Indeed the county magnates were so intent on keeping the companies under their control that the results verged on the ludicrous; Sir William Spring commanded the forces of the hundreds of Blackbourne and Thedwastre, so Sir Robert Jermyn, who also lived in that area, was constrained to take command of the bands of Lothingland, Mutford, and Wangford, 'the most remote places from his habitacion of all that country'. The Privy Council was not blind to the failings of this system; in giving Jermyn the Blackbourne and Thedwastre command after Spring's death it rather acidly commented on the Lothingland captaincy that 'the said Sir Robert ys nowe growne into yeres, and so neither so fytt for travell nor (in our opynions) so nere to attende a chardge so farr dystant from him'.[79] However, it would take more than the Privy Council's 'opinion' to work any great alteration in the ways of the Suffolk muster commissioners.

Both in 1597 and 1598 as the ship money dispute dragged on, the commissioners could secure reductions in troops demanded by the Privy Council, and only once did they suffer any check on their activities. In July 1598 the Council ordered the commissioners to send up £120 for furnishing Horse for Ireland; five months later despite both letters and personal reminders the money had still not been paid, and the commissioners were dragging their feet over another payment for the Irish war.[80] The Council summed up years of frustration in its dealings with Suffolk in a rebuke worthy of the tongue of its royal mistress:

Theis kinde of dealinges in matters concerninge her Majesty's speciall service beinge so full of careless negligence hath bin made knowne to her Majestie, as reason ys her Highnes should knowe those who have care of her service and suche as so slightly regard the same, and therfore as you shewe smale respect of our letters and earnest sollicytacion unto you, so wee deale plainly with you to let you knowe that wee perceive evidently you affect more that tytle to have authorety to deale in theis matters for your private credites and respectes in the contry and not for anie regard or care you have of her Majesties service . . .

The commissioners were commanded to appear before the Council board or face dismissal.[81] It is astonishing that after this diatribe there is no evidence of any dismissals. There is no good evidence that even

---

[78] Smith, pp. 287–8.   [79] *APC* XXXI, pp. 373, 389.
[80] *APC* XXVII, p. 105; XXIX, pp. 276, 343.   [81] Ibid., p. 395.

Sir Nicholas Bacon, prime gadfly of patentees and Privy Councillors alike since the 1580s, was dismissed; although he does not reappear among a list of muster commissioners in 1601 it is possible that the list is incomplete, and no other lists appear to have survived for the period after 1598.[82] Perhaps the commissioners paid up, but still their ship money debt remained outstanding. Against passive resistance of such consistency the Council had little redress, for all its bluster; in a county whose magistracy was as united as that of Suffolk had become, it would be a dangerous task to seek 'others that shall shew better care in theis occacions of publique and important services'.[83]

A combination of factional disputes, religious disagreements, obstinate traditionalism and some genuinely constitutionalist idealism was responsible for a high degree of opposition to central government's demands from the county establishments of Norfolk and Suffolk by the 1590s. While in Norfolk the leaders of that opposition were still not able wholly to dominate their strife-torn county, in Suffolk they had reached a degree of eminence in which there was little overt opposition at least to their conduct of county affairs, even when one half of the county continued to enjoy fruitful contacts with leading courtiers like Lord Hunsdon and the Howards. In the stresses created by the wars and economic dislocation of the nineties, the image of 'country' was coming to maturity for the county leaders.

[82] Folger Xd. 30/31.   [83] *APC* XXIX, p. 395.

PART IV

POPULAR POLITICS

Introductory

THIS book has concentrated on the world of the nobility and the gentry, its rhythms of life, the shifts of power and changes of belief within it, and the emergence of a Protestant power bloc which effectively ran the county by the death of Elizabeth. However, there was another world of politics alongside the great houses of East Anglia; we have glimpsed it at work in the disruption of East Anglian life which followed the downfall of the Howards in 1549, and in the areas of the county which developed a vigorous grass-roots Protestantism on the basis of earlier Lollardy. Not only gentlemen and clergy were able to express themselves or carry out the work of local administration. The Tudor landscape did not reveal merely the rich man in his castle, the poor man at his gate: in East Anglia there were three types of community, the purely agricultural, the manufacturing, and the market centre, and power was diffused through these in different ways. In the countryside there were gradations of yeoman, husbandman, and labourer below the level of the gentleman. In Suffolk, inland manufacturing communities were almost exclusively concerned with cloth production, and so the power in such classic examples of the type as Lavenham, Glemsford or the Waldingfields would be concentrated in the hands of clothiers, with below them tradesmen of varying levels of prosperity, and once more at the bottom of the pile the labourers who sustained the cloth industry. On the coast, fishing communities like Lowestoft or Orford were similarly dominated by the shipowners, the men who organized the industry, and their poorest men were mariners. Some market centres overlapped with cloth towns, particularly at Hadleigh, Sudbury, and Long Melford, but there was a whole range of market centres where the cloth industry was of minor significance in the Tudor period: at one end of the scale, giants like Ipswich or Bury St Edmunds, ranging through smaller places like Stowmarket, Beccles or Bungay, but all characterized by an élite of merchants and tradesmen.

Wealth was the obvious mode of differentiation in subtle shades of status in these diverse communities. One early sample of occupations in the hundreds of Babergh and Cosford, the list of 'rebels' in 1525 discussed below, fails to differentiate between yeomen and husbandmen in the communities which it lists, classing the two groups together as husbandmen; nevertheless, when compared with the valuation for the Subsidy of 1524, it reveals how this class, with its valuations in goods or lands ranging between £2 and £20 *per annum*, was sharply differentiated from labourers and weavers, overwhelmingly assessed at the minimum rate of a pound.[1] However, the assessment of status by wealth only complicated the problem of relating the status of different groups within the different types of community. The small group of men from whom the bailiff leadership of the great chartered borough of Ipswich was drawn was as wealthy as the leading county gentlemen and lawyers who formed the county commission of the peace, yet the leadership in a small borough like Eye or even a fairly substantial one like Sudbury was emphatically not on the same social level, even if it could boast a royal charter just as much as Ipswich. How did town tradesmen of varying degrees of wealth relate in status to country yeomen, husbandmen or labourers? Contemporary commentators were vague about this; they were mostly drawn from the armigerous landed classes, and their main interest in classification stayed at that exalted level. It was difficult for them to relate groups like gentry, yeomen, and husbandmen, identified by their social status, to groups like tradesmen and manufacturers, identified by their economic activity; classification of the clergy presented a further puzzle.

What was clear throughout the Tudor period was that power in the communities of the county was not confined to men of coat armour. The towns which had achieved a chartered corporation were the most obvious example of this, but it was true of many a village too, where yeomen represented the summit of the village hierarchy, and no gentleman would regularly appear. The listing of the 1524 Subsidy suggests that at that period, 67 per cent of Suffolk communities apart from Bury and Ipswich lacked a resident gentleman or influential monastic house.[2] Forty years later, when the definition of gentle status

---

[1] Cf. *1524 Subsidy* pp. 1–46, 152–66, with PRO, KB 29/157, mm. 5–6.

[2] 312 out of 466 communities for which statistics can be deduced; the 1524 Subsidy returns have suffered some damage. Towns with more than one parish, Sudbury, Bungay, and Dunwich, are taken as single communities. This percentage is lower than that quoted by other writers (e.g. Hoskins, p. 56), but this is because they have not taken into account the fact that not all gentlemen are listed as such in the Subsidy; the names in the listing have to be examined with reference to the Anticipation returns (pr. *1524 Subsidy* pp. 402–8) and other sources.

was becoming more generous, the percentage of Suffolk communities without a resident gentleman in the 1568 Subsidy was still 58 per cent.[3] This percentage might not have been so significant if gentlemen had been evenly distributed throughout the county, but in practice they were concentrated in the most pleasant and economically attractive areas. This meant that they were thin on the ground in the light-soil regions outside the wood–pasture area: hundreds with lower-than-average concentrations of gentlemen in 1524, 1568, and in the listing of county gentry in 1578 were the fenland and Breckland hundred of Lackford and the Sandlings hundreds of Blything, Carlford, Wilford, Lothingland, and Mutford. Robert Ryece, writing at the end of Elizabeth's reign, was conscious of the relative unpopularity of the Sandlings among his fellow-gentry, and explained it in terms of the current wisdom on health, rather remote from our own ideas on sea breezes: 'the aire here is nott esteemed so pure by reason of those winds which blow from the sea, and so are deemed unwholesome'.[4]

Yet also within the wood–pasture area, there were noticeable variations in gentry residence. Tudor gentlemen seem to have felt uneasy outside the well-watered river valleys. As a result, wide areas of upland parishes contained few gentlemen's residences throughout the century: whole groups of parishes on the plateau of central south Suffolk in particular, stretching from the high open landscape of Rede in the west some twenty miles, almost to Ipswich in the east, intersected by only a few valleys which account for the gentle families who did appear there. For an upland parish of this area like Stanstead near Glemsford, it was natural for the early seventeenth-century Chorographer of Suffolk to record without further comment that 'there have no gent. dwelled in the towne', yet in the valley village of Monks Eleigh, the lack of any symbols of the gentry's presence was a matter for surprise: 'in the church is not one escutcheon or monument and yet in the towne are many fayre houses and sweet dwellings for ayer'—air, one notes again, signifying protection from the breezy uplands. When the heralds came into the county seeking gentlemen to quiz about lineage and coat armour, the gaps in their itineraries are

---

[3] This figure is within 1 per cent of the figure which can be deduced from the 1561 listing of freeholders in the Geldable (BL Lansd. 5/7). The list of Suffolk gentlemen in 1578, Hatfield 139/214–18, suggests a higher percentage of communities without a resident gentleman, at 65 per cent, but it may exclude some lesser gentry.

[4] Ryece, p. 24.

significant; they reflect this combination of light-soil and upland parishes.[5]

Such unevennesses meant that something like a majority of Suffolk townships were accustomed to running their affairs with little intervention from the world of the gentry. Yet is this fact enough to justify speaking of 'popular politics'? Politics is about aims and objectives, and about results; can we trace any lines of action or achievement which forced the political nation of gentry and nobility to pay heed to the opinions of the wider community? There are indeed such traces. The story of popular protest in East Anglia shows that in the first half of the century, the members of the yeoman oligarchies throughout the region were prepared to unite with humbler folk in direct action to express their will, and only with the failure of the greatest attempt of all at such action, the stirs of 1549, did they concentrate on other means of getting things done.

  [5] *Chorography* pp. 63, 51; on the heralds, cf. the map of itineraries in Corder, *1561 Visitation* I, opposite p. viii.

10

The Age of Rebellions 1525–1570

To talk of rebellions raises problems of definition. One man's rebellion is another's responsible protest, and most rebels in Tudor England would have been highly indignant so to be termed; a more neutral word might be that frequently used at the time: 'commotion'. A whole range of serious disturbances faced successive Tudor governments, and the intention behind these disturbances was by no means always to topple the existing regime. When it was, it usually signified the involvement of aristocracy and gentry in the organization of the affair; only two 'commotions' in Tudor East Anglia, Mary's 1553 *coup* and the 1570 Norfolk rising, unambiguously had such an intention and such an involvement. Nevertheless, there is a certain convenience in keeping to the terms rebel and rebellion in the discussion which follows, although they are used with due apologies to the sensibilities of those who were involved; in doing so, some amends can be made by searching for the real motives behind the disturbances.

Most Tudor rebellions were distinguished by their lack of success: looking through the melancholy story of such affairs as the Cornish rebellion of 1497, the Lincolnshire Rising and the Pilgrimage of Grace, or Wyatt's Rebellion and the Rising of the Northern Earls of 1569, one is tempted to wonder why the rebels bothered, when the odds seemed so consistently stacked against them. However, there were two exceptions to this general picture: two rebellions which succeeded. Their very success has indeed obscured their character as rebellions, following Sir John Harrington's maxim that if treason prosper, none dare call it treason. One rebellion succeeded in annulling one of the most punitive taxes which a Tudor government ever attempted to levy, the Amicable Grant of 1525; the other succeeded in substituting the Lady Mary for Lady Jane Grey on the throne of England. Both these rebellions had their focus in East Anglia, and they cannot be viewed in isolation from each other; they form part of a sequence of East Anglian rebellions which also came to a head in 1549 and 1569–70. To investigate the continuities which lie behind the sequence we need to examine each of these in turn.

Lt. Walsingham

• Castle Rising

N. Elmham
Gayton Thorpe
King's Lynn •

Fincham

Woodrising   Norwich   Gt. Yarmouth

Downham Market

Wymondham   Hales
Griston

R.*Waveney* Lowestoft

Little *Ouse R.*   Kenninghall   Bungay• Beccles Carlton
                                                          Colville
I. OF ELY   S. Elmham •
                                                      Sotterley
        Mildenhall   Hinderclay•   Eye   Laxfield   Walberswick
        Flempton   Sibton
           • Fornham   Cotton   •Dunwich
Bury St. Edmunds•   Kenton
                         Mendlesham   •Theberton
CAMBRIDGESHIRE •Rushbrooke   Benhall • •Leiston
                         Crowfield
        Rede• Cockfield Stowmarket Letheringham   •Aldeburgh
        Lawshall Lavenham   Glemham Farnham
        Stanstead •Brent Eleigh   Orford
Glemsford•   •Monks' Eleigh ʌ   Melton .
   Clare Long   •Hadleigh   Ipswich
        Melford Waldingfields
Stansted   Sudbury• Stoke by Tattingstone *Orwell*
Mountfitchet   Nayland
              Nayland & • •E. Bergholt   •Felixstowe
              Wissington R.*Stour*
                         Boxted   Brantham
       County boundaries   ESSEX
  - - - Approximate boundaries of sheep-corn
       and wood–pasture farming areas
<u>Norwich</u> Places with camps in 1549

VII. Popular politics and East Anglia 1525–1570

    The Amicable Grant of 1525 was a drastic and grotesquely-named attempt to finance Henry VIII's aggressive foreign policy by a levy of one-sixth of the goods of the laity and one-third on the goods of the clergy. This followed hard on the heels of a very substantial money grant in the Parliament of 1523, and shortage of ready money was exacerbated by a flow of specie abroad; throughout April 1525, the month after the announcement of the new exaction, there were reports from areas as far apart as Huntingdonshire, East Anglia, London, and

Kent of reluctance to pay.[1] In East Anglia the two Dukes were charged with the organization of the collection, and whatever their private opinions might have been about the wisdom of Wolsey's desperate fund-raising venture, there is no indication that they showed any slackness in pressing ahead with the collection. To minimize the possibility of resistance to the Grant, the Duke of Norfolk postponed the assessing in Norfolk to coincide with that of Suffolk.[2] Nevertheless, discontent grew to dangerous levels right across England. By the beginning of May Wolsey was proposing to modify the original demand by abandoning the idea of a fixed sum and instead negotiating with the taxpayers as to what they might pay. It may have been this sign of weakness that precipitated the most dramatic stage of the crisis in East Anglia.

According to Hall's Chronicle, it was the agreement which the Duke of Suffolk negotiated with the rich clothiers which caused the trouble. They claimed to their workers that the demand for money would force them to lay off labour. 'Then began women to wepe and young folkes to crie, and men that had no woorke began to rage, and assemble theimselves in compaignies.' On 9 May the Earl of Essex and Lord Fitzwalter reported to Wolsey that they had succeeded in persuading the freeholders assembled at the county town at Chelmsford to assent to the Grant, but had met with total failure at the north-west Essex town of Stansted. The reason was 'an unlaufull and a heyghnous assemble of a thowsand personys at the lest lately commytted in the countye of Souffolke in the border of the same next adioyneng to the hundred of Hynkford where we do now sytte'. Hall reports an even more alarming story: the Duke of Suffolk attempted to disarm the crowds,

but when that was knowen, then the rumour waxed more greater, and the people railed openly on the Duke of Suffolke, and Sir Robert Drurie, and threatened them with death, and the Cardinall also, and so of Lanam,

---

[1] Hall, pp. 698–9. Woods, 'The rioting crowd', pp. 9–11, convincingly relates coin shortage to international exchange rates; however, his ingenious attempt to show that Wolsey intended the Amicable Grant to discredit the war policy advocated by the Dukes of Norfolk and Suffolk while knowing that there was no real need for money, is based on an incomplete survey of the Crown's financial position at the time (R. L. Woods, 'The Amicable Grant: some aspects of Thomas Wolsey's rule in England, 1522–26', Univ. of California Los Angeles Ph.D. 1974). Dr. G. W. Bernard's important article on the Amicable Grant was unpublished at the time of writing.
[2] BL Cott. Cleop. F VI, fos. 336–8 (*LP* IV pt. i, no. 1235).

Sudbery, Hadley, and other tounes aboute, there rebelled foure thousande men, and put theimselfes in harnes, and rang the belles *Alarme,* and began to gather still more . . .³

The Dukes of Suffolk and Norfolk were in no doubt that they were facing full-scale rebellion. If Hall talks of four thousand, the chronicler Ellis Griffith mentions ten thousand gathered at Lavenham.⁴ Even after they had brought matters under control, and there was time for cooler reflection, the Duke of Suffolk could let Wolsey know that the great assembly in the Lavenham area was only the centre of a much wider phenomenon: 'the confederacie . . . extanded to many places not oonly in this shire and Essex but in Cambridge shire the towne and unyversite of Cambridge and dyvers other contryes lay herkenyng to here'.⁵ The two Dukes had even raised the possibility that representatives of the old White Rose grouping among the aristocracy, Lord Bergavenny and the late Duke of Buckingham's son Lord Stafford, might be drawn into a nation-wide uprising if Wolsey did not take swift action. Even if this frightening combination of popular and aristocratic discontent did not materialize, within a few days of the gathering at Lavenham, a priest was circularizing the news of commotion in Huntingdonshire, to the alarm of Bishop Longland of Lincoln.⁶ It was therefore vital to suppress the Lavenham stirs before they spread further; apart from anything else, the two Dukes' credibility as the masters of East Anglia was at stake. They gathered their own force of four thousand, gentry and their tenantry, which took up a position just outside the area affected by open defiance, but the chances of their achieving a settlement by brute force were slim; their followers were reluctant to do open battle against 'their kindred and companions, who, they deemed, were suffering from utter injustice.'⁷

The Dukes would therefore have to proceed as much by diplomacy as by coercion, much to the disgust of the Duke of Suffolk; equally, however, the demonstrators were split between militants and those who sought conciliation. According to Ellis Griffith, who was relying

---

³ Hall, p. 699; PRO, SP 1/34/192–3 (*LP* IV pt. i, no. 1321). The demonstration took place on 5 May, being preceded by a similar outbreak on 4 May at Lavenham (PRO, KB 9/497, mm. 7–10).
⁴ Griffith, p. ii.
⁵ PRO, SP 1/34/196 (*LP* IV pt. i, no. 1329).
⁶ Dukes: SP 1/34/190 (*LP* IV pt. i, no. 1319). Longland: SP 1/34/198 (*LP* IV pt. i, no. 1330).
⁷ Griffith, pp. ii–iii, and cf. Hall, pp. 699–700.

on eyewitnesses of the affair from among the local gentry, the militants failed to sway the crowds to their purpose only because a rich townsman of Lavenham had had the foresight to remove the clappers of the bells of Lavenham church, which would have been rung to alert those waiting in the great swathe of country commanded by the newly-finished tower; this would have been the signal to go on the attack. It was this crucial loss of initiative among the militants which enabled negotiations to go ahead and for the Dukes to exploit their opponents' sense of deference to established order.[8] Within two days of the Dukes gathering their forces outside Lavenham, the demonstrators had caved in; over a two-day period, at setpiece confrontations at Lavenham and Long Melford, they were forced to sue for pardon in their shirts and were formally indicted of riot and unlawful assembly after the Dukes had threatened them with the far more menacing charge of high treason.[9] The rebellion had been crushed, without a single life being lost, as far as we know; nevertheless the rebels had in effect won. The money demand was withdrawn, and when the rebel leaders appeared before Star Chamber at the end of May, they were pardoned after the King's Council Learned in the Law had 'laied sore to theim their offence'. More importantly, Wolsey ostentatiously sought their pardon and stood surety for them as a fellow-Suffolk man, obtaining a royal grant to pay the expenses which they had incurred while imprisoned in the Fleet, plus a present in silver for each of them. The Amicable Grant had been quietly dropped.[10]

What organization lay behind this extraordinary outburst of feeling? It is easy to assume that everything was a spontaneous expression of anger, without any further form of organization. Superficially, both Hall and Griffith concur in suggesting this, writing from the point of view of the gentry; they both describe the Lavenham crowd at its first meeting with the Dukes as all speaking at once 'with the characteristic indiscretion of the ignorant . . . like a flock of geese in corn' in Griffith's vivid phrase.[11] Both chroniclers also record the famous retort of the rebel spokesman John Grene, when asked who their captain was, that they knew no other captain but Poverty. However, this is the

---

[8] Griffith, pp. iii–iv. Woods, 'The rioting crowd', pp. 21–4, misses this point, and his interpretation of the affair therefore differs from mine in playing down the potential danger of the situation.
[9] PRO, SP 1/34/209–10 (*LP* IV pt. i, no. 1343).
[10] Hall, p. 702; Griffith, p. v.
[11] Hall, p. 700; Griffith, p. iii.

answer of a natural orator. Griffith makes it clear that Grene did not just emerge out of the crowd; he was chosen as spokesman by a delegation of sixty representatives. This wizened little Melford weaver must have been an impressive figure; Sir Humphrey Wingfield, then *custos* for the county and one of the leading lawyers of his day, asserted to Griffith (an old employee of his brother Robert), that 'no four of the ablest lawyers in the kingdom, even after a week's consultation, could make an answer so meet as did the weaver within less than two hours' space'. Grene was among those fourteen singled out for imprisonment and Star Chamber appearance because they had 'caused' the affair.[12] Who was this leadership, and whom did it organize?

We are exceptionally fortunate to have a detailed memorial of the heart of the stirs not merely in the narratives of Hall and Griffith or in the self-justificatory accounts given by the Dukes to the Cardinal and to the King, but also in the form of the list of those indicted for riot and unlawful assembly by Chief Justice Brudenell at a special sessions; for convenience, we will refer to this document as the 'rebel list'.[13] It extends to 525 men each named with his residence and occupation, drawn from nineteen communities in the area of south Suffolk around Lavenham, on the Essex border; there are representatives from the three towns of Lavenham, Sudbury, and Hadleigh named by Hall. We are therefore able to take a closer look at those who took part in the rising. They came from a single block of communities round the clothing town of Lavenham, but it is quite clear that the traditional picture of a rising of cloth trade workers is an over-simplification. Only three of the nineteen communities involved, Lavenham and Great and Little Waldingfield, were overwhelmingly concerned with the cloth trade, the large village of Long Melford to a lesser extent; these contributed 289 names to the rebel list. The others, apart from the market towns of Sudbury and Bildeston (33 names between them) were purely agricultural, with hardly any direct involvement with cloth manufacture, but they still numbered 203 rebels in the list.[14]

It is a further stroke of luck that we can easily compare the rebel list

---

[12] Ibid., pp. iv–v. Woods, 'The rioting crowd', p. 4, is mistaken in doubting Green's existence.

[13] PRO, KB 29/157, mm. 5–6. Dr Woods came on a different but very similar version of the same list (PRO, KB 9/497, mm. 7–10) before my own discovery, and I am grateful to him for alerting me to his find (cf. Woods, 'The rioting crowd', pp. 5–6, 12–21).

[14] Lawshall, Cockfield, Thorpe Morieux, Brettenham, Hitcham, Alpheton, Preston, Kettlebaston, Brent Eleigh, Monks Eleigh, Milden, Chelsworth, and Acton.

with the very full Subsidy returns of the previous year; we can therefore gauge the wealth of participants as well as their geographical distribution. In doing this, an interesting contrast emerges between the clothing communities and the agricultural villages involved, as can be seen in Table 2. In the cloth towns it was mostly the very poor who took part, the one-pound tail-end of the subsidy list, nearly all weavers and labourers in the rebel list; these were the sort of labourers described in Hall's narrative, presumably scared of the consequences of unemployment. At Lavenham only three people out of 169 participants were valued at more than £5 per annum in 1524, one a tailor at £12 and two fullers, one with a valuation of £10 but the other (Roger Grome senior) wholly exceptional with a valuation of £140.[15] A group of seven tilers at Long Melford may well have been employees of a single business threatened with lay-off in the same manner as their fellows in the cloth industry; certainly two of them were close companions, for they appeared next to each other both in the 1524 Subsidy listing and in the rebel list.[16]

Table 2. *Wealth of 1525 'rebels' identifiable in the 1524 Subsidy*

Type of community	£20+	(%)	£10–14	(%)	£5–9	(%)	£3–4	(%)	£2 (%)		£1 (%)		Total
A	2	1.5	8	6	21	16	9	7	25	19	64	50	129
B	1	0.5	3	2	9	6	8	5	22	15	108	71	151
C	0		0		3	15	4	21	1	5	11	58	19
Total	3	1	11	4	33	11	21	7	48	16	183	61	299

Key to types of communities
A   Agricultural communities: Acton, Alpheton, Brent Eleigh, Brettenham, Chelsworth (no useable data), Cockfield, Hitcham, Kettlebaston, Lawshall, Milden, Monks Eleigh, Preston, Thorpe Morieux.
B   Cloth-producing communities: Lavenham, Long Melford, Great and Little Waldingfield.
C   Market towns: Bildeston, Sudbury.

However, the agricultural villages were far more united in their protest in 1525, showing a social cohesion which was in striking

[15] Hugh Sotyll, tailor; Philip Rogyll, fuller. Woods, 'The rioting crowd', p. 15, names two men of the clothing village of Little Waldingfield as unusually prosperous, but these are wrong identifications.
[16] Thomas Sparowe, Geoffrey Style.

contrast to the division revealed in the cloth townships. A comparison
of the rebel list with the 1524 tax return shows that the rebels from
these villages included the substantial men, those who paid the most in
1524; significantly, these were nearly all villages without any resident
gentlemen, and they were therefore used to running their own affairs
in a communal manner. At Alpheton, for instance, the five rebels
included the first four names on the village's tax list, all husbandmen;
Cockfield's twenty-five rebels included two 'husbandmen' (more likely
men of yeoman status) worth £20 per annum.[17] At Thorpe Morieux,
Thomas Spynk, top of the list in 1524 at £20, was not among the
rebels, but Thomas Spynk the younger was, together with a
husbandman worth twenty marks a year,[18] and eight members of a
village clan of husbandmen and labourers called Bixby; altogether the
village contributed eighteen rebels, as against twenty-five male
taxpayers in the previous year. At Sudbury there were only two weavers
and two labourers among the twenty-four rebels; one of the Sudbury
rebels, Thomas Stevenson, tailor (£4 in 1524), was listed during the
decade after 1525 as one of the four-man oligarchy of 'rulers of the
town' who assisted the mayor.[19]

The contrast between the clothing and the agricultural communities
involved is well illustrated by the two places which the Dukes of
Norfolk and Suffolk named as particularly central to the rebellion:
Lavenham and Brent Eleigh. The communities make an odd pair.
Lavenham was the prodigy cloth town, with its remarkable industrial
prosperity making it the second highest contributor in Suffolk to the
1524 Subsidy. But why was Brent Eleigh paired with it? Then as now,
it was a very ordinary agricultural village, apparently like any other in
the neighbourhood, with 28 male taxpayers in 1524 as opposed to
Lavenham's 185. Nevertheless, a year later it managed to muster no
fewer than forty males to join the rebellion, one of only two among the
nineteen communities with more rebels than listed taxpayers, and they
included most of the prosperous men of the village, for instance
husbandmen of £12 and £10 and a carpenter of £10; only four people
connected with the cloth trade were among them. Here, in contrast to
the list of humble rebels at Lavenham, was a community united in
protest; yet the two places clearly had some special affinity, for reasons

[17] John Ildreyard senior, John Rede.
[18] Thomas Fordham.
[19] PRO, C1/605/58.

which remain obscure. The first identifiable instance of this was a violent incident in 1493, when a full-scale battle broke out between the two communities (a friendly football match, perhaps) in which James Spring, the brother of the rich clothier Thomas, was killed.[20] After this the evidence is of a more harmonious relationship; we shall find that not only in 1525 but also in 1549 and 1569, the two communities were associated in moves of protest.

The events of 1525 thus revealed that in the hub of the rebellion in the hundreds of Cosford and Babergh, very diverse communities united round a single political issue. What brought them all together? Perhaps the husbandmen of the surrounding villages and the tradesmen of Sudbury were worried about a slump in their sales of goods and food to the cloth towns. Perhaps their readiness to make common cause with the labourers and weavers of the clothing communities reveals a pattern of life in which young people left their farming communities to make a living at the cloth trade in Lavenham, Waldingfield or Melford, and so in the protest of 1525 the cloth workers were uniting with angry friends and relatives from home. Whatever the reason, the agricultural communities demonstrated their capacity for action across the social barriers which separated relatively prosperous husbandmen or yeoman from humble labourers. Only the gentry, who were marching under the banner of the two Dukes, and the wealthy clothiers took no traceable part.[21] The leadership of the agricultural villages contrasted with the disruption of leadership among the clothiers of Lavenham. The town's prosperity had been largely built up on the spectacular achievements of the Spring family, in particular through the Thomas Spring who had died two years before the Amicable Grant; Spring's widow was locked in a bitter dispute with his executor Thomas Jermyn about the control of the family fortune.[22] If Spring had been alive Lavenham might not have exploded in 1525 as it did; as it was, it was Spring's son John and his executor Jermyn who were chosen by the Duke to bargain with the

---

[20] Howard, I, p. 201.

[21] Only two yeomen are named in the rebel list: Nicholas Thorne of Lavenham and Andrew Kyng of Lawshall. Thorne does not make a particularly convincing yeoman, since he was only assessed on £1 goods in 1524. This absence, coupled with the substantial subsidy assessments of several of those described as husbandmen, indicates that the rebel list subsumed those who might have been described otherwise as yeomen in the category of husbandmen.

[22] PRO, REQ 3/38, Bill of Thomas Jermyn, and PRO, C4/25, fragment of another Bill of Jermyn, both against Alice Spring.

assembled crowds.[23] And in the end, without having received any support from gentry or clothiers, those crowds could be conscious that they had won an important political point.

Popular discontent was never very far from the surface for the rest of the 1520s. 1523–5 had been years of relatively low food prices, and it had been the government's folly which had incited people to desperate protest, but from 1526 there were additionally steep price rises as a consequence of a run of poor harvests. In late 1526, with Suffolk suffering more severely from grain shortages than Norfolk, there was trouble in Stowmarket which resulted in several people being imprisoned, and the Duke of Norfolk's immediate thought was to send for 'the most substanciall men' of Lavenham to reassure himself that all was well there; both he and the Duke of Suffolk fervently pleaded with Wolsey to relax the ban on food exports other than grain to make it possible to raise cash to relieve famine with grain purchases in the Low Countries.[24] In early 1528, with the government threatening war with the Emperor, East Anglia's vital trade in cloth and agricultural produce with the Netherlands was once more being disrupted, and the two Dukes and Sir Robert Drury had to step in to quell disturbances in Norwich and Bury St Edmunds; the Duke of Norfolk acted to control grain prices and enforce the sale of grain stored at Colchester. He also begged the clothiers not to risk a repetition of 1525 by laying off clothworkers, only narrowly avoiding being faced with a planned demonstration at Stoke Park by two or three hundred women on behalf of the threatened workers.[25] Wolsey took the Duke's hint and prevailed upon the London merchants to press ahead with purchases of East Anglian cloth and thus to encourage the clothiers to listen to Howard's pleas. Even so, two months later, the clothiers were still alarmed by the lack of trade, and by the interruption of oil supplies from Spain needed in cloth manufacture; they were still raising the spectre of a lay-off.[26] A combination of food shortages and the collapse of the cloth trade had even greater potential for danger than the situation of 1525.

[23] PRO, SP 1/34/209–10 (*LP* IV pt. i, no. 1343).

[24] Stowmarket: SP 1/45/189–90 (*LP* IV pt. ii, no. 3664, there misdated to 1527). Lavenham: SP 1/45/266–7 (*LP* IV pt. ii, no. 3703, likewise misdated to 1527). Suffolk: SP 1/46/50 (*LP* IV pt. ii, no. 3760, there misdated to 1528, but January 1527). The redating is derived from a reference in the second letter above to Sir Lewes, a Welsh priest, also referred to in depositions of 15 December 1526 (SP 1/40/77–80, *LP* IV pt. ii, no. 2710).

[25] SP 1/47/59, 1/47/83 (*LP* IV pt. ii, nos. 4012, 4044).

[26] Hall, p. 745; PRO, SP 1/48/1A (*LP* IV pt. ii, no. 4239). Cf. Hoskins, pp. 184–5.

This time, however, the regime rode the storm, and when it was next faced with open rebellion with the Lincolnshire Rising and the Pilgrimage of Grace, East Anglia held firm under the Howards' leadership. There were rumblings of trouble, 'many light personys' taking heart from the Lincolnshire stirs, but here it was not religion but once more the state of the cloth industry which seemed to be the potential flashpoint; the county's leading men assured the Duke of Norfolk in October 1536 that a proclamation on the cloth industry had only just saved the day, and Sir Thomas Rush was of the opinion that 'the young clothiers be very light'. Howard thought it likely that the Lincolnshire rebels would try and advance from Boston 'trustyng upon the clothyers of Suff.'; in both cases, this was a loose application of the word clothier, implying the workers of the industry rather than the leading men who had stood aloof from their employees' discontent in the 1520s.[27]

In the end, fears of trouble from the cloth industry proved groundless, but the fact that at no stage in the 1530s did East Anglia experience any major attempt at rebellion does not mean that there was not real cause for alarm. It is noticeable that the recorded incidents of unrest in this decade show that the potential for trouble extended well beyond cloth-producing districts. In fact there is only one mention of a major cloth-producing town, Norwich—in any case, a city with many more strings to its bow than simply the cloth trade: in 1537 a drunken Norwich clothworker could see a rising as the only answer to the cloth industry's troubles.[28] Other incidents during 1536 and 1537 had no connection with cloth production, and were concentrated in the centre of the East Anglian region away from the cloth areas: John Walter of Griston urging a *jacquerie* against the East Anglian gentry while their leaders were away fighting the northern rebels; a wandering minstrel circulating a song in the Diss area presenting a subversive view of events in the north; a Bungay man discussing ideas for a rising with a man he happened to meet in a wood; a May game in the same area with ad-libbed speeches against gentlemen.[29] There were risings planned at

[27] PRO, SP 1/107/83–4, 1/107/118–19 (*LP* XI, nos. 603, 625). Never one to avoid self-congratulation, the Duke assured Cromwell that his own arrival in East Anglia had been as important to the gentry there as the cloth proclamation.
[28] Elton, *Policy and Police*, p. 143. Elton's reference (ibid., p. 137) to Lavenham should in fact be to Lakenham, near Norwich.
[29] Walter: PRO, SP 1/160/157–8 (*LP* XV, no. 748; the report is of 1540, but the incident clearly took place in autumn 1536). Diss minstrel: SP 1/116/30–1 (*LP* XII pt. i, no. 424). Bungay man, play: SP 1/120/100–4 (*LP* XII pt. i, no. 1212).

Walsingham and at Fincham in Norfolk during 1537, both nipped in the bud before they achieved anything; nevertheless Professor Elton can characterize the Walsingham affair as 'the most serious plot hatched anywhere south of the Trent in those years'.[30] 1536–8 were anxious years for the government as far as Norfolk and Suffolk were concerned, but there was much else to worry Cromwell: the last phase of the assault on monasteries and shrines, widespread conflict between religious progressives and conservatives, and finally during 1538, the wholesale eviction from his native county of the Duke of Suffolk, one of the two men who had done most to secure East Anglia's peace, not only in 1525 but also during the unrest of 1536–7.

By 1549 not merely the Brandons but also the Howards had been removed from the East Anglian scene. In successive articles in *Past and Present* I sought to demonstrate that the East Anglian troubles traditionally known as Kett's Rebellion were far more widespread than has been previously realized; they united Norfolk and Suffolk, and they probably had a still wider reference. A concentration on a narrow range of sources has obscured this in the past, in particular the focus on a narrative by Nicholas Sotherton which has the clear intention of whitewashing the Norwich hierarchy from the suspicion of having co-operated with the rebels, and on a schoolboy Latin textbook written a quarter century after the event by Alexander Neville. The speed and efficiency with which the East Anglian region was taken over in less than a week, and various prominent gentry rounded up for internment, are the best arguments for a co-ordinated move behind this great explosion, rather than a series of spontaneous outbreaks of violence.[31] How widely did the co-ordination extend? In all the early sixteenth-century popular protest, it is difficult to recover evidence of planning over a wide area—not surprisingly, since there would be every reason to conceal it. The Dukes of Suffolk and Norfolk were sure that the 1525 stirs had included links with Essex and Cambridgeshire, while the chronicler Ellis Griffith asserted that Kent had been included in the plans to rise at the ringing of bells.[32] In 1549, quite apart from the earlier troubles in Hampshire and the great rising in the west, there is again evidence of very similar trouble to that in East Anglia in Kent and Essex and also in the Thames Valley, but little direct evidence of co-ordination, apart from a hint that the Lady Mary may have been

---

[30] Elton, *Policy and Police*, pp. 144–51.
[31] MacCulloch, 'Kett's Rebellion', especially pp. 39–40, 42–3, 68–9.
[32] PRO, SP 1/34/196 (*LP* IV pt. i, no. 1329); Griffith, p. ii.

testing the waters by sending agents to see what advantage the troubles held for her.[33]

One might easily dismiss the accusations of widespread conspiracy in 1525 and 1549 as upper-class paranoia, but certain considerations should give us pause. First, such links were perfectly possible in theory. Prominent, for instance, among the recorded participants in the stirs were men in the butcher's trade: among leading figures, Robert Kett's brother William, Captain Levet at Bury St Edmunds, and Robert Pawling at Orford, and seven among the forty-seven individuals involved in the commotions for whom Bindoff could trace trades.[34] Butchers and other men in the meat trade, if their business was on a large enough scale, would travel over long distances and would be ideally placed to spread ideas and make suggestions for future plans; Pawling himself, in a legal case of 1540, emphasized the necessity of a horse for carrying on his victualling trade.[35] One fascinating case of 1545 in Requests, for instance, describes a Glemsford man who specialized in dealing in sheep, the victualling trade, and shoemaking being used as an agent by a syndicate of men from his area to spend a season travelling round the Worcestershire fairs getting the best bargain for animals to replenish East Anglian stocks depleted by disease.[36] Secondly, there are indeed indisputable instances of large-scale contacts among dissident groups, although they concern the Lollards rather than the sequence of rebellions under discussion: during the 1510s and 1520s, such figures as Thomas Man, Thomas Risby, and John Hacker were revealed by ecclesiastical investigations as travelling and maintaining contacts between groups over wide areas of south-eastern England: East Anglia and as far west in the Thames basin as Newbury—much the same area as was affected by the stirs of 1525 and 1549.[37] This may have some bearing on the negligible interest in Catholicism displayed by the rebels of eastern England in 1549.

Perhaps the most suggestive characteristic of the 1549 troubles was the fact that they exhibited common features not only throughout East Anglia but also beyond. Most obvious was the deliberate choice to

[33] PRO, SP 10/8/30, and for Mary's reply to this Council accusation, G. Burnet, *History of the Reformation*, ed. N. Pocock (7 vols., Oxford, 1865), VI, p. 283; cf. MacCulloch, 'Kett's Rebellion', p. 61.
[34] Levet: PRO, STAC 3/9/82. Pawling: STAC 2/21/93. Bindoff, p. 20.
[35] PRO, STAC 2/17/236, deposition of Pawling.
[36] PRO, REQ 3/27, *John Marsh* v. *Baldwin Sheldon*.
[37] Foxe, IV, pp. 209, 213–14, and see above, pp. 148–9.

make the rebellion static by setting up camps: so characteristic was this that the rising became known by contemporaries as 'the campyng tyme', and as early as 19 July 1549, the Provost of Eton could refer to the rebels far away from East Anglia in the Thames Valley as 'the camp men'.[38] The contrast with the determined march eastward by the Western rebels of the same year is striking, despite the Westerners' diversion to besiege Exeter; nor do camps seem to have been a prominent feature of other Tudor rebellions. Yet in 1549, we can find references to them in Kent, Sussex, and Berkshire as well as in East Anglia, and this creation of static foci for the movement must say something about the intentions of the insurgents.[39]

The message of the camps was that they had no aggressive intentions towards the government; they simply sought justice and good governance, as was symbolized by the Oak of Reformation which was the centrepiece of the Norwich camp at Mousehold.[40] S. T. Bindoff long ago identified this concern in his study of the Mousehold camp, but it was equally true of the other East Anglian camps; several of the surviving references to the Suffolk camps are to do with the rebels' interventions in long-standing legal disputes to secure summary justice for one side, and further, with their obstinate pursuit of justice after the commotion had ended. For instance, the captain of the Bury camp put one George Swinbourne, a pursuivant of the King, into possession of his stepchildren's property in the town, and the captain himself assumed custody of the children from a rival claimant; Swinbourne's name will recur in our examination of popular politics. At the Melton camp in east Suffolk, we have a rare chance to eavesdrop on one of the rebels themselves, as Thomas Nottingham, merchant of Aldeburgh, demanded compensation for an old trespass from one of the gentry interned there, and said 'Naye, I wyll have yt now or [ere] I go or ells I wyll complayne, for I know I shall have remedye here'.[41] His words bear us a faint resonance of the exuberant

---

[38] PRO, STAC 3/4/7, Answer of Robert Browne. Eton: PRO, SP 10/8/33, and on the invention of the word 'inkennel', see MacCulloch, 'Kett's Rebellion', pp. 47–8. It is tempting to trace a link between 'the campyng tyme' and the East Anglian variant of football, also known as 'camping', for which many villages set aside special 'camping pightles'; trying to establish such a connection would alas probably be a vain effort.

[39] MacCulloch, 'Kett's Rebellion', p. 47; on Sussex, see *The Gentleman's Magazine*, CIII pt. ii (1833), p. 14.

[40] For a reference to the Oak of Reformation outside the Sotherton/Neville narrative tradition, see PRO, C1/1264/62. On Mousehold, cf. Bindoff, pp. 16–23.

[41] Swinbourne: PRO, STAC 3/9/82, interrogatories for and deposition of George

confidence which must have characterized those summer weeks, just as a casual remark in a Star Chamber deposition five years later sends us a faint echo of the sound of the drum which beat to escort Lord Willoughby's bailiff of Orford, as the 1549 rebels took him away in triumph to Melton gaol.[42] The camps had after all started in a summer festival of plays at Wymondham, and they celebrated the downfall of the oppressive Duke of Norfolk; they resounded with talk of 'remedy' and 'reformation', and at Norwich at least there were guest preachers and a church choir on hand.[43] As fiestas of justice, the nearest relatives to the camps of 1549 may well have been the camp meetings of the Primitive Methodists two and a half centuries later, when humble folk once more asserted their dignity and identity in a troubled and threatening world.

Who led these strange specimens of revolutionaries? The names of the rebel leaders which have survived from Suffolk show them coming from the same world of yeoman prosperity just below the gentry class as the Norfolk leaders Robert and William Kett. John Levet, butcher, captain of the Bury rebels, was a nephew of Giles Levet, a minor gentleman and one of the bailiffs of Bury, and he survived the excitements of 1549 to receive a twenty shillings bequest from his uncle in 1552.[44] Robert Brand of the Ipswich camp held second-rank offices in the borough of Ipswich in the 1540s; in his will, made in 1558, he could leave a house, lands, and weir at Felixstowe together with several hundred pounds in cash to his family, and stipulate that his eldest son Josias should be sent to St Anthony's School in London and go on to an apprenticeship.[45]

The other Ipswich captain whose name we know was Robert Brand's 'trustie and derely beloved' brother-in-law and executor John Harbottle; the two men were sufficiently close for Harbottle to adopt the same slightly unusual formula for commending his soul to the Trinity when making his will two decades after Brand.[46] Harbottle is the most interesting character of the three known Suffolk leaders. He started on the ladder of success as a minor Ipswich merchant, an immigrant from Norfolk; in 1538 we find him snapping up the lead

Swinbourne: see *APC* II, p. 315, for his appearance before the Council. Nottingham: PRO, STAC 2/34/139, deposition of Edward Glemham.

[42] STAC 4/10/76. For other cases and their aftermaths, see MacCulloch, 'Kett's Rebellion', pp. 48–9, 69.

[43] Russell, p. 65.

[44] *Bury Wills* pp. 140–3.

[45] Bacon, pp. 222, 225, 227; PCC 25 Welles.

[46] PCC 6 Langley.

from Babwell Friary at Bury. Like his brother-in-law, he served as a chamberlain of Ipswich in the 1540s, and went on steadily to accumulate a comfortable fortune. Already before 1549, he had bought two manors in central Suffolk, Crowfield and Kenton, and devoted a good deal of his energies to fighting lawsuits with his tenants.[47] By the time he died in 1578, he was wealthy enough to be termed an esquire, although in view of the memories of 1549, it is perhaps not surprising that he never achieved the honour of inclusion in the county commission of the peace. His widow's marriage to one of the Wingfields of Letheringham, though a personal disaster for her, showed how far this former rebel had travelled up the social scale; Harbottle's granddaughter and coheir married an official of the court of Star Chamber, and it was appropriate that he should lend his name to his great-grandson, that ambiguous revolutionary of the Civil War period, Sir Harbottle Grimston.[48] In summary, the increasingly prosperous and successful careers of Brand and Harbottle were exactly what one would have expected of Robert Kett, had he shown their adroitness in surviving the upheavals of 1549.

However, there is something more remarkable still about the men who were prominent in the stirs of 1549 in Suffolk. It is perhaps not surprising that the two leaders of the Ipswich camp, Brand and Harbottle, should be closely related, but a chance discovery in the surviving pocket book of the Clerk of Star Chamber for 1525 widens the net of relationships. In it, in entries associated with July 1525, occurs the following note: 'George Swynborne Roger Swynborne and John Harbotell be committed to Marshalsey'.[49] George Swinbourne, as we have seen, was one of those who benefited from the direct action carried out by the rebel captain at Bury St Edmunds in 1549. In other words, men who were to have a central involvement in the two camps set up in Suffolk some thirty-five miles apart in 1549 had known each other for at least a quarter of a century. We cannot know directly whether the offence for which they suffered imprisonment in 1525 was connected with the Amicable Grant, but to find the relationship is telling enough in itself.

John Harbottle may have had closer connections with west Suffolk

---

[47] Babwell: PRO, SP 5/3, fo. 129ᵛ (*LP* XIII pt. ii, no. 1213). Ipswich: Bacon, p. 219. Crowfield and Kenton: PRO, REQ 2/20/96; PRO, C1/1277/20, 24; C1/1424/26, 30; PRO, C3/96/19; C3/188/4; PRO, REQ 2/23/28, 102.

[48] Wingfield marriage: PRO, C2 ELIZ G14/50; on the Harbottles, see Corder, *1561 Visitation* I, p. 161.

[49] PRO, STAC 10/4/2 (316–27), fo. 6ʳ.

than at present can be recovered. His interest in the lead of Babwell Friary may merely have been the action of a sharp businessman, but it might equally well have been connected with Katherine Harbottle, a widow of some property and sister-in-law of Abbot Reve of Bury, who made her will in 1546 as of Fornham St Genevieve, a mile from Babwell; her link with John Harbottle cannot yet be demonstrated.[50] However, one marriage alliance in the Harbottle family is unmistakably resonant of the continuities in East Anglian popular protest: the wedding in 1554 of John Harbottle's daughter and heir Joan to Thomas Risby, son of a wealthy Lavenham clothier. What is significant about this was that Lavenham was once more a centre of rebellion in 1549. A wandering Norfolk parson turned up in Colchester on 6 August 1549 and started spreading stories about the various East Anglian camps with which he had had contact. Of the Bury camp, he said that it numbered 'as he thought vii thowsand of the townes of Bury, Hadley, Lanham, Brend Ely with other townes therabowt'.[51] One need not trust the priest's statistics, but the very confusion and wild exaggeration of his remarks as dutifully detailed by his Colchester audience make the coincidence of places with the centre of the 1525 stirs reported by the two Dukes and by Hall's Chronicle all the more striking. In particular, Lavenham and Brent Eleigh, that same ill-matched pair of communities which were so prominent in 1525, were here again singled out for special mention.

The leaders of the 1549 stirs were building on patterns of protest already in existence, and moreover, patterns which had met with success a quarter of a century before. They associated their grievances with the misdeeds of their social superiors, notably the Howards, but the only direct insight which we have into their political programme, the demands of the Mousehold camp, shows that their distaste for the world of gentlemen went further than the ducal family.[52] They were determined to create a world in which gentlemen would be kept at arm's length, recapturing an imaginary past where society had been divided into watertight social compartments, each with its own functions: a sort of medieval social apartheid. Their articles demanded that lords should take on the payment of certain free rents and castleward payments (articles 2, 9) and keep their beasts off the commons (3 and 11); the rights of mesne lords and private leet

---

[50] Muskett III, pp. 5, 10.
[51] BL Lansd. 2/25; cf. MacCulloch, 'Kett's Rebellion', p. 52.
[52] BL Harl. 304, fos. 75–8, pr. Russell, pp. 48–56.

jurisdictions were to be abolished (24, 13) and the effects of the feudal rights of the Crown restricted to the gentry (18). In return the magistracy's privileges of keeping dovecotes and having unrestricted rights of warrenage were to be protected (10, 23). Everyone should know his place in this tidy world: priests should neither be landowners nor officers to the gentry (4, 15), and gentlemen should not hold spiritual livings (26); lords of manors should not be bailiffs to other lords, and royal officers should protect their impartiality by avoiding other men's service (25, 12). This was affirming and strengthening existing social institutions, not attacking them; yet the Mousehold rebels' intentions were lost in the tragic mishandling of the situation which led to the massacres of Dussindale.

Such a programme of 'separate development' is consistent with the common social level from which the 1549 leadership was drawn, the social grouping just outside the orbit of the East Anglian magistracy as represented by the armigerous county gentry and the oligarchies which ran the greater towns of the region. John Levet of Bury was one step away from the tiny élite of Bury's community leaders; the offices which Brand and Harbottle held in Ipswich in the 1540s were of the second rather than the first rank, and in 1543 Harbottle turned his back on further advancement in the Ipswich hierarchy of office by purchasing a life discharge from all further official responsibilities in the borough.[53] The leaders of a great town like Ipswich, the annually-elected pair of bailiffs, were as likely to be targets of hostility for the rebels as the county gentry whose status, power, and wealth were similar to their own. A witness of this can be found in a scandalized memorandum of 1549 scribbled in the otherwise severely impersonal record of court business at Ipswich; the rebel Richard Wade, it records, 'seid to Mr. Bayliffes openly in the [borough] halle that there was small favour shewyd to ther pore neybores'.[54]

Leaders in a lesser borough were more likely to throw in their lot with the rebels; at Orford the arrest of Lord Willoughby's bailiff Thomas Spicer and his imprisonment by the rebels at Melton was only one episode in a feud in the town which had arisen out of the dispute over the Willoughby inheritance in the 1520s, and which would continue at least into the reign of Mary. Those who humiliated Spicer in 1549 would do so again, by a second time committing him to the

---

[53] Bacon, p. 221.
[54] SROI, C5/12/9, p. 548; on Wade's appearance before the Privy Council, see *APC* II, pp. 316–7.

stocks in 1554; they were no rural anarchists, but the representatives of a ruling group in the town who had previously supported the rival claimant to Lord Willoughby's property, and who sought to maintain their independence of his claims to the town as a seigneurial borough by emphasizing their series of royal charters 'from and before the tyme of king Edward the Second'.

When Spicer was arrested again in 1554 by the leader of the Orford royal charter party, Robert Pawling, Pawling significantly asserted that he ordered him to the stocks by virtue of the fact 'that he was the quenes offycer and the other was but the lords balyff'.[55] No doubt Pawling had felt precisely the same justification when he had used the Melton rebels against Spicer four years earlier. Not only did these 'rebels' seek to recall their social superiors to their duty and to a shared sense of justice and 'remedy', but they felt that they represented the Crown in their actions against the misdeeds of the magisterial class; there was therefore no scandal in officers like constables or churchwadens joining the East Anglian stirs. The churchwardens of the Waveney valley village of Carlton Colville collected a major debt owed to the parish together with other town monies and marched off with them to help the cause at Mousehold; similarly, the parish officers of North Elmham in Norfolk kept a careful record among the parish papers of their disbursements about business in the Mousehold camp. Protector Somerset and the Privy Council reluctantly acknowledged this disturbing paradox in a proclamation of 22 July 1549 which lamented that bailiffs, constables, and headboroughs, far from suppressing the popular disorders, had become 'the very ringleaders and procurers' of the risings.[56]

When considering Kett's Rebellion and its leaders, we are therefore very far from the unflattering portrait of crazed barbarous wretches painted in the narratives of Nicholas Sotherton and Alexander Neville. The leaders were responsible, sophisticated men, often used to carrying on large-scale businesses or to leading communities which had no resident gentry: they were men like Robert Brand, with his insistence on a first-class education for his son. Behind their surviving list of demands, at first sight so chaotic and disorganized, lies a

---

[55] PRO, STAC 4/10/76. Charter claim: PRO, REQ 3/6, petition of burgesses and inhabitants of Orford. Cf. MacCulloch, 'Kett's Rebellion', p. 51. Pawling was sufficiently reconciled to Spicer by 1555 as to be one of the burgesses who made the indenture for his election to Parliament (PRO, C219/24/148).

[56] Carlton Colville: PRO, C1/1264/62. North Elmham: Russell, pp. 181–4. *Tudor Royal Proclamations* I, no. 342.

consistent programme of ideas, dominated by the longing for order and good governance in an area which had been politically disrupted by the fall of the Duke of Norfolk from political power in 1547 and by the subsequent dismemberment of the great Howard estates. The East Anglian stirs related as much to a celebration of the Howards' downfall as to the disruption caused by Protector Somerset and his encouragement of hostility to enclosures; enclosures were in any case an issue of secondary concern to East Anglia, with its pattern of early medieval enclosure and its peculiar local farming customs.[57] The famous Mousehold article praying for the manumission of bondmen, often seen as irrelevant to the main aims of the rebellion, may in fact be said to have produced the affair's only success, for the Howard bondmen who were the main group referred to in the article were indeed 'made fre'. Ironically it was not Somerset but the man who destroyed Kett's army, the Duke of Northumberland, who was responsible for the manumissions of former Howard tenants to be found on the Patent Rolls between 1550 and 1553.[58] The process was continued by the fourth Duke of Norfolk when his lands were restored by Mary, in a series of manumission charters and fictitious legal actions right up to the year of his execution in 1572, and owners of lesser numbers of East Anglian bondmen followed suit at the same time.[59]

It is not surprising given this animus against the Howards, that one can find no evidence of sympathy among the rebels for the sort of Henrician conservatism in religion represented by the third Duke of Norfolk. The more one examines the accounts of the Mousehold camp in particular, the more prominently does the figure of the Norwich Protestant preacher Robert Watson emerge; while the future Elizabethan Archbishop of Canterbury Matthew Parker never satisfactorily explained what he was doing preaching to the Mousehold rebels.[60] No doubt the conservative gentry of East Anglia would have been only too pleased to exploit the rebellion to harass or even destroy the regime of Protector Somerset. At the heartland of the East Anglian protests, the Lady

[57] MacCulloch, 'Kett's Rebellion', pp. 53–6.

[58] *CPR Edward VI* III, p. 316; IV, p. 153; V, pp. 78, 407; cf. above, Ch. 2, n. 75, and MacCulloch, 'Kett's Rebellion', p. 59.

[59] Duke's manumission of Thomas Wyard, one of those who had petitioned Somerset (PRO, C1/1178/9): BL Add. Ch. 17637. Manumission by legal fiction: NRO, SUN 3, fos. 111–62. Cf. the forthcoming discussion in D. N. J. MacCulloch, 'Bondmen under the Tudors', in *Government and Law under the Tudors*, ed. D. M. Loades *et al.* (Cambridge, 1986).

[60] On Watson, cf., e.g. 'The commocyon in Norfolk, 1549', ed. B. L. Beer, *Journal of Medieval and Renaissance Studies* VI (1976), p. 82.

Mary was lodged in the former Howard palace at Kenninghall, and it was not surprising that the Privy Council believed that she was heavily involved in the stirs. There are indeed signs that she had contacts with the rebels, and there are connections between the Kett family and the conservative magnate Sir Richard Southwell of Woodrising in Norfolk which remain to be explained.[61] Yet the Spanish ambassador, eager to find any sign of support for the Lady Mary against the government, could detect nothing stronger than a general sympathy with her personal plight among the East Anglian insurgents: they felt sorry for her, but they still broke down her fences around Kenninghall, presumably in a further defiant gesture at the memory of the Howards.[62] A movement whose published demands so emphasized its efforts to keep its distance from the gentry community could have little to offer gentlemen of any political persuasion.

Given this lack of conservative motivation in the 1549 stirs, it is at first sight unexpected that the third in the sequence of rebellions in Tudor East Anglia should have the effect of placing a determinedly Catholic monarch on the English throne instead of a Protestant one. Indeed, the *coup d'état* based in East Anglia which defeated Northumberland in 1553 seems very different from the rebellions so far considered. The best account of the *coup*, by the eyewitness Robert Wingfield of Brantham, was written as a celebration of the role of Wingfield's East Anglian gentry circle in putting Mary on the throne; what this son of the Speaker of the Reformation Parliament wanted to achieve was to provide a monument to the loyalty and legitimism of gentlemen of coat armour. He himself had been a victim of the rebels from the camp near Ipswich in 1549 over a dispute with the heirs of John Mannyng of Tattingstone, who had denounced him to the rebel leaders; with this in mind, it was not surprising that the only good word that he had for the Duke of Northumberland in his treatise was for the part which Northumberland had played in suppressing the Mousehold rebels.[63] However, despite this, a notable feature of his account is the way that it reveals how Mary enjoyed strong popular support throughout the *coup*. When she fled to Kenninghall, it was the 'countryfolk' of Norfolk and Suffolk who first flocked to join her; when conservative and Protestant gentry alike agreed to proclaim Jane at Ipswich, it was the 'common people' who objected with 'murmurs of

[61] MacCulloch, 'Kett's Rebellion', pp. 60–1, 74–5.
[62] *CSPSpan.* IX, p. 405.
[63] Mannyng: PRO, C1/1279/78; *'Vita Mariae'* pp. 244–5.

discontent and great indignation'; when a squadron of five ships was sent up the East Anglian coast to threaten Mary, it was the crews who mutinied for her against their officers; and most dramatically of all, when the Earl of Oxford was being persuaded to stand by Jane, it was his servants who forced that ineffectual peer to support Mary and to imprison Northumberland's agents: 'if their lord did not wish to give his backing to this cause, the most righteous of any, they threatened immediately to throw off their liveries and set out for Princess Mary'. The Londoner's-eye-view of the same events in the *Chronicle of Queen Jane and Queen Mary* tells the same story, and conveys the alarm which this popular intervention in politics brought to the nation's leaders: quite apart from news of the mutiny of the sailors in the Orwell, 'worde of a greater mischief was brought to the Tower—the noblemen's tenauntes refused to serve their lordes agaynst quene Mary'.[64] For the various ambassadors in London, accustomed to the more aristocratic character of Continental civil strife, it was all very puzzling.

Was this popular reaction mainly legitimism, as it clearly was with so many East Anglian gentry? Equally powerful must have been the memory of Northumberland's commanding role in the destruction of the Mousehold camp four years earlier. In the commons' hatred of Northumberland, it must have been easy to forget that Mary's accession to the throne would inevitably bring the Howards back to favour; and no one outside Mary's immediate circle, gentry or people, could foresee the extent of her commitment to a papalist religious settlement. The East Anglian people who hastened to support Mary in her bid for the throne were the same people who had risen in the stirs of 1549, but this time they were acting in conjunction with the gentry whom they had terrified four years before. In doing so, they took their revenge for the débâcle of summer 1549, and helped to create the second of Tudor England's two successful rebellions.

After this heady story of victory, the tale of the 1569 rebellion in Suffolk has a dying fall. It seems to have achieved nothing, its participants were apparently humble men who have left virtually no trace on the records, and what we know of it is confused, probably reflecting its character as an ill-planned and ill-coordinated rising. Just like Kett's Rebellion and Mary's East Anglian *coup*, it took place in July: in other words, well before full-scale trouble broke out in the North and well before the Duke of Norfolk lost his nerve amid the

---

[64] Ibid., pp. 253, 255, 258, 263–4; *The Chronicle of Queen Jane, and of two years of Queen Mary*, ed. J. G. Nichols, Camden Society Old Series XLVIII (1850), p. 9.

tensions of Court politics and fled to East Anglia to rally support in late September. It seems therefore to have no connection with the other risings of 1569 and with their ramifications in high politics; if there is a connection, it is probably merely that the participants were aware of the feelings of confusion and anxiety among the country's ruling élite, and were trying to exploit the chance of disruption while it was offered. Even De Spes, the Spanish ambassador, normally so sanguine in his perception of support for the Catholic faith, could detect no more enthusiasm for Catholicism among the rebels of Suffolk than could his predecessor in the East Anglian troubles of 1549: no more than the evidence suggests for 1553. After hearing initial confused reports, he came up with a more accurate analysis which was confirmed by the less partisan Venetian ambassador: this was a rising of clothworkers and agricultural labourers in protest against the economic dislocation brought about by the government's confrontation with Spain—the same combination of groups as in 1525.[65] De Spes talked of the rebels' animus against royal officers and their grievances against royal and private parks, which took up good agricultural land; he asserted that they 'attempted to kill the keepers of the Queen's parks and the owners of the private ones'. A correspondent of Sir James Crofts, presenting much the same picture, repeated these hints that the rebels felt very bitter against their social superiors: 'their intent', he said, 'was playnlie to have spoiled all the gentlemen and welthie personages that they mighte overtake, begynnynge with Sir Ambrose Germayne . . .'[66]

Mention of Jermyn gives us our first clue as to the focus of this rising; Sir Ambrose lived at Rushbrooke, just south of Bury St Edmunds, and hence the rebels were likely to be concentrated in the west of the county. However, we can be more precise than that. One of the rebels betrayed the whole plot to the authorities before the rising had fully begun, and as a result won himself a pardon for a speech he had made to gather support. Predictably, he came from Lavenham; he was James Fuller, a sawyer.[67] His speech, meticulously preserved in the pardon, confirms the impression of violence and class animus in the rebels' minds, which otherwise we might consider resulted from the gentry bias of our sources: his plan, spelled out in lurid detail, was to hang all the 'riche churles', sparing only 'the gentlemen of old contynuance'. Here again we see the curious disapproval of social mobility already noted in connection with the Mousehold articles:

---

[65] *CSPSpan., Elizabeth I* II, pp. 179, 181; *Calendar of State Papers, Venetian* VII, p. 437.
[66] BL Cott. Titus B II, fos. 488–93.   [67] *CPR Eliz.* V, no. 1818.

those who were to die were those who were 'newe comme uppe and be heardemen'. Additionally, it suggests that the community at Lavenham was as split in 1569 as the 1525 rebel list indicated that it had been then, for it implied that the wealthy clothiers would be prime targets.

However, there are two more remarkable features to Fuller's pardon. First, he was described in it as aiding and abetting John Porter of Lavenham, weaver, who was the intended leader of the rebellion. A John Porter of Lavenham, weaver, had been among those indicted for riot and unlawful assembly in 1525; in December the following year, when the Duke of Norfolk became nervous about renewed restlessness at Lavenham, he was assured by the town leadership that 'they never knew one that dyd mysbehave hym selff save one person called John Porter, whom for his ill ordre they had put out of the towne'; the Duke proposed to examine Porter and at the very least, bind him to be of good abearing.[68] Even if one objects that John Porter of 1525 might be rather old to be the doyen of Lavenham revolutionaries in 1569, the second noteworthy feature of Fuller's pardon brings us unquestionably back to the continuities of East Anglian popular protest. Fuller explained to his listeners that having gathered a crowd from Lavenham, 'we will goe to the towne of Brent Illeigh and rayse up the people in that towne, and from thens to Lanham [Lavenham] and there to rynge the bells'. A rising in Elizabethan Suffolk had taken on almost the qualities of a ritual; memories of past disturbances were still fresh. A Colchester weaver had proved this three years before, in 1566, when he had outlined his own plans for a rising in Essex and Suffolk, and drawn his audience's attention to the time of year which had seen the outbreak of protest in 1549 and 1553, and would see it again in 1569: 'thus wyll I doe at mydsomer next', he proclaimed, 'for that wylbe the best tyme, for at that tyme beganne the last commotion.'[69]

Nothing came either of these efforts in 1566, or of the rising of 1569. Two days after Fuller had raised himself from anonymity, he found himself indicted before the justices of assize in Bury St Edmunds; it was an unfortunate time to choose to launch a rebellion, in the middle of Bury assizes. We have traced continuities through half a century of East Anglian rebellions, but where did those continuities lead? Apparently not in the direction of further risings. No one forgot

    [68] PRO, SP 1/45/266–7 (*LP* IV pt. ii, no. 3703, there misdated to 1527).
    [69] *Calendar of Assize Records, Essex Indictments, Elizabeth I*, ed. J. S. Cockburn (1978), no. 289.

the drama of 1549: the expression 'a Mousehold captain' passed into local usage, mightily annoying Lord Keeper Bacon's son when it was used forty years later to describe his arrival at an unfriendly neighbour's house;[70] when Robert Kett's son Richard died in 1601, several hundred people turned out for the funeral.[71]

The name of Kett was to be heard once more in the abortive rising in the Waveney and Yare basins in 1570; Robert Kett's sons Loye and George played a small part in this, Loye having a marginal role in concealing the scheme or aiding the conspirators, and George being forced to reveal to the government what he knew of the plans. Yet these Ketts were very small beer in the affair compared with their father in 1549. The leadership included their cousin John Appleyard, which may be why they were involved at all, but most of the leading figures were discontented Catholic gentry like Anthony Nolloth, James Hobart of Hales, Walter Jerningham or Christopher Playters of Sotterley.[72] Although the conspirators aimed to capitalize on popular resentment against immigrant Dutch settlers, their real aims were to free the Duke of Norfolk and challenge the Protestant settlement: more in the tradition of Mary's challenge to Northumberland than of the 1549 stirs, still less the Suffolk popular rising of summer 1569. Their efforts were in any case stillborn. No one of the stature of the 1549 yeoman leadership attempted to repeat the effort during Elizabeth's reign. The shadowy Suffolk revolutionaries of 1569 seem hardly to have been in the mould of the village worthies of Brent Eleigh and their fellows of 1525, or of John Harbottle and Robert Brand in 1549.

The success of the responsible protest of 1525 may well have spurred East Anglians on to try again in 1549; the bloody débâcle at Mousehold may have deterred any further independent forcible action on a large scale again. When the common people of East Anglia resorted to arms in 1553, it was in partnership with the area's gentry, and when an attempt was made to arouse popular militancy once more in 1569, it seems to have met with a limited response. The gentry-led rising of 1570 was equally ineffectual. The next time that the patterns of 1525 and 1549 were repeated would be in the national crisis of

---

[70] PRO, STAC 5 B19/37.
[71] L. M. Kett, *The Ketts of Norfolk: A Yeoman Family* (1921), pp. 81–2 (I am indebted to Mr Gary Hill for this reference).
[72] Details of the rising: PRO, SP 12/71/61, and see above, Ch. 2, n. 149. On the Kett genealogy, see L. M. Kett, n. 71 above.

1642. The continuities between the world of the Eastern Association and of the earlier tradition of popular direct action may well yield fruitful results to investigation, but for Elizabeth's reign we must look elsewhere for the expression of popular politics. In this period, the age of rebellions was at an end, and the story of East Anglia's tradition of protest was more bound up with the story of John Harbottle's and Robert Brand's steadily more prosperous careers than with the bloodthirsty harangue of James Fuller.

Alternative Patterns of Politics

In 1577 John Chapman alias Barker, yeoman of Sibton in central east Suffolk, was reported as saying that if he might have three or four of the chiefest yeomen in the county assured to him, he 'wold not care for never a justyce of them all'. Chapman was well placed to express this breezy contempt for the county magistracy; he lived at the heart of High Suffolk, home of 'very many yeomen of good credit and great liberalitie, good housekeepers', and in 1568 his yeoman father had been assessed at £20 in goods, which put him on the level of the lesser gentry.[1] Yet by the time that John's son Edmund added his tomb to the collection of family monuments in Sibton church in 1626, the Chapmans were styled gentlemen, and their yeoman pride was forgotten. No doubt this story could be paralleled many times over; writing in 1642, Thomas Fuller described yeomen as 'gentlemen in ore, whom the next age may see refined'. However, it serves as a significant pointer to changes of attitude among the yeomanry which ensured that 1549 was the last time that East Anglian yeomen, tradesmen, and merchants led a popular commotion without the co-operation of a section of the gentry. Yeomen remained tough and independent-minded. Edward Chamberlayne, writing in the 1660s, could still castigate them from the gentleman's point of view for this: yeomen 'at their ease and almost forgetting labour, grow rich and thereby so proud, insolent and careless that they neither give that humble respect and aweful reverence which in other kingdoms is usually given to nobility, gentry and clergy'.[2] Yet the characteristics which Chamberlayne so deplored were probably those which ensured that gentry and yeomen interests would never again diverge as disastrously as they had done in 1549.

One significant factor in this was that by the end of the sixteenth century, yeoman culture was nearer that of the gentry than of their social inferiors; the particular mark of this was in their acquisition of

[1] PRO, STAC 5 C49/12, interrogatories. *Chorography* p. 19. *1568 Subsidy* p. 48.
[2] Fuller and Chamberlayne qu. in D. Cressy, *Literacy and the Social Order* (Cambridge, 1980), pp. 126, 225.

literacy. Dr Cressy's work has shown that by the end of the century, status in society was clearly related to literacy, both within the traditional status groups of the countryside and within the groups differentiated by their economic activity. After 1580, clergy and gentry and the retailers/distributors (for Suffolk, the merchants in the market centres) shared a common level of literacy of 90 per cent or over; specialist crafts in all urban communities and yeomen both achieved levels of more than two-thirds literacy within their groupings; manufacturers and processors came next down the scale 37–52 per cent illiterate), with village crafts lower still (53–68 per cent illiterate); at the bottom of the pile both in literacy and socially were husbandmen, labourers, and heavy manual trades, with illiteracy rates of 73–100 per cent.[3]

This picture remained broadly the same from 1580 to 1720, but it was a pattern achieved in the decades of the mid-sixteenth century. Dr Cressy has detected signs of advance in literacy in the 1530s, followed by a falling-back in the 1540s and 1550s which he associates with the political upheavals of the Edwardian and Marian period and the dissolution of chantries, which had provided appreciable resources for elementary education; the stirs of 1549 throughout east and west in the lowland zone may have played their part in this setback. However, the really significant advances in acquisition of literacy were made among yeomen of southern England educated from the late 1550s into the 1570s; Cressy's results for the diocese of Exeter are remarkably similar to those for the diocese of Norwich. It was in these decades after the 1549 commotions that yeoman illiteracy fell from about 75 per cent to about 35 per cent in Exeter diocese and from about 60 per cent to about 30 per cent in Norwich diocese; from then on, most yeomen could participate in the world of reading and writing, unlike the majority of their social inferiors among the small tradesmen, husbandmen, and labourers.[4]

From the mid-sixteenth century, virtually all gentlemen in the south of England were literate, and by the 1620s, they had been joined by their fellows in the extreme north as well. From then on, power and politics would inevitably be expressed within the framework of a literate culture since this was the culture of the powerful. Once the broad consensus of belief which had existed within the late medieval English church had been burst apart, one of the main items on the

---

[3] Ibid., Ch. 6, especially p. 136.   [4] Ibid., Ch. 7.

political agenda would be the future shape of English religion; within this debate, Protestantism in particular emphasized the Word, especially through the assimilation of complex structures of ideas conveyed in the sermon, and without the ability at least to read, it would become increasingly difficult to enter this world of ideas. In 1555 an illiterate husbandman of the Stour valley village of Wissington, Robert Wade, used a literate neighbour to write quite a sophisticated statement of his moderate Protestant faith, very much along lines which would have been approved by Archbishop Cranmer. Wade's illiteracy seems only to have extended to writing, for he could probably read; however, even this degree of distancing from literate culture would become increasingly rare among those who discussed polemical theology.[5]

By acquiring literacy, mid-sixteenth-century yeomen were gaining access to the culture of literate political discussion. Their lifestyle reflected their acquaintance with the prosperity of the gentry world; Nesta Evans, studying the wills of yeomen of South Elmham parishes, in the middle of High Suffolk yeoman country, notes that bequests of silver were quite common; books also appeared as legacies, along with musical instruments like virginals and even one instance of a viola da gamba: illustration of a rather specialized side of literate culture.[6] This degree of integration with their social superiors would combine with memories of the messy end to the aspirations of 1549 to deter the yeoman successors of Robert Kett, John Harbottle, and Robert Brand from seeking to lead popular politics in mass demonstrations or armed violence.

What were the alternatives? From the mid-sixteenth century, one new way of expressing public activism was in what Professor Collinson has termed 'voluntary religion': the promotion of godly Protestantism in one's own locality.[7] This had advantages: to a certain extent at least, it coincided with the intentions of Elizabethan central government, and even when it did not, it could be sure of sympathy from the leading gentlemen who were dominating Suffolk politics by the 1590s. Popular Protestantism could draw on the Lollard tradition preserved in the sixteenth century, particularly in such communities as Stoke by Nayland and Mendlesham. Before the reign of Elizabeth it had known nothing but official persecution and opposition, except for the brief

---

[5] Davis, pp. 39–40, and BL Harl. 421, fo. 187ʳ.
[6] Evans, 'South Elmham', p. 194.
[7] Collinson, *Religion of Protestants*, Ch. 6.

interval of Edward VI's reign; even then it had had to work within the constraints imposed by a largely hostile local ecclesiastical hierarchy (above, Ch. 5). Now, however, for the first time, godly professors could identify with the establishment and find a secure and permanent place within it, at much the same time as the yeomanry were being drawn nearer the gentry world of literacy and prosperity. By 1561 Robert Wade, the illiterate Protestant husbandmen of Wissington so lately interrogated and forced to abjure by the Marian regime, was one of the two parishioners appointed as sequestrators after the rector had been ejected for neglect of the cure and decay of the church.[8]

Such identification with and acceptance by the Elizabethan establishment was an ambiguous phenomenon, particularly as the hotter sort of Protestants grew increasingly impatient with the defects of the 1559 Settlement. At Bury, for instance, as early as 1565 a significant section of the townsfolk backed the Puritan preacher George Withers in his refusal to wear the cornered clerical cap, a rag of Popery; Withers claimed that it was their 'offence' that he chiefly feared in agreeing to wear the cap, and said that he had only given way because they urged him to conform rather than 'to forsake them'.[9] In the Bury stirs over religion in 1582, two successive petitions on behalf of the Puritan faction could respectively gather 174 and 147 signatures from a town whose population was between four and five thousand: a substantial although by no means an overwhelming group.[10] Ordinary layfolk affected by such Protestant enthusiasm retained their strong views on the issue of clerical dress long after the first Vestiarian controversy had died down; when in 1589, the minister of Nayland in the Stour valley went off to Boxted in Essex to preach, accompanied by a party of Suffolk layfolk, the vicar of Boxted felt constrained to leave off his surplice, since 'some that came owt of Suffolke syde would have liked hym the worse yf he had worn it'.[11]

Such people were determined to secure clergy who would do justice to their religious needs. This concern was of course hardly new. We have already noted that before the Reformation, the parishioners of St Clement's Ipswich were accustomed to act forcefully and independently in choosing their parish priest (above, p. 175), and the Mousehold articles of 1549 were also concerned with the quality of the clergy.

---

[8] SROB, IC 500/5/1, fo. 110[r]; cf. Davis, p. 114.
[9] Petyt 538 vol. 47, fo. 320.
[10] PRO, SP 12/155/5; *HMC Salisbury* XIII, p. 210.
[11] Collinson, *Religion of Protestants*, p. 259.

Where it was possible, parishes continued to follow the example of St Clement's. East Bergholt, for instance, was able to exercise a choice of pastor because of the anomalous status of its great parish church, in legal terms a mere chapel of ease to the church of Brantham nearby. A remarkable letter of 1592 signed by 141 inhabitants of the village survives in transcript. It completes the negotiations for employing William Jones, a new minister: and employment it was. The letter described how it had 'pleased god to move us hertofore to send for you' to begin a trial period in the parish, which had proved successful; the letter then became a veritable congregational covenant, promising before God that the inhabitants would submit themselves 'to all that counsayle of God which you shall truly deliver to us out of his written word'. This was not a document which would readily have commended itself to the hierarchy of the Church, and many gentlemen would have found it fairly threatening as well.[12]

Even where the workings of the traditional patronage system prevented a parish from having any say in the choice of its pastor, it was possible for the godly to do their own pastoral work and encourage the shepherd of the flock to improve himself. For instance, at Hinderclay, a north Suffolk village which did not boast a resident gentleman during the sixteenth century, a visitation of the time of Bishop Freke noted that although the parson was 'no graduat nor precher nor Latenest, he hath given him selfe to the studye of divinitie xx yeres provoked by the goodwill of the townesmen therunto'.[13] Moreover, if the incumbent proved beyond redemption, groups of parishioners might be forced to make alternative provision for their spiritual needs. The case of Lawshall has already been mentioned; here the Protestant faction in the village reacted against the inadequacies of the parson and the religious conservatism patronized by the recusant gentry family of Drury at Lawshall Hall by maintaining an extraordinary lecture, which regularly attracted an attendance of fifty.[14]

The case of Lawshall clearly shows how Protestant religious activism could stand over against the wishes of a local gentleman and survive, particularly if it was given help from more sympathetic

---

[12] NRO, letter transcribed by Francis Blomefield, Accession Mrs C. M. Hood, 31.5.73, shelf P186D.
[13] NRO VIS 1, list of clergy in the deanery of Blackbourne dateable to Freke's time on internal evidence, no foliation.
[14] BL Add. 38492, fo. 107, and cf. above, p. 203.

members of the county gentry; in this case the Puritan squire Edward Lewkenor championed the cause of the Lawshall godly when their enemies harassed them. Catholic religious activism, however, was even more dependent on gentry support than its Protestant counterpart; without the protection of some great house, less powerful Catholics could not survive in Elizabethan East Anglia, and the pattern of Catholicism which did continue into the seventeenth century was overwhelmingly a matter of seigneurial strongholds. This process can be clearly observed at work if one examines the lists with which central government sought to identify Catholic activists in the county. The earliest such list can be dated between 1575 and 1577, and is remarkable in two ways when compared with lists of the 1590s to be found in the Recusant Rolls and elsewhere.[15] First, it contains nearly all the main Catholic gentry centres of later years: the names of Timperley, Hare, Cornwallis, Bedingfield, Jerningham, Norton, Everard, Jetter, Mannock, Martin, Sulyard, Rookwood, Drury, and Yaxley already mark out those who would form the backbone of Suffolk Catholic survival in later years.

Secondly, the list is remarkable for the number of names and places in it which do not recur in the history of Suffolk recusancy: just over half. These were places where no Catholic gentlemen lived to give patronage to the humbler Catholics as times got harder. Nicholas Stannard, yeoman of Laxfield in the heart of High Suffolk yeomam country, for instance, was a notorious local religious conservative in the earlier part of Elizabeth's reign, having taken a leading part in the arrest of his Laxfield neighbour the martyr John Noyes under Mary; he figured in the earliest recusant list and was constantly in trouble for papist opinions, seditious words and the possession of Catholic literature. Yet when he died in 1581, leaving an aggressively Catholic will, he found no successors in his strident activism; no one would protect the next generation of potential Catholics in Laxfield.[16] There were many other conservatives like him in east Suffolk, filling such offices as churchwarden as late as the 1580s, but they did not have enough gentry support to sustain their religious viewpoint.[17] It was

---

[15] Hatfield 2/21–3; on dating, see MacCulloch, 'Catholic and Puritan', p. 249 n.

[16] On Stannard, cf. Hatfield 2/21–3; Foxe VIII, p. 424; *CPR Eliz.* VI, no. 1501; PRO, E178/2133; *Parkhurst* p. 120.

[17] Cf., e.g. the churchwardens of Debenham (above, Ch. 3, n. 19); the case of John Chapman alias Barker of Sibton, or of Thomas Brampton at Kenton (MacCulloch, 'Catholic and Puritan', p. 254).

therefore in the world of Protestantism that the yeomen élites of Suffolk were to find an identity and a use for their energies and their organizational ability, in a form that would bring them into harmony with the hopes and beliefs of Puritan county magnates like Sir Robert Jermyn or Sir John Higham.[18]

Another way in which ordinary people could assert themselves alongside gentlemen of coat armour was through use of the law. There was nothing novel about this in Tudor East Anglia. The area had long been notorious for its addiction to the law. In 1460 Friar John Brackley had suggested to John Paston during his time in Parliament that legislation ought to be introduced to curb the number of attorneys in Suffolk and Norfolk, a theme which was repeatedly taken up (with complete lack of success) during the fifteenth and sixteenth centuries. The early seventeenth-century Chorographer took up the subject of Norfolk's litigiousness with relish:

the inhabitants . . . are so well skilled in matters of the law, as many times even the baser sort at the plough-tail will argue *pro et contra* cases in law, whose cunning and subtiltie hath replenished the shire with more lawyers than any shire whatsoever though far greater, and made themselves suspected of most shires of the realm and given the beginning unto the common word Norfolk wyles many a man beguiles.[19]

The same attention to the law had, after all, been a feature of the 1549 protest: so strong was the desire among the Mousehold leaders to preserve the King's authority even in the highly unpopular practice of purveyance that when they arrested one of the royal purveyors in Norfolk, they were persuaded to issue their own commission of purveyance to his deputy to preserve the grain already collected for the Scottish armies. Most striking of all was the way that so many of them pursued grievances in the King's courts after they had attempted to remedy them through the commotions of 1549.[20]

An awareness of the value of law was naturally at its most acute in those places which had obtained legal privileges and become chartered corporations: the bigger the corporation, the greater its reliance on and use of the law. Ipswich was Suffolk's greatest borough, and from at least the fifteenth century it had retained two attorneys, one in the

[18] Cf. K. Wrightson and D. Levine, *Poverty and Piety in an English Village. Terling 1525–1700* (1979), pp. 156–62, 173–85.

[19] *Paston Letters* II, p. 214, and cf. Richmond, p. 181; Smith, p. 3; *Chorography of Norfolk* p. 68.

[20] MacCulloch, 'Kett's Rebellion', pp. 48–9.

common law courts and one in the Exchequer, to look after its legal business. By 1572, the town felt it sufficiently important to have the legal services of its Town Clerk constantly available that it substantially increased his fee on condition that he give up his private legal practice.[21] Underlying this was an acute awareness of the importance of constant vigilance over the town's privileges in the face of attempted depredations both by private individuals and by the county as a whole. Francis Nunn, the town's legal counsel, hammered this point home to the bailiffs in a letter just before the election of their successors in 1570; those elected must be 'learnyd menn' who would be vigilant for the town's liberties

which I doe muche feare if they be not ernestly defendyd and maynteyned wilbe muche hindred. Yo have no walls no bullwarkes no gates by strength to defend yower towne, but yower towne standyth and resteth to be defendyd by the meyntnaunce preservinge and well kepinge of yower lybertys fraunchyses and customes . . .[22]

Every Suffolk borough would have recognized this as a statement of the obvious. The records of every chartered borough are full of suits to defend its liberties: at Sudbury, for instance, one can trace the town as being involved in seventeen separate law-cases concerned with its privileges between 1558 and 1603.[23] What is clear, however, is that major conflicts were becoming more common as the century went on. Only two serious quarrels began in the first three decades of the century. One was the total breakdown of relations between the leading men of Bungay and the Duke of Norfolk's gentleman steward there, Richard Wharton, leading between 1514 and 1519 to a massive but ultimately unsuccessful campaign of harassment against him, carried out largely in the form of Star Chamber suits brought by individuals.[24] The other was the feud over the nature of the corporation at Orford, which as we have already seen took its roots in the disputes of the late 1520s over the Willoughby inheritance, and was prolonged into the 1540s and 1550s. Trouble only subsided in Elizabeth's reign, when the Willoughby family who asserted the seigneurial character of the

---

[21] Bacon, pp. 118, 130, 174; *HMC* IX pt. i, p. 254.

[22] SROI, HD 36/2672/55.

[23] PRO, DL 1/43/M6, 70/A2, 103/B32, 105/S6, 110/B26, 137/S10, 148/S28, 153/G4; PRO, STAC 5 B31/3, G19/2; SROB, EE 501/1, fos. 108ᵛ, 179ᵛ, 193ᵛ; EE 501/3, fos. 5ʳ, 146ʳ, 149ʳ; EE 501/4, fo. 149ʳ.

[24] Guy, *Cardinal's Court*, p. 66, and additionally, PRO, STAC 2/11/17–22, 13/51–63, 4/39, 15/36, 15/74.

borough became absentees to East Anglia, and Orford secured the privileges which its 'royal charter' party had always claimed through its new charter in 1579.

From the 1540s, great setpiece confrontations developed between boroughs and their enemies, usually local gentry, confrontations which habitually reached the level of Star Chamber. These confrontations contrasted with the decline in conflict among the county's leading gentry which took place in the reign of Elizabeth, and also provided a very different picture to the tale of ever-growing conflict among the gentry which dominates the story of Elizabethan Norfolk. Change was at the root of most of these disputes: how to adapt liberties and privileges to changing circumstances. Any burgess of Dunwich could have pointed this out, for the continual conflicts waged between that hapless borough and its gentry and community neighbours since the early fourteenth century arose from the cruellest change of all: the erosion of the town's very ground and the shifting coastline which continually harassed its harbour and river-mouth haven. However, the reason for the growth in such conflicts in mid-century was the greatest change to occur in the ownership of land and privilege for many centuries: the dissolution of the religious houses. Wherever monastic houses had been substantial landowners in a borough, the legal and physical disputes which played so prominent a part in borough life in the second half of the century had the Dissolution at their root. A *modus vivendi* worked out doubtless with much pain over a long period by two corporate bodies was suddenly under challenge from a gentleman who had bought up the monastic property, and who might well be an outsider to the town.

Typical of this sort of case was the confrontation at Ipswich, which generated most of the important legal business in the town from mid-century. The town's leading religious house had been the Augustinian priory of Holy Trinity; by 1546 it had been sold to an eminent London merchant of Shropshire origins, Paul Withipoll, who during the rest of the decade rebuilt it in the most up-to-date style as Christchurch House. It was his son Edmund who came into conflict with the town as he tried to make the most of the former monastic status of his home and the manor attached to it. During the reign of Mary a variety of complaints from the townsfolk about his depredations on the revenues of three parishes and on the fabric of St Margaret's church, next door to his own property, led to the Privy Council intervening against him.[25]

[25] *APC* V, p. 105.

Tension continued with a series of lawsuits during the early sixties. Withipoll claimed that his house was outside the liberties and leet jurisdiction of the town by virtue of its former monastic status, and he attempted to reassert all the rights of the old priory; these included the collection of tithe in certain parishes, fishing privileges in the Orwell, rights of public thoroughfare, and most importantly, control over the annual Holy Rood Fair held on 14 September in the parish of St Margaret.[26]

It was this last issue which led to the most dramatic stage of the conflict, at the Fair of 1565. The bailiffs of Ipswich claimed that they and their officers had held court for the Fair at least since the Dissolution; their consequent clash with Withipoll provided some extra free entertainment for the countryfolk who had come to the Fair. On the night before the Fair's opening, Withipoll sent a message to the bailiffs advising them not to attend, and adding provocatively that 'in times past the maces of the towne have, uppon the Faire even, bein delivered up to the Trinity, and there have remained till the next day after the Faire'. True or false—and one can cite parallel cases even from such a proud corporation as York—this was a declaration of war to which the town officials readily responded.[27] The next day both sides met at the Fair, each with a large crowd of supporters, the bailiffs in their full official regalia with their sergeants carrying the disputed town maces. Each side charged the other in the Queen's name to keep the peace, the bailiffs as the town's rulers and Withipoll as a justice of the county. They then committed the minimum of violence necessary to bring their grievances within the cognizance of Star Chamber, and the bailiffs restored their self-esteem by binding Withipoll over to keep the peace.[28]

Whatever the comic-opera qualities of this exchange, there was a genuine and bitter dispute at stake; this was illustrated in the following April, when Withipoll (whose hobby was designing ornamental waterworks) let the water out of the ponds in his grounds into the town below with such force that it broke up the street-paving and drove much gravel into the town harbour.[29] Disputes between Withipoll and

[26] PRO, STAC 5 J8/5, W9/38.
[27] Bacon, p. 277; cf. Palliser, p. 182.
[28] PRO, STAC 5 J8/5.
[29] PRO, STAC 5 J4/7, interrogatories; cf. Redgr. 4090, where Lord Keeper Bacon notes that he had asked his 'frend' Mr Withipoll to inspect his new ornamental lake.

the town over the ownership of land dragged on into the 1570s.[30] The motto '*mortui sine hoste*' which Withipoll placed on his tombstone in St Margaret's church was either an extraordinary piece of self-deception or a wry acknowledgement of the fact that his enemies in the town were not one but many. Trouble eased after his death in 1582, but the town cannot have forgotten his threat to buy the fee-farm of the town, 'for then [he] shoulde rule'.[31]

Similar disputes wracked the borough of Sudbury and the town of Beccles. At Sudbury, conflict was with the family of Eden, the Bury St Edmunds family who had bred two clerks of the King's Council. The first of these clerks, Richard Eden, Archdeacon of Middlesex, surrendered his mastership of Sudbury College in 1544, but the other clerk of the Council, Thomas Eden, had already bought Sudbury's Dominican friary in 1539, and had transformed it into his home in the same thoroughgoing way as Paul Withipoll had done with Holy Trinity Ipswich.[32] It was his son, also Thomas, who came into conflict with the town: although Thomas the younger sat as MP for the town as late as 1558, the regular gifts of wine which the Edens were receiving in the 1570s did not continue later, and from the 1580s there was a series of clashes which became increasingly bitter and violent.[33] The focus of all these was the former extra-parochial status of the friary and all the rights and exemptions that this might imply: for instance, the loss to the parish poor rate contribution of a rich man like Eden was a serious matter.

As a leading gentleman of the county, Eden was in a good position to harass the town. In his year as Sheriff, 1596/7, he was involved in the row over the election of one of Sudbury's burgesses of Parliament which we have already seen so ruthlessly resolved by the Chancellor of the Duchy of Lancaster (above, p. 33). Also during his shrievalty he sent one of his servants who was a free burgess of the town, provocatively attired in the Eden livery rather than his burgess's gown, to order the Mayor to suspend his court because he needed a county

---

[30] Bacon, pp. 288, 300, 309, 313, 318, and cf. D. N. J. MacCulloch and J. M. Blatchly, 'An Ipswich conundrum: the Withipoll Memorials', *Transactions of the Monumental Brass Society* XII (1977), pp. 240–7.

[31] PRO, STAC 5 J21/40, interrogatories for Withipoll.

[32] *LP* XIV pt. ii, no. 435/27; for Eden's early destruction of the church, cf. PRO, STAC 5 B31/3.

[33] Gift of wine, e.g. SROB, EE 501/1, fo. 180ʳ; lawsuits, EE 501/3, fo. 5ʳ; PRO, DL 1/137/S10; PRO, STAC 5 B31/3, B56/1, G37/10. For further details, MacCulloch, 'Power, Privilege and the County Community', pp. 311–14.

JP present to make the proceedings valid, a contention which does not seem to be borne out by the terms of the town's charter. He termed the corporation a 'scraplation' and was heard to wish that the town was 'a greene before his howse'.[34]

Beccles suffered an equally turbulent resident, and with a much weaker corporate body than Sudbury, its struggle to maintain its liberties was all the greater. The quarrel between the townsfolk and the family of Rede, lasting as it did for a full fifty years, had a good claim to be considered the main *cause célèbre* of Tudor Suffolk. Here the monastery at the root of the trouble was Bury Abbey. By the fifteenth century, after previous disagreements, Bury had come to an understanding with the townsfolk over the management of the extensive and valuable common land known as Beccles Fen. However, this reasonably benevolent absentee regime ended in 1539, and the people of Beccles were determined not to be the losers by the Dissolution. They sought to have their administration of the Fen enshrined in letters patent; unhappily for their plans, although understandably, they selected William Rede, one of a family of Norwich merchants, but resident in Beccles and a JP in Suffolk, to negotiate for the purchase of the Fen. It is quite clear from the mass of subsequent evidence that Rede was out for his own profit; the townsfolk considered the first patent that he had obtained to be so unsatisfactory that they compelled him to sue out a fresh patent. Nevertheless the Redes still secured the surveyorship of the Fen for themselves and kept the deeds concerning it.[34]

Trouble had certainly occurred once more by 1562, when the inhabitants of Beccles brought an action against William Rede's grandson and the widow of his son to obtain possession of the Fen deeds;[35] by this time the deeds were in the hands of Sir Thomas Gresham, who had married the widow of another of William Rede's sons, and of her son, another William, who was to become the chief protagonist in the Elizabethan disputes over the Fen.[36] The compromise reached three years later was only a temporary palliative, and during the 1570s the conflict broke out with renewed bitterness. A bewildering variety of suits in the common law courts, Chancery, Star Chamber, and even the ecclesiastical courts culminated in the

---

[34] PRO, STAC 5 B31/3; cf. the provision for the Mayor to be a JP within the town in the 1559 charter (*PSIA* XIII, 1909, p. 264).
[35] PRO, C3/30/4.
[36] Ibid., C3/29/109; Metcalfe, p. 59.

inhabitants suing out a new grant of incorporation by stealth in 1584, much to Rede's fury.[37]

By the drastic device of claiming the Fen to be concealed Crown lands, also insinuating that the new grant endangered the interests of the poor, Rede brought the case into the Exchequer Court, where he received more support than the weakness of his case deserved; the Exchequer seems to have taken a long time to react to the impressive and repeated testimony of leading members of the Suffolk Bench in support of the townsfolks' claims, perhaps because of Rede's marriage links with Lord Treasurer Burghley.[38] A disastrous fire devastating the town in 1586 does not seem to have dampened the ardour of the combatants even in the face of widespread moralizing about this divine judgement on community 'discord and debate', and it is unlikely that the compromise reached by the Exchequer in 1588 was as significant in the townsfolks' eventual triumph as the death of William Rede.[39] The date of the 1584 patent became a prominent element in the design of the town seal; no gentry heraldry for them. The whole affair was a triumph for the persistence of the townspeople and in particular for William Downing, a Puritan common attorney born in the town. The Puritan JPs brought in to examine the case frankly expressed their admiration for their social inferiors' stubbornness: 'we have not knowne men of ther caling to have holden out so well in so unkynde and chargeable trobles'. Perhaps if Rede and his fellows had not been such aggressive religious conservatives, and their opponents had not been so firmly godly in religion, the JPs' admiration might have been tempered by unease at this evidence of political energy among the lower sort.[40]

The disappearance of Bury Abbey caused at least two further significant disputes of the same type: at Mildenhall and at Bury itself. Mildenhall was not a corporate borough, but it was a very large parish on the edge of the Fens with no prominent gentry family of long standing, and parish government had devolved on the leet; within the

---

[37] Lawsuits: PRO, STAC 5 R6/14, S10/12; Bec. A4/14, A4/12, A4/82–5, A4/24–6, A4/36–42, A4/73, A4/67; PRO, E134/28 Elizabeth/Easter 21. Grant: PRO, C66/1251, m. 1.

[38] Exchequer case: Bec. A4/36–42. JPs' letters and drafts of letters: PRO, E134/28 Elizabeth/Easter 21; Bec. A4/51, A4/56, A4/72. Burghley links: Bec. A4/36.

[39] Renewed suit 1586: PRO, E133/4/658. Cf. two broadside ballads on the fire preserved in Hengr. 18, fo. 70ʳ. Exchequer compromise: PRO, E134/30 Elizabeth/Hilary 23.

[40] Bec. A4/56, and cf. MacCulloch, 'Power, Privilege and the County Community', pp. 306–7.

leet, effective control rested on an elected body of leading yeomen known as the Twenty-Four. Theirs was an important community, which seems to have taken the dissolution of Bury Abbey as the chance to drain the drowned fenland, reclaiming, it was said, more than four thousand acres, half the extent of the manor, in sixty years and swelling the population through the parish's scattered hamlets to a formidable two thousand.[41] The problem facing the Twenty-Four was to maintain and extend their authority over this boom town in the face of the dispersal of the Abbey's old authority in two different directions: the lordship of the manor had eventually passed to the Duchy of Lancaster, but various lands and tithes had been leased to Lord Keeper Bacon.[42] He sublet to successive gentlemen who came to live in Mildenhall.

It was these latter gentlemen, William Pope and Henry Warner, who played the role of Withipoll at Ipswich, Eden at Sudbury, and Rede at Beccles, and found themselves entangled in a complicated web of litigation over the control of commons, the collection of tithe, and the making of by-laws.[43] All the gentry who were associated with the Duchy's local administration consistently supported the Twenty-Four through these disputes: the local Puritan magnate Sir John Higham, who was Steward to the Duchy just as his father before him had been Steward to the Abbot of Bury, and the family of Lord North, who leased the profits of the leet courts from the Duchy in 1587; one of North's sons came to live at Mildenhall thereafter. In 1600 Sir Henry North went so far as to demonstrate his friendship with and trust in the Twenty-Four by selling them the leet profits.[44]

The case of this proto-corporation is instructive. Here was no class conflict; gentlemen were perfectly prepared to support an oligarchy of yeomen when they felt that right and custom were on their side. Everyone in this world was obsessed not by class but by law. As long as the Twenty-Four could substantiate the claim of one of their number that they had 'as good power to make lawes and to taxe ... as the parlament might do', no conscientious local gentleman could gainsay them.[45] It all depended on meticulous investigation of precedent and

[41] PRO, DL 1/164/H22; PRO, STAC 5 W26/27, Answer of John Clarke.
[42] PRO, DL 1/71/F21, 1/120/C8.
[43] For details, see MacCulloch, 'Power, Privilege and the County Community', pp. 299–300.
[44] Cf., e.g. PRO, DL 1/107/F3, 1/150/N1; PRO, STAC 5 W26/27, deposition of Sir Henry North. North's lease: PRO, DL 1/203/H14, and sale of profits: DL 1/203/H14.   [45] BL Harl. 98, fo. 126ʳ.

custom, a process of retrieval from the accidents of memory and the profound upheavals of the Dissolution: the same impulse which led the town of Sudbury to commission research like a pedigree of the mesne lords of their town, and an investigation of the patent rolls in Chancery.[46]

The feelings of the gentry might be very different where a community was actually trying to initiate change in custom. The gentry did not want further islands of privilege in their midst, however logical such an alteration of custom might seem to a disinterested outsider. Such was the case of Bury St Edmunds. Although it was the county assize town and the undoubted capital of the Liberty of St Edmund, the sway which the Abbey had exercised over it had left it with no proper corporation at all. Instead, administration was divided between the governors of the Grammar School, the feoffees of the various town charities and property, and a separate commission of the peace, which was in practice dominated by the town's handful of resident gentlemen and the local magnates on the county Bench. The town's first attempt to remedy this situation was made in 1562, and it is interesting to note that the four knights and gentlemen then on the Bury commission of the peace supported the request. The friendly but discouraging reply that they received from Lord Keeper Bacon led to the proposal being shelved. Bacon told them that 'men of wisdom and understanding' felt that there were already too many corporations, the implication being that although nothing could be done to lessen these existing privileges, 'it were not mete nor convenyent to have that nombr encreassed with any mor'.[47]

The second recorded attempt, made in 1601, contrasts sharply with the first. The gentry county community and in particular the Puritan leadership of the Bury area, had gained in unity and coherence in the forty intervening years; by 1601 the leading JPs around Bury looked with extreme disfavour on the idea of the assize town with its many amenities and attractions falling from their grasp. Sir Robert Jermyn and Sir John Higham embodied their protest in a letter to Sir Robert Cecil which represents one extreme interpretation of what a corporation might mean to its neighbours.[48] They referred scornfully to the

[46] SROB, EE 501/1, fos. 188ᵛ, 196ᵛ.

[47] SROB, C4/1. On government in Bury, see Lobel, *passim*.

[48] Hatfield 87/118 (*HMC Salisbury* XI, p. 351). The letter has only Sir Robert Jermyn's signature, but uses the plural throughout and was sealed with a signet bearing the Higham arms.

townsfolk of Bury as 'mechanicall and trades men' who wished to 'wring the authoritie that now is out of the handes of Sir H. Northe, Sir N. Bacon, Mr. Mawe and Mr. Smithe bothe Cowncelers of the Lawe, Mr. Barber, Mr. Dandy and our sealves commissioners for her Majesties peace in that towne'; seeing that Robert Mawe was Sir Nicholas Bacon's lawyer, James Smith was Sir John Higham's son-in-law and that Roger Barber had succeeded Lord Keeper Bacon's servant Thomas Andrews as county feodary, one can gauge how tight an oligarchy of county magnates dominated Bury.[49] The writers also suggested that the townsfolk were trying to evade 'the common charges of the contrie' and that they would attempt to impose 'suche impositions and colours of forfeitures' in Bury market 'as can not but either greave and impoverishe the contry Neighbors upholders of the said Merkett, or bringe an utter ruine and decaye uppon the wholl towne'. In view of Sir Nicholas Bacon's attempt to wrest the stall-rents of the market from the control of the bailiffs of Bury seven years earlier by legal action, this latter comment looks suspiciously like a piece of special pleading.[50] The last fear that they expressed was for the safety of the godly Puritan commonwealth, to the fostering of which they had devoted so much energy, 'which we feare the Corporation wil not or shall not be able to beare out'.

This appeal was successful in blocking the townsfolk's efforts, and Jermyn and Higham wrote their profuse thanks to Cecil.[51] However, James I proved more accommodating than his predecessor, and Bury got its charter only five years after the county magnates' success, appropriately expressing its gratitude with a generous expenditure of £40 on portraits of its royal benefactor and of two eminent townsfolk of the past. Even as late as 1623, however, Sir Nicholas Bacon was still carrying on the feud in an attempt to preserve his old criminal jurisdiction as lessee of the Liberty of St Edmund against the new powers of the corporation.[52]

In all the disputes which we have considered, it was the townsfolk and not their opponents who eventually won; the sheer persistence which their collective effort could sustain would eventually win through. However, such persistence was not just the quality of a

---

[49] Mawe: Redgr. 4157, 4163, 4170, 4175. Smith: PCC 125 Clarke. Barber: PRO, C66/1256, m. 5d.

[50] PRO, E134/36 Elizabeth/Easter 12.   [51] *HMC Salisbury* XI, p. 396.

[52] PRO, E134/20 James I/Easter 3. On the portraits, see *PSIA* XXXI (1970), pp. 148–9. For Hadleigh's similar efforts to gain a charter, also successful under James I, see MacCulloch, 'Power, Privilege and the Community', p. 301.

mighty chartered corporation like Ipswich; a charter was a highly useful weapon, but lesser communities could fight long and determined battles too. When Robert Browne clashed with the people of Leiston and Theberton in the 1540s and 1550s about fold-course rights in his newly-acquired abbey lands, he was inheriting litigation which had harassed the Abbot of Leiston before him.[53] Yeoman communities might club together to finance a formidable series of suits against a gentleman who was offending against local custom, as Francis Colby of Benhall discovered to his cost when trying to assert his rights to former glebeland in Benhall and Farnham in the 1580s, or as did Matthew Crispe and the incoming London alderman Robert Brooke when successively confronting the people of Walberswick over claims to common rights in the following decade.[54] Faced with similar action from the tenants of Cotton Hempnalls in his attempts to recover the valuable demesnes of his newly-acquired manor, Sir John Tyrell's reaction was one of extreme irritation; this prominent religious conservative saw his tenants' litigation as an offence to the created order, and said so forcefully and at length:

by the sufferauns of suche as have the occupyinge of the dymeanes of the said mannor they be growen to be of such substauns as they lyve farre above the degrees of their Auncestors that have been auncyent tenauntes of the said mannor and been the more able to lyve in their degree and above their degrees then the said Sir John Tyrrell and suche others as have [been] Lordes of the said mannor have been able to lyve in their degrees. And the same Sir John further saithe that in case he and suche as he is beinge Lordes of mannors shuld be enforced to suffer their dymeanes to be occupied by comminers and meane tenauntes and not to occupie the same theymselffes for the mayntenauns of their hospitalitie and commodite, they shuld therebie come to great povertie and decaye, and therebie the astate of gentlemen and men of worship shuld come to suche ruyne as the cyvill and quyett governement of the common welthe shulde therebie be moche hindered and decayed . . .[55]

Behind all these corporate actions great and small lay a strong sense of tradition, of justice and of common responsibility. We have seen Francis Nunn spelling this out for the bailiffs of Ipswich in 1570, yet we can also find traces of the same attitude in much smaller-scale communities. The village people of Flempton with the aid of

[53] PRO, STAC 2/25/4, 2/34/4, 3/2/6, 3/4/7.
[54] Colby: PRO, STAC 5 C16/34, C74/8, H62/37, H75/38. Crispe, Brooke: STAC 5 B96/39.
[55] PRO, C3/47/11, 105/3, 141/64, 154/6 (from which the quotation comes).

surrounding communities waged a massive but ultimately unsuccessful campaign against the might of the Hengrave Hall estates in an effort to stop the permanent enclosure of Flempton's former demesne lands by Sir Thomas Kitson's leasehold tenants.[56] When Sir Thomas's servant in the village reported the throwing open of the demesnes by the village to his master, he made it clear that he was anxious not to take sides openly against the rioters 'because I am a townesman'.[57] His conflict of loyalties was not easily to be resolved in favour of social deference.

Did political awareness in a place like Flempton stop merely at the level of parochialism, or did it have a wider focus? The scale of the action in 1525 and 1549 suggests that for many, the wider focus was there. The conflicts over religion which successive Tudor government policies served to precipitate can only have helped to encourage the process, which was also spurred by the mid-century advances in literacy and the output of printed books. In the following century, the English Civil War would be a war of the written word, of broadsheets and pamphlets, as no other previous disturbance in English history had been. In the meantime, one can find traces of concern for and participation in the affairs of Parliament beyond the small world of gentry politics: the process of involvement which Derek Hirst has identified as so clearly at work in the early seventeenth century.[58]

Widespread interest in parliamentary affairs was in fact nothing new. The famous statute of 1430 which created the forty shilling freeholder qualification was, after all, a response to the large numbers of people who were liable to turn up in county elections, and the disorder which they might cause. The knights of the shire were peculiarly the county's representatives. Parliament could pass legislation which affected everyone's well-being, and it was only natural for a broad cross-section of the population to be concerned for the choice of an appropriate knight of the shire. Margaret Paston reported to her husband in 1460 that he had the prayers of 'the poer pepyl' for his candidature for the shire in Norfolk, both for measures to bring peace to the county and to control the wool trade; whatever her partisanship for her husband, clearly there was nothing unusual in such popular

---

[56] PRO, STAC 5 M6/20; *HMC Salisbury* VIII, p. 566. The chief Flempton defendants Gregory Brett and Tobias Chapman appeared as having been fined in 1601 in the index of *Fines in the Court of Star Chamber 1596–1641* (computer print-out compiled by T. G. Barnes, available in the Round Room of the PRO).

[57] Tanner 97, fo. 73ʳ.   [58] Hirst, *passim*, especially Chs. 6 and 7.

concern for the intentions of the knight of the shire. Likewise, popular sensibilities were upset when the Norfolk under-sheriff tried to avoid accepting the election result in 1461: 'the comynnes throw all the shyer be movyd agayn hym for cause of his lyght demeanyng towardes them for this elexsyon of knygttes of the shyer', John Berney told John Paston.[59]

We have no way of knowing how large a number of this fifteenth-century sample of the 'comynnes' might be. In a comparatively small county, Huntingdonshire, the rare phenomenon of a surviving poll from 1450 totals the substantial number of 424 or 430 freeholders, 85 per cent of them apparently forty shilling freeholders below the level of named members of the armigerous classes.[60] No figures of total county polls survive for comparison in sixteenth-century Suffolk. The disputed Norfolk election of 1586 produced an estimated 3,000 freeholders assembled at Norwich while Edward Coke at least claimed to have been elected by 7,000 as first Norfolk knight of the shire in 1593.[61] Neither figure is entirely trustworthy, but each implies an electoral turnout which was numbered in thousands rather than in hundreds. East Anglia, like Kent, was an area where the accidents of tenure meant that there were plenty of freeholders to draw on. The surviving list of freeholders for the Geldable of Suffolk in 1561 numbers 1,282 names in 203 townships outside the parliamentary boroughs of Ipswich and Dunwich. Projected across the 500 or so townships of the county as a whole, this gives a potential freeholder electorate for the county at the very beginning of Elizabeth's reign of over 3,000.[62] This was a stark contrast with the very restricted franchises of the county's parliamentary boroughs; it implied that a large number of people might have a say in a county election.

Could such a potentially large number of county voters have been effectively manipulated by their social superiors? Manipulation might be aided by the strong sense of community which the electorate displayed: voting was not so much an individual matter but an obligation laid on some for the sake of others, just as the fifteenth was a tax laid on communities rather than on individuals. Partly it was a matter of the ceremonial nature of the occasion; those voting were

[59] *Paston Letters* I, p. 259; II, p. 243.
[60] J. R. Lander, *Government and Community* (1980), p. 57.   [61] Smith, p. 314.
[62] BL Lansd. 5/7. The projection can only be approximate; it is likely that the Geldable had a higher proportion of freeholders than elsewhere (above, Ch. 1), but this is likely to be offset by the large number of freeholders in Bury St Edmunds.

undertaking a solemn duty for the community, and they would expect to show that they were acting on behalf of their lesser community in a body. In January 1483 we catch a glimpse of 'the feleschippe of Clare' on their journey to Ipswich for the county election, being given a lodging *en route* at Stoke by the first Howard Duke of Norfolk; Howard was not their lord or in any sense their feudal superior, but he could take advantage of their travelling together as a group to provide a little influence in the form of entertainment.[63]

Among such groups would naturally be the groupings of tenantry. All the surviving references to canvassing at elections in sixteenth-century Suffolk testify to the importance of marshalling bloc votes from the estates of individual gentlemen. It was in this way that Lord Keeper Bacon surveyed the county scene for his son in the 1572 election, even regarding the tenants of the Exchequer in the county as a potential bloc vote to be influenced by the county receiver, Thomas Badby.[64] In 1593 Sir John Higham called on his friend Thomas Clopton of Melford to utilize the potential of the two-centuries-old unit of the Clopton family estates: Clopton, in a politely but firmly worded circular, ordered his tenants to assemble at the edge of Ipswich between seven and eight in the morning, some eighteen miles' journey for his Melford tenants at least, to vote for Higham's son, adding that he would 'take yt as thankfullie as if yt weare done to my self or my owne sonne'.[65] Naturally, a gentleman's influence need not merely be directly through his tenants: 'proquer all your frehouldurs in Suffoke and your frendes' wrote Anthony Gawdy to his half-brother Bassing-bourn to secure their 'woyesis' on behalf of Sir William Drury in the tense electioneering of 1584.[66]

All this might indicate that the Suffolk electorate was fairly passive; certainly it still accepted a royal recommendation for the two knights of the shire in January 1553, and when John Southwell discussed the choosing of knights of the shire in Mary's last Parliament of 1558, it was entirely in terms of deals among the leading Catholic gentry.[67] However, could it be that simple in later years? Not only was the electorate expanding through the process of inflation on the forty shilling franchise, and there was increasing confusion as to what the freehold qualification might mean, but it is likely that the old corporate notion of voting was breaking down; with the introduction of religion

---

[63] Payne Collier, *Household Books*, p. 337.
[64] Redgr. 4118.
[65] BL Harl. 385, fo. 177ʳ.
[66] BL Eger. 2713, fo. 63ʳ.
[67] BL Lansd. 3/19. fo. 36; on Southwell, above, pp. 81–2.

as an issue in politics, as was clearly the case in the 1584 election, individual conscience might well be a more significant factor than in the days when the 'feleschippe' of Clare had marched to Ipswich. Moreover, contested elections were becoming a regular feature of Suffolk life, and if the county gentry could not reach a consensus on a candidate among themselves before the county court, it might well be the opinions of their social inferiors which proved decisive in swinging the result.

In Norfolk, Dr Smith could work from private letters to reach the conclusion that almost every Elizabethan county election was contested.[68] In Suffolk the evidence is simply not there for most elections, but four election contests out of ten Elizabethan elections have left traces, involving the 1584, 1586, 1597, and 1601 county courts. The 1584 contest was that in which the Puritan leaders confronted Sir William Drury and were partly defeated; the 1586 contest can be inferred from the fact that Sir John Higham once more took out an 'insurance policy' in the form of a borough seat at Ipswich, a precaution which in the end proved unnecessary. We know of the two later contests on the strength of a single letter to Sir Nicholas Bacon from Henry Warner of Mildenhall, a few days before the 1601 election.[69] Warner had been the second of the successful candidates in 1597, and he referred darkly to 'sume that were put by ther expectation' at that election, who were now opposing the candidature of his friend and future cousin by marriage Sir Henry Glemham. Warner named as his chief opponent the veteran county administrator Sir Robert Jermyn, who was supporting the candidature of Sir Philip Parker's eldest son Calthorpe; for his own side, Sir Anthony Wingfield, Sir Robert Wingfield's heir and successor, Warner's old Cambridge contemporary and brother-in-law, was campaigning with enthusiasm for Glemham, who was in any case his cousin.

At first sight it is difficult to relate these alignments to any ongoing dispute within the county, or indeed to account for west Suffolk Jermyn's alliance with the east Suffolk Parkers. However, Jermyn's

[68] Smith, p. 314. The only surviving indication of an election contest in Suffolk in the first half of the sixteenth century is the exceptional number of people to be named in the county election indenture of 1545: PRO, C219/18C/110. Sir Anthony Wingfield, previously one of the knights of the shire, sat for Horsham borough in this Parliament.

[69] For the detailed argument about these elections, see MacCulloch, 'Catholic and Puritan', pp. 282–3, 285. On the 1597 and 1601 elections, see Redgr. 4171. The 1597 contest can be inferred additionally from Sir William Waldegrave's provision for an alternative seat for himself at Ipswich: Bacon, p. 389.

motive may have been resentment at interference in the top level of county affairs by a pair of relative outsiders like Warner and Glemham. While he himself and Sir Philip Parker had for many years been colleagues as muster commissioners and deputy lieutenants, and had respectable roots in Suffolk, Warner was a settler in the county from Norfolk, although he had been on the Bench since 1585; in no Tudor election for the county before 1597 had any knight of the shire been returned who did not come from a Suffolk family of respectable antiquity, with the pardonable exceptions of the Master of the Rolls in January 1558 and later two sons of Lord Keeper Bacon.[70] With his home in the eponymous village of Glemham, Glemham's Suffolk background was unexceptionable, as was that of his supporter Sir Anthony Wingfield, but no member of the Glemham family had sat on the Suffolk Bench since the death of Henry's father Thomas in 1571, and his cousin Edward of Benhall had recently disgraced the family name by his bankruptcy and cowardice in the Algiers expedition of 1595.[71] Henry achieved a knighthood, a place on the Suffolk Bench and inclusion in the muster commission all in the election year of 1601, a triple achievement doubtless related to his marriage to the daughter of Lord Treasurer Buckhurst.[72] His sudden rise may well have raised eyebrows among older members of the county élite, and disposed them against his election candidature in the same fashion as they had been against Warner's in 1597. In the event, Glemham was to add the honour of first knight of the shire to his other trophies of 1601, despite Warner's forebodings. Either there was a compromise or neither side could sweep the board with two candidates, for Calthorpe Parker appeared as second MP for the county. Just as in 1584, the 1601 election result produced successes for representatives of two different groupings in the county. It is also of interest to note that just as in 1584, when the county electorate was presented with a chance to back members of the Suffolk Puritan establishment against candidates with 'Court' associations, the response was hardly an overwhelming endorsement of the 'Country' cause.

The disagreements of their social superiors thus gave the electorate a genuine choice of representative in more and more county elections; if the evidence were as abundant for Elizabethan Suffolk as for

[70] Nicholas Bacon in 1572 and Edward in 1593. Warner was the son of Sir Edward Warner of Plumstead (BL Add. 19172, fo. 57ᵛ).

[71] PRO, C2 ELIZ G15/38; *APC* XXX, pp. 157, 283, 422.

[72] Metcalfe, p. 140.

Elizabethan Norfolk, further evidence of contests might well emerge. Moreover, one did not necessarily need an electoral contest to bring forth boisterous expressions of political opinions at a county election; Dr Hirst comments of early seventeenth-century Suffolk county elections that they produced 'extensive disruption in years when there was possibly no contest'.[73] Disruption this may have been, but it was a different sort of disruption from the sequence of commotions from 1525 to 1569. The emphasis in conflict moved from direct action in the countryside to alternative arenas: the common law courts, the prerogative courts, and the High Court of Parliament—traditional areanas, and all the more effective because of that in siphoning off popular protest. Each embodied aspects of that immense respect for law which was so deep-rooted in Tudor society, and which was perceptible even in the popular rebellions of earlier years. Between 1640 and 1642 it would take the growth of a general feeling that the Crown itself had lost its respect for law, and that the whole fabric of English liberties was in danger from the threat of popish Irish invasion, for a significant number of ordinary people to be tempted once more into direct action.

[73] Hirst, p. 227.

Conclusion

DURING the sixteenth century, Suffolk was transformed in political terms. From being part of an East Anglian region dominated by great noblemen, first the Earl of Oxford, then the Dukes of Norfolk and Suffolk, it became an increasingly self-contained county whose day to day running was in the hands of an oligarchy of Puritan-minded gentry; they took immense pride in their work of government. Dr Richmond has given us the portrait of John Hopton, a fifteenth-century Suffolk gentleman who wanted little to do with the faction-fighting of the magnates above him: Hopton's late sixteenth-century successors would be only too willing to be emancipated from the interference which his generation had known.[1]

Central government could also claim its successes. Henry VII had restored the power of the Earl of Oxford, and Henry and his son did the same for the house of Howard. Henry VIII created the power of the Duke of Suffolk, and just as surely removed him from the East Anglian scene; the Duke of Norfolk was next to go. In an informal sense these noblemen had been the forerunners of the Crown-appointed lords lieutenant later in the century. The government also retained the whip-hand over the commission of the peace, knowing that it had a surplus of applicants for the justices' Bench to choose from. Every Tudor reign began with a review of the commission of the peace and a removal of men considered undesirable or unnecessary for whatever reason. The 'purges' of justices in 1553 and 1558 additionally reflected the new importance of ideology in deciding who the Crown's local agents would be, and they were more thoroughgoing than any previous efforts (above, Chs. 7 and 8). Periodic reviews could take place on other occasions as well; the earliest one detectable is in 1514 and 1515, perhaps associated with a review of local administration in East Anglia following the creation of the two new Dukes. In Elizabeth's reign, concern at the 'overgreat number' of JPs, a favourite theme of Lord Burghley, led to a succession of cuts in numbers on the Bench, notably in 1561, 1564, 1587, and 1595.

What is notable about the last two of these attempts is that as far as Suffolk was concerned, cuts were made on a largely mechanical basis:

---

[1] Cf. especially Richmond, Ch. 3.

in 1587 nearly all those who can be detected as having been omitted came from the eastern half of the county, presumably reflecting the conclusion of central government that the area was overweighted with JPs. In 1595 those who went were either the last names in the list of those in commission, the most recently appointed JPs or those with a poor record of attendance at quarter sessions, and of twenty justices dismissed on this occasion, only three cannot be accounted for by such mechanical explanations. One of these was a crypto-Catholic, the other a notorious usurer—two obvious targets for official disapproval. When the government chose to, it could assert its will quite effectively.[2]

On the other hand, even with an operation based in Westminster like the choice of JPs, it might not always be politic or possible to achieve the perfect commission. The most notorious example of this discussed above (Ch. 2) was the influence of the Duke of Norfolk during the 1560s, which resulted in many religious conservatives remaining in commission when Westminster ideally would have seen to their dismissal. In a parallel sphere, by the 1590s the government had little room for manœuvre in its choice of county muster commissioners; one group of leading knights had made themselves so indispensable to the county's military organization that there was little alternative to making them muster commissioners, even while two of them had been ejected from the commission of the peace for excessive Protestant enthusiasm, and while many of them successfully obstructed Westminster's demands for extra military spending (above, Chs. 6 and 9). The accidents of high politics had given Puritan magnates like Sir Robert Jermyn, Sir John Higham, Sir Robert Wingfield and Sir Nicholas Bacon their chance. Those accidents had removed the great noblemen and discredited the conservative gentry who had taken their lead from the circle around the Duke of Norfolk and Sir Thomas Cornwallis. Sir Arthur Heveningham's effort to rally the remains of the Howard clientage and place it in the service of the Court and lord lieutenant was never wholly effective, although it could not be ignored and was not necessarily without a popular following; the equivocal results of the county elections of 1584 and 1601 are reminders of this (above, Ch. 11). By the 1590s there were signs of the revival in Howard fortunes which would gain such rapid momentum under

[2] Cf. Appendix III, and for a detailed discussion of dismissals and purges of the Bench under Elizabeth, MacCulloch, 'Power, Privilege and the County Community', pp. 89–97. See also Smith, pp. 76–81.

James I: from 1589, the recovery of part of the Howard inheritance through the legal skill of Edward Coke (above, Ch. 8), the associated appearance of the Howard trustees Roger Townshend and Robert Buxton in the Norfolk commission in 1590 (short-lived though Townshend's tenure was) and from 1598 the appearance of the fourth Duke of Norfolk's son Thomas, newly promoted to be Lord Howard de Walden, in the Essex and Norfolk commissions.[3] Nevertheless, despite the tragedy of Charles Brandon's ducal line ending in untimely death, and despite all Sir Arthur Heveningham's efforts, it was the descendants of the east Suffolk Brandon circle and the west Suffolk gentry outside the Howard grouping who would lead Suffolk by the end of Elizabeth's reign.

The government would find it considerably more awkward to deal with an oligarchy like this than with single great men like Vere, Howard or Brandon. To begin with, Protestant religious enthusiasm increasingly created a common identity for this network of gentry families which was totally different from the identities within the shifting factions of fifteenth-century East Anglia; these were 'the godly'. As early as 1575 Roger Lord North, an associate of the developing Puritan group in Suffolk, could further a suit for a friend of Robert Jermyn's pious stepmother to Seckford, the Suffolk-born Master of Requests, although he did not know the lady concerned. He promoted her case on the joint grounds of county feeling and Puritan solidarity: 'she ys of Suffolke: and I suppose of Godds flocke because my good Lady Jarmin doth commend hir to me.'[4] Already, therefore, the party who would take over county government by the end of the century could feel that they were distinguished from their gentry neighbours by being God's flock.

God's flock was built up among the gentry by youthful experiences at University or in years spent in London at the Inns of Court; increasingly, also, a University-trained clergy strengthened the godly with a shared network of piety and practice at home: parish life, the market-day lecture and exercise. 'Godliness' therefore involved the

---

[3] Townshend and Buxton appear in commission in the *liber pacis* BL Eger. 3788, fo. 25ᵛ; this was not discovered until after Dr Smith had compiled his lists of Norfolk JPs. Wimond Carey, a cousin of Lord Hunsdon, became a Norfolk JP later the same year (Smith, Appendix I).

[4] PRO, REQ 3/37, a file of letters relative to Requests business, Jan./Feb. 1575, North to Thomas Seckford, 20 January. Lady Jermyn, Sir Ambrose Jermyn's second wife, was Dorothy, daughter of William Badby of Layer Marney, and married Sir Ambrose after 1568 (*Rushbrook Registers* pp. 201, 206–7).

Puritan gentry at both a national and a local level, but nationally, the one forum which grew increasingly remote from the concerns of the godly party was the Court. As Elizabeth's reign wore on, the Puritan county leadership was finding fewer and fewer contacts at Court, while it was battling with central authority over religion and over civil and military administration. This was not a healthy development; those who did have strong Court contacts and promoted the interests of the Court and of central government departments like the Exchequer, such as Lord Hunsdon and Sir Arthur Heveningham, were not so certainly of God's flock, to say nothing of their links with the old Howard circle.

Equally alarming for the Elizabethan regime in the capital was the fact that the fragile Henrician ecclesiastical consensus had failed to survive the traumas of the Edwardian and Marian regimes; the uneasy peace which had preserved the illusion of an all-embracing national church in the 1560s had broken by 1569. Within the gentry there was developing a group which was increasingly marked out from its neighbours, a group not merely conservative in religion out of habit, but Catholic out of considered conviction. The group emerged out of the circle which had affectionate memories of great churchmen of the past like Bishop Nix and Abbot Reve of Bury, and it was sustained by sophisticated and well-informed members of the gentry like Sir Thomas Cornwallis and Michael Hare. This Catholic group was increasingly subject to official harassment and financial hardship, but nevertheless it was never wholly alienated from its gentry neighbours. In a small society, family ties with non-Catholics remained strong throughout the Elizabethan period; older Catholics could never quite shake off their respect for the structures of the established Church in which they had grown up, and we have already noted the ties which bound some of them to non-Puritan Anglican clergy (above, Ch. 6). Moreover, several prominent Catholics continued to take a paradoxical interest in the fabric of their parish churches, sometimes to provide discreet family side-chapels to withdraw from participation in uncongenial Anglican services, but sometimes apparently out of sheer goodwill: all this at a time when very little was in general being done to make improvements to the corpus of parish church building accumulated up to the 1540s.[5]

It was not simply at a local level but also in their relations with

<hr>

[5] MacCulloch, 'Catholic and Puritan', pp. 251–6.

central government that Catholics were kept from desperation with their position and hence were discouraged from armed rebellion. Prominent Catholics like Sir Thomas Cornwallis could exploit old relationships with leading politicians of very different views from their own, like Leicester and Burghley, while lesser officials might prove equally useful. We have already seen the way in which the Exchequer proved useful to East Anglian Catholics (above, Ch. 8), and even leading recusants who were singled out for punishment according to the law found that mitigation was possible. Only three Suffolk gentlemen elected to pay the statutory £20 a month fine for non-churchgoing for any length of time: Edward Sulyard, Edward Rookwood, and Michael Hare. All received special consideration from time to time to make sure that they could still go on paying; this was after all, a good source of income for the government. Compassionate leave for family or health reasons was also common for leading Catholic gentry in prison. Gentlemen remained gentlemen, to be treated with respect; in the worst years of anxiety around fears of foreign invasion, the government confiscated the armouries of leading Catholics, but it seems to have taken good care to return them once the crisis had passed.[6] Here was an untidiness of government which was partly involuntary, partly deliberate: a considerably modified apparatus of repression which ensured that the Catholic gentry of East Anglia were never tempted into rebellion after the fiasco of the small-scale attempt in 1570. For all the revolutionary hopes of a minority of the Catholic clergy whom they sheltered at considerable common risk, the Catholic gentry remained loyal subjects of the Queen first and Catholics second. Michael Hare, one of the most courageous and long-suffering of the Suffolk recusant community and the son of Mary's Master of the Rolls, summed up the ambiguity of his position in advice to his young kinsman Arthur Everard: 'serve God, be not rashe nor reckles'.[7]

The same dilemma confronted enthusiastic Puritans who were disgusted with the incomplete nature of the 1559 Settlement and who found themselves during the 1570s and 1580s drawn into bitter conflict first with the Bishop of Norwich and later with the Archbishop of Canterbury. They were deeply involved with the 'advanced' clergy who were attempting to produce a nationwide clandestine alternative

---

[6] Ibid., pp. 257–61.

[7] Aylsham 175, Hare to Everard, 1595; for examples of similar sentiments, see MacCulloch, 'Catholic and Puritan', p. 256.

system of church government to that of episcopacy, and when elected to Parliament, they were active in support of efforts to bring religious change through legislation. How far could they carry this opposition to the Queen's policy?

The Puritan county magnates had in fact given the answer to this question in their celebrated letter of protest to the Privy Council in 1583, describing their sense of anguish and frustration at the actions of the justices of assize in humiliating both leading ministers and gentlemen of the county.[8] How could loyal county magistrates adequately protest against such gross interference in the pursuit of godliness without causing further disruption? By criticizing the assize judges, they would be by implication attacking the fabric of English law:

... we that be magestrates under hir maiestie, are as we think equivalent of voice and knowe that law and justice is one and may not be devyded, do forbeare to speake what we knowe lest by owr severance in opinion law shuld be rent and Justice cut in twayne, and so the mynds of the people whiche ar so easely distracted be caried hether and thether to the movynge of further inconveniences and so by our licence ministery and magestracye is brought into open contempte ...

The reference to 'equivalence of voice' was the nearest that the authors came to a direct reference to Wray and Anderson in the course of their letter, for it was an echo of the comment that the Suffolk delegation had made to the assize judges on their visit earlier in the year. The sense of bewilderment and outrage that they felt on discovering that the agents of central authority had not merely ceased to support them but were actively working against their sense of justice was sharpened by the perennial fear of the Tudor gentleman: the popular anarchy which awaited any rent in the seamless robe of authority and the rule of the better sort. It was this fear which saw the threat of widespread disorder in 1640–2 as a signal to withdraw obedience to the Crown; in those circumstances, many of the East Anglian gentry would come to feel that the Crown had forfeited its right to be obeyed.[9]

However, things were very different in 1583. The petitioners went on to emphasize their obedience to the law:

This is owr course, we serve hir maiestie in the contry, not accordynge unto

---

[8] The quotations are taken from the text in BL Harl. 367, fo. 24.
[9] Holmes, pp. 48–52.

our fancyes as the worlde falcely beareth us in hand, but accordynge to the lawes and the lawe makars. Law spekethe and we kepe silence, law comaundithe and we obey. Without law no man can pocesse his owne in peace, by law we procede agaynste all offendars, we towche none that lawe sparethe, we speare none that law towchethe.

In fact, when Robert Jermyn, Robert Ashfield, John Higham, and Thomas Andrews had drawn up regulations for Bury St Edmunds in 1579, they had displayed an extraordinarily cavalier attitude to the law insofar as it was the statute law of'the lawe makars'.[10] Their regulations had made constant references to 'the Statute' but more than once laid down punishments on matters of supposition that could never be covered by any equitable system of law, for example, for merely being 'voyced commonlie' to be a papist or a conjuror. However, the petitioners' emphasis on the law was not merely hypocrisy or special pleading. In his efforts to promote godly reformation within his locality, the Puritan justice put himself in an anomalous position. He was part of the recognized establishment of his area, fearful of social change, socially and politically conservative in every respect except one: the sphere of religion. Here he was the innovator, a potential agent of disruption in Church and State. A stronger inner tension between social conservatism and religious radicalism lay behind the 'orthodox' Puritan gentry's disapproval and embarrassment when faced with the yet more radical challenge of separatism, and drove them back on to the certainties of the law that they administered locally. The easy suppression of the '*classis*' movement by the central authorities was to demontrate that as yet the respectable radical Protestant was not prepared to step decisively away from the law. 'Law comaundithe and we obey.'[11]

The compromise ending of Whitgift's campaign against the Puritan ministers showed that there were still enough sympathetic ears at Council level for the Puritan gentry of the county to make themselves heard; like the Catholic group at the other end of the religious spectrum, they had contacts through the system. In effect, neither side got what it wanted; for the Puritans, there was no further structural reform of the Elizabethan Church, while with the departure of Bishop Freke in 1584, the Catholic hope of retaining a place of influence in local politics was at an end. While the Catholics lapsed into political

[10] Rose, pp. 160–2, discussing the regulations, BL Lansd. 27/70.
[11] For similar comments on the Civil War period, see D. Underdown, *Pride's Purge* (Oxford, 1971), pp. 3, 8.

passivity, the Puritan élite gradually renounced its aggressive stance against the objectionable features of the Anglican Settlement in return for a position in county government which the late Elizabethan Council hardly ever saw fit to challenge.

What part did lesser folk play in the religious transformation? We have seen that they had minds of their own. In 1525 they had shown their mettle by being at the centre of the only successful large-scale popular protest of the Tudor age. In 1549 the same group below the level of the armigerous gentry had succeeded in temporarily paralysing government in East Anglia; in 1553, in co-operation with the East Anglian gentry, they had been at the heart of the explosion of popular indignation which had toppled the regime in Westminster: again, a unique occurrence in the Tudor period. Yet it is noticeable that none of these upheavals was designed to promote the cause of religion one way or the other; even in the 1553 affair, legitimism and resentment of Northumberland seems to have been the prime motivation outside the ranks of the conspirators who generated the *coup* from Mary's household.[12] It is possible that popular disturbance utilized the same contacts which sustained the Lollards over wide areas of southern England, but even if this was the case, an animus against the traditional church never emerged in times of commotion. To the ordinary people of late medieval England, the Church meant their parish church, the place that in the compact parishes of East Anglia dominated their everyday life; and the evidence shows that for most of them, the parish church was a place to be cherished, a place on which they lavished affection and money. Perhaps the doctrines which these buildings enshrined were secondary to the buildings themselves. The Mousehold rebels listened to sermons from Protestant preachers; Archbishop Parker tells us that they also delighted in a choral performance of the *Te Deum* in English, but significantly, Robert Kett's great enemy John Flowerdew was a man who had given himself a lasting place of contempt in Norfolk folk-memory for his looting of Wymondham and Hethersett churches.[13]

Why did the iconodulic religious life of late medieval East Anglia wither? Lollardy would not have brought it down single-handed, despite recent efforts to underline the vigour of Lollard survival into the Tudor age. One of the old Church's problems was that its

[12] *'Vita Mariae'* p. 191.
[13] On the Te Deum, Russell, p. 20. Cf. Bindoff, pp. 3, 11, and for John Flowerdew's outrages at Hethersett, *Chorography of Norfolk* p. 113.

leadership was flawed. Richard Nix was among the best of late medieval bishops—resident, energetic, conscientious if unimaginative. However, his subordinates as Archdeacons were on the whole far from being *oculi episcopi:* local clergy like John Bailey and Thomas Pells hardly compensated for the lack of personal supervision from characters like Thomas Larke or Thomas Winter. The system might be efficient, but it was impersonal: Richard Nix, for all his virtues, could not be everywhere, and with this vacuum in local religious life between the bishop and the parishes, it was easy for charismatic dissidents to fulfil a need. Thomas Bilney's personal crusade of the 1520s, a blend of Lollardy and Cambridge Erasmianism, was probably of great importance in stimulating popular disenchantment with traditional Catholicism, and his death at the hands of the local religious hierarchy was probably of greater importance still. Nix and his circle, desperately lashing out to defend themselves against growing royal attack, could not have made a worse move to alienate popular sympathy from their cause, as the campaign of iconoclasm and the slump in devotion at Gracechurch in the aftermath of Bilney's death showed (above, Ch. 3).

After this, the support of influential local men like the Duke of Suffolk, Lord Wentworth, and Sir William Waldegrave would provide encouragement for popular Protestantism to develop strength on the basis of the beleaguered outposts of Lollardy. Humanist Catholicism, so elegantly nurtured in the household of Sir Humphrey Wingfield and in the great secular colleges, could find no such long-term support from above. With Elizabeth's accession, with the mighty labours of John Laurence of Fressingfield, John Knewstub of Cockfield, and many lesser figures, with the gradual establishment of the county alliance between Protestant 'magistracy and ministry', the world of devotion which seemed so unchallengeable when Bishop Nix arrived in East Anglia was irretrievably lost. One curious survival from it, never to be eradicated for all Puritan disapproval of the practice, was the East Anglian enthusiasm for change-ringing as a pastime. The splendid bell-towers of the region would not go to waste. It is particularly appropriate that one of the earliest known written change-ringing schemes, and probably the oldest in existence to have a single bell's course traced through it, survives among the papers of Sir Arthur Heveningham; Sir Arthur took a characteristically ruthless interest in the rebuilding of the bell-tower of his parish church at Ketteringham in Norfolk when it collapsed in 1608.[14] Perhaps the pastime was an appropriate memorial of a lost world: a custom owing more to social enjoyment and good fellowship than to any doctrine of the Church.

Last words on the Suffolk gentry community at the end of the Tudor age can go to its contemporary historian and to its sovereign. Robert Ryece, born and bred in the county, discussed the fortunes of his fellows in a guileless anticipation of the conclusions of the twentieth-century 'storm over the gentry', and like his twentieth-century successors, concluded that there was not much useful that one could say.[15] Yet it is the very blandness of his prose which gives the clue to the mood of the Suffolk county community by 1600. It was self-confident, it had an identity, and it had no immediate superiors to challenge that identity. For all the stresses of the 1590s, the future of the Suffolk gentry was assured.

. . . for all expences if they can make even att the yeares end with their receipts, they think they have sufficiently thryved, howbeit all are nott of this mind, because there bee many which with a very wise and wary foresight do much yearly improve and increase their estate, whilest others nott so provident, butt overtaken with too well meaning and good nature, doe become depressed with the alternate vicissitude of this world, and so are inforced sometimes to suffer a revolution.

As we have seen already (Ch. 3), Queen Elizabeth in folk memory at least had set her seal of approval on the county gentry who caused her ministers so many headaches. Their descendants and their Puritan ministers looked back with nostalgia in the Interregnum to her pronouncement on Sir Robert Jermyn and his like: 'Now I have learned why my country of Suffolk is so well governed, it is, because the magistrates and ministers go together.'

---

[14] The ringing scheme is on a loose sheet in Aylsham 175; I am indebted to Professor Frank King of Churchill College, Cambridge for pointing out the significance of the single bell's course. On Sir Arthur and Ketteringham, cf. Smith, p. 159, although the restoration was not to repair storm damage as Smith states: see *NA* III (1852), p. 307. On bell-ringing in the region, see E. Morris, *The History and Art of Change Ringing* (1974), pp. 182–215, and R. W. M. Clouston and G. J. W. Pipe, *Bells and Bellringing in Suffolk* (Suffolk Historic Churches Trust, 1980).
[15] Ryece, p. 60.

APPENDIX I

The Careers of Suffolk JPs and their attendance at quarter sessions 1485–1603

The system of charting devised by Dr Hassell Smith to record the careers of
JPs has not been bettered, and for this reason as well as for the sake of
uniformity his method is reproduced here without modification (see his
explanatory notes, Smith, p. 344).

Key to symbols used in the chart

√ indicates positive evidence that a justice was in commission, but the source
gives no information about the order of precedence. Otherwise the career
of each justice is indicated by two annual numbers. The upper number
indicates his placing in the commission; the smaller and lower number
indicates the number of days that he attended quarter sessions during each
year as given on the Pipe Rolls.

II indicates year of death. Where the date of death falls outside the scope of
this chart it has been indicated in the final column.

C indicates the *custos rotulorum*.

S indicates the year in which the justice was sheriff.

→ indicates continuation to a further chart.

List of JPs: sources

This list of sources follows that in Smith, p. 344–50; the numbering is of the
list column in the charts, which includes 'dummy' numbers for regnal years in
which there are no lists extant. Where a Suffolk list suggests a variant date
from that given by Dr Smith I have indicated my own opinion; otherwise I have
followed his suggestions, which are the dates italicized. I am also most
grateful to Dr R. L. Woods for giving me a computer print-out of his
compilation of quarter sessions attendances from the Pipe Rolls up to 27
Henry VIII.

1	(20 Sept. 1485) PRO, C66/561, m. 4d. An enrolled commission, as are all the following lists down to no. 32.	3	(8 July 1486) C66/561, m. 6d.
		4	(2 Henry VII) None extant.
		5	(28 Mar. 1488) C66/567, m. 2d.
		6	(9 Mar. 1489) C66/569, m. 2d.
2	(29 Nov. 1485) C66/561, m. 2d.	7	(19 Sept. 1489) C66/570, m. 2d.

8	(30 Nov. 1489) C66/570, m. 1d.	21	(9 July 1500) C66/585, m. 2d.
9	(5 May 1490) C66/570, m. 2d.	22	(20 Nov. 1500) C66/587, m. 3d.
10	(4 Dec. 1490) C66/571, m. 2d.	23	(12 Feb. 1501) C66/587, m. 4d.
11	(14 May 1492) C66/572, m..1d.	24	(17 Henry VII) None extant.
12	(8 Henry VII) None extant.	25	(23 July 1503) C66/591, m. 3d.
13	(20 Feb. 1494) C66/575, m. 3d.	26	(19 Henry VII) None extant.
14–15	(10–11 Henry VII) None extant.	27	(27 Nov. 1504) C66/595, m. 2d.
16	(20 Nov. 1496) C66/579, m. 3d.	28	(30 Nov. 1504) C66/595, m. 2d.
17	(16 Feb. 1497) C66/579, m. 6d.	29	(12 Mar. 1506) C66/598, m. 2d.
18	(14 Dec. 1497) C66/581, m. 2d.	30	(28 June 1507) C66/601, m. 2d.
19	(14 Henry VII) None extant.	31–2	(23–4 Henry VII) None extant.
20	(11 Sept. 1499) C66/582, m. 1d.		

1 (8 July 1509) C66/610, m. 4d. An enrolled commission, as are all the following lists down to no. 30.

2 (18 Nov. 1509) C66/610, m. 8d.

3 (28 June 1510) C66/612, m. 2d.

4 (8 July 1510) C66/612, m. 6d.

5 (20 Nov. 1510) C66/612, m. 6d.

6 (6 June 1511) C66/615, m. 4d.

7 (24 Feb. 1512) C66/617, m. 7d.

8 (24 May 1512) C66/618, m. 2d.

9 (29 Apr. 1513) C66/620, m. 1d.

10 (4 Feb. 1514) C66/620, m. 5d.

11 (28 May 1514) C66/622, m. 2d.

12 (18 Oct. 1514) C66/622, m. 6d.

13 (1 Mar. 1515) *LP* II pt. i, no. 207.

14–18 (7–11 Henry VIII) None extant.

19 (12 Nov. 1520) *LP* III pt. i, no. 1081.

20–2 (13–15 Henry VIII) None extant.

23 (6 May 1524) *LP* IV pt. i, no. 390.

24 (20 Dec. 1524) Ibid., no. 961.

25 (11 Feb. 1526). Ibid., no. 2002.

26–7 (18–19 Henry VIII) None extant.

28 (26 Jan. 1529) *LP* IV pt. iii, no. 5243.

29 (21 Henry VIII) None extant.

30 (2 Feb. 1531) *LP* V, no. 119/2.

31 (23 Henry VIII) None extant.

32 (1532) *LP* V, no. 1694. A *liber pacis*.

33 (20 Apr. 1534) *Butley Chronicle*, p. 62: a list of commissioners to take the oaths to uphold the Act of Succession, from which the

commission of the peace can be extrapolated.

34 (20 Feb. 1535) PRO, E371/300, m. 48; an enrolled commission. I am grateful to Dr Amanda Bevan for letting me know of this.

35–6 (27–8 Henry VIII) None extant.

37 (28 Nov. 1537) *LP* XII pt. ii, no. 1150/42.

38 (12 Feb. 1538) *LP* XIII pt. i, no. 384/64. An enrolled commission as are all the following lists down to no. 55.

39 (29 May 1538) *LP* XIII pt. i, no. 1115/67.

40 (24 May 1539) *LP* XIV pt. i, no. 1056/51.

41–2 (32–3 Henry VIII) None extant.

43 (24 Feb. 1543) *LP* XVIII pt. i, no. 226/85.

44 (27 Feb. 1544) *LP* XX pt. i, no. 622 VII.

45 (29 Oct. 1545) *LP* XX pt. i, no. 623 VI.

46–7 (37–8 Henry VIII) None extant.

48 (26 May 1547) *CPR Edward VI* I, p. 89.

49–54 (2–7 Edward VI) None extant.

55 (18 Feb. 1554) *CPR Philip and Mary* I, p. 24.

56 (1555) PRO, SP 11/5, fos. 48ᵛ–49ᵛ. A *liber pacis*.

57–60 (2 & 3 to 5 & 6 Philip and Mary) None extant.

1 (*Dec. 1558 or Jan. 1559*) BL Lansd. 1218, fols. 27–28. An undated *liber pacis*.

2 (2 Eliz.) None extant.

3 (*Nov/Dec. 1561*) BL Lansd. 1218, fols. 78–9. *A liber pacis*, dated 1562.

4 (11 February 1562) *CPR Eliz.* II,

p. 442. An enrolled commission.

5   (5 Eliz.) None extant.

6   (1 June 1564) *CPR Eliz.* III, p. 141. An enrolled commission.

7–11   (7–11 Eliz.) None extant.

12   (30 December 1569) PRO, SP 12/60/62. Not a *liber pacis*, but a signed undertaking of JPs and former JPs of the county to observe the contents of the Act of Uniformity. Residents only.

13–15   (13–15 Eliz.) None extant.

16   (November 1573) PRO, SP 12/93 pt. ii, fols 25–6. A dated *liber pacis*.

17   (Dec. 1573/January 1574) BL Eger. 2345, fols. 31–32. A *liber pacis* dated 16 Eliz. Omits Sir William Cordell unlike previous lists, but includes Robert Gosnold, whose will was proved 4 February 1574.

18   (2 June 1574) BL Harl. 309, fols. 79–80. A copy of the letters patent for a muster commission. Omits non-resident state officers and the Bishop.

19   (Mid-autumn 1574) BL Add. 19172, fo. 95^v. A copy by D. E. Davy of a 'MS pen. R. Sparrow Arm. 1814', probably an original commission. Later than the three last, for it includes not only Sir William Cordell but Edward, Earl of Oxford.

20   (24 June 1575) PRO, SP 12/96, fo. 58; SP 12/104, fo. 117; BL Stowe 570 (identical copies). Not a *liber pacis*; arranged by Hundreds and 'divisions', residents only. Compiled in response to a Council order, *APC* VIII, p. 398.

21   (18 Eliz.) None extant.

22   (*Late 1577*) PRO, SP 12/121, fols. 28 ff. A *liber pacis* dated 19 Eliz. With annotations of autumn 1578, which are not tabulated.

23   (*Late 1577–early 1578*) Hatfield 223/7. A *liber pacis* dated 20 Eliz. With emendations to the end of the decade, not tabulated.

24   (21 Eliz.) None extant.

25   (End of 1579) PRO, SP 12/145,

fo. 37. A *liber pacis*. Cf. SP 12/133/13, fo. 29 ff, of December 1579, which lists those JPs present at or absent from the last summer assizes; the names are identical.

26   (23 Eliz.) None extant.

27   (Mid 1582) BL Lansd. 35, fols. 135–6. Not a *liber;* non-residents and state officers missing. Some emendations, not tabulated.

28   (Early 1583) BL Royal 18 DIII, fo. 37^r. List in Lord Burghley's atlas; not a *liber pacis;* state officers are omitted.

29   (?July 1583) BL Harl. 474, fols. 34–5. A miniature *liber pacis*.

30   (Early 1584) PRO, E163/14/8. A *liber pacis*. Annotations into 1587 are not tabulated.

31   (Mid-late 1584) BL Lansd. 737, fols. 155–6. An undated *liber pacis*. Emendations into 1585 are not tabulated.

32–36   (27–31 Eliz.) None extant.

37   (7 April 1590) BL Eger. 3788, fols. 32–3. A *liber pacis*.

38   (Mid 1591) Hatfield 278. Not a *liber pacis*.

39   (34 Eliz.) None extant.

40   (Mid 1593) Kent Record Office U. 350. 03, unpag. A miniature *liber pacis*.

41   (Late 1593 or early 1594) Hatfield 278. Not a *liber pasis*. Probably the list used by Lord Burghley to work out the dismissals of 1595.

42   (5 July 1594) PRO, C66/1421 m. 13d. An enrolled commission.

43   (February 1595) Northants Record Office, Wingfield (Tickencote) Collection, Box X, 511. Not a *liber pacis*.

44   (10 July 1595) PRO, C66/1435 m. 7d. An enrolled commission.

45   (Early 1596) PRO, SP 13 F11. An undated *liber pacis*.

46   (10 July 1596) PRO, C66/1468 m. 14d. An enrolled commission.

47   (10 July 1597) C66/1469 mm. 28d–29d. An enrolled commission.

48   (10 July 1598) C66/1482 m. 16d. An enrolled commission.

49 (10 July 1599) C66/1493 m. 24d. An enrolled commission.

50 (23 May 1600) C66/1523 m. 26d. An enrolled commission.

51 (12 June 1601) C66/1549 m. 25d. An enrolled commission.

52 (4 June 1602) C66/1594 m. 31d. An enrolled commission.

53 (15 February 1603) Ryece p. 89; a list of the resident justices at the assizes of 21 February 1603, in order of precedence. This must be the commission issued on 15 February, PRO, C231/1, fo. 150^r.

1	2	3	4	5	6	7	8	9	10	11	12	13	14	15	16	17	18	19	20
1	1	1	2	3	4	5	5	5	6	7	8	9	10	11	12	12	13	14	15
20 Sept. 1485	29 Nov. 1485	8 July 1486		28 Mar. 1488	9 Mar. 1489	19 Sept. 1489	30 Nov. 1489	5 May 1490	4 Dec. 1490	14 May 1492		20 Feb. 1494			20 Nov. 1496	16 Feb. 1497	14 Dec. 1497		11 Sept. 1499
							·24_2	·26_2	·28_2	·26_4		·26_5			·28	·30_1	·28_1	1	·27
		22_2	1	·21_1	·22_1	·23_1	·21_1	·23_2	·26_2	·23		·23			·25_1	·27_1	·23_1	1	·22_1
														1	20_1	21_1	S_1		
																		3	15_2
				·24	·26_1	·23_1	·25^2_6	·27^2_6	·24_3		3	·24_1			·26_1	·28^1_1	·26^1_1	$\tfrac{1}{2}$	·25_2
									5	5			||				–		
			S								3	15			||				
							1	10_1	11_1	||									
										S								2	16_1
9	11	13	2	12_2	13^1_3	13^1_2	13^2_2	15^2_2	16	||									
															11	12	12		10
	2	2		1	1	1	1	2	2	2		2			2	2	2		2
							1	17_1	15			S			15	16	17		14
		·7	||																
		23_2	3	·22	·23_3	·24_3	·22_3	·24	||										
										·25		·25			·27	·29	27		·26
·12_1	12_1	14_1	1	13	14	14	14_1	16_1	18	16		16			18	19	||		·26
																	21		·20
						22	20_1	·22_1	·25	·22		·22	||						
11																					
						·17_2	·17_2	·19_1	·21_1	·18_2	$^4_4$	·18^4_4			·21_1	·22_1	·16	/	·13
14_1	14_1	·17_1		·16	·17										||				
																			·28_1
				3	3	3	3	4	4	4		4			4	4	4		3
															14	15	15_1	1	12
						·8	8	·9	10	·10		·10			·5	·7	·7		·6
4	5	5		6	6	6	6	7	8	8		8									
		·18		·17	·18	·18											||		
					8														
10	10	11		10	11	11	11_1	13_1	14_1	13_2	1	14_1	1		12	13	13		

21	22	23	24	25	26	27	28	29	30	31	32	
15	16	16	17	18	19	20	20	21	22	23	24	
9 July 1500	20 Nov. 1500	12 Feb. 1501		23 July 1503		27 Nov. 1504	30 Nov. 1504	12 Mar. 1506	28 June 1507			
·29	·29	·29	1	·29$_1$	3	·22	·23	·20	·18			ALEYN, JOHN →
·23	·23	·23		·26		·27	·29	·30	·28‖			APPLETON, THOMAS
												ARUNDEL, EDMUND →
16$_3$	14$_3$	14$_2$	1	12$_4$	2	2						AUDLEY, JOHN →
				·31	1	·29$_1$	·31$_1$	·32	·29			AYLOFFE, WILLIAM →
·27‖												BACHELER, GILBERT
												BEDFORD, JASPER, D. OF
												BEDINGFIELD, EDMUND I
26$_3$	27$_3$		2 3	18		17	18$_5$	17	S			BOOTH, PHILIP →
												BOURCHIER, THOMAS
17	15$_1$	15$_1$	2	11$_2$	2					S	S	BRANDON, ROBERT →
												BRANDON, WILLIAM
11	9	9		9		10	11	10	‖			BROUGHTON, ROBERT
				1	‖							CANTERBURY, HENRY DEANE, ABP. OF
·2	‖											CANTERBURY, JOHN MORTON ABP. OF
						2	2					CANTERBURY, WILLIAM WARHAM ABP. OF
15$_1$	12$_1$	13	‖									CAREW, WILLIAM d. 1532
												CATESBY, JOHN
												CHEKE, JOHN
	20	20		21								CHITWOOD, ADAM
·28	·28	·28		·28	‖							CLERK, CLEMENT
												CLOPTON, JOHN I
·21	·21	·21		·15$_1$	1	15$_2$	16	15	14			CLOPTON, WILLIAM I →
												COKET, JOHN
												DARCY, THOMAS
·14	·13	·12	1	13$_1$	4	·13$_4$	·14	·13	·9			DRURY, ROBERT I →
												DRURY, ROGER
30$_4$	·30$_1$	·30$_5$	3	·30$_5$	5	5	‖					EDGAR, GREGORY
4	‖											ELY, JOHN ALCOCK, BP OF
					4	·24$_4$	·23	‖				EYRE, WILLIAM
13	11	11		10		11	12	11	11	‖		FIENNES, ROBERT d. 1509
·7	·5	·5		·5		·7	·8	·7	·7	‖		FINEUX, JOHN
												FITZWALTER, JOHN RADCLIFFE, LD
												GEDDING, WILLIAM
												HAUGH, JOHN
‖												HEVENINGHAM, JOHN I
							26	24				HEVENINGHAM, JOHN II →

1	2	3	4	5	6	7	8	9	10	11	12	13	14	15	16	17	18	19	20
1	1	1	2	3	4	5	5	5	6	7	8	9	10	11	12	12	13	14	15
20 Sept. 1485	29 Nov. 1485	8 July 1486		28 Mar. 1488	9 Mar. 1489	19 Sept. 1489	30 Nov. 1489	5 May 1490	4 Dec. 1490	14 May 1492		20 Feb. 1494			20 Nov. 1496	16 Feb. 1497	14 Dec. 1497		11 Sept. 1499
$.13_5$	$.13_5$	$.15_5$		$.14$	$.15_2^1$	$.15_2^2$	$.15_2^2$	$.17_2$	$.19_2$	$\|\|$									
	6	$.16_6$	3	$.15_3^3$	$.16_2^3$	$.16_2^3$	$.16_2^3$	$.18_7^{10}$	20_7^{10}	17_{10}^{13}	8	$.17_8$			$.17$	$.18_9$	$.19_9$	I_6	$.18_6^7$
$.5$	$.6$	$.6$		$.7$	$.7$	$.7_1$	$.7_1$	$.8$	$.9$	$.9$		$.9$	$\|\|$						
16_3	$.17_3$	21_3	2	$.20$	$.21$	$.21_6$	$.19_6$	$.21_4$	$.24_4$	$.21_5$	3	$.21_1$			$.23_6$	$.24_6$	$.22_5$	4	$.21_6$
															$.24$	26_1	$.25_1$	$\tfrac{1}{1}$	$.24$
$.6$	$.7$																		
1	1	1		2	2	2	2	3	3	3		3			3	3	3		$\|\|$
													$?$						
3	4	4		5	5	5	5	6	7	7		6			5	5	5		4
																$.8$	$.8$	$/$	$.7$
													S						
												7			6	6	6		
2	3	3		4	4	4	4	5	6	6	$\|\|$								
$.7_4$	$.8_4$	$.8_4$	5	$\|\|$															
															25	24_3		4	23_3
															13	14	14		11
																			8
															19	20	20		19
								1	1	1		1			1	1	1		1
		12		11	12	12_1	12_1	14_1	15	14		13			10	11	11		$\|\|$

21	22	23	24	25	26	27	28	29	30	31	32		
15	16	16	17	18	19	20	20	21	22	23	24		
9 July 1500	20 Nov 1500	12 Feb 1501		23 July 1503		27 Nov 1504	30 Nov 1504	12 Mar 1506	28 June 1507				
												HIGHAM, THOMAS	
.19$_7$	.17$_7$	.17$_8$	9	.23$_6$	/$_{12}$	.12$_{12}$	13$_{10}$	.12	.12			HOBART, JAMES	→
							6	6	6			HOWARD, THOMAS LD.	→
												HUSSY, WILLIAM	
.22$_7$	.22$_8$	.22$_8$	/$_7$	S^{16}	S	.21	.22	.21$_5$	.19			JENNY, EDMUND	→
						.25	.27	.28	.26	‖		JERMYN, THOMAS I	
.25$_1$	.25$_1$	.25		.24	1	.26	.25	.24	.22			LUCAS, THOMAS	→
												NEEL, RICHARD	
												NORWICH, JAS GOLDWELL, BP. OF	
3	‖											NORWICH, THOS. JANE, BP OF	
				2		3	3	2	2			NORWICH, RICHD. NIX, BP. OF	
												OXENBRIDGE, THOMAS	
2	2	2		3		4	4	3	3			OXFORD, JOHN VERE EARL OF	
				32$_3$	/	30$_4$	.32$_4$	33$_3$	30			PLAYTER, WILLIAM	→
.8	.6	.6		.6	2	.8$_2$	.9	.8	.8			REDE, ROBERT	
26$_2$	26$_2$	1		20$_2$	2	19$_2$	20$_3$	19	17			SAMPSON, THOMAS	d. 1512
						.20	.21	.22$_2$	.20			SOUTHWELL, ROBERT I	→
								.27	.25			SOUTHWELL, ROBERT II	→
3	3											SUFFOLK, EDM. DE LA POLE E. OF	d. 1513
												SUFFOLK, JOHN DE LA POLE D. OF	
												SULYARD, JOHN I	
								34	.31			SULYARD, JOHN II	→
						5	5	4	4			SURREY, THOMAS HOWARD, E. OF	→
24$_5$	24$_5$	24$_2$		17$_1$		16	17$_2$	16	15			TILNEY, PHILIP I	→
				19$_1$		18	19	18	16			TIMPERLEY, JOHN	d. 1522
12	10	10	‖									TYRRELL, JAMES	
9	7	7		7	‖							VERE, GEORGE	
20	18	18		14		14	15	14	13			WALDEGRAVE, WILLIAM I	→
1	1	1	‖									WALES, ARTHUR PRINCE OF	
						1	1	1	1			WALES, HENRY, PRINCE OF	d. 1547 →
												WENTWORTH, HENRY I	

No.	No.	Date	WENTWORTH, RICHARD ↑	WILLOUGHBY, CHRISTOPHER I	WILLOUGHBY, WILLIAM LD. I ↑	WINGFIELD, HUMPHREY ↑	WINGFIELD, JOHN	WISEMAN, JOHN ↑	WISEMAN, SIMON	YAXLEY, JOHN	TOTAL IN COMMISSION
32	24										
31	23						=				
30	22	28 June 1507	21		5	27	10	28			31
29	21	12 Mar. 1506	23_4		5	29_6	9	31_5		=	34
28	20	30 Nov. 1504	26_4		7	28_6	10	30_5		24_3	32
27	20	27 Nov. 1504			6	26	9	28_1		23	30
26	19			2			1	1		2 / 9	
25	18	23 July 1503	24_1		4		8_1	27_4		22_4	31
24	17		1		⁄			1			
23	16	12 Feb. 1501	19_2		4		8_2	27		16_5	30
22	16	20 Nov. 1500	19_2		4		8_1			16_6	30
21	15	9 July 1500			6		10_1			18_6	30
20	15	11 Sept. 1499	=		5		9			17_4	28
19	14						1			1_4	
18	13	14 Dec. 1497		9_1			10_1		2	18_5	28
17	12	16 Feb. 1497		9_1			10_1		23_1	17_5	30
16	12	20 Nov. 1496		8			9		22‖	16_6	28
15	11										
14	10									8	
13	9	20 Feb. 1494		11			12		19_3	20_{10}	26
12	8						5		5	9	
11	7	14 May 1492		11			12		19	20_9	26
10	6	4 Dec. 1490		12_1			13_1		22_2	23_8	28
9	5	5 May 1490		11_1			12_1		S_2	20_8	26
8	5	30 Nov. 1489		9_1			10_1		S	18_4	24
7	5	19 Sept. 1489		9			10_1		18	20_4	25
6	4	9 Mar. 1489		9			10_1		19	20_4	24
5	3	28 Mar. 1488		8			9		18_1	19	22
4	2						1		1	4	
3	1	8 July 1486		9_3			10		19	20	23
2	1	29 Nov. 1485		3			9		15	16	17
1	1	20 Sept. 1485					8		15		16

	1	2	3	4	5	6	7	8	9	10	11	12	13	14	15
	1	1	2	2	2	3	3	4	5	5	6	6	6	7	8
	8 July 1509	18 Nov. 1509	28 June 1510	8 July 1510	20 Nov. 1510	6 June 1511	24 Feb. 1512	24 May 1512	29 Apr. 1513	4 Feb. 1514	28 May 1514	18 Oct. 1514	1 March 1515		
ALEYN, JOHN ←	.8	.8	.8	.8	.8	9_3	9_3	10_3	.10 ‖						
ASHFIELD, ROBERT I															
AUDLEY, JOHN ←												21	21		
AUDLEY, THOMAS, LORD															
AYLOFFE, WILLIAM ←	.18	.19	.19	.20	.21	.22	.23	.24	.24	.22	.24	.28	28		
BACON, NICHOLAS I															
BALDWIN, JOHN															
BARNADISTON, THOMAS I															
BARNADISTON, THOMAS II															
BARNARD, PHILIP															
BATH, JOHN BOURCHIER, E OF															
BEDINGFIELD, EDMUND II															
BEDINGFIELD, HENRY															
BLENNERHASSET, JOHN															
BOHUN, NICHOLAS															
BOOTH, PHILIP ←				.15	.17	$.18_1$	$.18_1$	$.20_1$	.19	.19	20_1	23_1	23		
BRANDON, ROBERT ←	S									10	9_1	11_1	12_1	1	2
BREND, JOHN															
BREWSE, JOHN															
BREWSE, ROBERT ←		.17	.17	.18	.19	$.21_4$	$.22_1$	$.22_1$	.23‖						
BROMLEY, THOMAS															
BROOKE, RICHARD															
BROOKE, ROBERT															
BROWN, ROBERT															
BRUDENELL, ROBERT															
BURGH, THOMAS, LORD															
BURY, JOHN REVE. ABBOT OF															
CANTERBURY, THOMAS CRANMER ABP. OF															
CARYLL, JOHN															
CAVENDISH, RICHARD I							29	35	33	32	34	26	26		
CAVENDISH, RICHARD II															
CHAMBERLAIN, RALPH															
CLERK, EDWARD															
CLERK, WALTER															

	16	17	18	19	20	21	22	23	24	25	26	27	28	29	30	31	32	33	34
	9	10	11	12	13	14	15	16	16	17	18	19	20	21	22	23	24	25	26
				12 Nov. 1520				6 May 1524	20 Dec. 1524	11 Feb. 1526			26 Jan. 1529		2 Feb. 1531		1532	20 Apr. 1534	20 Feb.1535
ALEYN, JOHN																			
ASHFIELD, ROBERT I																			
AUDLEY, JOHN																	||		
AUDLEY, THOMAS , LORD																	1	1	2
AYLOFFE, WILLIAM	||																	
BACON, NICHOLAS I																			
BALDWIN, JOHN																			
BARNADISTON, THOMAS I									25	26	1		21	2	34	1	32_3	28	3
BARNADISTON, THOMAS II																			
BARNARD, PHILIP																			
BATH, JOHN BOURCHIER, E OF																			
BEDINGFIELD, EDMUND II														S					
BEDINGFIELD, HENRY																			
BLENNERHASSET, JOHN																			
BOHUN, NICHOLAS																			
BOOTH, PHILIP																			
BRANDON, ROBERT								||											
BREND, JOHN																			
BREWSE, JOHN																			
BREWSE, ROBERT																			
BROMLEY, THOMAS																			
BROOKE, RICHARD			/	11	/	/	/	13	11	11_1	/	/	10||						
BROOKE, ROBERT																			
BROWN, ROBERT																			.
BRUDENELL, ROBERT				10	1	/	/	12	/	10_1	/	/	9	/||					
BURGH, THOMAS, LORD																			
BURY, JOHN REVE. ABBOT OF				7				7	6	8			8		12			12	13
CANTERBURY, THOMAS CRANMER ABP. OF																			1
CARYLL, JOHN		/																	
CAVENDISH, RICHARD I	||																	
CAVENDISH, RICHARD II																			
CHAMBERLAIN, RALPH																			
CLERK , EDWARD																			
CLERK, WALTER																			

36	37	38	39	40	41	42	43	44	45	46	47	48	49	50	51	52	53	54	55	56	57	58	59	60	
28	29	29	30	31	32	33	34	35	36	37	38	1	2	3	4	5	6	7	1	2	3	4	5	6	
28 Nov. 1537	12 Feb. 1538	29 May 1538	24 May 1539				24 Feb. 1543	27 Feb. 1544	29 Oct. 1544			26 May 1547							18 Feb. 1554	1555					
												54	✓$_1$		‖										
	2	2	2	2			1	1	‖																
												24	✓						·33	30					→
✓	12	12	12	13	✓				‖																
	27	27	27	24	‖																				
								25	26						✓	‖									
38_2	38	38_3	‖																						
																			·3	2	✓				→
												16					‖								
																			·12						d. 1583
															✓	✓	✓		$.48_3$	44_2	✓$_3$	4	6		→
			49_3			2	47	49_1	48		1														d. 1561+
			‖																						
																			$.45_3$	40_2	✓$_3$	2	5	1	→
							21	22	22	$\frac{2}{1}$	1	23					✓		25	23_4	✓$_4$	✓$_3$	1		→
							8	8	9	✓		9					‖								
																				13				‖	
2	43_3	43_3	43_3	39	1	3	35_3	37_1	36	$\frac{1}{1}$	$\frac{1}{4}$	36	✓$_3$	✓	✓	✓			$.28_1$	24_8	✓$_6$	✓$_7$	5		d. 1559
												6				‖									
	11	11	11	11	‖																				
	1	1	1	1																		‖			
															✓	✓			21	‖					
																✓			24	22_2					
																			48			3	✓$_2$		d. 1575
																			51	‖					d. 1578+

	1	2	3	4	5	6	7	8	9	10	11	12	13	14	15
	1	1	2	2	2	3	3	4	5	5	6	6	6	7	8
	8 July 1509	18 Nov. 1509	28 June 1510	8 July 1510	20 Nov. 1510	6 June 1511	24 Feb. 1512	24 May 1512	29 Apr. 1513	4 Feb. 1514	28 May 1514	18 Oct. 1514	1 March 1515		
CLOPTON, FRANCIS I															
CLOPTON, WILLIAM I ←	.13	.13	.13	.13	.14	.15_1	.15_1	.17_1	.16	.16_1	.15_1	.17_1	17		
COCKET, EDWARD															
COLT, GEORGE I															
CONINGSBY, WILLIAM															
CORDELL, WILLIAM															
CORNWALLIS, JOHN															
CORNWALLIS, THOMAS															
CRANE, ROBERT I															
CURZON, ROBERT LD.													7		2
CUTLER, NICHOLAS															
DANIEL, THOMAS															
DOWNES, JAMES															
DOWNES, ROBERT															
DOYLE, HENRY															
DRURY, ROBERT I ←	.10	.10	.10	.10	.10_2	.11_2	.11_4	.11_4	.12	.12_3	.11_3	.13_3	14		1
DRURY, ROBERT II															
DRURY, WILLIAM I															
ECHINGHAM, EDWARD															
EDEN, GEORGE															
EDEN, THOMAS I															
ELY, THOMAS GOODRICH BP OF															
ELY, NICHOLAS WEST BP OF															
ESSEX, THOMAS CROMWELL E. OF															
EYER, JOHN															
FELTON, THOMAS															
FINEUX, JOHN ←	.6	.6	.6	.6	.6	.7	.7	.7	.6	.7	.7	.7	.8		
FITZHUGH, THOMAS															
FORTH, WILLIAM I															
FOSTER, WILLIAM															
FRAMLINGHAM, JAMES										1	19_1	22_1	22		
FRESTON, RICHARD															
FULMERSTON, RICHARD															

16	17	18	19	20	21	22	23	24	25	26	27	28	29	30	31	32	33	34	35	36	37	38	39	40	41	42	43
9	10	11	12	13	14	15	16	16	17	18	19	20	21	22	23	24	25	26	27	28	29	29	30	31	32	33	34
			12 Nov. 1520				6 May 1524	20 Dec. 1524	11 Feb 1526			26 Jan. 1529		2 Feb. 1531		1532	20 Apr. 1534	20 Feb 1535			28 Nov. 1537	12 Feb. 1538	29 May 1538	24 May 1539			24 Feb 1543
			17				18	16	16			14		21	||												
																	27										
																	33	33	29	$/_1$	37	37	37	33		2	27
																				/					||		
																25		24	25	28	24	24	24_1	20			17
																35		34	35	32	40	40	40	35			29
1			9_7	2			11	10	9			7		10		10	10	11||									
																					47	47	47	43			40
																		.31	$/_2$	2	39_3	39	39_3	34		3	28_3
																				4	49_6	49	49_3	45	1	7	42_6
1	1		14_1	1	1		14	12	12_1	1	4	11_2	3	15_3	3	15_{10}	15_3	16_2	||								
								33_1	1	1	2	30_2	5	42	2	41_4	29_4	32_2	$/_2$	S_3							
								19	20_3	4	2	||															
																				9	9	9	9	9			5
			3				3	3	3			3				8	8	8||									
																					5	5	5	5	||		
									||																		
	||																										
																				/	56	56_4	53_8		1	7	52_6
																											30

	44	45	46	47	48	49	50	51	52	53	54	55	56	57	58	59	60	
	35	36	37	38	1	2	3	4	5	6	7	1	2	3	4	5	6	
	27 Feb. 1544	29 Oct. 1544			26 May 1547							18 Feb. 1554	1555					
CLOPTON, FRANCIS I	50	49	1_1		48	√		√	√									d. 155
CLOPTON, WILLIAM I																		
COCKET, EDWARD																		
COLT, GEORGE I	29	30_1				√		√	√			30_2	27	$√_3$				→
CONINGSBY, WILLIAM																		
CORDELL, WILLIAM												.27	25					→
CORNWALLIS, JOHN	17	‖																
CORNWALLIS, THOMAS					31				√		S	.13	10					→
CRANE, ROBERT I	31							‖										
CURZON, ROBERT LD.																		
CUTLER, NICHOLAS																$√_1$		→
DANIEL, THOMAS	42	41			38							42	36_2	$√_2$	√	2		→
DOWNES, JAMES					32											‖		
DOWNES, ROBERT	30_1	31_1	2_1			‖												
DOYLE, HENRY	44_5	43	$√_5$	4	42		1	√	√			23_8	20_8	$√_7$	$√_6$	S	S	→
DRURY, ROBERT I																		
DRURY, ROBERT II									√			38_2	3	1	‖			
DRURY, WILLIAM I		S			12	√		√	√			$.10_4$	8_3	$√_7$	$√_4$	‖		
ECHINGHAM, EDWARD																		
EDEN, GEORGE													42			‖		
EDEN, THOMAS I												.43	37			1		→
ELY, THOMAS GOODRICH BP OF	5	5			4							‖						
ELY, NICHOLAS, WEST BP OF																		
ESSEX, THOMAS CROMWELL E. OF																		
EYER, JOHN					51			√	√									→
FELTON, THOMAS								√	√			39_1	33_2	$√_2$	$√_3$	2		→
FINEUX, JOHN																		
FITZHUGH, THOMAS			√			√		√	√									
FORTH, WILLIAM I								√	√									d. 15
FOSTER, WILLIAM	55_5	54_1	$√_1^4$	$√_3$	52	1	$√_1$	√	√			$.46_1$	41_2	√	$√_3$	$√_4$		→
FRAMLINGHAM, JAMES																		
FRESTON, RICHARD	32	32										.14	11		2		‖	
FULMERSTON, RICHARD			√	1	46													d. 15

	1	2	3	4	5	6	7	8	9	10	11	12	13	14	15	16	17	18	19
	1	1	2	2	2	3	3	4	5	5	6	6	6	7	8	9	10	11	12
	8 July 1509	18 Nov. 1509	28 June 1510	8 July 1510	20 Nov. 1510	6 June 1511	24 Feb. 1512	24 May 1512	29 Apr. 1513	4 Feb. 1514	28 May 1514	18 Oct. 1514	1 March 1515						12 Nov. 1520
GATES, HENRY																			
GLEMHAM, CHRISTOPHER																			
GLEMHAM, EDWARD																			
GLEMHAM. JOHN							30	36₁	34	33	21	24	25						
GOLDINGHAM, CHRISTOPHER																			
GOLDINGHAM, JOHN, JN.								.34	.32	.31₁	.33₁	.36₁	36		‖				
GONVILLE, RICHARD																			
GOODRICH, HENRY																			
GOODRICH, JOHN																			
GOSNOLD, JOHN																			
GOSNOLD, ROBERT I																			
GRESHAM, RICHARD																			
GRIFFIN, EDWARD																			
GRIMSTON, EDWARD																			
GURDON, ROBERT																			
HARE, NICHOLAS																			
HARMAN, JOHN, JN.																			
HATFIELD, HENRY																			
HERVEY, JOHN																			24₈
HEVENINGHAM, ANTHONY																			
HEVENINGHAM, JOHN II ←	19	20	20	21	S	S	S	25			1	1	1						23₃
HIGHAM, CLEMENT																			
HOBART, HENRY																			
HOBART, JAMES ←	.9	.9	.9	.9	.9	.10₃	.10₃	.9₂	.11	.11	.10	.12	13			‖			
HONNINGS, WILLIAM																			
HOPTON, ARTHUR											1	10₁	11₁·	1			3	2	13₂
HOPTON, OWEN																			
JENNY, CHRISTOPHER																			
JENNY, EDMUND ←	14	14	14	14	15	16	16	18	17	17	.16	.18	18				1		18
JENNY, FRANCIS I																			
JENNY, JOHN																			
JERMYN, AMBROSE																			
JERMYN, THOMAS																			
JERNINGHAM, GEORGE																			
JERNINGHAM, HENRY																			

	20	21	22	23	24	25	26	27	28	29	30	31	32	33	34	35	36	37	38
	13	14	15	16	16	17	18	19	20	21	22	23	24	25	26	27	28	29	29
				6 May 1524	20 Dec. 1524	11 Feb. 1526			26 Jan. 1529		2 Feb. 1531		1532	20 Apr. 1534	20 Feb. 1535			28 Nov. 1537	12 Feb. 1538
GATES, HENRY																			
GLEMHAM, CHRISTOPHER																			
GLEMHAM, EDWARD																			
GLEMHAM. JOHN														$\|\|$					
GOLDINGHAM, CHRISTOPHER																			
GOLDINGHAM, JOHN, JN.																			
GONVILLE, RICHARD																			
GOODRICH, HENRY															26			36	36
GOODRICH, JOHN															25			35	35
GOSNOLD, JOHN																			
GOSNOLD, ROBERT I																			
GRESHAM, RICHARD																			
GRIFFIN, EDWARD																			
GRIMSTON, EDWARD																			
GURDON, ROBERT																			
HARE, NICHOLAS																			
HARMAN, JOHN, JN.																	/	44_1	44
HATFIELD, HENRY															27				
HERVEY, JOHN	6		1	27	30	31_1	5	2	26_3	3	37_2	4	36_3	36_4	33_2	1	$/_2$	41_3	41
HEVENINGHAM, ANTHONY																			
HEVENINGHAM, JOHN II	2	1	S	26_5	29	30	3	1	25		20_1	3	20_4	20_2	22_1	1	$\|\|$	18	18
HIGHAM, CLEMENT								1	29_1	3	40	3	39_4	42_5	42	$/_2$	2	54_4	54
HOBART, HENRY											41_1	3	40_4	43	43		2	55	55_1
HOBART, JAMES																			
HONNINGS, WILLIAM																			
HOPTON, ARTHUR		1		15	13	13_1		5	12_5	6	17_2	3	17_4	17	20_3	2	2	16_1	16
HOPTON, OWEN									17										
JENNY, CHRISTOPHER															/				
JENNY, EDMUND		$\|\|$																	
JENNY, FRANCIS I																			
JENNY, JOHN																			
JERMYN, AMBROSE																			
JERMYN, THOMAS					27	28_1	1		23_1	2			S				1	30_4	30
JERNINGHAM, GEORGE																			
JERNINGHAM, HENRY																			

39	40	41	42	43	44	45	46	47	48	49	50	51	52	53	54	55	56	57	58	59	60	
30	31	32	33	34	35	36	37	38	1	2	3	4	5	6	7	1	2	3	4	5	6	
29 May 1538	24 May 1539			24 Feb. 1543	27 Feb. 1544	29 Oct. 1544			26 May 1547							18 Feb. 1554	1555					
									49													
	36	l_1	7	31_6	33_3	33_1		1	35		‖											
													l			53_2	50_4	l_3	l_3	4		→
																						→
				.					55				l_2									
												l		l		‖						
36	32			26	28	29			29											‖		
35	31	l		25	27	28																
		1	. 8	50_4	53_3	52_1	2/2	7	$c25$	l_1	1	l	l			$.34_3$						
												l	l			36_3	32_7	l_1		4		→
				15	15_1	16					‖											
																$.15$	14					d. 1569
												l						l				→
									56													→
									$11.$			l	l			$.8$	7			‖		→
44_5	40_4		1	36	38	37																
																						→
41_5	37_4	1	3	33_3	35_2	‖																
									23		21					20	19_3					
18																						
54_2	51		1	49_3	51_2	51_1	4/2	1	33	l_1		l	l			$.26_3$	12_3	l_7	l_4	3		→
55_1	52			51	54	53			S	S			$?l$									
																56						→
16_1	15_2		1	11	11	12		1	14			l	l			16_1	16	‖				→
					20_1	20	3/2	4	22	l_3		l	l			31_3	28_4	l_5	7	6		→
				‖																		
												l	l			47_3	43_3	l	3	3		→
			S						18			l	l			22_6	1	l_2				→
												l					21_5	l_5	5	3		→
30_1	25	S_2	l											‖								
																38	l_2	1	6			→
																$.7$	6					→

	1	2	3	4	5	6	7	8	9	10	11	12	13	14	15	16	17	18
	1	1	2	2	2	3	3	4	5	5	6	6	6	7	8	9	10	11
	8 July 1509	18 Nov. 1509	28 June 1510	8 July 1510	20 Nov. 1510	6 June 1511	24 Feb. 1512	24 May 1512	29 Apr. 1513	4 Feb. 1514	28 May 1514	18 Oct. 1514	1 March 1515					
JERNINGHAM, JOHN I																		
JERNINGHAM, JOHN II																		
KEMP, ROBERT																		
KENE, ROBERT																		
LEE, EDMUND								33_1	31	30	32_3	35_3	35_3		2	1		
LISTER, RICHARD																		
LUCAS, JOHN																		
LUCAS, THOMAS	17	18	18	19	20	20_2	21_2	23	22	21	23_1	27_1	27_1		1	1		
MONTAGUE, EDWARD																		
MORE, THOMAS																		
MORGAN, RICHARD																		
NEWTON, ALEXANDER																		
NORFOLK, THOS. 2nd D. OF	3	3	3	3	3	3	3	3	2	2	2	2	2					
NORFOLK, THOS. 3rd D. OF	5	5	5	5	5	5	4	4	3	4	4	4	4					
NORWICH, ROBERT																		
NORWICH, JOHN HOPTON, BP. OF																		
NORWICH, RD NIX, BP. OF	1	1	1	1	1	1	1	1	1	1	1	1	1					
NORWICH, THOS. THIRLBY BP. OF																		
NUNN, FRANCIS																		
NUNN, HENRY								30	28	27	29_2	32_2	32_2		1	1		
OXFORD, JOHN VERE 13th E. OF	2	2	2	2	2	2	2	2	‖									
OXFORD, JOHN VERE, 15th E. OF									20	20	22	25	24					
PAYNE, HENRY																		
PEYTON, CHRISTOPHER																		
PLAYTERS, THOMAS I																		
PLAYTERS, WILLIAM	24	25	25	26	26	27_2	28_2	32_1	30	29	31_1	34_1	34_1		2	‖		
POPE, THOMAS																		
REDE, ROBERT	7	7	7	7	7	8_1	8_1	8	7	8	8_1	8_1	9_1				‖	
REDE, WILLIAM																		
REYNOLD, ROBERT, JUN																		
ROCHESTER. ROBERT																		
ROOKWOOD, NICHOLAS																		
ROOKWOOD, ROBERT																		
ROUS, ANTHONY																		

20	21	22	23	24	25	26	27	28	29	30	31	32	33	34	35	36	37	38	39	40	41	42	43	44	45	46
13	14	15	16	16	17	18	19	20	21	22	23	24	25	26	27	28	29	29	30	31	32	33	34	35	36	37
			6 May 1524	20 Dec. 1524	11 Feb. 1526			26 Jan. 1529		2 Feb. 1531		1532	20 Apr. 1534	20 Feb. 1535			28 Nov. 1537	12 Feb. 1538	29 May 1538	24 May 1539			24 Feb. 1543	27 Feb. 1544	29 Oct. 1544	
			23	24		1	2	19_3	3	31_2	5	29_7	27_5	30_3	1	2	26_3	26	26_3	23_4			19_3	19_3	19	$\frac{3}{2}$
1	1	1	28	31	32_1	1	.	27_1	1	38	2	37_5	38	.36	$/_2$		45	45	45	41			37	39	38	
										14		14	14	.15	/		13	13	13							
			22	22	23			18_1	1	29‖	1															
																					12	/	7	7	7	/
										1			‖													
			4	‖																						
			6	4	4			4		2		2	2	.3			3	3	3	3			2	2	2	
										13		13	13	.14	‖											
			2	2	2			2		7		7	7	8	‖											
												5	5	6			6	6	6	6	‖					
																				57	54	1	53_2	56	55	1
													38	37			46_3	46	46_2	42_4		2	39_1	41_3	40	
			29	32	33_1	1		28	1	39		38	41	41			52	52	52	48		1	46	48	47	1
													37	34			42_2	42	42_1	38		1	34_1	36	35	$\frac{1}{2}$
															1											
																	29	29	29	26			20	21	21	

	47	48	49	50	51	52	53	54	55	56	57	58	59	60	
	38	1	2	3	4	5	6	7	1	2	3	4	5	6	
		26 May 1547							18 Feb. 1554	1555					
JERNINGHAM, JOHN I	3	19	$\checkmark_3$		$\checkmark$		$\checkmark$		18_4	17_3	$\checkmark_1$	$\checkmark_2$	4		→
JERNINGHAM, JOHN II											1				→
KEMP, ROBERT													$\checkmark_2$		156-
KENE, ROBERT									55_1	51	$\checkmark$		$\checkmark_4$	||	
LEE, EDMUND															
LISTER, RICHARD								||							
LUCAS, JOHN		39											||		
LUCAS, THOMAS															
MONTAGUE, EDWARD		8			$\checkmark$	$\checkmark$							||		
MORE, THOMAS															
MORGAN, RICHARD									.9		$\checkmark$				
NEWTON, ALEXANDER		30													1569
NORFOLK, THOS. 2nd D. OF															
NORFOLK, THOS. 3rd D. OF									.1	||					
NORWICH, ROBERT															
NORWICH, JOHN HOPTON, BP. OF										3				||	
NORWICH, RD NIX, BP. OF															
NORWICH, THOS. THIRLBY BP. OF									.4						1570
NUNN, FRANCIS		28		1	$\checkmark$	$\checkmark$			$.50_1$	46_4	$\checkmark_3$	$\checkmark_7$	$\checkmark_6$		→
NUNN, HENRY															
OXFORD, JOHN VERE 13th E. OF															
OXFORD, JOHN VERE, 15th E. OF															
PAYNE, HENRY		50	$\checkmark_2$		$\checkmark$	$\checkmark$			$.52_2$	49_3	$\checkmark$	$\checkmark_3$	4		→
PEYTON, CHRISTOPHER									54	3	$\checkmark_2$		1		→
PLAYTERS, THOMAS I						$\checkmark$	$\checkmark$								→
PLAYTERS, WILLIAM															
POPE, THOMAS	1	53	$\checkmark_1$		$\checkmark$	$\checkmark$									
REDE, ROBERT															
REDE, WILLIAM		37	3			$\checkmark$									
REYNOLD, ROBERT, JUN		46				|?									
ROCHESTER, ROBERT									.6	5			||		
ROOKWOOD, NICHOLAS									.41	34			||		
ROOKWOOD, ROBERT						$\checkmark$	$\checkmark$		40_2	35_3	$\checkmark_1$	2	2		→
ROUS, ANTHONY	||														

	1	2	3	4	5	6	7	8	9	10	11	12	13	14	15	16	17	18	19
	1	1	2	2	2	3	3	4	5	5	6	6	6	7	8	9	10	11	12
	8 July 1509	18 Nov. 1509	28 June 1510	8 July 1510	20 Nov. 1510	6 June 1511	24 Feb. 1512	24 May 1512	29 Apr. 1513	4 Feb. 1514	28 May 1514	18 Oct. 1514	1 March 1515						12 Nov. 1520
ROUS, EDMUND																			
ROUS, THOMAS I																			
ROUS, THOMAS II																			
ROUS, WILLIAM																			
RUSH, ARTHUR																			
RUSH, THOMAS																			
RUSSELL, JOHN, LORD																			
RYECE, ROBERT																			
ST. JOHN, WILLIAM, LORD																			
SAUNDERS, EDMUND																			
SECKFORD, THOMAS																			
SOMERSET, EDWARD, D. OF																			
SOMERSET, GEORGE																			
SONE, JOHN																			
SOUTHAMPTON, THOMAS, E. OF																			
SOUTHAMPTON, WILLIAM, E. OF																			
SOUTHWELL, JOHN																			
SOUTHWELL, ROBERT I	11	11	11	11	11	12	12	12	9	9	||								
SOUTHWELL, ROBERT II	21	22	22	23	23	24_6	25_6	27_4	26	25_2	27_2	||							
SOUTHWELL, ROBERT III																			
SPENCER, MILES																			
SPRING, JOHN																			
STOCKHEATH, HENRY																			
SUFFOLK, CHARLES BRANDON, D. OF							19	15	8	3	3	3	3						5
SULYARD, JOHN II	23	24	24	25	25	26_3	27_3	31_4	29	28	30_3	33_3	33_3		1				22_6
SULYARD, JOHN III																			
SULYARD, WILLIAM																			
SUSSEX, HENRY, RADCLIFFE, E. OF																			
SUSSEX, ROBERT, RADCLIFFE, E. OF						6	5	5	4	5	5	5	5						8
TASBURGH, JOHN I																			
TEY, THOMAS																			
THURSTON, JOHN																			
TILNEY, PHILIP I	15	15	15	16	16	17_2	17_2	19_2	18	18	17_3	19_3	19_3		1		2		20_6
TILNEY, THOMAS																			
TOLLEMACHE, LIONEL I	22	23	23	24	24	25_5	26_5	29_2	S	24	26_4	30_4	30_4	5	3	1	7		21_8
TOLLEMACHE, LIONEL II																			
TYRELL, JOHN I																			
TYRELL, JOHN II																			

	20	21	22	23	24	25	26	27	28	29	30	31	32	33	34	35	36	37	38
	13	14	15	16	16	17	18	19	20	21	22	23	24	25	26	27	28	29	29
				6 May 1524	20 Dec. 1524	11 Feb. 1526			26 Jan. 1529		2 Feb. 1531		1532		20 Apr. 1534	20 Feb. 1535		28 Nov. 1537	12 Feb. 1538
ROUS, EDMUND																			
ROUS, THOMAS I																			
ROUS, THOMAS II																			
ROUS, WILLIAM											24_1	3	23_3	24_4	27_1			23_2	23
RUSH, ARTHUR														34_2	.30		5	$\|\|_2$	
RUSH, THOMAS				25_6	28_6	29_4	2	4	24		36_4	4	35_5	S_6	.25	$/_2$	$/_7$	$\|\|_3$	
RUSSELL, JOHN, LORD																			
RYECE, ROBERT																		53_1	53_1
ST. JOHN, WILLIAM, LORD																			
SAUNDERS, EDMUND																			
SECKFORD, THOMAS															39			50	50
SOMERSET, EDWARD, D. OF																			
SOMERSET, GEORGE															19	/		15	15
SONE, JOHN																			
SOUTHAMPTON, THOMAS, E. OF																			
SOUTHAMPTON, WILLIAM, E. OF											11		11	11	12			8	8
SOUTHWELL, JOHN														40_1	.38	2	2	48_2	48_2
SOUTHWELL, ROBERT I																			
SOUTHWELL, ROBERT II																			
SOUTHWELL, ROBERT III																			
SPENCER, MILES																			
SPRING, JOHN											32		30_1	30	33	/	1	32_2	32_2
STOCKHEATH, HENRY															.28				
SUFFOLK, CHARLES BRANDON, D. OF				5	5	5			5		3		3	3	.4			4	4
SULYARD, JOHN II	1		1	24	26	27			22	2	20	1	25_1	31				34	34
SULYARD, JOHN III																			
SULYARD, WILLIAM															17				
SUSSEX, HENRY, RADCLIFFE, E. OF																			
SUSSEX, ROBERT, RADCLIFFE, E. OF				8	7	6			6		6		6	6	7			7	7
TASBURGH, JOHN I																			
TEY, THOMAS					20	21	1	2	16_2	4	23_1	2	22_2	23_3	26	1	2	22_4	22
THURSTON, JOHN																			
TILNEY, PHILIP I	2	3		20	18	18_1	1	S	19		19	$2\|$	19_2	19					
TILNEY, THOMAS																			
TOLLEMACHE, LIONEL I	2	3	2	23	24	25_4	2	3	20_5	7	33_2	4	31_3	32_7	$.34_1$	$/_1$	1	33_2	33_2
TOLLEMACHE, LIONEL II																			
TYRELL, JOHN I																			
TYRELL, JOHN II																			

39	40	41	42	43	44	45	46	47	48	49	50	51	52	53	54	55	56	57	58	59	60	
30	31	32	33	34	35	36	37	38	1	2	3	4	5	6	7	1	2	3	4	5	6	
29 May 1538	24 May 1539			24 Feb. 1543	27 Feb. 1544	29 Oct. 1544			26 May 1547							18 Feb. 1554	1555					
				43	45	44	1/1	4	43				/									157-
												/	/	/		32_4	29_4	$/_4$	4	6		→
																			2			
23																						
				4	4	4			3								‖					
53_1	50		1	48_1	51	50_1	‖															
									2													
												/		/								1572
50	46		2	44	46_2	45		1	44			/	/			49_2	45_4	$/_1$	/			1575
									1				‖									
15	14			10	10	11			13									$/_1$				→
								4	34			/	/	‖								
				1									‖									
8	8		‖																			
48_4	44_7	$/_1$	6	41_2	43_3	42_1	1/2	$/_2$	40		$/_2$	/	/			.44_2	39_6	$/_1$	2	$/_4$		→
				8					7							15						1559
																	1					1570
32_1	28		4	23_2	24_1	25	3	1	20		‖											
4	4			3	3	3	‖															
34	30	‖																				
																29_2	26	S		$/_6$		→
	‖															.2	1			‖		
7	7		‖																			
														‖								
22_1	20		‖	16	16	17																
																	47	$/_1$	$/_2$	$/_3$		→
				38_6	40	39_1	1/1	1														1559
33_2	29_3	1	2	24_2	26_4	27	2/2	$/_3$	26			$/_1$		‖								
																35_1	31_3	$/_5$	$/_4$	$/_5$		→
																19_1	18_5	$/_7$	$/_6$	$/_5$		→
																3						

	1	2	3	4	5	6	7	8	9	10	11	12	13	14	15	16	17	18	19
	1	1	2	2	2	3	3	4	5	5	6	6	6	7	8	9	10	11	12
	8 July 1509	18 Nov. 1509	28 June 1510	8 July 1510	20 Nov. 1510	6 June 1511	24 Feb. 1512	24 May 1512	29 Apr. 1513	4 Feb. 1514	28 May 1514	18 Oct. 1514	1 March 1515						12 Nov. 1520
TYRRELL, THOMAS I																			
WADLAND, WALTER																			
WALDEGRAVE, EDMUND																			
WALDEGRAVE, WILLIAM I ←	12	12	12	12	.13	14_1	14_1	16	15	15	14	16	16				1		1
WALDEGRAVE, WILLIAM II																			
WENTWORTH, RICHARD ←	16	16S	16S	S				13	13	13	12_3	14_3	15_3		S_2				19
WENTWORTH, THOMAS, LORD I																			
WENTWORTH, THOMAS, LORD II																			
WHARTON, RICHARD																			
WILLOUGHBY, CHRISTOPHER																			
WILLOUGHBY, JOHN																			
WILLOUGHBY, WILLIAM, LORD	4	4	4	4	4	4	6	6	5	6	6	6	6						
WILTSHIRE, THOMAS BOLEYN, E. OF					.12	.13	.13	.14	.14	14	.13	.15	15						
WINGFIELD, ANTHONY			17	18	19	20	21_2	21			18_1	20_1	20_1	S					1
WINGFIELD, HUMPHREY ←	.20	.21	.21	.22	.22	$.23_7$	$.24_7$	$.26_2$	.25	.23	$.25_6$	$.29_6$	$.29_6$	5	3	2	7		S
WINGFIELD, RICHARD I																			
WINGFIELD, ROBERT																			
WISEMAN, JOHN								28	27	26	28	31	31						
WISEMAN, THOMAS																			
WYNDHAM, THOMAS												9	10						1
YORK, THOMAS WOLSEY AB. OF																			
188 TOTAL	24	25	25	26	26	27	30	36	34	33	34	36	36						2

20	21	22	23	24	25	26	27	28	29	30	31	32	33	34	35	36	37	38	39	40	41	42
13	14	15	16	16	17	18	19	20	21	22	23	24	25	26	27	28	29	29	30	31	32	33
			6 May 1524	20 Dec. 1524	11 Feb. 1526			26 Jan. 1529		2 Feb. 1531		1532	20 Apr. 1534	20 Feb. 1535			28 Nov. 1537	12 Feb. 1538	29 May 1538	24 May 1539		
					19			15_1	2	22	1	21_3	21_1	23_2	1	2	19	19	19	17		
														40			51	51	51_2	47_5		3
			16	14	14		||															
										30		28	26	29	2	3	25_2	25_2	25	22		
3			19	17	17_1	1	$\|\|_2$															
										9		9	9	10	/		10	10	10	10		
																	31_1	31_1	31_4	27_4		2
										16		16	16	18			14_1	14_1	14	1		
																	21_3	21_3	21_1	19		
			9	8	7		||															
										4		4	4	.5						||		
1			17	15	15_3	1		13_4	4	18_2	2	18_5	18_3	21_3	$/_2$	5	17	17	17_2	16_4	/	
S	1	3	21	21	22_5	3	4	17_7	7	28_3	5	27_6	22_7	$.24_3$	$/_4$	$/_{12}$	20_{10}	20	20_{11}	18_{15}	/	$/_5$
			10	9			||															
																	28	28	28			
	||																					
			1	1	1			1		||												
			29	33	33			30		42		41	?	43			55	56	57	54		

	43	44	45	46	47	48	49	50	51	52	53	54	55	56	57	58	59	60
	34	35	36	37	38	1	2	3	4	5	6	7	1	2	3	4	5	6
	24 Feb. 1543	27 Feb. 1544	29 Oct. 1544			26 May 1547							18 Feb. 1554	1555				
TYRRELL, THOMAS I	12	12$_1$	13$_1$			15				||								
WADLAND, WALTER	45$_3$	47$_1$	46	$_1$		45		||$_1$										
WALDEGRAVE, EDMUND													.11	9					c
WALDGRAVE, WILLIAM I																		
WALDEGRAVE, WILLIAM II	18	18	18		$_1$	17			/S				17	||				
WENTWORTH, RICHARD																		
WENTWORTH, THOMAS, LORD I	6	6	6			5			/	||								
WENTWORTH, THOMAS, LORD II													.5	4				
WHARTON, RICHARD	22$_2$	23$_1$	24	1/1	$_1$	27			/	/			37$_3$					
WILLOUGHBY, CHRISTOPHER																		
WILLOUGHBY, JOHN	14	14	15															
WILLOUGHBY, WILLIAM, LORD																		
WILTSHIRE, THOMAS BOLEYN, E. OF																		
WINGFIELD, ANTHONY	9	9	10			10		1			||							
WINGFIELD, HUMPHREY	13$_6$	13$_{11}$	14$_1$	/$^\beta_3$	||													
WINGFIELD, RICHARD I																		
WINGFIELD, ROBERT								3	/									
WISEMAN, JOHN																		
WISEMAN, THOMAS	32	34	34															
WYNDHAM, THOMAS																		
YORK, THOMAS WOLSEY AB. OF																		
188 TOTAL	53	56	55			56							56	51				

	1	2	3	4	5	6	7	8	9	10	11	12	13	14
	1	2	3	4	5	6	7	8	9	10	11	12	13	14
	Dec '58/Jan '59		Nov./Dec. 1561	February 1562		June 1564						December 1569		
ALINGTON, GILES	8													
ANDERSON, EDWARD														
ANDREWS, THOMAS												√	√₁	1
ARUNDEL, HENRY FITZALAN, E. OF	3		4	4		4								
ARUNDEL, PHILIP HOWARD, E. OF														
ASHFIELD, ROBERT II		√	37₄	36₄	√₄	40₅	3	2	3	3	4	√₄	√₄	3
BACON, EDWARD														
BACON, NICHOLAS I ←	1		1	1		1								
BACON, NICHOLAS II														1
BADBY, THOMAS						2	√	1	3	√₁	4	√₃	√₃	2
BARKER, ROBERT OF TRIMLEY														
BARKER, ROBERT OF PARHAM														
BARNADISTON, THOMAS III														
BATH, BOURCHIER, JOHN E. OF ←	5		||											
BEDINGFIELD, THOMAS OF REDLINGFIELD														
BLENNERHASSET, JOHN ←	34₅	5	19₅	19₃	5	22₆	7	√₅	4	3	√₆	√₆	2	
BLENNERHASSET, THOMAS														
BOCKING, EDWARD														
BOHUN, FRANCIS														
BREND, JOHN ←	17₁		||											
BREWSE, JOHN ←	15		15	15		16		√₁	√₇	3		√₁	1	1
BROMLEY, THOMAS														
BROWNE, ANTHONY		√	11	11	√	12	√	√	√	||				
BROWNE, JOHN										2	√₆	√₇	4	4
BROWNE, PHILIP														
BUCKENHAM, EDMUND														
BUCKHURST, THOMAS SACKVILLE LORD														
BURGHLEY, WILLIAM CECIL LORD														
CALTHORPE, WILLIAM III												1	2	3
CATLYN, ROBERT		√	9	9	√	10	√	√	√	√	√	√	√	√
CAVENDISH, CHARLES														
CAVENDISH, WILLIAM	30₃	√₂	29₆	29₁₀	√₈	31₃	√₆	√	√₅	2	3	√₁		||
CHITTING, HENRY	46	||												
CLENCH, JOHN														
CLERKE, ROBERT														
CLOPTON, FRANCIS														
CLOPTON, JOHN II														

	15	16	17	18	19	20	21	22	23	24	25	26	27	28	29	30
	15	16	16	16	16	17	18	19	20	21	22	23	24	25	25	26
		November 1573	? January 1574	June 1574	Mid-autumn '74	June 1575		Late 1577	Late '77/Early '78		End of 1579		Mid 1582	Early 1583	? July 1583	Early 1584
ALINGTON, GILES																
ANDERSON, EDWARD												/	/	/	9	9
ANDREWS, THOMAS		40_2	40_2	40_2	41_2	/		41_1	42	$_1$	40_3	$_1$	40_2	36	35	36
ARUNDEL, HENRY FITZALAN, E. OF												‖				
ARUNDEL, PHILIP HOWARD, E. OF														4	3	3
ASHFIELD, ROBERT II	4	27_3	26_3	26_3	28_3	$/_3$	S	27_4	28_4	4	30_4	$_3$	28_6	26_6	25_6	26_4
BACON, EDWARD																
BACON, NICHOLAS I		1	1	1	1			1	1	‖						
BACON, NICHOLAS II		18_2	17_2	18_2	19_2	/	$_1$	18_2	18_2		22_1	$_3$	S	$_3$	20_3	22_2
BADBY, THOMAS	2	37_2	36_2	36_2	38_2	/	$_1$	37_3	38_1	$_2$	37_4	$_3$	44_2		‖	
BARKER, ROBERT OF TRIMLEY																
BARKER, ROBERT OF PARHAM																
BARNADISTON, THOMAS III		42_7	42_7	42_7	43_7	/		44_1	46_1		20	S	21	21	19	21
BATH, BOURCHIER, JOHN E. OF																
BEDINGFIELD, THOMAS OF REDLINGFIELD																
BLENNERHASSET, JOHN	‖															
BLENNERHASSET, THOMAS																
BOCKING, EDWARD							6	43_5	44_2	9	42_3	6	47_5	42_4	42_4	43_1
BOHUN, FRANCIS																
BREND, JOHN																
BREWSE, JOHN	$/_3$	15_2	14_2	15_2	16_2	$/_3$	$_2$	16_5	16_4	$_1$	16	$_3$	13_1	13	13	14
BROMLEY, THOMAS /											1				1	1
BROWNE, ANTHONY																
BROWNE, JOHN	$/_5$	35_9	34_9	34_9	36_9	$/_8$	6	34_5	35_5	6	34_4	$_1$	41_6	37_8	36_8	37_8
BROWNE, PHILIP													51_3		46_4	48_1
BUCKENHAM, EDMUND																
BUCKHURST, THOMAS SACKVILLE LORD																
BURGHLEY, WILLIAM CECIL LORD		2	2	2	2			2	2		2				2	2
CALTHORPE, WILLIAM III	10	43_{14}	42_{14}	43_{14}	44_{14}	$/_8$	7	45_8	47		45_1	/	60			
CATLYN, ROBERT	/	8	8	8	9	‖										
CAVENDISH, CHARLES													34_2			
CAVENDISH, WILLIAM																
CHITTING, HENRY																
CLENCH, JOHN															11	11
CLERKE, ROBERT																
CLOPTON, FRANCIS	1	33_7	32_7	32_7	34_7	$_2$	$_4$	32_5	33_1	‖						
CLOPTON, JOHN II																

31	32	33	34	35	36	37	38	39	40	41	42	43	44	45	46	47	48	49	50	51	52	53	
26	27	28	29	30	31	32	33	34	35	36	36	37	37	38	38	39	40	41	42	43	44	45	
Mid-late 1584				April 1590		Mid 1591		Mid 1593	Late 93/Early '94	July 1594	February 1595	July 1595	Early 1596	July 1596	July 1597	July 1598	July 1599	May 1600	June 1601	June 1602	February 1603		
		||																					
9	$/$																						d. 1605
37	||																						
3												||											
27_4	$/_6$	4	$/_3$	$/_8$	4	24_6	23_4	5	27_4	27_7	26_7	24_5	22_5	23_7	23_7	21_5	21_5	22_6	22_8	23	22	21_5	d. 1613
								2	47_7	46_5	45_5	42_7	34_7	36_8	36_8	35_8	34_9	34_8	34_6	S34	32_6	31_7	d. 1618
22_2	$/_2$	$/_3$	$/_3$	$/_3$	3	19_6	18_3	4	18_4	17_6	16_6	16_4	15_4	14_5	15_5	13_5	14_4	14_5	13_8	13	12	12_2	d. 1624
																		43	44	44	42		d. 1618
																				43	41	40	
21						18	17		17	16	15	15		18	14	12	13	13	12	12	11	11	d. 1619
41						31	29		33	32	31	28											d. 1613
					6	50_8	48_7	7	57_5	59_7	61_7	58_4						||					
48_1	3	||																					
								2	51_8	2											|→		
14	||																						
1			||																				
40_8	7	8	6	$/$																			
53	||																						
											64	61					50	50_8	50_8	51_4	50_2	48_1	d. 1618
																		2	2	2	2		d. 1608
2						2	2		2	2	2	2	2	2	2	2	||						
																							d. 1617
12	$/$		$/_3$			9_1	9	1	8_2	6_1	5_1	5	7	7	7	6	7	7_2	7	6	5	5	d. 1607
													6	6	6	5	6	6	6	5	4		d. 1607
											2	2											

	1	2	3	4	5	6	7	8	9	10	11	12	13	14	15
	1	2	3	4	5	6	7	8	9	10	11	12	13	14	15
	Dec. '58/Jan. '59		Nov./Dec. 1561	February 1562		June 1564						December 1569			
CLOPTON, THOMAS															
CLOPTON, WILLIAM II															
CLOPTON, WILLIAM III															
COKE, EDWARD															
COLBY, THOMAS								2	5		$/_2$	4	5	4	$/_7$
COLT, GEORGE I ←	21		21	21		25						/			
COLT, GEORGE II															
CORDELL, EDWARD															
CORDELL, WILLIAM ←	7		10	10		11						/			
CORNWALLIS, THOMAS ←		/													
CRANE, ROBERT II	41_2	$/_4$	32_7	31_6	/	36_5	5	1	2	$/_2$	2	$/_2$	2	2	2
CROCHROOD, MATTHEW															
CROFTS, THOMAS															
CUTLER, NICHOLAS ←	38_4	$/_3$	34_9	33_3	5	38_4	/	4	5	||					
DANIEL, THOMAS ←	26		25	25		29	||								
DARCY OF CHICHE, JOHN, LORD															
DOYLE, EDWARD															
DOYLE, HENRY ←	16_8	$/_5$	3												
DRURY, ROBERT III															
DRURY, WILLIAM II															
DUKE, EDWARD															
EDEN, THOMAS I ←	19		18	18		20			||						
EDEN, THOMAS II															
EGERTON, THOMAS															
EVERARD, EDWARD															
EYER, JOHN ←	32_1	$/_3$	2	||											
FELTON, ANTHONY															
FELTON, THOMAS ←		2	23_3	23_3	14	27_{12}	4	$/_2$	4	5	12	$/_5$	4	4	5
FENNER, EDWARD															
FORTH, ROBERT														1	10
FORTH, WILLIAM II															
FOSTER, WILLIAM ←	1					/									
FRAMLINGHAM, CHARLES															
FROBISHER, MARTIN															
GARDINER, JOHN															
GARDINER, ROBERT						~									
GARNEYS, NICHOLAS															

16	17	18	19	20	21	22	23	24	25	26	27	28	29	30	31	32	33	34	35	36	37	38	39
16	16	16	16	17	18	19	20	21	22	23	24	25	25	26	26	27	28	29	30	31	32	33	34
November 1573	? January 1574	June 1574	Mid-autumn '74	June 1575	Late 1577		Late '77/Early '78				End of 1579	Mid 1582	Early 1583	? July 1583	Early 1584	Mid-late 1584					April 1590	Mid 1591	
																					1	33	3
											2	49	2	49_4	44_4	44_2	46_3	51_1	S	l_2	2	||	
																						38	
29_8	28_8	28_8	30_8	l_4	5	29_6	30_8	6	31_4	l_4	38_8	34_8	33_8	34_8	35_8	l_7	8	l_8	l_8	||			
20	19	20	21	l		21	22	||															
										2	1	35	32	31	32	33		1	S	1	27_2	26_2	3
												39	35	34	35	36					30				
9		9	10	l		9	9		9	||													
26_7	25_7	7	27_7	l		26	27		29		29_3	27	26	27	28							||	
																					42_1	40	1
										3	58_3	51_5	54_5	56_4	61_4	2	4	l_3	l_2	4	47_3	45_3	2
6		6	7			6	6		6																
																						49_1	1
													41	42_2	47_2	3	2	l_3	l_4	3	35_4	34_2	3
					1	14_2	14_3		14		15_1	15_5	22_5	16_2	16_2	2	1			1		||	
																				5	41_8	$39_{?}$	8
																				1	45_1	43_3	3
																							8
22_4	21_4	21_4	23_4	l_s	5	22_2	23	||															
46_8	45_8	46_8	47_8	l_4	3	50_4	51_6	1	51_3	5	50_6	45_2	45_2	47_3	52_3	l_3	l_2	3	5	6	39_4	37_3	4
																				1	52_1	53_4	6
							2	3	44_6	3	24_6	23_4	21_4	23_5	23_5	1	2	l_3	l_4	5	20_4	19_5	5
									53	4	54_4	48_2	49_2	51_3	56_3	1					22	21	
																					43_1	41_7	S

Name	40 / 35 / Mid 1593	41 / 36 / Late 93/Early '94	42 / 36 / July 1594	43 / 37 / February 1595	44 / 37 / July 1595	45 / 38 / Early 1596	46 / 38 / July 1596	47 / 39 / July 1597	48 / 40 / July 1598	49 / 41 / July 1599	50 / 42 / May 1600	51 / 43 / June 1601	52 / 44 / June 1602	53 / 45 / February 1603	d.
CLOPTON, THOMAS	37_4	36_7	35_7	32_4	25_4	27	27	26	$\|$						
CLOPTON, WILLIAM II															
CLOPTON, WILLIAM III									53_1	53_7	53_4	54	53	51_1	d. 1619
COKE, EDWARD		23	22_1	20_1	19_2	19	19	17	17	19	19	20	19		d. 1634
COLBY, THOMAS															
COLT, GEORGE I															
COLT, GEORGE II	30	30	29	27_2											
CORDELL, EDWARD															
CORDELL, WILLIAM															
CORNWALLIS, THOMAS															d. 1604
CRANE, ROBERT II															
CROCHROOD, MATTHEW	44_1	43_2	42_2	39	31	33	33	32_1	31_2	32_2	31_2	31	29	28	d. 1615
CROFTS, THOMAS	54_1	56_3	57_3	54_S	S	42_2	42_2	42_4	41_5	41_7	41_8	41	39	38_2	d. 1612
CUTLER, NICHOLAS															
DANIEL, THOMAS															
DARCY OF CHICHE, JOHN, LORD															
DOYLE, EDWARD	58_2	60	62	59											d. 1612
DOYLE, HENRY															
DRURY, ROBERT III	38_4	37_7	36_7	33_5											d. 1625
DRURY, WILLIAM II															
DUKE, EDWARD	43_6	42_8	41_8	38_2	30_2	32_2	32_2	31	30	$\|$					
EDEN, THOMAS I															
EDEN, THOMAS II	42_4	54_3	54_3	51_3	40_3	40_6	40_6	40_S	39_1	39_6	39_6	39	37	36	d. 1614
EGERTON, THOMAS						1	1	1	1	1	1	1	1		d. 1617
EVERARD, EDWARD			56_2	53_6						$\|$					
EYER, JOHN															
FELTON, ANTHONY	49_3	48_4	47_4	44_1				36_4	35_4	35_5	35_S	35	33	32_3	d. 1614
FELTON, THOMAS															
FENNER, EDWARD	9	7	6	6											d. 1612
FORTH, ROBERT	41_4	$_S40$	$_S39_1$	36	28	30_{10}	30_{10}	29_7	28_8	30_6	29_4	$\|$			
FORTH, WILLIAM II	60_6	62_6	63_6	60_7		47_7	47_7	48_{13}	48_{13}	$\|_9$					
FOSTER, WILLIAM															
FRAMLINGHAM, CHARLES	20_4	19_4	18_4	18_2	$\|$										
FROBISHER, MARTIN	22	21	20	$\|$											
GARDINER, JOHN		64	65_3	63_3	$\|$										
GARDINER, ROBERT	23	22	21	19	18	17	18	16	16	16	15	16	15	15_2	d. 1620
GARNEYS, NICHOLAS	45_1	44_1	43_1	40_2	32_2	34_9	34_9	33_8	32_9	33_9	32_8	32_8	30_9	29_9	d. 1623

	1	2	3	4	5	6	7	8	9	10	11	12	13	14	15
	1	2	3	4	5	6	7	8	9	10	11	12	13	14	15
	Dec '58/Jan. '59		Nov./Dec. 1561	February 1562		June 1564						December 1569			
GAWDY, BASSINGBOURN															4
GAWDY, HENRY															
GAWDY, THOMAS															
GERRARD, GILBERT	√								√	√	√	√	√	√	√
GILBERT, HENRY															
GILBERT, JOHN															
GLEMHAM, EDWARD ←	43_1	1	||												
GLEMHAM, HENRY															
GLEMHAM, THOMAS			4						1			4	||		
GOLDINGHAM, CHRISTOPHER ←	36_4	√||													
GOSNOLD, ROBERT I ←		1	22_3	22_2	1	26						√			
GOSNOLD, ROBERT II															
GOSNOLD, ROBERT III															
GRESHAM, WILLIAM															
GRIMSTON, EDWARD ←							6	$√_8$	$√_4$	11	$√_7$	11	8	6	
GRIMSTON, WILLIAM															
GURDON, JOHN															
GURDON, ROBERT ←	42_3	$√_4$	39_4	38_5	$√_6$	41_1	5	2	3	$√_3$	2	$√_4$	2	1	3
HARE, MICHAEL	28_5	2	26_4	26_{10}	5	30_2	4		4		2				
HATTON, CHRISTOPHER															
HEVENINGHAM, ARTHUR															
HIGHAM, CLEMENT ←	$√_{16}$	$√_{20}$	12_{20}	12_{20}	$√_{19}$	13_{23}	$√_{20}$	20	$√_{18}$	$√_{13}$	20	$√_{14}$	$√_1$	||	
HIGHAM, JOHN													2	4	4
HIGHGATE, REYNOLD															
HONNINGS, EDWARD															
HONNINGS, WILLIAM ←	35		35	34_1	$√_5$	32_{11}	$√_1$	√	$√_6$	5	9||				
HOPTON, ARTHUR															
HOPTON, OWEN ←	22_9	9	16_5	16_7	6	17_8	S		8	$√_4$	$√_{13}$	$√_8$			
HUMBERSTON, WILLIAM				3	$√_4$	45_4	$√_2$	1				$√_4$	3	1	4
JENNY, ARTHUR															
JENNY, FRANCIS I ←	31_5	5	4												8
JENNY, FRANCIS II															
JENNY, JOHN ←	14		||												
JERMYN, AMBROSE ←	S	$√_5$	13_4	13_5	$√_5$	14_9	$√_5$	4	$√_3$	$√_3$	4	$√_4$	4	3	S
JERMYN, JOHN .					1	43_4	5	3	2	3	4	$√_3$	2	1	4
JERMYN, ROBERT															
JERNINGHAM, HENRY ←	9														

	16	17	18	19	20	21	22	23	24	25	26	27	28	29	30	31	32
	16	16	16	16	17	18	19	20	21	22	23	24	25	25	25	26	26
	November 1573	? January 1574	June 1574	Mid-autumn '74	June 1575		Late 1577	Late '77/Early '78		End of 1579		Mid 1582	Early 1583	? July 1583	Early 1584	Mid-late 1584	
GAWDY, BASSINGBOURN	44_8	48_8	44_8	45_8	$\vert_8$	5	46_4	48_5		46_1	$\vert_3$	33_2	31_6	30_6	31_8	32_8	4
GAWDY, HENRY																	
GAWDY, THOMAS												4	10	10	10	10	
GERRARD, GILBERT	10	9	9	11	/	/	10	10	/	10	/						
GILBERT, HENRY																	
GILBERT, JOHN																	
GLEMHAM, EDWARD																	
GLEMHAM, HENRY																	
GLEMHAM, THOMAS																	
GOLDINGHAM, CHRISTOPHER																	
GOSNOLD, ROBERT I	21	20	$\Vert$	22													
GOSNOLD, ROBERT II												43_3	39_5	38_5	39_9	44_9	9
GOSNOLD, ROBERT III																	
GRESHAM, WILLIAM																38	
GRIMSTON, EDWARD	24_8	23_8	23_8	25_8	5	5	24_7	25_6	5	27_3	5	30_7	28_5	27_5	28_7	29_7	6
GRIMSTON, WILLIAM																	
GURDON, JOHN								45	2	43_1	3	48_6	43_3	43_3	44_3	49_3	S_2
GURDON, ROBERT	30_3	29_3	29_3	31_3	$\vert_1$	1	30	31	$\Vert$								
HARE, MICHAEL																	
HATTON, CHRISTOPHER																	
HEVENINGHAM, ARTHUR								19	6	21_1	3	18	18	17	19_6	19_6	5
HIGHAM, CLEMENT																	
HIGHAM, JOHN	32_4	31_4	31_4	33_4	$\vert_4$	4	$_531$	32_4	2	32_2	3	22_6	22_3				
HIGHGATE, REYNOLD												37_2					
HONNINGS, EDWARD																	
HONNINGS, WILLIAM																	
HOPTON, ARTHUR																	
HOPTON, OWEN	14	13	14	15	/		13	13		13	/	14	14	14	15	15	
HUMBERSTON, WILLIAM	31_5	30_5	30_5	32_5	$\vert_7$	$\Vert$											
JENNY, ARTHUR																	
JENNY, FRANCIS I	34_7	33_7	33_7	35_7	$\vert_3$	4	33_3	34_2	3	33_3	1	31_2	29	28	29_2	30_2	1
JENNY, FRANCIS II																	
JENNY, JOHN														·			
JERMYN, AMBROSE	12_4	11_4	12_4	13_4	$\vert_4$	1	$\Vert$										
JERMYN, JOHN	41_2	40_2	41_2	42_2	$\vert_4$	4	42_2	43_3	2	41_2		46_5	41_4	40_4	41_4	46_4	$\vert_2$
JERMYN, ROBERT							19_3	20_3	S_2	18		4	19_4	4			
JERNINGHAM, HENRY	$\Vert$																

33	34	35	36	37	38	39	40	41	42	43	44	45	46	47	48	49	50	51	52	53	
28	29	30	31	32	33	34	35	36	36	37	37	38	38	39	40	41	42	43	44	45	
				April 1590	Mid 1591		Mid 1593	Late 93/Early '94	July 1594	February 1595	July 1595	Early 1596	July 1596	July 1597	July 1598	July 1599	May 1600	June 1601	June 1602	February 1603	
2	/	/	$\|\|$																		
						5	24_3	24_2	23_2	21_6	20_6	20_6	20_6	18_7	19_{11}	20_8	20_4	21_2	20_9	19_2	d. 1621
	$\|\|$																				
							$\|\|$														
				50_4		5	59_3	61$\|\|$													
															52_2	52_{10}	52_2	53	52	50	d. 1613
																		15	14	14	d. 1632
$/_8$	2																				
																54	55	56	55	53	d. 1615
																					d. 1624
6	6	$/_5$	6	25_4	24_5	4	28_7	28_6	27_6	25_6	23_6	24_4	24_4	22_6	22_6	23_6	$\|\|$				
						2	61_5	63_7	59_7	56_6					49_4	49_9	49_8	50_8	49_9	47_9	
$/_3$	/		4	36_4	35_2	5	39_4	38_5	37_5	34_5	26_5	28_8	28_8	27	26_5	28_7	27_8	28_2	26	25_2	d. 1621
																					d. 1611
		1	1	$\|\|$																	
6	8	$/_6$	4	16_8	15_6	7	15_5	13_4	12_4	12_6	12_6	11_5	11_5	9_8	10_9	10	10_4	10_4	9_9	9	d. 1630
/			3			4	19_4	18_5	17_5	17_5	16_5	15_8	16_8	14	15_5	15_7	14_8	14_2	13	13_2	d. 1634
	$\|\|{\rightarrow}$																				
												45_2	45_2	46_8	46_9	47_{11}	47_2	48_2	47_4	45_2	d. 1609
1	$/_8$	$/_8$	6	23	22		26	26	25	23											d. 1614
				13	12		13	11	10	10	$\|\|$										
							48_6	47_5	46_5	43_{10}	35_{10}	6	6								d. 1605
1	2	S	$\|\|$																		
																24_6	23_6	24	23	22_3	
3	3	6	3	34_2	32	4	36_3	35_5	34_5	31_7	24_7	26_7	26_7	25_4	25_5	27_7	26_6	27	25	24_2	d. 1606
				16				c14	c13	c13	c13	c12	c12	c10	c11	c11	c11	c11	c10	c10	d. 1614

	1	2	3	4	5	6	7	8	9	10	11	12	13	14	15
	1	2	3	4	5	6	7	8	9	10	11	12	13	14	15
	Dec '58/Jan. '59		Nov./Dec. 1561	February 1562		June 1564						December 1569			
JERNINGHAM, JOHN II ←	10	||													
JERNINGHAM, JOHN, OF BELTON III ←															
JOHNSON, RICHARD															
KEMPE, RICHARD														2	5
KEMPE, THOMAS															
KITSON, THOMAS						19_1	4	$/_3$	2	2	1				
LANY, JOHN															
LE HUNT, JOHN															
LEWKENOR, EDWARD															
MACKWILLIAM, HENRY															
MERES, LAURENCE			38_5	37_9											
HOWARD, THOMAS, DUKE OF NORFOLK ←	4		3	3		3								||	
NORTH, EDWARD, LORD	6		8	8		9	||								
NORTH, HENRY															
NORTH, JOHN															
NORTH, ROGER, LORD															
FREKE, EDMUND, BISHOP OF NORWICH															
PARKHURST, JOHN, BISHOP OF NORWICH						6									
REDMAN, WILLIAM, BISHOP OF NORWICH															
SCAMBLER, EDMUND, BISHOP OF NORWICH															
NUNN, FRANCIS ←	37_2	$/_{11}$	33_{12}	32_{11}	15	37_{12}	$/_6$	$/_{13}$	$/_8$	$/_{10}$		/			
VERE, EDWARD, EARL OF OXFORD															
PARKER, PHILIP													2	3	2
PAYNE, HENRY ←	1	2	24_3	24_4	4	28_5	2			||					
PEMBROKE, WILLIAM, EARL OF								/	/	/	/				
PENNING, ARTHUR/ANTHONY															
PERIAM, WILLIAM															
PEYTON, CHRISTOPHER ←	39_2	||													
PLAYTERS, THOMAS, I ←	45_5	6	4		5	44_6	2	5	5	4	$/_6$	$/_6$	5	3	||
PLAYTERS, THOMAS, II															
POLEY, EDMUND															
POLEY, THOMAS							2	3	2	$/_3$	4	$/_4$	$/_2$	3	3
POLEY, WILLIAM															
POPHAM, JOHN															
PUCKERING, JOHN															
REDE, WILLIAM															
RIVETT, JAMES	44_2	/	40_5	39_6	8	42_8	$/_3$	$/_5$	$/_7$	$/_2$	10	$/_3$	7	6	7
RIVETT, JOHN															3

16	17	18	19	20	21	22	23	24	25	26	27	28	29	30	31	32	33	34	35	36	37	38	39
16	16	16	16	17	18	19	20	21	22	23	24	25	25	26	26	27	28	29	30	31	32	33	34
November 1573	? January 1574	June 1574	Mid-autumn '74	June 1575		Late 1577	Late '77/Early '78		End of 1579		Mid 1582	Early 1583	? July 1583	Early 1584	Mid-late 1584						April 1590	Mid 1591	
					5	48_5	49_5	8	48_4	3	57_8		53_4	6									
45_8	44_8	45_8	46_8	$/_6$	7	49_3	50_4	4	50_4	$/_4$	52_4	46_7	47_7	49_7	54_7	4	6	1					
												52	55_4	60_4	$/_5$	6	7	$/_7$	9		46_7	44_{10}	9
			$/$			52	53_2	1	55_2	2	59_2	52	55	57_2	62_2	2		$/_1$	$/_7$	3	49_3	47_2	4
												24	26	25	24	25	26	‖					
																				2	11_3	11_4	4
																				1	10_2	10	
7	7	7	8			7	7		7	$/$		7	7	7				$/$			6	6	
						3	4		4			4	5	5								‖	
4		4	5	‖																			
															5			$/$			4	4	
‖																							
			3																				
39_4	39_4	39_4	40_4	$/_1$	3	40_5	41_4	1	s17	2	17_4	17_2	16_2	18_5	18_5	$/_5$	$/_6$	6	$/_5$	6	15_5	14_6	5
																	$/$	$/$	$/$	$/$	8	8	$/$
																	1	1	$/_8$	7	48_6	46_3	7
38_3	37_3	37_3	39_3	$/_5$	4	38_5	39_4	3	38_2	2	45_4	40_2	39_2	40_2	45_2	6		2	$/$				
																							$/$
			$/$			47			47		62												
c16_{14}	c15_{14}	c16_{14}	c17_{14}	$/_{17}$	12	c17_{12}	c17_8	10	c23_7	c7	c25_{13}	c24_{13}	c23_{13}	c24_{10}	c25_{10}	10		$/$	$/$	‖			
47_6	46_6	47_6	48_6	$/_6$	4	51_6	52_9	3	52_5	2	53_2	47_2	48_2	50_3	55_3	1	2	1					

	40	41	42	43	44	45	46	47	48	49	50	51	52	53	
	35	36	36	37	37	38	38	39	40	41	42	43	44	45	
	Mid 1593	Late 93/Early '94	July 1594	February 1595	July 1595	Early 1596	July 1596	July 1597	July 1598	July 1599	May 1600	June 1601	June 1602	February 1603	
JERNINGHAM, JOHN II															
JERNINGHAM, JOHN, OF BELTON III									$\|$						
JOHNSON, RICHARD		52_2	51_2	48_6	37_6			$\|$							
KEMPE, RICHARD												$\|$			
KEMPE, THOMAS								49	51_9	51_{10}	51_{10}	52_2	51_4	49_5	d. 1623
KITSON, THOMAS															d. 1603
LANY, JOHN	53_8	55_7	55_7	52_5		41_3	41_3	41_{10}	40_{11}	40_8	40_8	40_8	38_8	37_8	
LE HUNT, JOHN	56_4	58	60	57_5	43_5			44	44	45_5	45_6	46	44	42	d. 1606
LEWKENOR, EDWARD		51_1	50_1	47	36	37_2	37_2	37_5	36_4	36_5	36_8	36	34	33_5	d. 1605
MACKWILLIAM, HENRY															
MERES, LAURENCE															
HOWARD, THOMAS, DUKE OF NORFOLK															
NORTH, EDWARD, LORD															
NORTH, HENRY	11_4	9_6	8_6	8_5	9_5	9_7	9_7	7_5	8_1	8_5	8_8	7	6	6_6	d. 1620
NORTH, JOHN	10	8_2	7_2	7	8	8	8	$\|$							
NORTH, ROGER, LORD	6	4	3	3	4	4	4	3	4	4	4	$\|$			
FREKE, EDMUND, BISHOP OF NORWICH															
PARKHURST, JOHN, BISHOP OF NORWICH															
REDMAN, WILLIAM, BISHOP OF NORWICH					3	3	3		2	3	3	3	$\|$		
SCAMBLER, EDMUND, BISHOP OF NORWICH	4	3	$\|$												
NUNN, FRANCIS															
VERE, EDWARD, EARL OF OXFORD															d. 1604
PARKER, PHILIP	14_3	12_5	11_5	11_7	11_7	10_8	10_8	8_4	9_9	9_8	9_8	9_8	8_4	8_2	
PAYNE, HENRY															
PEMBROKE, WILLIAM, EARL OF															
PENNING, ARTHUR/ANTHONY												60	58	55_2	
PERIAM, WILLIAM															d. 1604
PEYTON, CHRISTOPHER															
PLAYTERS, THOMAS, I															
PLAYTERS, THOMAS, II				62_6		44_2	44_2	45_8	45_8	46_9	46_8	47_8	45_9	43_9	d. 1638
POLEY, EDMUND	55_6	56_4	58_4	55_7	42_7	43_9	43_9	43_6	42_9	42_8	42_{10}	42_6	40_8	39_7	d. 1613
POLEY, THOMAS															
POLEY, WILLIAM												19	18	18	d. 1629
POPHAM, JOHN	7	5	4	4	5	5	5	4	5	5	5	4	3	$/$	d. 1607
PUCKERING, JOHN	1	1	1	1	1	$\|$									
REDE, WILLIAM															
RIVETT, JAMES															
RIVETT, JOHN			52	49_7	38_7	38_5	38_5	38_7	37_4	37_6	37_4	37_2	35_4	34_9	d. 1624

Name	1	2	3	4	5	6	7	8	9	10	11	12	13	14	15
	1	2	3	4	5	6	7	8	9	10	11	12	13	14	15
	Dec '58/Jan. '59	Nov./Dec. 1561	February 1562	June 1564								December 1569			
RIVET, THOMAS I															
RIVET, THOMAS II															
ROBERTS, WILLIAM															
ROLFE, ROBERT															
ROOKWOOD, ROBERT ←	24_4	4	$/_2$					||							
ROUS, THOMAS I ←	24_5	$/_1$													
ROUS, THOMAS II															
SECKFORD, CHARLES															
SECKFORD, THOMAS	18	/	17	17	/	18					/		/		
SOMERSET, GEORGE ←	12	||													
SONE, FRANCIS	33_5	$/_9$	31_{12}	||											
SOUTHWELL, JOHN I	29_6	$/_5$	28_7	28_4	3	34									
SOUTHWELL, JOHN II															
SOUTHWELL, ROBERT IV															
SPRING, JOHN II															
SPRING, WILLIAM													2	2	4
STANHOPE, MICHAEL															
STEYNINGS, THOMAS						24_2	7	6	4	4	4	$/_7$	6	1	1
STUTEVILE, THOMAS															
SULYARD, JOHN III ←	13														
RADCLIFFE, HENRY, EARL OF SUSSEX															
RADCLIFFE, THOMAS, EARL OF SUSSEX			5	5		5									
TASBURGH, JOHN II															
THURSTON, JOHN ←	40_4	5	36_8	35_4	10	39_9	$/_1$	$/_9$	$/_8$	$/_6$	11	$/_{13}$	10	3	4
TILNEY, PHILIP II															
TIMPERLEY, THOMAS	1														
TOLLEMACHE, LIONEL II ←	20_2	$/_4$	20	20_1	1	23_6	$/_2$		S	1		/		||	
TOLLEMACHE, LIONEL II															
TYRRELL, JOHN I						/									
TYRRELL, THOMAS II ←															
WALDEGRAVE, GEORGE															
WALDEGRAVE, WILLIAM III						21_3	2		1		S	/	2	3	3
WARNER, HENRY															
WARREN, THOMAS															
WENTWORTH, HENRY II	23_1		2									|—→			
WENTWORTH, HENRY I, LORD															
WENTWORTH, JOHN, OF SOMERLEYTON															

	16	17	18	19	20	21	22	23	24	25	26	27	28	29	30	31
	16	16	16	16	17	18	19	20	21	22	23	24	25	25	26	26
	November 1573	? January 1574	June 1574	Mid-autumn '74	June 1575		Late 1577	Late '77/Early '78		End of 1579		Mid 1582	Early 1583	? July 1583	Early 1584	Mid-late 1584
RIVET, THOMAS I							36	37		36		23	||			
RIVET, THOMAS II																
ROBERTS, WILLIAM																
ROLFE, ROBERT																
ROOKWOOD, ROBERT																
ROUS, THOMAS I	||															
ROUS, THOMAS II																43
SECKFORD, CHARLES										1	5	55_7	49_6	50_6	52_9	57_9
SECKFORD, THOMAS	11	10	11	12	/		11	11		11			11	10	12	11
SOMERSET, GEORGE																
SONE, FRANCIS																
SOUTHWELL, JOHN I																
SOUTHWELL, JOHN II																
SOUTHWELL, ROBERT IV																24
SPRING, JOHN II																
SPRING, WILLIAM	28_5	27_5	27_5	29_5	$/_3$	4	28_5	s29	1	19_1	3	20_2	20_6	18_6	20_5	20_5
STANHOPE, MICHAEL																
STEYNINGS, THOMAS	19_6	18_6	19_6	20_6	$/_3$	1	20_2	21_1	2	25_2	3	27_3	1			
STUTEVILE, THOMAS								1	1	54_1		56_1	50	51	54	59
SULYARD, JOHN III		||														
RADCLIFFE, HENRY, EARL OF SUSSEX													3	4	4	4
RADCLIFFE, THOMAS, EARL OF SUSSEX	3	3	3	4			3	3		3		||				
TASBURGH, JOHN II																
THURSTON, JOHN	36_{10}	35_{10}	35_{10}	37_{10}	$/_6$	5	35_5	36_5	9	35_4	$/_4$	42_8	38_8	37_8	38_8	42_8
TILNEY, PHILIP II		38_4	38_4	4	$/_4$	5	39	40_1	5	39_1	1	32_7	30_7	29_7	30_5	31_5
TIMPERLEY, THOMAS																
TOLLEMACHE, LIONEL II																
TOLLEMACHE, LIONEL II																
TYRRELL, JOHN I				||												
TYRRELL, THOMAS II																
WALDEGRAVE, GEORGE																
WALDEGRAVE, WILLIAM III	17_5	16_5	17_5	18_5	$/_2$	3	15_6	15_2	1	15		16_1	16_6	15_6	17_5	17_5
WARNER, HENRY																
WARREN, THOMAS															45_3	50_3
WENTWORTH, HENRY II																
WENTWORTH, HENRY I, LORD																6
WENTWORTH, JOHN, OF SOMERLEYTON																

33	34	35	36	37	38	39	40	41	42	43	44	45	46	47	48	49	50	51	52	53	
28	29	30	31	32	33	34	35	36	36	37	37	38	38	39	40	41	42	43	44	45	
			April 1590	Mid 1591		Mid 1593	Late 93/Early '94	July 1594	February 1595	July 1595	Early 1596	July 1596	July 1597	July 1598	July 1599	May 1600	June 1601	June 1602	February 1603		
															2	43_{13}	44_{10}	45_6	43_4	41_3	
		6	51_6	52	‖																
																55_1	56_8	57	56		d. 1622
2	6	*I*	1	40_8	$_s38$	4	42_5	41_6	40_6	37_4	29_4	31_5	31_5	30_8	29_9	31_9	30_8	30_6	28_9	27_7	d. 1603
4	5				‖																
				‖																	
				‖																	
			2	32_2	30_5	4	34_5	33_4	32_4	29_3											d. 1612
				21	20		21	20	19		17	16	17	15	‖						
																58_2	59	‖			
4	I_3	I_3	4	17_4	16_4	4	$17_4^{\cdot}$	15_7	14_7	14_7	14_7	$_s13$	$_s13$	11_4	12_5	12_5	2	‖			d. 1622
							25	25	24	22	21	21	21	19	20	21	21	22	21	20	
2	I_4	6	4	44_3	42_4	3	51_1	53	53	50_6	39_6	39_7	39_7	39_2	38_5	38_5	38_4	38	36	$_s35$	d. 1606
		‖→																			
				3	3		3	‖													
																46_9	44_7				
2	I_2			33	31		35	34	33	30		25	25	24	24	26	25	26	24	23	d. 1606
4	1	I_4	S	26_4	25_6	6	29_5	29_4	28_4	26_5			23_4	23_9	25_8	24_6	25_6	‖			
									‖												
			2	$_s46$	45	44	41_4	33_4	35_8	35_8	34_6	33_4	2	33	33_6	31	30				d. 1612
															6	54_8	55	54	52		
																56	57_9	58	57	54	
2	I_1	5	3	$_s14$	13_2	5												8	7	7_4	d. 1614
3	I_3	I_4	4	37_3	36_4	4	40_2	39_7	38_7	35_7	27_7	29_5	29_5	28_5	27_4	$_s29$	28_6	29	27	26_2	d.1617
							50	50_3	49_3	46_2											d.1628?
			$_c5$	$_c5$		$_c5$	‖														
												46_2	46_2	47_8	47_9	48_{11}	48_8	49_8	48_9	46_7	d. 1619

Appendix I

	1	2	3	4	5	6	7	8	9	10	11	12	13	14	15
	1	2	3	4	5	6	7	8	9	10	11	12	13	14	15
	Dec '58/Jan. '59		Nov./Dec. 1561	February 1562		June 1564						December 1569			
WENTWORTH, THOMAS LORD II			6	6		7	/					/			
WILLOUGHBY, WILLIAM LORD OF PARHAM			7	7		8									
PAULET WILLIAM MARQUIS OF WINCHESTER ←	2		2	2		2								||	
WINGFIELD, ANTHONY II															
WINGFIELD, HENRY															
WINGFIELD, RICHARD II	27	3	27_4	27_9	$/_6$	33_6	$/_6$	$/_6$	4	4	8	$/_8$	9	7	4
WINGFIELD, ROBERT ←	11_4	7	$s14$	14_8	$/_3$	15_{12}	$/_{14}$	$/_{15}$	$/_4$	$/_7$	9	$/_9$	11	10	8
WITHIPOLL, EDMUND I		4	30_5	30_3	2	35_2	$/_1$	2		2	4	$/_3$	S	1	2
WITHIPOLL, EDMUND II															
WRAY, CHRISTOPHER															
WROTT, ROBERT															
TOTAL IN COMMISSION	46		40	39		45						?41			

16	17	18	19	20	21	22	23	24	25	26	27	28	29	30	31	32	33	34	35	36	37	38	39
16	16	16	16	17	18	19	20	21	22	23	24	25	25	26	26	27	28	29	30	31	32	33	34
November 1573	? January 1574	June 1574	Mid-autumn '74	June 1575		Late 1577	Late '77/Early '78		End of 1579		Mid 1582	Early 1583	? July 1583	Early 1584	Mid-late 1584						April 1590	Mid 1591	
5	5	5	6			5	5		5		/	7	6	6	||								
	||																						
															39	1	4	5	/	1	29_5	28_4	4
25_{10}	24_{10}	25_{10}	26_{10}	$/_6$	7	25_1	26_2	3	26_3	2	36_2	33_9	32_9	33_6	34_6	/	/	10	8	6	28_8	27_3	
13_{13}	12_{13}	13_{13}	14_{13}	$/_{13}$	2	12_6	12_5	8	12_9	3	12_5	12_7	12_7	13_8	13_8	$/_3$	$/_7$	$/_8$	$/_9$	4	12_3	4	3
23_6	22_6	22_6	24_6	$/_2$	1	23_1	24_4	2	26_1		||												
			/	/		8	8	/	8		/	/	/	10	8	8	/	/	/	/	7	7	/
								2			56_1	$/_4$	61_4	53_6	56_6	53_8	58_8	8		2	$/_8$	4	||
47	46	47	48			52	53		56		62	53	56	57	62						52	53	

	40	41	42	43	44	45	46	47	48	49	50	51	52	53	
	35	36	36	37	37	38	38	39	40	41	42	43	44	45	
	Mid 1593	Late 93/Early '94	July 1594	February 1595	July 1595	Early 1596	July 1596	July 1597	July 1598	July 1599	May 1600	June 1601	June 1602	February 1603	
WENTWORTH, THOMAS LORD II															
WILLOUGHBY, WILLIAM LORD OF PARHAM															
PAULET WILLIAM MARQUIS OF WINCHESTER															
WINGFIELD, ANTHONY II	32_1	31_4	30_4		41_4	22_{10}	22_{10}	20_4	$s17$	17_{11}	16_{10}	17_8	16_8	16_{10}	d. 1606
WINGFIELD, HENRY	1	49_3	48_3	45_2						‖→					
WINGFIELD, RICHARD II	31														
WINGFIELD, ROBERT	12_1	10_2	9_2	9_6	10_6	‖									
WITHIPOLL, EDMUND I															
WITHIPOLL, EDMUND II										18	17	18_6	$s17$	17	d. 1606
WRAY, CHRISTOPHER	‖														
WROTT, ROBERT															
TOTAL IN COMMISSION	61	64	65	63	43	47	47	49	53	56	58	60	58	55	

APPENDIX II

The careers of Norfolk JPs and their attendance at quarter sessions 1485–1558

This table is included because of the intimate links between Norfolk and Suffolk throughout the century, and it forms the complement to the Norfolk listing of 1558–1603 in Smith, pp. 351 ff.; as in Appendix I above, it follows the same conventions. In the listing of sources below, it is worth noting that the references for pre-Elizabethan JPs given by Smith, p. 360, appear to be incorrect and to refer to listings of Suffolk JPs.

Lists of JPs: sources

1	(7 Dec. 1485) PRO, C66/561, m. 5d. An enrolled commission, as are all the following down to no. 29.	16	(12 Feb. 1497) C66/579, m. 5d.
		17	(19 Feb. 1497) C66/579, m. 1d.
		18	(8 May 1497) C66/579, m. 7d.
		19	(13 Henry VII) None extant.
2	(6 Jan. 1486) C66/561, m. 5d.	20	(6 Dec. 1498) C66/582, m. 4d.
3	(12 Mar. 1486) C66/561, m. 7d.	21	(8 June 1499) C66/582, m. 3d.
4	(9 Sept. 1486) C66/565, m. 1d.	22	(15 Henry VII) None extant.
5	(30 Aug. 1487) C66/565, m. 2d.	23	(10 Feb. 1501) C66/587, m. 4d.
6	(30 Aug. 1487) C66/567, m. 1d.	24	(18 Feb. 1501) C66/589, m. 6d.
7	(4 Henry VII) None extant.	25	(12 Feb. 1502) C66/589, m. 5d.
8	(17 Aug. 1490) C66/570, m. 3d.	26	(6 Feb. 1503) C66/591, m. 3d.
9–11	(6–8 Henry VII) None extant.	27	(11 May 1503) C66/591, m. 8d.
12	(9 May 1494) C66/575, m. 4d.	28	(27 June 1504) C66/593, m. 2d.
13	(10 Henry VII) None extant.	29	(30 Nov. 1504) C66/595, m. 3d.
14	(14 May 1496) C66/577, m. 4d.	30–3	(21–4 Henry VII) None extant.
15	(12 Nov. 1496) C66/579, m. 5d.		

1	(1 Henry VIII) None extant.	20	(23 Feb. 1524) LP IV pt. i, no. 137.
2	(20 Nov. 1510) C66/612, m. 6d. An enrolled commission, as are all the following down to no. 27.	21	(16 Henry VIII) None extant.
		22	(11 Feb. 1526) LP IV pt. i, no. 2002.
3	(6 June 1511) C66/615, m. 4d.	23–6	(18–21 Henry VIII) None extant.
4	(11 Nov. 1511) C66/615, m. 3d.	27	(4 Mar. 1531) LP V, no. 166/12.
5	(24 Feb. 1512) C66/617, m. 7d.	28	(23 Henry VIII) None extant.
6	(22 Sept. 1512) C66/618, m. 3d.	29	(1532) LP V, no. 1694. A liber pacis.
7	(24 Nov. 1512) C66/618, m. 4d.	30	(25 Henry VIII) None extant.
8	(5 Henry VIII) None extant.	31	(24 Nov. 1534) PRO, E371/300, m. 46. An enrolled commission, as are all the following up to no. 51.
9	(28 May 1514) C66/622, m. 2d.		
10	(12 Nov. 1514) C66/622, m. 3d.		
11	(1 Mar. 1515) LP II pt. i, no. 207.		
12	(14 Nov. 1515) Ibid., no. 1152.		
13–19	(8–14 Henry VIII) None extant.		

32–4   (27–9 Henry VIII) None extant.
35   (13 July 1538) *LP* XIII pt. i,
        no. 1519/50.
36   (31 Henry VIII) None extant.
37   (26 Nov. 1540) *LP* XVI,
        no. 305/68.
38   (33 Henry VIII) None extant.
39   (23 May 1542) *LP* XVII,
        no. 362/66.
40   (11 May 1543) *LP* XX, no. 622.

41–3   (36–8 Henry VIII) None extant.
44   (26 May 1547) *CPR Edward VI* I,
        p. 87.
45–50   (2–7 Edward VI) None extant.
51   (18 Feb. 1554) *CPR Philip and
        Mary* I, p. 22.
52   (1555) PRO, SP 11/5. fo. 42^v.
        A *liber pacis*.
53–6   (2 & 3 to 5 & 6 Philip and Mary)
        None extant.

1	2	3	4	5	6	7	8	9	10	11	12	13	14	15	16	17	18	19	20
1	1	1	2	3	3	4	5	6	7	8	9	10	11	12	12	12	12	13	14
7 Dec. 1485	6 Jan. 1486	12 Mar. 1486	9 Sept. 1486	30 Aug. 1487	30 Aug. 1487		17 Aug. 1490				9 May 1494		14 May 1496	12 Nov. 1496	12 Feb. 1497	19 Feb. 1497	8 May 1497		6 Dec. 1498
											5		||						
12	13	12	11	S	S		12				12		11	||					
13	15	14	13	12	15		15				15		14	12	12	12	12		11
16	18	18	18	17	18		19		S		20		19	17	17	17	17		
											29		29	27	26	29	31		26
													23	25	23	22	22		S
2	2	2	2	1			2				2		2	2	2	2	2		2
														24	26	27			23
											22		20	18	18	18	18		14
														29	28	31	33		30
			2	3			4				4		4	4	4	3	4		4
											30		30	28	27	30	32		28
19	21	21	20	20	22		24				26		27	||					
							10				10		8	8	8	8	8		7
6	6	6	6	6	7		7				8		||						
	14	13	12	11	14		14				14		13	11					
21	23	23	23	22	24		26				28		28	26	25	28	30	||	
			21	23			25				27	||							
10	10	10	9	9	12	||													
					9														
14	16	15	14	13	16		16				16		16	15	13	13	13	13	12
20	22	23	22	16	19		20				21		22	21	19	21	21		19
			15	14	17		18				19		18	16	16	16	16		13

21	22	23	24	25	26	27	28	29	30	31	32	33		
14	15	16	16	17	18	18	19	20	21	22	23	24		
8 June 1499		16 Feb. 1501	18 Feb. 1501	12 Feb. 1502	6 Feb. 1503	11 May 1503	27 June 1504	30 Nov. 1504						
													BEDFORD, JASPER TUDOR D OF	
													BEDINGFIELD, EDMUND I	
10	S	8	8	10	10	/	12	12	||				BOLEYN, WILLIAM	
											S		BRANDON, ROBERT	→
				28		/	31	30					BREWES, ROBERT	→
26		24	24	28	27	/	30	29					CALIBUT, FRANCIS	→
S		13	12	15	13	/	15	16					CALTHORPE, PHILIP I	→
				2	2	||							CANTERBURY, HENRY DEANE ABP OF	
2		||											CANTERBURY, JOHN MORTON ABP OF	
							2	2					CANTERBURY, WILLIAM WARHAM ABP OF d. 1532	
22		S	S	18	16	/	18	||					CATESBY, HUMPHREY	
13		11	S	13			14	15					CLERE, ROBERT	→
30		25	25	29	30	/	33	31					ELLIS, WILLIAM	→
3		||											ELY, JOHN ALCOCK, BP OF	
29		27	27	31	29	/	34	32		||			EYER, WILLIAM	
													FINCHAM, JOHN	
6		4	4	5	5	/	7	7					FINEUX, JOHN	→
													FITZWALTER, JOHN RADCLIFFE LD	
													FITZWALTER, ROBERT RADCLIFFE LD	→
													GIGGS, THOMAS	
													GREY, WILLIAM	
													HASTINGS, HUGH	
													HAWES, THOMAS	
11		9	9	11	11	/	||						HEYDON, HENRY	
							26	25					HEYDON, JOHN	→
18		17	16	20	18	/	13	13					HOBART, JAMES	→
25		22	21	25	24	/	27	26					HOBART, WALTER	→
12		10	10	12	12	/	19	14					HOGARD, HENRY	→
				8	9	/	10	10					HOWARD, EDMUND LD	→

1	2	3	4	5	6	7	8	9	10	11	12	13	14	15	16	17	18	19	20	21	22	23	24
1	1	1	2	3	3	4	5	6	7	8	9	10	11	12	12	12	12	13	14	14	15	16	16
7 Dec. 1485	6 Jan. 1486	12 Mar. 1486	9 Sept. 1486	30 Aug. 1487	30 Aug. 1487		17 Aug. 1490				9 May 1494		14 May 1496	12 Nov. 1496	12 Feb. 1497	19 Feb. 1497	8 May 1497		6 Dec. 1498	8 June 1499		16 Feb. 1501	18 Feb. 1501
7	7	7	7	7	8		8				9	||											
5	5	5	5	5	6		6	||															
11	11	11	10	10	13		13				13		12	10	11	11	11		10	9		7	7
																							22
											S				25	26			22	21		20	19
																17	16					15	14
					S		22				24		25	24	22	24	25		16	15		14	13
15	17	16	16	15	11		11				11		10	9	10	10	10		9	8		6	6
8	8	8																					
1	1	1	1	1	2		3				3		3	3	3	4	3		3	||			
																					||		
													9										
4	4	4	4	4	5		6				6		5	5	5	5	5		5	4		2	2
S	S	S	S								17		16	14	14	14	14						
															9	9	9		8	7		5	5
	12										21		19										||
													7	7	7	7	7		||				
		17	17		S		17				18		17	15	15	15	15		||				
																	34		27	28		28	28
17	19	19	19	18	20		21				23		24	22	21	23	23		20	19		18	17
														S	23		24		21	20		19	18
18	20	20	21	19	21		23				25		26	||									
																			29	27		26	26
											7		6	6	6	6	6		6	5		3	3
3	3	3	3	3	4		5	||															
																32	29		25	24		23	23
9	9	9	8	8	10		9			||												21	20
											1		1	1	1	1	1		1	1		1	1
																19	19		15	14		12	11
														20	20	20	20		18	17		16	15
																			27	28	||	24	23
21	23	23	23	22	24		26				30		30	29	28	31	34		30	30		28	28

25	26	27	28	29	30	31	32	33		
17	18	18	19	20	21	22	23	24		
12 Feb. 1502	6 Feb. 1503	11 May 1503	27 June 1504	30 Nov. 1504						
				5					HOWARD, THOMAS LORD	→
									HUSSEY, WILLIAM	
									KENT, EDMUND GREY, E OF	
9	8	/	11	11					KNYVET WILLIAM	→
.26	.25	/	.28	27					L'ESTRANGE, JOHN	→
23	22	/	21	20	||				L'ESTRANGE, ROGER	
17	15	/	17	18	||				LOVELL, GREGORY	
.16	.14	/	.16	.17					LOVELL, ROBERT	→
.7	.7	/	.9	.9					LOVELL, THOMAS	→
	.21	/	.24	.23					LUCAS, THOMAS	d. 1531
									NEEL, RICHARD	
									NORWICH, JAMES GOLDWELL, BP OF	
									NORWICH, THOMAS ,JANE BP OF	
3	3	/	3						NORWICH, RD NIX BP OF	→
||									OXENBRIDGE, THOMAS	
4	4	/	4	3					OXFORD, JOHN VERE, 13th E OF	→
		||							PASTON, JOHN	
	.32	/						||	PINKNEY, ROBERT	
.6	.6	/	.8	.8					REDE, ROBERT	
									ROBSART, TERRY	
									SCROPE, JOHN LORD ,OF BOLTON	
									SHELTON, RALPH	
32	33	/							SKIPWITH, WILLIAM	
.21	.19	/	.23	.22				||	SOUTHWELL, RICHARD I	
22	20	/	20	.19					SOUTHWELL, ROBERT I	→
									SPELMAN, HENRY	
.30	.31	/	.32	33					STUBBS, WALTER	→
									SUFFOLK, EDM DE LA POLE, E OF	d. 1513
									SUFFOLK, JOHN DE LA POLE D OF	
.27	.26	/	.29	28					SULYARD, ANDREW	→
			5	4					SURREY, THOMAS HOWARD E OF	→
.24	.23	/	.25	.24					TOWNSHEND, ROGER I & II	→
1	||								WALES, ARTHUR, PRINCE OF	
	1	/	1	1					WALES, HENRY, PRINCE OF	d.1547
		/	6	6					WILLOUGHBY, WILLIAM LD I	→
14	||								WYNDHAM, JOHN	
.19	.17	/	.22	.21	||				YAXLEY, JOHN	
									YELVERTON, WILLIAM	
32	33	33	34	33					TOTAL	

	1	2	3	4	5	6	7	8	9	10	11	12	13	14	15
	1	2	3	3	3	4	4	5	6	6	6	7	8	9	10
		20 Nov. 1510	6 June 1511	11 Nov. 1511	24 Feb. 1512	22 Sept. 1512	24 Nov. 1512		28 May 1514	12 Nov. 1514	1 March 1515	14 Nov. 1515			
APPLEYARD, NICHOLAS			22	21	22	24	25		24	21	22	23		||	
AUDLEY, EDMUND															
AUDLEY, JOHN		17	18	18	18	20	21		18	18	19	19			
AUDLEY, THOMAS															
BALDWIN, JOHN															
BANYARD, RICHARD															
BARNEY, JOHN OF LANGLEY															
BARNEY, ROBERT															
BATH, JOHN BOURCHIER E OF															
BEAUPRE, EDMUND															
BEDINGFIELD, EDMUND II															
BEDINGFIELD, HENRY															
BEDINGFIELD, JOHN															
BEDINGFIELD, THOMAS I															
BEDINGFIELD, THOMAS II															
BERNERS, JOHN BOURCHIER LD															
BILLINGFORD, EDWARD															
BOLEYN, JAMES			24	22	23	25	26		25	20	21	22			
BRAMPTON, WILLIAM															
BRANDON, ROBERT ←	S					14	14		12	12	13				
BREWES, ROBERT ←	/	26	29	27	28	30	30	||							
BROMLEY, THOMAS															
BROOKE, RICHARD															
BROOKE, ROBERT															
BRUDENELL, ROBERT															
BUTTS, WILLIAM															
CALIBUT, FRANCIS ←	/	27	30	28	30	32	32		30	24	25	26	||		
CALIBUT, JOHN															
CALTHORPE, EDWARD															
CALTHORPE, PHILIP I ←															
CALTHORPE, PHILIP II															
CARYLL, JOHN															/
CATLYN, RICHARD															
CAVENDISH, RICHARD I					35	23	24		23					||	
CAVENDISH, RICHARD II															
CLERE, CHARLES															
CLERE, JOHN															
CLERE, ROBERT ←	/	14	15	15	15	18	19		16	16	17	17			
CLERE, THOMAS															
COCKET, EDWARD															

16	17	18	19	20	21	22	23	24	25	26	27	28	29	30	31	32	33	34	35	36	37	38	39
11	12	13	14	15	16	17	18	19	20	21	22	23	24	25	26	27	28	29	30	31	32	33	34
				23 Feb. 1524		11 Feb. 1526					4 March 1531		1532		24 Nov. 1534				13 July 1538		26 Nov. 1540		23 May 1542
													‖										
													1		1				1		1		1
																			9		9	/	
																						/	
																			42	3			'42
						20					S		20						18_1	$/_{11}$			17_5
															27	/	/	/	30_9	2	28_1	8	25_1
		S									18		19		18				17	‖			
											8		8	‖									
																			44		43		43
			19			21					12				.13	/			18	$/_3$	19_1	4	18_5
			‖																				
																							10
				11		12			‖														
				10		11				‖													
						13					15		16			‖							
															25						27		24
				‖																	27		21
																					26		
																			36		33		

	40	41	42	43	44	45	46	47	48	49	50	51	52	53	54	55	56	
	35	36	37	38	1	2	3	4	5	6	7	1	2	3	4	5	6	
	11 May 1543				26 May 1547							18 Feb 1554	1555					
APPLEYARD, NICHOLAS																		
AUDLEY, EDMUND												30						
AUDLEY, JOHN																		
AUDLEY, THOMAS	1	||																
BALDWIN, JOHN			||															
BANYARD, RICHARD	||																	
BARNEY, JOHN OF LANGLEY													29_4	$/_{10}$		/		→
BARNEY, ROBERT			/	48	/							32_7				9		→
BATH, JOHN BOURCHIER E OF												.3	2					d. 1561
BEAUPRE, EDMUND	45_1	4	2	6	42	2						34_{11}	28_4	$/_7$	6			→
BEDINGFIELD, EDMUND II	20_1		1		16					||								
BEDINGFIELD, HENRY	29_1				31							$.10_5$	11		$/_6$	12		d. 1583
BEDINGFIELD, JOHN					39													
BEDINGFIELD, THOMAS I																		
BEDINGFIELD, THOMAS II	41																	
BERNERS, JOHN BOURCHIER LD																		
BILLINGFORD, EDWARD	54	/												→			||	
BOLEYN, JAMES	21_6	$/_1$	2	2	17	/		$/_6$	/			19_6	14	4		4		→
BRAMPTON, WILLIAM	51														3			
BRANDON, ROBERT																		
BREWES, ROBERT																		
BROMLEY, THOMAS	11				8								||					
BROOKE, RICHARD																		
BROOKE, ROBERT													8				||	
BRUDENELL, ROBERT																		
BUTTS, WILLIAM					27	/	2		11									→
CALIBUT, FRANCIS																		
CALIBUT, JOHN					53							35_8	←||					
CALTHORPE, EDWARD													30				||	
CALTHORPE, PHILIP I																		
CALTHORPE, PHILIP II	28				29			||										
CARYLL, JOHN																		
CATLYN, RICHARD					52	$/_3$	7		/	$/_5$		5	20	||				
CAVENDISH, RICHARD I																		
CAVENDISH, RICHARD II												.23	||					
CLERE, CHARLES														→				d. 1572
CLERE, JOHN	25		1		22	$/_3$				12				→	/	||		
CLERE, ROBERT																		
CLERE, THOMAS						/	/	/										
COCKET, EDWARD																		
													8				||	

	1	2	3	4	5	6	7	8	9	10	11	12	13	14	15
	1	2	3	3	3	4	4	5	6	6	6	7	8	9	10
		20 Nov. 1510	6 June 1511	11 Nov. 1511	24 Feb. 1512	22 Sept. 1512	24 Nov. 1512		28 May 1514	12 Nov. 1514	1 March 1515	14 Nov. 1515			
CONINGSBY, WILLIAM									34	27	28	29			
CORBET, JOHN SENIOR															
CORDELL, WILLIAM															
CURZON, JOHN															
CURZON, ROBERT II											7	7			
CURZON, ROBERT II															
DAVY, GREGORY															
DEY, THOMAS															
DOWNES, JAMES															
DUDLEY, ROBERT															
ELLIS, WILLIAM		29	32	30	31	34	34		33	26	27	28			
ELY, THOMAS GOODRICH BP OF															
ELY, NICHOLAS WEST BP OF															
ESSEX, THOMAS CROMWELL E OF															
FARMER, HENRY I															
FARMER, HENRY II															
FARMER, WILLIAM															
FINEUX, JOHN ←		6	7	7	7	7	7		7	7	8	8			
FITZWALTER, THOMAS RADCLIFFE LD															
FRAMLINGHAM, JAMES									20						
FULMERSTON, RICHARD															
GAWDY, THOMAS II															
GAWDY, THOMAS III															
GLEMHAM, JOHN					36	37	37		21						
GODSALVE, JOHN															
GOODRICH, JOHN															
GOODRICH, JOHN															
GRESHAM, PAUL															
GRESHAM, RICHARD															
GREY, EDMUND															
GRIFFIN, EDWARD															
GUYBON, THOMAS															
HARE, NICHOLAS															
HEYDON, CHRISTOPHER I															
HEYDON, CHRISTOPHER II															
HEYDON, JOHN ←	/	19	20	19	19	21	22		19	S	S	S			
HEYDON, RICHARD															
HOBART, HENRY															
HOBART, JAMES ←	/	11	12	13	13	16	16		13	13	14	14		‖	
HOBART, WALTER ←	/	22	25	23	24	26	27		26						

	16	17	18	19	20	21	22	23	24	25	26	27	28	29	30	31	32
	11	12	13	14	15	16	17	18	19	20	21	22	23	24	25	26	27
					23 Feb. 1524		11 Feb. 1526					4 March 1531		1532		24 Nov. 1534	
CONINGSBY, WILLIAM	/				24		30					29		30		.33	
CORBET, JOHN SENIOR																	
CORDELL, WILLIAM																	
CURZON, JOHN																	
CURZON, ROBERT II																	||
CURZON, ROBERT II												36		36		40	
DAVY, GREGORY																	
DEY, THOMAS																	
DOWNES, JAMES																	
DUDLEY, ROBERT																	
ELLIS, WILLIAM	/				21		22					22		23		||	
ELY, THOMAS GOODRICH BP OF																7	
ELY, NICHOLAS WEST BP OF					2		3					7		7		||	
ESSEX, THOMAS CROMWELL E OF																	
FARMER, HENRY I												31	S	/			
FARMER, HENRY II																	
FARMER, WILLIAM																28	/
FINEUX, JOHN						||											
FITZWALTER, THOMAS RADCLIFFE LD																	
FRAMLINGHAM, JAMES	||																
FULMERSTON, RICHARD																	
GAWDY, THOMAS II																	
GAWDY, THOMAS III																	
GLEMHAM, JOHN																	||
GODSALVE, JOHN																	
GOODRICH, JOHN														30			
GOODRICH, JOHN														29			
GRESHAM, PAUL																	
GRESHAM, RICHARD														·			
GREY, EDMUND																	
GRIFFIN, EDWARD																	
GUYBON, THOMAS							·										
HARE, NICHOLAS												35		35		.38	
HEYDON, CHRISTOPHER I																	
HEYDON, CHRISTOPHER II																	
HEYDON, JOHN	S	S			16		S					16		17		16	
HEYDON, RICHARD																	
HOBART, HENRY																	
HOBART, JAMES																	
HOBART , WALTER												33		33		.21	

33	34	35	36	37	38	39	40	41	42	43	44	45	46	47	48	49	50	51	52	53	54	55	56	
28	29	30	31	32	33	34	35	36	37	38	1	2	3	4	5	6	7	1	2	3	4	5	6	
				13 July 1538		26 Nov. 1540	23 May 1542	11 May 1543			26 May 1547							18 Feb. 1554	1555					
/	/	28_5	6	$\parallel$																				
				41	3	40_4	50_{10}	$/_{15}$	$/_{19}$	$/_{26}$	46	$/_{16}$	$/_{19}$	3	/			•25_{10}	$/_{16}$	$/_{19}$	$/_6$	8	$\parallel$	
																			21					d. 1581
				34	2	31_1	36_2		2					$\parallel$										
		43		38		36_5	44							$\parallel$										
						45	55_5	1	3	4	49	2		4									$\parallel$	
						53																		
																					6	$\parallel$		
														/	/						→			d. 1588
		7		7		6	7				5							$\parallel$						
		4		$\parallel$																				
																					→			
/	/	31_6	4	1			19	1		2	15	2	/	$/_7$	/	$/_{30}$		16_{12}	1		3	$/_6$	$\parallel$	
																		•5	4	/				→
											51													→
				44	/	44_1	49_2	$/_8$	$/_4$	$/_6$	45	$/_6$	$/_8$	$/_9$	/	$/_9$		•22_{21}	19_{14}	$/_{13}$	$\parallel$			
																				$/_7$	$/_8$	/		
											24							•17_3	18	/		$\parallel$		
		33		30		28	31				33											$\parallel$		
		32		29		27	32																	
											54	2				4								
		19	$/_3$	20	3	19	22_2				20		$\parallel$											
				40	3	38	47				44	$\parallel$												
																		•12	9					d. 1569
														6		7		10	32_{18}	$/_{10}$	6	8		→
/	/	24		15		14	16				13							•8	7			$\parallel$		
		21_3		22	$\parallel$	20																		
											30	2		8	/	$/_{21}$		13_{13}	10_{23}	$/_{19}$	/S	11		→
/	/	15_{10}	$/_5$	14_4		13	15				12			$\parallel$										
				39		37_2	46				42							$\parallel$						
						26	30		/	S_3	$_S32$							•28_3	23		4	$/_9$		→
S			2	$\parallel$																				

		1	2	3	4	5	6	7	8	9	10	11	12	13	14	15
		1	2	3	3	3	4	4	5	6	6	6	7	8	9	10
			20 Nov. 1510	6 June 1511	11 Nov. 1511	24 Feb. 1512	22 Sept. 1512	24 Nov. 1512		28 May 1514	12 Nov. 1514	1 March 1515	14 Nov. 1515			
HOGARD, GEORGE																
HOGARD, HENRY	←	/	12	13												
HOLDICH, ROBERT																
HOLLIS, THOMAS																
HOWARD, EDWARD	←		9	10	10	10	10	10	‖							
HUNSTON, HENRY										32						
HUNSTON, WILLIAM																
JENNEY, CHRISTOPHER																
JENNY, JOHN																
JERMY, JOHN																
KERVILE, ...																
KNYVET, EDMUND																
KNYVET, THOMAS																
KNYVET, WILLIAM I & II	←		10	11	12	12	13	13		11	11	12	12	‖		
L'ESTRANGE, JOHN	←	/	24	27	25	26	28	28		27	22	23‖	24			
L'ESTRANGE, NICHOLAS																
L'ESTRANGE, THOMAS																
LISTER, RICHARD																
LOVELL, FRANCIS																
LOVELL, ROBERT	←	/	15	16	16	16	19	20		17	17	18	18			
LOVELL, THOMAS I	←		8	9	9	9	9	9		9	9	10	10			
LOVELL, THOMAS II																
MONTAGUE, EDWARD																
MORE, THOMAS																
MORGAN, RICHARD																
MORLEY, HENRY, LORD																
MOUNDFORD, FRANCIS										37	29	30	31			
MOUNDFORD, OSBERT																
NORFOLK, THOMAS HOWARD 2nd D OF	←		3	3	3	3	3	3		2	2	2	2			
NORFOLK, THOMAS HOWARD 3rd D OF	←		4	5	4	6	6	4		4	4	4	4			
NORFOLK, THOMAS HOWARD 4th D OF																
NORWICH, ROBERT																
NORWICH, JOHN HOPTON BP OF																
NORWICH, RD NIX BP OF	←		1	1	1	1	1	1		1	1	1	1			
NORWICH, THOMAS THIRLBY BP OF																
NORWICH, ROBERT																

16	17	18	19	20	21	22	23	24	25	26	27	28	29	30	31	32	33	34	35	36	37	38	39
11	12	13	14	15	16	17	18	19	20	21	22	23	24	25	26	27	28	29	30	31	32	33	34
				23 Feb. 1524		11 Feb. 1526					4 March 1531		1532		24 Nov. 1534				13 July 1538		26 Nov. 1540		23 May 1542
						25					24		25		23		√	√	26_7	$√_{11}$	25	$√_{11}$	23_8
																‖							
				26		32					32		24		.22		√		12	$_2$	11	√	
															.19		√		20_5	$_3$	21	$_3$	
				27																			
																			38		36		33
											20		21	S			√	√	$_6$		16		15
											11		11		.11				10				
									S		21		22		20				22				
			‖	15																			
					‖																		
																						8	7
											1					‖							
				25		31					30		31		.34		‖						
				4	‖																		
				6		4					2		2		2				2		2		2
											10		10		.10	‖							
				3		2					6		6		6	‖							
						10																	

	40	41	42	43	44	45	46	47	48	49	50	51	52	53	54	55	56	
	35	36	37	38	1	2	3	4	5	6	7	1	2	3	4	5	6	
	11 May 1543				26 May 1547							18 Feb. 1554	1555					
HOGARD, GEORGE	37				36													→
HOGARD, HENRY																		
HOLDICH, ROBERT	27$_7$		8	√$_9$	28	√$_9$		√$_9$		√		.24$_8$	22$_{12}$	√$_{11}$	√$_7$	√$_5$	‖	
HOLLIS, THOMAS					26	4		2		3		3	4					
HOWARD, EDWARD																		
HUNSTON, HENRY																		
HUNSTON, WILLIAM								2		3								→
JENNEY, CHRISTOPHER		‖																
JENNY, JOHN															2	8		d. 1575
JERMY, JOHN																		d. 1560
KERVILE												→						
KNYVET, EDMUND	24				21		‖											
KNYVET, THOMAS												26	→					→
KNYVET, WILLIAM I & II																		
L'ESTRANGE, JOHN																		
L'ESTRANGE, NICHOLAS	39				37	S												→
L'ESTRANGE, THOMAS	17$_1$	1	‖															
LISTER, RICHARD													‖					
LOVELL, FRANCIS	23	S			18					‖								
LOVELL, ROBERT																		
LOVELL, THOMAS I																		
LOVELL, THOMAS II												21	17		6	√		→
MONTAGUE, EDWARD	8				7			√								‖		
MORE, THOMAS																		
MORGAN, RICHARD												.9			‖			
MORLEY, HENRY, LORD												.6	5					d. 1578
MOUNDFORD, FRANCIS																		
MOUNDFORD, OSBERT	43	7	2		41			4		2		.29	24$_9$	6	2	6		→
NORFOLK, THOMAS HOWARD 2nd D OF																		
NORFOLK, THOMAS HOWARD 3rd D OF	2											.1	‖					
NORFOLK, THOMAS HOWARD 4th D OF																√		→
NORWICH, ROBERT																		
NORWICH, JOHN HOPTON BP OF													3					
NORWICH, RD NIX BP OF																		
NORWICH, THOMAS THIRLBY BP OF												.4						d. 1570
NORWICH, ROBERT																		

	1	2	3	4	5	6	7	8	9	10	11	12	13	14	15
	1	2	3	3	3	4	4	5	6	6	6	7	8	9	10
		20 Nov. 1510	6 June 1511	11 Nov. 1511	24 Feb. 1512	22 Sept. 1512	24 Nov. 1512		28 May 1514	12 Nov. 1514	1 March 1515	14 Nov. 1515			
NUNN, HENRY		28	31	29	31	33	33		31	25	26	27			
OXFORD, JOHN VERE, 13th E OF ←		2	2	2	2	2	2	‖							
OXFORD, JOHN VERE 14th E OF															
PASTON, THOMAS															
PASTON, WILLIAM														S	S
PENNINGTON, WILLIAM															
PLUMSTEAD, JOHN															
RAGLAND, THOMAS															
REDE,ROBERT ←		7	7	8	8	8	8		8	8	9	9		‖	
REPPS,JOHN															
ROBSART, JOHN															
ROBSART, ROBERT															
RUSSELL, JOHN LD															
ST. JOHN, WILLIAM PAULET, LORD															
SANDALL, RICHARD															
SHARNBOURNE, HENRY												20			
SHELTON, JOHN I	/	20	21	20	20	22	23		22	19	20	21			
SHELTON, JOHN II															
SOMERSET, EDWARD D OF															
SOUTHAMPTON, WILLIAM FITZWILLIAM,E OF															
SOUTHAMPTON, THOMAS WRIOTHESLEY,E OF															
SOUTHWELL, RICHARD II															
SOUTHWELL, ROBERT I ←		16	17	17	17	12	12		‖						
SOUTHWELL, ROBERT II															
SPELMAN, JOHN ←					29	31	31		29	23	24	25			
STUBBS, WALTER		30	33	31	33	35	35		35	‖					
SUFFOLK, CHAS.BRANDON D OF					21	15	15		3	3	3	3			
SULYARD, ANDREW ←		25	28	26	27	29	29		28						
SURREY, HEN. HOWARD E OF															
SUSSEX HEN. RADCLIFFE E OF															
SUSSEX, ROBERT RADCLIFFE E OF ←			6	5	4	4	5		5	5	5	5			
SYMONS, RALPH															
THWAITES, ANTHONY															
TILNEY, PHILIP	/	13	14	14	14	17	18		15	15	16	16			
TOWNSHEND, GILES															
TOWNSHEND, ROBERT															
TOWNSHEND, ROGER ←	/	21	23	S	S	S									S
TYNDALL, JOHN															
TYNDALL, THOMAS I															

	16	17	18	19	20	21	22	23	24	25	26	27	28	29	30	31	32
	11	12	13	14	15	16	17	18	19	20	21	22	23	24	25	26	27
					23 Feb. 1524		11 Feb. 1526					4 March 1531		1532		24 Nov. 1534	
NUNN, HENRY																	
OXFORD, JOHN VERE, 13th E OF																	
OXFORD, JOHN VERE 14th E OF							6	||									
PASTON, THOMAS																	
PASTON, WILLIAM					17		16				S	14		15		15	/
PENNINGTON, WILLIAM												19		||			
PLUMSTEAD, JOHN																	
RAGLAND, THOMAS																	
REDE, ROBERT																	
REPPS, JOHN																	
ROBSART, JOHN														28		31	
ROBSART, ROBERT																	
RUSSELL, JOHN LD																	
ST. JOHN, WILLIAM PAULET, LORD																	
SANDALL, RICHARD																	
SHARNBOURNE, HENRY																	
SHELTON, JOHN I				S	18		17					17		18		17	
SHELTON, JOHN II																	
SOMERSET, EDWARD D OF																	
SOUTHAMPTON, WILLIAM FITZWILLIAM, E OF												9		9		9	
SOUTHAMPTON, THOMAS WRIOTHESLEY, E OF																	
SOUTHWELL, RICHARD II												27		27			S
SOUTHWELL, ROBERT I																	
SOUTHWELL, ROBERT II																	
SPELMAN, JOHN	/				23		24					23		12		12	
STUBBS, WALTER																	
SUFFOLK, CHAS.BRANDON D OF					5		5					3		3		3	
SULYARD, ANDREW																	
SURREY, HEN. HOWARD E OF																	
SUSSEX HEN. RADCLIFFE E OF																8	
SUSSEX, ROBERT RADCLIFFE E OF					7		7					5		5		5	
SYMONS, RALPH																	
THWAITES, ANTHONY																	
TILNEY, PHILIP					13		14			S					||		
TOWNSHEND, GILES																	
TOWNSHEND, ROBERT							34					34		34		37	
TOWNSHEND, ROGER	S				20		18	S				13		14		14	
TYNDALL, JOHN							28					26		26		26	
TYNDALL, THOMAS I																	

33	34	35	36	37	38	39	40	41	42	43	44	45	46	47	48	49	50	51	52	53	54	55	56	
28	29	30	31	32	33	34	35	36	37	38	1	2	3	4	5	6	7	1	2	3	4	5	6	
		13 July 1538		26 Nov. 1540		23 May 1542	11 May 1543				26 May 1547							18 Feb. 1554	1555					
											19															
√	√	14₅	√₁₃	13	9	12₆	14	3	√₃	3	11		11			15		15	||					
																√₄		11						d. 156
																					6	6		
																√		8	6					d. 156
√	√	34₄	3	31	3	29	33				25	S			S√			||						
														3										
				4		4					3															
											2													d. 157
															4			7	4				:	
		16₃	||																					
						35				√₃	23	√₃		6	√	√₈		.11₆	S	√	√₅	√	||	
											1															
		6		4																						
						?								||										
√	√	25₂₅	25	17₂	√₂₅	16₁₈	12₂₁	15	19	26	9	√₂₄	21		√	√₃₂		.7₃₂	6₃₄	c√₃₃	√₁₉	√₂₁	√_c	d. 156
		39	2	23		8	9				6													d. 155
	√	:1		10		9	10		||															
		3		3		3	3																			
							ii																	
		6		5	5																				
		8	√				6				4			√				.2	1	√		/||		
		5		5																						
															4	4										
																						5		
						34₆	40₃	1		√₇	38	4				2		ii						
√	√	41₉	√₉	24	√₅	22₉	26₄	3	√₁		14											||		
√	√	13₂₀	√₂₅	12₂	22	11₁₃	13₁₀	7	12	√₂₂	10	√₁₃	20	√₂₀	√		||							
√	23	||																						
															2	7		27	15₁₄	8	6			→

	1	2	3	4	5	6	7	8	9	10	11	12	13	14	15
	1	2	3	3	3	4	4	5	6	6	6	7	8	9	10
		20 Nov. 1510	6 June 1511	11 Nov. 1511	24 Feb. 1512	22 Sept. 1512	24 Nov. 1512		28 May 1514	12 Nov. 1514	1 March 1515	14 Nov. 1515			
WALPOLE, JOHN															
WARD, HENRY															
WHITE, EDWARD												32			
WILLOUGHBY, WILLIAM LD ←		5	4	6	5	5	6		6	6	6	6			
WILTSHIRE, THOMAS BOLEYN E OF		18	19	11	11	11	11		10	10	11	11			
WINGFIELD, RICHARD															
WINGFIELD, THOMAS															
WOODHOUSE, ROGER															
WOODHOUSE, THOMAS II															
WOODHOUSE, THOMAS II															
WOODHOUSE, WILLIAM															
WOTTON, JOHN															
WOTTON, WILLIAM	/	31	34	32	34	36	36		36	28	29	30			
WYNDHAM, EDMUND															
WYNDHAM, THOMAS		23	26	24	25	27	17		14	14	15	15			
YELVERTON, WILLIAM II (Jun.)															
YELVERTON, WILLIAM III (Sen.)															
YORK, THOMAS WOLSEY ABP OF															
TOTAL		31	34	32	36	37	37		37	29	30	32			

16	17	18	19	20	21	22	23	24	25	26	27	28	29	30	31	32	33	34	35	36	37	38	39
11	12	13	14	15	16	17	18	19	20	21	22	23	24	25	26	27	28	29	30	31	32	33	34
				23 Feb. 1524		11 Feb. 1526					4 March 1531		1532		24 Nov. 1534				13 July 1538		26 Nov. 1540		23 May 1542
																							41_1
				27		33																		
				8		9																		
				12		8					4		4		4										
				9																				
						29																	
												28	29		32		/		35		32		30
						19																	
																							39
															.35		/	/	37		35	8	32
				22		23																		
						26						25		26	24		/	/	S				
															36		/	/	42_5	2	2		||
													32		.39	/	/	/	40_{13}	9	37_2	$/_{19}$	35_{10}
				1		1																			
				27		34					36		36		40				44		44		45

	40	41	42	43	44	45	46	47	48	49	50	51	52	53	54	55	56	
	35	36	37	38	1	2	3	4	5	6	7	1	2	3	4	5	6	
	11 May 1543				26 May 1547							18 Feb. 1554	1555					
WALPOLE, JOHN					50					8		33_{26}	26_{19}	$√_{33}$	$√_{13}$			→
WARD, HENRY	52	$√_1$	2		47	√		3		2		31_{18}	25_{10}	15		||		
WHITE, EDWARD																		
WILLOUGHBY, WILLIAM LD																		
WILTSHIRE, THOMAS BOLEYN E OF																		
WINGFIELD, RICHARD																		
WINGFIELD, THOMAS																		
WOODHOUSE, ROGER	34				34							20	16	√	$√_2$	√	√	→
WOODHOUSE, THOMAS II																		
WOODHOUSE, THOMAS II	48	$√_5$			35		9	√		15		S	13_{16}	$√_8$	3	$√_6$		→
WOODHOUSE, WILLIAM						√						18		$√_8$	√			→
WOTTON, JOHN	38		2	||														
WOTTON, WILLIAM																		
WYNDHAM, EDMUND	18		2	S	√		S			$√_{23}$		14_4	12_{23}	$√_{33}$	$√_6$	√	√	→
WYNDHAM, THOMAS																		
YELVERTON, WILLIAM II (Jun.)																		
YELVERTON, WILLIAM III (Sen.)	42_7	6	4	10	40	$√_8$	$√_2$	4		$√_{15}$			31_{14}	$√_{19}$	4	$√_{17}^{16}$		→
YORK, THOMAS WOLSEY ABP OF																		
TOTAL	55				54							35	32					

APPENDIX III

Norfolk and Suffolk JPs dismissed 1485–1603

The figures below consider only genuine residents of the two counties, and therefore omit not only national figures who did not have an East Anglian base, but also those local men who were omitted from the commission because they had left the area: for instance, Robert Gardiner of Elmswell on his being made Chief Justice of the Irish Queen's Bench in 1585. In constructing this table I have used data on the careers of Suffolk and Norfolk justices in Appendices I and II: to make comparison of the Norfolk figures with Suffolk as close as possible, I have not used Smith's Appendix II charting dismissals in Norfolk 1540–1656 (Smith, pp. 359–60) as it now needs to be amplified in a number of points from further information; instead I have worked out my own figures from his table of Norfolk justices' careers (Smith Appendix I, pp. 343–58), adding the information given in his three footnotes to Appendix II, the recently discovered *liber pacis* for 1590 (BL Eger. 3788), the Ancient Indictments (PRO, KB 9) and estreats of fines in the Exchequer (PRO, E137/42/4). None of the figures except those in the twelfth division below can claim to be exact, owing to the incompleteness of our information as to who was on the Bench at any one time; this is particularly true of the first half of the period, making events at the especially crucial stages of 1515, 1524, 1543, and 1547 impossible to recover. It is not until the first Docquet Book of the Crown Office noting issues of commissions including those of the commission of the peace was begun in 1595 (PRO, C231/1) that we have an exact record of all the commissions issued and the reason for the issue. The figures before 1595 are therefore certainly an underestimate, and there may be some justices whose careers on the Bench were too brief to figure in surviving records.

The dismissals are set out in two periods. For second or third dismissals, the names are italicized. Totals for the two counties are tabulated at the end.

SUFFOLK	NORFOLK

I. 1485–1509 *(reign of Henry VII)*

| 1485 | Robert Fiennes, Ralph Willoughby, Christopher Willoughby I, Robert Clere, Gilbert Debenham, Henry Wentworth, William Hopton, Alexander Cressener, Thomas Appleton | William Calthorpe, Ralph Willoughby, Henry L'Estrange, John Wyndham, Robert Clere, John Heveningham, Henry Heydon, Thomas Earl of Surrey, Terry Robsart, Thomas Jenny, John Earl of Lincoln, Ralph Shelton |

SUFFOLK	NORFOLK
1486	*Terry Robsart*
1489 William Gedding, Robert Drury	
1494?a Edmund Bedingfield I	
1496	*Terry Robsart*, Robert Lord Fitzwalter
1497 Edmund Arundel	John Paston, Robert Southwell, Robert Brandon
1499 John Heveningham I	
1501 Edmund Earl of Suffolk, Philip Booth	Edmund Earl of Suffolk
1503	*Robert Clere*, Robert Pinkney
1504 John Audley, Robert Brandon, Richard Wentworth	Richard Bishop of Norwich, William Skipwith

2. 1509–1529 (*accession of Henry VIII to fall of Wolsey*)

SUFFOLK	NORFOLK
1509 Thomas Sampson, John Timperley, John Wiseman, *Philip Booth*, Thomas Jermyn I	Philip Calthorpe
1510 *Richard Wentworth*	
1512 John Heveningham II	Roger Townshend
1514 Anthony Wingfield I	Richard Cavendish, James Framlingham, John Glemham, Walter Hobart, Henry Hunston, Andrew Sulyard
1515	John Audley, *Robert Brandon*, Robert Lord Curzon
1515?a *John Audley, Philip Booth*, John Glemham, *John Wiseman, John Heveningham II*, Thomas Boleyn, John Vere, William Lord Willoughby	
1516 *Robert Brandon*	
1517 Thomas Lucas	
1524	Thomas Lovell
1529?a	Philip Tilney

3. 1530–1540 (*Wolsey's fall to Cromwell's fall*)

SUFFOLK	NORFOLK
1530? Owen Hopton	
1531?a	James Boleyn
1532?a Thomas Jermyn II	
1533?a Edmund Cocket	Edmund Bedingfield II, Philip Calthorpe, Richard Southwell
1535?a Henry Hatfield, Henry Stockheath	
1536 William Drury	

	SUFFOLK	NORFOLK
1538		Thomas L'Estrange
1539	John Abbot of Bury	
1539?a		Edmund Wyndham

4. 1540–1547 (*Cromwell's fall to Henry VIII's death*)

1540		William Farmer, Francis Lovell, Henry Lord Fitzwalter
1541		John Jenny
1542		Christopher Jenny, Richard Banyard
1543		Robert Barney
1544	*Thomas Jermyn*	

5. 1547–1553 (*reign of Edward VI*)

1547?	Thomas Barnadiston II, George Colt, Robert Crane, Richard Freston, Thomas Duke of Norfolk, Thomas Tilney, Richard Gresham, Robert Downes, Robert Rookwood	Edward Billingford, William Brampton, John Curzon II, Robert Curzon II, Thomas Dey, Thomas Duke of Norfolk
1550?a	Richard Fulmerston	Richard Fulmerston

6. 1553–1558 (*reign of Mary I*)

1553	Francis Clopton, James Downes, John Eyer, William Forth, Henry Gates, Christopher Goldingham, Henry Goodrich, Edward Grimston, Robert Gurdon, John Lucas, Alexander Newton, George Somerset, Robert Southwell, Robert Wingfield, Thomas Playters, Henry Hobart	Thomas Clere, William Butts, John Clere, Gregory Davy, Henry Goodrich, Thomas Guybon, Lord Robert Dudley, George Hogard, Thomas Hollis, Nicholas L'Estrange, William Hunston, Robert Southwell, Robert Townshend, Ralph Symonds, Robert Robsart, John Plumstead
1554	William Honnings, Ambrose Jermyn, Christopher Peyton, John Jenny, Henry Bedingfield	*William Farmer*, Thomas Knyvett
1558	*Edward Grimston*	

7. 1558–1569 (*Elizabeth's accession to flight of Duke of Norfolk*)

1558	*Henry Bedingfield*, John Jerningham II, Robert Kempe, Miles Spencer, Thomas Cornwallis, Robert Gosnold, Thomas Timperley, John Tyrrell, Robert Browne, Edward Clerke, Thomas Felton, William Foster, George Jerningham, Henry Payne, Thomas Seckford I, Edward Waldegrave	Edmund Audley, Charles Clere, Henry Farmer, Thomas Guybon, *Lord Robert Dudley*, John Jenny, Thomas Lovell, ... Kerville, Anthony Thwaites, Thomas Ragland, *Richard Southwell*, John Repps, John Walpole

	SUFFOLK	NORFOLK
1559	Giles Alington, Henry Jerningham, John Sulyard	John Barney
1560	*Thomas Cornwallis*	
1561	*Thomas Playters I*, Thomas Rous	John Appleyard, Thomas Brampton, *William Brampton*, Edward Clere, William Cocket, *Richard Fulmerston*, Thomas Gawdy II, Martin Hastings, *Thomas Knyvett, Thomas Lovell*, Thomas Thrower, Thomas Barrow, Francis Thoresby
1562	Thomas Glemham, Francis Jenny, *Robert Rookwood*, Henry Wentworth I	
1563	Laurence Meres	
1564	John Southwell I, *John Tyrrell, William Foster*	
1564?a		*George Hogard*, Thomas Tyndall

8. 1569–1575 (*flight of Duke of Norfolk to death of Bp. Parkhurst*)

1569	Michael Hare, Thomas Kitson	*Nicholas L'Estrange*, William Yelverton I
1571?a	Thomas Duke of Norfolk	Thomas Duke of Norfolk
1574	Philip Tilney	Henry Woodhouse

9. 1575–1584 (*episcopate of Bishop Freke*)

1576		Thomas Townsend
1577?a		Osbert Moundford
1578	William Rede	Charles Calthorpe
1579		*William Hunston*
1581?a		*John Walpole*
1582	Reynold Highgate	
1583	Nicholas Bacon, Thomas Badby, Philip Browne, Charles Cavendish, John Higham, Robert Jermyn, *William Rede*, Thomas Steynings	Edward Flowerdew, Arthur Heveningham, John Reynolds, Henry Weston, Roger Woodhouse
1584	*John Jerningham II*	

10. 1584–1595 (*coming of Bishop Scambler to eve of 1595 'purge'*)

1585		Philip Parker
1585?a	Robert Crane, William Gresham	
1586		Robert Wood
1587	Robert Gosnold, Richard Kemp, John Rivet, William Waldegrave, *John Higham*, Charles Seckford	*Thomas Barrow, Thomas Gawdy II*, Nicholas Hare II, Robert Kemp II, Thomas Knyvett II, Edward Lord Morley, Philip Woodhouse, William Woodhouse, Henry Yelverton

	SUFFOLK	NORFOLK
1588		Miles Hobart, John Steward, William Gresham
1589		Thomas Farmer, Thomas Lovell II
1590	*Robert Wingfield*	*Philip Woodhouse, Henry Yelverton, Henry Woodhouse*
1591	William Clopton	Christopher Heydon, Roger Townsend
1592	*William Waldegrave*	Thomas Knyvett III
1593	Francis Bohun	
1594		Wimond Carey

11. 1595 *'purge'*

| 1595 | Thomas Barnadiston, Thomas Blennerhasset, Edmund Buckenham, John Clopton, George Colt, Edward Doyle, Robert Drury, Edward Everard, Anthony Felton, William Forth, William Grimston, Arthur Hopton, Richard Johnson, John Lany, Thomas Playters II, John Southwell II, John Thurston, *Philip Tilney*, Thomas Warren, Henry Wingfield, Arthur Jenny | Martin Barney, Thomas Barney, Henry Clere, Thomas Clere II, *Thomas Farmer*, Richard Freston, William Gresham, William Hatton, John Le Hunt, John Repps, James Scambler, Clement Spelman, *Henry Yelverton*, Gregory Pratt, *Henry Woodhouse* |

12. 1596–1603

1596	John Le Hunt, *Arthur Jenny*	*John Le Hunt*
1598		Humphrey Guybon, Robert Buxton
1599	Lionel Tollemache	*Martin Barney*, Thomas Guybon
1600		*Christopher Heydon*, Robert Mansell, John Townshend
1601	Robert Barker I, Robert Rolfe	Edward Lord Cromwell, Thomas Dove, Edward Bartlett
1602		William Kemp
1603		*Thomas Barney*, Thomas Bennett, John Jay

Totals of dismissals per period (second or third dismissals are given in brackets beside main figure)

PERIOD	SUFFOLK	NORFOLK
1.	19	23 (3)
2.	18 (7)	13 (1)
3.	7	6
4.	1 (1)	7
5.	10	7
6.	22 (1)	18 (1)
7.	30 (6)	29 (7)
8.	4	4 (1)
9.	11 (2)	10 (2)
10.	12 (3)	23 (5)
11.	21 (1)	15 (3)
12.	5 (1)	15 (4)

Total JP's	467	425
Total dismissal cases	160	170
Total individuals involved	138	143

The Suffolk gentry and their marriages
1558–1603

The following sample of 635 marriages among the Suffolk gentry for the period *c.* 1550–1612 is taken from the three Visitations of 1561, 1577, and 1612 and the additional pedigrees as edited by Walter Metcalfe. The principle chosen has been to list and analyse the marriages of eldest sons, heirs, heads of families, and of cadet branches in all cases where the wife's place of origin could be traced. Where the marriage was with a widow it has been classified by the residence of the previous husband rather than by the wife's original home.

Figures are for marriages, not for individuals. They are given compositely, the second figure being for those marriages which took place from recusant gentry families. Separate analyses are given for east and west Suffolk, and then combined for the county as a whole.

Key to symbols used:

Local: Marriages which took place between families within the same area, i.e. either in the east or the west only.
E/W: Marriages where the wife came from the other half of the county.
Nf: Marriages where the wife came from Norfolk.
Ess: Marriages where the wife came from Essex.
Cam: Marriages where the wife came from Cambridgeshire.
Lon: Marriages where the wife came from London.
Other: Marriages where the wife came from some other county.

	East Suffolk families	%	West Suffolk families	%	Total	%
Local	195 + 14	52	95 + 5	44	355 + 23	60
E/W	38 + 3	10	27 + 1	12		
Nf.	49 + 11	15	22 + 1	10	71 + 12	13
Ess.	29 + 1	7	25 + 3	12	54 + 4	9
Cam.	4 + 0	1	12 + 2	6	16 + 2	3
Lon.	12 + 0	3	6 + 0	2	18 + 0	3
Other	37 + 12	12	27 + 4	14	64 + 16	12
Total	405		230		635	

Analysis of marriages of JPs included in the sample

	East Suffolk families		West Suffolk families		Total	
		%		%		%
Local	26 + 3	42	16 + 1	39	57 + 5	60
E/W	11 + 1	20	4 + 0	10		
Nf.	4 + 1	9	3 + 0	8	7 + 1	7
Ess.	3 + 0	6	9 + 0	20	12 + 0	11
Cam.	0		0		0	
Lond.	2 + 0	3	1 + 0	3	3 + 0	2
Other	8 + 4	20	7 + 2	20	15 + 6	20
Total	63		43		106	

The figures in the second table indicate that the upper levels of the gentry class shared the attitudes of more minor gentry about marriage within their own area; it was normal in any case for Suffolk men to seek a wife within the county. However, the magistracy of west Suffolk showed a tendency to marry into the élite of their neighbours in Essex which may have been more pronounced than among the lesser gentry of the Liberty. In both halves of the county the magistracy were more inclined than lesser men to look beyond the bounds of East Anglia for a wife, presumably because they had more opportunities, perhaps more university or Inn-of-Court contacts, to do so.

APPENDIX V

Origins of Suffolk borough MPs 1504–1601

In compiling this table, I follow in the main the descriptions of the Tudor volumes in the History of Parliament series (individual biographies and *1509–58* I, pp. 190–3, *1558–1603* I, pp. 246–50). I disagree with or would wish to supplement their analyses in numerous details, but the following are our most significant differences:

(*a*) I contest *HP*'s identification of John Harrison (1547 Dunwich) who is surely the resident burgess of that name. If so, Thomas Heydon cannot have been MP for Dunwich in a by-election in 1548.

(*b*) *HP* fail to stress that Humphrey Wingfield (Ipswich 1523) was an habitual Ipswich resident.

(*c*) *HP* miss the important fact that Edward Coke (Aldeburgh 1588) was lawyer for the Howard family (above, Ch. 8, n. 29).

(*d*) Anthony Wingfield I (Orford 1571) is wrongly identified; he was brother-in-law of Francis Sone (PCC 41 Pyckering) and brother of Sir Robert Wingfield of Letheringham.

(*e*) Philip Gawdy (Sudbury 1601) was a relative of the Fortescue family and resident at Chilton-by-Sudbury at the time, so he should not be regarded as an absentee courtier (PRO, STAC 5 S1/6, S26/11, S28/19).

(*f*) Francis Hervey (Aldeburgh 1597) is wrongly identified by *HP*: see above, Ch. 8, n. 46.

Key to symbols used in table

Figures in brackets are percentages.

A 'True' burgesses
B Resident or local gentlemen, or men elected through their influence
C Gentlemen from elsewhere in Suffolk, or men elected through their influence
D Outsiders to the county elected through outside influence

	Number of known election results	A	B	C	D
IPSWICH					
1504–58	34	22 (64)	8 (24)	4 (12)	0
1559–1601	20	8 (40)	6 (30)	3 (15)	3 (15)
DUNWICH					
1504–58	20	10 (50)	7 (35)	1 (5)	2 (10)
1559–1601	21	4 (19)	8 (38)	0	9 (43)
ORFORD					
1504–58	23	6 (26)	12 (52)	3 (13)	2 (8)
1559–1601	20	1 (5)	13 (65)	4 (20)	2 (10)
SUDBURY					
1559–1601	20	2 (10)	8 (40)	5 (25)	5 (25)
EYE					
1571–1601	16	0	14 (88)	1 (6)	1 (6)
ALDEBURGH					
1571–1601	16	4 (25)	3 (19)	3 (19)	6 (38)
TOTAL 1504–58	77	38 (49)	27 (35)	8 (10)	4 (5)
1559–1601	113	19 (17)	52 (46)	16 (14)	26 (23)
TOTAL IN ALL	190	57 (30)	79 (42)	24 (13)	30 (16)

Index

All places are in Suffolk unless otherwise indicated. For the laity, date of death is given wherever possible to aid identification. For the clergy, ultimate preferment is given. Headings with more than five entries have been sub-divided wherever possible.